Guide to Documents and Manuscripts in the United Kingdom Relating to Russia and the Soviet Union

Guide to Documents and Manuscripts in the United Kingdom Relating to Russia and the Soviet Union

Janet M. Hartley

Mansell Publishing Limited

London and New York

First published 1987 by Mansell Publishing Limited
(A subsidiary of The H. W. Wilson Company)
6 All Saints Street, London N1 9RL, England
950 University Avenue, Bronx, New York, 10452, U.S.A.

British Library Cataloguing in Publication Data

Hartley, Janet M.
  Guide to documents and manuscripts in the
  United Kingdom relating to Russia and the
  Soviet Union.
  1. Soviet Union—History—Bibliography
  I. Title
  016.947   Z2506

  ISBN 0-7201-1805-0

Library of Congress Cataloging-in-Publication Data

Hartley, Janet M.
  Guide to documents and manuscripts in the United
Kingdom relating to Russia and the Soviet Union.

  "Result of a three-year research project undertaken
at the School of Slavonic and East European Studies,
University of London, from 1982 to 1985"—Introd.
  Bibliography: p.
  Includes index.
  1. Soviet Union—Library resources—Great Britain.
  2. Soviet Union—Archival resources—Great Britain.
  3. Libraries—Great Britain—Directories. 4. Archives—
Great Britain—Directories. I. Title.
  Z2491.H37 1986   016.947   [DK3]   86-18148
  ISBN 0-7201-1805-0

Printed in Great Britain by
Whitstable Litho Ltd., Whitstable, Kent

Contents

Contents

Contents

Dundee

Durham

Edinburgh

Exeter

Folkestone

Forres

Glasgow

Gloucester

Grantham

Grimsby

Guildford

Contents

Contents

Introduction

This *Guide* is the result of a three-year research project undertaken at the School of Slavonic and East European Studies, University of London, from 1982 to 1985. The director of the project was Professor J. E. O. Screen, Librarian of the School, and the research fellow and compiler was Dr Janet M. Hartley. They were assisted by an advisory committee comprising Professor M. A. Branch, the Director of the School, Professor A. G. Cross, Dr Georgette Donchin, Mr N. E. Evans, Mr J. D. Morison, Dr G. P. M. Walker and chairmen of the departments of Russian and History in the School. The index was prepared by Dr Helen Szamuely. The project was made possible by the generosity of the Leverhulme Trust, which funded the project for three years. A two-month grant from the Nuffield Foundation covered the cost of the final preparation of the text. All those associated with the publication of the *Guide* would like to express their gratitude to the Leverhulme Trust and the Nuffield Foundation for their support.

The aim of the project was to record systematically for the first time the location of documentary material relating to Russia and the Soviet Union in the United Kingdom. It is hoped that this will open up the possibility of many new areas of research in Russian and Soviet studies. The diversity of the contacts between Britain and Russia has resulted in extensive material relating to Russia being deposited in many repositories including record offices, libraries, museums and professional, religious and cultural organizations. Apart from the obvious value of locating this material for the study of Russian and Soviet history and Anglo-Russian relations, it was felt that it was particularly useful to locate material in this country in view of the difficulties sometimes experienced in gaining access to archives in the Soviet Union.

The material was recorded during the period between September 1982 and July 1985. As well as official and private papers, there has been an attempt to locate manuscript literary papers, maps, plans and musical scores, photographs and typescripts and proofs of published works. There has been no systematic attempt to locate or make tape recordings of personal experiences in Russia but tapes have been included when cited in catalogues. Newspaper cuttings and privately published books have been noted when they form part of a larger collection relating to Russia or the Soviet Union. Manuscript codices have not been included as these are the subject of a detailed study by R. Cleminson, *Union Catalogue of Cyrillic Manuscript Codices in British and Irish Collections* (forthcoming).

Over eight hundred enquiries were sent to repositories, including all county and municipal record offices, university libraries, major public libraries, specialist libraries and museums known to have large manuscript collections, museums of the armed forces, banks, firms with trading connections with Russia or the Soviet Union, political parties, major trade unions, and learned, scientific, artistic, religious, missionary, cultural and charitable organizations which could have had contacts with Russia or the Soviet Union. The response was poor only from industrial and trading companies, whose policy generally seems to be to destroy old papers and to not give access to recent papers for reasons of commercial confidentiality. Even large firms with their own archives often proved unwilling to be included in the survey and the amount of material recorded in the possession of firms in the *Guide* is disappointing. Some of the repositories which returned negative replies are listed following this introduction. There was no systematic attempt to locate papers in private ownership but notices were placed in journals and newsletters of cultural organizations to advertise the project and encourage owners of private papers to make them known. It proved difficult to locate papers in private hands and the list of such papers (Appendix 2) does not claim to be comprehensive or necessarily to cover the most important private collections in this country.

Pressure of time meant that it was not feasible to visit all the repositories which held material relating to Russia. All repositories were visited which held extensive collections or which were unable to supply the information by post. Over one hundred repositories were visited and over half the material in the *Guide* was recorded through a visit rather than by post. The general principle has been to rely on the information in calendars, catalogues and handlists, whether published or unpublished, and, although original material has been examined where no finding aids exist, it has usually been assumed that the finding aids are accurate. Drafts of the entries were sent back to the repositories for comments and amendments in the summmer of 1985. Although doubtless far more material would emerge if all the collections were to be examined thoroughly, such an approach would have required many years of funding and it was felt that the priority should be the completion of the *Guide* within as short a time as possible so that the more readily accessible information could be made available to scholars.

In particular, there has been no attempt to itemize the Russica in the Public Record Office, the House of Lords Record Office and the India Office Library and Records. It was felt that as these collections are generally well known to scholars, priority should be given to locating and describing the less familiar holdings of smaller repositories. A brief description has been given of the public records relating to Russia and the Soviet Union in these three repositories and appropriate finding aids have been listed. In order to limit the length of the *Guide* the size of entries was deliberately restricted and further information in handlists and catalogues has been noted. There are some inevitable inconsistencies in the amount of description given in the *Guide*; large collections relating to Russia are briefly summarized in a paragraph while individual items which are deposited singly or which constitute the only item relating to Russia in a collection are described in full and thus given a prominence which they do not necessarily deserve.

The repositories are arranged in the *Guide* in alphabetical order by town. Within a repository, unless clearly inappropriate, collections are arranged in alphabetical order by name of the collection followed by miscellaneous items listed in numerical order according to their class mark or accession number. There has been no attempt at any arrangement by subject as this was considered to be too complex, and it is anticipated that the index to the *Guide* will be used for this purpose. Where it is known that the document has been published this has been noted, but otherwise there has been no attempt to ascertain this or to find where the originals of copied material are located. The language of the material is noted when indicated in the finding aids. Conditions of access are laid down according to the stipulations of the repository concerned, but researchers should be aware that all documents are made available at the discretion of the custodians or owners and inclusion of an item in this *Guide* does not necessarily mean that it will be made readily available, or that it may be published or reproduced without permission. It is always preferable, and essential in the case of papers in private ownership, to write before making a visit.

The British Standard form of transliteration of Russian has been used. Russian names have normally been left in the form adopted by the repository unless only minor changes were required ('ov' instead of 'off' etc) with the standardized spelling after the word in brackets. Where the proper spelling is uncertain the standardized spelling of the name in brackets is preceded by a question mark. In general, European names which have been russified are given in their original form with the Russian version in brackets. The names of Emperors, Tsars and members of the Russian Imperial family have been anglicized, and the commonly accepted spelling of well-known Russians (Tchaikovsky etc) has been retained. Alternative spellings are cross-referenced in the index. Russian dates have been recorded as they appear in the finding aids; it is not always clear whether dates are Old or New Style.

The *Guide* could not have been prepared in the time available without the co-operation and assistance of the custodians of the collections who supplied information by post and who gave much useful advice when the repositories were visted. Gratitude must be expressed to all the custodians and owners of papers who responded to enquiries, including those who had to make a negative reply. Thanks are also due to the following people who assisted at various stages of the project : Dr J. Appleby, Professor Geraldine M. Phipps, Dr W. F. Ryan, Mr J. S. G. Simmons, Miss Pamela Willetts, members of the advisory committee, the staff of the Palaeography Room in the University of London Library and to the many people who advised upon the location of materials and the presentation of the text.

For the reasons given above, the *Guide* cannot claim to be exhaustive in listing all documentary material in this country relating to Russia and the Soviet Union. The approach to this project was pragmatic and concerned less with completeness or finality than with the more limited aim of making the coverage of repositories, and collections within repositories, as wide as possible. In a work of this nature it is impossible to avoid errors and omissions. Further information on the location of material and corrections would be welcomed as it is hoped that it may be possible in the future to publish a supplement to the *Guide*. Correspondence should be addressed to the Librarian, School of Slavonic and East European Studies, University of London, Senate House, Malet Street, London WC1E 7HU.

Société Guernesiaise (St Saviour), Somerville College Library (Oxford), South Glamorgan County Libraries (Cardiff), South Wales Borderers Museum (Brecon), Southwark Libraries, Staffordshire County Libraries (Stafford), Stirling University 'Library, Strathclyde University Archives (Glasgow), Strathclyde University Library (Glasgow), Surrey County Library (Dorking), Surrey University Library (Guildford), Tameside Libraries (Ashton-under-Lyne), Theosophical Society, Tower Hamlets Local History Library, Trinity College Library (Oxford), Trinity Hall Library (Cambridge), Truro County Museum and Art Gallery, Tyne and Wear Archives Department (North Shields), Ulster Museum (Belfast), United Reformed Church History Society, University College of North Wales Library (Bangor), University College of Wales Library (Aberystwyth), University College of Wales Library (Cardiff), University of Manchester Institute of Science and Technology Library, University of Wales Institute of Science and Technology Library (Cardiff), Veteran's Car Club (Ashwell), Wadham College Library (Oxford), Waltham Forest Libraries, Walsall Libraries, Wandsworth Libraries, Warrington Local Studies Library and Local Record Office, Warwickshire Central Divisional Library (Leamington Spa), Wellington Museum, Whipple Library (Cambridge), Wiener Library, Wigan Reference Library, Willesden Libraries, Wiltshire Regimental Museum (Devizes), Winchester Cathedral Library, Winchester City Record Office, Winchester College Library, Wirral Archives (Birkenhead), Wolfson College Library (Cambridge), Wolfson College Library (Oxford), Wolverhampton Borough Archives, Worcester Cathedral Library, Worcester College Library (Oxford), Worcestershire & Sherwood Foresters Regimental Museum (Worcester), York City Archives, Yorkshire Regiments Museum (Strensall), Zoological Society Library.

Bibliography

Repositories in the United Kingdom are listed in *Record Repositories in Great Britain* (7th ed., 1982) (and supplements in *Archives*, vol. 14 no. 63 (Spring, 1980), pp. 163-77 and vol. 15 no. 67 (April, 1982), pp. 157-168). The holdings of many of the repositories in this *Guide* are described briefly in J. Forster and J. Sheppard, *British Archives : a Guide to Archive Resources in the United Kingdom* (London, 1982) and C. Cook, edit., *Sources in British Political History, 1900-51*, vol. 1 'A Guide to the Archives of Selected Organisations and Societies' (London, 1975). Library holdings relating to East European and Slavonic materials are described in G. Walker, edit., *Resources for Soviet, East European and Slavonic Studies in British Libraries* (Birmingham, 1981). The following guides have been used in the preparation of this *Guide* : J. S. Batts, *British Manuscript Diaries of the Nineteenth Century* (Totowa, New Jersey, 1976); G. D. R. Bridson, V. C. Phillips, A. P. Harvey, comp., *Natural History Manuscript Resources in the British Isles* (London, New York, 1980); C. Cook, edit., *Sources in British Political History, 1900-51*, vols 2-5 (1975-85); C. Hazlehurst and C. Woodward, comp., *A Guide to the Papers of British Cabinet Ministers, 1900-51*; P. Hudson, *The West Riding Wool Textile Industry : a Catalogue of Business Records from the Sixteenth to the Twentieth Century* (Pasold Occasional Papers, 3) (Edington, 1975); P. Mathias and A. W. H. Pearsall, edit., *Shipping : a Survey of Historical Records* (Newton Abbot, 1971); S. L. Mayer and W. J. Koenig, *The Two World Wars. A Guide to Manuscript Collections in the United Kingdom* (London, New York, 1976). The series of guides to sources for British history based on the National Register of Archives by the Royal Commission on Historical Manuscripts includes *Papers of British Cabinet Ministers, 1782-1900* (Guides to Sources for British History, 1) (London, 1982), *The Manuscript Papers of British Scientists, 1600-1940* (Guides to Sources for British History, 2) (London, 1982) and *Private Papers of British Diplomats, 1782-1900* (Guides to Sources for British History, 4) (London, 1985). There are several guides to documentary material in the United Kingdom relating to other countries and the most relevant for material relating to Russia are the two volumes compiled by N. Matthews and M. D. Wainwright, *A Guide to Manuscripts and Documents in the British Isles relating to the Far East* (Oxford, 1977) and *A Guide to Manuscripts and Documents in the British Isles relating to the Middle East and North Africa* (Oxford, 1980). Publications relating specifically to the holdings of particular repositories are listed under that repository.

Repositories

1.1

ABERDEEN CENTRAL LIBRARY

Local Studies Department, Rosemount Viaduct, Aberdeen AB9 1GU

1.1 Journal of George Ross, representative of Gordon, Barron and Co., cotton manufacturers, describing his travels and business transactions in Russia, Poland and Germany, 1824.

2.1-9

ABERDEEN UNIVERSITY LIBRARY

Manuscripts and Archives Section, King's College, University of Aberdeen, Aberdeen AB9 2UB

Preferably by appointment.

2.1 J. M. BULLOCH: GORDON COLLECTION
Copies of letters re the Gordon family in Russia, 1666, 1668 (**MS 3051/1/2-9**).

2.2 DUFF OF BRACO COLLECTION
Papers of William, later Lord Braco and 1st Earl Fife, include letters of Jean, Dowager Countess Fife, to Arthur Duff, 1776-7, including re visit of a Russian princess to Edinburgh (**MS 2727/1/155**) and letter from J. E. Gordon Cumming to Wharton Duff re trouble in India and the possibility of Russian involvement, 12 Aug. 1857 (**2/17**).

2.3 KEITH, James Francis Edward (1696-1758)
TS lives of Keith by A. W. Keith-Falconer and H. Godfrey (**MS 2707; MS 3163**); copies of correspondence of Keith in the Berlin State Library and the British Library (**MSS 2709, 2711**).

2.4 KEITH OF KINTORE COLLECTION
Collection includes charter of Empress Elizabeth of Russia granting lands to James Francis Edward Keith, 1742, and other papers re Keith (**MS 3064/Bundles 146, 198, 329, 335**); 'Diary 1913. Turkey, Mesopotamia, Persia, Russia' (**Bundle 327 vol. 136**).

2.5 A. D. McLEAN COLLECTION
Collection of news-cuttings, pamphlets, correspondence etc. re Russian affairs, *c.* 1940-60 (**MS 2399/1-2**).

2.6 REE COLLECTION
Copy of 'Origin of the familie and sirname of Leslie', including references to members of the Leslie family in Russia (**MS 805, MS 2493**).

2.7 T. REID COLLECTION
Letter from Archibald Leslie to unknown correspondent mentioning the Leslie family in Russia, 26 Jan. 1894 (**MS 2814/6/41**).

2.8 R. WILSON COLLECTION
Travel account of visit to Russia by Robert Wilson MD, 19th century (**MS 425**).

2.9 Stereoscopic photographs of Russian scenes, n.d., probably late 19th century (**MS 2408**).

3.1
CITY OF ABERDEEN DISTRICT ARCHIVES

The Charter Room, The Town House, Aberdeen AB9 1AQ

3.1 The records of the city of Aberdeen contain a few references to trade with Russia and to Scotsmen who settled there, but most of the records are unindexed and there are no other finding aids to locate this material.

4.1-40
NATIONAL LIBRARY OF WALES

Department of Manuscripts and Records, Aberystwyth, Dyfed SY23 3BU

Handlist of Manuscripts in the National Library of Wales 4 vols (1943-) describes material acquired up to 1940 in the general series of National Library of Wales MSS; handlists of family papers and major collections; person, place and subject indexes. Acquisitions are listed in the *Annual Reports* (1909-). A brief guide to the Department of Manuscripts and Records is under preparation.

4.1 ANWYL MSS (**NLW MSS 2421-2505**)
Notebooks and papers of Sir Edward Anwyl (1866-1914), Professor of Welsh and Comparative Philology at the University College of Wales, Aberystwyth, include exercises in Russian (**NLW MS 2459-60C**).

4.2 ASTON HALL COLLECTION
Deeds and documents include press cuttings re the Crimean War (**No. 4406**). Correspondence includes letter from Wm. Mac... from Warsaw to William Lloyd of Aston including an account of the sender's travels into Russia, 7 Nov. 1819 (**1171**), and many letters re the Crimean War, including letters by Lady Sarah Cholmondeley, 1854 (**1667-8**) and Charlotte Piggott, 1854 (**6089, 6098-104**), and letters from the Crimea by Robert Drummond, 1854-5 (**7788-98, 7822-3**). *See handlist for details.*

4.3 CWMGWILI MSS AND DOCUMENTS
Papers re the Cwmgwili estate of the Philipps family include detailed instructions, printed with MS additions, re an expedition (in the Crimean War) endorsed by Lt Philipps (**484**).

4.4 LORD DAVIES OF LLANDINAM PAPERS
Papers of Lord David Davies, 1st Baron Llandinam (1880-1944), Liberal MP, include: memo on his visit to Russia, Jan. 1918; reports on the situation in Russia in early 1917, particularly re transport, supplies, resources and the economy; notes on the political situation in early 1917; printed report by the Conference of the Allies at Petrograd re munitions, Jan.-Feb. 1917; an eyewitness account of the Revolution by George Bury; report by Davies on the effect of the Revolution; report by P. Vinogradoff on Russian POWs in Germany and Austria; copy of report by Douglas Young on British Official Activities in Archangel, 1917; reports and notebook by Alexander Proctor on the intervention (**C3/11-25**).

4.5 JOHN HENRY DAVIES PAPERS
Principal of the Mining and Technical Institute, Pontardare. Journals of visits to Russia and galley proofs of L. and J. H. Davies, *A Trip to Soviet Russia* (1933).

4.6 DESMOND DONNELLY PAPERS
Papers of Desmond Donnelly (1920-74), MP, include a letter from Svetlana Allilueva, 1967. Papers not fully catalogued. Permission to consult this collection must be obtained from Mrs Rosemary Donnelly, Bodmor, Newport Road, Lower Town, Fishguard, Dyfed.

4.7 ELIS O'R NANT MSS (NLW MSS 8573-612)
Miscellaneous collection including a short history of Russia by G. Jones, 19th century, Welsh (**NLW MS 8595B**).

4.8 GEORGE EYRE EVANS BEQUEST (NLW MSS 13271-13585)
A volume of letters from David Ivon Jones to Evans includes letters from Moscow and Yalta, and a few items re the death and burial of Jones in Russia, 1924, English and Welsh (**NLW MS 13580C**).

4.9 FRANCIS GREEN PAPERS
Papers of Francis Green (1854-1942), antiquary, include papers re the fund for orphans and widows of those killed in the Crimean War, Nov. 1854 (**164-5, 167**).

4.10 JAMES GRIFFITHS PAPERS
Papers of James Griffiths (1890-1975), Labour MP, include notes, printed material and newspaper cuttings re the visit to Britain of Bulganin and Khrushchev in 1956 (**B7**).

4.11 HARPTON COURT PAPERS
Letters from George Cornewall Lewis to his father, Sir Thomas Frankland Lewis, commenting on the Crimean War, 1854-5 (**C/473-7**).

4.12 HERALDRY (NLW MS 12221E)
Much of the draft notes, extracts, memoranda etc. by C. F. Egerton Allen on the arms of Pembrokeshire families is written on the back of a variety of printed sheets relating to the disarmament conference summoned by Nicholas II of Russia, 1899.

4.13 LORD HOOSON PAPERS
Collection of Hugh Emlyn Hooson, Lord Hooson, while Liberal MP, 1962-79, includes a file of papers and correspondence re political prisoners in the USSR, 1976 (**Box no. 37**). Permission to consult this collection must be obtained from Lord Hooson, Summerfield, Llanidloes, Powys.

4.14 D. E. JENKINS MSS (NLW MSS 12731-12853)
Papers of Revd David Erwyd Jenkins (1864-1937), Calvinistic Methodist minister and schoolmaster, include a letter to Joseph Tarn, Assistant Secretary of the British and Foreign Bible Society, re the Society's intention of setting up a printing office in Russia, 1814 (**NLW MS 12776B**).

4.15 R. O. JENKINS MSS(NLW MS 20753E)
Papers relating to his service as a captain attached to the White Russian forces in Archangel in 1919, including military documents, maps, Bolshevik posters, leaflets and newspapers, correspondence in English and Russian re White Russian resistance around Archangel and the first two years of Bolshevik rule.

4.16 DR THOMAS JONES, C.H., COLLECTION

Papers re foreign affairs include a volume on the USSR, 2 Feb. 1918 - Oct. 1927, containing: a report by Capt. Alexander Proctor from Archangel, Feb. 1918; memo by A. E. Zimmern on Russia, 1918; printed 'Memorandum on the Russian Situation and a Suggestion as to British Policy' by A. G. Marshall, Oct. 1927; letter from E. G. Wise following his visit to Russia, 2 July 1925; letters re the Soviet Union published in the *Manchester Guardian*, Feb. 1927; press cuttings (**Class E, vol. 2**). Permission to consult parts of this collection must be obtained from the Librarian.

4.17 THOMAS GWYNN JONES PAPERS

Two letters to Jones from O. Rozitis, Secretary of the Latvian Legation in London, 18 Sept., 30 Oct. 1941; postcard from Thomas Evan Nicholas from Russia, ?1935.

4.18 DR HENRY LEWIS PAPERS

Professor of Welsh at University College of Wales, Swansea. Papers include letters re a Russian translation of his book, *Supplement to a Concise Celtic Grammar*.

4.19 J. HERBERT LEWIS PAPERS

Papers include material re the diplomat Sir Charles Hanbury Williams, including a contemporary copy of a note delivered by the Russian government to Wahrendorff (Konrad Heinrich Warendorf), the Prussian Envoy, re the maltreatment of Russian subjects in Prussia, 4 Dec. 1750, German. Papers not fully catalogued.

4.20 LLOYD GEORGE, David, 1st Earl Lloyd George of Dwyfor (1863-1945) (NLW MS 21009E)

Dossier of papers includes notes of speeches made in a debate in the House of Commons re a proposed trading agreement with Russia, 1921.

4.21 LLOYD-JONES, Herbert (NLW MS 10779D)

TS copy of his article, 'The Ukrainian Minority in Poland', *c.* 1935.

4.22 MILITARY STANDING ORDERS (NLW MS 10907D)

Collection includes a copy of the Tsar's Order of the Day to his troops, 15 Sept. 1824, picked up in Sebastopol in 1855, and a list of events and prizes at the Scutari games, held on 16 Apr. 1856.

4.23 MYDDELTON FAMILY PAPERS

Correspondence to unidentified recipients includes 2 letters from John Yorke, Oct. 1854, and 2 letters from ?E. J. Stracey, Oct., Dec. 1854, all from the Crimea.

4.24 NICHOLAS, Revd T. E.

Papers of Revd Nicholas (1879-1971), communist and poet, include: letters from Sh. Saklatvala, 1928, and Molinov at the Soviet Embassy, 1942; satirical poem by Ivy Litvinov on 'The Death of the Tsar'; a receipt signed by Trotskii for a parcel which he had sent to the Moscow branch on the International Workers' Famine Relief Committee, 1924.

4.25 NOYADD TREFAWR COLLECTION

Papers relating to the Lewes family include notes by Capt. Thomas Lewes (1742-95) on the geography, population, society, trade, ethnography, religion and national character of Russia, n.d., ?*c.* 1776.

4.26 G. E. OWEN COLLECTION
Includes 3 bundles of papers re the Macey family in Russia. Mr N. Macey was a teacher of English language at the St Petersburg School of Commerce, and his children worked in Russia as tutors in noble families. The papers are unsorted and unlisted, but comprise family letters, certificates of proficiency in foreign languages, poems, and translations of literature, commercial agreements, memoranda books, MS musical score and some printed material, mostly 1830s and 1840s with some earlier material. Mainly English, some Russian, German and French. Apply to the Keeper.

4.27 PENNANT, Thomas (**NLW MS 21692C**)
Miscellaneous notes include notes on the time allowed the courtiers who attended the Russian Embassy to China to go from Irkutsk to St Petersburg.

4.28 E. G. B. PHILLIMORE PAPERS
Papers include 32 letters, 1747-72, to Dr James Mounsey, physician to Empress Elizabeth of Russia. Correspondents from Russia include Robert Keith, John Rogerson, John Thomson and Joseph Canning. Papers not yet fully catalogued.

4.29 PLAS YOLYN MSS (**NLW MSS 1140-11481**)
Poems in Russian and English and a Russian vocabulary, n.d., 18th century (**NLW MS 11469D**).

4.30 RAMSAY MSS (**NLW MSS 11574-11593**)
Papers of Sir Andrew Crombie Ramsay (1814-91), Director-General of the Geological Survey, include a letter from him to his brother, William Ramsay, re the reception for the Russian Tsar at the Foreign Office, n.d. (**NLW MS 11590D**).

4.31 REID, Douglas A., M.D. (**NLW MS 8475C**)
Letters from the Crimea, 1855-6.

4.32 RENDEL PAPERS
Letters to Stuart Rendel, 1st Baron Rendel (1834-1913) include references to the Russo-Japanese War.

4.33 REPORTS ON EDUCATION (**NLW MS 12133D**)
A composite volume of the period *c.* 1764-5 containing transcripts and drafts of reports on education in England, Wales, Ireland and elsewhere, collected by a Russian commissioner with a view to establishing an educational system in Russia. Reports include: 'Reflexions sur l'utilité de deux Sociétés de Traducteurs, établies à St Petersbourg & à Moscou', 'Doutes touchant le Projet pour avoir 4 différentes sortes de Grandes Ecoles', 'Projet de deux Grandes Ecoles, ou Séminaires Séculiers, l'un à St Petersbourg, & l'autre à Moscou'.

4.34 RYLAND, John (**NLW MS 14348**)
Copy of letter from John Ryland, founder of the Baptist Missionary Society, to the Empress of Russia, describing the work of the Baptist Mission in India, n.d., 19th century.

4.35 NASSAU SENIOR PAPERS
Papers of Nassau William Senior (1790-1864), Professor of Political Economy at Oxford, include his travel journals which comment upon the Crimean War, the Eastern Question, Alexander II and Russian policies in general, 1851-63 (**A7, 10, 16, 19-20, 28-30, 33, 35, 38, 41, 50**). *See card index for details.*

4.36 SLEBECH PAPERS

Papers of the de Rutzen family include: letter from --- to the Baroness de Rutzen, referring to the death of the writer's husband at Inkerman, 28 Feb. 1857 (**2486**); pedigree charts of the Romanov dynasty (**3359**); notes on genealogy of the de Rutzen family of Courland (**4087, 4092, 6204-36, 6261-79, 6365-8, 7467**).

4.37 SUMMERS, J. A. (**NLW Misc. Vol. 318**)

MS and TS copies of Summers' book, *The Red and the Black* (1979), in which he describes his visit to Russia and impressions of the Soviet Union.

4.38 LLEUFER THOMAS MSS (**NLW MSS 3601-3640**)

Papers of Daniel Lleufer Thomas, Secretary of the Welsh Land Commission, include 2 lists of Welsh families in 'Hughesofka' (Yuzovka, now Donetsk), Russia, sent to him by John I. Hughes, son of John Hughes who founded the colony, and the Russian Embassy, together with correspondence, 1896 (**NLW MS 3617E**).

4.39 TREDEGAR COLLECTION

Includes letters from the Crimea, 1854-5, by Godfrey Charles Morgan, afterwards 2nd Baron Tredegar (1831-1913), and by Frederic Courtenay Morgan. TS copies of the letters are available in the Search Room.

4.40 WIGFAIR MSS (**NLW MSS 12401-12513**)

Letters to John Lloyd of Wigfair (1749-1815) from William Davies Shipley, Dean of St Asaph, introducing a ?Russian traveller, and from Willie Wynne re Napoleon in Russia (**NLW MS 12422D**).

5.1-2

ARMY MUSEUMS OGILBY TRUST

Connaught Barracks, Duke of Connaught Road, Aldershot, Hampshire GU11 2LR

By appointment.

5.1 HAWLEY, Gen. Robert Beaufoy (*c.* 1820-98)

66 letters written from the Crimea, 1854-6.

5.2 SPENSER WILKINSON PAPERS (**Reg. No. OTP 13**)

Papers of (Henry) Spenser Wilkinson (1853-1937), military historian and journalist, include letter from Gen. Sir Ian Hamilton re Russia, 30 Mar. 1904 (**/23/12**) and typescripts and notes re Count H. von Moltke's plans against Russia and France, n.d. (**/52**).

6.1

QUEEN ALEXANDRA'S ROYAL ARMY NURSING CORPS MUSEUM

Regimental Headquarters Q.A.R.A.N.C., Royal Pavilion, Farnborough Road, Aldershot, Hampshire GU11 1PZ

By appointment.

6.1 Letters and pictures relating to Florence Nightingale's work during the Crimean War.

7.1-2

REGIMENTAL MUSEUM OF THE ROYAL CORPS OF TRANSPORT

Regimental Headquarters, Buller Barracks, Aldershot, Hampshire GU11 2BX

By appointment.

7.1 Ledger containing the record of Crimean War shipments, 1854-7.

7.2 Report of the Commission of Inquiry into the Supplies of the British Army in the Crimea, 1855.

8.1-28

ROYAL ARMY MEDICAL COLLEGE HISTORICAL MUSEUM

Keogh Barracks, Ash Vale, Aldershot, Hampshire GU12 5RQ

By appointment by application to the Curator. Cyclostyled catalogue, 1958, with later supplements; handlists of major collections. Documents with the classmark **801/** form part of the Mytchett Collection of documents and photographs relating to the Army Medical Services accumulated at the Royal Army Medical College Historical Museum, 1951-71.

Crimean War Papers

8.1 BRACEBRIDGE MSS (**271, 494**)
Papers of Charles Bracebridge include: 6 folders of letters to Florence Nightingale at Scutari re supplies, missing relatives, remedies for certain illnesses, and letters of thanks, 1854-5; 'Women at Crimea' containing lists of donations for soldiers' wives and widows and supplies of clothing, *c.*1855; account of conditions of soldiers' wives and widows at Scutari and Constantinople and attempts at relief; extracts of letter by the officer commanding the Royal Engineers re the supply of water to the Hut Hospital, Balaclava, 2 Nov. 1855 (**271**). *See handlist for details.* Letter by Bracebridge describing conditions in Scutari Hospital, Nov. 1854 (**494**).

8.2 SIR JOHN HALL MSS (397)

Inspector-General of Hospitals and Chief of the Medical Staff during the Crimean War. Papers re the Crimean Expedition, 1854-5, including papers on medical personnel, patients, casualties, admissions and discharges, medical supplies and equipment, ambulances, sanitary conditions, proceedings of the Board of Survey, Committees of Medical Officers and Courts of Inquiry, letter-books of correspondence between Hall and the War Office and re supplies and hospital ships (**F/25-95**); Crimean diaries, 1854-6 (**F/104-6**). *See handlist for details.*

8.3 LONGMORE MSS (1139, 637)

Papers of Inspector-General Sir Thomas Longmore in the Crimea include: medical memos re stores and transport, returns of the sick and wounded, notes on the Medical Department, 1855-6 (**1139/LP.9-12**); correspondence including letters from the Crimea, 1855-6 (**L.21/1-29**); correspondence with John Birkett from the Crimea, 1855-6 (**L.34/1-26**); press cuttings re the Crimean War and other campaignss (**L.105/1-12; 110/1-5**). Correspondence from Longmore and others in the Crimean War (**637**).

8.4 Press cuttings re the Crimean War (**27**).

8.5 TS copies of letters from Asst Surg. A. H. Taylor to his parents from the Crimea, 1854-6 (**156; 801/1/8**).

8.6 Records of No. 1 Pathological Board Balaclava of case notes and post mortem reports from the General Hospital, Balaclava, 1856 (**192**).

8.7 Medical Register of certain cases treated in London, 1855-6 (**193**).

8.8 Pathological register of cases in the Camp before Sebastopol by Asst-Surg. J. H. Ross, 1856 (**194**).

8.9 Pathological registers of cases in the Camp before Sebastopol by Surg. D. G. Greig (**195-6**).

8.10 Pathological register of cases in the Highland Division in the Crimea, 1856 (**197**).

8.11 Letters and Crimean diary of D. M. Greig (**226**); copies of the Crimean letters (**801/6/7**).

8.12 Papers of Surg.-Maj. T. E. Hale re the Crimea including account of the assault on the Redan (**270**).

8.13 Photocopy of letter from Sir A. Smith to Sir John Hall from the Crimea, 24 Dec. 1855 (**322**).

8.14 Letters of Pte W. Hudson of the Rifle Bde from the Crimea (**339**).

8.15 Photocopy of letter by Surg. H. T. Sylvester from Scutari, 4 Sept. 1854 (**348**).

8.16 Memoirs of Dep.-Surg. Gen. W. Cattell covering the Crimean War (**391**).

8.17 TS copies of letters by F. Reynolds from before Sebastopol, 1855 (**399**).

8.18 Copies of Crimean letters of William Markham of the Rifle Bde (**436**).

8.19 'Reminiscences of Scutari Hospitals' by S. Terrot (**532**).

8.20 Crimean diary of Surg.-Maj. William M. Calder, July 1855 - Mar. 1856 (**701**).

8.21 Crimean War diary of Surg.-Maj. A. M. Tippetts (**703**).

8.22 Medical returns of the 46th Regt in the Crimea by Asst-Surg. R. R. Scott (**751**).

8.23 MS articles re the death of Asst-Surg. J. Thomson in the Crimea (**801/6/2**).

8.24 Copies of correspondence of Florence Nightingale (**801/9/1-2**); letters from Florence Nightingale to Staff Surg. G. M. Beatson in the Crimea, Nov. 1855, Apr. 1856 (**902**). *See also* **Bracebridge MSS, 8.1**.

8.25 Copies of papers, notes and pictures of Sgt E. Baker covering his service with the 34th Foot in the Crimea (**801/11/1**).

8.26 Collection of photographs of the Royal Army Medical Services from the Crimea to the present day (**801/24**).

Post-Crimean War Papers

8.27 Newspaper cutting re medical work in Murmansk, 1918 (**842**).

8.28 Booklet, 'From Gulf to Caspian (3 MAC abroad 1916-19)' with photographs and autographs (**1152**).

9.1

WYE COLLEGE LIBRARY

Wye College (University of London), near Ashford, Kent TN25 5AH

By appointment.

9.1 RUSSELL, Sir E. John (1872-1965)
Chemist, Director of Rothamsted Experimental Station, 1912-43. 3 vols of notes on visits to the USSR , 1934, 1937, 1939, and 1 vol. on visit to Poland and Russia, 1930; TS of his book on agriculture in the USSR, *Russia's Changing Farms and Farmers*; notes on Poland and Russia.

10.1-5

BUCKINGHAMSHIRE RECORD OFFICE

County Hall, Aylesbury, Buckinghamshire HP20 1UA

Notice should be given of intended visits to avoid delays.

10.1 BATESON-HARVEY (LANGLEY PARK, SLOUGH) MSS (**D 31**)
Russian passport of Sir Robert Grenville Harvey, landowner and big-game hunter, 1902 (**/H/11**).

10.2 ARCHIVES OF THE EARLS OF BUCKINGHAMSHIRE (D/MH/H/War)

Papers of Robert, Lord Hobart, 4th Earl of Buckinghamshire, (1760-1816) include: memos and reports on the political state of Russia (**R**); intelligence reports from Sir Charles Stuart, Baron Stuart de Rothesay, at Vil'na and St Petersburg, 1801-5 (**S**); copies of treaties with Russia and diplomatic notes (**T**). Papers of Vere Henry, Lord Hobart, (1818-75) include letters on the Crimean War to various correspondents including W. E. Gladstone.

10.3 CURZON (HOWE OF PENN) MSS

11 letters from William Henry Curzon of the 17th Lancers with members of his family from the Crimea, July-Sept. 1855 (**Temporary reference: Box 1, part 1**).

10.4 FREMANTLE MSS (D/FR)

Crimean War papers and correspondence of Adm. Sir Charles Howe Fremantle (1800-69), 1855-6 (**/208-12**).

10.5 HOWARD VYSE (OF STOKE POGES) MSS (Additional) (**D 121**)

Russian tickets, photographic negatives, letter and printed items relating to H. Davidson's trip to Omsk in 1903 (**/67/3**).

11.1

MUSEUM OF THE ROYAL ARMY CHAPLAINS' DEPARTMENT

Royal Army Chaplains' Department Centre, Bagshot Park, Bagshot, Surrey GU19 5PL

By appointment.

11.1 FRASER, Revd Alexander

Scottish Free Church Minister. Diary covering service in the Crimea, 15 Jan. - 7 Sept. 1855.

12.1

NATIONAL UNION OF MINEWORKERS (YORKSHIRE AREA)

Huddersfield Road, Barnsley, South Yorkshire

By appointment.

12.1 Printed reports of delegates to foreign congresses including to the USSR, 1951-6 (**4/544**); report of the Yorkshire Miners' delegation to the USSR, 1956 (**4/545**).

13.1

CUMBRIA RECORD OFFICE, BARROW-IN-FURNESS

140 Duke Street, Barrow-in-Furness, Cumbria LA14 1XW

13.1 MOWAT PAPERS
Papers of J. Mowat include correspondence files, circulars and ephemera relating to the Anglo-Russian Friendship Committee, 1941-46.

14.1-11

BEDFORDSHIRE COUNTY RECORD OFFICE

County Hall, Bedford MK42 9AP.

Handlists; name, place and subject card indexes.

14.1 BARNARD MUNIMENTS (BD)
Letter from Robert Halpin to Lady Catherine Long re the death of her son, Col. Cowell, at Inkerman, 19 Feb. 1855 (**1390/2**).

14.2 BURGOYNE MUNIMENTS (X143)
Diary of Sir John Montague Burgoyne covering his service in the Crimea (**/20**) (published in *Bedfordshire Historical Record Society,* vol.XL, pp. 163-86); letters relating to the Crimean War, *c.* 1854 (**/21**).

14.3 CLAPHAM PARISH RECORDS (P117)
Prayer and thanksgiving for the end of the Crimean War, 1856 (**/1/22**).

14.4 LADY LUCAS' COLLECTION (L)
Project for an answer to the Empress of Russia's declaration, n.d. (**29/558**); 57 letters from Sir James Harris to Thomas Robinson, 2nd Baron Grantham, 1782-3 (**29/559**); summaries of reports from embassies, including Russia, 1782 (**29/598C**). Letters from A. Campbell to Henry Grey, 11th Earl of Kent, re the Tsar causing apprehension, Apr. 1721 (**30/8/8/16**), plot to betray Norway to the Tsar, Apr. 1723 (**30/8/8/21**), the Muscovite raid in Bothnick Bay, 1721 (**30/8/10/21**) and the Tsar, 1722 (**30/8/10/42,44-6,54**). Letter from Thomas Philip Robinson, 3rd Baron Grantham, Earl de Grey, to his aunt Countess de Grey from St Petersburg, 1801 (**30/11/243/2**); letters from James Harris, Ambassador in St Petersburg, to the 2nd Baron Grantham, 1771-82 (**30/14/176/1-49**); de Grey's diaries in Russia, 1801 (**31/114/4,5**). No publication or photocopying of the documents is allowed without the written permission of Lady Lucas. *See handlist for details.* See also **14.9**.

14.5 POTTON PARISH RECORDS (P64)
Special forms of prayer for the capture of Sebastopol, 30 Sept. 1855 (**/7/3**).

14.6 WHITBREAD PAPERS (W)
Letter from J. B. Pettigrew to Samuel Whitbread II re proposed invitation to anniversary festival of Royal Humane Society which was going to present the Tsar with a medal for saving the life of a Russian peasant, 16 May 1814 (**1/3322**); letters re financial difficulties of R. Sutherland, member of Sutherland, Brown Whishaw, Court Bankers in Russia, June-Nov. 1800 (**1/4474-81**).

14.7 Invitation to service of thanksgiving for success in the Crimea, Bedford, 27 Sept. 1855 (**AD 3207**).

14.8 TS copy of medical history of the 55th Regiment in the Crimea in 1855 by Surgeon E. Blake (**CRT 180/374**).

14.9 TS copy of memoirs of Thomas Philip Robinson, 3rd Baron Grantham, Earl de Grey, including his stay in Russia (**CRT 190/45/2**). See also **14.4**.

14.10 Journal, probably of Francis Pym, includes entries re trade with Archangel, 1737-8, Dutch (**PM 2745**).

14.11 Permit to hunt granted to Godfrey Courtney, 1913, Russian with English transl. (**X 649/1-2**).

15.1-35

PUBLIC RECORD OFFICE OF NORTHERN IRELAND

66 Balmoral Avenue, Belfast BT9 6NY

Records are divided into original documents on deposit (prefix **D.**), administrative papers relating to Northern Ireland (prefixed according to department), microfilms (**MIC.**) and transcripts and copies (**T.**). Acquisitions are described in the *Deputy Keeper's Reports* 1966-72 (*Report* for 1972-8 is in progress). Card indexes of persons, places and subjects.

Northern Ireland Official Papers

15.1 CABINET SECRETARIAT SUBJECT FILES (**CAB**)
Papers of the Ministry of Commerce include: convention between the United Kingdom and Lithuania, 1934, and Latvia, 1940, re legal proceedings in civil and commercial matters (**CAB9F/29/22, 26**); correspondence with HM ambassadors in the Baltic re Baltic flax crop, 1924-5 (**CAB9F/52/1**).

15.2 MINISTRY OF COMMERCE DEPOSITS (**COM**)
Articles on Soviet Russia by Harry Sacher of the *Manchester Guardian*, Oct. 1930 - Sept. 1932 (**COM18/8**); application from Russian national for naturalisation, 1948 (closed for 75 years) (**COM87/95**).

Private Papers

15.3 ANNAGHMAKERRIG (CO. MONAGHAN) PAPERS (**D.3585**)
Papers of William Power (1819-*c.* 1916) include: papers re military career including the Crimean War, 1841-76 (**/B/2/1-85**); letter from the Crimea, 6 Sept. 1854 (**/B/3/1**); press cuttings on countries in which he served, *c.* 1840-75 (**/B/8/2**).

15.4 ANNESLEY PAPERS (**D.1503, D.1854**)
Press cuttings, press reports and sketches re Crimean War, *c.* 1855 **D.1503(/11/146, 149**). Albums of photographs of the Crimean War, *c.* 1855 **D.1854** (**/6**); journal of Lt R. J. Annesley describing his voyage to the Crimea, 1854 (**/9/5**)).

15.5 BEECHEY, Richard (T.2479)
Midshipman in HMS *Blossom.* Transcript of notebooks describing voyage to Petropavlovsk and the Behring Straits, 1826.

15.6 BOYLE PAPERS (D.1943)
Papers re Lt-Col. Joe Boyle's service in Rumania, *c.* 1916-19, include references to Russian affairs.

15.7 CARSON PAPERS (D.1507)
Cabinet papers from Col. Blain in Petrograd containing reports on the Russian situation, 1917. Carson papers are in the process of being arranged and re-calendared. Papers not generally available but may be made available by special arrangement. Apply to Archivist.

15.8 CASTLEREAGH PAPERS (D.3030)
Papers of Robert Stewart (1769-1822), Lord Castlereagh and 2nd Marquess of Londonderry, include: letters from British diplomats in Russia whilst Foreign Secretary, 1812-22; references to Russian military activities on Indian border as President of Board of Control, 1802-06. *See handlist for details.* Letters to Frances Anne, Lady Londonderry from Alexander I, French, *c.* 1820s (/NN), and from Prince A. M. Gorchakov and others, *c.*1840s (/JJ1). Letters to Gen. Sir C. W. Stewart from Alexander I (/BB1); letter from Robert Stewart, 1st Marquess of Londonderry, to Castlereagh with account of a visit by a Russian Grand Duke to Mount Stewart, *c.* 1812 (/H); TS copy of letter of condolence from Alexander I (/T2).

15.9 DONOUGHMORE PAPERS (T.3459)
Transcripts of papers of Gen. the Hon. John Hely-Hutchinson, Lord Hutchinson, later 2nd Earl of Donoughmore include: correspondence with Richard Hely-Hutchinson, 1st Earl, re Russia, from Memel and Pillau 1807-08 (/D/42/39-42); papers re mission to Prussia and Russia to negotiate subsidy treaties, Nov. 1806 - Nov. 1807 (/E/26-303), including letters to Donoughmore from Charles Stuart, Secretary of the Embassy in St Petersburg, and Count Stroganov, draft minutes of conversations between Donoughmore and the Tsar, 23? Aug./ 4 Sept. 1807, declaration by the Tsar on dispute with Britain, 26 Oct. 1807, letter from Gen. A. Budberg a copy of letter from George III to the Tsar, n.d. *See list for details.*

15.10 DUFFERIN PAPERS (D.1071)
Papers of Frederick Temple Hamilton-Temple Blackwood, 1st Marquess of Dufferin and Ava, include: references to Russia in papers re his period as British Commissioner on the Great Powers Commission, 1860-1, (H/C); papers and correspondence re his ambassadorship in St Petersburg, 1879-81 (H/J), including diary (H/V/19); references to Russia in Indian Viceregal papers (H/M); private correspondence, including a number of Russian correspondents, *c.* 1855-1902 (H/B/F and MIC.22); TS draft article by Dufferin re Russian experiences, centred on assassination of Alexander II, published in *Youth's Companion,* 1899 (H/W1/16). Papers of Lady Dufferin include: journals during her husband's ambassadorship in Russia, 1879-81, published as *My Russian and Turkish Journals* (J/C1/2); daily journal of guests entertained, 1873-96, including in Russia (J/E/17); account of interviews between Dufferin and Alexander II and Russian officials (J/B/7).

15.11 DUNRAVEN PAPERS (D.3196)
Four letters from Augustus Stafford to Augusta, Countess of Dunraven, from Turkey, the Crimea and Malta re the Crimean War, Sept. ?1854 - Nov. 1855 (/E/13/63, 67, 68, 76).

15.12 EMERSON TENNENT PAPERS (D.2922)
Letters to James Emerson Tennent about some company's (P&O?) trading relations with Russia; the principal correspondent is Charles Manby, 1851, 1867 (/F/2/1-4).

15.13 PAPERS OF MESSRS L'ESTRANGE & BRETT, SOLICITORS (D.1905)
Papers of John Finlay, flax merchant of Belfast, inlude notes of main flax districts and ports on the White Sea and Baltic, *c.* 1853 (/1/91). Documents of Messrs. Carter including note about debtors in Russia, *c.* 1876 (/2/10B).

15.14 FERGUSON, Andrew (D.1130)
General merchant, Londonderry. Out-letter books include references to trade with Russia, 1775-80, 1783-7 (/1,2). *See Mic. 460 for copy.*

15.15 GLENDINNING, LEISH & CO. PAPERS (D.2424)
Linen merchants, Belfast. Papers re County Down Weaving Company include papers re R. Lewin and L. Thal, Riga, 1931-4 (/G/2/11).

15.16 HOLLAND HOUSE PAPERS (MIC.227)
Microfilms of letters from George, later Lord, Macartney to Lord Holland from Russia, 1765-6; microfilm copies of letters received by Macartney re his departure for Russia.

15.17 HUTTON FAMILY PAPERS (D.636)
Letter from Mrs L. Hutton to Henry Dix Hutton mentioning Emperor of Russia (Nicholas I), 8 Dec. 1845 (/18).

15.18 LONDONDERRY ESTATE OFFICE PAPERS (D.654)
Papers of the Stewart family. The commercial papers of Alexander Stewart include correspondence with Stewart *et al.* from agents and concerns in Narva and St Petersburg, and in particular from Michael Thomas from St Petersburg and J. Plowman from Narva, 1726-7 (/B.2./41, 67, 75, 78-9, 81, 86, 90, 106, 106A, 124).

15.19 MACARTNEY PAPERS (D.572, D.2225, MIC.382, T.2513)
Papers of Lord George Macartney (1737-1806), Envoy Extraordinary to St Petersburg, include: letters to him from various people re Russian affairs, 1769-70, 1795, 1801 (/2/106, /2/109, /3/138, /6/108, /21/50); copy of petition by a bankrupt addressed apparently to Catherine II, French (8/7/63); letter to Macartney, unsigned, may be from Catherine II, French, *c.* 1767 (/19/2) (D.572). Copy of articles IX-XVI of a treaty between Russia and Denmark, n.d. (/1/1); copy of address from the members of the British factory at St Petersburg to Macartney on the completion of the Treaty of Commerce with Russia, *c.* 1767 (/1/2) (D.2225). Microfilm of commonplace book of Lord George Macartney comprising 'Abrégé de l'Histoire Anecdote de l'Académie Imple de Sciences de St Peterbourg par M. Stehlin', 'Short account of little Russia or Ukraine' (/2) (MIC.382). Transcripts of two vols of dispatches sent by Macartney from Russia, 1765-6 (T.2513).

15.20 MEADE-CLANWILLIAM PAPERS (D.3044)
Papers of the Meade family include many references to Russia. The Woronzow (Vorontsov) papers include 4 volumes of autobiographical and biographical material on Count, later Prince, Mikhail Semenovich Vorontsov (son of Semen Romanovich Vorontsov), 1803-56 (/C/1-4); letters to Vorontsov from his sister Catherine, and re Russian affairs, newspaper cuttings re Vorontsov and Russian affairs, miscellaneous papers, mostly in Russian, autobiographical and biographical papers re Count Simon (Semen Romanovich) and Prince Mikhail Vorontsov, 1815-56 (/C/5). *See summary list for details.* Papers of Richard George Francis Meade, 3rd Earl of Clanwilliam include: memo

on Tsar Alexander, his administration and army, by Maj. Karl Josef Clam-Martinez (**/F/15-16**); letter from Baron P. Brunnow, Russian Minister in London (**/F/18**). *See calendar for details.* Papers of Sir Robert Henry Meade include : letters from M. Vorontsov, Princess D. Lieven (**/J**). *See summary list for details.* Autographs of Russian Princes and Catherine, Grand Duchess of Russia, sister of Alexander I (**/R/3-4**).

15.21 MONTGOMERY PAPERS (T.1638)
Transcripts of papers of Capt. Robert James Montgomery include copies of his letters from the Crimean War to his family, related letters and copies of various papers re Crimean War, Apr. 1854-?Aug. 1855 (**/18/1**).

15.22 O'KANE (SOLICITORS) PAPERS (D.3239)
TS (corrected) of a portion of a draft of *With the Cossacks, being the story of an Irishman who rode with the Cossacks throughout the Russo-Japanese War* by Francis McCullagh, published 1906 (**/4/8**).

15.23 MISCELLANEOUS PAPERS PURCHASED FROM J. W. PARKER (D.1222)
Letter from E. F. V. Knox to George Nathaniel Curzon, Lord Curzon, re distrust of the British Embassy in Petrograd, 7 Aug. 1915? (**No. 62**). Letter from I. Kamehomoctckin (?Kamenomostskii), Vladivostok, to S. Tolkovskii, President of the Zionist Organization re formation of a Jewish Legion in Siberia and Russia, 12 Nov. 1918 (**No. 64**).

15.24 ROSS OF BLADENSBURG PAPERS (D.2004)
Papers of David Ross of Bladensburg include: article and notes on the Turkish Question; papers re Russian foreign policy, Russian church and religion, 1835-53 (**/2**). Papers of Sir J. F. G. Ross of Bladensburg include material re Russia and the Balkans, 1878-9 (**/4/19-22**).

15.25 SAVAGE PAPERS (D.618)
Letter from Capt. Francis W. E. Savage enclosing corrected printer's proofs of an eye-witness account of the battle of Chernaya, 16 Aug. 1855 (**/144**).

15.26 SHARMAN CRAWFORD MANUSCRIPTS (D.856)
Letter from Richard Cobden to William S. Crawford re Cobden's opposition to the Crimean War fever, 27 Jan. 1855 (**/D/125**).

15.27 SMILES PAPERS (D.3437)
Letter from Sir Walter Smiles to his mother re Russian experiences, 27 May 1916; Russian identity pass, 1917; press cutting and pamphlet (**/B/1-5**).

15.28 SMILEY, Capt. Samuel (D.2723)
Captain of merchant ship *Lady Russell*, engaged in carrying supplies in the Crimean War. Letters, lists of supplies, wages for crew, *c.* 1855-6 (**/1/27-33, /2/3-5**).

15.29 WILSON FAMILY PAPERS (D.2133)
Four notebooks by Charles Monck Wilson re service in the Crimean War, 1851-6 (**/Box 3**).

15.30 Journal of Robert Thompson of trip to Eastern Mediterranean, including visit to Scutari, 1854 (**D.1559/6**).

15.31 Microfilm of out-letter book of John Cooke, shipping agent in Londonderry, Jan. 1837 - Mar. 1847, inluding letters to Riga (**MIC.112**). *See handlist for details.*

15.32 Microfilm of letters from J. Beatty, civil engineer, to his wife describing the construction of military supply railways in the Crimea, 1854-5 (**MIC.166**).

15.33 Transcripts of testamentary papers relating to the death in Moscow of Capt. James Waughope and the provisions under his will for his widow Helen Maxwell also Waughope, Ballygraffan, County Down, 1632-8 (**T.1256**).

15.34 Transcript of letter from R. A. Gracey to his cousin from the Crimean War, 26 Jun. 1855 (**T.1752/4**).

15.35 Transcript of two letters to William Yeames, Consul in Taganrog, 1818, 1823 (**T.2857**).

16.1-5

HUMBERSIDE COUNTY RECORD OFFICE

County Hall, Beverley, North Humberside HU17 9BA

16.1 MISS L. BIRD OF BEVERLEY MSS (**DDBD**)
Account book of Chevalier John Paul Bezerra of Haya and Seixas, Portugal, with clients in Amsterdam, London and St Petersburg, 1793-1814 (**87/18**).

16.2 CHICHESTER-CONSTABLE OF BURTON CONSTABLE MSS (**DDCC**)
Map of Russia and Turkey 'shewing the various places of interest connected with the Seat of War', n.d. 1850s (**152/9**); plan of Kronstadt with details of fortifications and inset map of Kronstadt and St Petersburg, 1854 (**Acc. 1749**).

16.3 GRIMSTON OF KILNWICK MSS (**DDGR**)
Papers of Lady Waechter de Grimston include: remarks on Count S. Algarotti's letters mainly re St Petersburg, *c.* 1770 (**38/158**); letters re William Maister going to St Petersburg to enter into partnership there, 1753 (**42/3**); letter re death of Maister in St Petersburg, 5 Dec. 1758 (**42/8**). Papers belonging to Lady Du Cane include letters from Sir John Norris to Capt. Medley re endeavours to attack and destroy Russian ships in the Baltic, 8, 13 May 1720 (**39/10**).

16.4 MACTURK & SON, SOLICITORS, SOUTH CAVE MSS (**DDMT**)
Fragment of a letter from John Pulleine to his wife from Moscow, n.d. *c.* 1800 and letter from Bayley in St Petersburg to Smith in Moscow re copy of Joseph Smith's will, 1817 (**296**).

16.5 TRUSTEES OF THE SALTMARSHE ESTATE MSS (**DDSA**)
Correspondence and diary of Harry Denison covering service in the Crimea, 1854-6 (**1077, 1122**).

17.1

BIRMINGHAM CHAMBER OF INDUSTRY AND COMMERCE

PO Box 360, 75 Harborne Road, Birmingham B15 3DH

Access by appointment for *bona fide* researchers.

17.1 The manuscript minutes of the Council of the Chamber are held from 1813. The minutes for 1903 contain references to the impact of the Russian customs tariff.

18.1-3

BIRMINGHAM REFERENCE LIBRARY, ARCHIVES DEPARTMENT

Chamberlain Square, Birmingham B3 3HQ

18.1 BOULTON & WATT COLLECTION
Letters from John Robinson to Jasper Watt from St Petersburg, 1768, 1771.

18.2 MATTHEW BOULTON PAPERS
2 boxes of letters containing *c.* 200 items re Matthew Boulton's dealings with the Russian Mint, 1796-1805 (**Russian Mint 1 & 2**); 3 letters from Alexander Baxter, Russian Consul in London, to Boulton re commissioning of works on the Mint in St Petersburg and offering an introduction for Mr Novosetzoff (?Novosil'tsev), 1896-98 (**Letters 'B' 282-85**).

18.3 GLASTON FAMILY PAPERS
Diary of Pte Thomas Berry of the 47th Regiment of Foot covering his service in the Crimea, 1854-5 (**612500**).

19.1-4

BIRMINGHAM UNIVERSITY LIBRARY

Special Collections Department, Main Library, University of Birmingham, PO Box 363, Birmingham B15 2TT

Access to *bona fide* researchers by written appointment.

19.1 CARR PAPERS
Papers of Professor E. H. Carr will eventually be transferred to the University Library, but are closed at the moment while his biography is being written. Apply to Librarian for Special Collections.

19.2 DOLGORUKOV LETTERS
43 letters from Vasilii Dolgorukov to Count Pavel Benkendorff, 1915-16.

19.3 PASHKOV LETTERS
Letters to Col. Vasilii Pashkov, ?late 19th century. In the process of being catalogued. Not available until catalogue is completed.

19.4 SHISHKIN PAPERS

Papers of Nikolai Pavlovich Shishkin, diplomat. Material re Balkans, Near-Eastern and Far-Eastern affairs includes: memos, documents, letters and reports on the Balkans, 1853-61, 1864-6, French and Russian; copies of reports from the Asiatic Department of the Foreign Ministry to Alexander II, 1856-7; report on western Siberia, 1882 (**SP 1-13**); documents, reports and copies of letters re Balkan and Serbian affairs, 1853-73, French and Russian (**SP 13**); Shishkin's passports and visas, 1880-1914 (**SP 14/1-7**); miscellaneous souvenir programmes, menus etc., 1883-98 (**SP 15/1-26**); correspondence arranged by name, 1876-1902 (**SP 31-52**); letters, telegrams and documents addressed mainly to Shishkin from many parts of the world, 1876-1902 (**SP 53-6**). Literary manuscripts consist mainly of letters and writings of N. V. Gogol', but also include MS copies of writings of Konstantin Sergeevich Aksakov and Ivan Sergeevich Aksakov, and miscellaneous royal letters including a secret instruction to Prince A. A. Vyazemskii by Catherine II and letters from M. Speranskii, N. M. Karamzin and Count F. V. Rostopchin to Alexander I (**SP 53-6**). *See handlist for details.*

20.1

CENTRE FOR RUSSIAN AND EAST EUROPEAN STUDIES

The University of Birmingham, PO Box 363, Birmingham B15 2TT

20.1 The Centre holds microfilms of selected items from the United States' Department of State relating to the internal affairs of Russia and the USSR, 1910-39, copied from the US National Archives.

21.1

SELLY OAK COLLEGES LIBRARY

Birmingham B29 6LE

Holds the archives of the British Council of Churches. Access by appointment.

21.1 FELLOWSHIP OF ST ALBAN AND ST SERGIUS (TATLOW'S PAPERS)

Papers include: Tissington Tatlow's correspondence with and on behalf of Nicolas Zernov, 1932-7; memoranda etc re Archpriest Sergei Bulgakov's scheme for inter-communion, 1933-5; annual reports, executive committee minutes by Zernov; papers re visit of Professor G. Florovskii, 1933; papers re Anglo-Orthodox work undertaken by Zernov's committee, 1932; minutes of Russian Clergy Aid fund, 1935.

22.1

WOODBROOKE COLLEGE, BEVIN-NASH LIBRARY

1046 Bristol Road, Birmingham B29 6LJ

By appointment.

22.1 Letter from Daniel Wheeler, from '5 Virst Moscow Road', to the Friends of Balby Monthly Meeting, 1823.

23.1-10

ROYAL SIGNALS MUSEUM

Blandford Camp, Blandford, Dorset DT11 8RH

By appointment.

23.1 Diagram of signal communications, North Russian Expeditionary Force, 1918 (**331.21/20**).

23.2 Circuit diagrams of Sebastopol, n.d., the Volunteer Army, HQ Rostov, May 1919, and the 3rd Corps, Don Army, 17 Aug. 1919 (**331.21/21**).

23.3 Letter from GHQ North Russian Expeditionary Force awarding service medal to Sgt H. B. Nield, 12 Nov. 1917 (**331.21/22**).

23.4 First report on signals with the British Military Mission to South Russia, *c.* 1919 (**331.21/23**).

23.5 Visual signals between British Military Mission HQ and HQ of the Military Governor of Novorossiisk, 24 Mar. 1920 (**331.21/24**).

23.6 Memo on signal service; diary and stores account for South Russia and Constantinople, 1919 (**331.21/25**).

23.7 Communications plan of the Allied forces in Archangel, July 1919 (**331.21/26**).

23.8 Miscellaneous papers re communications in South Russia, 1919-20 (**331.21/27**).

23.9 Second and third official report on the signal service in South Russia, May 1919 - Mar. 1920 (**131.21/28**).

23.10 Rules and notes for guidance for the British Military Mission, South Russia (**331.21/29**).

24.1-2

REGIMENTAL MUSEUM OF THE DUKE OF CORNWALL'S LIGHT INFANTRY

The Keep, Bodmin, Cornwall PL31 1EG

By appointment.

24.1 Album of water-colours of the Crimea by Lt W. J. Foster, 46th South Devon Regt.

24.2 Diary of a Russian officer picked up afer the fall of Sebastopol, containing a number of small prints.

25.1-6

BOLTON METROPOLITAN BOROUGH ARCHIVES

Central Library, Civic Centre, Le Mans Crescent, Bolton BL1 1SA

By appointment.

25.1 AINSWORTH FAMILY OF MOSS BANK AND SMITHILLS, NEAR BOLTON **(ZAH)**
Letter from Asst-Surg. Matthew Combe from the Crimea, 1855.

25.2 FARNWORTH MUNICIPAL BOROUGH ARCHIVES **(AF)**
Correspondence of the Secretary of Farnworth and Kearsley Aid to Russia Fund with the National Council for British-Soviet Unity and the Joint Committee for Soviet Aid, together with accounts and memos re fund-raising activities, 1942-4.

25.3 HEYWOOD FAMILY OF BOLTON **(ZHE)**
Papers of Robert Heywood (1786-1868) include: account of journey to Russia, 1858; MS and printed copy of paper given by him on his return from Russia to the Bolton Mechanics' Institute; letters from family and friends to Heywood in St Petersburg; tickets for the vessel *Vladimir*; handbill containing illustration of a Russian paddle steamer.

25.4 HICK, HARGREAVES & CO., SOHO IRONWORKS, BOLTON **(ZHH)**
Engineers, formerly Benjamin Hick & Son. Business records, *c.* 1820-1950, include a letter from a millwright re the difficulties of working near Moscow, 1854, and drawings and plans of machinery, mainly for use in the textile industry, exported to firms in Russia including De Jersey & Co., Baltic Spinning and Weaving Co., Egerton, Hubbard & Co., Narva Flaxco, Nevsky Paper Mill, Nevsky Manufacturing Co., and Steiglitz. *See handlist for details.*

25.5 JOHN MUSGRAVE & SONS, GLOBE IRONWORKS, BOLTON **(ZZ/311)**
Photocopy of millwright's agreement and account for the erection of engines supplied to the Catherinehoff Manufactury, St Petersburg, 1873.

25.6 JOHN & EDWARD WOOD, VICTORIA FOUNDRY, BOLTON
(ZWO)
Engineers and millwrights. Business records, include engineering drawings and catalogues of machinery supplied to firms in Russia including Bardiggan, Chadwick, A. & G. Chludow (?Khludov), Koenig, New Samson Mill Co., Russian Imperial Cotton and Jute Co. and Zotoff (Zotov), 1875-1913.

26.1

BRADFORD UNIVERSITY LIBRARY

University of Bradford, Bradford BD7 1DP

26.1 Diary, with photographs, of Mrs Joyce Redman who visited Leningrad in 1932 as the Bradford representative of the Independent Labour Party.

27.1

WEST YORKSHIRE ARCHIVE SERVICE, BRADFORD

15 Canal Road, Bradford, BD1

27.1 POSSELT & CO. LTD
Yarn exporters. Ledgers of Yarn Failures and Debtors include references to firms in Russia and Eastern Europe, 1885-1907, 1936-50.

28.1-2

SUSSEX UNIVERSITY LIBRARY

University of Sussex, Brighton BN1 9QL

28.1 KINGSLEY MARTIN PAPERS (Sx MS 11)
Papers of (Basil) Kingsley Martin (1897-1969), journalist and editor of the *New Statesman*, include: diaries and travel notebooks covering East European visits, 1945-53; address book in the USSR; correspondence re USSR; files re the Cold War, Communism, Russia and World War Two; draft of autobiography including material on Russia and the Cold War; broadcasts re Russia and Trotskii.

28.2 MULTIMEDIA RESOURCE COLLECTION: RUSSIA 1905 - *c.* 1925
500 slides of cartoons, maps, photographs, paintings and posters; 76 filmstrips and 30 sound recordings re Russia and USSR.

29.1-5

BRISTOL RECORD OFFICE

The Council House, College Green, Bristol BS1 5TR

29.1 COURAGES (WESTERN) LTD PAPERS **(35740)**
Brewers. Foreign letter book of Georges, Ricketts and Co. includes 2 letters to Thornton Cayly & Co., St Petersburg, re sales of beer, 1818, 1821.

29.2 ELLISON FULLER EBERLE PAPERS **(28049)**
Include menu cards, programmes for dinners, list of royal inspections and photographs of the Bristol Crimea and Indian Mutiny Veterans Association, 1907-14 **(/29a)**.

29.3 PETER GEORG GUSTAV NEBENDAHL PAPERS, 1847-1952 **(21132)**
Vice-consul in Bristol for Sweden, Norway and Russia. Official appointments, naturalization papers, birth, marriage and death certificates.

29.4 SOLDIERS' DEPENDANTS' RELIEF FUND (CRIMEA), 1854-5 **(00369/1-70, 04150/1-2)**
Papers re administration of fund, orders for payments, receipts and donations; treasurer's accounts and bank pass book.

29.5 Account book of the *Snow Fanny*, 1777-91, covering voyages to Kronstadt **(12162)**; bill of lading **(AC/MU/2/17)**.

30.1-5

BRISTOL UNIVERSITY LIBRARY

University of Bristol, Tyndall Avenue, Bristol BS8 1TJ

By appointment.

30.1 LONDON, Heinz (1907-70) **(DM 510)**
Physicist. Correspondence re the 10th International Conference on Low Temperature Physics, Moscow, 1966, includes correspondence with P. L. Kapitsa **(85)**.

30.2 POWELL, Cecil Frank (1903-69) **(DM 517)**
Physicist. TS article re his visit to Russia, 1955 **(131)**; TS paper re opening of final session of the Cosmic Ray Conference, Moscow, ?1959 **(146)**; TS introduction of Professor A. G. Masevich, Feb. 1960 **(151)**; TS article for *Pravda*, 1967 **(177)**; TS draft address to the Soviet Academy of Sciences, 1968 **(178)**.

30.3 TEICHMAN FAMILY PAPERS
Travel diaries of Emil Teichman include references to Miles Lampson's appointment as Acting Commissioner for Eastern Siberia and the Bolsheviks, 1919 **(DM 317)**; travel diary in the Crimea of Maj. Oskar Teichman, 1902 **(DM 317)**; TS draft of life of Ivan Stefanovich Mazeppa and description of the Cossacks in the Ukraine, 1928, 1931 **(DM 518)**; TS diaries of journeys in Eastern Europe, 1902, and through Russia to the Levant by Oskar and Eric Teichman, 1904 **(DM 518)**; letters, 1926-30, re Emil Teichman's diary of journey to Alaska in 1868 **(DM 556)**.

30.4 UNWIN COLLECTION (**DM 851**)
Collection of Emma Jane Catherine Cobden Unwin and Thomas Fisher Unwin includes items re the Society of Friends of Russian Freedom, the Committee for the Relief of Russian Exiles in Northern Russia and Siberia and the Russian Club, 1894-1909.

30.5 12 colour prints of Moscow and St Petersburg, 1799; 2 watercolour paintings of Russian birds, n.d., 18th century.

31.1

THE SOCIETY OF MERCHANT VENTURERS

Merchants' Hall, The Promenade, Bristol BS8 3NH

By appointment. Indexes to the Society's records.

31.1 There are a few references to Russian trade in the indexes to the Society's records, for example, on 11 March 1791 the complaint of merchants against the seizure of cargoes of Russian iron was recorded, and on 12 April 1855 it was resolved to present petitions to Parliament praying for a vigorous prosecution of the Crimean War and for the prevention of trade in Russian produce passing through Persia. The series of Wharfage Books, 1654-1840, list all the ships coming into Bristol and their cargoes, but the port from which they sailed is only given from the late eighteenth century.

32.1

BROMLEY PUBLIC LIBRARIES, ARCHIVE DEPARTMENT

Central Library, High Street, Bromley, Kent BR1 1EX

By appointment.

32.1 4 letters from Prince Petr Kropotkin, 1884-1905, 3 to unnamed correspondents and 1 to Mr Collins (**621/1-4**).

33.1

TOWNELEY HALL ART GALLERY AND MUSEUMS

Towneley Hall, Burnley, Lancashire BB11 3RQ

By appointment.

33.1 GENERAL SCARLETT COLLECTION
Papers of Sir James Scarlett, leader of the Charge of the Heavy Brigade in the Crimean War include: lithograph views of the Crimea; commissions and citations of Sir James; letter from Sir James to James Thomas Brudenell, 7th Earl of Cardigan, with account of the Charge of the Light Brigade, 28 June 1863.

34.1

BURY REGIMENTAL MUSEUM

The Lancashire Headquarters, The Royal Regiment of Fusiliers, Wellington ·
Barracks, Bury, Lancashire BL8 2PL

By appointment.

34.1 Diary of William Govett Romaine, Judge Advocate to the Army in the East, covering
the Crimean War, 17 June - 17 Nov. 1855.

35.1-5

SUFFOLK RECORD OFFICE, BURY ST EDMUNDS BRANCH

Raingate Street, Bury St Edmunds, Suffolk IP33 1RX

35.1 GRAFTON MANUSCRIPTS (413; HA 513)
Letters from various members of the family serving in the Crimea, 1854-5 (**433/30; HA
513/11/11, 14-19, 21-22; HA 513/26/22**); journal of Lady Frederick FitzRoy in the Crimea
and other related items, 1854-5 (**HA 513/11/93, 105-18**).

35.2 HERVEY FAMILY PAPERS (941)
9 letters from Count S. Vorontsov, formerly Russian ambassador to Britain, to members
of the Hervey family, 1800-26 (**/52/7; /56/14, 73**); 11 letters from British envoys in St
Petersburg to Frederick William Hervey, 5th Earl of Bristol, as Under-Secretary of State
for Foreign Affairs, 1801-3 (**/56/5, 10, 13**).

35.3 FREDERIC POCKLINGTON PAPERS (695, 1878)
Trench passes, 1855 (**695/1-2**); entries re Crimean War in his diaries, 1853-1914
(**1878/5/8/1-13**).

35.4 Log-book kept by Sir John Wood on a cruise which included St Petersburg, 1891
(**405/2**).

35.5 Letter from J. Death of the Coldstream Guards from Balaclava, and award of medal
to him, 1854 (**1970**).

36.1

CAERNARFON AREA RECORD OFFICE

County Hall, Shire Hall Street, Caernarfon, Gwynedd LL55 1SH

36.1 NEWBOROUGH PAPERS (XD2)
Letters, *c.* 1808-25, of Maria Stella Chiappini, wife first of Lord Newborough and then of
Baron Ungern-Sternberg of Estonia, include references to Estonia. Catalogue in
preparation.

37.1-14

REGIMENTAL MUSEUM OF THE ROYAL WELCH FUSILIERS

Caernarfon Castle, Caernarfon, Gwynedd

The museum and library are undergoing reorganization and there are no research facilities at present. Apply to Curator.

37.1 Diary of Sgt George Newman covering service in the Crimea, Nov. 1854 - Oct. 1855.

37.2 Various documents and photographs re Sgt (later Maj.-Gen.) Sir Luke O'Connor, VC, KCB.

37.3 Regimental Orders of the 1st Bn Royal Welch Fusiliers, 19 Mar.-11 Sept. 1855 **(270)**.

37.4 Newspaper cuttings and copy letter re the capture of the Russian guns at Alma by Capt. E. W. D. Bell, VC **(279, 1859)**; 5 letters from Bell to his family from the Crimea, 1854 **(315/1-5)**; letter from William Russell to Bell, 19 Apr. 1856 **(315/5-6)**; copy of claim by Bell for award of the VC, n.d. **(774/3)**.

37.5 Digest of service of the 1st Bn Royal Welch Fusiliers covering details of action, casualties, troop dispositions etc. in the Crimean War, 1854-6 **(286)**.

37.6 Diary of Lt B. Granville covering service in the Crimea, 4 Apr. 1854 - 25 Dec. 1858 **(380)**.

37.7 Report of officers and men claiming the award of the Victoria Cross, n.d. **(460)**.

37.8 General Orders from Headquarters before Sebastopol, 1855 **(753)**.

37.9 Letters to Lt-Col. Bunbury from Lord Dynevor and W. P. Forster re strength of the regiment, 1856; statement of casualties, 4 Apr. 1854 - 4 Apr. 1855 **(785/1-5)**.

37.10 40 letters from 2nd Lt B. T. Griffith to his parents from the Crimea, 8 July 1855 - 25 Jan. 1856 **(1707)**.

37.11 Memorials to Lt H. Anstruther and booklet 'A Flower Plucked from the Banks of the Alma', 1856 **(1864)**.

37.12 11 photographs by R. Fenton of Sebastopol and vicinity, 1854-5 **(2260-70)**.

37.13 Copy letter re death of Lt Douglas Dynely, 1855 **(2604)**.

37.14 Medal Roll in the Crimean War of the 1st Bn Royal Welch Fusiliers, including biographical details of those awarded medals **(WO 100/28)**. Research is currently being undertaken on this roll with a view to publication.

38.1-66

CAMBRIDGE UNIVERSITY LIBRARY

West Road, Cambridge CB3 9DR

A Catalogue of the Manuscripts preserved in the Library of the University of Cambridge, 5 vols (1856-67) (photographic reprint 1980); A. E. B. Owen, *Summary Guide to Accessions of Western Manuscripts (other than medieval) since 1867* (1966); R.P. Blake, 'Catalogue of the Georgian Manuscripts in the Cambridge University Library', *Harvard Theological Review,* vol. XXV, no. 3, July 1932, pp. 207-76. Card indexes of names; handlists of major collections.

38.1-59 Western Manuscripts

38.1 ACTON COLLECTION (Add. MSS 4607-5021, 5347-8, 5381-710, 5751-76)
Order book at the British Embassy, Moscow, 19 Aug.-22 Sept. 1856 (Add. MS 4872).

38.2 BALDWIN PAPERS
Papers of Stanley Baldwin, 1st Earl Baldwin of Bewdley, include: papers re Russia, 1923, 1926-9, Russian loan, 1924, Armenia, Nov. 1924 (F.1 /113); letters re Russia, 1923-4, 1926-7, 1929, 1931-2 (F.2 /114-118); letters re arrest of Metro-Vickers engineers, 1933 (F.2 /120). *See index to correspondents for details* and A. E. B. Owen, *Handlist of the Political Papers of Stanley Baldwin* (1973).

38.3 BERNAL PAPERS (Add. MS 8287)
Papers of Prof. J. D. Bernal contain many references to USSR including: papers re science in the Soviet Union, 1950, 1954 (Box 53 B.4.60, 69); paper 'On the death of Joseph Stalin', 1953 (Box 53 B.4.65); papers re life in the USSR, 1956, 1958 (Box 53 B.4.78, 81); broadcasts re USSR, 1957-9 (Box 56 B.5.44, 48); peace papers re USSR, 1949, 1962, n.d. (Box 61 E.1.54, Box 62 E.2.3, Box 66 E.14.7); papers re British-Soviet Society, 1946-67 (Box 77 I.15) and Society for Cultural Relations with the USSR, 1948-58 (Box 79 I.39); correspondence with N. Khrushchev, 1961-2 (Box 83 J.115) and the Soviet Embassy, 1951-67 (Box 87 J.220); papers re visits to USSR, 1931-2, 1949, 1951, 1953-4, 1956 (Box 90 L.4-5, 31, Box 91 L.38-9, 44, 46, 56); papers re Lenin Peace Prize, 1953 (Box 100 O.7); scroll of Academy of Sciences of USSR, 1958 (Box 100 Q.1).

38.4 BLORE, Edward (1787-1879) (Add. MS 8170)
Letter from S. R. Vorontsov to Blore, n.d. (/91).

38.5 CHOLMONDELEY (HOUGHTON) MSS
Sir Robert Walpole's archive includes: warrant for payment of expenses to Samuel Holden for sending horses to Russia, n.d. (79/39); memorial of James Spilman for money lent to a Mr Weber in Russia, 31 Aug. 1725 (80/30); memorial of Russia Company re trouble at Copenhagen, 20 Feb. 1729/30 (80/46,1-3); petition of Samuel Holden for a contract with Russia to be enforced, n.d. (80/264); petition of Russia Company for a Bill to allow import of Persian silk via Russia, n.d. (80/483-4); account of charges for shipping 12 horses, 22 May 1733 (89/13); observations on a British factory at St Petersburg, n.d. (89/31); case of the Russia Company re trading to Persia through Russia, n.d. (89/53); note of a conference of E. M. da Costa and Prince Cantemir (Antiokh Kantemir) re trade and Russia, 1735 (91/87,1-2). *See,* G. A. Chinnery, *Handlist of the Cholmondeley (Houghton) MSS: Sir Robert Walpole's Archive* (1953).

38.6 CREWE PAPERS
Papers of Robert Crewe-Milnes, Lord Crewe include: papers re Economic Conference of Allies at Paris, 1916 (**M/6**); Anglo-Russian agreement in Persia, 1912-13 (**I/14/9**); terms for an understanding with Russia re Tibet, 1913-14 (**I/16/5**). *See index to correspondents for details.*

38.7 DARWIN PAPERS
Correspondence between Charles Darwin and Prof. A. Kovalevskii, 1870, and V. Kovalevskii, 1867-81 (**DAR. 169**).

38.8 DICKEN, Adm. Charles G. (**Add. MS 7351**)
Memoirs cover service in the Mediterranean Fleet during the Russo-Turkish War, 1878-9.

38.9 EVANS, Ulick Richardson (1889-1980) (**Add. MS 8352**)
Metallurgist. Correspondence with F. G. Mann includes recollections of P. L. Kapitsa, 1976 (**D.17**).

38.10 GERHARDI, William Alexander (1895-1977) (**Add. MS 8292**)
Correspondence with his relatives in the USSR.

38.11 GUILLEMARD, Francis H. H. (**Add. MSS 7783, 7957**)
Journals and photographs of visits to the East Indies, Japan and Kamchatka, 1882-3.

38.12 HARDINGE PAPERS
Papers of Charles Hardinge, 1st Baron Hardinge of Penshurst, include: correspondence, letter book, papers, diary as Ambassador in St Petersburg, 1904-06 (**/3, 5-7**). Hardinge's letters, 1907-15, are indexed and include many references to Russia, including letters from Sir Arthur Nicolson, Ambassador in St Petersburg, Sir Cecil Spring-Rice, Chargé d'Affaires in St Petersburg, Count A. K. Benkendorff, Russian Ambassador in London, H. O'Beirne, Councillor of Embassy in St Petersburg, Sir George Buchanan, Ambassador in St Petersburg, Maj. C. J. M. Thornhill, serving in the British Army in Russia, Sir Charles Eliot, Consul-General in Siberia, copy letters by Nicholas II and Nicholas, Grand Duke of Russia, memos re Russia by various authors, photographs of Kiev. *See indexes of correspondents for details* and N. J. Hancock, *Handlist of Hardinge Papers at the University Library Cambridge* (1968).

38.13 HURST, Charles Chamberlain (**Add. MS 7955**)
Geneticist. There may be correspondence and papers re USSR and Soviet scientists. Collection uncatalogued.

38.14 JENKINSON, F. J. H. (**Add. MS 6463**)
Letter from Ivan Kazanou (?Kazanov) to the University, 30 Jan. 1892, Russian (**/1963**).

38.15 KEILIN, David (1887-1963) (**Add. MS 7953**)
Biochemist. Scientific correspondence including with Russian scientists, 1911-38 (**/177-99**).

38.16 KELVIN PAPERS (**Add. MS 7342**)
Papers of William Thomson, Lord Kelvin. Correspondence with Russian scientists, 1890s. *See,* D. B. Wilson comp., *Catalogue of the Manuscript Collections of Sir George Gabriel Stokes and Sir William Thomson, Baron Kelvin of Largs, in Cambridge University Library* (1976).

38.17 KENNET PAPERS
Papers of Rt Hon. Edward Hilton Young, 1st Lord Kennet of the Dene, include: letter from Young to William Allen Jowitt, Earl Jowitt, re visit of delegation of the Supreme Soviet, 20 Feb. 1947 (39/1-2); letter from Young to Lloyd George re Russian treaty, 25 Sept. 1924 (45/7); log of HM Armoured Train in command of the Vologda campaign in North Russia, 1918 (75/6); copy letters from Young to Katherine Marjory Stewart-Murray, Duchess of Atholl, re her book on Russia, 5 Oct. 1931 (80/8). Access to papers by authority of Lord Kennet.

38.18 THE MAYO PAPERS (Add. MS 7490)
Papers of Richard Southwell Bourke, 6th Earl of Mayo, include: Sir A. Buchanan's correspondence re trade, explorations, visits, military organization and expeditions in Central Asia (6.II. a-e); papers re Central Asian trade, routes and agreements (7. III); papers re relations between Persia, Russia and Britain (7. IV); papers re expedition to Bukhara (8. V. b); letters re Sir Thomas Douglas Forsyth's mission to Russia (9. VI. a).

38.19 MIGULIN, Prof. P. P. (Add. MS 5944 no. 73, Add. MSS 7212-15)
Collections of papers mainly re Russian financial policy and literary figures, *c.* 1935-7, Russian.

38.20 MINNS PAPERS (Add. MS 7722)
Papers of Sir Ellis Hovell Minns (1874-1953) include correspondence with Russian and Soviet archaeologists, art historians, historians and numismatists, including: V. M. Alekseev, P. P. Efimenko, V. A. Gorodtsov, B. Grekov, I. E. Grabar', N. P. Kondakov, N. P. Likhachev, V. F. Minorskii, A. V. Oreshnikov, M. I. Rostovtsev, S. P. Tolstov, A. N. Zograf.

38.21 NAPIER SHAW COLLECTION (Add. MS 8124)
Papers of Sir William Napier Shaw, meteorologist, include photograph of Upper Air Commission in St Petersburg, 1904.

38.22 NEEDHAM PAPERS
Papers of Dr Joseph Needham, biologist, include: correspondence with Soviet scientists and re USSR, 1926-42 (6/1-2, 5-6); papers re visit to USSR, 1935-6 (6/3-4); correspondence and articles re Soviet polar expeditions, 1938 (6/7); correspondence and articles re genetics controversy, 1936-41 (6/8); cuttings and correspondence re Russian science in wartime, 1941-2 (6/9); correspondence re *Science in Soviet Russia*, 1941-2 (6/10-11); papers re Moscow celebraton of 220th anniversary of Academy of Sciences, 1945 (6/12-13); paper, 'Visits to Poland and Russia in 1936' (10/6); papers re Cambridge Anglo-Soviet Friendship Committee, 1941-2 (13/2-3).

38.23 NORRISH, Ronald George Wreyford (1897-1978) (Add. MS 8370)
Chemist. Folder of material re Russia and Yugoslavia, n.d. (C.12).

38.24 OGDEN PAPERS (Add. MSS 8309-8314)
Letters from Ivy Litvinov to C. K. Ogden, *c.* 1930-37 (Add. MS 8312).

38.25 SIR HENRY PARKES PAPERS
Memo re Russia (I/4); letters from Baron Nicholas Wrangel (Vrangel'), 2nd Secretary at the Russian Legation in Peking, n.d. (V/2); extracts from treaty between Russia and Japan (VI/b12). Access by prior permission from Matheson & Co., 3 Lombard Street, London EC3.

38.26 PITT, William (**Add. MS 6958**)
Copies of correspondence include: correspondence between A. R. Vorontsov and Count S. R. Vorontsov, 1786-7, French (**/104, 120, 433***); letter from Count I. A. Osterman to S. R. Vorontsov, 17 July 1786, French (**/167**).

38.27 PLUMPTRE PAPERS (**Add. MSS 5784-5867**)
Drafts of letters from J. Plumptre to Alexander I, 28 July, 22 Dec. 1817, and to Count C. Lieven, 28 July, 2 Dec. 1817 (**Add. MS 5864/419, 473**); letter from Lieven to Plumptre, 7 Aug. 1817 (**Add. MS 5864/420**).

38.28 W. ROBERTSON SMITH COLLECTION (**Add. MSS 7449, 7476**)
Letter from Prince Petr Kropotkin to Robertson Smith, n.d. (**Add. MS 7449/D.334**).

38.29 RUTHERFORD PAPERS (**Add. MS 7653**)
Papers of Ernest Rutherford, Baron Rutherford of Nelson, include correspondence with P. L. Kapitsa, 1925, 1927, 1931, 1933 (**K7-K15**), Lenin Electro-Technical School in Kiev (**K27**), K. Yakovlev, 1912 (**Y1**).

38.30 SEDGWICK PAPERS (**Add. MS 7652**)
Papers of Prof. Adam Sedgwick (1785-1873), geologist, include letters from the the Chief of the Corps des Mines re fossils sent from St Petersburg, n.d. (**/100, 112**).

38.31 SEEBOHM, Henry (**Add. MS 4471-6**)
Ornithological journals and travel diaries, including re rivers Pechora, 1875, and Yenisei, 1877.

38.32 SEVER, C. (**Add. MS 7949**)
Diary of a cruise to St Petersburg, 1895.

38.33 THE STOKES COLLECTION (**Add. MS 7656**)
Papers of Sir George Gabriel Stokes. Correspondence with Russian scientists, 1869-97. *See*, D. B. Wilson comp., *Catalogue of the Manuscript Collections of Sir George Gabriel Stokes and Sir William Thomson, Baron Kelvin of Largs, in Cambridge University Library* (1976).

38.34 SUTHERLAND, Sir Gordon Brims Black McIvor (1907-80) (**Add. MS 8353**)
Physicist. Correspondence re visit to Moscow to attend meetings of the Joint Commission for Spectroscopy, Aug. 1958 (**F.6**).

38.35 TEMPLEWOOD PAPERS
Papers of Sir Samuel John Gurney Hoare, 2nd Bt, Visc. Templewood, include: papers of the British Intelligence Mission, Petrograd, 1915-17 (closed) (**II/1**); papers re Russian situation, 1917-24 (**II/2-5**); papers re *The Fourth Seal* and other publications re Russia (**II/5-8, XVIII/3, XXI/1-5**); copy letter from F. A. Golovin to Sazonoff (S. D. Sazonov), 1919; paper, 'The League and the Russian Refugees in Constantinople' n.d. (**D.1**); papers re Sam Hoare's visit to Russia (**P.2, S.1**); letters re wartime Russia, 1916-22 (**S.10**); photographs of Russian Army at Gallipoli, *c.* 1921 (**Ph.2**).

38.36 THOMSON PAPERS (**Add. MS 7654**)
Papers of Sir Joseph John Thomson, physicist, include letters from I. I. Borgman, Aug. 1910 (**B60**); G. A. Brodskii (**B67**); V. Evreinov, Feb. 1913 (**E15**).

38.37 VICKERS LTD
The archive of Vickers Ltd contains material re shipbuilding business with Russia. *See catalogue for details and* E. R. Goldstein, 'Vickers Limited and the Tsarist Regime', *Slavonic and East European Review*, vol. 58, no. 4, October 1980, pp. 561-71.

38.38 WALLACE PAPERS (Add. MS 7341)
Papers of Sir Donald Mackenzie Wallace including re Russian foreign policy, 1908-09, the Russian Revolution of 1905, the agrarian movement, zemstvos and Finland.

38.39 WHIPPLE, Francis John Welsh (Add. MS 8075)
Meteorologist. Paper, 'Siberian Meteor Notes and Taylor's Wave Theory' (/18).

38.40 Copy letters from Elizabeth I to Ivan IV and Theodore, 1570-85/6 (**Dd. III. 20 ff. 27, 37, 41, 43, 44v, 78v, 89, 104, 105v, 230v, 258v, 264**) (copies of the same in **Mm. I. 43**). *See,* A. E. B. Owen, 'Sir John Wolley's Letter-Book as Latin Secretary to Elizabeth I' *Archives*, vol. XI, no. 49, (Spring 1973) pp. 16-18.

38.41 Letter to Robert Carr, Lord Rochester, re Russian trade, *c.* 1613 (**Dd. III. 63 no. 4**).

38.42 Copies of documents re negotiations of Elizabeth I include: 'Instructions for Denmark from her Majesty re treating with Denmark for the opening of trade to Russia', ?1583 (**ff. 27-8**); 'Instructions for Denmark from the Company of Russia, for Mr Harbert' (**f. 31**) (**Dd. IX. 2**).

38.43 State papers including: 'Instructions given by her Majesty the --- of May, 1575, to Daniell Sylvester, beinge then sent to the Emperour of Russia' (**pp. 33-9**); 'Instructions given to Mr Dr Rogers [Daniel Rogers] and Mr Jenkinson [Anthony Jenkinson], beinge sent to Embden to treate with the Kinge of Denmarks Commissioners' re Russian trade (**pp. 150-2**) (**Gg. V. 36**).

38.44 5 letters by John Browne of Trinity from St Petersburg, 1783-5, Latin (**Oo. VI. 95/4**).

38.45 Letter by Reginald Cust from Moscow, Sept. 1853 (**Oo. VI. 97/48**).

38.46 Passport granted to John Lent and John Hebdon by Tsar Alexis, 1652 (**Add. MS 152**).

38.47 Petition to go to Kakhovka to buy horses and leave granted, Sept. 1851. Brought from Sebastopol, 1856. (**Add. MS 4166 no. 63**).

38.48 Collection of letters includes P. Tchaikovsky to John Peile, 16 Dec. 1892, French (**Add. MS 4251/1409**).

38.49 Transcript notes of diplomatic correspondence re Russia, 1619-1764, made from Foreign Office Records by Miss A. E. Seeley, 1895 (**Add. MSS 4288-97, 4305 f. 61v**).

38.50 Notes by Sir Ellis Minns on P. V. Postnikov and I. F. Kopievskii, 25 May 1920 (**Add. MS 4403 no. 266**).

38.51 Notebook by Wladimir Nikonowicz, Polish teacher, re electro-magnetic theory, 1947, Russian (**Add. MS 5959(5)**).

38.52 Papers in Russian for the Mediaeval and Modern Languages Tripos, 29-31 May 1916, 27-29 May 1918 (**Add. MSS 5968/2, 5969**).

38.53 Numismatic album including sketches of Russian coins, 19th century (**Add. MS 5980**).

38.54 University Library Visitors' Book including signatures of V. Kuznetzov and N. K. Krupskaya (**Add. MS 6370**).

38.55 Copies of orders, dispatches, resolutions etc. of Adm. Sir James Dundas and Adm. Sir Edmund Lyons during their command of the Mediterranean Fleet, 1852-6 (**Add. MS 6658**).

38.56 Log of HMS *Hannibal* in the Crimea, 1855-6 (**Add. MS 6659**).

38.57 Copy of *Ulozhenie* of Tsar Alexis, *c.* 1700 (**Add. MS 7352**).

38.58 Military journal and account book of the garrison at Kinburn, 1853, Russian (**Add. MS 7952**).

38.59 '*O razorenii Tsarstva Moskovskago i Knyaze Pozharskom ... 1612-1684*'. A MS history of Russia containing texts of petitions submitted by the streltsy and charters and letters of the Tsars, n.d. (**Add. MS 8291**).

See also Armenian, Georgian and Mongolian manuscripts in the Oriental manuscript section.

38.60 Map Room

38.60 Topographical Postcards Collection and Peck Collection of postcards include views of various Russian cities in 1920s and 1930s.

38.61 University Archives

38.61 Papers relating to individual Slavists; board minutes of the Faculty of Modern and Medieval Languages, 1874-1924; records of inter-services Russian language courses, 1945-60.

38.62-66 ARCHIVES OF THE BRITISH AND FOREIGN BIBLE SOCIETY

The archives of the BFBS consist primarily of the minutes of the Committee and sub-committees, correspondence and financial records. The main series of incoming letters for the years 1857-1900 and 1906-31 are missing, as are some of the early Committee minutes. The basic arrangement of the archive is chronological, not geographical, so that material relating to Russia has to be extracted through use of the subject and name indexes. Individual volumes of minutes are indexed by name, subject and language, and there are separate indexes to volumes of correspondence by name only. Handwritten lists of all correspondents from Russia, mainly missionaries but also including merchants and officials, are available. Amongst these names can be found the following BFBS agents in Russia: Revd Richard Knill (St Petersburg, 1826-33), Revd John Brown (St Petersburg, 1833-40), Revd Thomas S. Ellerby (St Petersburg, 1840-53), Archibald Mirrielees (St Petersburg, 1853-40), William Mirrielees (St Petersburg, 1857-65), Adalbert Eck (St Petersburg, 1865-9), Revd William Nicolson (St Petersburg/Petrograd, 1897-1918), John Melville (Odessa, 1839-67), James Watt (Odessa, 1867-82), Michael Morrison (Odessa, 1882-95), Walter Davidson (Ekaterinburg, 1889-1918). Papers concern the activity of missionaries in Russia, their finances, the staffing and administration of agencies, and bible translation and distribution. The relevant series are:

38.62 COMMITTEE AND SUB-COMMITTEE MINUTES
The minutes of the Committee run from 1807 with some gaps in the early years. The Committee exercised overall control over the Society's operations. Minutes for 1812-26 cover the period of the Imperial Russian Bible Society's existence; later records include material on BFBS agents in Russia. The minutes of the Editorial Sub-Committee run from 1830. This dealt with all questions of bible translation, and oversaw the preparation and publication of the Society's own Russian Bible. There are records of bible translation into Armenian, Estonian, Georgian, Ukrainian and several Turkic languages of peoples of the Russian Empire, and material relating to prominent Russian translators, including V. A. Levisohn, D. A. Chwolson (Khvol'son), N. I. Il'minskii and V. V. Radlov. Other sub-committees dealt with Russian matters from time to time. There are references in the minutes of the Depository and Printing Sub-Committee (from 1817) to the printing of Russian Bibles in England, and in the minutes of the Foriegn Depots Sub-Committee (from 1852) to the administration and staffing of depots and colportage work.

38.63 GENERAL CORRESPONDENCE
Incoming correspondence, 1804-56, 1901-05, is indexed by name of writer, 1804-56, and includes letters from A. N. Golitsyn, V. M. Popov, Count C. Lieven, K. K. von Pol' and BFBS agents in Russia. Outgoing correspondence, 1819-80, 1900-06, 1919-31, will also include letters to BFBS agents in Russia. In addition, there are 2 files of Secretaries' Correspondence : Russia, 1919-27, relating to bible distribution in Russia and account and closure of the Leningrad Depot, and 4 vols of Agents' Books : Russia, 1869-74, comprising copies of letters, principally from W. Nicolson and J. Watt, BFBS agents in St Petersburg and Odessa.

38.64 CORRRESPONDENCE ON TRANSLATIONS
Editorial Correspondence Inwards, 1858-97, and Editorial Correspondence Outwards, 1832-1908, consist of copies of letters relating to translation matters and are indexed by translator and language. Editorial Subject Files run from 1909 and include files on Russian (including Belorussian), Ukrainian and other languages spoken in the USSR. Papers relating to Russian émigré translation work are subject to a 50-year closure period.

38.65 PATERSON PAPERS
Memoirs (1805-50, 4 vols) and papers (1808-47, 3 vols) of John Paterson, BFBS agent and major figure in the formation and activity of the Russian Bible Society. Much, though not all, of this material was published in Paterson's *The Book for Every Land*. Letters to Paterson are listed in a card index.

38.66 WISEMAN PAPERS
Correspondence of W. Wiseman, Secretary for North-East Europe, 1925-9. Wiseman was based in Helsinki, but the collection includes material on the fate of the Leningrad and Siberian depots after the Revolution and on bible distribution and pensions for BFBS workers in Russia. Rough file list.

39.1-2

CAMBRIDGESHIRE COUNTY RECORD OFFICE

Shire Hall, Cambridge CB3 OAP

39.1 COTTON FAMILY OF LANDWADE AND MADINGLEY COLLECTION
Approx. 30 letters from Col. J. H. King and Maj. W. A. King mainly to their mother, Lady Philadelphia King of Madingley Hall, from the Crimea, 1854-5. The collection is in the process of being catalogued.

39.2 THOMAS WALE POCKET-BOOKS
38 pocket-books covering Wale's business interests in Riga, 1724-94, covering journals, personal and business memos, commonplace books, letters and minutes and register of letters, shipping insurance papers and shipping notes, memos on journeys to Riga, accounts of business trips to Moscow and St Petersburg, Riga Commissioners' accounts, notes on Russian politics and trade. *See list for details.* Extracts from the pocket-books have been published in *My Grandfather's Pocket-Book. From A.D. 1701 to 1796* (London, 1883) by Revd H. J. Wale.

40.1-47

CHURCHILL COLLEGE ARCHIVES CENTRE

Churchill College, Cambridge CB3 0DS

By appointment. Documents subject to thirty-year rule. TS *Guide to the Holdings of the Churchill College Archives Centre*; handlists of major collections.

40.1 AGNEW, Stair Carnegie (1872-1940) (**AGNW**)
Company lawyer. Approx. 200 letters from Russia, 1888-1915.

40.2 ARCHIVES OF LORD ALEXANDER OF HILLSBOROUGH (**AVAR**)
Papers of A. V. Alexander include: speeches re Russia, 1943, 1945 (**12/98, 167**); notes on conversations with Ivan Maiskii, 1940, 1941 (**5/4/31, 5/6/5**); correspondence with Edward F. L. Wood, 1st Earl of Halifax, re Russian situation and conquest of the Baltic States, July, Aug. 1940 (**5/4/36, 48**); correspondence with Sir Alexander Cadogan re conversations with Maiskii, 1940, 1941 (**5/4/53, 57, 5/5/17**); TS article on visit of Dynamo football team, Dec. 1945 (**5/10/75**).

40.3 BEVIN, Ernest (1881-1951) (**BEVN**)
Trade unionist, Labour M.P. Papers re Labour Party delegation to USSR, Aug. 1943 (**2/11**); letter to Ivan Maiskii re relief of Leningrad and reply, 19, 22 Jan. 1943 (**3/3**); speech re Soviet delegation visit to Ministry of Labour, 9 Jan. 1942 (**4/3**).

40.4 BRIMELOW, Thomas, Baron (b.1915) (**BIMO**)
TS of interview re his experiences in the Russian section of the Foreign Office, 1945-7.

40.5 BULL, Rt. Hon. Sir William (1863-1931) (**BULL**)
Chairman London Unionist MPs, 1910-29. Letters from Walter Long re Russian trade delegation and Russian policy re Poland, July-Dec. 1920 (**5/2**); letters and reports, largely by Boris Said, re Russian trading relations with Germany and Austria, L. B. Krasin and

the situation in Russia, 1921-2 (**5/8**); press cuttings re Leningrad, 1925 (**5/14**). Consent of the depositors is required before any publication quoting or deriving from these papers.

40.6 CARRON, William John, Baron of Kinston-upon-Hull (1902-70) (CARN)
Trade unionist. Itinerary of visit to USSR, 1955 (**1/9**); report of Amalgamated Engineering Union delegation's visit to USSR, 1955 (**1/10**); photographs of Carron's trip to Moscow, 1955 (**7/3**).

40.7 CHURCHILL, Sir Winston Leonard Spencer (1874-1965) (WCHL)
Additional items include recorded speech re the German invasion of Russia, 22 June 1941 (**WCHL 3/4**). Main collection of papers closed until 10 years after official biography has been completed.

40.8 COCKCROFT, Sir John Douglas (1897-1967) (CKFT)
Nuclear physicist. Papers re Kapitza club including photographs of Petr Leonidovich Kapitsa (**7/1-7**); papers re visits to USSR, 1931, 1936, 1945, 1959, 1965 (**11/1, 4, 6, 10, 15**); papers re I. V. Kurchatov, 1961, 1967 (**18/24**); correspondence with and re Kapitsa, 1921-56, 1962-7 (**20/15-17, 40-44**). Lady Cockroft's permission is needed to consult Sir John's papers.

40.9 CUNNINGHAME GRAHAM, Adm. Sir Angus E. M. B. (1893-1981) (ANCG)
Papers, correspondence and report of a trip to Murmansk with Anthony Eden, 1941 (**II 3/5**).

40.10 DAVIS, Adm. Sir William Wellclose (b.1910) (WDVS)
Vols. 5 and 6 of his memoirs contain references to Russia. Adm. Davis's permission is required to consult his papers.

40.11 DILKE-ENTHOVEN-ROSKILL COLLECTION (DILK+REND)
Dilke papers include: letters to Ashton W. Dilke to his family from Russia, 1869-73 (**6/3-6**); letters to him from Russians including Turgenev, 1872-86 (**6/11**); letter from Prince P. Kropotkin to Virginia Mary Crawford, 15 Oct. 1898 (**9/2**); Russian death certificate and passport of Charles Wentworth Dilke, 1869 (**10/14**); galley proofs of book by Ashton Dilke, *Russian Power,* which was to have been published in 1875 and notes and correspondence about this (**15/1-4**). Enthoven papers include: notes by V. M. Crawford on Germany and Russia, 1886 (**5**); notes on interview with Petr Lavrov (**7**).

40.12 DIRAC, Prof. Paul Adrian Maurice (b.1902) (DRAC)
Physicist. Letters from P. L. Kapitsa, N. W. Timofeev-Ressovskii, Boris Podolskii (**3/7, 11**).

40.13 EDWARDS, Adm. Sir Ralph Alan Bevan (1901-64) (REDW)
Account of Yalta Conference by a WRNS officer, n.d. (**2/20**). Not open to general inspection. Apply to archivist.

40.14 FEATHER, Prof. Norman (1904-78) (FEAT)
Physicist. Correspondence with Soviet physicists. *See catalogue for details.*

40.15 FELL, Capt. William Richard, RN (1897-1981) (FELL)
Private log of Sub-Lt and Lt in the Black Sea, 1919-20 (**1/6**); report on demonstration of X craft for Adm. Kharlamoff (N. M. Kharlamov), USSR Navy, 3 Dec. 1943 (**3/1**).

40.16 FOOT, Sir Dingle (1905-78) **(DGFT)**
Labour MP. Correspondence and papers re Soviet invasion of Hungary, 1956-8 **(5/9)**.

40.17 GODFREY-FAUSSETT, Capt. Sir Bryan Godfrey, RN (1863-1945) **(BGGF)**
Naval equerry to George V. Photograph of Russian Imperial Yacht *Standart* **(3/5)**. Apply to archivist for access.

40.18 GRIGG, Sir Percy James (1890-1964) **(PJGG)**
Secretary of State for War, 1942-5. Correspondence with FM Lord Montgomery re relations with USSR, 1944-5 **(9/8/18, 36, 9/9/36)**.

40.19 HALDANE, T. G. N. (1897-1981) **(TGNH)**
Scientist. Diary, letter and report of his firm re his visit to USSR touring power stations, 1932 **(3/1-3)**.

40.20 HANKEY, Maurice Pascal Alers, 1st Baron (1877-1963) **(HNKY)**
Secretary to the Cabinet, 1912-40. PM's (Lloyd George) statement on Russia, 13 Nov. 1919, in Cabinet Office papers **(8/19)**.

40.21 HARRIS, Theodore (Feodor Minorskii) (b.1916) **(HARS)**
TS account of service in French Foreign Legion, 1940-42, including photograph of himself in Leningrad.

40.22 INGRAMS, William Harold (1897-1975) **(IGNS)**
Diplomat. Briefing notes on local goverment systems in USSR and other countries, 1943-5 **(1/1)**.

40.23 IVANENKO, Prof. D. **(IVAN)**
Box of photographs.

40.24 IVERMEE, Lt R. W. A. **(IVRM)**
Photographs of North Russia and Russian ships, 1918-19. *See list for details.*

40.25 JAMESON, Margaret Storm **(JMON)**
Writer. Diary of visit to Poland, 9-19 Sept. 1945 including references to USSR.

40.26 KENNEDY, Aubrey Leo **(LKEN)**
Diplomatic correspondent of *The Times*, 1919-42. Journals of his experiences in Eastern Europe and the Baltic States, 1919-20, 1938-9 **(1-2, 21-22)**; journal including sketch of Hitler's plan to overrun Turkey and seize Baku and the Ukraine, 1941 **(24)**.

40.27 KNATCHBULL-HUGESSEN, Sir Hughe Montgomery (1886-1971) **(KNAT)**
British Minister to the Baltic States, 1930-4. Diary, 1930-4 **(1/6-9)**.

40.28 LLOYD, George Ambrose, Lord Lloyd of Dolobran (1879-1941) **(GLLD)**
Report on mission to Russia, Oct. 1915 **(9/7)**; subject file on Russia, 1907-12 **(16/37)**.

40.29 McLACHLAN-BEESLY COLLECTION (**MLBE**)
Papers of Donald McLachlan include unsigned papers 'The Naval Mission to Russia 1943-45' (**1/7**) and 'North Russia Convoys 1942-3' (**1/16**). Papers of Patrick Beesly include letters to him from J. C. K. Everett re his experiences in North Russia (**2/40**).

40.30 MEITNER, Prof. Lise (1878-1968) (**MTNR**)
Nuclear physicist. Correspondence with Soviet scientists. Not open to general inspection. Apply to archivist.

40.31 MILLINGTON-DRAKE, Sir Eugen (1889-1973) (**MLDK**)
Diplomat. Scrapbook of photographs including Russia, 1913-15 (**10/1**). Diaries and letter books closed at present but include letters and diaries written in St Petersburg, 1913-14.

40.32 NOEL-BAKER, Philip John, Baron (1889-1982) (**NBKR**)
Labour MP. Many records relating to Russia including: notes and cuttings on Zinoviev letter, 1966-7 (**3/254**); newspaper cuttings re USSR (**4/92, 252, 277, 533, 714**); correspondence and papers of the League of Nations' Russian Refugees Conference, 1921-2 (**4/450**); correspondence on minority groups in Poland and the Ukraine, 1931-3 (**4/560-1**); papers re USSR and disarmament, 1940-60s (**5/110, 115**); papers re League of Nations and Russian and Lithuanian refugees, 1920-21, 1927 (**4X/43, 90**). Section **4/605-52** all relates to USSR and mainly consists of material on Russian refugees, the famine, papers and pamphlets on conditions in the 1920s and 1930s, reports on trials, cuttings and correspondence on Soviet foreign policy and papers re Noel-Baker's visit to Moscow in 1960. *See list for details.*

40.33 O'CONOR, Sir Nicholas (d.1908) (**NIOC**)
Ambassador to Russia and Turkey. Papers, *c.* 100 boxes, closed.

40.34 PHIPPS, Sir Eric Clare Edmund (1875-1945) (**PHPP**)
Diplomat. Draft agreement, with instructions, for Sir W. Seeds for negotiations with USSR, June 1939 (**5/9**).

40.35 THE PHYSIOLOGICAL SOCIETY (**PHYS**)
Archives 1897-1967. References in the minutes to and letter dated 2 May 1927 from Ivan Petrovich Pavlov. Permission to consult the records must be sought from one of the officers of the Society.

40.36 PLUNKETT-ERNLE-ERLE-DRAX, Adm. Sir Reginald A. F. (1880-1967) (**DRAX**)
Draft of article re visit to Moscow, n.d. (**6/5**).

40.37 POUND, Adm. Sir (Alfred) Dudley (1877-1943) (**DUPO**)
Notes on Russian convoys and PQ17, Dec. 1941 - July 1942 (**5/6**).

40.38 ROSKILL, Capt. Stephen Wentworth, RN (1903-82) (**ROSK**)
Historian. Cabinet papers re Zinoviev letter, 1924 (**7/115**); papers re USSR and Soviet Navy, n.d. (**7/191**).

40.39 SPEARS, Gen. Sir Edward Louis (1886-1974) (**SPRS**)
Letters from Russian anti-Bolsheviks, 1919-20 (**1/19**); correspondence with Corporation of Mines and Steamship Owners in Russia, 1920-54 (**1/53**), with I. Maiskii, 1936, 1945 (**1/221**), and with various correspondents re USSR, 1966-7 (**1/301**).

40.40 SPRING-RICE, Sir Cecil Arthur (1858-1918) **(CASR)**

1st Secretary, St Petersburg, 1903-04. Letters to Spring-Rice from Neville Henderson, R. Ronald MacDonald, Leslie Urquhart and others from various cities in Russia, 1905-06 **(1/44, 46, 50, 53, 69)**; letters, memos and copies of letters from Spring-Rice to various correspondents from St Petersburg, 1905-06 **(4/1, 2, 9/4)**; 2 Russian broadsheets, 1904, n.d. **(8/3)**; letters mainly from N. Hartwig, head of the Imperial Russian Legation to Spring-Rice, 1906-07 **(10/3)**.

40.41 STRANG, William, 1st Baron of Stonefield (1893-1978) **(STRN)**

Letters from one of the Metro-Vickers defendants and from Vladimir Poliakoff (Polyakov) describing the situation in the USSR in 1931 **(4/2)**; photographs of the Metro-Vickers Trial in Moscow, 1933, of Eden's visit to Moscow in 1938 and of the Tripartite Conference in Moscow in 1943 **(6/4)**.

40.42 SWINTON, Philip Cunliffe-Lister **(SWIN)**

TS copy and cutting of Zinoviev letter, 1966 **(174/16/4)**; copy letter from Swinton to his wife re Lloyd George and Russia, 1921 **(313/1/1)**; letters from Swinton to Stanley Baldwin from Genoa re negotiations with USSR, 6, 14 May 1922 **(313/1/2)**.

40.43 VANSITTART, Robert Gilbert, Lord Vansittart of Denham (1881-1957) **(VNST)**

Cabinet papers re Russia, 13 Jan.-30 Apr. 1939 **(3/2)**. Not open to general inspection. Apply to archivist.

40.44 WESTER-WEMYSS, Adm. Lord Rosslyn (1869-1959) **(WMYS)**

Papers and lecture notes on the Russo-Japanese War **(2/3)**; papers and letters re operations in the Baltic and Black Sea, 1919 **(5/3, 6/2-3)**.

40.45 WILKINSON, Gerald Hugh (1909-65) **(WILK)**

Report by William B. Ballis on the economic potential of Eastern Siberia as a base for offensive military action, 1942 **(3/3)**; report from the Bitish Embassy, Washington, on Japanese-Soviet relations, Apr. 1945 **(3/4/4)**.

40.46 WILLIS, Adm. Sir Algernon (1869-1959) **(WLLS)**

Diary of Baltic operations against the Bolsheviks, 1918-19 **(3/1)**.

40.47 ZVEGINTZOV, M. (1904-78) **(ZVEG)**

Pre-war papers on a variety of industrial and economic subjects including USSR **(2/4)**; wartime and post-war letters and papers on relations with USSR **(2/5)**; family letters in Russian **(8/4)**.

41.1-8

THE FITZWILLIAM MUSEUM

Cambridge CB2 1RB

Apply in writing to the Keeper. M. R. James, *A Descriptive Catalogue of the Manuscripts in the Fitzwilliam Museum* (1895); F. Wormald, P. M. Giles, *A Descriptive Catalogue of the Additional Illuminated Manuscripts in the Fitzwilliam Museum* vol. 1 (1982); J. A. Fuller-Maitland, A. H. Mann, *Catalogue of the Music in the Fitzwilliam Museum, Cambridge* (1893). Indexes of writers, correspondents and composers.

41.1 Letter from Alexander I to Bentinck (?Lord William Cavendish Bentinck), 2 July 1812 (**MS 24-1961. Voltaire Letters 305**).

41.2 Poem by Herman James Elroy Flecker, 'The Golden Journey to Samarkand'.

41.3 2 letters from Frances Parthenope Nightingale to Mrs Strutt re departure of her sister Florence for the Crimea and recruitment of nurses for the Crimea, Oct. 1855, n.d. (**MS 63-1947, 64-1947**).

41.4 Letter from P. S. Pallas to --- describing travel routes in central Russia, 8 Mar. 1781 (**Perceval Bequest, J.115**).

41.5 Letter from Jane Porter to Sir Richard Philips re a publication on Russian history (**MS 2-1966. Philips Collection**).

41.6 I. Stravinskii, MS musical score, 'Dance of the Lilac Fairy' (**MV MS 1373**).

41.7 Letter from L. N. Tolstoi to Aylmer Maude, 19 May 1901.

41.8 Copy letters from Voltaire to Count I. I. Shuvalov, 13 Aug. 1762, 27 July 1772, 28 Mar. 1775 (**MS 6-1961. Letters of Voltaire ff. 117, 154-5**).

42.1

KING'S COLLEGE LIBRARY

Cambridge CB2 IST

By appointment.

42.1 LOPOKOVA, Lydia (Lady Keynes)
Correspondence and papers including some letters in Russian from her family in Russia and from Russian émigrés and figures in the world of ballet. Apply to the Modern Archivist for conditions of access.

43.1

MAGDALENE COLLEGE, PEPYS LIBRARY

Cambridge CB3 OAG

By appointment.

43.1 Credentials for Charles Howard, 1st Earl of Carlisle, on his appointment as Ambassador to the Court of Muscovy in 1663.

44.1

QUEENS' COLLEGE LIBRARY

Cambridge CB3 9ET

By appointment. M. R. James, *A Descriptive Catalogue of the Western Manuscripts in the Library of Queens' College, Cambridge* (Cambridge, 1905).

44.1 Giles Fletcher, 'Of the Russe Common Wealth', *c.* 1589.

45.1-2

ST JOHN'S COLLEGE LIBRARY

Cambridge CB2 1TP

By appointment. M. R. James, *A Descriptive Catalogue of the Manuscripts in the Library of St John's College, Cambridge* (Cambridge, 1913).

45.1 BROWN, John (d. 1766)
Copy of letter from Brown to the Empress of Russia suggesting a scheme for sending young Russians abroad to be educated, 28 Aug. 1766.

45.2 CLARKSON, Thomas
Papers include a copy of 'Conference with the Emperor of Russia at Paris in September 1815' (Alexander I).

46.1-6

SCOTT POLAR RESEARCH INSTITUTE

University of Cambridge, Lensfield Road, Cambridge CB2 1ER

46.1 BREITFUSS, Leonid L'vovich **(SPRI MS 148-70)**
Administrator and historian of polar research. Papers include reports on Russian and Soviet expeditions and research projects in Artic regions, *c.* 1905-39.

46.2 JACKSON, Frederick George (1860-1938) **(SPRI MS 287)**
British polar explorer. Journals, observations, correspondence and miscellaneous papers re the Jackson-Harmsworth expedition to Franz Josef Land, 1894-7.

46.3 KUPSCH, Walter Otto **(SPRI MS 1029)**
TS photocopy report on visit to USSR under an exchange programme of the National Research Council of Canada and the Soviet Academy of Sciences, 10 Aug.-26 Sept. 1971.

46.4 POPHAM, Hugh Leybourne **(SPRI P48)**
Approx. 150 photographs, with negatives, taken during travels in Siberia, 1894-1900 **(/231)**.

46.5 ROBERTS, Brian Birley (1912-78) **(SPRI MS 1308)**
Polar explorer and administrator. Journal of a visit to the USSR including visits to organizations concerned with polar research in Leningrad and Moscow, 28 May - 9 June 1956 **(/8)**.

46.6 SWEENEY, Edward **(SPRI MS 1389)**
Diary of a voyage to the Yenisei in northern Siberia, July-Oct. 1911.

47.1-7

TRINITY COLLEGE LIBRARY

Cambridge CB2 1TQ

By appointment. M. R. James, *Catalogue of the Western Manuscripts in the Library of Trinity College, Cambridge*, 3 vols (Cambridge, 1900-04); card index of modern manuscripts.

47.1 DAVIES, James Arthur **(R.2.53)**
Papers include notes on national music and instruments of China, India, Egypt, Russia and other countries, dating from *c.* 1860.

47.2 FRISCH, Otto Robert (1904-79)
Physicist. Journal of and correspondence re trip to Moscow and Novosibirsk, Sept. 1970 **(E.43)**.

47.3 LAYTON, Walter Thomas, 1st Baron Layton
Papers on the Milner Mission to Russia, Jan.-Mar. 1917 **(Box 7)**; Ministry of Supply papers on supplies to the USSR, 1941 **(Box 30)**.

47.4 TAYLOR, Sir Geoffrey Ingram (1886-1975)
Aerodynamicist. Telegrams re his foreign membership of the USSR Academy of Sciences, 1966 **(A.63)**; correspondence with P. L. Kapitsa, 1963-73, and photograph with Kapitsa, ˙66 **(D.36; E.12)**; invitations to the jubilee session and 250th anniversary celebrations of t. ˙JSSR Academy of Sciences, 1971, 1975 **(D.101)**.

47.5 THOMSON, Sir George Paget (1892-1975)
Physicist. Notes on 'The Russian Atomic Explosion', *c.* 1948 **(F.167)**; MS and TS draft of 'Soviet thermonuclear scheme with Joffré windings' **(F.201)**.

47.6 8 letters by G. Mathew, consular official in Odessa, 1858 and n.d.

47.7 'Certen notes touchinge the benefitt that may grow to England by the trafficque of English marchaunts into Russia, 1575' signed M. Tok **(R.5.15)**.

48.1

UNIVERSITY BOTANIC GARDEN

Cambridge CB2 IJF

By appointment.

48.1 The files contain letters re visits from Russian and Soviet scientists, the exchange of seeds and the borrowing of herbarium specimens, but there are no indexes or other finding aids for locating these records.

49.1-2

THE BUFFS REGIMENTAL MUSEUM

The Royal Museum and Art Gallery, High Street, Canterbury, Kent

Museum is under reorganization and material is not generally available. Apply to Curator.

49.1 Album of photographs includes photographs of Russia, *c.* 1910 **(Acc. No. 33)**.

49.2 Photograph of New Year greetings sent by the 3rd Narva Regt to the 3rd East Kent Regt, *c.* 1916 **(filed under Imperial Russia)**.

50.1

UNIVERSITY OF KENT LIBRARY

University of Kent, Canterbury CT2 7NU

50.1 JOHNSON ARCHIVE

Papers of Hewlett Johnson, Dean of Canterbury, 1930-63, include much correspondence relating to the USSR covering topics such as support for the USSR during the War, friendship messages to the USSR, the Berlin blockade, the Hungarian rising, the Stalin Peace Prize, Russian visitors to Canterbury and Johnson's visit to the USSR, the relations of the USSR with Britain, Finland, Poland and Korea, economic and military policies of the USSR, and religion, persecution of the Jews, position of women, education, youth policy, secret police, psychiatric abuse and slave labour in the USSR. The collection is only partly listed and access is restricted until the listing is completed. Apply to Librarian.

51.1

COMPANIES REGISTRATION OFFICE

Companies House, Crown Way, Maindy, Cardiff CF4 3UZ. London Search Room, Companies House, 65-71 City Road, London EC1

51.1 Microfiche copies of original documents on all live companies, as well as for most companies dissolved since 1976, can be consulted in Cardiff and London. Files containing the original company documents for live companies and files relating to companies dissolved since 1964 are kept by the Cardiff office, although such records can be sent to London. Material relating to companies dissolved before 1964 has been transferred to the Public Record Office. Indexes are available in the search rooms in Cardiff and London of all live companies (updated monthly) and of dissolved companies, 1964-83. Microfiches and files can be ordered by researchers (a fee is charged) and contain documents relating to the structure of the company, changes of directors, secretaries and registered offices, annual returns and accounts, lists of principal shareholders, details of mortgages or charges and appointments of receivers and liquidators where appropriate. There is no topographical index but records can be found under the names of companies with trading contacts with the USSR or Soviet companies registered in Britain. Telephone and written enquiries about the Postal Search Service should be made to the Postal Service Section of the Office. *For Scottish companies, see entry for Companies Registration Office, Edinburgh, 78.1.*

52.1-3

GLAMORGAN ARCHIVE SERVICE

Glamorgan Record Office, County Hall, Cathays Park, Cardiff CFI 3NE

52.1 DILLWYN & JONES (D/D DJ)
Mining engineers. The papers of Rice Mansel Dillwyn [Nicholl], 1891-1919, include letters received by him while in Russia, later correspondence with Russians, postcards, photographs, a notebook re collieries and coke works on Nicolaieffka (?Nikolaevka) property in southern Russia, and a geological plan of Almaznyi district.

52.2 DOWLAIS IRON COMPANY (D/D G)
C. 24 letters re export of locomotive rails to Russia, including the order of 1843 for the St Petersburg-Pauloffsky Railway Co., the Great Southern Railway of Russia and the Volga-Don Railway Co. Letter books mention the visits of Russian dignitaries, including Prince I. I. Baryatinskii, 1802, and the Grand Duke Constantine, June 1847. *See list and published calendar of the letter book series for details.*

52.3 Copies of 8 photographs of the family and friends of the Hughes family who founded the iron town of Yuzovka in southern Russia (**D/D X 409/1-8**).

53.1-2

THE WELCH REGIMENT MUSEUM

The Black and Barbican Towers, The Castle, Cardiff CF1 2RB

By appointment; apply to Curator.

53.1 Court Martial Book for the period when the 41st Regt of Infantry was in Sebastopol, Oct. 1855 - Mar. 1856.

53.2 Regimental Order Book includes 3 routine regimental items written while the 41st Regt was in Sebastopol.

54.1-23

THE BORDER REGIMENT AND THE KING'S OWN ROYAL BORDER REGIMENT MUSEUM

Queen Mary's Tower, The Castle, Carlisle CA3 8UR

Records relating to the 34th (Cumberland) Regt and the 55th (Westmorland) Regt.

54.1 Plans of the British Camp before Sebastopol, 1855 **(01/A4/001/1A, 002/1A)**.

54.2 Extracts from Maj. (later Gen.) Charles George Gordon's diary in the Crimea, 13 May, 26-8 Nov. 1855 **(01/A4/003/1A)**.

54.3 Statement of strength of 'G' Company of 34th (Cumberland) Regt on parade in readiness for attack on the Redan, 7 Sept. 1855 **(01/A4/004/1A)**.

54.4 Distinguished service list of 34th and the 55th (Westmorland) Regt for Sebastopol, 1855-6 **(01/A4/005/1A; 02/A2/005/3A)**.

54.5 Extracts from the *Illustrated London News* re the 34th and 55th Regts, 1855-6 **(01/A4/006/1A; 02/A2/007/3A)**.

54.6 Letter from William Stray of the 34th from the Crimea to his sister and mother **(01/A4/007/1A)**.

54.7 Records of Hospital Sgt Edward Baker of the 34th in the Crimea **(01/A4/008/1A)**.

54.8 Medals list for the 34th and 55th Regts for the Crimea, 1854-6 **(01/A4/009/1A; 02/A2/001/3A, /003/3A, /014/3A, /016/3A)**.

54.9 Map of the country from the Alma to Balaclava **(01/A4/010/1A)**.

54.10 Newspaper cuttings re the 34th in the Crimea **(01/A4/011/1A, /012-13/1A, /015/1A, /017-18/1A)**.

54.11 Copy of letter from Lord Raglan to Lord Panmure re sortie of the 34th of 22 Mar. 1855 **(01/A4/014/1A)**.

57.1-37

THE ROYAL ENGINEERS MUSEUM

Brompton Barracks, Chatham, Kent

By appointment. Card indexes and accession lists.

57.1 BURGOYNE, Sir John (**5401-59, -136,**)
Papers re the Crimean War include: passport, 12 Aug. 1854 (/1); original report on Sebastopol by Lt C. G. Gordon, 8 June 1858 (/2); 21 letters from Sir Harry Jones to Willoughby (/3); letters to Sir John from Sir George Cathcart, 2 Nov. 1854 (/4), George William Frederick Charles, 2nd Duke of Cambridge, (/5), Omer Pasha, in German and transl. (/6); memo on the attack on the Malakoff Tower (/7) (**5401-59**). 4 files of letters and memoranda whilst serving in the Crimea (**5401-136**). *Indexes to letters in files 1-3, contents list for file 4. See also 57.24.*

57.2 GORDON RELICS (**4801, GR**)
Copy of letter from C. G. Gordon at Khartoum to the Consuls-General of Austria, Germany, Italy and Russia, 15 Apr. 1884 (**4801-51, GR 51**); notes after visiting the Crimea, notes on fortifications, 3 photographs of Sebastopol, sketches of the Crimea (**4801-68, GR 68-78**); plans of Sebastopol dockyard showing project for demolition bearing C. G. Gordon's signature (**4801-158, GR 158**).

57.3 Notification of award of Médaille Militaire, certificate of service and award of British Crimean War medal, award of Legion of Honour to Cpl Brou, French Engineers, in the Crimean War (**3801-186**).

57.4 Notebook of Col. H. Sandham covering service in the Crimean War, 1856 (**3901-20**).

57.5 Letters of Sir H. Jones, 1854-6 (/4); biography of Jones by Lt-Gen. H. Sandham covering his service in the Crimea (/5) (**4201-371**).

57.6 Duty roster of RE officers during the siege of Sebastopol, 1854-5 (**5401-01**).

57.7 Drawing of sledge used at Bomarsund to move naval cannon ashore (**5401-55**).

57.8 Pocket ledger of French soldier picked up at Balaclava; letter from Gen. Niel of the French Army to Sir John Burgoyne re the attack on Sebastopol (**5401-57**).

57.9 Sketch of Balaclava by Maj. Biddolph (**5401-72**).

57.10 Sketches of the Malakoff Bastion and Redan by Lt C. G. Gordon, 1855-6 (**5401-84**).

57.11 Rough sketch of a Russian rifle pit (**5401-87**).

57.12 Plan of advanced English trenches and the 'Quarries', sketch of the lines near Balaclava, plan of the counter mines in front of the Bastion du Mat, by Lts H. C. Elphinstone and E. R. James, RE (**5401-88**).

57.13 Drawing and plans of attacks in the Crimean War (**5401-91**).

57.14 Sketch of the fortress of Kars by Col. H. A. Lake (**5401-94**).

57.15 Sketches of 'Camp of Slobodzie entrenched by Lt-Col. Simmons Aug. 1854' (/1) and Silistria (/2); letter to Col. Simmons describing the state of affairs in Kars during the siege (/3); report on the condition of the Turkish hospital at Varna by S. D. Bird (/4) (**5401-99**).

57.16 Field telegraph letter book and 5 field telegraph message books from the Crimea (**5401-113**).

57.17 3 maps of the Crimea by Maj. Jarvis (**5401-115**).

57.18 Narrative of the defence of Kars in 1855 by Lt-Gen. Georg Kmety Ismail Pasha of the Turkish Army, written 1856 (**5401-116**).

57.19 Crimean sketches by Capt. Eyre Massey, 95th Regt (**5401-117**).

57.20 Notebook of Gen. Sir Lothian Nicholson when in the Crimea mainly re demolitions at Sebastopol, some engineering field notes (/1); Corps order book (/2); published maps and charts of the Crimea (/3-/6); War Department sketches of Kars and the Malakoff Tower (/7,/8) (**5401-118**).

57.21 Photographs of serving officers in the Crimea, *c.* 1854-6 (**5401-138**).

57.22 19 maps and sketches re the Crimean War (**5401-140,-141**).

57.23 Drawings of Sebastopol by H. C. Elphinstone, including instructions to the engineer by William Mack, 1856 (**5401-142**).

57.24 4 letters from Sir John Burgoyne re demolitions of the docks at Sebastopol, 1855-6 (**5401-144**). *See also 57.1.*

57.25 Photograph of a cable-laying plough used in the Crimea for laying electric telegraph cables (**5401-145**).

57.26 2 photographs of Col. Simmons and Omer Pasha in the Crimea (**5401-146**).

57.27 File of letters of RE officers, mostly re the Peninsular campaign but including one from the Crimea (**5501-79**).

57.28 Report reputed to have been prepared for Gen. Strickland before the outbreak of the Crimean War re the potential of Turkey (**5905-02**).

57.29 Album of photographs taken in the Crimea shortly after the fall of Sebastopol (**6209-03**).

57.30 Maj.-Gen. P. Barry's sketch books of the Crimea (**6611-03**).

57.31 Photostat copies of 2 letters from Sir Gerald Graham to his family while serving in the Crimean War (**6707-04**).

57.32 Letter from F.M. Burgoyne to Douglas Cheape from Sebastopol, 1855 (**6906-05**).

57.33 French pass; sketch of part of Sebastopol defences; photograph of Crimean memorial (**7512-08**).

57.34 82 letters by Lt-Gen. George Bent from the Crimea (/1); 5 sheets dealing with his record of service and commendations for his work in Canada and the Crimea (/9) (7602-02).

57.35 4 tracings on linen showing areas of operation in the North Russian campaign, 1919 (6402-08).

57.36 Letter from GHQ North Russian Expeditionary Force to Lt Wilken re his award of MC (7503-04).

57.37 Russian bank notes; proclamation 'Why we are fighting in North Russia'; copy of citation of Sup. Sgt Nield issued by Gen. Ironside in North Russia, 12 Nov. 1918 (8209-13).

58.1-2

CHELMSFORD AND ESSEX MUSEUM

Oaklands Park, Moulsham Street, Chelmsford, Essex

Holds material relating to the Essex Regt.

58.1 5 framed 'examples of official correspondence of the Committee of the Docks of Sebastopol' picked up in Sebastopol in 1855, Russian.

58.2 Duplicated letter by Capt. W. Scott Watson, Mess President of Essex Regt Depot, re 'Easter Greetings and answers' to the 44th Kamchatskii and 56th Zhitomirskii Regts, 5 Oct. 1916.

59.1-10

ESSEX RECORD OFFICE

County Hall, Chelmsford, Essex CM1 1LX

F. G. Emmison, *Guide to the Essex Record Office* (1969).

59.1 BROGDEN PAPERS (D/DSe)
Papers of Daniel Bayley, consul-general and agent for the Russia Co., 1814-15, include letters commenting on Russian foreign policy, Russian trade and tariff policies and American policy towards Russia, list of imports and exports entered at the St Petersburg Custom House and the duty paid, printed lists of goods exported in British ships from St Petersburg and the names of British firms, printed circular letter requesting aid for building an English Church in St Petersburg (15). Account of the battle of Austerlitz (17); letter describing the visit of Queen Victoria to the wounded returning from the Crimea, 22 Mar 1855 (29).

59.2 BULLOCK PAPERS (D/DVv)
Copy of letter re description of audience with Tsar Nicholas II at Tsarskoe Selo, 1904 (107).

59.3 DU CANE PAPERS **(D/DDc)**
Papers of Peter Du Cane may include accounts of trade with and voyages to Russia, 1st half 18th century **(A1-8, 10-11, 16-17, 78)**.

59.4 GEPP AND SONS, SOLICITORS **(D/DGg)**
12 bundles of accounts and correspondence re Crimean Patriotic Fund, 1854-5 **(7)**.

59.5 LUARD PAPERS **(D/DLu)**
Copies of letters by Capt. Thomas Harvey Bramston of the Rifle Bde from the Crimea, 27 Oct. - 17 Nov. 1854 **(12)**; newscutting re Russian nurses at the front, 26 Feb. 1915 **(55/9/6)**; letter from Clementine Churchill to Katherine Evelyn Luard thanking her for her contribution to the Aid to Russia fund, 11 Dec. 1944 **(79)**.

59.6 MARSHALL AND SUTTON, SOLICITORS **(D/DMb)**
Log-book of Capt. H. E. Laver, Master of the SS *Kalgan* of the China Navigation Co. Ltd, includes reference to reactions of the Russian postmaster at Chefoo to the early stages of the Russian Revolution **(B2)**.

59.7 OXLEY PARKER PAPERS **(D/DOp)**
Circular of Essex Patriotic Fund to raise money for Crimean widows and orphans, 1854 **(B123/135)**; letter from Sir George Brooke-Pechell, Bt, suggesting that troubles in Ireland, Russia, France and Spain, socialism, nihilism etc. are all a result of Jesuit machinations, 1880 **(B123/255)**; letters from Revd Charles Fanshawe mentioning relatives in Russia and the possibility of a chaplaincy at the factory in St Petersburg, 1814-18 (extracts published in J. Oxley-Parker, *The Oxley Parker Papers* (Colchester, 1964) **(B123/530-88)**.

59.8 RUSSELL PAPERS **(D/DRu)**
Summary of letter from Ann Eliza Branfill to her son Benjamin A. Branfill in the Crimea, 3 Oct. 1859 **(C4/3)**.

59.9 JOHN SADD AND SONS LTD **(D/F)**
Bill of lading for timber shipped by Surkow and Schergold from Archangel to Maldon, and letter claiming for timber lost during that voyage, 1887 **(4/8/8, 9)**.

59.10 SPERLING PAPERS **(D/DQl; D/DGd)**
Ledger of Henry and John Sperling, furriers of London, includes papers on trade with Russia, 1719-58 **(D/DQ1)** and letter from Thomas Gemer to James Sperling re attempt of the Russian Ambassador to the States General to secure reconciliation between the United Provinces and England, 1781 **(D/DGd F60)**.

60.1-5

CHESHIRE RECORD OFFICE

Duke Street, Chester, Cheshire CH1 1RL

TS *County Record Office and Chester Diocesan Record Office, Summary Guide.*

60.1 BAKER-WILBRAHAM COLLECTION **(DBW)**
Memo, notes and dispatches re military actions in the Crimea, 1854-6 **(/N/G/A, B)**.

60.2 R. V. H. BURNE'S PAPERS (DDX 545)
Diary, photographs and lecture notes re Baltic cruise in which Memel, Riga and Reval were visited, 1933 (/72-4).

60.3 HIBBERT OF BIRTLES PAPERS (DHB)
3 bundles of letters by Capt. Hugh Hibbert from the Crimea, 1854-6 (temp. ref. D/2618)

60.4 LEICESTER-WARREN OF TABLEY COLLECTION (DLT/C)
30 letters by Rudolph de Salis from the Crimea, 1854-61 (11/11-40).

60.5 JOSEPH LEIGH & CO. RECORDS (D/1698)
Liverpool merchants. Order Book, 1829-47, (/5), and Foreign Letter Book, 1795-6, (/7) include references to St Petersburg, Kronstadt and Finnish and Baltic ports. German and English.

61.1

CHESTER CITY RECORD OFFICE

Town Hall, Chester, Cheshire CH1 2HJ

61.1 STOLTERFOTH COLLECTION (S)
The collection of the Stolterfoth family, 1784-1929, which originated in Lithuania, consists mainly of personal papers, but also includes a letter from Alderman J. N. Stolterfoth of Liverpool to Dr Henry Stolterfoth of Chester re the fate of a cousin in Moscow (S/97), and papers re the family history (S/107).

62.1-9

WEST SUSSEX RECORD OFFICE

County Hall, West Street, Chichester, West Sussex PO19 1RN

62.1 BUCKLE PAPERS
Papers of Adm. Matthew Buckle (1770-1855) include correspondence from the Crimean campaign (237). Papers of Adm. Claude Henry Mason Buckle (1803-94) include records re his command of HMS *Valorous* during the Crimean War (159-63, 505, 507-8). Papers of Adm. Charles Matthew Buckle (1828-1914) include diary and correspondence re his service in HMS *Vengeance* during the Crimean War (248, 267). *See* A. E. Readman edit., *The Buckle Papers* (Chichester, 1978).

62.2 COBDEN PAPERS
Papers of Richard Cobden (1804-65), statesman, politician, and advocate of free trade and disarmament, include: extracts of a narrative journey to Russia by Capt. James Abbott, 1843 (214); papers on commercial policy of Britain and Russia, 1854-5 (228, 231); notes by Cobden on the Crimean campaign, 1854-5 (229); diary of journey to Russia by Cobden, 1846-7 (454-62); notes by Cobden for speeches on Russia, n.d. (992); scrapbook of T. Fisher Unwin including material on Russia (1104). *See* F. W. Steer, edit., *The Cobden Papers* (Chichester, 1964), P. Gill, edit., *The Cobden and Unwin Papers* (Chichester, 1967).

62.3 COWDRAY ARCHIVES
Account book of Newdigate Owsley, London merchant, trading to Archangel, Danzig and Lisbon in cloth, linen, leather, hemp and wine, Jan. 1712 - Sept. 1714 (**1829**). *See* A. A. Dibben, edit., *The Cowdray Archives* 2 vols (Chichester 1960, 1964).

62.4 THE GOODWOOD ARCHIVES
Parliamentary papers of Charles Henry Gordon-Lennox (1818-1903), 6th Duke of Richmond, include memo on Russian advances in Asia, Jan,. 1868 (**854**). *See* F. W. Steer, J. E. A. Venables, edit., *The Goodwood Estate Archives* (Chichester, 1972).

62.5 LENNOX, Gen. Sir Wilbraham Oates (1830-97)
Intelligence maps of the Crimea, 1854-6 (**Add. MSS 15,471-5**) and for the Russo-Turkish War, 1877-8 (**Add. MSS 15,598-607**).

62.6 LYONS PAPERS
Papers of Adm. Sir Edmund Lyons (1790-1858), 1st Baron Lyons, include: correspondence on political affairs including references to Russia; naval papers, reports, memos re Crimean War; correspondence from ships, squadrons, ambassadors and consuls during the Crimean War. Papers of Richard Bickerton Pemell Lyons (1817-87), 2nd Baron and 1st Earl Lyons, diplomat, include correspondence, political papers, diaries and journals with references to Russia. The collection is being catalogued and access will be by prior appointment only until the catalogue is completed.

62.7 MAXSE PAPERS
Letters from Adm. Frederick Augustus Maxse to his parents from the Crimea, 1854-5 (**175**), and diary, Jan.-June 1855 (**179**). *See* F. W. Steer, edit., *The Maxse Papers* (Chichester, 1964).

62.8 RECORDS OF THE ROYAL SUSSEX REGIMENT (R.S.R. MSS)
Diary of L/Cpl James Justin, 11th Bn, the Royal Sussex Regt, in North Russia, Sept. 1918 - Apr. 1919 (**7/60**); diary of Sgt W. C. Chessum, 11th Bn, the Royal Sussex Regt, in North Russia, Sept. 1918 - Aug. 1919 (**7/61**); photograph albums compiled by Lt Lashmer Gordon Whistler, 45th Bn, The Royal Fusiliers, in North Russia, May-Sept. 1919 (**9/42**). Catalogue to be published shortly.

62.9 SMITH, John Abel (1802-71)
Letters from Jervoise Smith to his father, John Abel Smith, from the Crimea, 1855 (**Add. MS. 22,391**); journal and account book of Jervoise of his visit to the Crimea on behalf of the Commissioners of the Crimean Army Fund, 1854-5 (**Add. MSS 28,583-4**).

63.1-3

ULSTER UNIVERSITY LIBRARY

University of Ulster, Cromore Road, Coleraine Co., Londonderry, Northern Ireland BT52 1SA

63.1 Letter from Count Aleksandr Andreevich Bezborodko to Fedor Ivanovich ---, St Petersburg, 19 May 1795. Published in *Solanus*, vol. 7.

63.2 Letter from A. G. Lizakevich, Russian Envoy to Sardinia, to Tsar Alexander I, 27 Feb./11 Mar. 1807. Published in *Solanus*, vol. 7.

63.3 Letters to A. Pavlov from Yurii Kazakov and V. Maksimov.

64.1-2
COVENTRY CITY RECORD OFFICE

Broadgate House, Broadgate, Coventry CV1 1NG

By appointment.

64.1 Photocopy of TS diary by Thomas Bushill covering the Crimean War, 30 Nov. 1855 - 10 Feb. 1856 **(Acc. 554/1)**.

64.2 Vol. 'from the Women of Stalingrad to the Women of Coventry' relating the role of the women of Stalingrad in the War, appealing for solidarity, and including signatures of many Stalingrad women **(Acc. 827/1)**.

65.1-25
MODERN RECORDS CENTRE

University of Warwick Library, Coventry CV4 7AL

R. A. Storey, J. Druker, *Guide to the Modern Records Centre, University of Warwick Library* (1977), R. A. Storey, S. Edwards, *Supplement to the Guide to the Modern Records Centre, University of Warwick Library* (1981). New accessions described in the biannual *Information Bulletin* and in annual *Reports*. There are handlists for most collections.

65.1 LADY ALLEN OF HURTWOOD PAPERS (MSS 121)
TS of an article by Donald Gill, mining engineer, of a journey from Ridder Mine, West Siberia, to England to enlist, 1914-15 **(/F/3/5/1)**.

65.2. AMNESTY INTERNATIONAL PAPERS (MSS 34)
Files of publications re the USSR, 1970- **(/4/1/USSR 1-)**; letter from Andrei Sakharov to Amnesty re abolition of the death penalty, 1979 **(/4/6/15)**; news releases re USSR, Dec. 1972- **(/4/NR/USSR 1-)**.

65.3 J. ASKINS PAPERS (MSS 189)
Secretary of the North Western Regional Council for Peace in Vietnam. Documentation re international peace conferences at Budapest, 1971, Leningrad, 1975, Patna, 1975 and York, 1976.

65.4 ROWLAND BARRETT PAPERS (MSS 83)
Papers of R. Barrett (1877-1950), socialist, journalist and campaigner, include copy of letter from Barrett to Nicholas II urging him to stop persecuting socialists, 26 Sept. 1914 **(/3/APP/27)** and correspondence re Barrett's attempts to get a visa to visit the USSR, 1937-9 **(/3/GEN/11-17)**.

65.5 CLARA COLLET PAPERS (MSS 29)
Photocopies of correspondence of Karl Marx with Collet Dobson Collet, Clara's father, include references to Russian émigrés in London, 1866.

65.6 CONFEDERATION OF BRITISH INDUSTRY ARCHIVES (**MSS 200**)
Records of the Federation of British Industries (**F**) include: FBI Russian Committee
papers, 29 Apr. 1930 - 19 Dec. 1935 (**/F/1/1/80**); papers of R. Nugent including
correspondence with Sir W. Peter Rylands re the Russian question (**/F/3/D1/2/1**) and
statement on Anglo-Soviet trade, 1932 (**/F/3/D1/9/3**); papers of N. Kipping including
subject files on Anglo-Soviet trade, 1943-64 (**/F/3/D3/6/95-7, 119-20**); Economic
Directorate papers including papers re Russian sub-committee of the FBI International
Trade Policy Committee, 1938-50 (**/F/3/EI/15/26**) and papers re trade with the USSR,
1922 (**/F/3/EI/16/9**); Overseas Directorate (General Series) papers re USSR, 1943-58
(**/F/3/O5/4/73-86**); FBI Secretaries' papers (Walker) re Anglo-Soviet trade, 1943-8, 1955
(**/F/3/S1**); Secretary's Department (Gough) papers re Soviet delegation from the State
Committee for co-ordination of research, 1964 (**/F/3/S2/26/21**); papers of Sir William
McFadzean including file on Sino-Soviet trade strategy, 1959 (**/F/P/McFadzean/23/1**);
papers of Sir Harry Pilkington including lists of visits to Russia, 1954
(**/F/P/Pilkington/1/5**); papers of Sir Peter Runge including correspondence with the Soviet
ambassador, 1963-4 (**/F/P/Runge/1/3,4**). Records of the British Employers' Confederation
(**B**) include: report 'The re-entry of Soviet Russia into the International Labour
Organization', 1954 (**/B/3/2/C98 pt. A9**); correspondence, reports etc. re the USSR and
other communist countries, 1953-7 (**/B/3/2/C580, C761 pt. 5, C1181**). Records of the
Confederation of British Industry (**C**) include references to the USSR in the index to
papers of the CBI Council, 1966-75 (**/C/1**). Papers of the British Industrial Measuring &
Control Apparatus Manufacturers' Association, deposited by the CBI, include file of
correspondence and circulars re Soviet trade agreement, 1948-9 (**/BIMCAM/3/9/9**). CBI
papers are subject to the thirty-year rule, and researchers are required to show their work
to the CBI before publication. *See catalogues and indexes for details.*

65.7 CONFEDERATION OF SHIPBUILDING & ENGINEERING UNIONS
(**MSS 44**)
2 letters re visit of the Engineering Union of the USSR, 1960 (**/TBN.65 file 2**).

65.8 HUGO DEWAR PAPERS (**MSS 206**)
Papers by Dewar (1908-80), revolutionary socialist and writer, include study notes from
the International Lenin School, Moscow, and articles on and by Trotskii.

65.9 ETHERIDGE PAPERS (**MSS 202**)
Papers of R. A. Etheridge, shop steward, include: papers re Anglo-Soviet exchanges of
shop stewards and trade union officials; Etheridge's diary of an exchange trip to the USSR,
1958; accounts of the Austin Joint Shop Stewards Russian Hospitality Fund (temporary
reference **/S files 462, 611, 641, 741**). Collection is in the process of being catalogued; apply
to Archivist.

65.10 GOLLANCZ PAPERS (**MSS 157**)
Papers of Sir Victor Gollancz (1893-1967), publisher, include: letter from Centre d'Aide
aux Refugiés Russes en France, 1951 (**/3/CHI/1/8-11**); box-file of correspondence,
cuttings, pamphlets etc. re the Left Book Club, mainly after the German-Soviet pact and re
attitudes towards the Communist Party and the USSR, 1939-42 (**/3/DOC/1/1-21, 85-91**);
copy of letter from Gollancz to Igor Stravinskii, 25 May 1954 (**/3/MU/G/1/30**). Papers re
the USSR in the 1930s include correspondence with Ivan Maiskii, S. Vinogradov, Russia
Today Society, Congress/Committee of Peace and Friendship with the USSR, H. F. K.
Snell and E. Reckitt (**/3/RU/1/1-41**); papers re Save Europe Now movement include
correspondence re the USSR with W. J. Rose and Bertrand Russell (**/3/SEN/1/8-18**).
Papers of the Anglo-Soviet Public Relations Committee (later Association), of which
Gollancz was Secretary, consist of minutes, notices, files of donations, correspondence
etc., 1941-2 (**/3/ASP/1/1-193**). *See handlist for details.*

65.11 GROVES PAPERS (MSS 172)

Balham Group papers of R. Groves, journalist, screenwriter, historian, pioneer member of the British Section of the International Left Opposition, include 2 letters from the Marx-Engels Institute, 30 Mar., 26 Apr. 1930 (**/BG/2/12, 14**) and draft of letter from Groves after the Communist Party of Great Britain Secretariat's refusal of permission for him to go to Moscow, n.d. (**/BG/2/15**).

65.12 HALLSWORTH : RESEARCH PAPERS (MSS 70)

Papers of Sir Joseph Hallsworth (1884-1974), 1st General Secretary of the Union of Shop, Distributive & Allied Workers, include memo on agreement of the union with Russian Oil Products Ltd (**/3/15/60-81**).

65.13 HARBER PAPERS (MSS 151)

Papers of Denzil Harber (1909-66), active in the British Trotskyist movement 1932-49, include discussion documents re the USSR, 1941-2 (**file 9**) and miscellaneous Soviet publications, 1944-5 (**file 13**). Permission to consult the collection must be obtained from J. Harber on behalf of the depositors.

65.14 INTERNATIONAL TRANSPORT WORKERS FEDERATION (MSS 159)

Correspondence re shipments in connection with the Russo-Polish war, 1920 (**Box 15**); file of correspondence re supply of arms to counter-revolutionary forces in Russia, 1920 (**Box 16**); circulars, statements etc. re British-Russian conference, 1923-5 (**Box 22**); correspondence, reports etc. re Baltic States, 1929-37, 1939 (**Boxes 40, 69**); file re German-Soviet pact, 1940-2 (**Box 70**); file re the USSR and Italy, 1941 (**Box 71**).

65.15 IRON & STEEL TRADES CONFEDERATION (MSS 36)

Publications, reports, pamphlets re USSR including material re delegation to the USSR, 1945, and visit of Soviet delegation, 1947 (**R30**)

65.16 MAITLAND/SARA PAPERS (MSS 15)

Papers of Henry Sara (1886-1953), socialist activist, include: publications, statements, scrapbooks of press cuttings on and by Trotskii, 1915-36, 1948 (**/3/1/69-76; /3/5/111; /3/9/1-8**); press cutttings re the USSR (**/3/6, 7; /7/1/1, 3; /7/2/2; /7/3-4**); excerpts from letter from Max Schachtman re party policy towards the USSR in the War, 8 Aug. 1941 (**/4/4/14**); duplicated notes for students from the International Lenin School, Moscow, 1927-9 (**/5/1/1-4**); photographs of Russia/USSR, 1914-16, 1924-5 (**/7/5/1-128**). *See handlist for details.*

65.17 MINERS' MINORITY MOVEMENT (MSS 88)

Circular re Russian-Swedish Committee of Co-operation & Friendship (between miners' unions), Jan. 1928 (**/3/1**).

65.18 MODERN RECORDS CENTRE MISCELLANEOUS SERIES (MSS 21)

Leaflets, broadsheets, handbills, posters, printed circulars, booklets etc. re the USSR, 1920, 1946, 1959, 1962, 1977, n.d. *See handlist for details.*

65.19 NATIONAL UNION OF RAILWAYMEN (MSS 127)

Box-file of letters of condolence following the death of the NUR General Secretary J. Campbell in a road accident in the USSR, 1957 (**/NU/3**).

65.20 NATIONAL UNION OF SEAMEN (MSS 175)
TS description of a conference convened in Petrograd to create a world marine workers' union, n.d. (**/3/18**).

65.21 RAGOSINE OIL CO. (MSS 198)
Established in Moscow by Victor Ragosine; London interest bought out in 1882. Records include correspondence London-Moscow, 1882-1907. Collection is in the process of being catalogued; apply to Archivist.

65.22 SOCIALIST VANGUARD GROUP (MSS 173)
Founded in 1929 as the British Section of the Militant Socialist International in Germany. File re Russia (**Box 3**).

65.23 TARBUCK PAPERS (MSS 75)
Papers re the Workers' International League include statements on the USSR and Stalinism (**/3/2/31**). Papers re the Revolutionary Communist Party include: amendment by A. Francis to the Central Committee resolution on the Soviet economy, Aug. 1945 (**/3/4/36**); conference documents re the USSR, 1946 (**/3/4/58-9**); international discussion documents and papers re the 4th International and Stalinism, 1947 (**/3/4/114, 116, 119-21**); amendments to thesis on the USSR and Eastern Europe, 1947 (**/3/4/115**). Remarks on Stalinism by D. Jones and reply by E. Grant, 1949 (**/3/4/133-4**); list of motions re USSR by the Socialist Review Group, 21 Nov. 1950 (**/3/7/3**); articles and pamphlets re USSR. *See handlist for details.*

65.24 UNION OF CONSTRUCTION, ALLIED TRADES & TECHNICIANS (MSS 78)
Index to the correspondence of the Amalgamated Society of Carpenters & Joiners/Amalgamated Society of Woodcutters has references to Russia, 1919-28, Russia and the Council of Action, 1920, and Russian workers' appeal, 1921. *See handlist for details.*

65.25 HARRY WICKS PAPERS (MSS 102)
Duplicated study notes of Wicks from the International Lenin School, Moscow, re Marxist economics, history of the Russian Communist Party and other subjects (**/1-38**).

66.1-4
GWENT COUNTY RECORD OFFICE

County Hall, Cwmbran, Gwent NP44 2XH

W. H. Baker, *Guide to the Monmouthshire Record Office* (1959). Card indexes of subjects and personal names up to 1870; research guides.

66.1 NEWPORT LIBRARY COLLECTION (D43)
Passport issued to Thomas Cooke, a merchant's son from Newport, aged 17, to visit Russia, 1845 (**4845**).

66.2 ROLLS COLLECTION (D361)
Letter from Edmund White, seaman in the Black Sea Fleet, to Martha Macready (née Rolls), 1855 (**F/P.4.21**); 30 letters from Messrs Bell, Carnegie, Harcourt, Grimshaw and Vaughan to John Etherington Welch Rolls from the Crimea, 1854-6 (**F/P.4.21, 86**); 2 copies of account of Gen. Suvorov by Edward Nevill Macready, n.d. (**F/P.6.12-13**);

watercolour of Sebastopol (**F/P. Misc. 12**); captain's account of a cruise on the yacht *Santa Maria*, visiting Sweden, Russia and Germany, 1898 (**F6.15**).

66.3 TULLOCH COLLECTION (**D460**)
Crimean papers of Col. Sir Alexander Murray Tulloch, authorized to enquire about Commissary arrangements in the Crimea, consist of papers, reports, letters, and proceedings before the Court of General Officers, 1855-6.

66.4 Sketch-book of Maj. (later Gen. Sir) Arthur Herbert containing watercolour scenes in the Crimea (**Misc. MSS 1345**).

67.1

DERBY CENTRAL LIBRARY, LOCAL STUDIES DEPARTMENT

25b Irongate, Derby DE1 3GL

67.1 THE CATTON COLLECTION (**Dep. No.42**)
Letter from Sir Robert Wilmot to Thomas Waite mentioning the dethronement of Peter III, 29 July 1762; letter from ?Sir Robert re characters of Catherine II and her son, 27 Sept. 1770. Permission to make copies or quote from the collection must be obtained from Mr D. W. H. Neilson, Estate Office, Catton Hall, Burton-on-Trent, Staffordshire.

68.1

DONCASTER ARCHIVES DEPARTMENT

King Edward Road, Balby, Doncaster DN4 ONA

Guide to the Archives Department (1981).

68.1 Account of Thomas Clarkson's interview with Alexander I on 23 Sept. 1815 (**DD.CL/C3**).

69.1

DORSET COUNTY RECORD OFFICE

County Hall, Dorchester DT1 1XJ

A. C. Cox, *Index to the Dorset County Records* (1938).

69.1 ARCHIVE OF BRIDPORT-GUNDRY LTD OF BRIDPORT (**D203**)
Business papers of Joseph Gundry & Co. (**D.203/A**) include 2 letters from James Atkinson of London, 1800, 1801, with invoices for purchase of Russian grown hemp and flax, 1799-1800 (**/A34**) and bills of exchange and papers re shipment of Riga hemp into West Bay, 1912-14 (**/A51**).

70.1

THE DORSET MILITARY MUSEUM

The Keep, Dorchester, Dorset DT1 1RN

70.1 Letters from Maj.-Gen. Robert Newport Tinley from the Crimea, 1855.

71.1-7

DUNDEE DISTRICT ARCHIVE AND RECORD CENTRE

City Chambers, Dundee DD1 3BY

By appointment.

71.1 ALEXEEV (ALEKSEEV), Ivan **(GD/Mus 27)**
Letter from Ivan Alekseev to his son ?in the Crimea, 10/22 May 1854, Russian.

71.2 GREIG PAPERS **(GD/Mus 47)**
Copies of letter from Asst-Surg. David Greig to his family from the Crimea, 1854-6; TS
copy of military service of Asst-Surg. T. E. Hale, 1855-7; copy of letters from Asst-Surg.
Arthur Henry Taylor to his parents from the Crimea, 1854-6.

71.3 MUNRO FAMILY PAPERS **(GD/X113)**
Photographs of Narva including the port, flax mills, yachts, workers and peasants (**/1-19**).

71.4 REGISTERS OF SHIPS
4 vols recording entry of ships into the harbour of Dundee, giving master, port of origin
and nature of cargo, including ships from Baltic ports.

71.5 REID FAMILY OF NEWPORT PAPERS **(GD/Mus 43)**
2 letters and copies from Lizzie Janson to her parents describing her journey to Petrograd,
1919-20; short biography of Ludwig Janson, written by his wife Lizzie, describing his
service in the Russo-Japanese War.

71.6 TAYSIDE REGIONAL COUNCIL WATER SERVICES
DEPARTMENT
25 glass monochrome projection slides of views of the Russian campaign, *c.* 1920.

71.7 Account book of the brig *Tagus* covering voyages to Riga and St Petersburg, 1796-9
(GD/Mus 66).

72.1-8

DUNDEE UNIVERSITY LIBRARY

Archives Department, University of Dundee, Dundee DD1 4HN

Descriptive lists of holdings available in the Library.

72.1 BAXTER BROTHERS & CO. LTD (MS 11)
Linen and jute manufacturers of Dundee. Balance books and profit and loss accounts (32 vols) include calculations for flax from Riga and Archangel, 1854-*c.* 1917 (/1).

72.2 LEWIS C. GRANT & CO. LTD (MS 45)
Owners of Dunnikier Foundry of Dysart. List of rice mills installed in Europe including Russia, n.d. (/3/16).

72.3 J. P. INGRAM (MS 73)
Shipping correspondent of the Dundee *Courier*. Photocopies of his notebooks which include references to local ships sailing to Russian ports and ships built locally for Russian owners, mainly 19th and early 20th centuries.

72.4 LOW AND BONAR LTD (MS 24)
Jute and flax manufacturers of Dundee. Letter-book containing correspondence with Messrs Egermann and Bolotin in St Petersburg, Jules Gay and Messrs Segesser and Ericks in Odessa, Nikolai Novikov in Kiev and S. R. Randrup in Omsk, 1910-15 (/4).

72.5 JAMES F. LOW (ENGINEERS) LTD (MS 89)
Textile engineers of Monifieth, by Dundee. Machine description books and order index showing some Russian customers including James McGregor, St Petersburg, and firms in St Petersburg, Khar'kov, Narva and Riga, mainly early 20th century.

72.6 JULIUS SALOMON & CO. (MS 12)
Linen merchants of Dundee. Reports by B. Steinitz and A. Schapiro from Odessa, 1876-84 (/6).

72.7 SIDLAW INDUSTRIES LTD (MS 66)
Jute spinners and manufacturers of Dundee. Foreign sales ledgers include orders from the USSR, 1921-47 (/X/3/63, 65, 70-1).

72.8 Scrapbook of newspaper cuttings by Jamie Neish includes references to Russia, 1893-1925 (/87).

73.1-5

DURHAM COUNTY RECORD OFFICE

County Hall, Durham DH1 5UL

W. A. L. Seaman, *Durham County Record Office* (1969).

73.1 EDLESTON COLLECTION (D/Ed)

Drafts of article 'The Fall of the Russian Empire' by R. H. Edleston *c.* 1940, and newspaper cuttings re same (**15/6/405-8**); newspaper cuttings re Russia, 1919-28 (**15/6/409-36**).

73.2 HODGKIN PAPERS (D/Ho)

Quaker business family. Letters from Lord Tenterden to Edmund Backhouse re a memorial by the Society of Friends urging neutrality in the war with Russia, 1876 (**/C 1/1**); anarchist proclamation 'Saratov', *c.* 1919 (**/X 107**).

73.3 LONDONDERRY PAPERS (D/Lo)

Papers of Robert Stewart, Visc. Castlereagh (1769-1822), 2nd Marquess of Londonderry, include: précis of dispatches from Sweden re progress of the war with Russia, 1808 (**/C 5**); confidential memo replying to the Tsar's proposal for a Holy Alliance, 1816 (**/C 16**); papers re Vienna Congress including references to Russia, 1815-20 (**/C 20-4**); letter from Lord Cathcart in St Petersburg, 1816 (**/C 34/23**); copies of letters from Castlereagh to the Tsar, 1819 (**/C 36**). Papers of Charles William Stewart (1778-1854), 3rd Marquess of Londonderry, include: diplomatic papers re Russia, 1815-21 (**/C 37-8**); letters to Lord Stewart from representatives in St Petersburg, 1815-17 (**/C 45-52**); correspondence with Count Philip von Brunnow, Russian diplomat, 1847-8, 1850-4 (**/C 66, 445; Files 7, 39, 34**); papers re visit to Russia, 1836 (**/C 128**); correspondence with Sir George Lefevre, physician at the embassy in St Petersburg, 1837 (**/C 460**), Michel Michailoff (M. Mikhailov), 1837-8 (**/C 465**), Prince M. D. Gortchakoff (Gorchakov), 1826-7 (**File 12**), Prince Lieven and Princess Troubetzkoi (Trubetskoi) (**File 21**); papers re the Crimean War, 1853-5 (**Files 5, 11**). Letters by Lord Adolphus Vane-Tempest to his mother from the Crimea (**/C 180(4)**). Correspondence of Frances Anne, Marchioness of Londonderry, with Alexander I, 1813-24 (**/C 523**) and re Crimean War (**/C 530, 536**) and visit to Russia (**/C 550**). *See catalogues for details and for further correspondence.*

73.4 NATIONAL COAL BOARD RECORDS (NCB)

Correspondence of the Weardale Iron and Coal Company Ltd with the Grande Société des Chemins de Fer Russes of St Petersburg re guarantee to replace rails supplied, 1871-80 (**14/179**).

73.5 PEASE PAPERS (D/Pe)

Quaker business family. Letter re lecture by a Tartar on his country, 1853 (**2/31**); letter re effect of news from Russia on the City, 1857 (**3/35**); letters re Friends going to Russia to promote peace, 1854 (**10/8-10**); correspondence between Yearly Meeting of Women Friends and Queen Victoria re threat of war with Russia, 1878 (**10/24-5**).

74.1-5

DURHAM LIGHT INFANTRY MUSEUM & ARTS CENTRE

Aykley Heads, Durham DH1 5TU

By appointment.

74.1 Letter from Colour Sgt William Henry Foster, 68th Light Infantry, from the siege of Sebastopol, 10 Jan. 1855 (**Acc. No. 61**).

74.2 Photographs by Roger Fenton of members of the 68th Light Infantry in the Crimea, 1855 (**Acc. No. 632**).

74.3 Album including: letter from Capt. H. D. Torrens re the battle of Inkerman, 3 Aug. 1856; letter by Gen. Sir Arthur Torrens from the Crimea, 30 Sept. 1854; ink sketches of the Crimea by Capt. Torrens and Gen. Sir Arthur Torrens, 1854-6 (**Acc. No. 649**).

74.4 Proclamation to the British troops giving reasons for their presence in Russia, *c.* 1919; photograph of 27th Bn Light Infantry at Archangel, 1919; 13 postcards of Archangel, *c.* 1919 (**Acc. No. 2763**).

74.5 Diary by Capt. Stephen Croft, 68th Light Infantry, covering service in the Crimea, 1855 (**Letts No. 9**).

75.1-3

DEPARTMENT OF PALAEOGRAPHY AND DIPLOMATIC

University of Durham, 5 The College, Durham DH1 3EQ

75.1 THE EARL GREY PAPERS
Papers of Charles, 1st Earl Grey, (1729-1807), include copy of secret instructions re Russian contingent for the descent on Holland, May 1799. Papers of Charles, 2nd Earl Grey, (1764-1845) include: copies of dispatches from St Petersburg, 1834-7; correspondence of Charles, Baron Stuart de Rothesay, Secretary of the Embassy in St Petersburg, 1806; subject files on Russia; papers on Russian foreign policy, relations with Britain and trade, 1804-06, 1832-4; extracts from conventions and treaties between and involving Britain and Russia, 1798, 1815, 1831; correspondence re Russia with Prince Czartoryski, Palmerston, Lord Ponsonby and Count Stroganov. Papers of Gen. Charles Grey (1804-70) include correspondence and papers on the Crimean War. Papers of Henry George, 3rd Earl Grey, (1802-94), include notes on the Crimean War; notes, letters and newspaper cuttings re Russian policy in Afghanistan, 1878, 1885. Papers of Albert Henry George, 4th Earl Grey, (1851-1917), include: memos and papers re the Anglo-Siberian Trading Syndicate Ltd, 1884-93; papers re the transactions of British Union Oil Co. in Russia, 1917. *See catalogues of the papers of the 1st and 2nd Earls and Gen. Charles Grey and card indexes of the papers of the 2nd, 3rd and 4th Earls for details.*

75.2 PONSONBY PAPERS
Papers of John William Ponsonby (1770-1855), 1st Viscount Ponsonby, include: memos and reports on Russian policy towards Turkey, 1836-7, 1839; memos on Russian policy in Circassia, 1836-7, n.d.; newspaper cuttungs re the arrest of the British schooner *Vixen* in the Black Sea, 1836; papers of Ponsonby as British Ambassador in Turkey including references to Russia, 1841-3; letters from James Yeames, Consul-General in Odessa to

Ponsonby, 1834-41; an examination of treaties between Russia and Turkey from the reign of Peter I. The collection is in the process of being listed and access will be restricted until a full list is available.

75.3 THE SHIPPERDSON PAPERS
Correspondence of Edmund Hector Hopper re contributions to the Patriotic Fund for assisting widows and orphans of those killed in the Crimean War, Dec. 1854 **(1581-5)**.

76.1-3
DEPARTMENT OF RUSSIAN, UNIVERSITY OF DURHAM

Elvet Riverside, New Elvet, Durham DH1 3JT

By appointment. *Russian Research Collections in the University of Durham* (Durham, 1982) available on request from the Department.

76.1 THE BARRY HOLLINGSWORTH ARCHIVE
Mainly MS, with some TS and printed material re teaching, research and writing of the late Barry Hollingsworth.

76.2 THE PRELOOKER COLLECTION
Material collected by Jaakoff Prelooker includes: 247 magic lantern slides of Russian subjects; postcard album of Russian postcards; collection of Russian banknotes; TS 'Why Count Vassili Danilovitch became a revolutionist', 'Semite and Slav' and introduction to *Russian Flashlights*.

76.3 THE VOLKHOVSKY COLLECTION
Collection of Felix Volkhovsky (Feliks Volkhovskii) include: letters to his daughter Vera Volkhovsky from Franco Venturi and E. A. Taratuta, 1957, 1963; TS of Vera's translations from Saltykov-Shchedrin (published in book form in 1931); MS lecture by Vera on Russian literature.

77.1-4
DURHAM UNIVERSITY LIBRARY

77.1-2 Main Library

Palace Green, Durham DH1 3RN

D. Ramage, *Summary List of Additional Manuscripts Accessioned and Listed between September 1945 and September 1961* (1963).

77.1 SHARP, Sir Cuthbert
3 letters from Prince Aleksandr Lobanov-Rostovskii, 1840, 1843; letters from John Lambton, Earl of Durham, from St Petersburg, 1836.

77.2 SMITH, Samuel
Letters to Smith from his son Thomas Smith from the Crimean War and India.

77.3 Oriental Section

Elvet Hill, Durham DH1 3TH

77.3 3 albums of photographs of Russia collected by John Sharp when travelling for the British and Foreign Bible Society, 1890-5.

77.4 Sudan Archive

Elvet Hill, Durham DH1 3TH

Access to *bona fide* researchers by appointment.

77.4 WINGATE PAPERS
Papers of Sir Reginald Wingate (1861-1953), Governor-General of Sudan, 1899, High Commissioner of Egypt, 1916-19, include: reference to Russian capture of Erzinjian, July 1916 (**138/15**); telegrams and copies of telegrams re Russia, Mar., May 1917 (**145/3, 6-7**); paper re Anglo-Russian agreement of the Near East, July 1917 (**146/1-2**); paper re British evacuation of Baku, Sept. 1918 (**149/7-9**).

78.1

COMPANIES REGISTRATION OFFICE, SCOTLAND

102 George Street, Edinburgh EH2 3DJ

78.1 The office holds microfiche copies of original documents on all Scottish registered companies since 1856; information since 1976 is held on microfiche. The files on companies are open to the public and contain documents relating to the structure of the company, changes of directors, secretaries and registered offices, annual returns and accounts, lists of principal shareholders, details of mortgages or charges, and appointments of liquidators and receivers where appropriate. The office holds records of approximately 45,000 Scottish companies, listed alphabetically, some of which will have connections with Russia and the Soviet Union. *See also entry for the Companies Registration Office, Cardiff, 51.1.*

79.1-3

EDINBURGH CENTRAL LIBRARY

George IV Bridge, Edinburgh EH1 1EG

By appointment.

79.1 Contributions from St Petersburg for a monument to Sir Walter Scott, 1832 (**YPR 5339**).

79.2 TS diary by Lilias Mary Grant covering her service in the Scottish Women's Hospital in Rumania and Russia, Aug. 1916 - Apr. 1917 (**qYR 489 152**).

79.3 Letters and photographs of Ethel M. Moir covering her service in the Scottish Women's Hospital in Rumania and Russia, 1916-17; extracts from a diary of one of the women in the Scottish Women's Hospital in Rumania and Russia, 1918-19 (**YR 489 152**).

80.1
EDINBURGH CITY ARCHIVES

City Chambers, High Street, Edinburgh EH1 1YJ

By appointment.

80.1 There are scattered references to Russia and Russian trade in the Town Council Minute Books which run from *c.* 1600 and comprise approx. 500 vols. Individuals with connections with Russia can be traced through the indexes.

81.1-14
EDINBURGH UNIVERSITY LIBRARY

Special Collections Department, George Square, Edinburgh EH8 9LJ

Index to Manuscripts, Edinburgh University Library 2 vols (Boston, Mass., 1964), *Index to Manuscripts, Edinburgh University Library, First Supplement* (Boston, Mass., 1981).

81.1 BLACK, Joseph
Correspondence of Black with Princess Ekaterina Romanova Dashkova re the Russian Academy of Arts and Sciences and Russian students, 1783, 1786, 1788 (**Gen. 873/II/90-3, 102-3.139F, 274-5; 873/III/36-9, 73-5**); letters from George Blake to Black re Russian grain for brewing and the possibility of introducing beer into Russia, 1783 (**Gen. 875/II/115-6F, 125-6**).

81.2 LAING MANUSCRIPTS (**La.**)
Letters from John Drummond on Russian movements in the Caucasus and Central Asia, 25 Jan. 1765 (**II.127**) and the Russo-Turkish War, 20 Sept. 1771 (**II.511**). *See handlist for details.*

81.3 SAROLEA, Charles (1870-1953) (**Sar. Coll.**)
Academic and editor. Papers include: correspondence and papers re Russia, 1898-1940 (**81/1-2; 82/1-2**); letter from Mrs Alec Tweedie giving impressions of Russia, 9 July ?1925 (**138**).

81.4 Correspondence and part of a diary of Armand Leslie as surgeon with the Turkish army during the Russo-Turkish War, 1876-8 (**Dk.2.15**); letter book mainly on Russo-Persian relations, Apr. 1829- Apr. 1830 (**Dk.2.37**)

81.5 Papers re conditions in Scutari Barracks Hospital, 1854 (**Dk.4.987**).

81.6 Letter from J. J. Sederholm to Sir A. Geikie referring to Russian policy in Finland, 8 July 1900 (**Gen.527/2**); letters from Russian geologists to Sir A. Geikie, 1886-1903 (**Gen.527/5**).

81.7 C. 400 letters and 60 postcards from M. A. Landau (*pseud.* M. A. Aldanov) and his wife to I. A. Bunin, Russian poet and novelist, and Mrs Vera Bunin, 1921-57, Russian (**Gen.565**).

81.8 Letter by Prof. T. Chenery re Russian royal archives, 30 July 1873 (**Gen.715/7**).

81.9 Letter by Sir L. Mallet re Anglo-Russian policy in Central Asia, 2 Feb. 1875 (**Gen.715/7**).

81.10 Diary kept by Helena Marshall, a governess in St Petersburg, 1871-4 (**Gen.848**).

81.11 Letter from Dr E. Henderson to Revd Wardlaw describing Russia as a 'model state', St Petersburg, 29 Dec. 1816 (**Gen.863/3 f. 11**).

81.12 Letters from J. Dodson to J. Fergus re importation of flax from Archangel, 1 Aug. 1837, 1839 (**Gen.863/7 ff. 14-19, 51, 53**).

81.13 Correspondence of John Buchan about printing and publishing in Russia, 1915-17 (**Gen.1728/B/5-7**).

81.14 4 boxes pf papers of W. P. Earsman re the USSR, *c.* 1920-50 (**Gen.1949**).

82.1-102
NATIONAL LIBRARY OF SCOTLAND

Department of Manuscripts, George IV Bridge, Edinburgh EH1 1EW

Summary Catalogue of the Advocates' Manuscripts (Edinburgh, 1971), *Catalogue of Manuscripts acquired since 1925*, vols 1-4, 6 (Edinburgh, 1938-84), *Accessions of Manuscripts 1959-64* (Edinburgh, 1965), *Accessions of Manuscripts 1965-1970* (Edinburgh, 1971). Major recent accessions are listed in the *Annual Reports* and TS quarterly lists of accessions are also produced. Place, person and subject indexes and TS texts of vols 5 and 7-14 of manuscripts acquired since 1925 and of some of the additional Advocates' manuscripts are available in the Reading Room. TS lists of recent acquisitions are also available in the Reading Room but researchers should note that their accession number is only temporary and will eventually be replaced by a MS number.

Advocates' Manuscripts

82.1 J. F. CAMPBELL OF ISLAY PAPERS (**Adv. MSS 50.2.2., 50.2.4., 50.3.14.-50.5.8.**)
Journal of John Francis Campbell (1822-85) while travelling in Norway, Russia and Italy, 1873-4 (**50.4.8.**).

82.2 CORONATIONS (**Adv. MS 33.2.26.**)
Descriptions of the coronations of Tsar Theodor, 1582, and Catherine I, May 1724 (**ff. 58-9, 96-101v**).

82.3 MURRAY PAPERS (**Adv. MSS 46.1.1.-46.10.2.**)
Papers of Gen. Sir George Murray include: letter from Grand Duke Michael of Russia to Murray, 1844 (**46.5.7. ff. 193-255**); statistical returns of the Russian army of occupation in France, 1816-18 (**46.7.19. nos. 76-133**); note on punishment in the Russian army, *c.* 1825

(46.8.7. f. 224); copy of report re Russian army operations, 1799 **(46.9.19. f. 73)**; description of Russian campaign against the Swedes, 1808 **(46.9.19. f. 82)**.

82.4 PATON COLLECTION (Adv. MS 28.3.12.)
List of bronze medals presented to the University of Edinburgh by Princess E. R. Dashkova, 1779 **(f. 54)**.

82.5 REGISTER OF ROYAL LETTERS, 1615-35 (Adv. MSS 34.2.12.-13.)
Copies of letters from Charles I to Tsar Michael, 26 Feb., 4 May, 26 Nov. 1632; licence to Sir Alexander Leslie for levying soldiers in Scotland for Russian service, 28 Mar. 1633; warrant to Sir John Hay, Patrick Maull and others to form an association to trade in Muscovy, Nov. 1633. (Published in C. Rogers, edit., *The Earl of Stirling's Register of Royal Letters relative to the Affairs of Scotland and Nova Scotia from 1615 to 1635* vol. 2 (1885).)

82.6 Charter by Tsar Alexis attesting that Capt. Vilirres (?Villiers) from Scotland, who had served in his army and now wished to return home, was a skilled soldier, Russian with English notes and transl. **(Adv. Ch. A. 130)**.

82.7 Alphabetical list of commercial regulations, 17th-18th century, Russian **(Adv. MS 22.5.4.)**.

National Library of Scotland Manuscripts

82.8 ABBOTSFORD COLLECTION (MSS 851-938, 1549-634)
Copies of documents re Napoleon's campaign in Russia **(MS 883 f. 62)**; letters by Count Vladimir Davidov, 1828, 1839 **(MS 885 f. 108; MS 934 no. 61)**; letter by Prince Aleksandr Lobanov-Rostovskii, n.d. **(MS 926 no. 119)**; paper by Sir Walter Scott 'Nathalia Sherimenitef' re Natal'ya Borisovna Sheremeteva, afterwards Princess Dolgorukova **(MS 1582 f. 143)**.

82.9 ANDERSON PAPERS (MSS 14842-7)
Letter to Warren Hastings Anderson describing visit to Siberia, 1836 **(MS 14843 f. 69)**.

82.10 ADAM AND CHARLES BLACK AND WILLIAM TAIT (MS 3713)
Publishers. Letters by Prince Petr A. Kropotkin, 1882-3 **(MS 3713 ff. 331, 336-43)**.

82.11 BLACKIE PAPERS (2621-64, Chs 947-50)
Papers of Prof. John Stuart Blackie include letters from Prince Petr A. Kropotkin, 1886-7 **(MS 2636 ff. 289, 318, 323; MS 2637 f. 43)**.

82.12 BLACKWOOD PAPERS (MSS 4001-940)
Papers of publishing house of William Blackwood and Sons include: 'A Correct Account of the Escape of James Henry Attwood and his Family from the Odessa in the South of Russia' **(MS 4762)**; MS and proofs of part of *The Invasion of the Crimea* by A. W. Kinglake **(MSS 4810-11)**; corrected proofs of 'The Attaman : a Tale of the Kosaks' by J. E. de Laskowska, 1885 **(MS 4816 f. 25)**. *See index of correspondents for details.*

82.13 BROWN CORRESPONDENCE (MSS 1847-62, 2835-78, 3258-76, Chs 1441-9, 2478-513)
Correspondence of Sir George Brown relating to the Crimean War, including letters written to him from officers at the front, 1854-6 **(MSS 1849-52; MS 1859; MS 3261 ff. 56, 64-9, 84-9, 110)**; papers re Kinglake's account of the War, 1863 **(MSS 1862, 2858-9**

passim., 2877 no. XV); papers re the Crimean War (**MSS 1860-1, 2854** *passim.*); papers re prize money in the Crimean War, 1863-4 (**MS 2859 ff. 101-5, 116; MS 2860**).

82.14 CARLYLE COLLECTION (MSS 601-9, 665-6, 787, 1763-78)
Letters from Ivan Sergeevich Turgenev to Thomas Carlyle, 1856, 1871 (**MS 666 nos. 76, 102**); letters from the Crimean War, 1855 (**MS 1767 ff. 55-7, 60-3**).

82.15 CARMICHAEL AND GORDON PAPERS (MS 109)
'Sundry Anecdotes of Peter the first', 1779, ascribed to Lord Hyndford but written by Patrick Bell of Antermony, physician at St Petersburg (**ff. 10-28**).

82.16 CHARLESTOWN COLLIERY AND LIMEWORKS (MSS 9625-31)
Letters from the St Petersburg Lübeck Steam Navigation Co., London, 1846, 1849 (**MS 9629 f. 213; MS 9631 ff. 1, 58, 65**).

82.17 COCHRANE PAPERS (MSS 2264-505)
Papers of Adm. Sir Alexander Forrester Inglis Cochrane and his son Adm. Sir Thomas John Cochrane include letters and copies of letters from Andrei Dashkov, Russian Minister at Washington, 1814 (**MS 2333 ff. 50-1, 207-10, 213-16; MS 2337 ff. 34, 93, 144-9**).

82.18 DICKSON PAPERS (MSS 13501-97)
Correspondence and papers of Rear-Adm. Robert Kirk Dickson (1898-1952) include letters from Sebastopol, 1918 (**MS 13510 ff. 72-83**) and diary of service on HMS *Superb* in the Black Sea, 1918 (**MS 13571**).

82.19 ELIBANK PAPERS (MSS 8801-24)
Correspondence of Alexander Murray as Chief Liberal Whip includes memos and letter re Russia, 1907-9 (**MS 8801 ff. 66, 116, 188-95**) and report re Russia, 1915 (**MS 8803 f. 265**).

82.20 ELLICE PAPERS (MSS 15001-195)
Letters from Marie Moutcharoff (?Mucharova) to Marion Coleman from St Petersburg, 1840, 1842, n.d. (**MS 15096**); notebook of Edward Ellice containing notes of travels in Russia, 1832 (**MS 15143; MS 15144 f. 11; MS 15145 f. 24**); pencil sketches of Count K. R. Nesselrode, Russian Chancellor, n.d. (**MS 15175 nos. 27, 47**).

82.21 ARTHUR ELLIOT PAPERS (MSS 19420-571)
Papers of Sir Thomas Frederick Elliot, diplomat, include notes re the Crimean War, 1855 (**MS 19432 f. 203**).

82.22 ERSKINE MURRAY PAPERS (Ch. 4370)
Passport for Sir John Erskine, 3rd Bt, Earl Erskine, issued at St Petersburg, n.d.

82.23 GEDDES PAPERS (MSS 10501-657)
Papers of Sir Patrick Geddes (1854-1932) include letters from Prince P. A. Kropotkin, 1882, 1888, 1897 (**MS 10522 ff. 159v, 170; MS 10524 f. 218; MS 10529 f. 128**).

82.24 GIBSON LETTERS (MS 3017)
TS copy of letter from John Dobson, merchant in Danzig, to his mother re the Polish rising of 1794 (**f. 40a**).

82.25 GLEIG PAPERS (MSS 3869-72)
Papers of George Gleig and George Robert Gleig include correspondence re the Crimean War, 1856 (**MS 3871**).

82.26 GREENSHIELDS, John Blackwood (MSS 19768-80)
Scrapbooks contain a telegraph message re the fall of Sebastopol, 1855 (MS 19770 no. 325).

82.27 HALDANE PAPERS (MSS 20001-260, 20510-33)
Papers of Gen. Sir Aylmer Haldane include typed copies and extracts of his letters to his mother whilst an observer in Japan and Manchuria during the Russo-Japanese War, 1904-5 (MS 20255 f. 119).

82.28 HALKETT, Col. James (1822-70) (MSS 14200-19)
Diary written during the Crimean War, Apr. 1854 - Mar. 1856 (MS 14214).

82.29 LISTON PAPERS (MSS 5510-721)
Papers of Sir Robert Liston include: copies of projects for treaties between Russia and England and Sardinia, late 18th century (MS 5518 f. 176; MS 5524 ff. 67-88); correspondence of Vasilii Nikolaevich Zinov'ev, Russian senator, 1787 (MS 5548 ff. 69, 96, 106, 115, 132, 138, 160, 176; MS 5549 ff. 85, 91; MS 5560 ff. 292-9); reports on the war between Russia and Sweden, 1789 (MS 5563 ff. 9, 22); copies of correspondence of Count S. R. Vorontsov, 1792 (MS 5568 ff. 125-8); dispatches from Constantinople including references to Russia (MSS 5570-82; MSS 5625-63); account of events concerning the death of Paul I, 1801 (MS 5605 f. 250); 2 plans of the Russian frontiers, late 18th century (MS 5719).

82.30 LITHGOW PAPERS (MSS 2543-55)
Letter from Maj.-Gen. Stewart Lithgow from the Crimea, 1856 (MS 2543 f. 95).

82.31 PAPERS OF JOHN P MACKINTOSH MP (Dep. 323)
Notes from printed sources on Russian history (/36); 4 letters between Mackintosh and Sir Bernard Braine re letter to be sent to *The Times* on erection of a memorial in London to those forcibly repatriated to the USSR, 14 June - 27 July 1979 (/94). Permission of Dr U. MacLean-Mackintosh is required before any item or part of an item may be photocopied or published.

82.32 MAXWELL OF MONREITH PAPERS (Acc. 7043)
Letters from Edward Maxwell to his brother William whilst on active service during the Crimean War and Indian Mutiny.

82.33 MELVILLE PAPERS (MSS 1-67, 1041-79, 6524)
Papers of Henry Dundas, 1st Visc. Melville, and his son Robert, 2nd Visc. Melville, include: papers re Russian activity in Asia, 1807-8 (MS 1071 ff. 1, 72-94); papers on Russia and the Northern Confederation, 1789, 1800-1, n.d. (MS 1075 ff. 148-212); notes on Russia, *c.* 1793 (MS 6524 f. 112).

82.34 MINTO PAPERS (MSS 11001-3496, Chs 8971-10633)
Papers of Sir Gilbert Elliot Murray Kynynmound (1751-1814), 1st Earl of Minto, include: letter re Russian forces in Italy, 1799 (MS 11230 f. 301); copies of letters of Paul I, 1799 (MS 11237 ff. 85-91); diplomatic papers re Russia, 1799-1801 (MSS 11243-4 *passim*); letter re Russian influence in India, 1801 (MS 11249 f. 403); correspondence re Russian army operations on Corfu, 1799-1801 (MS 11252 f. 128; MS 11259 ff. 128-277). Papers of Gilbert Elliot Murray Kynynmound (1782-1859), 2nd Earl of Minto, include: letters describing service in the Crimean War, 1854-6 (MS 11751 ff. 223-6; MS 11760 ff. 118-241; MS 11764 ff. 164-254; MS 11765 ff. 1-67, 92-339; MS 11765A; MS 11787 ff. 299, 317, 332); letters re naval operations in the Far East during the Crimean War, 1854-6 (MS 11762 ff. 1-229); journals concerning military and diplomatic events of the Crimean War

(**MSS 12000-2** *passim.*). Papers of Gilbert John Elliot Murray Kynynmound (1845-1914), 4th Earl of Minto, include diary and papers re the Russo-Turkish War, 1877 (**MS 12504; MS 12531 ff. 71-83; MSS 12533-5**). Papers of Hugh Elliot (1752-1830), diplomat, include: account of Russian campaign against Turkey, 1771 (**MS 12976 f. 50**); intelligence re Russian troops in Sicily and Corfu, 1804-5 (**MS 13004 f. 18; MS 13051 ff. 109, 129**); project for a British treaty with Russia, 1778 (**MS 13020 f. 38**). *See index of correspondents for further details.*

82.35 MURRAY, Sir John Archibald, Lord Murray (1779-1859) (**MSS 19735-9**)
Letters re the MacNeill report on commissariat failures in the Crimea, 1857 (**MS 19736 ff. 225-33**).

82.36 PAUL PAPERS (**MS 5162**)
Corrected proofs of 'Letters and Documents relating to Robert Erskine, Physician to Peter the Great, Czar of Russia, 1677-1720' edited by Revd Robert Paul.

82.37 RENNIE PAPERS (**MSS 19771-968**)
Letters from Sir John Rennie (1761-1821), engineer, re the imperial mint at St Petersburg, 1815 (**MS 19822 ff. 114-31**) and the naval dockyard at Kronstadt (**MS 19966**).

82.38 RICHARDSON OF KIRKLANDS PAPERS (**MSS 3989-92**)
Correspondence of John Richardson concerning the Crimean War, 1855-6 (**MS 3990 ff. 138-231**).

82.39 ROBERTSON-MACDONALD PAPERS (**MSS 3942-88**)
Letters to the Robertson family from Princess E. R. Dashkova, 1776 (**MS 3942 ff. 265, 269, 281, 289**) and Prince P. M. Dashkov, 1783 (**MS 3843 f. 143**).

82.40 ROSE PAPERS (**MSS 3795-801, Chs 2595-629**)
Papers of Sir George Henry Rose, diplomat, include correspondence with Prince Aleksandr Lobanov-Rostovskii, 1845 (**MS 3797 ff. 217-22**). Papers of Hugh Henry Rose, Baron Strathnairn, include papers re the Crimean War, 1856 (**MS 3798 ff. 105-32**).

82.41 ROSEBERY PAPERS (**MSS 10001-241**)
Papers of Archibald Philip Primrose (1847-1929), 5th Earl of Rosebery, include: memo on Anglo-Russian relations, 1885-6 (**MS 10132 ff. 38, 79**); copies of telegrams of Alexander III, 1893 (**MS 10133 f. 165**); printed reports re the Russian army (**MS 10144 ff. 64-6, 200**). There could be further references to Russia in his papers as P.M. and as Secretary of State for Foreign Affairs.

82.42 RUTHERFORD PAPERS (**MSS 9686-728**)
Papers of Andrew Rutherford (1791-1854), Lord Rutherford, include letters from Count Vladimir Davidov, n.d. (**MS 9718 ff. 43-6**).

82.43 RUTHERFORD OF EGERSTON PAPERS (**Acc. 7676**)
Correspondence of Robert Rutherford of Fairnington, Baron of the Russian Empire, includes a letter from Gicca (Prince Gregory Ghika) at Leghorn re his stay in Russia and referring to Count Aleksei Orlov and Russian military commanders, 1777 (**/A/Bdl. 38**).

82.44 LETTERS TO SIR WALTER SCOTT (**MSS 3874-920**)
Letters from Vladimir Davidov, 1826-8 (**MS 3902 f. 189; MS 3904 f. 46**); letter from Aleksandr Evtimovich Izmailov, fabulist, 1828 (**MS 3907 f. 7**).

82.45 SCOTTISH FOREIGN MISSIONS (MSS 7530-8022)
Foreign mission records of the (Established) Church of Scotland and the United Free Church of Scotland include letter to the Russian Bank for Foreign Trade, 1905 (**MS 7718**) and letter to the Russian Famine Relief Fund, 1922 (**MS 7868**).

82.46 SCOTTISH MISSIONARY SOCIETY (MSS 8983-7)
Letter books of William Brown, the Secretary, contain correspondence with missionaries in the Crimea, 1820-32 (**MS 8984 pp. 1-84**), Orenburg, 1820-5 (**MS 8985 pp. 1-112**), Vladikavkaz, 1821 (**MS 8985 p. 115**) and Astrakhan', 1821-36 (**MS 8987 pp. 1-267**).

82.47 SEYMOUR, Adm. Sir Edward Hobart (MSS 9486-8)
Journal kept by Seymour as a naval cadet and midshipman on HMS *Terrible* in the Black Sea, 1854-6 (**MS 9486**); letters and copies of letters from Seymour to his family from the Black Sea, 1854-6 (**MS 9488 ff. 1-31**).

82.48 STUART DE ROTHESAY PAPERS (MSS 6160-246)
Papers of Charles Stuart, Baron Stuart de Rothesay, include report on relations between Russia and China, 1818 (**MS 6183 p. 861**) and copy of letter from Alexander I, 1821 (**MS 6210 p. 321**).

82.49 SUTHERLAND PAPERS (Dep. 313)
Copy of a speech by Peter I on the occasion of meeting King William III at Utrecht, n.d., Russian with English transl. (**no. 3655**).

82.50 THOMSON PAPERS (MSS 9235-7)
Correspondence of Allen Thomson includes letters from Sir William Aitkin, the pathologist, describing life in Scutari in 1855 (**MS 9237 ff. 123-65**).

82.51 WAR OF THE SECOND COALITION AGAINST FRANCE (MS 731)
Letters and copies of letters mainly to Gen. John Ramsay relating to the war against France and including dealings with Russia, 1796-1821.

82.52 WATSON COLLECTION (MSS 577-600)
English transl. of 'The Black Shawl' by Aleksandr Sergeevich Pushkin, n.d. (**MS 581 no. 465**).

82.53 WILSON, Prof. John Dover (1881-1969) (MSS 14306-400)
Shakespearian scholar. Lecture notes concerning Russia, 1916, n.d. (**MS 14365 ff. 128-71**); newspaper cuttings re Russia, 1905-14 (**MS 14369**).

82.54 ARTHUR WOODBURN PAPERS (Acc. 7656)
Papers re official visits from the Supreme Soviet of the USSR to Britain, July 1956, Nov. 1966 (**Box 7**); papers re the activities of the British, Soviet and other communist parties, *c.* 1928-69 (**Box 9**).

82.55 YESTER PAPERS (MSS 14401-827)
Correspondence of George Hay, 8th Marquess of Tweeddale, and Arthur Hay, 9th Marquess of Tweeddale, re the Crimean War (**MS 14448 ff. 157-87; MS 14464 ff. 3-12**). Papers of William Montagu, 10th Marquess of Tweeddale, include correspondence re the Crimean War (**MS 14466 f. 160**) and papers re Russia and Siberia, 1864-5 (**MS 14469 ff. 226-78**).

82.56 YOUNG, Douglas C. C. (**Acc. 7085**)
Correspondence and papers re his World Peace Appeal visit to Prague and Moscow, 1952 (**Box 6**).

82.57 Letters to Sergei Mikhailovich Kravchinskii (Stepnyak), 1893 (**MS 966 ff. 32-5**).

82.58 Letter from Elizabeth Mackenzie, a nurse at Therepia, 1855 (**MS 2224 f. 39**).

82.59 Letters by Sir Colin Campbell from the Crimea and on the Indian Mutiny, 1855-8 (**MS 2257 f. 312**).

82.60 Letter by Brig.-Gen. Thomas Graham (afterwards Lord Lynedoch) referring to the conduct of the Russians, Malta 1800 (**MS 2618 f. 63**).

82.61 19th-century copies of treaties made by Persia with Russia, Persian (**MS 2777 ff. 22v-30, 36v-40v**).

82.62 TS copies of letters from Sir Walter Scott to Princess Golitsyn, 1826, from originals in the Saltykov-Shchedrin Library and Academy of Sciences in the USSR (**MS 2980 f. 65**).

82.63 Photostat of the last will and testament of Col. George Mathesome in the Tsar's service, 1633 (**MS 3112 f. 2**).

82.64 Letter from Catherine II to the King of Poland, n.d., French (**MS 3873 p. 289**).

82.65 Documents relating to Robert Erskine, physician to Peter I (**MS 5163**).

82.66 Letter of Capt. Arthur Walker describing the Crimea, 1856 (**MS 5406 f. 39**).

82.67 Letter concerning the war in the Crimea, 1854 (**MS 5509 f. 140**).

82.68 Letters from Sir Charles Maitland to his mother concerning the Crimean War, 1854-5 (**MS 6294 ff. 157, 226v**).

82.69 Notebook containing a record of the campaigns of the 1st Bn, Scots Fusilier Guards, in the Crimea, 1854-6 (**MS 9319**).

82.70 Sketch-book containing drawings and watercolours of incidents in the Crimean War, 1854-6 (**MS 9489**).

82.71 Journal of travels of John Ivor Murray covering service as surgeon in the Crimean War (**MS 9843**).

82.72 Letters from Sir John McNeill to John Paget discussing Russia's policy towards Turkey and Afghanistan, 1877-83 (**MS 10982**).

82.73 Letters and diaries of Capt. (later Lt-Col.) Richard L. O. Pearson from the Crimea, 1854-5 (**MSS 10985-7**).

82.74 Photocopies of letters mostly from officers of the 34th Foot from the Crimea, 1854-5 (**MS 15385 f. 102**).

82.75 Letters from Asst-Surg. Thomas Ligertwood to his family from the Crimea, 1854-6 (**MS 15385 f. 177**).

82.76 Correspondence of Pte Noah Bullimore whilst on active service in the Crimean War (**MS 15385 f. 233**).

82.77 Letter from Gen. Sir George Brown to Gen. Sir James Kempt including a detailed account of the battle of Inkerman (**MS 15385 f. 237**).

82.78 Letters from Sir William Gordon, 6th Bt, to his mother and sisters from the Crimea and India, 1854-?8 (**MS 15385 f. 245ff.**).

82.79 Copy of diary and letters of Maj. Alexander Irving covering the early part of the Crimean War, 8 Aug. - 3 Dec. 1854 (**MS 15391**).

82.80 Diary of Lt-Col. (later Brig.-Gen.) James George Smith Neill while in charge of the Turkish contingent in the Crimean War, 2 Sept. 1855 - 30 Sept. 1856 (**MS 15392**).

82.81 MS vol. entitled 'The Journey Rout[e] of Her Imperial Majesty from Charkoff thro' the Government of Kursk to Moscow ... . By the Governments Geometrician & Land Measurer Basshiloff 1787', relating to Catherine II's journey to southern Russia, and belonging to Dr Rogerson (**MS 19419**).

82.82 Collection of passports of Lt-Col. Robert Batty includes passports for Russia, 1817-30 (**Ch. 10660-8**).

82.83 MS of *Memoirs of a British Agent* (1932) by Sir Robert Bruce Lockhart (**Acc. 3176**).

82.84 Passport issued by the British Ambassador at St Petersburg to enable Arnold Churchill to travel home to England, 12 June 1917 (**Acc. 3663**).

82.85 MS chapter 'At the Beginning of Life' by S. Marshak, including translations of poems by Burns, Shakespeare and others into Russian, n.d. (**Acc. 3945**).

82.86 Galley proofs of the 'Battle of Inkerman' corresponding to chapter 5 of *The Invasion of the Crimea* by A. W. Kinglake, with extensive amendments (**Acc. 4270**).

82.87 21 poems by V. Mayakovskii translated into Scots by Edwin Morgan, 1959-60 (**Acc. 4535**).

82.88 TS of *Red Peak : a Personal Account of the British-Soviet Pamir Expedition 1962* (London, 1964) by Malcolm Slesser (**Acc. 5090**).

82.89 Prints from original photographs of events in Russia, *c.* 1920 (**Acc. 5435**).

82.90 Photocopy of letter from Sir Walter Scott to Gen. D. Davidov, 1826, from the original in the Lenin Library (**Acc. 5692**).

82.91 Passport of Revd Robert Boog Watson, chaplain to the Scottish troops in the Crimea, 1854 (**Acc. 6182**).

82.92 TS of diary of a trip to Russia by T. G. N. Haldane, 1932 (**Acc. 6317**).

82.93 Journals by Mary Lee Milne of service with the Scottish Women's Hospitals in Russia and Rumania, 1916-17 (**Acc. 6318**).

82.94 3 letters from Sir Archibald William Crichton to Dr Hamel from Tsarskoe Selo and St Petersburg on personal and medical matters, 1830-6 (**Acc. 7365**).

82.95 9 letters from Prince P. A. Kropotkin to William Duff in Glasgow, 1896-1909 (**Acc. 7868-9**).

82.96 Letter from FM Sir Donald Martin Stewart to the Duke of Cambridge mostly re the Russo-Afghan frontier question, 1884 (**Acc. 7878**).

82.97 Draft memo compiled possibly by Lord Augustus Loftus to Arthur Philip Primrose, 5th Earl of Rosebery, concerning Russian pretentions in Afghanistan, n.d. (**Acc. 8151**).

82.98 MS vol. containing maps and statistics re the districts of northern Russia presented to Dr John Rogerson, 1811 (**Acc. 8180**).

82.99 *C.* 180 letters from Gen. Sir Frederick W. Hamilton written mostly from the Crimea, 1847-55 (**Acc. 8218**).

82.100 Letter from William Schaw Cathcart, 1st Earl Cathcart, Ambassador at St Petersburg, to Charles Stuart, Baron Stuart de Rothesay, n.d. (**Acc. 8317**).

82.101 Letter from Adm. Sir Samuel Greig of the Russian Navy to Sir Charles Douglas re the American War of Independence, 1777 (**Acc. 8389**).

82.102 Album of photographs by N. V. Poggenpol re a mountaineering expedition to the Caucasus, July-Aug. 1904 (**Acc. 8563**).

83.1

ROYAL BOTANIC GARDEN LIBRARY

Inverleith Row, Edinburgh EH3 5LR

By appointment.

83.1 Letters to the Royal Botanic Garden, and in particular to Prof. I. B. Balfour from George Carrick, physician at the British Embassy in St Petersburg, 13 Dec. 1874, B. A. Fedtschenko (Fedchenko), 15 May 1913, W. Kesselring from the Imperial Botanic Gardens in St Petersburg, May 1913, C. J. Maximowisz (Karl Ivanovich Maksimovich) from St Petersburg, 25 July 1890, Dr E. L. Regel, Director of the Imperial Botanic Garden in St Petersburg, 19 Aug. 1890, D. N. Sokalskii, 12 Nov. 1907 and Fischer de Waldheim, Director of the Imperial Botanic Gardens in St Petersburg, 1913.

84.1-2

ROYAL COLLEGE OF PHYSICIANS' LIBRARY

9 Queen Street, Edinburgh EH2 1JQ

84.1 Certificate of Empress Elizabeth of Russia in favour of Dr North Vigor on his leaving Russian service, 28 June 1755.

84.2 Rescript by Nicholas I in favour of Sir James Basil Wylie, Bt, with a note of his distinguished service, 1851, and Latin transl. of same, 1852.

85.1

THE ROYAL SCOTS' REGIMENTAL MUSEUM

Regimental Headquarters, The Royal Scots (The Royal Regiment), The Castle, Edinburgh EH1 2YT

85.1 'Account of Service in 2nd/10th Bn The Royal Scots 1918-1919' by John Stewart covering service in North Russia (**Library A43**).

86.1-104

SCOTTISH RECORD OFFICE

HM General Register House, Edinburgh EH1 3YY

M. Livingstone, *Guide to the Public Records of Scotland* (Edinburgh, 1905) covers older historical records. A new *Guide* to the Scottish Record Office is under preparation. Non-public records are listed in the *List of Gifts and Deposits in the Scottish Record Office*, 2 vols (Edinburgh, 1971, 1976) (covering collections GD1 - GD96). Details of new accessions are given in the *Annual Report of the Keeper of the Record of Scotland*. Several source lists covering various topics are available in the Search Rooms. *Source List no. 22, Russia* is more detailed version of this entry, and reference to material relating to Russia can also be found in *Source List no. 8, Sweden, Source List no. 9, Naval and Mercantile,* and *Source List no. 23, Germany*. There are inventories for most classes of records in the Search Rooms; also card index of plans. Source lists are periodically revised and advice should be sougt from the Record Office on the most recent revision available. Main holdings are kept in HM General Register House, Princes Street, Edinburgh but modern departmental records, the records of nationalised industries and some private industrial concerns, maps and plans are kept in the West Register House, Charlotte Square, Edinburgh.

British Railways (BR)

86.1 PORT OF BO'NESS HARBOUR COMMISSION (**BR/BNH**)

Records include references to goods imported from and exported to Russian ports, particularly in the class Bo'ness Harbour Export Book, 1883-93 (**/4/1**) and to ships sailing to and from Baltic and Russian ports, particularly in the class Arrivals and Sailing Book for Bo'ness Harbour and Dock, 1889-97 (**/4/2**). *See inventories for details.*

Commissary Courts (CC)

86.2 The testaments (wills and intestate estates) of Scots living abroad were registered for the years 1601-1829 in the Commissary Court of Edinburgh. Names are listed alphabetically by year in printed *Registers of Testaments*. The wills of some, but not all, Scots who lived and worked in Russia can be traced through these registers including: James Smith, sometime merchant in London, thereafter in Archangel, 29 Oct. 1731; James Hewitt, Councillor of Commerce in St Petersburg, 15 Jan. 1747; William Freer, formerly Surg.-Maj. in the Russian Army, 29 Jan. 1768. *See Registers for further names.*

Exchequer (E)

86.3 CUSTOMS ACCOUNTS (E504)

Copies of quarterly accounts by customs collectors of merchants' entries of goods exported and imported arranged by port, 1742-1830, including details of ship, captain, owner, cargo, origin and destination. The records of the port of Leith (/22) include references to Russian ports and there may be further references in the records of other Scottish ports. *See inventories for details.*

Gifts and Deposits (GD)

86.4 ABERCAIRNY MSS (GD24)

Letter from George Mackenzie to Dr Erskine in St Petersburg, 1715 (**/1/449**); correspondence of Sir Henry Stirling in St Petersburg, 1721, 1729, 1732 (**/1/450-1, 464/F-M**); papers re Mungo Graham, apprenticed to George Napier, merchant in St Petersburg, 1736-64 (**/1/454**); letter from Mainwaring and Taylor, merchants in Archangel, 1711 (**/1/464/F-M**); letter from James Mounsey, physician to the Russian Empress (Elizabeth), 1762 (**/1/846**); papers re the career of Adm. Thomas Gordon of the Russian Navy including commissions in the Russian Navy, letter books and notes, 1720-37, logs and notebooks, papers re his estate and house in Russia and his will (**/1/854-62**). *See inventory for details.*

86.5 AIRTH WRITS (GD37)

Copies of letter to Gen. J. D. Bruce in Russia, 1720, and from Bruce in Åbo, 22 Apr. 1721 (**/328-9**).

86.6 J. & F. ANDERSON COLLECTION (GD297)

Letter from John P. Curran to Lady Charlotte Rawdon re Vorontsov (?S.), n.d. (**/2**).

86.7 BUCCLEUCH MUNIMENTS (GD224)

5 envelopes of correspondence including letters of Charles, Earl of Dalkeith, while travelling in Russia, 1793.

86.8 D. & J. H. CAMPBELL W.S. (GD253)

Letters re Russian rhubarb to Dr John Hope, Professor of Botany and Materia Medica at Edinburgh University from James Mounsey, physician to Empress Elizabeth of Russia, 1765 (**/144/5/4**), John Bell, 1765 (**/144/5/9**), P. Pallas, 1777 (**/144/5/10**); note concerning the sale and price of Russian, Indian and Scottish rhubarb, n.d. (**/144/5/12**).

86.9 CARRON COMPANY (GD58)

Vol. containing particulars and drawings of guns supplied to the Russian government, 1779-97 (**/16/24**).

86.10 CLERK OF PENICUIK (GD18)

Passport belonging to Sir George Douglas Clerk of Penicuik with Russian visa, 1872 (**/2079**); letters from Dr John Rogerson to John Clerk of Eldin commenting on life in Russia, 1773 (**/5121**).

86.11 CUNNINGHAME GRAHAM OF ARDOCH (GD22)

Transl. of a patent of 1665 by Tsar Alexis to Lt-Col. Thomas Dalyell allowing him to return to Scotland, 1762 (**/1/195**); letters from Douglas Graham from the Crimean War (**Section I no. 350**).

86.12 DALHOUSIE MUNIMENTS (**GD45**)
Papers of Fox Maule (later Lord Panmure), Secretary for War, re the Crimean War (**/8/2/126-501**); copy of letter from Florence Nightingale from the Crimea (**/8/337/3**); printed memo, with sketch-map, by William Spottiswoode to Lord Clarendon re a journey on the Asiatic frontier of Russia, 1856 (**/8/401**). *See inventory for details.*

86.13 DALQUHARRAN PAPERS (**GD27**)
Request from John Johnston for letters of safe conduct to travel from Danzig to Russia, 1710 (**/3/2**).

86.14 DAVIDSON & SYME, W.S. (**GD282**)
Letter from Sir Justin Sheil to J. P. Riach instructing him to find out about Russian movements on the shores of the Caspian, 1841 (**/13/242**).

86.15 DUNDAS OF OCHTERTYRE MUNIMENTS (**GD35**)
Letter from A. Carlton Cumberbatch to William Dundas re Russian policy and HMS *Vixen*, June 1837 (**/195**); letter from John Dundas to Sir David Dundas referring to the bribing of Russian officials in the Baltic trade, 5 Aug. 1864 (**/236/6**).

86.16 DUNDONALD MUNIMENTS (**GD233**)
Letters from Sir Alexander Malet to Thomas, Lord Cochrane, 10th Earl of Dundonald, referring to relations between Turkey and Russia, 1828-32 (**/13**); papers re the action of Britian and Russia regarding Greek independence, 1827 (**/44/XX**).

86.17 ELPHINSTONE MUNIMENTS (**GD156**)
Letters addressed to Adm. John Elphinstone re his service in the Russian Navy, 1766-83 (**/69**). *See inventory for details.*

86.18 GILMOUR OF LUNDIN AND MONTRAVE (**GD383**)
Letter from John Baird, Governor-General of Australia, to Sir John Gilmour deploring the unions' use of Soviet contributions in the General Strike, 1926 (**/22/7-9**); correspondence of Sir John Gilmour with Capt. J. M. Ritchie re the German-Soviet alliance, 1939 (**/73/1-4**).

86.19 GORDON CASTLE (**GD44**)
Letter from Adm. Thomas Gordon to Cosmo George, 3rd Duke of Gordon, from Kronstadt, 1737 (**/43/13**).

86.20 HAMILTON BRUCE PAPERS (**GD152**)
Letters from Moscow and St Petersburg including a description of a visit to the Russian Court, 1813-14 (**/53/1**).

86.21 HOPE OF CRAIGHALL MUNIMENTS (**GD377**)
Letter from Thomas Hope to Alicia Hope with news of the Crimean War, 1855 (**/284/1**).

86.22 HOPE OF LUFFNESS (**GD364**)
Letters and ship's log by George Hope from HMS *Royal Albert* in the Crimean War (**/1/632; /2/111**); staff papers re British and Russian prisoners in enemy hospitals, 1799 (**/1/1095**); papers re the Russian army in Holland, 1799 (**/1/1099-100**); letters and reports on Russian reactions to the Peninsular Expedition, 1808 (**/1/1175, 1178**); map showing the position of the Russian army, 1812 (**/1/1227**); letters re Russo-German Legion in Finland, 1813 (**/1/1232-4, 1241**); copies of treaties of between Britain and Russia and Russia and Prussia, 1812-13 (**/1/1237, 1240**); copy of correspondence on negotiations between Denmark, Sweden, Russia and Britain, 1813 (**/1/1239**); letter from Capt. G. Brown

commending the Russian troops, 1813 (**/1/1243**); plans and orders of Russian review by Sir George Murray, 1815 (**/1/1271**); part of a pocket diary covering tour in Eastern Europe, including Russia, 1867 (**/2/155**). *See inventory for details.*

86.23 HUME OF MARCHMONT MSS (GD158)

Papers of Alexander, 2nd Earl of Marchmont, as Ambassador to Copenhagen, include: memo by B. Oxenstierna on the Russo-Swedish War, 1702 (**/1488**); note on conference between Danish and Russian ministers, 1716 (**/1517**); copy of convention re Danish, English and Russian fleets, Aug. 1716 (**/1519**); line of battle of the Danish, English and Russian fleets, 1716 (**/1524**); letters from F. C. Weber, Hanoverian Resident at St Petersburg, to Sir Patrick Hume, Lord Polwarth, 1717-18 (**/1597**); list of the Russian fleet, 1743 (**1643**); letters from Capt. James Jefferyes to Polwarth from St Petersburg, 1718-21 (**/1696**); copy of letter from Peter I to Sir John Norris and his reply, copy letter from Count F. A. Golovin to Norris, 1719 (**/1721**); copy of declaration by Peter I re Baltic trade, 17/28 June 1719 (**/1727**); copy of treaty between Russia and Sweden, 30 Aug. 1721 (**/1959**).

86.24 MESSRS HUNTER, HARVEY, WEBSTER & WILL (GD298)

Letter from John Agnew to Vans Hathorn discussing decline of business and that Russia would not assist Britain in a war with the Dutch, 1780 (**/38/7**).

86.25 HUNTLEY MUNIMENTS (GD312)

Letter from Douglas Gordon Halyburton of Pitur to John Frederick Gordon referring to the explorer James Burness who travelled through Bukhara to Persia, 16 June 1834 (**/46**).

86.26 KINLOCH OF KILRIE MUNIMENTS (GD1/931)

Papers of John Kinloch as Inspector-General of the British Foreign Legions (German and Swiss) enlisted for service in the Crimean War, 1855-7 (**/24**).

86.27 LEITH HAY MUNIMENTS (GD225)

Diary of Col. Alexander Leith-Hay whilst serving in the Crimean War, 1854 (**Box 39/9**).

86.28 LEVEN AND MELVILLE MUNIMENTS (GD26)

Letters from Edmund Bayley, merchant at St Petersburg, 1801 (**/13/842**); letter from John Leslie Melville from St Petersburg to his brother Visc. Balgonie, giving details of a journey through Denmark and Sweden to Russia, 3 July 1807 (**/13/861**).

86.29 LOCH MUNIMENTS (GD268)

Letter from Joseph Robinson answering queries about the Gordon family in Russia, 1850 (**/87**).

86.30 LOTHIAN MSS (GD40)

Papers of Philip Kerr, 11th Marquess of Lothian, include: files entitled 'Russia', 1917-21, whilst he was Private Secretary to Lloyd George (**/17/26-31**); letters and memos from prominent Russians and non-Russians re Russia including J. H. Bratiano, T. Keyes, A. W. A. Leeper, Dr F. Nansen, Prof. B. Pares, A. Ransome, Gen. Shokal'skii, Prof. J. Y. Simpson (**/17/206-20**); papers re Russia, 1917-20 (**/17/746-820**); A. F. Kerenskii papers, 1918 (**/17/821-31**); Bullitt papers re Russia, 1919 (**/17/832-7**); Prof. J. Y. Simpson papers re Russia, 1919 (**/17/834-64**); papers re Poland including references to Russia, 1917-20 (**/17/872-916**); papers re Russia at peace conferences, 1918-19 (**/17/1173**). *See inventory for details.*

86.31 SIR JOHN MCNEILL PAPERS (GD1/928; GD371)

Crimean Commission papers include: letters between McNeill and Fox Maule, Lord Panmure, 1855-6 (**GD1/928/2**); letters re the Crimean Commission (**/3-12**); letter book of copy letters from and re McNeill covering his voyage and arrival at Balaclava, 1855 (/13); memo by McNeill on reactions to the Crimean report, 1856, n.d. (/14). Correspondence addressed to McNeill while in service of the East India Company in India and the Legation in Persia, 1819-35, and then as Envoy and Minister Plenipotentiary in Persia, 1835-43, includes references to Russian expansion and relations with Persia and Britain (GD371/1-225); general correspondence referring to Russian policy, 1843-6, 1853 (/270/2; /276/2; /278; /297/2; /371; /374); memo by J. N. R. Campbell on Persia referring to Russian ambitions, n.d. (/373); memo by McNeill on Russian ambitions as they affect Persia, 1835 (/379). *See inventory for details.*

86.32 MACPHERSON OF CLUNY PAPERS (GD80)
Copy of genealogical memorial of the family of Verson in Estonia sent by Count F. A. Golovin to Sir John Erskine of Alva, 15 Oct. 1725 (/967).

86.33 MAR AND KELLIE (GD124)
Letter from Dr Robert Erksine to the Earl of Mar (John Erskine) from Moscow, 20 Jan. 1708 (/15/773).

86.34 MELVILLE CASTLE (GD51)
Papers and correspondence of William Eaton re Russian foreign policy and commerce, 1796, 1803, 1805 (/1/508; /1/812; /1/817/1-3); correspondence of Henry Dundas re relations between Russia and England, 1797-1899 (/1/529/4-7; /1/545/1-2; /1/548; /1/712/1-5); letter from Thomas Bruce, Earl of Elgin, to William Pitt on Russia and Turkey, 1800 (/1/550); printed papers re Russia and Malta, 1803 (/1/558); memo by Sir John Dalrymple on Russia and Sicily, 1803 (/1/560); letters from Dalrymple to Henry Dundas, Lord Melville, re possibility of a naval alliance with Russia, 1807 (/1/569); letter from Sir Stephen Shairp to Robert Dundas containing statistics of Russian trade in the Caspian Sea, 1808 (/1/572). *See inventory for details.*

86.35 MURRAY, BEITH & MURRAY W.S. (GD374)
Abstract of contract of marriage between Sir Robert Pollock Somerville Head, Bt, and Grace Margaret Robertson, signed by both parties at Petrograd, 1915 (/78).

86.36 MURRAY OF POLMAISE MSS (GD189)
Letter from John Murray to William Murray of Polmaise describing a review of troops in Paris attended by Alexander I, 30 Sept. 1815 (/2/591); receipt for officers' packages for the Crimea, 13 Dec. 1854 (/2/855); letters from John Murray to his father John Murray of Polmaise from the Crimea, 1854-5, and family letters commenting on the war (/2/857-1069 *passim*). *See inventory for details.*

86.37 PAPERS OF SIR CHARLES AUGUSTUS MURRAY (GD261)
Journal covering the visit of the Russian Emperor (Nicholas I), June 1844 (/5); journals of journey from Teheran to Tiflis, 1859 (/8); journal at Poti on the Black Sea, 1859 (/9); TS copies of letters from G. Stevens, Acting Consul at Trebizond, to Lord Clarendon chiefly re Russian operations on the shores of the Black Sea, 1858 (/14a); letters from Sir James Redhouse to Murray re Russia and the Eastern Question, 1879-80 (/26); copy letters from C. A. Stevens, Acting Consul in Tabriz, re a ban on ships sailing to Circassian ports and anti-Russian riots, 1858 (/60).

86.38 NAPIER, George (GD1/850)
Merchant in St Petersburg. Letters from George in St Petersburg to his brother James Napier, 1732-44 (/31-6, 38-9) and to Sir Henry Stirling, 15 Jan. 1743 (/37).

86.39 OGILVY OF INVERQUHARITY (**GD205**)

Correspondence of the 5th Duke of Leeds whilst Secretary of State for Foreign Affairs deals with Russian foreign policy and includes 2 letters from Charles Whitworth, Envoy at St Petersburg, 1791 (**/Box 50**).

86.40 ROGERSON PAPERS (**GD1/620**)

Correspondence of Dr John Rogerson of Dumcrieff (1741-1823), court doctor and Privy Councillor in Russia, 1767-1824 (**/1-35**). Papers of William Rogerson, merchant in St Petersburg, include: correspondence, 1788-1806 (**/48-52**); papers re his funeral and copy of his will (**/53-4**). Correspondence of Alexander Rogerson, merchant of St Petersburg re business, family and domestic matters, 1813-24, 1818-32 (**/55, 73, 76, 83, 85-6, 96-7, 99-114**). *See inventory for details.*

86.41 ROLLO OF DUNCRUE MUNIMENTS (**GD56**)

Papers re the trust estate of Dr John Rogerson, formerly physician to the Tsar, include a copy of his testament executed on 1 July 1816 at St Petersburg and accounts of Messrs Thomson and Bonar, merchants in St Petersburg, 1823-4 (**/164/3**).

86.42 SCOTT OF HARDEN MSS (**GD157**)

Letter from Francis James Scott to Hugh Scott re the Duchess of Kingston's estate in Livonia, 14 Dec. 1815 (**/2347**); letters from Prince P. Mestschersky (Meshcherskii), supervisor of the Greek Church in St Petersburg, to Harriet Scott, 12 Apr., 12 Dec. 1831, 16/28 May 1833 (**/2441, 2445**); letters from Count J. Ugartz (or Ugate) to Harriet Scott from St Petersburg, 22 Apr., 15 Sept. 1835 (**/2448**); letter from Princess Elizabeth, daughter of George III, to Harriet Polwarth re the fire at St Petersburg, 13 Jan. 1838 (**/2463**).

86.43 SCRYMGEOUR WEDDERBURN MUNIMENTS, EARL OF DUNDEE (**GD137**)

Letter from Anne Lobry from St Petersburg to Mrs Gressel Wedderburn, 16 July 1740 (**/140**).

86.44 SEAFIELD (**GD248**)

Letter from William and George Lyon to their mother describing their journey to, and arrival in, Russia, where they had gone to work under the direction of Charles Cameron, the architect, 1784 (**/518/6**).

86.45 SEAFORTH MUNIMENTS (**GD46**)

Document giving permission to William Mackenzie to leave the Russian Life Guards and passport issued by the 3rd Section of the Russian Chancellery for him to travel to England, 3 Mar 1740 (**/6/97A**); extracts from correspondence between Prince Hoare, Secretary for Foreign Correspondence to the Royal Academy of London, and the Academies of Vienna and St Petersburg on the cultivation of the arts, 31 May 1802 (**/16/7**).

86.46 SEMPILL OF CRAIGIEVAR MUNIMENTS (**GD250**)

Mitchell MSS include copies of treaty with the Empress of Russia (Elizabeth), 1747 (**/Bdl 7**).

86.47 SHAIRP OF HOUSTON (**GD30**)

Letter from Walter Shairp, merchant in St Petersburg, to Thomas Shairp referring to the coup of 1762 (**/1583**).

86.48 SINCLAIR OF DUNBEATH PAPERS **(GD280)**
Map of Europe illustrating a journey made to St Petersburg by Sir John Sinclair, Bt, 1786-7 **(/4/9)**.

86.49 SOCIETY OF ANTIQUARIES **(GD103)**
Letters patent under the great seal of Alexander I granting permission for a merchant to trade in Russian waters, 1814, Russian and Italian **(/2/489)**.

86.50 THE JOHN STEIN COLLECTION (SCOTTISH OILS LTD) **(GD367)**
Photographs, draft reports and publications re the shale oil industry in Estonia, 1918-28 **(/38-44)**.

86.51 THOMSON, David **(GD1/980)**
Marine engineer in Russian General Post Office Department, 1854-72. Papers, passport, testimonials and photograph.

86.52 WARING OF LENNEL PAPERS **(GD372)**
Letter from Sally MacNaughton to Lady Clementine Waring from her hospital service in Petrograd **(/94)**; letters from F. M. Cutler and Maj. L. H. Marriage serving with the North Russian Expeditionary Forces, 1918-19 **(/131-3)**; newscuttings and TS notes on trade with Russia by Walter Waring, 1923-30 **(/206)**.

86.53 3 letters between Sir A. Smith, Director-General of the Army Medical Department, and James Alexander, Divisional Medical Officer of the Light Division, re medical conditions during the Crimean War **(GD1/71)**.

86.54 Letters from James Young to his father from the Crimea, 1855-6 **(GD1/96/3)**.

86.55 2 letters from Lt Solfleet from the Crimean War, 1854 **(GD1/135/1)**.

86.56 Correspondence of John Gemmill from Moscow and St Petersburg re textile trade, 1851-4 **(GD1/504/2-4)**.

86.57 Letters from R. D. Buchanan, Seaforth Highlanders, from the Crimea, 1855-6 **(GD1/512/51)**.

86.58 Passports issued to Sir George Morison Paul and his wife, Lady Mary Morison Paul, and to Miss Georgina Eleanor Paul travelling in Europe, stamped with Russian visas, 18 July 1912 **(GD1/585/46)**.

86.59 Printed 'Memorial to His Britannick Majesty by the Minister from His Czarish Majesty [Peter I]' congratulating the King on his discovery of a Swedish conspiracy against him, 1717 **(GD1/616/41)**.

86.60 Notebook including a history of the Russian royal house, ?1762 **(GD1/616/213)**.

86.61 Printed copy of letter from John Bright re the Crimean War, 1854 **(GD2/119)**.

Privy Council (PC)

The following documents are published in *The Register of the Privy Council of Scotland*, 38 vols.

86.62 Decree concerning goods in a ship from Danzig, the goods including a history and description of Poland, Muscovy and Prussia, 29 Dec. 1595 (**PC1/16 p. 417**).

86.63 Order relating to the robbery of a Dutch ship wrecked on the Island of Uist when sailing from St Nicholas in Russia, 1627 (**PC1/31 ff. 258v-9**).

86.64 Reference to the supplication of Col. John Kinninmonth, governor of Nettenburg in Russia, for a certificate of his birth and family, 13 Oct. 1636 (**PC1/37 f. 173**).

86.65 Birth-brief granted to Lt-Col. [Alexander] Hamilton, serving under the Emperor of Russia, 1670 (**PC1/40 p. 326**).

86.66 Proclamation of Charles II for establishing a company for fishing, having the right to trade to 'Muscovia, Freezland Island, Greenland and other such northerne islands and continents ...' (**PC1/40 p. 356**).

86.67 Supplication by Lt-Col. Alexander Hamilton, who had served with the Emperor of Russia, for appointment as major in the new model of the militia, 27 Jan. 1681 (**PC2/20 pp. 525-6**).

86.68 Letter from Eric XIV, King of Sweden, to Queen Mary of England re regulations for navigation and commerce in the Baltic and including a reference to the Muscovites, 22 Oct. 1562, Latin (**PC5/2 ff. 19-20**).

86.69 Royal letter to Sir Alexander Leslie granting him licence to raise troops in Scotland for Russian service, 28 Mar. 1633, and copy of the same, 1 May 1633 (**PC5/4; PC11/5A ff. 214v-15**).

86.70 Letter from Sir Andrew Keith to Regent Morton referring to the castle taken from the King of Denmark by the Muscovites, 25 Feb. 1577/78 (**PC10/3**).

86.71 Proposals submitted to the Committee for Trade by the Provost of Linlithgow request that the improvement of the Muscovite trade should be considered, 1681 (**PC12/7**).

Register of Deeds (RD)

86.72 Procuratory by George Barnes and Andrew Judde and Anthony Huse, provosts of the college or society of merchants of England in Russia, to Laurence Huse, George Gilpin, John Lewes, John Bukelands, Edmund Roberts and Robert Best, 10 Dec. 1556 (**RD1/2 ff. 61r-63v**).

86.73 Procuratory by Owscheip Gregoryrech Nepera (Osip Nepea), ambassador of Ivan IV, to John Lewsche (Lewes), Edmund Roberts and John Buckland (?Bukelands), 5 Feb. 1557 (**RD1/2 ff. 64r-66v**).

Special Collections (RH)

86.74 BARGANY LETTER BOOKS (**RH4/57**)

Microfilm of letter from Miguel de Alava to Lady Emma Hamilton discussing the danger of the Russian taking Constantinople, 12 Sept. ---, French (**vol. 3/17**); letter from Count S. Vorontsov to ?Adam Duncan, 14 Oct. 1797, French (**vol. 3/47**). Readers wishing to use this microfilm must sign an undertaking to submit the relevant parts of any proposed publication based on these records to the owner, Sir Frederick Dalrymple Hamilton, for approval.

86.75 ROYAL SCOTS (**RH2/4/561**)

Photocopies of documents relating to the Royal Scots include: distribution of forces at Scutari, 1854 (**/40**); casualty returns from action at Alma and Inkerman (**/41-3**); papers re the siege of Sebastopol, 1855 (**/44-5**). Copied from class WO 1/368-9 in the Public Record Office, London.

86.76 TOWNSEND PAPERS (**RH4/98**)

Microfilms of papers re treaties include ones between Britain and Russia, 1742-62 (**Reel 7**); miscellaneous treaties including ones involving Russia, 1710-53 (**Reel 8**). Formerly **GD224**. No large scale publication, quotation or copying without the permission of William L. Clement, Library of Michigan, USA.

86.77 Microfilm of letter from FM HRH Edward, Duke of Kent, to E. Viale expressing hopes for the success of Viale's memorial to the Emperor of Russia, 3 May 1807 (**RH4/31/2**).

86.78 Microfilm of 'The notebook of a private soldier, or the 93rd Sutherland Highlanders in the Crimea' by Robert Sinclair; 'Tyneleachdin in the Crimea' by Donald Cameron (**RH4/141**). Originals in the Regimental Museum of the Argyll and Sutherland Highlanders, Stirling Castle.

Plans (RHP)

Some of the following may be published maps and plans.

86.79 Plan of the environs of Sebastopol, 1854 (**RHP 1630/1**).

86.80 Plan of the Crimea and the town and harbour of Sebastopol, 1854 (**RHP 1630/2**).

86.81 A sketch showing the function of investing corps of Allied Armies before Sebastopol, 1854 (**RHP 1630/3**).

86.82 A birds-eye view of part of the south-west coast of the Crimea, 1854 (**RHP 1630/4**).

86.83 Copy plan of the town of Revel, 1730 (**RHP 3198**).

86.84 Pictorial etching of Kronstadt, 1854 (**RHP 4977**).

86.85 Panoramic view of Sebastopol, 1855 (**RHP 4978**).

86.86 Panoramic view of external and internal defences of Sebastopol, 1855 (**RHP 4979**).

86.87 Sketches of Sebastopol by Lt M. O'Reilly, 1854, n.d. (**RHP 4981-2**).

86.88 Panoramic view of the entrenched position of the allied armies before Sebastopol, [1855] **(RHP 4982)**.

86.89 Map of the Kingdom of Poland and Grand Duchy of Lithuania showing their dismemberment, 1799 **(RHP 9839)**.

86.90 Map of the Empire of Russia, 1787 **(RHP 9842)**.

86.91 Plan of the environs of Sebastopol showing the positions of the besieging armies, 1854 **(RHP 12190)**.

86.92 Plan of the Sea of Azov, 1855 **(RHP 12192)**.

86.93 Bird's-eye view lithographed etching of the island of Kronstadt, mid 19th century **(RHP 12196)**.

86.94 Architectural elevations and sections of Fort Alexander at Kronstadt, mid 19th century **(RHP 12197)**.

86.95 Architectural elevations and sections of Fort Prince Menzikoff (Menshikov) at Kronstadt, *post* 1851 **(RHP 12198)**.

86.96 Pictorial coloured sketch of the town of Revel, 1854 **(RHP 12217)**.

86.97 Plan of the environs of Sebastopol with the batteries and approaches, 1854 **(RHP 30225)**.

86.98 Plan of Mamelon and the new Russian defences with the siege works of the Allies at Sebastopol, 1855 **(RHP 30226)**.

86.99 Map of Poland with its dismembered provinces, 1784 **(RHP 35217)**.

86.100 Map, with pictorial sketch, showing military positions at the battle of Alma, 16 Oct. 1854 **(RHP 41865)**.

86.101 Map of the environs of Sebastopol with the batteries and approaches, 10 Oct. 1854 **(RHP 41866)**.

86.102 Map of the environs of Sebastopol with the batteries and approaches and military positions, 3 Nov. 1854 **(RHP 41867)**.

86.103 Map of the environs of Sebastopol with the batteries and approaches and military positions, 28 Apr. 1855 **(RHP 41868)**.

Register of Sasines (RS)

86.104 Instrument of sasine by Gen. Patrick Gordon, C.-in-C. of the Russian forces, following on disposition dated at Moscow, 11 Jan. 1692, and signed in the presence of Maj.-Gen. Paul Menzies, Col. Alexander Livingstoun and Maj. Harry Gordon, all in Russian service. Registered, Aberdeen, 8 Sept. 1692. **(RS8/14)**.

87.1-10

SCOTTISH UNITED SERVICES MUSEUM

The Castle, Edinburgh EH1 2NG

By written appointment.

87.1 Letter by John Hawkins of the Scots Greys describing the action of the Heavy Brigade at Balaclava (**2. D. 852. 1.**).

87.2 Letter fron Col. Lenox Prendergast to Col. Williams re the Crimean War, Dec. 1906 (**2. D. 854. 2.**).

87.3 Copy of an extract from a letter from J. W. Fortescue to Col. Cator, re an incident that occurred at the Alma, 4 Oct. 1922 (**3. G. 854. 1.**).

87.4 *Letters from an Officer of the Scots Grey to his Mother during the Crimean War* (London, 1866) by Capt. George Buchanan of Drumpeller, being a book printed for private circulation (**947. 07.**).

87.5 'Reminiscenses of the 42nd Royal Highlanders, The Black Watch, in the Crimea and the Indian Mutiny' by David McAusland (**A. 242. 42.**).

87.6 List of Crimean and Indian mutiny veterans present at the occasion of the state visit of HM Edward VII to Edinburgh, May 1903 (**C. 126.**).

87.7 2 Russian postcards sent by the 79th Russian Regt to the 1st Bn of the 79th Highlanders in France, Easter 1916 (**C. 197.**)

87.8 Postcard sent by the 79th Russian Regt to the 2nd Bn of the 79th Highlanders in Salonika, Easter 1916 (**C. 202.**).

87.9 Letter of James Scott, No. 6 Co., 11th Bn Royal Artillery, re the battle of Inkerman, 20 Jan. 1855 (**R.A. 855. 1**).

87.10 3 letters from Rifleman (later Sgt) John Linton, 2nd Bn Rifle Bde, to his parents from the Crimea, 1855 (**R.B. 855. 1**).

88.1-8

DEVON RECORD OFFICE

Castle Street, Exeter EX4 3PU

88.1 ACLAND OF KILLERTON (**1148 M**)
Letters and papers of Stratford Canning, Lord Stratford de Redcliffe, re the Crimean War, 1856 (**/8/11**).

88.2 ANSTEY AND THOMPSON, SOLICITORS (**1926 B**)
Walrond family papers include a declaration and statement about shares in the Dünaburg and Vitebsk Railway Co., 1875-8 (**/W/E/30/4**).

88.3 PALK DEPOSIT (**Z 6**)
Letters from Laurence Palk to Sir Robert Palk mentioning Catherine II, 10 Apr. 1786 (**no. 435**) and referring to the declaration of war between Russia and Turkey, 8 Sept. 1786 (**no. 458**).

88.4 ROBINSON, Fred (**74**)
Passports issued in St Petersburg to Miss Annie Marshall, 1910, and Fred Robinson, 1917 (**/11/1-2**); TS copy of letter from W. Wulff to Robinson re events in Russia after the Revolution, 20 Sept. 1920 (**/11/3**); letter of appointment of Robinson as representative in Archangel of Frederick James Leathers, 1st Visc. Leathers, Minister of War Transport, 28 Aug. 1941 (**/11/4**); diary of Robinson in Archangel, 10 Oct. - 31 Dec. 1941 (**/11/5**).

88.5 SIDMOUTH PAPERS (**152 M**)
Letter from Prince William of Gloucester from St Petersburg to Henry Addington, Visc. Sidmouth, re his visit to Russia, 1802 (**/C 1802/OZ 154**); 'Mémoire sur les intérêts de la Russie relativement à la situation actuelle de l'Europe', 1803 (**/C 1803/OL 2**); letter from James Macpherson to Henry Addington re an alliance between Prussia and Russia, 1800 (**/M/OZ/59**); letter from Charles Addington in the Crimea, 1855 (**/M/49/14**); files re the United States, 1823-7, include material re the 1824 convention with Russia (**/Box 34. Public Office. 1-4**).

88.6 Letter from Ross Balfour Moore to Miss Anne Moore with news of the death of Paul I, 17 Apr. 1801 (**68/30/8**).

88.7 MS vol. in Russian, dated 1 Dec. 1849, found in a street in Sebastopol in 1856 (**MS 9**).

88.8 Journal and letters of Richard de la Bere Granville include references to Russia, 1847-54 (**MS 35**).

89.1

THE DEVONSHIRE REGIMENTAL MUSEUM

The Regimental Headquarters, The Devonshire and Dorset Regiment, Wyvern Barracks, Exeter

89.1 2 albums of photographs compiled by Lt-Col. N. A. Wilcox covering part of the service of the 1st Bn Oxfordshire and Buckinghamshire Light Infantry in North Russia, 1919 (**Acc Nos 1241-2**).

90.1

KENT ARCHIVES OFFICE, SOUTH-EAST KENT BRANCH

Central Library, Grace Hill, Folkestone, Kent

90.1 TS travel diaries of Alice M. Hunt include an account of a world tour encompassing Russia, 1909, and a vol., 'A Tour through Russia, 1913'.

91.1

MORAY DISTRICT RECORD OFFICE

Tolbooth, High Street, Forres, Moray, Grampian IV36 0AB

91.1 FALCONER MUSEUM ARCHIVE (**DAV**)
Letter from the palaeontologist Sir Roderick Impey Murchison to Lady Gordon Cumming of Altyre re his travels in Russia, 1841 (**ZF486**).

92.1-8

GLASGOW UNIVERSITY ARCHIVES

The University, Glasgow G12 8QQ

92.1 JOHN BROWN AND CO. LTD (**UCS 1**)
Contracts for the building of barges for the Russian Volunteer Fleet Association from 1898.

92.2 JAMES FINLAY AND SON (**UGD 117**)
Transcripts of letters from Christopher Aubin to James Finlay and Son on trade to Turkey via Russia, 1812 (**/1**).

92.3 HINDLE, Edward (1886-1973) (**DC 75**)
Zoologist. Press cuttings re T. D. Lysenko and Russian biological sciences (**A.20**); correspondence re the Darwin Medallion of the USSR, 1960 (**A.30**).

92.4 ROGIVUE AND CO. (**UGD 91**)
Letters and reports re Russian business, 1906-11 (**/122**).

92.5 Matriculation records for Russian students who studied naval architecture in the early 20th century.

92.6 Minutes of the Faculty of Law include references to S. Desnitskii who studied law at the University and became Professor of Russian Law in the University of Moscow, 1767-87.

92.7 Receipt for duty on bibles from the Russian Bible Society, 1822 (**GUA 9038**).

92.8 Memorandum mentioning suggestions for the promotion of closer relations of the city of Glasgow with Russia, 1916 (**GUA 31631**).

93.1-6

GLASGOW UNIVERSITY LIBRARY

Hillhead Street, Glasgow G12 8QE

Access for *bona fide* scholars by written application to the University Librarian. J. Young, P. H. Aitkin, *A Catalogue of the Manuscripts in the Library of the Hunterian Museum* (Glasgow, 1908), TS *TS Notes on Some of the More Important Collections, Glasgow University Library* (Glasgow, 1983), *Whistler-MacColl-Wright : Art History Papers 1850-1950 in Glasgow University Library* (Glasgow, 1979).

93.1 BAYER, Gottlieb Siegfred (1696-1738)
Professor of Greek and Roman Antiquities in St Petersburg, 1726-38. Papers include correspondence with Jesuits in Peking, papers re Chinese and other languages of Asia and Asiatic Russia, poems and other material in Russian.

93.2 CAMPBELL, Archibald
Journal of a voyage around the world, 1806-12, including descriptions of Kamchatka and Russian America, 19th century (published, Edinburgh, 1816).

93.3 ROBISON, John (1739-1805)
Teacher of mathematics at the Naval College in St Petersburg, then Professor of Natural Philosophy at Edinburgh University. Material written *c.* 1806 by Mr Porter, a merchant in St Petersburg, re Robison's stay in Russia, 1769-74.

93.4 SCHLESINGER, Rudolph (1901-69)
Director of the Institute of Soviet and East European Studies at Glasgow University. Papers include: editorials, articles and correspondence re his editorship of *Soviet Studies* and *Co-existence*; lectures; drafts and revisions for books and articles on Soviet history; unpublished memoirs; part of the records of the German Communist Party in the 1930s. Collection partially listed. The collection, the property of Mr J. R. Beerman, is housed in the Library of the Institute of Soviet and East European Studies within the University Library.

93.5 SCOTT, Alexander MacCallum (1874-1928)
Labour MP, author of several books on the Baltic countries and Russia. Political diaries (A) cover the following topics: parliamentary trip to Russia, 1912; trade with Russia, 1913-14, 1927; Russian Revolution; Krassin's agreement of 1921; situation in Russia, 1923; situation in Finland and the Baltic States, 1924. Notebooks (B) include description of Russia, 1906, and journey through the Baltic States, 1924. Political papers (D) include papers on: Russian Parliamentary Committee; Anglo-Finnish Society, 1905-11; Memorial to the Duma Committee, 1906-7; Finland, 1918; talks on Russia. *See catalogues for details.*

93.6 WHISTLER, James Abbott McNeill (1834-1903)
American painter, etcher and writer who spent some of his childhood in St Petersburg while his father was engaged in a railway construction. Correspondence when in St Petersburg of James Whistler, 1843-9; journal and letters written in St Petersburg by Anna Whistler, his mother; letters from St Petersburg by Maj. C. Whistler, his father; photographs of the Whistler family in St Petersburg; Russian school books owned by James Whistler. *See calendars, abstracts and index to correspondents for details.*

94.1-7

THE MITCHELL LIBRARY

201 North Street, Glasgow G3 7DN

94.1-4 Rare Books and Manuscripts Department

By appointment.

94.1 THE BOGLE PAPERS
4 letters from William Richardson, Secretary to Lord Cathcart while Ambassador at St Petersburg, to George Bogle, St Petersburg, 12 May 1769, 24 Mar. 1770, 26 Aug., 14 Dec. 1771.

94.2 A. S. D. COLQUHOUN PAPERS (392687-91)
'Notes of a Summer Tour to St Petersburg & Moscow. June 1875' by Maj. A. S. D. Colquhoun (**392688**).

94.3 OSTROUMOVA-LEBEDEVA, A. P. (59344)
Album of greetings from the women of Leningrad to the women of Coatbridge and Airdrie.

94.4 WILLIAM "CRIMEAN" SIMPSON COLLECTION
Papers of William Simpson (1823-99), artist and correspondent, especially for the *Illustrated London News*, include a scrapbook of notes, drawings and sketches from his visit to Russia to cover the coronation of Alexander III in Moscow, May-June 1883 (**128351**).

94.5-7 Strathclyde Regional Archives

94.5 RECORDS OF MESSRS, BARCLAY, CURLE & CO. LTD (TD 265)
Shipbuilders. Letters from Edward Barrie to Mr Sealls from Moscow, Feb. 1935 (**/40A**).

94.6 RECORDS OF FAIRFIELD SHIPBUILDING AND ENGINEERING CO. (UCS 2)
Photographs of the *Livadia* built for Alexander II and launched July 1880 (**/132/231/1-6**).

94.7 ARCHIBALD SMITH OF JORDANHILL (TD 1)
Letters to Smith, mainly re compasses and nautical science, from the following: Andrew Buchanan from the British Embassy in St Petersburg, 1866-7 (**/741, /825**); Adm. Nikolai Karlovich Krabbe, Minister of the Marine in St Petersburg, Sept. 1866 (**/819**); John Balavenety from the Compass Observatory in Kronstadt, 1866, 1870 (**/826, /840**). Letter of condolence on the death of Smith from Balavenety to Mrs Susan Emma Smith (née Parker), 1872 (**/921**); letters and postcards from Margaret Smith, A. Smith's daughter, to her mother describing visit to Odessa, Oct.-Dec. 1903 (**/970**).

95.1-4

REGIMENTAL MUSEUM OF THE ROYAL HIGHLAND. FUSILIERS

Regimental Headquarters, The Royal Highland Fusiliers (Princess Margaret's Own Glasgow and Ayrshire Regiment), 518 Sauchiehall Street, Glasgow G2 3LW

By appointment.

95.1 Letters from Lt-Col. Frederick George Ainslie, 21st Royal North British Fusiliers, to his family from the Crimea, 1854, and letters re his wounding.

95.2 Scrapbooks including material re the service of the 1st Bn Royal Scots Fusiliers in the Crimean War, 1855-6 (**N 40, N 41**).

95.3 Album of photographs compiled by F. de S. Shortt, 1st Bn Royal Scots Fusiliers, including photograph of Russian naval squadron off Portland, 1902 (**N 3**).

95.4 Scrap-books including material re the service of the 2nd Bn Royal Scots Fusiliers around the Black Sea, 1919-20 (**N 16**).

96.1-18

GLOUCESTERSHIRE RECORD OFFICE

Worcester Street, Gloucester GL1 3DW

A Short Handlist to the Contents of the Gloucestershire Record Office (Gloucester, 1979).

96.1 BELLOWS FAMILY PAPERS (**D4540**)
Papers of William Bellows (1873-1942) include: TS 'Russian Journey 1908' by Bellows with annotations by Countess Olga Tolstoi; autograph of a young Russian author later killed by the Bolsheviks; newscuttings re L. N. Tolstoi's death (**/5**).

96.2 BOWLY FAMILY PAPERS (**D4582**)
Correspondence of Col. Melchior Guy Dickens, Envoy Extraordinary at the Russian Court, 1749-54 (**/3/1-7**).

96.3 CHARLETON FAMILY PAPERS (**D4432**)
Papers of Henry Charleton include circular issued by the Royal Steam Packet Co. to its vessels containing instructions to avoid capture by the Russians, 1854 (**/4/8**).

96.4 CLIFFORD OF FRAMPTON-ON-SEVERN FAMILY ARCHIVES (**D149**)
Map of the Crimea, *c.* 1854 (**/P15**).

96.5 DYRHAM PARK ARCHIVES (BLATHWAYT FAMILY) (**D1799**)
Correspondence of Miss Charlotte A. Baker (married G. W. Blathwayt, 1856) includes references to the Crimean War (**/C35-7**); extract from letter by Capt. Edward Hibbert from the Crimea, Jan. 1855 (**/F251**).

96.6 GARDNER, James A. (1823-95) **(D1950)**
List of Cheltenham subscribers to the Patriotic Fund for the relief of Crimean War widows and orphans, 1854 **(/Z20)**.

96.7 HICKS BEACH PAPERS **(D2455)**
Papers of Sir Michael Hicks Beach include 2 maps of Turkish Armenia and Trans-Caucasia, 1877 **(PC/MP/5)**.

96.8 KINGSCOTE FAMILY PAPERS **(D471)**
Crimean journal of Col. R. N. F. Kingscote; printed notes of forces at Inkerman, 1854; list of surviving officers of the Bde of Guards, 1879 **(/F22)**.

96.9 MANSFELDT DE CARDONNEL LAWSON PAPERS **(D1022)**
Printed notice in Armenian signed by Sadet Bey, 1781 **(/23)**.

96.10 MORTON GRANGE ESTATE COLLECTION **(D4018)**
Map of European Russia, *c.* 1850 **(/F85)**.

96.11 MESSRS NICKS AND CO. (TIMBER) LTD, GLOUCESTER **(D3038)**
Lists of timber imports from the USSR, 1937-59 **(/3-4)**; list of customers including customers in Riga, Memel and Archangel, *c.* 1915 **(/5)**; invoice from Leningrad, 1934 **(/6)**.

96.12 SOTHERON-ESTCOURT FAMILY OF SHIPTON MOYNE PAPERS **(D1571)**
Papers, correspondence and diaries of Maj.-Gen. James Bucknall Estcourt (1802-55) covering his service in the Crimean War, 1854-5 **(/F485-93, 495-6, 498-505, 557-60)**. *See handlist for details.*

96.13 THURSTON FAMILY PAPERS **(D866)**
Printed letters from Thomas Kingscote of Kingscote to the Chairman of the Board of Guardians of Thornbury Union asking for collection of foodstuffs for the troops in the Crimea, 1854 **(/Q16)**.

96.14 UNITARIAN CHAPEL, GLOUCESTER, RECORDS **(D4270)**
Articles written in 1967 on Morgan Philips Price, special correspondent of the *Manchester Guardian* in Russia during the Revolution **(/7/5)**.

96.15 WHITMORE FAMILY PAPERS **(D45)**
Correspondence, diary and notebook of Maj.-Gen. Francis Locke Whitmore covering his service in the Crimean War, 1855-6 **(/X8/3-5, 7)**. Papers of Sir Edmund Augustus Whitmore include a request from a clergyman to join the expeditionary forces, 1854 **(/X9/5)**. Papers of Maj.-Gen. George Stoddard Whitmore include papers re his service with the Turkish contingent, 1855-7 **(/X10/1-3)** and Russian hospital entry certificates, 1854 **(/X11/3)**.

96.16 Copy letter re disposal of 2 guns from Sebastopol presented to the town of Cheltenham, 1858 **(D3893/6/12)**.

96.17 Scrapbooks of newspaper cuttings and pictures including of the Russian Army and the Russian Revolution **(D4180/1, 4)**.

96.18 Photostat of 'Memorandum of circumstances connected with Lt.-Col. Mayoo's services in the Crimea which it is hoped will establish a title to the Victoria Cross', *c.* 1860 **(D4198/3)**.

97.1-2

REGIMENTAL MUSEUM OF THE GLOUCESTERSHIRE REGIMENT

Regimental Headquarters, The Gloucestershire Regiment, Custom House, 31 Commercial Road, Gloucester GL1 2HE

By appointment.

97.1 Vol. containing documents re the service of the 28th Regt in the Crimean War includes: summary and narrative of service; letters by James Williams, Lt-Col. Frank Adams and Pte T. Miller from the Crimea; dispatches by Lt-Gen. Sir Richard England from the battle of Inkerman; maps of battles and of allied dispositions before Sebastopol; list of casualties in the Crimea; list of medals awarded to members of the 28th Regt (**Vol. 95**).

97.2 Album of 234 photographs by Col. J. W. A. Tweedie, 1st Bn Gloucestershire Regt, includes photograph of Russian troops, 1916 (**Acc. No. E 75**).

98.1

GRANTHAM REGIMENTAL MUSEUM OF THE 17TH/21ST LANCERS

Belvoir Castle, Grantham, Lincolnshire

By appointment.

98.1 2 letters written after the battle of Balaclava.

99.1

SOUTH HUMBERSIDE AREA RECORD OFFICE

Town Hall Square, Grimsby, South Humberside DN31 1HX

TS *South Humberside Area Record Office Summary Guide* (1984).

99.1 PARKINSON PAPERS
3 travel diaries of John Parkinson in Russia, 1790s.

100.1

THE QUEEN'S ROYAL SURREY REGIMENT MUSEUM

Clandon Park, Guildford, Surrey GU4 7RQ

By appointment.

100.1 TS vol., with 27 photographs, covering the arrival by sea, disembarkation and service of the 1st Bn East Surrey Regt in and around Murmansk, 1919 (**A/Q 70**).

101.1-3

SURREY RECORD OFFICE, GUILDFORD MUNIMENT ROOM

Castle Arch, Guildford GU1 3SX

By appointment. *Summary Guide to Guildford Muniment Room* (1967).

101.1 HUBAND COLLECTION (**77**)
Transl. from Russian of certificate of admission to the Free Economic Society of St Petersburg of Lannoy Richard Cousmaker, 21 Sept. 1789 (**/9/6**).

101.2 LOSELEY MSS (**LM**)
Copy of marriage service, invitation to W. More Molyneux, and papers, in Russian and French, re marriage of Alfred Ernest Albert, Duke of Edinburgh, and Grand Duchess Mariya Aleksandrovna of Russia, 1874 (**1963/1-10**).

101.3 ONSLOW PAPERS (**173**)
Papers of William Hillier Onslow (1853-1911), 4th Earl of Onslow, include: invitation to the baptism of the Tsarevich, 1904 (**/23/3**); Russian menus, 1904 (**/23/4-5**); memo by Onslow on the political situation in St Petersburg and Berlin, Dec. 1904 (**/13/24**).

102.1-7

ROYAL GREENWICH OBSERVATORY ARCHIVES

Royal Greenwich Observatory, Herstmonceux Castle, Hailsham, Sussex BN27 1RP

By appointment.

102.1 G. B. AIRY PAPERS (**RGO 6**)
Material and readings re Pulkovo Observatory (**/115, 147-8, 230, 239, 595, 634**); photographs of Moscow Observatory (**/149**); correspondence with Otto Struve on astronomy, late 19th century (**/176, 195, 230, 232, 235, 238, 259, 271, 366, 371-84, 412-17, 420, 445, 479, 744**); papers re pendulums in Russian observatories (**/244, 424**); letter from J. Ooschackoff (?I. Ushakov) from St Petersburg (**/256**); papers re steam hammers bought for Russia (**/453**); letter from Lt Pestchouroff (?Peshchurov) re purchase of chronometer for the Russian Government, 1858 (**/599**); papers re English compasses for the Russian

Navy (*/684, 689*); sanction by Russian Government for setting up an observatory in Peking (*/695*). *See list for details.*

102.2 CAPE ARCHIVES (RGO 15)

Letters sent to F. G. W. Struve from T. Maclear, 1853, 1858 (*/52/17, 260-5*). Letters from W. Knight, Russian Vice-Consul, to T. Maclear, 1867, 1871 (*/65/16, 172*). Letters sent to J. C. Kapteyn (Ya. K. Kaptein) from the following: D. Gill, 1896-1900 (*/73/289-91; /128 passim*); W. H. Christie, 1900 (*/76/296-7*); H. Outhwaite, 1896 (*/78/2, 4-5, 25-6*); W. H. Finlay, 1896 (*/128/626, 628*); J. L. Sirks, 1898 (*/128/686-8*). Letters from Kapteyn to W. H. Finlay, 1887, 1890, 1893, 1896-1900 (*/73/186-7, 284-5(A); /128 passim*). Letters sent to O. Backlund from D. Gill, 1896, 1898, 1902 (*/111/4-7; /129/548, 600-7*) and from R. T. A. Innes, 1899 (*/129/608*). Correspondence between Otto Struve and D. Gill, 1881, 1883-4, 1886-9, 1893, 1897-8 (*/125-9 passim*). Letter sent to F. A. Bredikhin from D. Gill, 1879 (*/125/98*). *See list for details.*

102.3 N. MASKELYNE PAPERS (RGO 4)

'A rigorous and easy rule of the nautical practice for reducing the observed distance of the Moon and the Sun or a fixed star into their true distance; presented by W. C. Krafft, Member of the Imperial Academy of Sciences at St Petersburg', St Petersburg, 22 July 1794 (*/177*).

RGO Twentieth Century Records

102.4 Correspondence with Maj.-Gen. E. Fedorov re magnetic data, 1937-48; correspondence re the visit of N. V. Pushkov to the Abinger Observatory, 1942 (**Part 1**).

102.5 Correspondence with Prof. A. A. Mikhailov re eclipse, 1945; copy of letter to Dr Subbotin re programme of the Institute for Theoretical Astronomy in Leningrad, exchange of material and asteroid ephemerides, 1946-8 (**Part 2**).

102.6 Correspondence re visit to Moscow by R. Woolley to attend the 10th General Assembly of the Astronomical Union, 1956-7; correspondence re the reopening of the Pulkovo Observatory, 1946-57; correspondence with Sir Frank Dyson re the visit of Prof. Solomon Mikhoels and Col. Hzik Feffer, 1943 (**Part 3**).

102.7 Correspondence with Dr E. P. Fedorov re motions of the stars, 1958; papers re co-operation with Russia concerning the Isaac Newton telescope, 1946-55; papers re Russian visitors to England, including Prof. A. A. Mikhailov, Prof. K. F. Ogorodnikov, Prof. B. A. Vorontsov-Vel'yaminov, Prof. A. B. Severnyi, Prof. M. S. Zverev, Prof. V. A. Ambartsumyan, Prof. Ya. K. Kharadze and Prof. T. A. Agekyan, 1955, 1959-63 (**Part 4**).

103.1-2
CALDERDALE ARCHIVES DEPARTMENT

Central Library, Northgate House, Northgate, Halifax, West Yorkshire HX1 1UN

Subject guide, persons and places indexes, lists and calendars.

103.1 HILL PAPERS (FH)
Papers of Samuel and Richard Hill, woollen manufacturers, include letter about trade with Russia, 1749 (**/441**) and letter from Weltden, Baxter and Freederickcz to Richard Hill from St Petersburg complaining about the quality of woollen goods sent, 1759 (**/451**).

103.2 SHIBDEN HALL MUNIMENTS (SH)
Travel notes and journal of Anne Lister while journeying from Sweden through Finland to Russia, Sept.-Oct. 1839 (**/7/ML/Tr.14; /7/ML/E/23-4**).

104.1
REGIMENTAL MUSEUM OF THE CAMERONIANS

Regimental Headquarters, The Cameronians (Scottish Rifles), Mote Hill, off Muir Street, Hamilton, Lanarkshire ML3 6BJ

By appointment.

104.1 Book of sketches by Lt-Gen. H. Hope Crealock whilst serving with the 90th Light Infantry in the Crimea.

105.1-4
CLWYD RECORD OFFICE, HAWARDEN BRANCH

The Old Rectory, Hawarden, Deeside, Clwyd CH5 3NR

A. G. Veysey, *Guide to the Flintshire Record Office* (1974).

105.1 ERDDIG MSS (D/E
TS letter from Gen. John Yorke in the Crimea, 1854 (**/1330**); printed resolutions of a meeting held to arrange for celebrations to mark the return of Gen. Yorke from the Crimea, 6 Oct. 1856 (**/1542/377**); daily journal kept by Ethelred Yorke of news received from her brother Gen. Yorke whilst in the Crimea, 4 Apr. 1854 - 8 Sept. 1856 (**/1543**); letters from Gen. Yorke to Ethelred Yorke from the Crimea, May-Dec. 1854 (**/1545**).

105.2 GLYNNE-GLADSTONE MSS, ST DEINIOL'S LIBRARY
Business correspondence and papers of Sir John Gladstone, 1st Bt, (1764-1851) include papers re 6 ships detained in Russian ports, 1801. Letters to Catherine Gladstone from various people re life of nurses in the Crimea and the death of Grey Neville, 1854-5. Papers of William Ewart Gladstone include political resolutions re the Eastern Question, 1877-8, and confidential memo of negotiations between the Russian government re the boundary of Afghanistan, 1885; letters to the Duke of Newcastle from A. W. Kinglake re

the Duke's Crimean correspondence. Lists under preparation. At least 2 days notice is required to bring papers from the muniment room of St Deiniol's Library in Hawarden where they are stored.

105.3 ISCOYD PARK (D/1P)
Journals and files of correspondence including references to Russian POWs in Germany and attempts by Britons to help them after the war, 1914-21 (**/609-10, 616, 620, 653**).

105.4 NANTLYS MSS (D/NA)
Newspaper cutting giving details of population and longevity in Russia, *c.* 1802 (**/922**).

106.1-2

HEREFORD RECORD OFFICE

The Old Barracks, Harold Street, Hereford HR1 2QX

106.1 AIREY FAMILY PAPERS (D52)
Crimean War correspondence of Maj.-Gen. Richard Airey (1803-81), 1st Baron (**/G/IV/A, E47**).

106.2 BIDDULPH, Capt. John (A87)
3 diaries describing military missions carried out on the North-West Frontier, 1866-76, including references to Russia.

107.1-2

HERTFORDSHIRE RECORD OFFICE

County Hall, Hertford SG13 8DE

Subject index of holdings available.

107.1 BLAKE FAMILY PAPERS (D/EX69)
Correspondence of Harriet Blake includes 4 letters from her husband, Frederic Blake, from the Crimea, letters to her sisters re his service in the Crimea, letter from C. Barrett in Sebastopol commenting on Frederic's condition, 1854 (**/F16**); Letters from W. Codrington, H. Marsh and H. D. Ellis from the Crimea, 1855 (**/F17**).

107.2 DIMSDALE, Dr Thomas, B.
TS list of collection and some transcripts of the correspondence of Thomas Dimsdale while physician to Catherine II. The originals are in the possession of Mr R. Dimsdale. *See Appendix 2, Dimsdale Papers.*

108.1-2
KIRKLEES DISTRICT ARCHIVES

Central Library, Princess Alexandra Walk, Huddersfield, West Yorkshire HD1 5SU

108.1 ARMITAGE AND NORTON COLLECTION (B/AN)
Chartered accountants of Huddersfield. Printed material re the Russian Petroleum and Liquid Fuel Co. including correspondence, reports re reconstruction proposals for the company and extracts from the chairman's speech, 1910 (**/41, 154**).

108.2 TOLSON PAPERS (DD/TO)
Papers of P. Tolson and Sons, woollen merchants of Leeds, include 2 letters from P. Tolson to his son, Richard, in Holland re trade with Russia, 15 Oct. 1776, 24 Apr. 1777.

109.1
TOLSON MEMORIAL MUSEUM

Ravensknowle Park, Wakefield Road, Huddersfield, West Yorkshire HD5 8DJ

By appointment.

109.1 British passport issued to Raymond Whiteley for a visit to Russia and other European countries, 1904 (**326**).

110.1-11
THE BRYNMOR JONES LIBRARY

The University of Hull, Cottingham Road, Hull HU6 7RX

By appointment.

110.1 CHICHESTER FAMILY PAPERS (DDCH)
2 diaries of Charles Raleigh Chichester kept in the Crimea, 1854-6.

110.2 DUESBERY FAMILY OF BEVERLEY PAPERS (DDDU)
4 letters from Robert Duesbery to his sister, Catherine Langwith, from St Petersburg, 1772-5.

110.3 ELLERMAN'S WILSON LINE (DEW)
Shipping firm of Hull. Files re Russian and Baltic trade, 1910-18, and Leningrad trade, 1925-8.

110.4 EVANS, Stanley George (DEV)
Churchman and Christian socialist. Files on Russia Today Society, 1941-6, National Council for British Soviet Unity, 1944-6, British-Soviet Friendship Houses Ltd, 1945-9, British-Soviet Friendship Society, 1951-6, churches, Christianity, religion and Evangelical Christians in the USSR, and a visit by a delegation of churchmen to the USSR, 1943,

1948, 1952, 1954-5, and the USSR, 1943-54; scrapbooks of material re USSR, 1940-62; diaries of visits to the USSR, 1946, 1955.

110.5 HORRABIN, Winifred (1887-1971) **(DWH)**

Authoress. Journal and letters to her husband, Frank Horrabin, covering her visit to the USSR, 1926.

110.6 INTERNATIONAL WOMEN'S CO-OPERATIVE GUILD **(DCX)**

'Report of a Group of Co-operators on a visit to Russia', 1930.

110.7 PAGE-ARNOTT, Robin **(DAR)**

Historian of the Labour movement and trade unionism in the mining industry. File of 35 letters, 'USSR Correspondence', 1957-67, including correspondence with Ivan Maiskii; address of Ivan Vladichenko, President of the Central Committee of the Soviet Coal Miners' Union, to the NUM Conference, 1960; report of visit of the representatives of the South Wales Area NUM to the USSR, 1961; account of Black Sea cruise of the British Peace Committee, 1966; file on the Society for Cultural Relations with the USSR, 1969-73; press cuttings and articles re the USSR.

110.8 SYKES FAMILY OF SLEDMERE PAPERS **(DDSY)**

Letter from Henry de Ponthieu to Revd Sir Mark Sykes from St Petersburg, 1761; diary of Tatton Sykes mentions Russian man-of-war in the river Humber, 1793; letter from the Crimea, 1855. Papers of Sir Mark Sykes include: notes and lectures on Anglo-Russian relations in the Middle East, 1915-17; material on the Anglo-Russian Friendship Society; papers re the visit to London of members of the Russian Duma, 1916-17.

110.9 UNION FOR DEMOCRATIC CONTROL **(DDC)**

Texts of messages from committees of the UDC to A. Kerenskii and Milyukov, 1917; copies of 3 letters between E. D. Morel and Walter Runciman re the British-Soviet negotiations, Sept. 1924; draft statement on the Finnish-Soviet War, 1940; pamphlets re Russia.

110.10 YOUNG, Cdr E. P. **(DYO)**

Politician and journalist. File on the Soviet War Veterans' Committee, 1960-71.

110.11 2 letters from Sebastopol, 1855 **(DX)**.

111.1

HULL INCORPORATED CHAMBER OF COMMERCE AND SHIPPING

Samman House, Bowlalley Lane, Hull HU1 1XT

111.1 Trust deed for endowment fund established in 1917 by Sir Henry Samman for awards to young men who wish to visit Russia to study Russian for the furthering of their careers in commerce and industry.

112.1-3

KINGSTON UPON HULL CITY RECORD OFFICE

79 Lowgate, Hull, Humberside HU1 2AA

G. W. Oxley, *Guide to the Kingston upon Hull Record Office* part 1 (1978), L. M. Stanewell, *City and County of Kingston upon Hull: Calendar of the Ancient Deeds, Letters, Miscellaneous Old Documents* (1951).

112.1 BROADLEY LETTERS (**DFB**)
4 business letters from Thomas Grundy in St Petersburg and Narva to Thomas Broadley in Hull, 1721-30.

112.2 RECORDS OF ROSEDOWNS PLC (**DBR**)
Manufacturers of oil milling machinery. Order books, 1875-43, include orders from Russia. *See name index of order books for details.*

112.3 WATER BAILIFFS ACCOUNTS (**WB**)
Records of taxation levied on ships using the port of Hull, 1569-1872, include ships from Archangel and Baltic ports with names of masters, tonnage of ships and some information about cargo.

113.1-2

CAMBRIDGESHIRE COUNTY RECORD OFFICE

Grammar School Walk, Huntingdon PE18 6LF

G. H. Findlay, *Guide to the Huntingdonshire Record Office* (1958). P. G. M. Richardson, *Maps in the County Record Office, Huntingdon* (1968).

113.1 PINKERTON, Revd Dr Robert
Missionary. Correspondence between Pinkerton in St Petersburg and Lady Olivia Bernard Sparrow on the education of his daughters during his absence on missionary work in Russia, 22 Mar., 3 June 1820 (**MS1B/3/1-2**).

113.2 4 printed maps of Russia, 1736-1854. *See* Richardson, *Maps in the County Record Office, Huntingdon* for details.

114.1-16
REGIMENTAL MUSEUM OF THE QUEEN'S OWN HIGHLANDERS

Regimental Headquarters, Queen's Own Highlanders (Seaforth and Camerons), Cameron Barracks, Inverness IV2 3XD

Access to the Library by appointment with the Regimental Secretary.

Records of the Seaforth Highlanders:

114.1 Regimental Order Book of the 72nd Highlanders, 1856-61, covering their service in the Crimean War **(72/14)**.

114.2 Letter from Lt J. C. Stewart to the Misses Stewart from the Crimea, 6 Aug. 1856 **(S 441)**.

114.3 Map of the siege of Sebastopol by Lt J. C. Stewart, 1856 **(S 443a)**.

114.4 Photocopy of the diary of William Parke, 72nd Duke of Albany's Own Highlanders, covering his service in the Crimean War, May 1855 - July 1856. The original is in the possession of Mr W. E. Sherston, Walnut Lodge, Stourton Castle, Sturminster, Newton, Dorset.

Records of The Queen's Own Cameron Highlanders:

114.5 MS (1857) and printed version (1863) of 'Historical Record of the 79th Regiment of Foot or Cameron Highlanders. By Quarter Master Jameson of the Depot Battalion, Fort George, late Quarter Master 79th Highlanders', covering the Crimean War **(79/119a, 133)**.

114.6 Crimean notebook of Capt. Adam Maitland, son of Lord Dundrennan, 1846-54 **(79/137)**. Published in *The 79th News* no. 255, Oct. 1949, pp. 264-6.

114.7 Regimental Order Book of the 79th Highlanders covering the Crimean War **(79/144)**.

114.8 38 letters from Lt F. G. Currie, 79th Highlanders, from the Crimea, 1854-6 (published 1899) **(79/700)**.

114.9 Casualty returns of the 79th Highlanders in Turkey and the Crimea, 1854-5 **(C 28)**.

114.10 Certificate of meritorious service and testimonials of Hosp.-Sgt Charles Halket with references to his service in the Crimean War **(C 40)**.

114.11 Letter from Pipe Maj. Richard Steuart, 79th Highlanders, to his wife from the camp before Sebastopol, 24 Feb. 1855 **(C 45)**. Published in *The 79th News* no. 169, Jan. 1925, pp. 47-8.

114.12 Copies of letters from Pte George Conn, 79th Highlanders, to his sister, Lillias Conn, and his uncle from the Crimea, 6 June - 7 Aug. 1855; letters re his death in action **(C 98)**. Published in *The 79th News* no. 275, Jan. 1956, pp. 42-8.

114.13 List of Crimean and Indian mutiny veterans present on the occasion of the state visit of Edward VII to Edinburgh, May 1903 **(C 126)**.

114.14 2 Russian postcards sent by the 79th Russian Regt (Kupinskii Infantry) to the 1st Bn, The Queen's Own Camerons in France, Easter 1916 (**C 197**).

114.15 Postcard sent by the Russian 79th Kupinskii Infantry Regt to the 2nd Bn, The Queen's Own Camerons in Salonika, Easter 1916 (**C 202**).

114.16 'Narrative of a soldier's life in the Crimea. 1854-6' by Pte David Reed.

115.1-3

SUFFOLK RECORD OFFICE, IPSWICH BRANCH

County Hall, Ipswich, IP4 2JS

115.1 ASHE PAPERS
Papers of Abraham Ashe, merchant of London and Moscow, include: bills of exchange and acquittances; wills and bonds of officers in the Tsar's service, 1619-1702; contract for trading voyage to Archangel, 1637 (**S1/1/77/1-65**). *See catalogue for details.* Access by appointment with the Archivist.

115.2 LONG FAMILY ARCHIVE
Letters from C. P. Long re actions at Balaclava and Sebastopol, 1855-6 (**HA 18/HG/7-75**). *See catalogue for details.* Access by appointment with the Archivist.

115.3 MARTIN FAMILY ARCHIVE
Letters from Col. Thomas Smith from the Crimea, 1855-6 (**HA 13/C/9**).

116.1-2

KEELE UNIVERSITY LIBRARY

University of Keele, Keele, Staffordshire ST5 5BG

116.1 GRAND DUKE MICHAEL BOX
12 photographs of the Grand Duke Michael, brother of Nicholas II, and his family and friends taken during his stay at Keele Hall, 1901-10.

116.2 WEDGWOOD ARCHIVES
Material re the dinner service made for Catherine II by Josiah Wedgwood, including lists of plates, expenses and wages paid to the workforce (**32/5184-328, 24187-202; 44/28759, 29055-6**).

117.1-2
KESTON COLLEGE

Heathfield Road, Keston, Kent BR2 6BA

By appointment.

117.1 RELIGIOUS SAMIZDAT COLLECTION
Collection consists of more than 4,000 items including correspondence, petitions, newsheets, symposia and memoirs. Among the religious groups and individuals represented are Adventists, Baptists, Jews, Pentecostals, Roman Catholics and Russian Orthodox. Items of special interest include: transcript of the trial of Aida Skripnikova (Baptist), handwritten on sheets of linen cloth; 'Chronicles of the Lithuanian Catholic Church'; 'Bulletins of Evangelical Christians and Baptists in the USSR'; correspondence of the Vashchenko and Chmykhalov families (Pentecostal) re their campaign to emigrate from the USSR; bound volumes such as 'Moskovskii sbornik', a collection of articles on religion and the nation compiled by L. Borodin in 1974. An index can be consulted at the college and a select bibliography is published in the college journal, *Religion in Communist Lands.*

117.2 PRESS ARCHIVE
Since its foundation in 1969 the college has maintained a file of press cutiings, pamphlets and references to articles in periodicals held by the college library. The collection is arranged thematically and covers many aspects of life in the Soviet Union with special emphasis on information relating to religious belief and practice. Sources include Soviet newspapers, Soviet religious publications, newspapers in English and other European languages and religious news services including the college's own publication, *Keston News Service.*

118.1-9
BRITISH GEOLOGICAL SURVEY

Keyworth, Nottingham NG12 5GG

By appointment. The British Geological Survey was previously named the Institute of Geological Sciences and the collection was formerly held in the Geological Museum in South Kensington. Handlist of records; card index of persons.

118.1 MURCHISON, R. I. (IGS1/12, 78, 396, 583, 663, 836, 1206)
Letters re Murchison's Russian specimens (/12) and swords (/78); letter to Murchison from V. Ya. Struve re heights for a map of Russia and xerox copies of letters to Murchison from Count E. F. Kankrin, P. K. Meyendorff (Meiendorf), K. V. Nesselrode and others, n.d. (/396); annotated proofs by Murchison of 16 of the plates from *Geology of Russia*, vol. 2, 1845 (/583); note from E. de Verneuil to Murchison with a description of *Leptena sarcinulata*, published in *Geology of Russia*, vol. 2 p. 242, 1843 (/663); four notices of safe passage used by Murchison during his travels in Russia, 1841-5 (/836); draft of an announcement of Murchison's Russian honours, 1845 (/1206).

118.2 MS maps and map sections, mostly connected with Russia (IGS1/126).

118.3 Anon., 'Outcrops of rocks in the district of Perm and its surroundings' with pen and ink drawings and annotations, n.d., *c.*1840 (IGS1/605).

118.4 A collection of photographic prints taken by E. O. Teale in Australia, New Zealand, Russia and many parts of Africa, 1888-1953 (**IGS1/955**).

118.5 Memo of agreement by A. L. Pearse re a visit to mines in Siberia, 1899 (**IGS1/1043**).

118.6 Letters and minutes re the attendance of Sir A. Geikie at the International Geological Congress at St Petersburg in August 1897 (**IGS2/186**).

118.7 Papers re scientific activity of Professor A. P. Karpinskii, 1916 (**IGS2/416**).

118.8 Papers re 17th session of the International Geological Congress in Moscow, 1937 (**IGS2/979**).

118.9 File re mica in Russia, 1929 (**IGS7/378**).

119.1
THE LYNN MUSEUM

Kings Lynn, Norfolk PE30 1NL

119.1 Correspondence with Radio Moscow and Dr S. P. Vorshovskii re the medieval explorer "Nicholas of Lynn".

120.1
SURREY RECORD OFFICE

County Hall, Penrhyn Road, Kingston upon Thames KT1 2DN

Prior notification of visits desirable.

120.1 GOULBURN PAPERS (**Accs 300, 319, 426, 1180**)
4 letters from Lord Henry Percy and Henry Robinson-Montagu, 6th Baron Rokeby, to Col. Edward Goulburn from the Crimea, 1855 (**Acc. 319 II/9**).

121.1-2
KIRKCALDY MUSEUMS AND ART GALLERY

War Memorial Gardens, Kirkcaldy, Fife KY1 1YG

By appointment.

121.1 Journal of a voyage from Kirkcaldy to St Petersburg and back kept by James Macdonald, 1835 (**Y44/6**); certificate of insurance for the vessel *Adriatic* for the voyage from Riga to Burntisland, 1879 (**Y44/25**).

121.2 Letters from David Malcolm to his father, Alexander, from Kronstadt, 21 Sept. 1840 (**Y54/6**).

122.1

ORKNEY ARCHIVES

The Orkney Library, Laing Street, Kirkwall, Orkney KW15 1NW

122.1 BALFOUR OF BALFOUR AND TRENABIE PAPERS
Fragment of unsigned letter describing the reason for the defeat of the British and Russian forces in Holland, 1799 (**8/14**); letter from Capt. William Manson on his arrival from St Petersburg, 1773 (**9/11**); letters of Maj.-Gen. Sir Evelyn Wood and Capt. Mitchell from the Crimean War (**17/7**).

123.1-4

LANCASTER DISTRICT CENTRAL LIBRARY

Market Square, Lancaster, Lancashire LA1 1HY

By appointment.

123.1 PORT COMMISSIONERS' ARCHIVE
Port Commissioners' Registers for the Port of Lancaster comprise records of ships visiting the port including name, master, port of origin and destination, port of register, charges and sometimes cargo. The following ships are listed for example in 1868 with a Russian port as port of origin or as port of register: *Astraca, Diligent, Frans, Mary Sophia, Storm Nymph, Stradstath, Therese.*

123.2 Log-book of the *Liberty* covering voyages to Kronstadt, Memel and St Petersburg, 1791-2 (**MS 5085**).

123.3 Log-book of the *Sisters* on voyage from Archangel to Lancaster, 1831 (**MS 5156**).

123.4 Photocopies of records of ships and events at Glasson Dock Graving Dock, 1841-1947, including work on ships registered at Russian ports.

124.1-2

LANCASTER MUSEUM

Market Square, Lancaster, Lancashire LA1 1HT

124.1 TS diary and letters of Capt. O. Y. Cocks, 4th King's Own Regt of Foot, from the Crimea, 1854-5 (**Acc. No. KO 870**). Access by appointment.

124.2 Letters from Capt. Jasper Hall, 4th King's Own Regt of Foot, to his sister and father from the Crimea, 1854-6. Published by E. Tyson, edit., *Letters from the Crimea*, Lancaster Museum Monograph Series.

125.1-106
THE BROTHERTON LIBRARY
University of Leeds, Leeds LS2 9JT

The Brotherton Collection

Applications for access should be made to the Keeper of the Brotherton Collection.

125.1 RANSOME PAPERS
Papers of Arthur Ransome (1884-1967), writer and correspondent in Russia for the *Daily News* and the *Manchester Guardian*. Papers re Russia include: diaries, 1909-1919, 1921-63, 1965-6; TS telegraphed dispatches, 1916-24; MS and TS of articles for newspapers; notes and drafts for his *Autobiography* and *Six Weeks in Russia*; MS and TS material re his Russian folk tales collections; correspondence; photographs; TS carbon copies of Russian documents, 1917-19, including reports, press-releases, speeches, memos by Lenin, M. Litvinov and Trotskii, press passes, 1916-19. Handlist in preparation.

125.2 MS poem, *Serenada* by Count V. A. Sollogub (1813-82), n.d. Published in *Moskvityanin*, VI, no. 11 (1841).

125.3 Letter from L. N. Tolstoi to P. I. Biryukov, 21 Feb. 1891. Published (with alteration) in Tolstoi Jubilee edition, vol. 65.

125.4 Letter from W. H. Twelvetrees to R. Damon from Voskresenskii Zavod near Orenburg, 3/15 Jan. 1879.

Special Collections

Applications for access should be made to the Sub-Librarian in Charge, Special Collections.

125.5 TUCKTON HOUSE COLLECTION
Papers re the Tolstoyan community and publishing venture at Tuckton House; correspondence of Vladimir and Anna Chertkov; Tolstoyan pamphlets, journals and monographs. Printed matter listed.

125.6 Copy of the will of John Cayley, merchant and British Consul-General at St Petersburg, 16 June 1794 (**MS 667**).

125.7 Fragment of reminiscences by Emily Susan Ford (1850-1930) include reminiscences of Russian acquaintances (**MS 371**).

125.8 Letter from Daniel Wheeler to Daniel Mallinson from the Moscow Road, 25 Oct. 1824 (**MS 436/86**).

125.9 215 letters and other documents of Aylmer Maude (1858-1938), translator, biographer and publicist of Tolstoi, mainly to George Herbert Perris and Charles F. Cazenove, re mainly translations from Tolstoi and the affairs of the 'Resurrection Fund', 1901-14 (**MS 553**). *See handlist 51 for details.*

125.10 Correspondence of Edmund Clifton Stoner (1899-1968), physicist, with P. L. Kapitsa (**MS 333/121, 135, 153, 164**).

125.11 Letters to Herbert Thompson, music critic, from A. K. Glazunov, St Petersburg, 30 June 1901, and S. V. Rakhmaninov, Rzhaksa, 26 June 1910 (**MS 361/116, 201**).

125.12 An anonymous account of the several deputations of members of the Society of Friends which met Frederick William III of Prussia and Alexander I of Russia, June 1814 (**MS 698**).

Special Collections, Leeds Russian Archive

Applications for access should be made to the Archivist, Leeds Russian Archive. R. Davies, *The Leeds Russian Archive 1982-1984 : A Progress Report* (Leeds, 1984); *The Leeds Russian Archive 1984-1985: Second Progress Report* (Leeds, 1985).

125.13 DANIIL ANDREEV PAPERS
MSS and TSS of political and philosophical works by Daniil Andreev (1906-59), including notebooks compiled in the Vladimir prison. Papers being sorted and listed.

125.14 LEONID ANDREEV PAPERS (MS 606)
Papers of Leonid Andreev (1871-1919) include: diaries for 1890-3, 1897-1901, 1914-19; correspondence with members of the Andreev family and others including A. Amfiteatrov, H. Bernstein, V. Burtsev, I. V. Gessen, M. Gor'kii, V. F. Komissarzhevskaya, A. V. Lunacharskii, P. N. Milyukov, V. I. Nemirovich-Danchenko, I. Ya. Repin, F. I. Shalyapin, I. S. Shmelov; correspondence of Anna Andreeva (1885-1948), 1919-39; photographs and autochromes. Listed in R. Davies, 'Leonid Andreev Manuscripts in the Collections of Vadim, Valentin and Savva Andreev' in W. Harrison, A. Pyman, edit., *Poetry, Prose and Public Opinion: Aspects of Russia 1850-1970: Essays Presented in Memory of Dr N. E. Andreev* (Amersham, 1984).

125.15 VADIM ANDREEV PAPERS
MSS and TSS of published poetry, prose works and memoirs by Vadim Andreev (1902-1976); letters from I. Bunin, B. L. Pasternak and M. I. Tsvetaeva. Papers being sorted and listed.

125.16 NIKOLAI BOKOV PAPERS (Acc. No. 2.4.94)
TSS of literary works by Bokov; editorial files and correspondence of the journal *Kovcheg*. Papers being sorted and listed.

125.17 IVAN BUNIN PAPERS (Acc. Nos. 2.4.45, 2.4.88, 2.4.113)
MSS and TSS of published and unpublished literary works by Bunin (1870-1953); diaries of Bunin and his wife, Vera Bunina; correspondence; photographs, portraits, posters, catalogues. Papers being sorted and listed.

125.18 CATTLEY PAPERS (Acc. No. 2.4.50)
Memoirs, letters, photographs and official papers of the Cattley family of St Petersburg, Pernau and Ealing, 18th-20th centuries. Listed.

125.19 ELIZAVETA FEN PAPERS (Acc. No. 2.4.56)
MSS and TSS of literary works, translations, diaries, correspondence and photographs of Elizaveta Fen (Lydia Jackson, née Zhiburtovich, 1900-83). Papers being sorted and listed.

125.20 NATAL'YA KODRYANSKAYA PAPERS (Acc. No. 2.4.38)
MSS, notebooks and TSS of literary works; correspondence (papers on short-term loan).

125.21 GEORGE LOMONOSSOFF (1908-54) PAPERS (MS 718)
Correspondence, personal documents and photographs. List under preparation.

125.22 GEORGE V. LOMONOSSOFF (1876-1952) PAPERS (MS 716)
Papers of Prof. Lomonossoff, railway engineer and administrator, include diaries, 1917-52, memoirs, photograph albums, official documents re Russian railway development, locomotive designs and correspondence including letters and memos from V. I. Lenin. List under preparation.

125.23 RAISSA N. LOMONOSSOFF PAPERS (MS 717)
Correspondence with Jane Adams, K. I. Chukovskii, A. M. Kollontai, T. G. Masaryk, B. L. Pasternak, A. N. Tolstoi, M. I. Tsvetaeva and others; TSS of her unpublished plays; personal documents, official papers and photographs. List under preparation.

125.24 DAVID MAGARSHACK PAPERS (Acc. No. 2.4.169)
TSS of published and unpublished works by Magarshack (1899-1977); press cuttings, programmes, posters, photographs and correspondence. Papers being sorted and listed.

125.25 HARVEY PITCHER PAPERS (Acc. No. 2.4.123.)
Files of correspondence re and photographs used in his published works.

125.26 RUSSIAN LITERATURE IN BRITISH PERIODICALS (MS 672)
Unpublished bibliographical compilation and related correspondence.

125.27 SMITH PAPERS (Acc. Nos. 2.4.76, 2.4.123, 2.4.170)
MSS memoirs and writings, diaries, correspondence, photographs and inventories of property of the Smith family of Moscow, early 20th century.

125.28 ZEMGOR PAPERS
Records of the charitable activities of the Zemgor organization, 1920s-60s; papers of the committee of former Imperial and Provisional Government ambassadors, 1920s; correspondence files, maps, photographs. Papers in the process of being transferred to Leeds.

125.29 Notebooks and MSS of literary and other writings by Aleksandr Aivazovskii (**Acc. No. 2.4.140**).

125.30 Telegram from and signed photograph of Anna Akhmatova (1889-1966) (**Acc. No. 2.4.11**).

125.31 MS of *Akafist Sergiyu Kameneostrovskomu*, *c.* 1915, by Aleksandr Amfiteatrov (1862-1938) (**Acc. No. 2.4.144**).

125.32 Letters to Gino Antonini re publication of Soviet literary works, 1934-8, 1946.

125.33 Letters written during the Allied intervention in Russia by Ernest Bush Appleyard (**Acc. No. 2.4.42**). Published in *Sbornik* 9, 1983.

125.34 Postcards, copies of photographs and official documents re Gilbert and Margaret Atack in Moscow, 1904-8 (**Acc. No. 2.4.82**).

125.35 Log-book of a visit to Borovoe meat-canning factory by Edward Percy Beavan, 1904-5 (**Acc. No. 2.4.25**).

125.36 Letter from Vasilii Belov to David Gillespie, Vologda, 9 Nov. 1983 (**Acc. No. 2.4.101**).

125.37 Copies of photographs of Aleksandr Bernardi (1867-1943) and his family and colleagues (**Acc. No. 2.4.25**).

125.38 TS of *Journey through Revolution* by Lucy Berzins (**Acc. No. 2.4.77**).

125.39 Legal documents re sale of property in Poland by Count A. A. and Countess N. A. Bobrinskoi, 1921 (**Acc. No. 2.4.83**).

125.40 Document issued by N. de Bokker to E. E. Dmitrievskaya on behalf of the Provisional Government of the Northern District (Archangel), 1919 (**Acc. No. 2.4.145**).

125.41 TS of *This Was Russia* by Marie Russell Brown (?1878-1956) (**Acc. No. 2.4.73**).

125.42 Copies of photographs of the Carr family of Archangel, 1890s-1918, and of the North Russian Expeditionary Force, 1918-19 (**Acc. Nos. 2.4.105, 2.4.163**).

125.43 Copies of official documents and photographs of L. G. Cheshire and his family in St Petersburg and Gurzuf (Crimea); copies of photographs of the North Russian Expeditionary Force and St Petersburg (**Acc. No. 2.4.120**).

125.44 Memoirs by Ethel Mary Christie of medical relief work in Russia, 1921-4 (**Acc. No. 2.4.39**).

125.45 Memoir, draft letter and photographs of Archangel environs by Samuel Church, serving in the North Russian Expeditionary Force, 1918; copy of letter to all ranks in North Russia, 26 Sept. 1918 (**Acc. No. 2.4.160**).

125.46 Copy of the family tree of the Coates family of St Petersburg; copy of memoirs of Percy Coates (mainly of New Zealand) (**Acc. No. 2.4.107**).

125.47 Copies of documents and photographs re trading and gold-washing activities of the Dieckmann and Langelutje families in Siberia, 1860s-1900s.

125.48 TS recollections by Mary Neva Eveleigh (daughter of Revd W. Nicolson); copies of photographs of the Nicolson family in St Petersburg, 1860s (**Acc. Nos. 2.4.105, 2.4.137**).

125.49 MSS of poems, newspaper cuttings of articles by Tatiana Fanshawe (d. 1945) (**Acc. No. 2.4.155**).

125.50 Copy of diary of Robert Leonard Fenton covering service in North Russia, 1918-19 (**Acc. No. 2.4.115**).

125.51 Copies of official documents and photographs of the Fullard, Isherwood and Matthews families, Vysokovskaya Manufactory, Klin, 1900s-1910s (**Acc. No. 2.4.111**).

125.52 Official documents and memoirs of the Gaubert and Manners families of Uglich and St Petersburg, 1820s-80s (**Acc. No. 2.4.75**).

125.53 Copies of photographs of the Giraud family of Moscow and of a military parade, 1890s-1910s (**Acc. No. 2.4.150**).

125.54 Text and notes for talks on the Soviet intelligentsia by Jeff Gleisner (**Acc. No. 2.4.31**).

125.55 Copy of MS memoir of Zinovii Isaevich Grzhebin and TS of unpublished biography of him (**Acc. Nos 2.4.93, 2.4.128, 2.4.156**).

125.56 Copy of Russian travel documents issued to John Hackworth, 1836 (**Acc. No. 2.4.129**).

125.57 Photographs, unsigned poems and letters to Salomee Halpern (née Princess Andronikova, 1888-1982) (**Acc. Nos 2.4.37, 2.4.91**).

125.58 Copy of notes made by E. C. Harris of the Neva Rope Works in Petrograd on the outbreak of the February Revolution, 1917 (**Acc. No. 2.4.133**).

125.59 Certificate of hereditary honorary citizenship granted by Alexander II to Vasilii Osipovich Govard (Howard) and his family, 1867 (**Acc. No. 2.4.83**).

125.60 Copies of postcards of Russia and photograph sent from Russia by Katherine Hughes, 1909-10 (**Acc. No. 2.4.62**).

125.61 Copies of photographs and letters of Margherita Johnson (1883-1973), formerly of St Petersburg (**Acc. No. 2.4.116**).

125.62 Official documents and photographs of Anna Kallin; Ms poem by Marek Kallin (under the assumed name of Belsch), 1920 (**Acc. Nos 2.4.143, 2.4.153, 2.4.162**).

125.63 Photographs of the ballerina Tamara Karsavina (1885-1978) and her family (**Acc. No. 2.4.96**).

125.64 Copy of official document issued to FM Francis Keith, 1742 (**Acc. No. 2.4.87**).

125.65 Correspondence and official documents re Georgina Kinnear who worked in Russia, 1860s-70s (**Acc. No. 2.4.35**).

125.66 Copies of family history, official documents and photographs of the Knox and Spearing families of St Petersburg and Odessa, 1890s-1910s (**Acc. No. 2.4.64**).

125.67 TS of monograph on Gogol' by Janko Lavrin (**Acc. No. 2.4.22**).

125.68 TS of 'An 'Ironside Boy' or Memoirs of a Sniper in Russia' by Maurice Lumb; copies of certificates (**Acc. No. 2.4.78**).

125.69 TS of Marvin Lyons, *Biographical Dictionary of the Corps of Pages: Outlines of the Project* (1984) (**Acc. No. 2.4.125**).

125.70 Copy of photograph album of the Lyzhin family of Vammelsuu (Karelian Isthmus), mainly 1910s-20s (**Acc. No. 2.4.157**).

125.71 Memoirs and photographs of Vera Marstrand (née Omelyanskaya) (**Acc. No. 2.4.1**).

125.72 Photographs and diary by Mark Mathers of the Allied intervention in Russia (**Acc. No. 2.4.79**).

125.73 Tape-recordings and TS transcriptions of interviews re D. S. Mirskii (**Acc. No. 2.4.6**).

125.74 Newspaper cutting, photograph and TS notes for memoirs of Leonid Grigor'evich Munshtein (1886/7-1947) (**Acc. No. 2.4.44**).

125.75 Certificates and photographs of and letters to M. S. Nappel'baum (1869-1958), photographer in St Petersburg (**Acc. No. 2.4.66**).

125.76 Photographs, bank statements, insurance policy documents and customs forms of Revd Herbert North, 1909-20 (**Acc. Nos 2.4.65, 2.4.123**).

125.77 Copy of memoirs of Katherine North of her work as an ambulance driver on the Rumanian and Galician fronts, 1916-17 (**Acc. No. 2.4.138**).

125.78 Copy of TS of F. M. Page, 'Steam Locomotives of the Russian Railways', 2 vols, 1984 (**Acc. No. 2.4.104**).

125.79 Copy of MS by Brian Pearce, '1941 and All That', 1984 (**Acc. No. 2.4.118**).

125.80 Copy of extracts from TS by Nina Petrova, 'Russian Memories' (**Acc. No. 2.4.110**).

125.81 TS of 'A Baltic Childhood' by Maud Radcliffe (**Acc. No. 2.4.74**).

125.82 Photographs of pipe-laying work in the environs of Baku by a member of the Reid family (**Acc. No. 2.4.29**).

125.83 MS of scenario by A. M. Remizov (1877-1957) for German Lovtskii's symphonic pantomine for orchestra, 1912 (**Acc. No. 2.4.33**).

125.84 Copies of notebooks and diaries of S. P. Remizova-Dovgello (1876-1943), 1930s and 1940s.

125.85 TS of memoirs on Russia by Prof. J. Henry Richardson, 1933 (**Acc. No. 2.4.69**).

125.86 Copies of photographs taken and postcards bought by Frederick Robinson on a journey on the (future) Trans-Siberian Railway, early 1910s (**Acc. No. 2.4.13**).

125.87 Press cuttings re the Romanov family, taken chiefly from émigré newspapers, 1921-33 (**Acc. No. 2.4.16**).

125.88 Letters from Archibald Campbell Ross to his wife from Nikolaev and St Petersburg, 1897-8, 1902 (**Acc. No. 2.4.99**).

125.89 Copy of TS of 'Our Russian Tale' by Mona Walkington (née Ross) and Charles Ross re childhood in Riga, Kurgan and Astrakhan', early 20th century (**Acc. No. 2.4.80**).

125.90 Glass transparencies of views of St Petersburg, 1910s (**Acc. No 2.4.92**).

125.91 Copies of photographs of Muriel Sara and her family in the Maikop oil fields, 1913-15 (**Acc. No. 2.4.57**).

125.92 Copy of MS of 'My Memories of the Russian Revolution' by Mrs R. G. Seaborn (**Acc. No. 2.4.86**).

125.93 Share certificates and dividend coupons of the Sibirskii Torgovyi Bank, 1910s **(Acc. No. 2.4.19).**

125.94 Copy of TS of memoirs of school-days in Russia by Evelyn Skempton (born 1892) **(Acc. No. 2.4.52).**

125.95 Letters from T. A. Smirnova-Maksheeva (1890-1982) to Richard Davies, 1977-81; TSS of poems **(Acc. No. 2.4.44).**

125.96 Letter from Charles Soloman to S. L. and T. L. Tolstoi, 1922 **(Acc. No. 2.4.89).**

125.97 Photographs and copy of memoirs of Ethel Stevenson as a governess in Russia, 1895-1902 **(Acc. No. 2.4.55).**

125.98 Copy of TS transcription of the diary of a journey to and sojourn in Murmansk by Z. Stiromirov, 1918.

125.99 Official documents and correspondence re the Tchengelek (Chengelek) Proprietory Co., 1904-22 **(Acc. No. 2.4.167).** Papers being sorted and listed.

125.100 Copies of photographs, official documents and TS correspondence re Thornton's Woollen Mills, St Petersburg, and the Thornton family, early 20th century **(Acc. No. 2.4.40).**

125.101 Cabinet portraits of Alica and Tom Tong (d. 1915 and 1921), Moscow **(Acc. No. 2.4.121).**

125.102 Letters to Vera Traill (then Suvchinskaya) from D. S. Mirsky (D. P. Svyatopolk-Mirskii) and M. I. Tsvetaeva, 1928-30 **(Acc. No. 2.4.7).**

125.103 Letters from Princess Varvara Trubetskaya to Sarah Rodger (née Stafford), 1845-8 **(Acc. No. 2.4.84).**

125.104 Photographs taken of Tolstoyans at Tuckton House, 1900s **(Acc. No. 2.4.171).**

125.105 TS of 'Some of My Experiences in Russia During the Revolution' by Helen Whitley (née Clarke), 1921 **(Acc. No. 2.4.36).**

125.106 Slides of works by unofficial Soviet artists, mainly Leningrad, 1970s-80s **(Acc. No. 2.4.106).**

126.1-4
LEEDS DISTRICT ARCHIVES

Chapeltown Road, Sheepscar, Leeds LS7 3AP

126.1 CLANRICARDE PAPERS
Papers of Hubert George de Burgh Canning (1832-1916), 2nd Marq. and 15th Earl of Clanricarde include: copy dispatch from John Wodehouse, 1st Earl of Kimberley, at St Petersburg to Lord Clarendon re a mission to Peking, Mar.-Apr. 1857 **(9)**; 2 letters from Peter Browne to Lord Malmesbury re the Russian occcupation of Villafranca, 24 Feb. 1859 **(10)**; register of dispatches sent from and received by the British Embassy at St Petersburg, 1838-41 **(52)**; dispatches from Lord Clanricarde at St Petersburg, mainly to

Lord Palmerston, 1838-41 (**53-60**); letters to Clanricarde: from George Canning re Russian affairs, 1825-7 (**62**); from J. W. Croker re provision for the Russian fleet, 1827 (**67**); re detention of Ulick Canning de Burgh (styled Lord Dunkellin) in Russia (**71**); from Sir Edward Baynes in St Petersburg re the Ionian Islands, 1847; miscellaneous letters re the Crimean War (**83**). These papers are part of Lord Harewood's records and can be seen on appointment on the understanding that no use is made of them in published work without the owner's consent.

126.2 FAIRBAIRN LAWSON LTD
Engineers of Leeds. Journals and ledgers re Baltic trade in the early 20th century may include references to ports in the Baltic States.

126.3 NEWBY HALL PAPERS (NH)
Letters from Thomas Philip Weddell, Lord Grantham, to his mother describing his tour of Europe and Asia, including St Petersburg and Moscow, *c.* 1801 (**2902**).

126.4 BATTIE WRIGHTSON PAPERS (BW)
Royal warrant permitting travel to Moscow, 1703 (**BW/L 39**).

127.1

YORKSHIRE ARCHAEOLOGICAL SOCIETY

Clarendon Road, Leeds LS2 9NZ

E. W. Crossley, *Catalogue of Manuscripts and Deeds in the Library of the Yorkshire Archaeological Society* (1931); S. Thomas, *Guide to the Archive Collections of the Yorkshire Archaeological Society 1931-1983 and to Collections Deposited with the Society* (1985).

127.1 DUKE OF LEEDS COLLECTION (DD5)
Diary of a grand tour, probably by Francis Godolphin Osborne (1777-1850), 2nd son of the 5th Duke of Leeds, covering Finland and Russia, 1797-8 (**/12/15**).

128.1

WIGAN RECORD OFFICE

Town Hall, Leigh, Lancashire WN7 2DY

By appointment. *Wigan Record Office* (1976)

128.1 EDWARD HALL COLLECTION (D/DZ EHC)
Journal of Thomas Moore, merchant, of journey to Riga, St Petersburg, Stockholm, Danzig, Copenhagen, Gothenburg etc, 20 Mar. 1806 - 18 Oct. 1806 (**57**); diary of Henry Francis Brown, June 1898 - Sept. 1909, referring to his friendship with Olga Novikov and the Russian artist Verestchegin (V. V. Vereshchagin) (**111**).

129.1-4

EAST SUSSEX RECORD OFFICE

The Maltings, Castle Precincts, Lewes BN7 1YT

129.1 RECORDS OF THE GAGE FAMILY OF FIRLE PLACE (**Gage**)
Illustrated and descriptive roll on the occasion of the funeral of Alexander I, 1825 (**acc. 737**).

129.2 RECORDS OF THE POOLE AND BLENCOWE FAMILIES OF THE HOOK, CHAILEY (**Hook**)
Letters from Gen. Hepburn to his aunt, Mrs Blencowe, from the Crimea, 1854-5 (**22/14/9-10**).

129.3 RECORDS OF THE EARL OF SHEFFIELD, OF SHEFFIELD PARK (**SPK**)
Letter from J. B. Stone to George Holroyd, 2nd Earl of Sheffield, re a request from Horace Solly, of the House of Isaac Solly & Sons, Russian merchants, to lease land at Newhaven, 1825, 5 letters from the Earl to his wife describing a visit to Russia in the summer of 1842, and invitation from the Tsar to attend military manoeuvres (**A 2714 (Newhaven correspondence no. 35)**).

129.4 RECORDS OF THE SHIFFNER FAMILY OF COOMBE PLACE, HAMSEY (**SHR**)
Letters from Capt. John Shiffner to his family from the Crimea, 1854-5 (**1323-30; 3157-77**); letter from Benjamin Cooke and John Watson in St Petersburg to Henry and John Shiffner re trade in Russia, 23 Nov. 1761 (**2796**); plan and views of St Petersburg, 1753 (**2875-900**); maps of the Crimea and Sebastopol, 1854-5 (**2918-9; 2921-4; 2926-30; 3680**); map and chart of the coasts between Ochakov, Nikolaev, Kherson and southern Russia by James Wyld, 1855 (**3681**). *See* F. W. Steer, *Shiffner Archives* (Lewes, 1959).

130.1

LICHFIELD JOINT RECORD OFFICE

Lichfield Library, Bird Street, Lichfield WS13 6PN

By appointment.

130.1 HINCKLEY & BIRCH, SOLICITORS (**D15**)
Papers re the children of John Jackson (d. 1827), painter of Lichfield, include the appointment of an attorney and certified extracts from the register of the British Church in St Petersburg, 1846 (**/12/33**).

131.1-7

STAFFORDSHIRE REGIMENT MUSEUM

Regimental Headquarters, The Staffordshire Regiment (The Prince of Wales's), Whittington Barracks, Lichfield, Staffordshire

By appointment.

131.1 Photograph by R. Fenton of the remains of the Light Co., 38th Regt, after the attack on Sebastopol (**80**).

131.2 MS copy of the 'Digest of the 38th Regt' covering the Crimean War (**935**).

131.3 'Passages in the Crimean War' by Richard Barnham, Light Co., 38th Regt (**1489**).

131.4 3 letters by Cpl J. Pritchard, 38th Regt, from the camp before Sebastopol, 1854-5 (**4068A**).

131.5 2 photographs of 38th Regt officers in the Crimea (**5022-3**).

131.6 Book containing 79 photographs of Russian soldiers in the field, 1914-16, being a gift from the 38th Tobol'skii Regt to the 1st Staffords (formerly the 38th Regt) (**902**).

131.7 MS copy of war diary of the 7th North Staffords Regt covering service at Baku, Balakhani and Zabrat, Aug. 1918 - June 1919 (**1075**).

132.1-9

LINCOLNSHIRE ARCHIVES OFFICE

The Castle, Lincoln LN1 3AB

By appointment. Summary list of accessions can be found in the annual *Archivists' Reports*.

132.1 ANCASTER FAMILY AND ESTATE PAPERS (**Anc**)
Correspondence of Peregrine, Lord Willoughby d'Eresby, (d. 1601) includes relation of Don Felipe Prenestain, Ambassador from the Emperor, to the Grand Prince of Muscovy, n.d. (**8 Anc I/9**).

132.2 DIXON FAMILY PAPERS (**Dixon**)
16 letters written by John Parkinson from St Petersburg, Astrakhan' and Moscow, Jan. 1793 - Feb. 1794 (**16/6/14-29**).

132.3 GRANTHAM LIBRARY COLLECTION (**G. L.**)
Copy of the log of the *Persian* during a voyage from Liverpool to Kronstadt and the return voyage to Hull, 1847 (**23**); letter in Russian picked up at Sebastopol (**51**).

132.4 MASSINGBERD OF GUNBY FAMILY DEEDS AND PAPERS (**M.G.**)
Business records of Thomas Meux, mercer and merchant in the firm of Cary and Meux of Narva, include: vol. containing household accounts, 1767-80, previously used for lists of goods sent to various persons in Moscow and the Governor of Archangel, probably by

Thomas Meux (**5/3/2**); ledger and day-book of disbursements of Thomas Meux at Narva, 1698-9 (**7/1; 7/3**); his ledger and day-book at London, 1700-16 (**7/2; 7/4**); book of invoices including ledger entries for 1699 for Narva and account of charges on his brother Samuel's goods received from Archangel, 1710 (**7/5**); draft letters from Thomas Meux re imports from Russia, 1716-17 (**7/6/4-6**); letter to Thomas Meux referring to Capt. Franklyn's return from Russia, 1720 (**7/6/8**).

132.5 MONSON FAMILY AND ESTATE PAPERS (Mon)
Papers, 1720-45, of the Hon. Charles Monson as Deputy Paymaster of the Forces include a project for trade with Persia via Russia, n.d. (**13/3/12**).

132.6 DEPOSIT FROM JOHN H RUNDLE LTD (Rundle)
Records of William Foster and Co. of Lincoln, agricultural engineers, include specification book with notes of foreign orders and requirements for Odessa, *c.* 1900, with extracts from agents' letters (**1/18**).

132.7 RUSTON AND HORNSBY LTD OF LINCOLN, ENGINEERS (Ruston)
Presentation album to Mr Jahn of Odessa, 1914.

132.8 RECORDS OF TAYLOR, GLOVER AND HILL OF EPWORTH, SOLICITORS (TGH)
Correspondence between Morris, Little & Son of Doncaster, sheep-dip manufacturers, and H. Lassen, their agent in Odessa, 1896-97 (**2/L Box 2**).

132.9 WORSLEY MANUSCRIPTS (Wors)
Travel journal of Sir Richard Worsley, Bt, through the Near East to Italy and Russia, 1785-7 (**24**).

133.1-11
LIVERPOOL CITY LIBRARIES

William Brown Street, Liverpool L3 8EW

133.1-10 Liverpool Record Office

133.1 DERBY FAMILY PAPERS (920 DER)
Letters from Eustace Clare Grenville Murray, Consul-General in Odessa, to Lord Stanley, 1866-8.

133.2 PAPERS OF HAROLD CHALONER DOWDALL (920 DOW)
Printed letter, and duplicate, re visit to England of members of the Russian Council of the Empire and the Russian Duma, 1909 (**2/24-5**).

133.3 PAPERS OF MATTHEW GREGSON (920 GRE)
Letter from David Samwell to Gregson referring to Travenon (Ya. I. Trevenen), Commander of the Russian fleet against the Swedes, 1788 (**2/17/1**).

133.4 LIVERPOOL CHAMBER OF COMMERCE
Papers from Russian Trade Section, Nov. 1902 - June 1912 (**3/6/1**) and Russian Trade Section and School of Russian Studies Joint Committee, Dec. 1917 - Apr. 1924 (**3/6/2**).

133.5 PAPERS OF JOSEPH MAYER (920 MAY)

Letter from Mary, Baroness de Bogouschevsky (Mariya Bogushevskaya, wife of Baron Nikolai) from Pskov to Mayer begging for financial assistance, Dec./Jan. 1881/2.

133.6 PAPERS OF WILLIAM ROSCOE (920 ROS)

Letter from William Frederick, Duke of Gloucester, re Russian Emperor (Alexander I) and the slave trade, 26 July 1814; copy of letter from Thomas Harrison to William Wilberforce re Russian Emperor's resolve to put an end to the piracies of the Barbary powers, 9 Oct. 1817.

133.7 Typewritten message of greeting from the Mayor of Odessa to the Lord Mayor of Liverpool, 26 Jan. 1972, Russian (**352 MD 32**).

133.8 Photostat of the log-book of the screw steamship *Andes* on voyage in government service carrying the 1st Royal Regt to the Crimea (**387 MD4**).

133.9 Journals of holiday travels in Europe, possibly by a member of the Kynaston family, includes extract re travels across Germany to Russia, 1886 (**920 MD 146**).

133.10 Material presented to the Civic Delegation to Odessa, June 1975, including pamphlets in Russian and copies of wartime photographs (**Acc. 2876**).

133.11 Hornby Library

133.11 Letters, postcards, greeting cards and photographs from Empress Alexandra, to Hon. Evelyn Moore, Maid of Honour to Queen Victoria, 1892-1916.

134.1-2

LIVERPOOL UNIVERSITY ARCHIVES

PO Box 147, Arts Reading Room, Bedford St South, Liverpool L69 3BX

By appointment.

134.1 PROFESSOR W. LYON BLEASE PAPERS (D.55)

Professor of Law at Liverpool University. Correspondence of Blease in Russian, 1919, 1922 (**/3**); script of BBC talk on Russia in revolt, 1956, essay on the Russian Revolution (**/6/1**); MS of book *Suvorof*, published 1930 (**/6/3**); 4 Russian newspapers, 1918-20, 1938 (**/10**); newspaper cuttings re war in Russia, 1919-21 (**/11**). *See list for details.*

134.2 VICE-CHANCELLOR'S PAPERS

Papers re the Bowes Chair of Russian, a Lectureship in Russian Legal and Institutional History, and the School of Russian Studies, 1906-13 (**4/1/16; 5/15, 26; 6C/16**). *See list for details.*

135.1-3

MERSEYSIDE COUNTY ARCHIVES

64-66 Islington, Liverpool L3 8LG

By appointment. TS *Preliminary Brief Descriptive Guide* (1976) with annual supplements.

135.1 BRYSON COLLECTION
Collection uncatalogued and not yet available to researchers, but will include material on Russian insurance claims.

135.2 DANSON ARCHIVES (**D/D**)
Letters from Prof. Bernard Pares, 1908-9, including one from Tavricheskoe, and others re visit of Russian representatives to Liverpool and compensation for the SS *St Kilda*, sunk by a Russian ship (**/V/2/32**); 13 letters, mainly from Prof. Pares, re the School of Russian Studies, 1910-11 (**/V/2/33C**).

135.3 OCEAN TRANSPORT AND TRADING CO. (**I.D.**)
Collection in the process of being sorted and listed but contains memoirs of Capt. J. B. Wilson, in Russia 1918-20 (**755, 1697**).

136.1-4

SYDNEY JONES LIBRARY

University Library, The University of Liverpool, PO Box 123, Liverpool L69 3DA

By appointment. *A Guide to the Manuscript Collections in Liverpool University Library* (1962).

136.1 GLASIER PAPERS
Correspondence, mainly of Prince Petr Kropotkin (**I.1.1880/2-3, 5-9; I.1.1886/4-5; I.1.1889/8-17; I.1.1891/8; I.1.1892/36; I.1.1893/80; I.1.1905/17-18; I.1.1906/46; I.1.1908/43; I.1.1911/6; I.1.1912/32; I.1.1917/5, 10, 27; I.1.1918/13-17; I.1.1920/98, 116; II.3**).

136.2 ELEANOR RATHBONE PAPERS
File on the deportation of Poles into the USSR, 1943-5 (**R.P.XIV.2.18(1-40)**).

136.3 Vol. of English newspaper cuttings on Russian affairs, 1880-1 (**K.11.7**).

136.4 Box of photographs of gypsies in Russia, n.d.

137.1

ALPINE CLUB LIBRARY

74 South Audley Street, London W1Y 5FF

By appointment.

137.1 The photographic collection includes photographs and slides of the Caucasus, mainly late 19th and early 20th century. Documentary collection on early mountaineering expeditions is in the process of being catalogued and may contain material on Russia.

138.1

BABCOCK INTERNATIONAL PLC

165 Great Dover Street, London SE1

Access to genuine researchers granted under exceptional circumstances. Apply to the Archivist.

138.1 Account by Henry Smith of his experiences working for Rodion Smith & Co. Boiler Works and then Babcock & Wilcox Ltd in Moscow including during the First World War (account used in Harvey Pitcher, *The Smiths of Moscow* (Cromer, 1984)).

139.1

BALLET RAMBERT ARCHIVE

Mercury Theatre Trust Limited, 94 Chiswick High Road, London W4 1SH

By appointment to genuine researchers.

139.1 The collection is in the process of being catalogued but contains correspondence, photographs, theatre programmes and other material relating to the career of Dame Marie Rambert (born in Warsaw in 1888), Russian ballet and Russian dancers visiting England.

140.1-3

BANK OF ENGLAND ARCHIVE

Archive Section, Bank of England, Threadneedle Street, London EC2R 8AH

By appointment. It is generally possible to see records over 30 years old although some records, owing to sensitivity (particularly where customers are involved), are closed for longer periods. Researchers may be required to submit texts to the Bank before publication for certain classes of records. Material relating to Russia and the USSR will be found in the following categories of records:

140.1 7 files re negotiations and operations of the Anglo-Russian Supplies Agreement, 1941-3 (**OV6/283-9**).

140.2 36 files covering relations with the Soviet state bank and other banks and general economic information, 1924-76 **(OV 111)**.

140.3 Records of customers' accounts dating from 1694 to the present, some of which will include dealings with Russian companies and individuals. Access to private accounts reqires the permission of the account holder(s) or his/their recognizable successor(s). If there is no successor, access is not allowed until the records are over 100 years old.

141.1

BARCLAYS BANK PLC ARCHIVE

54 Lombard Street, London EC3P 3AH

Access for accredited researchers by application in writing to the Archivist. A written undertaking is required from researchers that a draft of any proposed publication based on material in the archives will be submitted to the archive for approval before presentation to a third party or publication.

141.1 The records of Martins Bank Limited (formerly of 68 Lombard Street, London EC3) include specimens of new Northern Russia rouble notes and related correspondence between the Treasury and Allen Harvey & Rose, 1918/19 **(572)**. Apply to Archivist for terms of access to these records.

142.1

BBC HULTON PICTURE LIBRARY

35 Marylebone High Street, London W1M 4AA

142.1 The foundation of this collection was the library of the *Picture Post*, which ceased in 1957, and an important recent addition is the library of the former *Evening Standard*. The library holds some 9,000,000 pictures, mainly photographs but also engravings, lithographs, postcards, some original works of art and several runs of illustrated periodicals. The library is a commercial picture library and a scale of charges is supplied on request. Clients do not consult the files directly and material is assembled for them by the library's own picture researchers. Material relating to Russia and the USSR can be found in particular in the following categories: Russian History, Scythian to the 18th century; Russia in Ferment, 1800-1914; Russian Revolution; Portraits connected with the Revolution; Post-Revolution, Scientific Progress 1920s and 1930s, Everyday Scenes; Post-Revolution, Agriculture, War etc.; White Russian Emigrés; Crimean War. There are also substantial collections of pictures relating to the Soviet occupation of Austria at the end of the Second World War, the Berlin Airlift and the Hungarian Uprising of 1956.

143.1-12
BOARD OF DEPUTIES OF BRITISH JEWS

Woburn House, Upper Woburn Place, London WC1H OEP

By appointment. Archive catalogue.

Board Minute Books (A)

143.1 BOARD OF DEPUTIES AGENDA AND REPORTS (A4)
Vol. 2, 1922-6, includes reports of the Russian Dependants Committee. There may be further references to Russia in minutes where the content is not specified.

President and Secretaries Papers (B)

143.2 EMANUEL PAPERS (B2)
Papers of C. H. Emanuel, mainly TS, include: reports and correspondence re Russian would-be immigrants to South Africa, 1902, 1911 (**/1/12, 17**); letters of appeals, donations for Kishinev and Russian war victims, 1892-1913 (**/9/1, 5**); correspondence with the Foreign Office re Russian Jews in Palestine, 1887 (**/9/8**); correspondence re threatened expulsion of Jews from Russia, 1914 (**/9/14**); papers re the Beilis trial in Kiev, 1912-13 (**/9/16-16a**); reports on a naturalized subject expelled from Memel (**/10**). *See catalogue for details.*

143.3 CODED SERIES (B4)
Correspondence, mainly TS copies, re USSR including re: the Russian Rabbi Dayan Abramskii in London, 1931 (**/A2**); the USSR in general, 1925-36 (**/B31, /LE30, /ST27, /Y12**); Jewish victims of the war in Russia, 1928-32 (**/FR21**); foreign affairs and Estonia, 1929-37 (**/GL40**); the closure and election of the Deputy of the Poltava Synagogue, 1924-6 (**/PM17**); the Zinoviev letter, Jews in Russia (**/RU12**); persecution of Jews in the USSR, 1930 (**/RU13**; Ukrainian Jews, 1935-9 (**/U9**). *See catalogue for details.*

143.4 GREY SERIES (B6)
Papers, mainly TS carbon copies, including: memos, applications, correspondence re Jews in Russia and Eastern Europe, 1952-4, 1956-63 (**/2/11; /3/12**) (**/2/11** closed for 50 years); report on Soviet Jewry, 1955 (**/2/25**); papers on the Ukraine, 1959-60 (**/3/23**).

Committee and Departmental Papers (recent) (C)

143.5 AD HOC AND SUB-COMMITTEES (C1)
Minute book on Jews in Russia, 1844-56 (**/1**); minutes of the East European Relief Committee, 1920 (**/6**).

143.6 FOREIGN AFFAIRS COMMITTEES AND JOINT FOREIGN COMMITTEE (C11)
Correspondence, mainly TS carbon copies, with the Foreign Office, League of Nations, Anglo-Jewish Committee, World Zionist Organization, C. G. Montefiore, L. Wolf, M. Gaster, H. Samuel, L. de Rothschild, C. Adler, Edgar A. R. Gascoyne-Cecil, Visc. Cecil of Chelwood, Rufus Daniel Isaacs, 1st Marq. of Reading, and others re Russia and the USSR including re: Russia, 1915-1916 (**/2/7, 9**); Russian Jews, 1915, 1917-19 (**/2/11, 14; /3/1/1; /4/1**); Jews in Russia, the Ukraine and Poland, 1917-19 (**/3/13/3**); the International Committee for Help to Russia, 1921-4 (**/3/1/6**); proposed Jewish colonies in Russia and

the assassination of the Tsar, 1918-24 (*/3/4/2*); the Federation of Ukrainian Jews, 1920-4 (*/6/3*); Jews in the USSR and Soviet Jewish refugees during the Second World War (*/7/2/2, /3b/5, /3d/4; /13/38*); Bukharan refugees, 1934-48 (*/11/6/2; /13/2-3*); problems after the Revolution of 1905 (*/12/118*); Russian refugees, 1919-29 (*/12/120-1, 135*); religious situation in Russia, 1924-7 (*/12/121, 123*); Ukraine, Bessarabia and Russia, 1920-3 (*/12/122*); USSR in general, 1928-30, 1939, 1941-3 (*/12/124-5, 127*); emigration from the USSR, 1935, 1953-62 (*/12/126; /13/39*). There are references to the USSR in the papers of: the Co-ordinating Board of Jewish Organizations, 1951-3 (*/9/2/11*), Foreign Affairs Committee general correspondence and papers, 1925, 1953, 1964-5 (*/11/10; /11/15; /12/51*); C. D. Rappaport, 1962 (*/11/14*); Lithuanian Telegraphic Association, 1936, 1938-40 (*/12/52*); Alliance Délégation Polonaise, 1923 (*/12/71*); Cossack pogroms collection, *c.* 1916 (*/12/119*). *See catalogue for details.*

143.7 FOREIGN APPEALS COMMITTEE (C12)
TS carbon copies of appeals and correspondence re Bukharan refugees from Russia in Persia and Afghanistan, 1934-5 (*/4*).

General Correspondence (E)

143.8 GENERAL CORRESPONDENCE (FILE ORIGIN UNKNOWN) (E1)
Cable and correspondence re the Schtrake case re kidnapping of an Israeli child to prevent his parents returning to Russia with him, 1961-2 (*/80*) (closed for 50 years).

143.9 CLERK/ADMINISTRATIVE SECRETARY'S PAPERS (E2)
TS carbon copies of correspondence re Association of Baltic Jews in Great Britain, 1946-9 (*/22*); report on Estonia, 1944 (*/63*).

143.10 GENERAL CORRESPONDENCE (NUMBERED BOX SERIES) (E3)
Papers re: Kishinev Fund, 1903-13 (*/64*); Russian Zionist Organization, 1931-3 (*/121*); Jews in Lithuania, 1920-3, 1926-34 (*/167-8*); Russian refugees, 1904-16, 1929-35 (*/192, 506*); Latvia, 1921-34 (*/232*). L. Wolf correspondence re Russia, 1916 (*/195*). *See catalogue for details.*

Finance (F)

143.11 BANK ACCOUNT BOOKS (F(a))
Kishinev Relief Fund Account no. 64, 1903-23 (*/2*).

Publications (G)

143.12 Publications and reports re USSR and Soviet Jews. *See catalogue for details.*

144.1-15

THE BRITISH ARCHITECTURAL LIBRARY

Royal Institute of British Architects, 66 Portland Place, London W1N 4AD

By appointment.

144.1 2 letters from Count von Brunnow (Count Filipp Ivanovich Brunnov), Russian Ambassador in London, to Sir Charles Barry, and copy letter from Barry to Brunnow, re drawings of the new Houses of Parliament, Westminster, presented to the Tsar by Barry, Jan. 1845, and drawings of the interior of the Imperial Palace, St Petersburg, presented to Barry by the Tsar, Apr. 1849.

144.2 Copies of letters from Philip Tilden to the Queen, the Hon. Sidney Greville and M. Stolypin re arrest in St Petersburg of Nikolai Chaikovskii, social reformer, 1908, with copy of the memorial sent to Baron Rosen (Baron R. R. Rozen), Russian Ambassador to the USA, 14 Dec. 1907, and a copy of the memorial leaflet issued by Chaikovskii's English friends.

144.3 Report by A. L. T. Vaudoyer to the Académie des Beaux-Arts, 8 Feb. 1840, re memorial column to Alexander I at St Petersburg, built to designs by Auguste Ricard de Montferrand, 1831-4.

144.4 Design for the Vorontsov palace at Alupka, Crimea, by Edward Blore, 1837.

144.5 Drawing of the town theatre, Odessa, by Ferdinand Fellmer and Herman Helmer, n.d.

144.6 Perspective of equestrian monument to Tsar Nicholas I, St Petersburg, by Josef Sharleman.

144.7 Tracings of the Bourse, St Petersburg, by John Turner, n.d.

144.8 3 drawings of a town house, Moscow, 1870-3.

144.9 3 drawings by Evgenii Rosenberg (b. 1907) for a town planning competition in the Ukraine, 1932.

144.10 Photographs of the work of Charles Cameron in Russia.

144.11 Photographs of Russian architecture of the 1920s and 1930s, especially the work of Viktor A. Vesnin, I. A. Golosov and B. M. Iofan.

144.12 Collection of photographs of St Petersburg.

144.13 Photographs of work by William Walcot in Moscow. Not yet catalogued.

144.14 Early photographs by Berthold Lubetkin. Not yet catalogued.

144.15 Collection of photographs of architecture in Russia, 1977-84. Not yet catalogued.

145.1-2

BRITISH FILM INDUSTRY LIBRARY SERVICES

127 Charing Cross Road, London WC2H 0EA

145.1 EISENSTEIN EXHIBITION COLLECTION
File of correspondence and press cuttings re exhibition held at the Victoria and Albert Museum in 1963 and 7 vols of photographic reproductions of drawings by S. M. Eisenstein used in the exhibition.

145.2 DIMITRI TIOMKIN COLLECTION
5 albums of press cuttings, 1969-73; 2 folders of documentation re film *Tchaikovsky*; letters to Tiomkin from Laurence Harvey, Ken Hughes, Ronald Reagan when Governor of California and others.

146.1-497

BRITISH LIBRARY

Great Russell Street, London WC1B 3DG

146.1-470 Department of Manuscripts

Catalogues and indexes are listed, and their location in the Department of Manuscripts' Reading Room given, in M. A. E. Nickson, *The British Library : Guide to the Catalogues and Indexes of the Department of Manuscripts* (London, 1982). Some of the documents relating to Russia are described in V. Burtsev, 'Russian Documents in the British Museum', *Slavonic Review*, 4, no. 12 (March 1926) pp. 669-85, L. Loewenson, 'Russian Documents in the British Museum', *Slavonic (and East European) Review*, 14, no. 42 (April 1936) pp. 661-9, and G. M. Phipps, 'Manuscript Collections in British Archives Relating to Pre-Petrine Russia', *Canadian-American Slavic Studies*, 6, no. 3 (Fall 1972) pp. 400-15. Researchers should note that the indexes to individual catalogues often include the names of correspondents and other additional information not included in the descriptive text of the catalogue.

Additional Charters and Rolls (Add. Ch.)

Add. Chs. 1054-75892 are listed in the *Catalogues of Additions to the Manuscripts, 1836-1955*, and in the *Rough Registers of Acquisitions*. Add. Chs. 1-59845 are calendared in 38 volumes.

146.1 Certificate of a sale of a Russian female slave at Venice, 7 Feb. 1450 (**Add. Ch. 15340**).

146.2 Order from Adrian, Patriarch of Moscow, for the delivery of goods from his estate, n.d. (**Add. Ch. 71247**).

146.3 Appointment of James Simpson as Russian Consul at Gibraltar, 1788, Russian with French and Italian transl. (**Add. Ch. 75499**).

Additional Manuscripts (Add.)

This series comprises by far the largest collection of manuscripts in the Department. The *Catalogues of Additions to the Manuscripts, 1843-*, are listed in full in Nickson, *The British Library* p. 9. Manuscripts 5017-6665 are only indexed and not listed in the catalogues. Manuscripts acquired from 1956 (from Add. 48989) are described briefly in TS *Rough Registers* available in the Reading Room.

146.4 THE ABERDEEN PAPERS (**Add. 43039-358**)
Papers of George Gordon, afterwards Hamilton-Gordon, (1784-1860), 4th Earl of Aberdeen, PM, include: correspondence with Princess Dorothea Lieven, 1832-54 (**Add. 43052-5, 43268, 43271-2, 43278**), William A'Court, 1st Baron Heytesbury, Ambassador to Russia, July 1828 - Oct. 1830 (**Add. 43089**), British representatives in Russia, 1841-6,

Baron P. Brunnow, 1841-56, Count K. R. Nesselrode, 1844 (**Add. 43144**); letter-books of correspondence from Russia, May 1828 - Dec 1829, Oct. 1841 - Apr. 1846 (**Add. 43113-15, 43177-8**). *See index for details.*

146.5 D'ABERNON PAPERS (Add. 48922A-62)
Papers of Edgar Vincent (1857-1941), Baron then Visc. d'Abernon, diplomat, include: reports and correspondence re Russia, 1920-5, n.d. (**Add. 48927 B ff. 161-86**); diary at Warsaw (published), July-Aug. 1920 (**Add. 48953 A**).

146.6 'ALI PASHA PAPERS (Add. 46695-9)
Papers, mainly in French, of Mehmed Emin 'Ali Pasha (1815-71), Turkish statesman, include: correspondence with Halil Šerif Pasha as Envoy to Russia, 1870-1; copies of alleged correspondence of Russian diplomats in Austria, 1870; 2 letters from Gen. P. N. Ignat'ev, Russian Ambassador, 1865, 1871; copies of intercepted correspondence of Russian diplomats, 1847-67; letters from Riza Bey, Turkish Ambassador to Russia, to Mustafa Rešid Pasha, 1857; correspondence with Georgios Konemenos Bey, Secretary of the Turkish Legation in St Petersburg, 1864-70 (**Add. 46697**). Diplomatic papers, mainly copies, re chiefly the Russo-Turkish War and the Congress of Berlin, 1877-8 (**Add. 46699 ff. 23-56b**). *See index for correspondents.*

146.7 ARGENTI CHIOS PAPERS (Add. 46205-15)
Material collected by Philip P. Argenti includes dispatches from Russia, 1770 (from the Public Record Office and the Haus-, Hof- und Staats-Archiv, Vienna) (**Add. 46211**).

146.8 THE AUCKLAND PAPERS (Add. 34412-71)
Correspondence and papers of William Eden, 1st Baron Auckland, include: printed treaty of commerce of Russia with France, 1787 (**Add. 34425 f. 64**); copy of letter from Prince Charles of Hesse to Catherine II, 1789 (**Add. 34429 f. 387**); copies of letter to Count S. R. Vorontsov, 1789, French (**Add. 34429 ff. 511, 515**). *See index for further details.*

146.9 THE BALFOUR PAPERS (Add. 49683-962)
Papers of Arthur James Balfour (1848-1930) probably include material re Russia, especially in his correspondence on foreign affairs.

146.10 BANKS CORRESPONDENCE (Add. 8094-8100)
Includes letters to Sir Joseph Banks from Russians. *See separate published catalogue for correspondents.*

146.11 BARROW BEQUEST (Add. 35300-9)
Letters to Col. John Barrow from Lt Sherard Osborn from the Crimean War (**Add. 35306-7**).

146.12 BASHKIRTSEVA, Mariya Konstantinovna (Marie Bashkirtseff) (Add. 41863-5)
Notebooks, drawings etc., 1860-84, mainly French.

146.13 BELLINGHAM PAPERS (Add. 48216)
Papers of and relating to John Bellingham, executed in 1812 for the murder of Spencer Percival, PM, include correspondence with the British and Russian authorities re the grievances which led him to commit the murder.

146.14 BENTHAM, Jeremy and Sir Samuel (Add. 33537-64, 37520)
Papers include: correspondence between Jeremy and Samuel while the latter was in Russia (**Add. 33537-46**); journals, travel accounts and papers re Jeremy's journey to Russia,

1785-7, and travels of Samuel in Siberia, 1781-2 (**Add. 33552**); copies of letters and papers written by Samuel during his travels in Russia, 1781-3 (**Add. 33554**); copies of letters of introduction for Samuel in Russia and copies of his letters to Jeremy and his father, 13 July 1779 - 12 May 1789 (**Add. 33555-7**); diary of Samuel in Russia, 28 Sept. 1780 - 8 Jan. 1781 (**Add. 33564**); letter book re Samuel's employment in Russia and Jeremy's journey to join him at Krichev, 1784-9 (**Add. 37520**). *See index for details.*

146.15 BLATHWAYT, William (Add. 37979-92)
Correspondence of Blathwayt as Secretary in attendance on the King (William III) in the Netherlands, 1693-1701, includes references to Peter I (**Add. 37,992**).

146.16 BLENHEIM PAPERS (Add. 61101-710)
Papers of John Churchill, 1st Duke of Marlborough, include: letters from Charles Whitworth, partly as Envoy and Ambassador at Moscow, 1703-11 (**Add. 61149**), Peter I, 1707, Russian and French transl. (**Add. 61261 ff. 1-3b**), A.A. Matveev, Russian diplomat, 1706-8, French (**ff. 4-47b**), Johann Christoph von Urbich, Russian diplomat, 1708-9, French, Latin, German (**ff. 48-64b**), and Prince A. D. Menshikov, 1710, French (**ff. 65-73b**). Papers of Charles Spencer (*c.* 1674-1722), 3rd Earl of Sunderland, include letter from Peter I, 1709, Russian and transl. (**Add. 61491 ff. 27-30b**), and correspondence with envoys including those in Muscovy, 1707 (**Add. 61540 ff. 71-8b**). Account of a visit of Diego de Miranda to Prague, Vil'na and the Caspian Sea, 1601-4 (**Add. 61693**). *See separate handlist for details.*

146.17 BLIGH PAPERS (Add. 41268-87)
Papers of the Hon. Sir John Duncan Bligh (1798-1872) include drafts of dispatches as Minister Plenipotentiary *ad interim* to Russia, 25 Sept. 1832 - 5 Nov. 1835 (**Add. 41269-73**). *See index for details.*

146.18 VAN DEN BOSCH PAPERS (Add. 45895)
Letters of Johan Adriaan Van den Bosch while accompanying the Prince of Orange as Aide-de-Camp on travels in Russia etc., 1859-69, mainly Dutch (**Add. 45895 ff. 18-139**).

146.19 BOYD CARPENTER PAPERS (Add. 46717-65)
Papers of William Boyd Carpenter (1841-1918), Bishop of Ripon, include letters from Empress Alexandra of Russia, 1894-1915 (**Add. 46721 ff. 227-48**), and Revd Frederick Louis Wybergh, Chaplain of the English Church in Moscow, 1906 (**ff. 249b-50**).

146.20 BROUGHTON PAPERS (Add. 36455-83)
Correspondence of John Cam Hobhouse, Baron Broughton, includes: papers by Lord Palmerston on the attitude of Russia to Persia and Afghanistan in 1838 (**Add. 36469**); memo by Thomas Love Peacock on Central Asia, 1838 (**Add. 36470**); letters and papers from political officers in Central Asia, 1835-41 (**Add. 36473-4**).

146.21 BUNBURY, Col. Henry E. (Add. 37051-2)
Correspondence and papers as Under-Secretary of State for War, 1813-16, include letters from Visc. Cathcart, Ambassador to Russia, 12 July 1813 (**Add. 37051 ff. 84, 87**) and 'Supplies of arms, ammunition and military stores ... furnished to the Russian, Prussian and Swedish Governments ... ', June 1813 (**f. 82**).

146.22 BURRARD, Col. William (Add. 34097, 34274)
Military journals as 'a volunteer to Russia with Lord Crawford [John Lindsay, 20th Earl of Crawford] against the Turks', 18 Apr. - 24 July 1738 (**Add. 34097**); 5 letters from William to Harry Burrard describing his journey to and from Russia (**Add. 34274 ff. 105-18**).

146.23 BURTON COLLECTION (Add. 25613-75)
Notes by J. Burton on Russian travellers and scientific men, 19th century (**Add. 25673 f. 64**).

146.24 CAESAR, Sir Julius (**Add. 14027**)
Papers include 'A briefe narration of the discoverie of the Northerne Sea' by the Muscovy Company (**Add. 14027 f. 168**).

146.25 THE CAMPBELL-BANNERMAN PAPERS (**Add. 41206-52, 52512-21**)
Papers of Sir Henry Campbell-Bannerman (d. 1908), PM, include correspondence with Nicholas II, 1894 (**Add. 41206**). *See index for further details.* There may be further material re Russia in the Supplementary Campbell-Bannerman papers (**Add. 52512-21**).

146.26 CANCELLIERI, Abbate Francesco (**Add. 22885-96**)
Correspondence with François Gabriel, Comte de Bray, and Adam von Lebzeltern, Austrian Ambassador to Russia, St Petersburg 8/20 Sept. 1817, Italian and French (**Add. 22885 ff. 141-62**).

146.27 CARNARVON PAPERS (**Add. 60757-61100**)
Papers of Henry H. M. Herbert, 4th Earl of Carnarvon, statesman, include notes on Russia, 1860-?1887 (**Add. 60966**), and may contain further material re Russia.

146.28 CARTERET, Lord John, 1st Earl Granville (**Add. 22511-45**)
Secretary of State. Papers include correspondence with diplomats in Russia, 1742-4 (**Add. 22528**). *See index for correspondents.*

146.29 CECIL OF CHELWOOD PAPERS (**Add. 51071-204**)
Papers of Lord (Edgar Algernon) Robert Cecil, Visc. Cecil of Chelwood, may include material re Russia, especially amongst miscellaneous correspondence re foreign affairs.

146.30 CHAPMAN LETTERS (**Add. 60538**)
Transcripts of letters from Col. Frederick Edward Chapman to 'A' from the Crimea, 1854-5.

146.31 CLARKSON PAPERS (**Add. 41262-7**)
Papers of Thomas Clarkson, slave-trade abolitionist, include his appeal on behalf of Haiti to Alexander I at the Aix-la-Chapelle conference of 1818, similar to the published *Thomas Clarkson's Interview with the Emperor of Russia* (**Add. 41266 f. 43**).

146.32 CLIFFORD PAPERS (**Add. 59773-5**)
Papers of Maj.-Gen. Clifford mainly re his Crimean War service, 1855-*c.* 1888.

146.33 COXE, Archdeacon William (**Add. 9078-283**)
Traveller in Russia. Papers and correspondence re the history and state of Russia (**Add. 9254-7**).

146.34 DASHKOVA, Princess Ekaterina Romanovna (**Add. 31911**)
Autobiographical memoirs, with some differences from the published version; letters from Catherine II to Dashkova, *c.* 1762-94; address by Dashkova, as President, at the opening of the Imperial Academy of Sciences, 1783. *See index for further details.*

146.35 DAYROLLE, James (Add. 15866-75)

Diplomat. Papers include: project of an act of inclusion, comprehending among others the Empress of Russia, in the treaty signed at Vienna, 16 Mar. 1731, Latin and French (**Add. 15868 ff. 13, 19, 42**); copy of the convention between England and Russia, 12 June 1747, French (**Add. 15869 f. 105**); Act of Consent of the States General to the treaty of subsidy with Russia, 5 July 1747, French (**Add. 15869 ff. 151, 153**); letter from Melchior Guy Dickens at St Petersburg to Dayrolle, 16 Nov. 1751 (**Add. 15873 f. 45**); copy of letter from Sir George Macartney, Ambassador at St Petersburg, to Georgina Carolina Fox, Lady Holland, Feb. 1766 (**Add. 15875 f. 176**); correspondence of Dayrolle with the Count Maturov, Russian Ambassador at the Hague (**Add. 15876 f. 232**) and John Carmichael, Earl of Hyndford, Ambassador in Russia (**Add. 15882 f. 1**); treaty between Britain and Russia, 9 Dec. 1747, French (**Add. 15884 f. 75**); convention for the service of 30,146 Russian troops, n.d. (**Add. 15884 f. 91b**).

146.36 DILKE PAPERS (Add. 43874-967)

Papers of Sir Charles Wentworth Dilke, 2nd Bt., (1843-1911), include: letters on behalf of Helena Pavlovna, widow of the Grand Duke Michael of Russia, Oct.-Nov. 1869, French (**Add. 43874 f. 106**); lists of acquaintances in Russia, 1869-70 (**Add. 43964**).

146.37 DRAKE PAPERS (Add. 46822-38)

Papers of Francis Drake (1764-1821), diplomat, include letters from Joachim Lizakevicz (Ioakim E. Lizakevich), Russian Chargé d'Affaires at Genoa, 1793-6 (**Add. 46827 ff. 132-264b**).

146.38 DROPMORE PAPERS (Add. 58855-59494)

Papers of William Wyndham Grenville (1759-1834), Baron Grenville, Foreign Secretary, 1791-1801, PM, include: papers re Russo-Turkish peace negotiations, Apr.-May 1791 (**Add. 59069**); papers re Russia (**Add. 59076-7, 59080**); précis books of correspondence to and from Russia, 1789-1800 (**Add. 59190-204**); vol. entitled 'Russia', 1799 (**Add. 59227**). Pitt family papers include letters to Thomas Pitt, 2nd Baron Camelford, mainly re the Austro-Russian campaign of 1799 (**Add. 59491**).

146.39 FRANCES DUBERLY LETTERS (Add. 47218)

Wife of Henry Duberly, Paymaster of the 8th Hussars. Diary covering the Crimean War and the Indian Mutiny, 1852-64 (**Add. 47218 A,B**).

146.40 DUTCH STATE PAPERS (Add. 5124-36)

' ... declaratio super Milite Moscovitico etc.', 30 Mar. 1707 (**Add. 5131 f. 384b**); letter from Peter I re the powers granted to Baron J. C. von Urbich to treat with the Emperor of Germany, 24 Sept. 1707, Dutch (**f. 404**).

146.41 ELLIS, George (Add. 28099)

Letter to Ellis from Louis Phillippe, Comte de Ségur, St Petersburg, 26 July 1787 (**f. 3**).

146.42 ELLIS, John (Add. 28874-918)

Papers include correspondence with Charles Whitworth, Envoy to Russia (**Add. 28902-16**). *See index for details.*

146.43 ERSKINE COLLECTION (Add. 26603-21)

Philological collections by William Erskine include vocabulary for Catherine II, in Sanskrit, Mahratti, Kokani and Hindustani (**Add. 26604 ff. 9-26**).

146.44 ESCOTT PAPERS (Add. 58774-801)
Papers of Thomas Hay Sweet Escott (1844-1924) include correspondence with S. M. Kravchinskii, alias Stepnyak, 1885 (Add. 58794).

146.45 FOX PAPERS (Add. 47559-601)
Papers of the Hon. Charles James Fox (1749-1806), statesman, include: correspondence with Sir James Harris, Ambassador to Russia, 1782-3, and Alleyne Fitzherbert, chiefly as Envoy to Russia, 1783 (Add. 47562); miscellaneous papers as Foreign Secretary and on foreign affairs, 1779-1804 (Add. 47562-3); account of the diplomatic relations of the Great Powers before and during the Crimean War in the hand of Lord John Russell (Add. 47601 ff. 122-30). *See index for details.*

146.46 FRANKLIN PAPERS (Add. 47768-72)
Papers of John Franklin (1786-1847), Arctic explorer, include British and Russian passports issued to his wife, Lady Jane Franklin, née Griffin (d. 1875) (Add. 47769 ff. 16-33).

146.47 FRASER, Col. Alexander John (Add. 44912-13)
Papers re the Crimean War.

146.48 THE GLADSTONE PAPERS (Add. 44086-835)
Papers of William Ewart Gladstone (1809-98), PM, include: memos, many printed, re Russia and Afghanistan, 1881-5 (Add. 44190 ff. 191, 196; 44627 f. 93; 44628 ff. 60, 91, 96, 110, 116; 44631 ff. 11-77 *passim*; 44769 ff. 31-100 *passim*); papers, many printed, re Russian persecution of the Jews, 1881-2 (Add. 44474 ff. 34, 62, 85, 87, 106-23 123; 44627 f. 123; 44628 f. 64; 44669 f. 30); memo re Russian advance into Central Asia, 1885 (Add. 44480 ff. 33-5); papers, many printed, re the Crimean War (Add. 44585 f. 29; 44586 ff. 1, 3, 56, 59, 71, 81-4, 162; 44654 f. 201; 44743 f. 150; 44744 f. 70; 44746 ff. 26-31); memos re assassination of Alexander II, 1881 (Add. 44668 f. 41; 44765 ff. 99, 102); 'Russian Policy and Deeds in Turkestan', 1876, and 'The Friends and Foes of Russia', 1879, by Gladstone (Add. 44695 f. 187; 44698 f. 1); correspondence of Alexander III as Tsarevich with Gladstone, 1854 (Add. 44778 f. 186). *See separate catalogue and index for details.*

146.49 GENERAL GORDON PAPERS (MOFFITT COLLECTION) (Add. 51291-312)
Papers of Maj.-Gen. C. G. Gordon (1833-85) include letters from the Crimea, 1855-6 (Add. 51291).

146.50 GRAHAM OF DRYNIE PAPERS (Add. 48213-5)
Papers of Anne Pauline Camille Graham, née de Calvy de St André, include correspondence with Count Carlo Andrea Pozzo di Borgo, Russian Ambassador to France and Britain, 1820-1842, n.d. (Add. 48213).

146.51 GUAETERIO, Cardinal F. A. (Add. 20543-50)
Correspondence with Count de Rastrelli in St Petersburg, 26 Sept. 1724, Italian (Add. 20550 f. 267).

146.52 GUTHRIE, Matthew (Add. 14388-90)
Traveller in Russia. Papers include: 'A Supplementary Tour through the countries on the Black Sea conquered by Russia from the Turks, comprehending everything omitted in Mrs Guthrie's rapid Survey ...', 1804-5 (Add. 14388-9); 'Noctes Rossicae, or Russian evening recreations', including English transl. of text of Catherine's opera *Oleg*, 1800, and oration of Platon, Archbishop of Moscow, on the crowning of Alexander I, 15 Sept. 1801 (Add. 14390). See *Catalogue of Manuscript Maps ... in the British Museum* for details of maps.

146.53 HALE FAMILY PAPERS (**Add. 33571-**)
Letter from Thomas Hale to Bernard Hale with description of Peter I, 1702 (**Add. 33573 f. 178**).

146.54 THE HALIFAX PAPERS (**Add. 49531-93**)
Correspondence of Charles Wood (1800-55), 1st Bt, 1st Visc. Halifax, while 1st Lord of the Admiralty, 1855-8, is likely to include references to the Crimean War.

146.55 HAMILTON PAPERS (**Add. 48599-699**)
Papers of Sir Edward Walter Hamilton (1847-1908), Private Secretary to W. E. Gladstone, include diary of a cruise to the Baltic and St Petersburg (published), 1897-8 (**Add. 48671-2**).

146.56 THE HARDWICKE PAPERS (**Add. 35349-36278**)
Papers of the Earls of Hardwicke include: transcripts of diplomatic correspondence of Sir Joseph Yorke, when Ambassador at the Hague ,to Sir James Harris, Ambassador at St Petersburg (**Add. 35434**) and with Lord Cathcart, Envoy Extraordinary at St Petersburg, 1771-2 (**Add. 35444**); diplomatic correspondence of Robert Keith as Envoy Extraordinary at St Petersburg, 1757-74 (**Add. 35482-5, 35493-5**); extracts from the correspondence of Robert Gunning, Envoy Extraordinary to Russia, 1772-5 (**Add. 35502**). Letter from James Melville describing his travels in Russia and Poland, 25 Jan. 1562 (**Add. 35831 f. 121**); copy of a letter from Elizabeth I to Ivan IV, *c.* 1568 (**Add. 35831 f. 275**); copies and extracts from treaties including between Britain and Russia, 1742, 1755, and Prussia and Russia, 1762 (**Add. 35839 ff. 123, 134, 138, 276**); notes on duties laid on English manufacture since 1720 by Germany, Russia and Holland, *post* 1773 (**Add. 35906 f. 231**). *See index for further details.*

146.57 LORD HARVEY OF TESBURGH DIARIES (**Add. 56379-402**)
Diaries of Sir Oliver Charles Harvey (1893-1968), 1st Baron Harvey of Tesburgh, Private Secretary to Anthony Eden and Edward Wood, 1st Earl of Halifax, while Secretaries of State for Foreign Affairs, 1937-46, may contain material re Russia.

146.58 WARREN HASTINGS PAPERS (**Add. 39871-904**)
Papers include 'Journal of a journey from Peterburgh to Reshd', 26 Feb. 1740 - 28 June 1742, by George Thompson (**Add. 39892 f. 1**).

146.59 HÉKÉKYAN BEY, Joseph (**Add. 37448-71**)
Armenian in Egyptian service. Note on Russian foreign policy, 1858 (**Add. 37463 f. 1**).

146.60 HERZEN-HERWEGH PAPERS (**Add. 47664-8**)
Correspondence of Aleksandr Ivanovich Hertsen (Herzen), mainly with Georg Herwegh, 1858-70, French, German and Russian.

146.61 THE HEYTESBURY PAPERS (**Add. 41511-66**)
Official correspondence and papers of William A'Court, 2nd Bt., 1st Baron Heytesbury, diplomat, include Series F, correspondence as Ambassador to Russia with Lord Aberdeen and Lord Palmerston as Foreign Secretaries, June 1828 - Aug. 1832 (**Add. 41557-63**). *See index for details.*

146.62 HINDLEY COLLECTION (**Add. 6930-7005**)
Route taken by John Bell of Antermony from St Petersburg to Tobol'sk and Peking (**Add. 6933 f. 238**).

146.63 HOBART, John, 2nd Earl of Buckinghamshire (**Add. 22358-9**)
Correspondence and papers mainly re his embassy to Russia, 1762-6, including correspondence with Count N. I. Panin and Count Victor Frederick von Solms, Prussian Envoy at St Petersburg, notes on the commerce of the Narva and on the population and revenues of Russia, circulars sent to foreign envoys at the Russian Court (**Add. 22358**). *See index for details.*

146.64 HODGKIN PAPERS (**Add. 38846-57**)
Letters from Peter I to William III, Moscow, 29 July 1699, transl. (**Add. 38853 f. 21**).

146.65 HODGSON PAPERS (**Add. 50240-52**)
Journals of John Gilson kept in Germany and Russia, 1843-6 (**Add. 50245-8**).

146.66 THE HOLLAND HOUSE PAPERS (**Add. 51318-52254**)
Papers of Henry Fox, 1st Lord Holland, include: letter from Newcastle to Melchior Guy Dickens, Envoy to Russia, 2 Oct. 1753 (**Add. 51378 ff. 97-107b**); correspondence with George Macartney, partly as Envoy to Russia, 1762-70 (**Add. 51388 f. 195**); letter-book of Macartney, 1762-1801 (**Add. 51389**); correspondence with Sir Charles Hanbury Williams, partly as Ambassador to Russia, 1739-58 (**Add. 51390-3**). 'Observations sur la déclaration de S.M. L'Empereur de Russie du 7 Novembre 1807' by Gentz (**Add. 51949**); newsletters from Paris during the Crimean War, 1854 (**Add. 52066**); journal kept by John Allen including a note on Russian history, *c.* 1803 (**Add. 52198 ff. 56-7b**).

146.67 HOLLES, Thomas Pelham, Duke of Newcastle (**Add. 32684-33201**)
Statesman, Secretary of State for the Northern Department, 1746-54. Papers include correspondence while at the Northern Department, memoranda of Cabinet papers and diplomatic papers. *See index for details and correspondents.*

146.68 HUSKISSON PAPERS (**Add. 38734-70**)
Papers of William Huskisson (1770-1830), statesman, include memo on the Russian tariff on sugar, 1825 (**Add. 38746 f. 208**) and paper on British and American trade with Russia, 1825 (**f. 265**).

146.69 SUPPLEMENTARY HYNDFORD PAPERS (**Add. 45113-21**)
Papers of John Carmichael, 3rd Earl of Hyndford, diplomat, include papers re Russia, 1742-4 (**Add. 45115**), and papers as Ambassador to Russia, 1745-8 (**Add. 45116-17**). *See index for correspondents.*

146.70 THE IDDESLEIGH PAPERS (**Add. 50013-64**)
Papers of Stafford Henry Northcote (1818-87), 1st Earl of Iddesleigh, statesman, probably include material re Russia, especially in papers while Secretary of State for Foreign Affairs, 1866.

146.71 JARVIS, Sir John (**Add. 31192**)
Journals of Sir John Jarvis, Earl of St Vincent of tours into Russia returning through Denmark, 21 July - 23 Oct. 1774.

146.72 PAUL JONES COLLECTION (**Add. 25893-5**)
10 copy books, partly printed, 'Extracts etc. for a fair and impartial History of Paul Jones ... Collected by me, Richard Filkin, M.D. (of Richmond, Surrey), whose Father, Richard Filkin, was a Midshipman in the action of 23rd September 1799 of the Serapis' (**Add. 25893**); printed papers and MSS re the life of Paul Jones, collected and arranged by Dr R. Filkin, 19th century (**Add. 25894**); original letters of R. Filkin to Joseph Allen, of Greenwich Hospital, re the life of Paul Jones, 20 July 1842 - 12 Jan. 1851 (**Add. 25895**).

146.73 KAEMPFER, Engelbert (**Add. 5232**)
Drawings of views, antiquities, plants etc. in Muscovy, Persia and the East Indies. See *Catalogue of Manuscript Maps ... in the British Museum* for details of maps.

146.74 KEENE PAPERS (**Add. 43412-43**)
Papers of Benjamin Keene, diplomat, re *inter alia* foreign relations with Russia, 1730-57. *See index for correspondents.*

146.75 KOTELIANSKII PAPERS (**Add. 48966-75, 60489**)
Papers of Samuel Solomonovich Kotelyanskii (1880-1955), translator, include letters from Mme Fanni Kravchinskii, mostly re her husband Sergei M. Kravchinskii, alias Stepnyak, and papers re the Russian Revolution (**Add. 48974**); letters to Miss Mervyn Lagden and Miss Diana Wilbraham, 1936-44, n.d. (**Add. 60489**).

146.76 LAMB (MELBOURNE) PAPERS (**Add. 45546-56**)
Correspondence of the Lamb family includes letters to Lady Cowper (later Lady Palmerston) from Dorothea Lieven, 1822-56, French (**Add. 45555-6**).

146.77 LAUDERDALE PAPERS (**Add. 23,113-8, 35125**)
Letters to John Maitland (1616-82), 2nd Earl Lauderdale, from William Drummond and Patrick Gordon re their service in Russia (**Add. 23122 f. 146; 23125 ff. 122-3; 23126 f. 96; 23129 ff. 231-2**). Copies of letters from Sir John Meyrick, or Mericke, English Ambassador to Russia, to Gustavus Adolphus re negotiations for peace between Russia and Sweden, Moscow, 1616, Latin (**Add. 35125f. 38**).

146.78 THE LAYARD PAPERS (**Add. 38931-39164**)
Papers of Sir Austen Henry Layard (1817-94), diplomat, include: newsletters on the situation in Turkey during the Russo-Turkish War, 1877-80, French (**Add. 39054 ff. 30-263**); diary of a journey in Denmark, Sweden and Russia, 1838 (**Add. 39066 f. 1**); and draft of an article on Russia (**Add. 39066 f. 88**); 'Notice sommaire sur la puissance et la politique Russe en Orient' with map (**Add. 39141**); 'Russian Advances in Asia' compiled by Lt-Col. A. C. Cooke, 1865 (**Add. 39157 f. 71**); confidential print chiefly re the Russo-Turkish War of 1877-8 (**Add. 39161-3**); correspondence re Russian forward policy in Asia, 1877, 1879 (**Add. 39164**). *See index for details.*

146.79 C. G. LELAND COLLECTION (**Add. 37168-74**)
Fragment of notes on life in Russia, n.d., probably late 19th century (**Add. 37172 f. 31**).

146.80 LEXINGTON PAPERS (**Add. 46525-59**)
Papers of Robert Sutton (1661-1725), 2nd Baron Lexington, include an account of the battle between Sweden and Russia at Narva, 20 Nov. 1700, French (**Add. 46553 ff. 133-8**).

146.81 LIEVEN PAPERS (**Add. 47236-435, 58121-3**)
Papers of Prince Christoph Heinrich Lieven (1774-1839), Russian general and diplomat, include: correspondence with Alexander I, Nicholas I, other members of the Imperial family, Prince V. P. Kochubei, Count D. N. Bludov, Prince M. S. Vorontsov, Count A. A. Arakcheev, Prince (?V. A.) Dolgorukov, Prince P. M. Volkonskii, Count N. P. Rumyantsov, Count K. R. Nesselrode, Count S. R. Vorontsov and others (**Add. 47236-300**); awards of Russian honours, chart giving returns of shipping for Russian ports, plan of the village of Baki (**Add. 47300**); engagement diaries (**Add. 47321-40**). Papers of Princess Dorothea Lieven, née Benckendorff, include: correspondence with members of the Imperial family and other prominent Russian and British figures (**Add. 47341-78**); notes and diaries (**Add. 47379-94**); correspondence, mainly with Count Constantine Benkendorff, 1847-57 (**Add. 58121-3**). *See catalogue and index for details.*

146.82 THE LIVERPOOL PAPERS (**Add. 38190-489, 38564-81**)
Papers of the Earls of Liverpool include a proposed letter from Augusta, Princess of Wales, to Catherine on the accession of her husband Peter III (**Add. 38191**), and letters to British ministers at St Petersburg (**Add. 38395**). *See index for details.*

146.83 LOEWENBERG COLLECTION (**Add. 48305-11**)
Material re opera collected by Dr Alfred Loewenberg (1902-47) includes notebooks and miscellaneous notes on Russian opera (**Add. 48306 A ff. 123-74; 48306 B ff. 28-90**).

146.84 LOWE, Sir Hudson (**Add. 20107-33**)
Papers include: copies of official correspondence as Inspector of the Russian-German Legion, 1813 (**Add. 20111**); copy of correspondence with Alexander I, 1814 (**Add. 20112 f. 188**); returns of enlistments etc. of the Russian-German Legion, 1813-14 (**Add. 20193-4**); correspondence with Count Balmain (?Alexander Balmaine) re Russia (**Add. 20203 ff. 86-233**), Count Pozzo di Borgo, Russian Envoy Extraordinary at Paris (**Add. 20233 f. 165**) and M. de Tatishchev, Russian Ambassador at Vienna (**Add. 20233 ff. 257-8**).

146.85 MACARTNEY, Sir George (**Add. 33764; 58834**)
Copy of 'An Account of Russia, 1767' including 'The Present State of the Church of Russia, 1767' by Revd John Glen King, Chaplain to the English Factory at St Petersburg (**Add. 33764 f.51**); letter-book with copies of 10 documents re the commercial treaty between Britain and Russia, 20 June 1766 (**Add. 58834**).

146.86 MACGRIGOR PAPERS (**Add. 61991-2**)
Letters from Army Surg. Alexander MacGrigor to his brother chiefly re his service at the Barrack Hospital at Scutari, 19 Mar. 1854 - 12 Nov. 1855 (**Add. 61991**); TS 'The Chronicles of an Army Surgeon during the Crimean War' (**Add. 61992**).

146.87 MACMILLAN ARCHIVE (**Add. 54786-56035**)
Correspondence with authors includes with M. Y. Ostrogorskii, 1895-1914 (**Add. 55171**) and there may be further references to Russian authors in the general correspondence and letter books. *See card index for details.*

146.88 THE MARTIN PAPERS (**Add. 41346-475**)
Papers of Col. Samuel Martin (1714-88), MP, and Sir Thomas Byam Martin (1773-1854), Comptroller of the Navy, include MS copy with corrections of the pamphlet 'Deliberate thoughts on the system of our late treaties with Hesse Cassell & Russia', printed 1756 (**Add. 41355**, and papers re the Russian fleet and armed forces, 1812 (**Add. 41365-6**). *See index for further details.*

146.89 MEYERSTEIN BEQUEST (**Add. 47843-82**)
Letter from Muzio Clementi saying that he is leaving for Russia, 14 Sept. 1805, Italian and transl. (**Add. 47843 ff. 8-10**).

146.90 THE MIDDLETON PAPERS (**Add. 41803-46**)
Papers of Charles Middleton, 2nd Earl of Middleton, Secretary of State, include: letters to British representatives in Muscovy and elsewhere 1684-8 (**Add. 41823 ff. 79-106b**); papers re mainly Poland and Russia including letters from Patrick Gordon, general in Russian service, 17 Sept. 1686 - 3 July 1688, and papers re the Russian embassy sent to England in 1687, including credentials of V. T. Postnikov as Envoy, 16 Feb. 1687, Russian with transl. (**Add. 41842 ff. 159-93**). *See index for correspondents.*

146.91 MIRSKY, Prince Dmitrii Petrovich (**Add. 49530, 49597**)
Literary historian and critic, lecturer at the School of Slavonic and East European Studies.
Letters, 1929-37.

146.92 MITCHELL, Sir Andrew (**Add. 6804-71**)
British Envoy and Ambassador at Berlin. Papers include: correspondence with English
envoys and ambassadors in Russia, 1756-7, 1763-71 (**Add. 6805-6, 6810, 6824, 6826**);
letters from Prince ?A. Naryshkin and Prince Golitsyn (?M. M), 1745, 1762 (**Add. 6851**); 3
original letters from the Grand Duke Peter and Grand Duchess Catherine addressed to Sir
Charles Hanbury Williams, 1756-7 (**Add. 6864**); papers re Russia etc., 1751-64 (**Add.
6865**); papers re revenues, population and statistics of Russia, 1740-58 (**Add. 6871**).

146.93 MORLEY PAPERS (**Add. 48218-301**)
Papers of John Parker, 2nd Baron Boringdon and 1st Earl of Morley, include journal of a
tour in Russia, 1792-3 (**Add. 48251**). Papers of Edmund, Visc. Boringdon and 2nd Earl of
Morley, include letter on behalf of Alexander I (**Add. 48260 f. 50**).

146.94 WILLIAM MORRIS PAPERS (**Add. 45338-53**)
Papers of Morris (1834-96), poet and artist, include correspondence with P. A. Kropotkin
and S. M. Kravchinskii (alias S. Stepnyak). *See index for details.*

146.95 NAPIER PAPERS (**Add. 40018-55, 54510-64**)
Papers of Adm. Sir Charles Napier (1786-1860), commander of the fleet in the Baltic
during the Crimean War, include: list of Russian warships in the Black Sea, 1836 (**Add.
40020 f. 385**); report on the Russian Baltic fleet, 1853 (**Add. 40023 f. 408**); papers re the
Baltic expedition, 1854-6 (**Add. 40024-7, 40032**). Supplementary papers (**Add. 54510-64**)
may contain further material re Russia.

146.96 THE NELSON PAPERS (**Add. 34902-92**)
Papers of Adm. Horatio Nelson include: letters from Paul I, 1798 (**Add. 34907 f. 392** and
copy **Add. 34942 f. 273**); lists of the squadron under Adm. F. F. Ushakov, *c.* 1798-9 (**Add.
34908 f. 425; 34932 f. 82**); copy of Russian declaration of war with Spain, 1799 (**Add. 34945
f. 94**). *See index for further details.*

146.97 NIGHTINGALE PAPERS (**Add. 43393-403**, 45750-849)
Papers of Florence Nightingale (1820-1910) include general correspondence and accompts
during the Crimean War. *See index for details.*

146.98 NORRIS, Adm. Sir John (**Add. 28141-57**)
Correspondence with Peter I, 1715, 1719, Russian with transl. (**Add. 28154 ff. 133, 135;
Add. 28155 ff. 218, 220; Add. 28156 f. 1**). *See index for details.*

146.99 NORTH, Sir Dudley (**Add. 32522**)
Writings include 'Voyage to Archangel', 'Voyage from Archangel', early 18th century
(**f. 33**).

146.100 NORTH (SHEFFIELD PARK) PAPERS (**Add. 61860-76**)
Papers of Frederick North (1732-92), 2nd Earl of Guildford, PM, include political papers
by George III on the political alliance between Vienna, Russia and Berlin, ?1772 (**Add.
61860**).

146.101 NORTHCLIFFE PAPERS (Add. 62253-397)

Papers of Alfred Charles William Harmsworth (1865-1922), Visc. Northcliffe, journalist and newspaper proprietor, include correspondence with Russian correspondents R. Wilton, 1919-20 (**Add. 62253**), and S. Washburn, 1914-22 (**Add. 62254**).

146.102 NORTHCOTE, John (1746-1831) (Add. 47770-93)

Autobiography includes a portrait of Alexander I, 1803 (**Add. 47792 f. 150**).

146.103 NORTHCOTE PAPERS (Add. 57559-61)

Papers of Lt Dudley Stafford Northcote re his work in Mesopotamia and Armenia where he was Relief Officer for the Armenian Refugees' (Lord Mayor's) Fund, 1918-26.

146.104 O'HARA, FM James, 2nd Baron Tyrawly (Add. 23627-42)

Papers when Ambassador to Russia, 1742-5, include correspondence with the Duke of Newcastle, Lord Carteret, Edward Weston, Sir Thomas Robinson, Robert Trevor, the Hon. Thomas Villiers and others (**Add. 23630-1**) with entry books of the correspondence of the same, Oct. 1743-Nov. 1744 (**Add. 23632-3**). *See index for details.*

146.105 ONU PAPERS (Add. 45526-33)

Papers and collections on Russian history of Alexander Onu, or Aleksandr Mikhailovich Onu, Professor of Modern History at the University of Petrograd, Consul-General in London for the 1917 Russian Government include: articles and lectures on Russian history by Onu; MS of a supplement to *A Thousand Years of Russian History* by S. E. Howe; translated extracts from Russian newspapers; notebooks of extracts from the Public Record Office re Russo-Turkish War of 1877-8; extracts from the published *Zapiski* of Count Nikolai Pavlovich Ignat'ev; extracts from miscellaneous historical works. *See catalogue and index for details.*

146.106 OSBORNE, Thomas (Add. 28046-54)

Account by John Hebdon (the son) about the service of his father (John Hebdon) in Russia.

146.107 OVERBECK-NOVIKOV CORRESPONDENCE (Add. 47460-1)

Letters of Joseph Julian Overbeck (1821-1905) to Olga Alekseevna Novikov, née Kireeva, 1869-1900.

146.108 PAGET PAPERS (Add. 48383-416, 51205-41)

Papers of Arthur Paget (1771-1840), diplomat, include correspondence with the Chevalier Andrei Yakovlevich Italinskii, Russian Minister at Naples, 1800-8, French (**Add. 48398 B ff. 134-69b**), Charles Whitworth, mostly as Ambassador at St Petersburg and Paris, 1794-1805 (**Add. 48400 ff. 1-41b**), Benjamin Garlike as Secretary at Stockholm and St Petersburg, 1794-1804 (**ff. 42-67b**), Alleyne Fitzherbert, Baron St Helens, as Ambassador at St Petersburg, 1801-2 (**ff. 68-122**), Adm. Sir John Borlase Warren as Ambassador in St Petersburg, 1801-2 (**ff. 68-122**); Adm. Count Carlo Andrea Pozzo di Borgo, Russian diplomat, 1801-13, French (**ff. 169-212b**). *See index for details.* Correspondence of Sir Augustus Berkeley Paget (1823-96), diplomat, (**Add. 51205-41**) may include material re Russia amongst his correspondence with the Foreign Office and with ambassadors.

146.109 THE PALMERSTON PAPERS (Add. 48417-589)

Correspondence of Henry John Temple (1784-1865), 3rd Visc. Palmerston, as Secretary for War, Foreign Secretary and PM, includes Foriegn Office letter-books, copies, abstracts and drafts, for Russia, 1830-49 (**Add. 48483-5, 48534-6, 48565-8**). *See index for correspondents.*

146.110 PECHERIN, Vladimir Sergeevich (1807-85) (**Add. 59672-76**)
Classical scholar, poet. Letters and papers relating to him, Russian, English, Latin and French.

146.111 THE PEEL PAPERS (**Add. 40181-617**)
Papers of Sir Robert Peel (1788-1850), 2nd Bt, PM, include printed bulletin of operations at the battle of Borodino, 1812 (**Add. 40222**) and papers re foreign affairs while PM. *See index for further details.*

146.112 PIGGOTT PAPERS (**Add. 42525-54**)
Collection of Sir Francis Taylor Piggott (d. 1925) includes copies of and extracts from diplomatic correspondence concerning Anglo-Russian relations, 1806-7 (**Add. 42545 ff. 84-210**). *See index for correspondents.*

146.113 PLACE, Francis (**Add. 27789-859**)
Notes by Place on the Russian campaign, 1813, with map (**Add. 27822 f. 97**).

146.114 PORTER, Sir Robert Ker (**Add. 14758, 18282, 53791-99**)
MS of *Travels in Caucasus, Georgia, Persia, Armenia, Ancient Babylonia etc. in 1817, 1818, 1819, 1820* including more drawings than the published volume and military sketch of Russia, 1812 (**Add. 14758**); sketches, principally of costumes, made during his travels in Albania, Russia, Georgia etc., 1817-20 (**Add. 18282**); journals and notebooks of Sir Robert Ker Porter during his travels in Russia, the Caucasus, Persia and Mesopotamia, 1817-20 (**Add. 53791-9**). See *Catalogue of Manuscript Maps ... in the British Museum* for details of maps.

146.115 POWER PAPERS (**Add. 56093-8**)
Papers of Sir Arthur John Power (1889-1960), Admiral of the Fleet, include papers re the award of the Russian Order of St Stanislaus, 1920 (**Add. 56098**).

146.116 ROSE PAPERS (**Add. 42772-846**)
Papers of George Rose, statesman, include 'A Succinct Account of Russia' (**Add. 42780 ff. 96-107**). Papers of his son Sir George Henry Rose, diplomat, include correspondence with William Schaw Cathcart as Ambassador to Russia (**Add. 42792**), Louis Casamajor as Secretary of the Embassy and Sir Charles Bagot as Ambassador to Russia (**Add. 42793**). Papers of Hugh Henry Rose, Baron Strathnairn, include: correspondence with George William Frederick Villiers, 4th Earl Clarendon, and Fitzroy James Henry Somerset, Baron Raglan, in the Crimea (**Add. 42802-5**); sketch-map of part of the works before Sebastopol, 1855 (**Add. 42809 A**); instructions to and correspondence of Adm. the Hon. George Henry Douglas in HMS *Cruizer* during the Crimean War (**Add. 42846**). *See index for details.*

146.117 ROYAL HISTORICAL MSS (**Add. 45130 A**)
Map of Moscow (**f. 64**); envelope addressed by Alexander I to Count Aleksei A. Arakcheev, n.d. (**f. 67**).

146.118 ROYAL SOCIETY PAPERS (**Add. 4448**)
Account of the death by lightning of Georg Wilhelm Richman, Professor of Experimental Physics at St Petersburg, on 26 July 1753, German and English (**Add. 4439 ff. 229-39**); genealogical tree of Aleksandr Nevskii, 18th century, German (**Add. 4448 f. 14**).

146.119 R.U.S.I. MAPS (**Add. 57636-722**)
Maps include Russia, 18th century, and the Crimea during the War (**Add. 57691-4**).

146.120 SIR CHARLES SCOTT PAPERS (**Add. 52294-310**)
Papers of Sir Charles Stewart Scott (1838-1924), diplomat, include correspondence with Foreign Secretaries, members of the Royal family and diaries while Ambassador to Russia, 1898-1904.

146.121 SEYMOUR, Francis, 1st Bt (**Add. 41167**)
Correspondence includes letters from the Crimea, 21 Mar. 1854 - 3 Sept. 1855.

146.122 SEYMOUR DIARIES (**Add. 60290-312**)
28 vols of diaries, 1818-78, of Sir George Hamilton Seymour, diplomat, Private Secretary to Lord Castlereagh and Ambassador at St Petersburg at the outbreak of the Crimean War.

146.123 BERNARD SHAW LETTERS AND PAPERS (**Add. 46505-7, 50593-743**)
Letters from George Bernard Shaw to his wife Charlotte Frances, née Payne-Townsend, include letters written from Berlin and the Soviet Union, July 1931 (**Add. 46506 ff. 134-53**); TS 'The Rationalization of Russia?', 1932 (**Add. 50676**).

146.124 LETTERS TO GEORGE STEPNEY (**Add. 21551**)
Letter to Stepney, English Minister at Vienna, from Charles Whitworth, Envoy to Russia, 1704 (**ff. 27, 32**).

146.125 TELFER PAPERS (**Add. 47685**)
Correspondence and papers of Capt. John Buchan Telfer re his unsuccessful attempt to further the claim of his wife, Ekaterina Aleksandrovna, daughter of the Decembrist Aleksandr Mikhailovich Murav'ev, to a share of her family's property in Russia, 1868-92, English, French and Russian, and journal in St Petersburg, 1889 (**Add. 47685**).

146.126 THURLOE PAPERS (**Add. 4155-9**)
Proposition by Nicholas de Bye, Polish Envoy, to the Lord Protector that he should refrain from helping Russia, 29 Sept. 1655, Latin and English (**Add. 4157 ff. 38-42b**).

146.127 TOWNSHEND PAPERS (**Add. 38492-508, 48981-2**)
Papers of Charles Townshend, 2nd Visc. Townshend of Raynham, include: memoire of a conference between Catherine I and the French Minister, 1725 (**Add. 38503 f. 255**); copies of letters from William Bromley, Secretary of State, to Sir Benjamin Ayloffe, Governor of the Muscovy Company, 14, 18 June 1714 (**Add. 38507 ff. 114-27**); draft of letter to Prince Aleksandr Borisovich Kurakin, 1727, French (**Add. 48982 f. 100**).

146.128 VAN DER VLIET PAPERS (**Add. 49065-85**)
24 vols of papers of Senator Vasilii Yakovlevich Van der Vliet, Russian diplomat, 1894-1918, Russian, French and German. *See index for correspondents.*

146.129 VANSITTART, Nicholas (**Add. 31229-37**)
Diplomat. Papers include material on Russian finances, 1812, French (**Add. 31230 ff. 271, 290, 294, 298**). *See index for further material.*

146.130 VERNON PAPERS (**Add. 40771-850**)
Correspondence of James Vernon (d. 1727), Secretary of State, includes heads of letters to Peter I from William III, 1700, and letters from W. Blathwayt to Vernon re Russia, Sept.-Oct. 1700 (**Add. 40774**).

146.131 ALFRED RUSSEL WALLACE PAPERS (**Add. 46414-2**)
Letters to Wallace (1823-1913), naturalist, from Vladimir O. Kovalevskii, Professor of Geology at Moscow, 1872, *c.* 1880 (**Add. 46435 f. 244; 46436 f. 93**).

146.132 WALKER PAPERS (**Add. 49615-20**)
Correspondence of Lt-Col. Edward Walter Forester Walker mainly with his wife re mostly his service in the Crimean War, 1854-64.

146.133 WELLESLEY PAPERS (Series II) (**Add. 37274-318**)
Papers of Richard Colley Wellesley (1760-1842), 2nd Earl of Mornington, Marquis Wellesley, minister and diplomat, include memo of public service of Sir Gore Ouseley in India, Persia and Russia (**Add. 37285 ff. 319-25**), and correspondence re foreign affairs whilst Foreign Secretary, 1793-1840. *See index for further details and correspondents.*

146.134 WENTWORTH, Thomas, Lord Raby and Earl of Stafford (**Add. 31128-52**)
Diplomat. Papers include letters from Charles Whitworth, Envoy to Russia, with a few draft replies, 12 Jan. 1705 - 16 Feb. 1710/11 (**Add. 31128**). *See index for other correspondents.*

146.135 WESTON PAPERS (**Add. 57305-8**)
Diplomatic letters addressed to Edward Weston (1703-70), Under-Secretary of State for the Northern Department, 1742-6, may include material re Russia.

146.136 WHITWORTH PAPERS (**Add. 37348-97**)
Papers of Charles Whitworth, Envoy Extraordinary in Moscow, 1704-12, include: correspondence from Russia, referring to trade, the English Tobacco Co. in Moscow, and the arrest of the Russian Ambassador in London for debt; correspondence of L. C. Weisbrod, Secretary of the Legation in Russia; miscellaneous papers re trade and other matters (**Add. 37354-60**). *See index for further details.*

146.137 H. W. WILLIAMS PAPERS (**Add. 54436-76**)
Papers of Harold Whitmore Williams (d. 1928), journalist, and his wife Ariadna Vladimirovna, formerly Tyrkova, re mainly the activities of the Russian Liberation Committee in London, 1918-29, n.d., some Russian.

146.138 WILSON, Sir Robert Thomas (**Add. 30095-144**)
Papers include: journal as British Commissioner at the headquarters of the Russian Army and of his mission with Lord Hutchinson to Berlin, 24 Nov. 1806 - 2 Dec. 1807 (**Add. 30098**); journal while serving as Commissioner with the Russian, German and Italian armies, 12 Apr. 1812 - 22 July 1814 (**Add. 30100-1**); correspondence with William Schaw Cathcart, Ambassador to Russia, Prince Adam Czartoryski (**Add. 30106-7**), Count P. Stroganov, Count S. R. Vorontsov, M. Ivanovich, and Alexander I (**Add. 30133**); papers re Russia and Turkey, 1807-39 (**Add. 30132**); letters from Count S. R. Vorontsov, 1807 (**Add. 30147 f. 1**). *See index for details.*

146.139 WINDHAM PAPERS (**Add. 37842-935**)
Correspondence and papers of William Windham (d. 1810) include letters from Paul I re Russian affairs, 1799 (**Add. 37852 ff. 290-302**).

146.140 WODEHOUSE PAPERS (**Add. 46692-4**)
Papers of John Wodehouse (1826-1902), 3rd Baron Wodehouse, as Envoy Extraordinary and Minister Plenipotentiary to Russia, 1856-8 (**Add. 46692-4**). *See index for correspondents.*

146.141 HENRY WOOD PAPERS (Add. 56419-43)
Papers of Sir Henry Joseph Wood (1869-1944), conductor, include correspondence with Sergei Rachmaninov, 1936-9 (**Add. 56421**), Dmitrii Shostakovich, officials at the Russian Embassy and Soviet cultural institutions, 1942-6 (**Add. 56426**), Sergei Prokof'ev (**Add. 56429**) and Igor Stravinskii (**Add. 56430**).

146.142 HENRY WORSLEY OFFICIAL CORRESPONDENCE (Add. 15936)
Copy of the answer given by George I to the demand of Peter I, presented by his Resident, M. Vesselovskii, 11 Feb. 1719/20, French (**Add. 15936 f. 289**).

146.143 DOUGLAS YOUNG PAPERS (Add. 61855-55)
Papers of Douglas Young (1882-1967) re chiefly his experiences as Consul in Archangel, 1915-18, his criticism of British military intervention in Russia and his dismissal and reinstatement in the consular service.

146.144 ZAMBELLI PAPERS (Add. 46871-82)
Papers of Antonio Lega Zambelli and his family include correspondence with Marietta and Antonio de' Rossi in St Petersburg, Italian (**Add. 46875**).

146.145 An examination of 'le stile, dont les Roys de Grand Bretagne se sont servis, en écrivant aux Czars de Moscovie', *temp.* Elizabeth I - George I (**Add. 4193 ff. 249-51**).

146.146 Miscellaneous collection of papers mainly re foreign affairs includes article 4 of the Treaty of Neustadt between Russia and Sweden, 1721, French (**Add. 4299 f. 19**).

146.147 Beginning of a letter from Elizabeth I to Ivan IV, n.d., Latin (**Add. 4712 f. 94b**).

146.148 Letter from Peter I to Mr Noy, shipbuilder, 16 May 1722, Russian with transl. (**Add. *5015 ff. 98, 100**).

146.149 Pedigree of Peter I (**Add. 5822 f. 1b**).

146.150 Epitaph of Peter I (**Add. 5832 f. 68b**).

146.151 Letter from Ivan IV to Edward VI, 1554, transl. (**Add. 6113 f. 176**).

146.152 Diploma given to George Parker, 2nd Earl of Macclesfield, from the Imperial Academy in St Petersburg (**Add. 6180 f. 187**).

146.153 Account of audiences given to Russian ambassadors in England and Stockholm, Jan. and Apr. 1662 (**Add. 6308 pp. 71, 104**).

146.154 Letter from Tsarevich Paul to Sir W. Hamilton re the sale of a picture to Catherine II, 8 July 1784 (**Add. 6416 f. 4**).

146.155 Statistical memoir on Russia, apparently drawn up by the direction of the French Government, Aug. 1729 (**Add. 6900**).

146.156 'Relazione dello Stato Attuale delle Chiese Cattoliche nell' Impero Russo, etc.' by M. Arezzo, 1804 (**Add. 8777**).

146.156 'Douchinka, Poëme traduit de Russe d'Hyppolite Bogdanovitche [Ippolit F. Bogdanovich], avec des notes sur les traits de mythologie cités dans le Poëme, par L.C.C.A., Professeur extraordinaire à l'Université de Moscou', 1797 (**Add. 10325-7**).

146.157 Letter from Paul I to Charles Whitworth, 17 Aug. 1799, French (**Add. 12096**).

146.158 Letter from the translators of Marmontel's *Bélisaire* into Russian, signed by Catherine II *et al.*, St Petersburg, 11 Sept. 1768 (**Add. 12110**).

146.159 Papers re the Russia Company, 1710-81, in the papers of the Board of Trade and Plantations (**Add. 14035**).

146.160 2 plans of St Petersburg; map of the course of the Dniestr to the Black Sea; plan of the Moscow Kremlin; 'Route des troupes Russiennes en 1783, au travers les Montagnes de Caucase' (**Add. 15329**).

146.161 Map, 'La rade et ville de Petersbourg et du Fort de Cronslot', 1739, and a copy of the same (**Add. 15330**).

146.162 Views of Kamchatka by J. Webber, 1776-80 (**Add. 15514**).

146.163 2 letters from Baron M. I. von der Pahlen (Palen) to ---, St Petersburg, 15 Aug. 1790, Riga, 25 May 1792, French (**ff. 122-3**); letters from Count G. Stackelberg (Stakel'berg) to Count Grigorii Orlov, 27 July 1818, 4/13 Nov. 1821, French (**ff. 191, 225**) (**Add. 15945**).

146.164 Letter from John Carmichael, Earl of Hyndford, Envoy Extraordinary to Russia, to --- , St Petersburg, 14 June 1747 (**Add. 15946 f. 41**).

146.165 7 maps re the conquest of the Åland Islands by Russia, Russian with English transl. (**Add. 16366**).

146.166 'Lettera del Kzar di Moscovia al Cardinale Primate, et agl' altri entrati nella confederazione contro il Rè di Polonia', 15 Mar. 1704 (**Add. 16465 f. 78**).

146.167 Letter of Peter I to the Sultan (Ahmed III), St Petersburg, 24 July 1710, Latin (**Add. 16477 f. 112**).

146.168 Poem on the conquests of the Russians over the Turks in 1769-74, 'Johannis Baptistae de Bonis, Archerontini, viri Patritii, de Bello Odrysio; ad Catheriniam II Moschorum Imperatricem Augustissimam, libri V' (**Add. 16568**).

146.169 Sketches during Capt. J. Cook's 3rd voyage, 1776-80, by J. Webber, including a sketch of Pavlovsk (**Add. 172771 f. 38**). See *Catalogue of Manuscript Maps ... in the British Museum* for details of maps.

146.170 'Giornale del Viaggio da Londra a Petersbourg nel vascello The Augusta di Mylord Baltimore, nel mese di Maggio, v.s., l'anno MDCCXXXIX' by Count Francesco Algarotti (**Add. 17482**).

146.171 Treaty between China and Russia, 1727-8, Manchu (**Add. 18106**).

146.172 Arms of the princes and chief nobility of Russia, 16th century (**Add. 18610**).

146.173 Papers re the Navy (**Add. 19033-6**) include lists of Russian and Spanish fleets, 17th - 18th centuries (**Add. 19032**); account of the Russian fleet by M. Rosbee, 1735 (**Add. 19036 f. 31**); account of the disgrace of Prince A. Menshikov, n.d. (**Add. 19036 f. 33**).

146.174 Collection of original patents of Russian sovereigns, 1713-82, with signatures of ministers etc. (**Add. 19715**).

146.175 Copy of letter from James Edward, son of James II, to the Cardinal Acquaviva communicating a promise of the Courts of Russia and Sweden to aid in his restoration, 27 Jan. 1718, French (**Add. 20292 f. 184**).

146.176 Letter from Louis XVIII to Alexander I, 1813, French (**Add. 20669 ff. 10, 12**).

146.177 Reception given at Königsberg to the first Russian embassy sent to Brandenburg, Peter I being in its train, 18/28 May - 8/18 June [1697], German (**Add. 20806 f. 352**).

146.178 'Notes on the Invasion of India by Russia', 1830, by Sir John Malcolm (**Add. 21178 f. 71**).

146.179 Letter from the Tsar Alexis to Charles II, Feb. 1665, Russian (**Add. 21408**).

146.180 Draft of a letter from Jean François Marmontel to Catherine II, Aix-la-Chapelle, 12 Sept. [1768], French (**Add. 21514 f. 78**).

146.181 Autographs of Peter I, Catherine II, Alexander I (**ff. 68-9, 73, 79**); copy of letters from Catherine II and Paul I to Adm. Paul Jones, 11 May, June 1788, French (**ff. 74, 76**) (**Add. 21529**).

146.182 Maps of Russia and Poland, 18th century (**Add. 21596**).

146.183 Journal of William Blathwayt, Secretary-at-War in Holland, including comments on Peter I, Apr.-Oct. 1697 (**Add. 22031**).

146.184 Copies of letters from William Breton, English Minister at Berlin, to Thomas Wentworth, Earl of Stafford, include propositions made by the King of Prussia to the Tsar, 1714, French (**Add. 22209 f. 54**).

146.185 Letter from ?Antoine François Le Bailly to Count Orlov, 31 May 1823, French (**Add. 23102 f. 112**).

146.186 Drawings and plans of battles, chiefly executed by Lt-Col. Charles Hamilton Smith, include: 'A Sketch of the Action fought by the ... Anglo-Russian Army ... and the Gallo-Batavian forces, on the 2nd of October 1799, near Camper in Holland' (**f. 6**); 'Order of attack of the Russian Army ... on the fortified suburb Prague', 24 Feb. 1794 (**f. 16**); plan of the 'Siege of Narva, 1700' (**f. 64**) (**Add. 23618**).

146.187 Letter from J.-L. Pictet (Pikte), secretary to Catherine II, to François Marie Arouet de Voltaire, St Petersburg, 4/15 Aug. 1762, French (**Add. 24024f. 66**).

146.188 Music of Maksim S. Berezovskii, composer to Catherine II, includes Psalm 51 (**f. 1**) and 'Kontsert sochineniya berezovskaya' (**f. 97**) (**Add. 24288**).

146.190 Extracts and notes re the history, language etc. of Armenia, French, Latin and Armenian, early 19th century (**Add. 24634**).

146.191 History of Georgia, 1647-1757, compiled from the works of native writers, 18th century, Russian (**Add. 25325**).

146.192 'Ossetisch, Dugorisch, Kurdische Wörtersammlung verglichen mit Zend, Pehlvi, und Persisch nebst anderen Sprachen', Tiflis, 6 May 1808, by Heinrich Julius Klaproth (**Add. 25328**).

146.193 Account of engagements in Moldavia between the Russians and Turks, 18 July and 1 Aug. 1770, French (**Add. 25490 f. 30**).

146.194 Papers re the restoration of Louis XVIII include secret instructions for negotiating with the Emperor of Russia and the King of Prussia, 1814 (**Add. 26669 f. 17**).

146.195 Plan of the Russian siege of Ochakov, 1788 (**Add. 27392 I**).

146.196 Cipher from Lord John Carteret, Secretary of State, to Lord Tyrawly, Ambassador to Russia, 18 May 1744 (**Add. 27548 f. 16**).

146.197 Draft of 'the Marquis of Carmarthen's proposalls for his Imperiall Majesty the great Czar of Muscovy ...' for the establishment of a Russian navy, 1698 (published) (**Add. 28092 f. 53**).

146.198 Papers re chiefly the elections of the Emperors and of the Kings of Poland include conditions offered by Ivan IV for election to the Crown of Poland, *c.* 1572, Latin with Spanish transl. (**Add. 28384 f. 187**).

146.199 Letter from Mattia Stabinger to Pasquale Tamburini, Moscow, 4 Mar. 1790, Italian (**Add. 29300 f. 87**).

146.200 'Discorso della Moscovia', 1558 (**Add. 29444 ff. 185-206**).

146.201 Letter from Count N. N. Demidov to W. T. Raikes & Co., Florence, 16 Oct. 1823 (**Add. 29475 f. 68**).

146.202 Letter from Jean Charles Léonard Simonde de Sismondi to Alexander I, 24 Sept. 1814, French (**Add. 29747 f. 88**).

146.203 Dispatches from Bonet, Prussian Envoy in England, describing Peter's activities in England, Jan.-Apr. 1698 (**Add. 30000 B**).

146.204 Trading privileges granted between England and Russia, 1555-1620, French (**Add. 30571 ff. 234-63**).

146.205 'Traictés des Empereurs des Turcs avec les Papes, les Empereurs d'Allemagne, les Rois de France et de Pologne, et les Venitiens, Tunis et Arger, Perse, et grand Mogor [Mogul et] Moscovie', 1494-1630 (**Add. 30658 f. 99**).

146.206 Map of Tsarskoe Selo by Lt Roukavichnikeff (?Rukavichnikov) (**Add. 31322 F2**).

146.207 Map of the Black Sea, with the seas of Marmara and Azov, n.d. (**Add. 31865 B**).

146.208 Accounts of the Engineer force in the fortress of Bomarsund for the year 1843, Russian (**Add.31906**).

146.209 Deciphers of dispatches passing between foreign governments and their ministers in England include those of Russia, 1719-1853 (**Add. 32288-92**).

146.210 Portrait of Peter I (**Add. 32360 f. 95**).

146.211 Extracts etc. re Nicholas I, *c.* 1835 (**Add. 33501 f. 129; 33502 f. 139**).

146.212 Pass from Lt-Gen. Colin Campbell, afterwards Lord Clyde, for Lt Crowe to enter Sebastopol, 14 Sept. 1855 (**Add. 33610 f. 7**).

146.213 'Descrittione del Mar Negro, e della Tartaria, par il Dottor Emidio Dortelli d'Ascoli, Lett: Dom: Prefetto del Caffa, Tartaria, etc., 1634' (**Add. 33762**).

146.214 Letter from the Hon. Alexander Stanhope, Resident at the Hague, to James Vernon, Secretary of State, re Peter I, the Hague, 25 Sept. 1700 (**Add. 34348 f. 98**).

146.215 34 letters from William Aldersey, Agent at Hamburg, to William Blathwayt, Secretary at War, chiefly re the success of the Swedes in Courland and Livonia, 8 July - 2 Dec. 1701 (**Add. 34357**).

146.216 Proclamation of Catherine II encouraging foreigners to settle in Russia (**Add. 34713 f. 164**); letter from Thomas Newberry describing an imperial entertainment at St Petersburg and interviews with Catherine II, 26 Aug. 1766 (**f. 275**).

146.217 Letters from Lord William Cavendish Bentinck to Sir William Hamilton, Minister at Naples, on his appointment to the headquarters of Marshal A. V. Suvorov's army in the north of Italy, Alexandria, 15 July, 4 Oct. 1799 (**Add. 35230 ff. 53, 55**).

146.218 Project for a treaty of commerce between Sardinia and Russia, in the letter-book of copies of letters from Louis Dutens and Robert Liston, Chargés d'Affaires in Turin, to the Secretaries of State, 1780-3 (**Add. 36805**).

146.219 Official copies of State Papers include an account of the conspiracy against Peter III in 1762 (**Add. 36807 ff. 213, 231, 239**).

146.220 Letter from Richard Cobden to --- on the limits to the offensive power of Russia, 15 Oct. 1849 (**Add. 37053 f. 41**).

146.221 Letter-book of Henry Shirley, Chargé d'Affaires at Moscow and St Petersburg, 14 May 1767 - 15 July 1768 (**Add. 37054**).

146.222 Letters of Karl Marx and Friedrich Engels to N. F. Daniel'son, 1868-95 (published in Russian transl. by G. A. Lopatin); letter from A. Konskii to Daniel'son, 25 Feb. 1895, Russian (**Add. 38075**).

146.223 Printed notes by Philip Yorke, 1st Earl of Hardwicke, Lord Chancellor, on a speech on a motion for a vote of censure on the treaties with Russia and Hesse-Cassel, 10 Dec. 1755 (**Add. 38161 f. 91**).

146.224 'The Fortune of War, or a ten years Captivity in France, by Robert Bastard James, Lieut. in the Royal Navy' mentioning the *Sparrow*, in which he was master's mate and which brought over Count M. I. Platov and Prince M. B. Barclay de Tolly (**Add. 3886 f. 109b**).

146.225 Preliminary draft of the reply of the first Duma to the speech from the Throne, 1906 (**f. 8**); a list of documents re negotiations of Russia with Japan, 1903-4, Russian (**ff. 13-45b**) (**Add. 39325**).

146.226 Letters from Ivan Sergeevich Turgenev to Yakov Petrovich Polonskii, 27 Dec. 1859, 8 Jan. 1860, and to Petr Aleksandrovich Valuev, 21 Jan./2 Feb. 1868, Russian (**Add. 40015 f. 5, 7**).

146.227 Letter from Ivan Aleksandrovich Goncharov to Mikhail Nikolaevich Pokhvisnev and his sister, Ludmila Nikolaevna, 8 Dec. 1868, Russian (**Add. 40015 f. 9**).

146.228 'Steno', a dramatic poem in Russian blank verse by Ivan Sergeevich Turgenev, 1834, with some marginal criticisms attributed to P. A. Pletnev (**Add. 40640**).

146.229 Drafts of a passage of an earlier version of *Resurrection* by L. N. Tolstoi, discarded in the printed edition, and part of a letter on military service, 1 Sept. 1896, Russian (**Add. 40688**).

146.230 Letters to Sir William Hamilton while Envoy at Naples include copies of correspondence between Catherine II and the Grand Master of Malta, 1770, French (**Add. 41197 ff. 157, 159**).

146.231 2 letters from Adm. Sir Erasmus Ommanney to William Hepworth Dixon, author of *Free Russia*, protesting against his account of the British action against the Solovetskii monastery in the White Sea in 1854, and reply by Dixon, 29-30 Apr., 5 May 1870 (published in *The Times*) (**Add. 41340 ff. 146-55**).

146.232 Letters from Charles Cavendish Fulke Grenville, the diarist, to Maj.-Gen. Charles Ash Windham while Chief of Staff in the Crimea, 1855-6 (**Add. 41760**).

146.233 Copy of a letter from Miss Mary Fenner to Count L. N. Tolstoi with his reply, 18, 28 Jan. 1909, French (**Add. 42711 ff. 135-7**).

146.234 Correspondence addressed to Dr James Mouat of the Army Medical Department re the Crimean War including 3 letters from Florence Nightingale, 19 July 1855 - 23 June 1856, and letter from Joseph Mazonowski, Russian army doctor, 10 June 1859 (**Add. 42711 ff. 139-46**).

146.235 'Rodoslovnaya rodu Oznobishinykh', being transcripts of genealogical evidences re the Oznobishin family as members of the nobility on the province of Penza, 1805, Russian (**Add. 43508**). *See index for details.*

146.236 Russian passport of Johann Engmann, 29/11 July 1833 (**Add. 43688 ff. 185-6b**).

146.237 The Russian Steam Navigation and Trading Company papers include a descriptive list of the 42 steamships of the Company compiled by Oswald Papengut, 1860, Russian (**Add. 43855**).

146.238 'Reminiscences of Thirty-Five Years of my Life' by Sir Joseph Archer Crowe includes references to the Crimean War (**Add. 44059-60**).

146.239 4 official letters to Gen. Kokhanovich, Commandant of the fort of Kinburn, during the Crimean War, 1854-5, Russian (**Add. 44085 ff. 57-64**).

146.240 Letter from Princess Catherine de Menshikov (Ekaterina Nikolaevna Menshikova) to ---, Moscow, 25 Apr. 1821, French (**Add. 44919 f. 6**).

146.241 Letters to Mrs Hannah Florence Dryhurst from P. A. Kropotkin, 14 Feb. 1897, 21 Feb. 1898, and S. M. Kravchinskii, alias Stepnyak, 26 Feb. 1890, 13 Nov. 1891 (**Add. 45498 ff. 72-8**).

146.242 Letter from Maksim Litvinov, Plenipotentiary of the Russian People's Commissary for Foreign Affairs, to the Director of the British Museum, 24 July 1918 (**Add. 45680 f. 1**).

146.243 2 letters from George Coombs to his sister from the Crimean War, 1 Aug. 1854, 26 Apr. 1855 (**Add. 45680 ff. 151-3**).

146.244 Copies of Admiralty papers and correspondence re the introduction of a revised scale of diet and comforts for Russian POWs at Sheerness, Lewes and Millbay, 26-7 Sept. 1854 (**Add. 45982 ff. 13-20b**).

146.245 Accompts and inventories of the Krestnyi Monastyr (Monastery of the Cross) on the island of Kio in the Gulf of Onega, 1658-1725, including register of monastic dues in the Kargopol' and Turchasovskii districts, 1600, and inventories of the treasure and sacristan, 1658, 1666, Russian (**Add. 46124 f. 165 ff**).

146.246 English transl. of Russian documents re Joseph Noy, Master Builder of Ships to the Tsar, including: letters from Peter I to Noy, 27 June 1700, 16 May 1722; order of Catherine I, 23 Nov. 1725; petition from Noy to Empress Anne, 1737-48 (**Add. 46362 ff. 2-2b**).

146.247 Copy of 'Narrative of a Journey from Tabriz along the shores of the Caspian Sea to Tehran by Keith Edward Abbott Esqre', 4 Nov. 1843 - 13 Feb. 1844, *post* 1860 (**Add. 46409**).

146.248 Letters from P. A. Kropotkin and others to Alfred Robert Dryhurst (**Add. 46473 ff. 1-33**).

146.249 Letter from Florence Nightingale to Miss Elizabeth Pringle recalling the landing at Scutari and the battle of Inkerman (**Add. 46839 f. 7b**).

146.250 Choreographic score of the ballet by Vaslav Nijinsky to Debussy's 'Prélude à l'après-midi d'un faune', 1915, with notes in Russian (**Add. 47215**).

146.251 Letter from Grigorii Efimovich Rasputin, n.d., Russian (**Add. 47841 ff. 1-2**).

146.252 Letters to Grand Duke Vladimir, 3rd son of Tsar Alexander II, from Count Pavel Petrovich Shuvalov and Lt-Gen. Nikolai Ivanovich Bobrikov, 1873-93, Russian (**Add. 47841 ff. 75-116**).

146.253 2 Russian documents picked up in Sebastopol re the Naval Hospital there, 1840, 1844 (**Add. 48212 ff. 18-20**).

146.254 Letters from Count Giovanni Antonio Capo d'Istria as Russian Secretary of State to Count Gustav Ernst Stackelberg, Russian Minister to Austria, 6/18 Oct. 1816, French (**Add. 48590 f. 61**).

146.255 Decree of the Court of Pinsk re a student Karol Byalozor, 7 Mar. 1682, Belorussian (**Add. 49597 ff. 78-83**).

146.256 Letter from Florence Nightingale re the welfare of the men of the Land Transport, Scutari, 22 Dec. 1855 (**Add. 49977 O**).

146.257 Letter from Petr Ilich Tchaikovsky (Chaikovskii) to Anna Yakovlena Aleksandrovna Levenson, 15 Apr. 1881, Russian with English transl. (**Add. 50483 ff. 141-7**).

146.258 Musical scores by Glazunov and others (**Add. 50505**).

146.259 Documents re James Simpson, Russian Consul at Gibraltar, 1788-1814 (**Add. 50483 ff. 96-114**).

146.260 3 letters, a postcard and a copy of a poem by Empress Alexandra, wife of Nicholas II (**Add. 50850 G**).

146.261 Copies of letters and journal of Lt Thomas Molyneux Graves from the Crimea, 1854 (**Add. 54483**).

146.262 2 letters from Vladimir Ilich Lenin (1870-1924), signed Joseph Richter, and other correspondence re his application for a BM Reading Room ticket, 1902, and issue slips, 1902-3 (**Add. 54579**).

146.263 Draft manifesto by Peter I to the Christian peoples of the Balkans, 8 May 1711, Russian (**Add. 57303**).

146.264 Copy-book of letters by James Brogden from Russia, Berlin, Dresden and Paris, 1787-8 (**Add. 57304**).

146.265 MS copy of a poem by Sergei Konstantinovich Makovskii, n.d. (**Add. 57486 G**).

146.266 Soviet wall newspaper, *c.*1927 (**Add. 57556**).

146.267 3 letters from D. H. Lawrence to S. S. Kotelyanskii, 10 Mar. 1919, 3 Mar ?1924 (**Add. 58372 H**).

146.268 Score of 'Capriccio' for piano and orchestra by Igor Stravinskii, 1929 (**Add. 58431**).

146.269 Signature of Vladimir de Pachmann (1848-1933), Russian pianist, with 2 bars of music, n.d. (**Add. 59652 B**).

146.270 Photograph of Igor Stravinskii and Ernest Roth at Venice, 1957 (**Add. 59652 I**).

146.271 Diary of Capt. Jasper Hall covering service in the Crimea, 30 May 1855 - 27 Jan. 1856 (**Add. 59776**).

146.272 53 letters from Joseph Samuel Prendergast, surgeon to Lord Raglan, to his brothers and sisters from the Crimea, 31 Dec. 1854 - 3 July 1855 (**Add. 59849**).

146.273 Correspondence of Lt-Gen. Sir Harry D. Jones during the Crimean War, 1854-5 (**Add. 59892 I**).

146.274 Letter from Walter James Hore-Ruthven, 8th Baron Ruthven of Gowie, to his mother while serving in the Crimean War, 24 Aug. 1855 (**Add. 60391 P**).

146.275 Map of St Petersburg and the Kronstadt ship canal (**Add. 60511**).

146.276 Documents re the Russian garrison at Kherson, 1786, Russian (**Add. 60753 U**).

146.277 2 share certificates of the Moscow Merchants' Bank, 1873, 1913 (**Add. 62551 A**).

146.278 Record of the baptism of Mariya, daughter of Vasily Iosofor Govard (Howard) of the Moscow Merchants' Guild, 4 Jan. 1754, and of Yuliya Stefanovna, at Vzdyna church in Kaluga guberniya, 8 Dec. 1860 (**Add. 62559 H**).

Burney Manuscripts (Burn.)

Catalogue of Manuscripts in the British Museum, New Series, vol. 1, part 2, *The Burney Manuscripts* (London, 1840). Indexed jointly with the Arundel MSS in vol. 3.

146.279 Extract of the instructions to Daniel Silvester sent to the Emperor of Russia by Queen Elizabeth I, May 1575 (**Burn. 390 f. 41**).

Cotton Manuscripts (Cotton)

A Catalogue of the Manuscripts in the Cottonian Library Deposited in the British Museum (London, 1808-12), 3 vols and index volume. Many of the royal letters have been published in Yu. Tolstoi, *Pervyya sorok let snoshenii mezhdu Rossieyu i Anglieyu* (St Petersburg, 1875).

146.280 The effect of the patent granted by Frederic II (King of Denmark) to the English merchants trading to Muscovy, 24 June 1582 (**Cotton Nero B iii f. 247**).

146.281 An abstract of the privileges granted by the King of Denmark to the English merchants trading in Muscovy, taken out of his letters patent of 22 June 1582 (**Cotton Nero B iii f. 255**).

146.282 A convention between English and Danish commissioners concerning the Muscovy trade, reciting patents of both Frederic II and Elizabeth I, 22 June 1583, Latin (**Cotton Nero B iii f. 258b**).

146.283 The patent of Frederic II concerning the Muscovy trade, recited in the above convention, 22 June 1583, Latin (**Cotton Nero B iii f. 263**).

146.284 A paper entitled 'An elucidation annexed unto the treaty which was agreed on by Mr Herbert' being a declaration of Elizabeth I on the subject of the trade to Muscovy, 12 Oct. 1583, Latin (**Cotton Nero B iii f. 263**).

146.285 Letter from Ivan IV to Elizabeth I, 10 Apr. 1567, German (**Cotton Nero B viii f. 1**).

146.286 Licence by Tsar Theodore to English merchants to trade, Russian (**Cotton Nero B viii f. 2**).

146.287 Letter from Philip and Mary to Ivan IV (Tsar Vasily in the catalogue), Apr. 1557, Latin (**Cotton Nero B viii f. 3**).

146.288 The reply of the governors of the merchant adventurers to the answers of W. and G. Bond and John Foxall and those partners trading to Narve (Narva) (**Cotton Nero B viii f. 11**).

146.289 Grant of privileges by Tsar Theodore to Rowland Howard 'with comrades' for trading in Russia, 1586 (reference to in Burtsev, *op. cit.* p. 3, another entry in BM catalogue) **(Cotton Nero B viii f. 4)**.

146.290 Letter from Ivan IV to Elizabeth I, 1562 **(Cotton Nero B viii f. 16b)**.

146.291 2 notes of speeches held by the Emperor of Russia (Ivan IV) to Daniel Silvester, 29 Nov. 1575, 29 Jan. 1576 **(Cotton Nero B viii f. 18b)**.

146.292 Letter from Tsar Theodore to Elizabeth I, Jan. 1592 **(Cotton Nero B viii f. 21)**.

146.293 Letter from Boris Godunov to Elizabeth I, Jan. 1592 **(Cotton Nero B viii f. 22b)**.

146.294 Letter from Lord Burleigh to Boris Godunov, May 1592 **(Cotton Nero B viii f. 24** copy at **viii f. 11)**.

146.295 The privilege granted by Boris Godunov to the English merchants, Sir John Hart and his company, Dec. 1598 **(Cotton Nero B viii f. 26)**.

146.296 Elizabeth I's instructions to Sir Jerome Bowes, 19 June 1583 **(Cotton Nero B viii f. 29)**.

146.297 Elizabeth I's instructions to Sir Richard Lee, sent to the Emperor of Russia (?Boris Godunov), June 1600 **(Cotton Nero B viii f. 32)**.

146.298 Minute from Elizabeth I to the Emperor of Muscovy (?Boris Godunov), 17 Sept. 1600 **(Cotton Nero B viii f. 33)**.

146.299 A particular declaration of the entertainment and usage of John Merrick at Moscow, 1603 **(Cotton Nero B viii f. 35)**.

146.300 Letter from Ferdinand I to Elizabeth I concerning the Tsar of Muscovy's attempt upon the Teutonic Order in Livonia, 28 July 1560, Latin **(Cotton Nero B ix f. 96)**.

146.301 2 papers in Russian (one being the original of **Nero B viii f. 4**) **(Cotton Nero B xi f. 316)**.

146.302 Letter from Tsar Michael to James I **(Cotton Nero B xi f. 320)**.

146.303 Instructions of the governors of the Russia Company, William Garrard and Rowland Hayward (?Howard) to one of their ambassadors or agents, 18 Apr. 1567 **(Cotton Nero B xi f. 321)**.

146.304 A note of one year's apparel for an apprentice in Russia and Persia **(Cotton Nero B xi f. 329)**.

146.305 Letter from Ivan IV to Elizabeth I, Nov. 1567 **(Cotton Nero B xi f. 332)**.

146.306 Report by Thomas Barnester and Mr Duckett from Vologda to the Council concerning new favours from the Tsar (Ivan IV) to the Company, 25 June 1569 (Burtsev *op. cit.*; catalogue only refers to Persia) **(Cotton Nero B xi f. 333)**.

146.307 Letter from the Russian Ambassador to the Secretary of State, 6 May 1570 (published by Tolstoi) **(Cotton Nero B xi f. 335)**.

146.308 Letter from Tsar Theodore to Elizabeth I, 1589 (**Cotton Nero B xi f. 337**).

146.309 Various requests from the Russian Ambassador re trade (**Cotton Nero B xi f. 339**).

146.310 Letter from Elizabeth I to Ivan IV, 18 May 1570 (**Cotton Nero B xi f. 341**).

146.311 Letter from Ivan IV to Elizabeth I, ?1567 (**Cotton Nero B xi f. 343**, original is at **Nero B viii f. 1**).

146.312 A treaty of alliance between Elizabeth I and Ivan IV, May 1570 (**Cotton Nero B xi f. 345**).

146.313 Letter from Ivan IV to Elizabeth I, 24 Oct. 1570 (**Cotton Nero B xi f. 347**).

146.314 Instructions from Elizabeth to Daniel Silvester, May 1570 (**Cotton Nero B xi f. 3**).

146.315 Note of 2 conversations between Ivan IV and Daniel Silvester in Moscow, 29 Nov. 1576, 29 Jan. 1577 (**Cotton Nero B xi f. 353**).

146.316 Letter from Elizabeth I to the Tsar (Ivan IV), 8 June 1583, Latin (**Cotton Nero B xi f. 355**).

146.317 A note on the improper behaviour of Richard Relph, one of the Company's apprentices in Russia and letter from Relph to English merchants in Kazan', Aug. 1584 (**Cotton Nero B xi f. 359b**).

146.318 A discourse on the employment of Sir Jerome Horsey, sent by Elizabeth I to the Emperor of Russia (Theodore), 1585, 1589 (**Cotton Nero B xi f. 363**).

146.319 Letter from Elizabeth I to Tsar Theodore, 9 June 1585, Latin (**Cotton Nero B xi f. 375**).

146.320 Letter from Boris Godunov to Elizabeth I, 1599, English transl. (**Cotton Nero B xi f. 379**).

146.321 A discussion on the trade in the Baltic and Russia (**Cotton Nero B xi f. 382**).

146.322 Letter from Elizabeth I to the Emperor of Russia (Ivan IV), 16 Sept. 1568, Latin (published by Tolstoi) (**Cotton Nero B xi f. 385**).

146.323 Letter from the Emperor of Russia (?Boris Godunov) to Elizabeth I, Apr. 1603 *[sic]*, English transl. (**Cotton Nero B xi f. 392**).

146.324 Rough draft of instructions from Elizabeth I to Daniel Silvester (**Cotton Nero B xi f. 393**).

146.325 Account by Dr Timothy Willis of his journey in Russia (**Cotton Nero B xi f. 400**).

146.326 Letter from the Emperor Ferdinand to Elizabeth I concerning an attack by the Duke of Muscovy on Livonia, 17 Aug. 1559, Latin (**Cotton Galba B xi f. 234**).

146.327 Letter from Adamus Tracigerus, Chancellor of Holstein, to Lord Burleigh re the invasion of Livonia by the Muscovites, 17 Oct. 1560, Latin (**Cotton Galba B xi f. 258**).

146.328 Copies of charters, patents etc. to the corporations of merchants of Spain, Portugal and Russia, n.d. 16th century **(Cotton Otho E iii)**.

146.329 Account by John Dee of journey to Cathay by the North Sea **(Cotton Otho E viii f. 77)**.

146.330 Letter to Henry VIII about the victory of the King of Poland over the Muscovites etc., 16 Jan. 1515, Latin **(Cotton Vitell. B ii f. 117)**.

146.331 Letter from the first false Dmitrii to James I, 28 Dec. 1605 **(Cotton Vesp. F iii f. 113)**.

146.332 The form of a letter which the priests in Russia put into the coffins of the dead, Latin transl. from Russian **(Cotton Vesp. F v f. 189b)**.

Egerton Manuscripts (Eg.)

Catalogued with the *Catalogues of Additions to the Manuscripts*, listed in full in Nickson, *The British Library* p. 9., and since 1956 **(Eg. 3725 ff.)** in TS *Rough Registers*. Further details and names of correspondents may be found in the index to each volume of the catalogue.

146.333 ELPHINSTONE, John (Eg. 3009)
Papers of John Elphinstone, Rear-Adm. in Russian service, include a warrant signed by Catherine II for payment to Elphinstone, 11 Sept. 1769, and 2 letters from Count Aleksei Orlov, 8, 10 Aug. 1770, Russian with English transl. **(ff. 22-8b)**.

146.334 FORSYTH, William (Eg. 3715-17)
Material collected by Forsyth for *History of the Captivity of Napoleon* includes a portrait of Alexander I **(Eg. 3715 f. 75)** and engravings of Moscow, 1814 **(Eg. 3716 f. 84; 3717 f. 42)**.

146.335 GUNNING PAPERS (Eg. 2696-2706)
Papers of Robert Gunning, Envoy Extraordinary at St Petersburg, 1772-6, include: correspondence with the Secretaries of State, 1772-7 **(Eg. 2701-3)**; letter-books containing copies of letters from Gunning while at St Petersburg to Henry Howard, Earl of Suffolk, Secretary of State, 1772-6 **(Eg. 2705-6)**. *See index for details.*

146.336 JOMINI-ONU PAPERS (Eg. 3166-3243)
Papers of Gen. Baron Antoine Henri Jomini (Genrikh Venyaminovich Zhomini) (d. 1869), in Russian service from 1813, Baron Alexandre Michel Jomini (Aleksandr Genrikhovich Zhomini) (b. 1817), served in the Russian Foreign Office from 1835, Michael Onu, served at the Russian Embassy in Constantinople, and the Smirnov family. Papers include correspondence with Russian representatives abroad, dispatches, material re the Crimean War and the Russo-Turkish War of 1877-8, political tracts, records of conferences, patents of Russian orders and decorations. *See catalogue and index for details.*

146.337 LEEDS PAPERS (Eg. 3324-3508)
Papers of Robert Darcy (1718-78), 4th Earl of Holdernesse, diplomat and Secretary of State, include: correspondence with English representatives in Russia, 1749-61 **(Eg. 3417, 3463)**; letters to George II from Catherine, later Empress Catherine II, and copies or drafts of his replies, mostly French **(Eg. 3425)**. Papers of Francis Godolphin Osborne (1751-99), Marquis of Carmarthen, include: correspondence with Alleyne Fitzherbert, Baron St

Helens, Envoy to Russia, 1784-6 (**Eg. 3500 ff. 1-17b**); copy of regulations for the Russian Navy, 1788, Russian with English transl. (**Eg. 3503**). *See index for correspondents.*

146.338 PANIZZI PAPERS (**Eg. 3677**)
Letters mostly addressed to Sir Anthony Panizzi, Principal Librarian at the British Museum, include a letter from Petr Aleksandrovich Saburov, 1863, French (**Eg. 3677 f. 178**).

146.339 TITLEY PAPERS (**Eg. 2680-95**)
Correspondence of Walter Titley, Chargé d'Affaires, afterwards Resident and Envoy Extraordinary at Copenhagen, with the Secretaries of State etc. include a treaty with Russia, 1736 (**Eg. 2683 f, 145**) and a declaration by Empress Anne, 1740 (**Eg. 2687 f. 260**). *See index for details.*

146.340 2 letters from Peter I to Brigadier Balk, n.d. and 26 Dec. 1711 (**Eg. 24**).

146.341 Extract from a letter re the discoveries by the Russian on the north-west coast of America, 23 Sept. 1764, French (**Eg. 1717 f. 117**).

146.342 Protocol re the movements of the Imperial Russian troops, 1748, French (**Eg. 1756 f. 160**).

146.343 Transl. of 'Beschreibung aller Nationen des russischen Reiches ... ', 1780-3, by Johann Gottlieb Georgi (**Eg. 1922**).

146.344 Notes from 'Vue générale de l'Empire de Russie' by Pierre Simon Pallas, late 18th century (**Eg. 2233 f. 104**).

146.345 Instructions to Daniel Silvester on a mission to Russia, 1575 (**Eg. 2790 f. 178**).

146.346 Map of the Black Sea, with the seas of Azov and Marmara and the Caspian (**Eg. 2803 f. 2**).

146.347 Correspondence of Sir John Gaspard Le Marchant, colonial administrator, re the raising of a force in North America to fight in the Crimea (**Eg. 2972**).

146.348 'Petite suite' etc. for piano by Aleksandr Porfirevich Borodin and notes and drafts in Russian (**Eg. 3087**).

146.349 Letter from Petr Ilich Tchaikovsky (Chaikovskii) to Frau Marie von Bülow, 24 Jan. 1888, French (**Eg. 3246 ff. 1-2b**).

Harleian Manuscripts (Harl.)

A Catalogue of the Harleian Manuscripts (1-7639) in the British Museum, 3 vols (London, 1808-12). Manuscript descriptions of Harl. 7640-60 are added to vol. 3 in the Reading Room.

146.350 Instructions from Elizabeth I to Daniel Silvester, May 1575 (**Harl. 36 f. 231**).

146.351 Answer delivered to Silvester to be made by him in the name of Elizabeth I to the Emperor of Russia (Ivan IV) and secret instructions sent by Anthony Jenkinson, May 1575 (**Harl. 36 f. 234**).

146.352 'Concerning the Burning of Moscow by the Crimme-Tartar etc.' by John Stow (**Harl. 247 f. 208**).

146.353 First draft of 'Notes of the benefyte that may growe to England, by Traffyke to Russia, throughe a firme Amitie betwene bothe the Prynces', 8 May 1575 (**Harl. 296 f. 189**).

146.354 Copy of letter from Ivan IV for craftsmen to be sent from England to Russia, Sept. 7070 (**Harl. 296 f. 194**).

146.355 Order observed in a funeral, sent by the Ambassador of Muscovy to England, *temp.* Elizabeth I (**Harl. 296 f. 195**).

146.356 Account given by Sebastian Livius of Vil'na of his brother Paulus Livius who was taken with his family as prisoner into Muscovy (**Harl. 424 f. 117**).

146.357 Notes made by Michael Lok concerning the possible benefit to England from the activities of English merchants in Muscovy, 8 May 1579 (**Harl. 541 f. 165**).

146.358 Circular letter of Ephraim Pagett to the Archbishop of Moscow, 1638 (**Harl. 825 f. 29**).

146.359 Treaties of England with Poland and Russia (**Harl. 1217 f. 143**).

146.360 Papers re transactions with Tripoli, Tunis, Turkey, Muscovy etc. (**Harl. 1217 f. 163**).

146.361 Account of the lineage of William Smith, servant to the Russian Emperor (**Harl. 1471 f. 98**).

146.362 Extract of a letter from Moscow concerning John Hebdon, 20 Feb. 1677, French (**Harl. 1516 p. 51**).

146.363 A project for a separate act for including the Grand Duke of Muscovy in the treaty between Sweden and the Empire, 9 July 1679, Latin (**Harl. 1517 f. 159**).

146.364 'A Relation or Memoriall, abstracted out of Sir Jerom Horsey his Travells ...' which includes his travels in Russia, 16th century (**Harl. 1813**).

146.365 Pass from Tsar Michael for Sir Arthur Aston, 1614 (**Harl. 2149 f. 139**).

146.366 16th century vol. including 'On the Kingdome of Muscovie' (**Harl. 2334 f. 30**).

146.367 'Relatione dell' Eccmo Sigr D. Filippo Pernisten Imperial Ambasciare della Maesta Cesarea al Gran Prencipe di Moscovia l'anno 1579' (**Harl. 3553 f. 501**).

146.368 'Traictez des Empereurs des Turcs avec les Papes, les Empereurs d'Allemagne, les Rois de France et de Pologne, et les Venetiens, Tunis, et Alger, Perse, Grand Mogul, Moscovia', 1494-1618 (**Harl. 4571**).

146.369 Account of printing in Russia, Turkey, East and West Indies, 17th century (**Harl. 5910 vol. 4 no. 38**).

146.370 Account of the great bell in the city of Moscow (**Harl. 6030 f. 1**).

146.371 Folio book entitled 'France, Britain, Denmark, Sweden, Poland, Moscovy, Germany, styled "The Roman Empire"' (**Harl. 6249**).

146.372 Text for the New Trade Statute with Russia of 1667 (**Harl. 6356**).

146.373 Miscellaneous Russian papers (**Harl. 7013 ff. 100-10**).

146.374 Letter from Peter I to Queen Anne, 30 Nov. 1705, and Latin copy (**Harl. 7016 f. 55-6, 59**).

King's Manuscripts (King's)

Catalogue of Western Manuscripts in the Old Royal and King's Collections vol. 3 (London, 1921).

146.375 Convention between Russia and Great Britain and the States General of Holland for the supply of 30,000 Russian troops, 19 Nov. 1747, French and Dutch (**King's 75 ff. 35, 43**).

146.376 'An Account of Russia, 1767' by George Macartney (**King's 189-90**) including 'The Present state of the Church in Russia, 1767' by Revd John Glen King (**190 f. 42**) and other papers re Russia.

146.377 Coloured drawings of Russian costumes etc., 18th century (**King's 191**).

146.378 'Extrait d'une lettre concernant les operations de la campagne de l'an 1739' referring to the Russian victory over the Turks at Jassy, 1739 (**King's 233**).

146.379 Journals of Gen. James Francis Keith while commanding the Russian troops in Finland against Sweden, 1741-3.

Lansdowne Manuscripts (Lansd.)

A Catalogue of the Lansdowne Manuscripts in the British Museum (London, 1819).

146.380 An account of the offence given to Mr T. Randolph, the Queen's Ambassador in Russia, 1568 (**Lans. 10 n. 34**).

146.381 'William Borrough's voyage for discovery of the coast and coast beyond Pechora, and to find an open passage to Cathaya' (China), 1568 (published in the *English Voyages* of Hakluyt) (**Lansd. 10 no. 35**).

146.382 Copy of letter from Mr Randolph in Moscow to the Emperor of Russia (Ivan IV), 12 Apr. 1568 (**Lansd. 10 no. 36**).

146.383 Privileges granted to the Merchant Adventurers by the Emperor of Russia (Ivan IV), 10 July 1569 (**Lansd. 11 no. 16**).

146.384 Mr Randolph's account and the balance due to him on his return from his embassy in Russia, 1569 (**Lansd. 11 no. 34**).

146.385 Copies of 2 letters from Mr Randolph to the Emperor of Russia (Ivan IV) and the Emperor's Council, 7 May 1569 (**Lansd. 11 no. 35**).

146.386 Letter from the Earl of Leicester (Lord Robert Dudley) to Mr Randolph, Ambassador in Russia, 1 May 1569 (**Lansd. 11 no. 36**).

146.387 Letter from the Russia Company to Mr Randolph, 26 Apr. 1569 (**Lansd. 11 no. 37**).

146.388 Letter from Eliseus Bomelius, physician, to Sir William Cecil, desiring either to continue as the Queen's physician or to be released to serve the Prince of Russia, 1570, Latin (**Lansd. 12 no. 73**).

146.389 Letter from William Smithe to James Wodcote with postscript in Russian, 15 May 1572 (**Lansd. 15 no. 76**).

146.390 Supplication from the Russia Company to the Council against infringers of their privileges, 17 Jan. 1573 (**Lansd. 16 no. 20**).

146.391 Representation to the Lord Treasurer (Sir William Cecil) from the Russia Company re trade with Russia, 1573 (**Lansd. 16 no. 58**).

146.392 Copy of letter from Richard Relph, member of the Russia Company, to some of his colleagues at Casan (Kazan'), 12 Aug. 1584 (**Lansd. 42 no. 23**).

146.393 Copy of an Act of Court of the Russia Company, 8 Apr. 1586 (**Lansd. 48 no. 40**).

146.394 Letter from Christopher Borough to the governors of the Russia Company re Russian trade, Nov. 1587 (**Lansd. 52 no. 37**).

146.395 Copies of 2 letters re trade sent by the Russia Company merchants to the Master of the Horse and to the Private Secretary of the Great Duke of Russia (Theodore), Dec. 1587 (**Lansd. 53 no. 19**).

146.396 Letter from John Uden and Philip Düring, German travellers, to Sir William Cecil requesting recommendatory letters to the King of Persia (or to the Grand Duke of Muscovy?), 1591, Latin (**Lansd. 67 no. 109**).

146.397 Letter from Robert Dow to Sir William Cecil re the Queen's letter to Russia, 23 Nov. 1597 (**Lansd. 85 no. 38**).

146.398 Account of wares exported from England and imported from Russia etc., n.d. (**Lansd. 110 no. 51**).

146.399 Enquiries to be made by Anthony Marshe on behalf of the merchants trading with Russia, ?1588 (**Lansd. 112 no. 31**).

146.400 Instructions for Mr Gardner on behalf of the merchants trading with Russia (**Lansd. 112 no. 32**).

146.401 Account of Elizabeth I's letters to the Emperor of Russia (?Ivan IV) on behalf of the Russia Company (**Lansd. 112 no. 33**).

146.402 Letter to Boris Fedorovich, Master of the Horse (**Lansd. 112 no. 34**).

146.403 The number of miles and stages between St Nicholas and Moscow by water and land (**Lansd. 112 no. 35**).

146.404 The Emperor of Russia's allowance for every flesh day, n.d. (**Lansd. 112 no. 36**).

146.405 Supplication to the Emperor of Russia by Mr Bennet, n.d. (**Lansd. 112 no. 37**).

146.406 Draft of the Council's instruction for Mr Cherry, a London merchant, to sail to Russia and obviate the reports spread there against Queen Elizabeth (**Lansd. 112 no. 38**).

146.407 Representation to Sir William Cecil by some merchants trading with Russia concerning Dr Fletcher's 'History of Russia' (**Lansd. 112 no. 39**).

146.408 Representation to Sir William Cecil from merchants trading with Russia showing the damage they have suffered through Mr Hieron (Jerome) Horsey (**Lansd. 112 no. 40**).

146.409 Petition of the Russia Company to the Emperor against Glover, Rutter etc. (**Lansd. 112 no. 41**).

146.410 2 representations from the Russia merchants to the Lord Treasurer (Sir William Cecil) re Mr Horsey (**Lansd. 112 no. 42**).

146.411 Observations of the Russia merchants on a letter sent by the Emperor of Russia (?Ivan IV) to Elizabeth I (**Lansd. 112 no. 43**).

146.412 Account of the voyages of Ochther, a Norman, in the time of King Alfred, referring to the passage by sea to Muscovy, transl. (published in Hakluyt's *Voyages,* vol. 1, p. 4) (**Lansd. 119 no. 1**).

146.413 Privileges granted by Ivan IV to the English merchants (**Lansd. 141 no. 54**).

146.414 Privileges from Russia granted when Mr Randolph was Ambassador (**Lansd. 141 no. 57**).

146.415 'The Humble Peticion and Remonstrance of the Fellowshippe of English Merchants for discovery of newe Trades, concerning their priviledges, the supportinge of the Trade to Russia, and the Whale fishing at Greeneland and in the Northerne Seas', 22 Jan. 1617 (**Lansd. 142 no. 69**).

146.416 A representation from the Tsar of Muscovy (Peter I) to the Queen of England (Anne), 1703, Latin (**Lansd. 849 no. 78**).

Royal Manuscripts (Royal)

Catalogue of Western Manuscripts in the Old Royal and King's Collections, vols 1-2 (London, 1921).

146.417 Versions of the beginning of a letter from Ivan IV to Elizabeth I, 1567 (**Royal 13 B i f. 10**).

146.418 Copies of letters from Elizabeth I to Ivan IV, 1561-8, Latin and English (**Royal 13 B i ff. 47, 119b, 160b-241** *passim*).

146.419 Copy of letter from the Muscovy Company to Anne, Countess of East Friesland, 1564, Latin (**Royal 13 B i f. 83b**).

146.420 Copy of letter from John Marshe, governor of the Muscovy Company, to Anne, Countess of East Friesland, 1564, Latin (**Royal 13 B i f. 103b**).

146.421 Letter from Sir William Cecil to Albert Knopper, Councillor to the King of Denmark, on behalf of merchants sailing to Russia, 21 Apr. 1565 (**Royal 13 B i f. 127**).

146.422 Copies of letters from Elizabeth I to Frederic II, King of Denmark, on behalf of the Muscovy Company, 1567-8, Latin (**Royal 13 B i f. 176**).

146.423 Copy of letter from Elizabeth I to Eric XIV, King of Sweden, on behalf of the Muscovy Company, 1567, Latin (**Royal 13 B i f. 176b**).

146.424 Copies of letters from the Muscovy Company to the Senate etc. of Hamburg, 1567, Latin (**Royal 13 B i ff. 178-178b**).

146.425 Account of the criticisms of the Muscovy Company by English subjects in Russia, 1567, Latin (**Royal 13 B i f. 189b**).

146.426 Copy of commission to T. Randolph as Ambassador to Russia, 1568, Latin (**Royal 13 B i f. 227**).

146.427 Letter from Elizabeth I to the magistrates of Narva asking them to dispatch her letter to the Tsar, 16 Sept. 1568 (**Royal 13 B i f. 249**).

146.428 Account of Muscovy, anon., n.d. ?*c.* 1555, Italian (**Royal 14 A xiii f. 97**).

146.429 Account of Muscovy, anon., n.d. ?*c.* 1555, Italian (**Royal 14 A xv ff. 1-40, 88-90b**).

146.430 Maps including the Black Sea and the Sea of Azov (**Royal 14 C v**).

146.431 Table of distances from the river Thames to St Nicholas and Moscow in Russia, 16th century, and map of the north-west coasts of Russia by W. Borough, *c.* 1573 (**Royal 18 D iii ff. 123-4**).

Sloane Manuscripts (Sloane)

S. Ayscough, *A Catalogue of the Manuscripts Preserved in the British Museum* (London, 1782) lists the manuscripts by subject; there is a second copy in the Search Room arranged in numerical order. Sloane manuscripts are indexed in E. J. L. Scott, *Index to the Sloane Manuscripts in the British Museum*(London, 1904).

146.432 KAEMPFER, E. (**Sloane 2907-8, 2910, 2912, 2914-17, 2919-21, 2923-4, 2929, 2937, 3060-4**)
Collection includes: remarks on the Russian mode of making the sign of the cross, 17th century, French and Russian (**Sloane 2910 ff. 2-3**); 'De invasione Tartarorum Usbekensium & Khalmukorum, in Persiam, annis 1667, 1668, 1669' (**2910 no. 3**); 'Excerpta ex itenere Jenkinsonii ad Astrakan, 1558' (**no. 4**); 'Variae de rebus Moscoviticis' (**no. 7**); diary by Kaempfer of a journey from Stockholm to Moscow, 17th century, German (**Sloane 2923 ff. 116-53b**); map of Muscovy (**Sloane 2926**); copy of a letter from Peter I and Ivan Alekseevich to their sister Sophia, *c.* 1682, Russian (**Sloane 3063 ff. 12-15b**). *See index for further material.*

146.433 Account by Nicholas Warkottsch of his embassy to Muscovy, 1593, Latin (**Sloane 232**).

146.434 Draft of a letter from Charles I to Tsar Michael re the purchase of wheat (Phipps *op. cit.* p. 410 notes that this is incorrectly listed in the catalogue as a letter from Charles II to Alexis), n.d. (**Sloane 856 f. 13b**).

146.435 'Relatione de Moscovia et Tartaria' by M. Contarini, n.d. (**Sloane 1826 ff. 82-8**).

146.436 Narrative of the war between Poland and the Cossacks, 17th century (**Sloane 1846 ff. 233-8b**).

146.437 Accounts of the travels of ambassadors into Muscovy, Tartary and Persia, n.d. (**Sloane 2350**).

146.438 Reflections upon Poland, Turkey and Tartary, n.d. (**Sloane 2440**).

146.439 Instructions from Elizabeth I to Daniel Silvester on being sent to the Emperor of Russia (**Sloane 2442 p. 201**).

146.440 Account of the boat given to Peter I, 18th century (**Sloane 3168 ff. 147-52b**).

146.441 Navigational textbook, ?1703, Russian (**Sloane 3227**).

146.442 Account of the introduction of the Embassy of the Grand Duke of Muscovy (Ivan IV) to the Emperor Maximilian, 1576, Latin (**Sloane 3299 f. 37**).

146.443 'Versus in classem Danico-Moscoviticam', 1716, by M. R. Dublar (**Sloane 3421 f. 29**).

146.444 A description of a Russian entertainment, n.d. (**Sloane 4164 no. 14**).

Stowe Manuscripts (Stowe)

Catalogue of the Stowe Manuscripts in the British Museum, 2 vols (London 1895-6).

146.445 CRAGGS PAPERS (Stowe 246-7)
Collection of letters from John Dalrymple, 2nd Earl of Stair, to James Craggs, Secretary at War, 1711-20, includes references to the affairs of Russia.

146.446 HANOVER PAPERS (Stowe 222-32)
Correspondence and papers of J. Robethon, Private Secretary to William III, George William Duke of Zelle and to George I, include: letter from Charles Whitworth, Ambassador to Russia, Moscow 9/20 Feb. 1709/10 (**Stowe 223 f. 302**); account of an audience of Whitworth with Peter I at Moscow, 9/10 Feb. 1709/10 (**Stowe 223 f. 304**); copies of letters from Baron P. P. Shafirov, Russian Ambassador to Turkey, to Prince B. I. Kurakin, 1 Dec. 1713 (**Stowe 226 f. 49**); letters from Johann Christoph, Baron de Schleinitz, Russian Envoy at the Hague, 2 Oct. - 16 Nov. 1714 (**Stowe 227 ff. 466, 468, 484, 508**); letter from Robert Areshkine (Erskine), Chief Physician to Peter I, to Adm. Sir John Norris, May 1717, French transl. (**Stowe 230 f. 122**); copies and abstracts of intercepted Jacobite correspondence from St Petersburg (**Stowe 232**); 'Memoire donné par Hooker à Schaffiroff', St Petersburg, 15/26 June 1718 (**Stowe 232 f. 110**). *See catalogue for further details.*

146.447 PHELPS PAPERS (Stowe 256-61)
Papers of Maj. Richard Phelps, Under Secretary of State for the Northern Department, 1744/5-68, include: letters to John Hobart, 2nd Earl of Buckinghamshire, Ambassador to

Russia (**Stowe 257 ff. 100, 121, 125, 141-7, 176, 198, 214**); letters from Sir George Macartney, Ambassador to Russia, 15/26 Mar. 1765, and from Baron A. L. Gross, Russian Minister, 14 Feb. 1765 (**f. 164**); letters to Macartney, 1765 (**ff. 126, 132, 170, 179, 183, 206, 211**).

146.448 STANHOPE, Alexander (**Stowe 243-5**)
Envoy to the States General, 1700-4. Papers include a letter in the hand of James Dayrolle, Resident at the Hague, referring to the designs of Peter I (**Stowe 243**).

146.449 WALSINGHAM, Sir Francis (**Stowe 162**)
Secretary of State. Papers include 'Repertoire of matters concerning Moscovia' (**f. 110**).

146.450 Passport from the Empress Elizabeth of Russia for John Owen, carrying dispatches to Prince I. A. Shcherbatov, Russian Minister in England, Moscow, 26 Aug. 1744, Russian with German transl. (**Stowe 142 f. 110**).

146.451 Jacobite references to Peter I under the pseudonyms of Smith and Dean, alias Dane, 1722 (**Stowe 250 ff. 14b, 31b, 48**).

146.452 Copies of official correspondence and papers chiefly re the commercial relations of Great Britain and Russia, 1732-65 include: correspondence re the negotiations for a treaty of commerce, 1732-4 (**f. 1**); copy of the treaty, 2 Dec. 1734 (**f. 42**); 'A state of the grievances and hardships the English Trade lies under in Russia', n.d. (**f. 52**); letters and papers re commercial relations and the proposed new treaty between the countries, c. 1765 (**ff. 81-143**) (**Stowe 252**). *See catalogue for details.*

146.453 Copies of historical letters re the Court of Russia, 1740-66, include: correspondence of Sir Charles Hanbury Williams, Ambassador to Russia, 23 June - 18 Nov. 1755 (**f. 3**); letter from John Hobart, 2nd Earl of Buckinghamshire, Ambassador to Russia, which recounts the overthrow and death of Peter III, 16 Apr. 1766 (**f. 26**); letter from the same containing an account of the death of Ivan VI, 26 July 1764 (**f. 37**); 2 letters from the Hon. Edward Finch-Hatton, Ambassador to Russia, giving an account of events in Russia on the death of Empress Anne in 1740 and on the accession of Empress Elizabeth (**ff. 41, 53**); letter by Robert Murray Keith with an account of the overthrow of Peter III, 12 July 1762 (**f. 58**) (**Stowe 253**). *See catalogue for further details.*

146.454 Transcripts of letters addressed to Sir Charles Hanbury Williams, Ambassador in St Petersburg, 1755-7 (**Stowe 263**).

146.455 Abstract of the travels of Adam Olearius in Muscovy, Tartary and Persia, 1634-7, French (**Stowe 988 f. 58**).

Loans

Manuscripts deposited on loan by their owners. Handlist of loans available in the Search Room.

146.456 BATHURST PAPERS (**Loan 57**)
Papers of Henry Bathurst, 3rd Earl Bathurst, (1762-1834) include 2 letters from the Earl of Aberdeen about the outcome of the Russo-Turkish War, 4 Sept., 15 Oct. 1829.

146.457 MUSIC MSS (Loan 75)
Include: score of Piano Concerto no. 3, opus 30, and copy of 'O Salutaris Hostia' by Sergei Rakhmaninov (/34-5); scores of many works by Igor Stravinskii, including 'Les Noces', 'Pulcinella', 'Chant des Bateliers du Volga' and 'Renard' (/36-56).

146.458 ROYAL PHILHARMONIC SOCIETY MSS (Loan 48)
Letters from musicians and composers including Mstislav Rostropovich and Dmitrii Shostakovich (/13/38).

146.459 STEFAN ZWEIG COLLECTION (Loan 77)
Collection of music includes 'Darling Savishna' and 'Aus meinen Thränen' by M. P. Musorgskii (/33).

Facsimiles (Facs.)
Catalogue of Additions to the Manuscripts lists Facs. 1-483 and Supplements I-VII. TS lists of Facs. 1-848 and Supplements I-XII are available in the Search Room.

146.460 'Mala Kinzka' by T. C. Shevchenko, Kiev 1963 (Facs. 623).

146.461 3 letters to the Lieven family and a biographical account of Visc. Castlereagh by Princess Dorothea Lieven (Facs. 650).

146.462 Score of P. I. Tchaikovsky's 6th symphony (Facs. 795).

146.463 Song, 'Akh, kogda by ya prezhde znala' by M. I. Glinka, 1855 (Facs. Suppl. x/22).

146.464 Document concerning the elevation of the 2 sons of the brothers Likhudy to the dignity of 'Stolniki', late 17th or early 18th century, Russian (Facs. Suppl. x/28).

146.465 Sketch of the song 'The Sun has Set' by P. I. Tchaikovsky (Facs. Suppl. x/46).

146.466 Letter from Count L. N. Tolstoi to Isaac W. Heysinger, 14 Apr. 1903 (Facs. Suppl. xii/14).

Microfilms (M)

Register of Microfilms and Other Photocopies in the Department of Manuscripts (London, 1976) covers microfilms acquired up to the end of 1975. TS registers of microfilms acquired since this date are available in the Search Room.

146.467 COVENTRY MSS (M/863 (1-65))
Papers of the Marquess of Bath at Longleat House include letter of Sir John Finch from the Levant, Poland and Russia, 1628-79 (reel 57).

146.468 HATFIELD HOUSE PAPERS (M/485)
Papers of the Marquess of Salisbury (127 vols) will include references to Russia.

146.469 PALLAS, Peter Simon (M/701)
German naturalist and traveller. Account of 3 voyages between Russia and America, 1762-72; letters and memoranda, 1766-81.

146.470 Imperial decree re the Likhudy brothers, 1692, Russian (M/635). *See 146.464.*

146.471-497 Map Library

Catalogue of the Manuscript Maps, Charts, and Plans, and of the Topographical Drawings in the British Museum, 3 vols (London, 1844-59, reprinted 1962). Maps of the Russian Empire can be found in vol. 3.

King's Library Collection (K.top.)

Catalogue of Maps, Prints, Drawings etc. forming the Geographical and Topographical Collection attached to the Library of His late Majesty King George the Third.

146.471 Drawn 'Mappa generalis Imperii Russici', 1745 (**K.top. 112.11**).

146.472 'Plan du canal de Ladoga' (**K.top. 112.32**).

146.473 'Grundriss der in Lieffland gelegenen Stadt und Vestung Revel, an der Oost See' by J. C. von Grünberg (**K.top. 112.57**).

146.474 'Plan of Riga and the river Düna, with the forts on Curland-Side, as it was in 1656, at the siedg by the Muscowits' by A. Beakman, 1700 (**K.top. 112.58**).

146.475 'Plan der Stadt Riga nebst der Cobrum Schantze' (**K.top. 112.59**).

146.476 'Grundiss der Dunamünder Schantz' (**K.top. 112.61**).

146.477 'Grundiss der Vestung Narva in Lieffland, nebst dem Schlosse Ivanogrod' by J. C. von Grünberg (**K.top. 112.62**).

146.478 Plan of part of the 'Golfe de Finlande. partie de l'Ingrie et Carélie, avec St Petersbourg, et Cronstadt' (**K.top. 112.67**).

146.479 Plan of the city of St Petersburg (**K.top. 112.73**).

146.480 'Plan de St Petersburg' (**K.top. 112.75**).

146.481 Bird's-eye view of the 'Palais de l'Ordre des Chevaliers Rouges de St Alexandre de sa Majesté Russienne, proche du Convent du Monastère Nevienne à St Peterbourg' (**K.top. 112.77.q**).

146.482 'Vue d'une addition faite par l'Impératrice à sa Maison de Campagne à Zarsko Zelo' (**K.top. 112.80c**).

146.483 'View in the English garden at Tzartzo Zelo, one of the palaces of the Empress Catherine' (**K.top. 112.80d**).

146.484 'View in the pleasure garden at Tzartzo Zelo' (**K.top. 112.80e**).

146.485 View of Varshelski (?), near Moscow (**K.top. 112.89**).

146.486 3 views near Kiev (**K.top. 112.92a-c**).

146.487 View of the church at Cirgoscher (?), between Kiev and Moscow (**K.top. 112.93**).

146.488 Plan of 'the town of Oxacow [Ochakov], and a Turkish Arsenal' (**K.top. 112.113**).

146.489 'Plan von Kinburn mit dem project' showing the place as surrendered to Russia in June 1736 (**K.top. 112.114**).

146.490 'Plan von Azoff ... ' by C. von Stoffeln, and copy of the same (**K.top. 112.115-16**).

146.491 'Carta derer Kalantzien, wie selbiege von denen Türken den 20ten. Martz crobert in 1736' of the forts on the Don near Azov (**K.top. 112.117**).

146.492 'Plan von Lutich von der Ottomanischen Pforte crobert den 23ten Martz in an. 1736' (**K.top. 112.118**).

146.493 Map of Siberia by Capt. Behring (**K.top. 114.43**).

King's Maritime Collection (K.Mar.)

Catalogues of the King George III Maritime Collection.

146.494 Chart of the harbour of St Petersburg and part of Lake Ladoga, with the adjoining country, n.d. (**K.Mar. ii 51.1**).

146.495 Hydrographical delineation of Lake Ladoga with its surroundings, *c.* 1730 (**K.Mar. ii 51.2**).

146.496 Plan of the situation and fortifications on the island of Retusari and the harbour for the Russian Navy, *c.* 1730 (**K.Mar. ii 51.3**).

146.497 'Plan de St Petersbourg et des ses environs', *c.* 1730, with an essay on 'the Present State of the Maritime Power of Russia' (**K.Mar. ii 51.4**).

147.1-40
BRITISH LIBRARY OF POLITICAL AND ECONOMIC SCIENCE

London School of Economics and Political Science, 10 Portugal Street, London WC2A 2AD

147.1-39 Manuscript Department

TS list of holdings; catalogues and handlists for some collections. J. Perceval, edit., *A Guide to Archives and Manuscripts in the University of London* vol. 1 (1984) pp. 1-35. Collections which are in the process of being catalogued may not be open to researchers.

147.1 BARRY, Sir Gerald (1898-1968) (BARRY)
Editor of the *News Chronicle*, 1936-47. Editorial correspondence from Andrew Rothstein re conditions in the USSR etc. *c.* 1940 (**/9**); paper by Barry to the Royal Institute of International Affairs on policy towards the USSR, *c.* 1940/41 (**/21**); articles, not by Barry, on the USSR, 1944-7 (**/65**).

147.2 BEAVER, Sir Hugh (1890-1967) (BEAVER)
Industrialist. Papers re trade mission to Moscow leading to 5-year trade agreement, 1959 (**B. 57**).

147.3 BERNAL, John Desmond (1901-71) **(BERNAL)**
Scientist; awarded the Lenin Peace Prize in 1953. Notes by Bernal re the organization of the International Economic Conference in Moscow, 1951 **(3)**.

147.4 BEVERIDGE, Sir William, Baron Beveridge (1879-1963) **(BEVERIDGE)**
Liberal MP; Director of the LSE. Reports and papers re the Crimea Conference, 1945 **(VII/51)**. There could be references to the USSR in papers re 'World Government and Peace Aims' **(VII/51-4)**.

147.5 WILLIAM BRANDT AND SONS CO. LTD **(BRANDT)**
Merchant bank. Papers include: Incoming Bill Payable E: Russian and Timber, 1924-51; Russian Accounts Current (13 vols), 1823-5, 1876-94, 1909-10, 1926; Russian Account Current A: St Petersburg (14 vols), 1891-1917; Russian Accounts Current B: Moscow (13 vols), 1890-1921. Summary list. Apply to Archivist.

147.6 BRITISH LABOUR DELEGATION TO RUSSIA (1920) **(COLL MISC 660)**
Collection of leaflets etc. re the British Labour Delegation to Russia, 1920, Polish and Russian.

147.7 BROADHURST, Henry (1840-1911) **(SR 151)**
Labour Leader and Liberal MP. Letter from W. E. Gladstone enclosing draft of a resolution, and amendments of the same, to be passed at a Russophile mass meeting at the Agricultural Hall, 18 Feb. 1878 **(vol. 1 ff. 45-8)**.

147.8 BUSSY, Jane Simone **(COLL MISC 527)**
Draft letter from Bussy to the Comité de Vigilance des Intellectuels Antifascistes protesting at the Moscow trials, n.d., and reply, 30 Jan. 1937.

147.9 CITRINE, Sir Walter, Baron Citrine of Wembley (1887-1983) **(CITRINE)**
Trade unionist. Papers include: diary of visit to the USSR, 1925 **(I.1/4)**; notes re mercantilism and Russia, 2 Dec. 1928 **(I.1/6)**; notes on Russia, 1927-8 **(I.2/3)**; correspondence with A. Duff Cooper re propaganda in favour of Anglo-Soviet co-operation, July 1941 **(I.4/7)**; papers, 'Russians in England' including memo on interview with V. M. Molotov, 23 Oct. 1941 and report on visit of Russian trade union delegation, 1941-2 **(I.4/9)**; papers on Anglo-Soviet Trade Union Committee, 1942 **(I.4/10)**; letters from Citrine and George Hicks in Moscow to Fred Bromley, Oct. 1925 **(I.4/20)**; notes on conversation with Churchill re Munich and Russia, 6 Apr. 1943 **(I.7/6)**; journal of tour in Russia, 1935 **(II.1/2-4)**.

147.10 COURTNEY, Leonard Henry, Baron Courtney of Penwith (1832-1918) **(SR 1003)**
Liberal MP. TS extract from address to the Tsar by Courtney *et al.*, 1899 **(B/6 f. 65)**.

147.11 DALTON, Hugh, Baron Dalton of Forest and Frith (1887-1962) **(DALTON)**
Labour MP and Minister. Papers include: diaries in the USSR, 1932 **(Diaies 53-4)**; notes of meetings with and conversations by and papers re I. Maiskii, 1939, 1943 **(3/2; 5/2; 8/1)**; and report of conversation between Eduard Beneš and P. Noel Baker re Russian policy, 1939 **(3/2)**; letter from Dalton to Ruth Dalton from Moscow, 1932 **(5/1)**; corrections by Dalton to his speech in Parliament re communism and the USSR, 18 May 1931 **(6/1)**;

copies of correspondence re clothing for Russia, June 1944 (**7/6**); note by Dalton on Eden's talks with Stalin, Dec. 1941 (**7/9**); letter from Dalton to H. N. Brailsford on post-war policy towards the USSR and Poland, 13 Mar. 1944, and correspondence with the Admiralty re purchase of Russian tanks for Egypt, 1940 (**8/1**); speeches by Dalton re the USSR, 1941 (**18/3**).

147.12 DELL, Robert (1865-1940) (DELL)

Foreign correspondent. 3 letters from Dell to Clifford Sharp including references to conditions in Russia, 1915-16 (**2/4**); letter from M. Litvinov, 21 Jan. 1935 (**2/7**); articles re USSR, 1939-40, n.d. (**5/4-6**).

147.13 GARDINER, Alfred George (1865-1946) (GARDINER)

Editor of the *Daily News*, 1902-19. Photocopies of 3 letters from Prince Petr Kropotkin, 28 Feb. - 6 June 1917 (**1/18**).

147.14 GIFFEN, Sir Robert (1837-1910) (SR 1016)

Civil servant at the Board of Trade. Letters to Giffin from Spenser Wilkinson and John Sterling re the Russo-Japanese War, 23 Mar. 1904, 18 Mar. 1905 (**vol. II/74,80**).

147.15 HARRISON, Frederic (1831-1923) (HARRISON)

Positivist. Letter from Prince Petr Kropotkin, 11 Feb. 1904 (**1/45 p. 42**).

147.16 HYNDMAN LETTERS (COLL MISC 429A)

2 letters from Henry Mayers Hyndman (1842-1921), socialist pioneer and propagandist, to Douglas Sladen with references to the Russian Revolution, 8 Nov. 1917, 9 Mar. 1919.

147.17 KNOWLES, Lilian (d. 1926) (COLL A)

Professor of Economic History at the LSE. Original corrected TS of 'Economic development in the nineteenth century : France, Germany, Russia and the United States' (**vols XI-XII**).

147.18 KROPOTKIN LETTERS (COLL MISC 530)

Letters from Prince Petr Kropotkin to Mrs Turin, P. S. Mel'gunov, Mr Colins and F. Volkovskii. Photocopies, pending cataloguing.

147.19 LANSBURY, George (1859-1940) (LANSBURY)

Leader of the Labour Party, 1931-5. Index cites correspondence with: the Anglo-Russian Democratic Alliance (**7.329**); D. V. Bogomolov (**9.242, 267**); Kliskko (of Odessa) (**8.171**); L. B. Krassin (**8.255, 262-4**); Princess Kropotkin (**3.256-7**); M. Litvinov (**12.88**); I. M. Maiskii (**13.143, 263; 15.273**); P. Petrov (**14.252-3**).

147.20 LEAGUE OF NATIONS UNION (LN4)

Moscow Conference Four Power Declaration (**VI.1**). There could also be material in the minute-books of committees.

147.21 LLOYD, Edward Mayow Hastings (1889-1968) (LLOYD)

Civil servant and author. Reports by Andrew Cairns on conditions in Russia, 1932 (**4/32-5**); memo on Russian agriculture by the Empire Marketing Board, June 1932 (**4/36**); letter from Lloyd to B. Webb re Russia, 20 Oct. 1920, and copy of agreement between the South East Russian co-operatives and the Co-operative Wholesale Society (**7/16**); letter from G. Lowes Dickinson to Lloyd and note by Lloyd re the proposed Anglo-Russian naval agreement of 1914 (**7/43**); TS articles on Russia, *c.*1932 (**9/4**); pamphlets on the Russian Revolution (**12/4**); correspondence of Margaret Lloyd re her visit to Russia and with friends in Russia, 1957-65 (**12/21**).

147.22 MEL'GUNOV, P. S. (MEL'GUNOV)
Russian émigré historian. Papers (225 boxes) re modern Russian history; letters; diary for 1914-18; printed material; émigré periodicals; papers on Russian students in France; letters from Kropotkin. Summary list.

147.23 MEYER, Ernst (1887-1930) (COLL MISC 494)
Chairman of the Polbüro of the German Communist Party. Photocopies of his reports, statements, resolutions and correspondence, including with G. Zinov'ev.

147.24 MILL-TAYLOR COLLECTION (MILL-TAYLOR)
Papers of John Stuart Mill (1806-83), philosopher. Letter by Mill on Russian women, 18 Dec. 1868 (**vol. XLV p. 85**); letters to *The Times* on the Russian note of 1870 and the Anglo-Russian treaty of 1856 (**pp. 114-17**).

147.25 MITRANY, David (1888-1975)
Functionalist and author. There may be material re Russia amongst his correspondence. Collection closed until catalogued.

147.26 NATIONAL PEACE COUNCIL (NPC)
Commission on East-West Relations, 1948-50 (**11/10**); reports on visits including to the USSR, 1950-69 (**11/13**); visit of the Soviet Peace Committee, 1972 (**11/64**).

147.27 NATSIONAL'NO-TRUDOVOI SOYUZ, 1935-61 (COLL MISC 675)
7 vols of pamphlets, mainly in Russian.

147.28 PARKER, Alwyn (COLL MISC M. 614)
Librarian of the Foreign Office. Material prepared for a biography of Cardinal Alberoni include MSS extracts from 'Papers of Prince B. I. Kuryakin' (published in St Petersburg, 1890) and correspondence between Peter I and Kuryakin, 1718 (**2/7**).

147.29 PASSFIELD PAPERS (PASSFIELD)
Papers of Beatrice, née Potter, Webb (1858-1943) and Sidney Webb (1859-1947), social reformers. Correspondence with I. M. Maiskii, Moscow Daily News, Moscow Radio Centre, National Council for British-Soviet Unity, Russia Today Society, N. Sokolnikova, L. Uspenskii, Society for Cultural Relations with the USSR (**II.4.j-c**); addressbook of persons in the USSR, ?1934 (**III.1.f**); financial papers re the USSR, 1933-43 (**III.4; III.5.U1 ff. 27-88**); photographs of the USSR, 1934 (**III.8.35-42**); drafts and reports of interviews and address by the Webbs re the USSR, 1931-3, 1938 (**VI.86-8, 90-1**); articles on the USSR by the Webbs (**VII.I.59-63b, 65-7, 69-73, 75, 77, 80-3, 85, 91, 93, 95-6, 99**); notes on visit to the USSR, 1932 (**VII.I.55-8**); memos of statements by I. M. Maiskii, Apr. 1933 (**VII.I.74**); TS Soviet notebooks by S. Webb, Barbara Drake and John Cripps, Sept.-Oct. 1934 (**VII.I.78-9**); TSS by S. Webb re the Soviet constitution, co-operative societies and agrarian problems (**VII.I.84, 87; XIV.12**); TS memo by B. Webb re Moscow trials, Feb. 1937 (**VII.I.87**); copy of notes by Dudley Amen, 1st Baron Marley, on visit to the USSR, 1936 (**XIV.11**); copy of letter from L. E. Hubbard to 'Mr Hoare' re Soviet agricultural problems, 16 May 1937 (**XIV.13**). *See catalogues for details.*

147.30 PIERCY, William Baron (1886-1966) (PIERCY)
Economist and business man. Papers as Managing Director of Pharoah Game & Co., importers of plywood from the USSR, Finland, Norway and Germany, 1925-33, include: notes on Julius Potempa Ltd, Riga 1930 (**4/26**); Russian and Finnish plywood prices, 1927-31 (**4/28**); negotiations with Finnish mills re Russian competition, 1931 (**4/31**); letter-book re Russian business, 1925-7 (**4/34**); papers re Russian timber business, 1926-32 (**4/35-6**); photographs of enterprises in Memel and Riga, 1929, n.d. (**4/40, 43**); essay, 'The

political and economic structure of Soviet Russia', *c.*1940 **(12/60)**. There could also be material in the firm's reports, accounting records and correspondence. Summary list only. Apply to Achivist.

147.31 POLITICAL AND ECONOMIC PLANNING (PEP)
Research organization. Broadsheets and reports include 'Economic Reform in the Soviet Union' **(P 53)**.

147.32 PRITT, Denis Noel (1887-1972) (PRITT)
Labour MP. Typed notes on activities as MP, mainly pro-Soviet, including discussions with Johnny (?Maiskii), 1941-2 **(1/3)**; diary notes including pro-Soviet activities, 1941-5 **(1/4)**; correspondence re anti-Russian army propaganda, 1944-5 **(1/7)**; note on Jean Valrin, alias Richard Krebs, an alleged Soviet agent, 1946 **(1/11)**; diaries of visits to the USSR, Sept. 1946, Sept. 1954, July 1961 **(1/13, 15-17)**; correspondence re publication/transl. of *Light on Moscow* and other books, 1943-8 **(3/6)**; introduction to paper on the 29th Congress of the Communist Party of the USSR and the invasion of Hungary, 1956 **(3/8)**; letter to 'Raji' on the Soviet position on China, 14 Sept. 1965 **(3/26)**.

147.33 SHAW, George Bernard (1856-1950) (SHAW BUSINESS PAPERS)
Business papers of Shaw including correspondence re the USSR **(15)**. Partly listed. Permission to publish Shaw material must be sought from the Society of Authors.

147.34 TARIFF COMMISSION PAPERS (TARIFF COMMISSION)
Papers re the new German commercial treaties with Russia etc. **(8 2/2 B13)**; questions re Russian tea duties, 1908 **(8 2/4 B237)**; lists of commercial arrangements and treaties with Latvia **(8 5/13)**; papers of W. A. S. Hewins re international trade and politics with references to the USSR, 1930-1 **(8 6/3)**; lecture on Russia, Feb. 1918 **(8 6/19)**; 6 vols of *Russia*, a journal of Anglo-Russian trade, 1916-18 **(10 3)**. There could also be material in the reports of various industries and committee meetings.

147.35 VOLKOVSKY LETTER (COLL MISC 493)
Letter from Feliks Volkovskii to Mrs Rossetti re the circulation in Germany of the periodical *Frei-Russland*, 5 May 1892.

147.36 WALLAS, Graham (1858-1932) (WALLAS)
Professor of Political Science at the LSE. Copies of 2 letters from N. Tchaikovsky to his daughter, 26 Aug. 5 Sept. 1906 **(1/28)**; letters appealing for help for friends in Russia, 1915 **(1/53)**; letter from P. W. Ward from the American Consulate in Warsaw re agrarian revolution in the USSR, 4 Mar. 1921 **(Box 7)**. There could also be material amongst his correspondence. Summary list only.

147.37 WEBSTER, Sir Charles Kingsley (1886-1961) (WEBSTER)
Professor of International History at the LSE. Memo on Russia etc., 1917-18 **(I.3/5-6)**; review of the Soviet press, 1940, 1945 **(I.10/2, 11/4)**; papers re USSR and the Dumbarton Oaks conference, 1944 **(I.11/9, 11; I.12/2, 5)**; memo re republics of the USSR **(I.13/2)**; papers re GB-USSR Society, 1959-61 **(I.19/43)**; correspondence re proposed conference on 'USSR: Second World War', 1960-1 **(I.19/45)**; papers re Webster's visit to the USSR, 1956 **(I.20/4)**; correspondence re the Anglo-Soviet conference of historians, Moscow 1960 **(I.20/5)**; diary of world tour including the USSR, 1929 **(II.8)**.

147.38 WELBY, Reginald Earle, Baron Welby (1832-1915) (SR 1017)
Treasury official. TS letter by George Peel re Russian monetary policy, 11 Aug. 1896 **(vol. VI/55)**.

147.39 WOMEN'S INTERNATIONAL LEAGUE FOR PEACE AND FREEDOM, BRITISH SECTION (WILPF)
Correspondence of Catherine E. Marshall re the Russian famine, 1921 (**4/4**); letter from W. G. Rinder to Marshall re famine relief in Russia, 27 Sept. 1922 (**4/6**); 'Note on conditions in the Baltic states' by the Institute of International Affairs, 27 Jan. 1948, and WILPF report on the Baltic States, *c.* 1948 (**4/20**); correspondence of Mary Nuttall including references to the relations of western powers with the USSR, *c.* 1932-54 (**Add. 3**).

Microfilms

147.40 Microfilms of manuscripts are treated as a special form of publication and are recorded in the general catalogue in the main Library. The following may contain references to Russia and the Soviet Union: Allied Commission for Austria; Auswärtiges Amt (German documents on the Balkans, 1867-1920); Reports by Prime Ministers to the Crown, 1837-1916; British Broadcasting Corporation; Labour Party; Office of Strategic Studies; Earl Browder papers (General Secretary of the US Communist Party).

148.1

BRITISH MUSEUM CENTRAL ARCHIVES

The British Museum, Great Russell Street, London WC1B 3DG

By appointment. Records over 30 years old are, with a very few exceptions, open to the public. Some indexing under names of individuals and some class handlists.

148.1 The Archives are the administrative records (up to 1926) of the former British Museum Reading Room and include minutes of Trustees' Meetings, registers of donations, copies of letters sent from the Director's Office, and records of the former British Museum Reading Room, now the Reading Room of the British Library. There may be references to gifts from Russian visitors and admissions of Russian visitors and émigrés to the Reading Room.

149.1-14
BRITISH MUSEUM (NATURAL HISTORY)
Cromwell Road, London SW7 5BD

By appointment to all departments. *Catalogue of the Books, Manuscripts, Maps and Drawings in the British Museum (Natural History)*, 5 vols and 3 supplementary vols (London, 1903-40); F.C. Sawyer, *A Short History of the Libraries and List of Manuscripts and Original Drawings in the British Museum (Natural History)* (London, 1971). Card indexes and indexes to correspondents. The British Museum (Natural History) houses a number of libraries and the location of the documents listed below is indicated as follows: **B**= Department of Botany, **E**= Department of Entomology, **L**= General Library, **P/M**= Department of Palaeontology and Mineralogy, **Z**= Department of Zoology. In addition, some items are held in the Sub-Department of Ornithology, Akeman Street, Tring, Herts. References to Russian scientists will also be found in the card indexes to letters, arranged by name of correspondent.

149.1 BANNERMAN, David Armitage
Collection of letters from E. Kozlova (23), N. Gladkov (7) and A.I. Ivanov (1), 1934, 1936, 1956-60 **(Tring)**.

149.2 BARBER, Horace George
Preliminary notes to 'Singilevo', marine fossil material from 'Singilei' Ul'yanovsk, 1961-?2 **(B Diatom Section)**.

149.3 CARRUTHERS, Alexander Douglas Mitchell
Notebooks re birds and mammals collected in Mongolia and Central Asia, 1910-11 **(Tring and Z 89 om)**.

149.4 CHANDOIR, Baron
List of specimens from the Crimea, n.d. **(M (477.7) MS)**.

149.5 DARWIN MUSEUM, MOSCOW
A collection of photographs in the Darwin Museum, Moscow, 1958 **(L MSS MUS)**.

149.6 ELLIS, William W.
Botanical drawing of Kamchatka locality from Cook's 3rd voyage **(B)**.

149.7 LOUIS, David Alexander
Diaries of expedition to Sakhalin Island, 1909 **(M (47) MS)**.

149.8 McLACHLAN, Robert
Notebook containing descriptions of *Odonata taxa*; 11 letters addressed to McLachlan, from Moscow, n.d. **(E)**.

149.9 MEIKLEJOHN, R. F.
Six field notebooks concerned with egg collecting in Algeria, Crete, Greece, USSR and Switzerland, 1919-39 **(Z 89 qm)**.

149.10 MUSSIN POUSHKIN (MUSIN-PUSHKIN), Count Apollon de
MS list of his collection of minerals from Russia **(M)**.

149.11 POPHAM, Hugh Francis Arthur Leyborne (1864-1943)
Diaries recording his travels and bird notes in Russia, Lapland etc. 7 vols, 1892-1914; notebook on birds collected in Siberia, 1895-1900 (**Tring**).

149.12 SILAN'TEV, A.
TS transl. of survey of hunting in Russia, n.d. (**Z 66 qs**).

149.13 TWELVETREES, William Harper (1848-1919)
101 mounted original drawings, mostly in pencil, of fossil plants, shells and bones from the Russian Permian cupriferous marls north of the town of Orenburg, 1877 (**P**).

149.14 WOODWARD, Arthur Smith (1864-1944)
3 letters to Woodward during his visit to Russia re exchange of fossils with the Reval Museum, Moscow University Zoological Museum and Dorpat University Museum, June 1892 (**P MSS**).

150.1-7

BRUCE CASTLE MUSEUM

Lordship Lane, London N17 8NU

150.1 Album of greetings from the women of Moscow to the women of Tottenham.

150.2 Prize certificate and lithograph by Alexander Rypinski, Belorussian poet and nationalist, while he was art master at Eagle House School in Tottenham in the 1850s.

150.3-7 Middlesex Regimental Museum

By appointment.

150.3 Approx. 100 letters by A. M. Earle from the Crimea, 1853-56.

150.4 5 letters by J. C. Ingham from the Crimea, 1854-5.

150.5 17 letters by William (later Gen.) and Raymond Inglis from the Crimea, n.d.

150.6 TS 'The Die Hards in Russia - an Unusual Campaign', being a précis of J. Wood, *With the Die-Hards in Siberia* (London, 1920).

150.7 Album from the 77th Tenginskii Infantry Regt presented to the 77th Middlesex, the Duke of Cambridge's, Regt containing mainly First World War photographs.

151.1-3
CABLE AND WIRELESS PLC ARCHIVES

Public Relations Department, Cable and Wireless plc, Mercury House, Theobalds Road, London WC1X 8RX

By appointment. Apply in the first instance to the Company Archivist. Handlist of holdings.

151.1 BLACK SEA TELEGRAPH COMPANY LIMITED
Corporate records, 1873-1926, comprise board minutes, shareholders' minutes, agreements, papers, correspondence and annual reports. Material relating to Russia includes Turkish and Russian concessions, 1874 (**1741/17**), photographs and plans of Odessa, log-books and charts of cable laying in the Black Sea.

151.2 THE GREAT NORTHERN TELEGRAPH COMPANY LIMITED
There could be references to Russia amongst the records of the Company which dealt mainly with cable laying to China, 1870-1927.

151.3 INDO-EUROPEAN TELEGRAPH COMPANY LIMITED
The Company was formed in 1868 to provide communications between England and India via Germany, southern Russia and Persia. There may be references to Russia in the board and shareholders' meetings, 1868-1932, and in other technical records and papers.

152.1-2
CHURCH MISSIONARY SOCIETY ARCHIVES

157 Waterloo Road, London SE1 8UU

By appointment. Indexes to archives.

152.1 BRITISH ISLES CORRESPONDENCE (G/AC 3)
Anonymous letter suggesting that a clergyman should be sent to Riga for the English community, 25 Jan. 1814; letter from Revd John Owen re communication from Russia by Revd John Pinkerton, 8 Feb. 1817; letter from Revd Thomas Sims re the possibility of missionary work in Russia, 16 May 1818.

152.2 NORTH INDIA MISSION ARCHIVES (C I 1/0)
Account of the Russian church by Revd James Long, *c.* 1873 (**185/107**).

153.1-2
CITY OF WESTMINSTER LIBRARIES

153.1 Central Music Library

160 Buckingham Palace Road, London SW1W 9UD

153.1 Letter from S. V. Rakhmaninov to Edwin Evans, 27 June 1922.

153.2 Archives Department, Marylebone Library

Marylebone Road, London NW1 5PS

153.2 HINDLEY COLLECTION
Furniture makers. Letter from Miles & Edwards (taken over by Hindley *c.* 1845) to Madame de Klupffell re bill for furniture delivered to the Empress of Russia, 2 Sept. 1841 **(494/25)**.

154.1

COMMUNIST PARTY LIBRARY, PICTURE LIBRARY & ARCHIVE

16 St John Street, London EC1M 4AL

Limited facilities for research; apply to the Librarian in the first instance. Much of the material in the Archive is as yet unsorted and unclassified.

154.1 7 boxes of visual material, mainly photographs but also newspaper cuttings and leaflets, relating to the USSR, Lenin and Stalin; box of early Soviet postcards; album of photographs and illustrations from the Civil War period including photographs of the Allied intervention; photograph albums presented to the Communist Party from Soviet workers and soldiers and on the occasion of Soviet anniversaries. There is also a large pamphlet collection relating to the USSR.

COMPANIES REGISTRATION OFFICE

London Search Room, Companies House, 65-71 City Road, London EC9

Microfiche copies of original documents on all live companies and of most companies dissolved since 1976. *See main entry for Companies Registration Office, Cardiff,* **51.1.**

155.1-6
CORPORATION OF LONDON RECORDS OFFICE
P.O. Box 270, Guildhall, London EC2P 2EJ

Apply in writing to the Archivist. Some records are subject to a closure period. P.E. Jones, *Guide to the Records in the Corporation of London Records Office and the Guildhall Library Muniment Room* (London, 1951), *Analytical Index to the Remembrancia 1579-1664* (London, 1878). There are subject indexes in nine MS volumes (to 1857) to the Repertories of the Court of Aldermen; thereafter the printed Court of Aldermen minutes are indexed. Card indexes to personal names, places and subjects. Further references might be found to Russia in the following classes of records for which detailed indexes are not available: Alien Entries, 1796-1800, Alien Imports, 1805-10, Aliens' Naturalisation, 1685-99, Package and Scavage.

155.1 ENTERTAINMENTS
Account of the visit of the Emperor of Russia (Alexander I) and King of Prussia, 4 June 1814 (**33B**); address on the presentation of a sword to FM Barclay de Tolly, 1814 (**RES.46**); address, programme, menu, committee papers etc. re the visit of the Emperor of Russia (Alexander II) to the Guildhall, 18 May 1874 (**specimen cards**); presentation of an address on board the Russian Imperial yacht at Cowes, 5 Aug. 1909 (**specimen cards**); invitation cards, programme, admission cards in connection with the visit of the Moscow City Soviet, 21 Oct. 1955 (**specimen cards**); letters, papers, press cuttings, menu, invitation and admission cards in connection with the luncheon at Mansion House for Marshal Bulganin and Khrushchev, 20 Apr. 1956 (**specimen cards**); admission cards, menu etc. for the reception and luncheon at the Guildhall for A. N. Kosygin, 8 Feb. 1967 (**specimen cards**).

155.2 HISTORICAL PAPERS
Letter from Sir George Grey, Home Secretary, to the Mayor notifying him of the peace treaty with Russia, 31 Mar. 1856 (**vol. I. 51, 113 A**).

155.3 HOUNSDITCH MURDERS PAPERS
3 boxes of papers relating to the investigation of the murders including material re Russian émigré suspects, 1910-18, 1933, 1945, including exchange of letters with French and Russian authorities and papers relating to Osip Federov, Peter Piaktow (Pyatkov, Peter the Painter), Nina Vasil'eva and others.

155.4 MANSION HOUSE PAPERS
Papers re the visit of A. N. Kosygin, 8 Feb. 1967 (**Box 58**).

155.5 REMEMBRANCIA
Volumes containing copies of letters exchanged between the City and the Privy Council *et al.* including: letter from the Lord Mayor to Thomas Radcliffe, 3rd Earl of Sussex, commenting that Botolph's Wharf had been granted to the Society of Merchants of Russia, 11 Feb. 1579 (**I.84**); letter from Thomas Howard, Earl of Suffolk, to the Lord Mayor informing him of the arrival at Gravesend of an ambassador from the Emperor of Muscovy, 21 Oct. 1613 (**III.112**); petition of Richard Cockes (?Cox) to the King stating that he had been driven from the City for free trading into Russia, *c.* 1623 (**VI.26**); letter from the Lords of the Council to the Lord Mayor, intimating that an ambassador from the Empire of Russia was expected, and that the King had commanded them to give order for his reception with fitting honour, 18 Nov. 1628 (**VI.188**); letter from Edward Montagu, 2nd Earl of Manchester, to the Lord Mayor and Aldermen re York House having been appointed for the residence of the Russian Ambassador, *c.* 1662-3 (**IX.55**).

155.6 REPERTORIES
Nine MS volumes individually indexed including: a lease of Somers' Key to be made to the governors of the Merchants of Muscovy (**Rep.17. f. 272, 1569-71**); motion for a lease of Botolph Wharf to the Merchants of Muscovy (**Rep.19 f. 232v, 1574-8**); committal for a misdemeanour concerning the Russian Ambassador's retinue (**Rep.69 f. 46, 1662-4**). *See indexes for further details.*

156.1-6

DR WILLIAMS'S LIBRARY

14 Gordon Square, London WC1H 0AG

K. Twinn, *Guide to the Manuscripts* (London, 1969). Handlists of collections and deposits. TS list of the archives of New College, London and the Coward Trust. Card index of persons.

156.1 LETTERS TO HENRY ALLON (MS 24.110)
Letters from Prince Petr Kropotkin to H. N. Dixon, 24 Dec. 1891, 2, 14 Jan. 1892 (**(347-9)**).

156.2 HEYWOOD, Robert (MSS 28. 157-64)
Manufacturer from Bolton. Journal of visit to Russia, 17 June - 23 July 1858 (**MS 28.161**); journal by his wife, Elizabeth, of the journey to Russia, June - July 1858 (**MS 28.162**).

156.3 NEW COLLEGE ARCHIVES
Divinity school, primarily for the training of men and women for the Congregational ministry. Letter from J. Lyon to Thomas Wilson re his entry to the medical college at St Petersburg and the patronage of Revd Richard Knill, 25 Oct. 1827 (**332/3**); letter from Knill to Wilson from St Petersburg re Mr Rutt, printer to the Russian Bible Society, 1827/8 (**335/27**), and re J. Lyon, *c.* 1829 (**341/28**).

156.4 THE SAY PAPERS (MSS 12.107 - 108)
Notes made by Samuel Say from Evert Ysbrants-Ides, *Three Years Travels from Moscow Overland to China*, 1706 (**MS 12.107 (252)**).

156.5 TOOKE, William (MS 24.47)
Traveller in Russia in late eighteenth century. Notebook containing English/Russian vocabulary; papers containing translations of Russian phrases and sentences, English prose translations of Russian poems and geographical references to the Russian Empire.

156.6 THE WODROW-KENRICK CORRESPONDENCE (MS 24.157)
Letters from Samuel Kenrick to James Wodrow re reading William Coxe's account of Poland and Russia, 21 Mar. 1785 (**(93)**), re Polish revolution, 10, 16 June 1791 (**(163-4)**), re Alexander I, 24 Sept., 10 Nov. 1802 (**(234, 236)**).

157.1-7

ENGLISH PROVINCE OF THE SOCIETY OF JESUS

Department of Historiography and Archives, 114 Mount Street, London W1Y 6AH

By appointment. There may be further references to Russia in the bound correspondence which is not yet indexed.

157.1 'Jesuits in Russia during the Suppression' by Charles Plowden, 1785, being a transcript of the Stonyhurst MS AIV. 6., 'Account of the preservation and actual state of the Society of Jesus in the Russian dominions 1783 and 1784'.

157.2 Envelope containing notes and transcripts re the Suppression period including references to Russia (**BB/7**).

157.3 Letter from the Russian Ambassador to the Apostolic Nuncio in Warsaw giving views of the Russian Court on the Suppression of the Jesuits, English transl. from Latin, 2 Aug. 1782 (**Foreign Correspondence 1776-1859**).

157.4 References to Russia and the Suppression will be found in the following original letters bound in volumes: William Strickland's letters, 1786-1811; Marmaduke Stone's letters; Nicholas Sewall's letters; George Connell's letters; Charles Plowden's letters.

157.5 'Catalogi Soc. Jesu in Imperio Rossiaco. 1803-5-8-9; 1811-17-19' referring to the Jesuit Generals Thaddaeus Brzozowski and Gabriel Grüber.

157.6 Correspondence between the Irish Mission and Jesuit General Thaddaeus Brzozowski (**SO/5**).

157.7 Exercise book containing prayers and hymns transl. from the 'Rites and ceremonies of the Greek Church in Russia' by Revd John Glen King, chaplain to the British factory in St Petersburg (published in 1722) and some 19th century holy picture cards (**48/11/7/2**).

158.1-3

FAWCETT LIBRARY

City of London Polytechnic, Calcutta House Precinct, Old Castle Street, London E1 7NT

158.1 ARCHIVE OF THE SCOTTISH WOMEN'S HOSPITALS FOR FOREIGN SERVICE
Archive comprises administrative records, letters from women working abroad and charity appeals. There may be material relating to nurses in Russia during the First World War.

158.2 Letter from Zinaida Mirovich to Edith Palliser, 1906.

158.3 TS 'The Price of Liberty' by Jessie Kenney based on a diary kept during a visit to Russia with Sylvia Pankhurst, June-Sept. 1917.

159.1
FRANCIS SKARYNA BELORUSSIAN LIBRARY

37 Holden Road, London N12 8HS

By appointment.

159.1 The Library has an extensive collection of books, periodicals and manuscript material relating to Belorussian culture, language, literature and history, including manuscripts, photocopies of manuscripts, and early printed books relating to Belorussia before incorporation into the Russian Empire in the late eighteenth century. Manuscript collections covering the period in which Belorussia was part of the Russian Empire include: records of the Pinsk Ecclesiastical Board (Arkhiv Pinskago Dukhovnago Pravleniya), 1793-1890, Russian (183 items; listed); a folder of manuscript verse and prose by Belorussian writers of the early twentieth century, including Yanka Kupala, Yakub Kolas and Eliza Ozheshko; unpublished TS by Vasil' Zakharka, 'Halounyya momanty Belaruskana rukhu' (The most significant moments of the Belorussian movement), written Prague, 1926. The Library also holds material relating to the following: the Belorussian Republic, 1918-19, Belorussian refugees, the German occupation of Belorussia in World War II, the Belorussian Democratic Republic in Exile. There is extensive material relating to Belorussian communities in Great Britain, France, USA, Canada, Australia and elsewhere.

160.1-7
GEOLOGICAL SOCIETY OF LONDON

Burlington House, Piccadilly, London W1V 0LQ

The Library is normally open only to Fellows of the Society. Other researchers should apply in writing to the Honorary Archivist. A handlist with name and subject indexes is under preparation.

160.1 Geological map and section of the country east of Lake Baikal by C. E. Austin, 1862 (**LDGSL 232**).

160.2 4 sketches of scenery and rocks around Sebastopol by C. F. Cockburn, 1857 (**LDGSL 188**).

160.3 Extracts from letters by Sir Alexander Crichton on a mammoth in ice and on meteorites, 1807.

160.4 Photograph album of Sir Archibald Geikie's visit to Russia and Europe, Sept.-Oct. 1897.

160.5 MS notes and geological colouring by G. B. Greenough on published maps of Russia, 1812 and 1837.

160.6 12 vols of field notebooks of R. I. Murchison recording his visits to Russia in 1840, 1841, 1844 and 1845; 7 vols of autobiographical journals of Murchison, written *c.* 1865, covering his visits to Russia; drawings and proofs of diagrams published in *Geology of Russia* by Murchison; MSS 'Facts respecting the Trubetskois', 'Tours in the Russian

Provinces' and 'Siberia and California' by Murchison (the last 2 being published in *Quarterly Review,* 1841 and 1850).

160.7 Drawing of strata on the lower rapids of the Msta above Borovichi (Pskov gub.) by W. T. H. F. Strangways, 1821 (**LDGSL 90**); geological map and sections of Russia by Strangways.

161.1-8

GREATER LONDON RECORD OFFICE

40 Northampton Road, Clerkenwell, London EC1 0AB

161.1 ANGERSTEIN PAPERS (Acc. 74.80)

Accounts from Thomson Bonar & Co. at St Petersburg, 1823; draft bond of John Angerstein re annuity to Gen. and Mrs Sabloukoff (?Sablukov), 1823 (**I Box 1 pt 1**); correspondence and trust re the Pokrofsky (Pokrovskii) estate, 1820-53 (**VII Box 2 pt 3**); papers re the annuity of the Sabloukoffs, 1848-9 (**IX Box 2 pt 5**). Interim box list only.

161.2 RECORDS OF THE DAUBENAY FAMILY (Acc. 1096)

Newspaper cuttings re the battle of Inkerman, 1854 (**/8-10**).

161.3 JERSEY ARCHIVES (Acc. 510, 1128)

Papers of the Earl of Jersey and his family include: letter from George Child-Villiers, later 5th Earl of Jersey, to his mother (Frances, Lady Jersey) re the preparations for the visit of the Grand Duke of Russia's (Alexander II) visit, 30 Apr. 1839 (**Acc. 510/317**); letters to Sarah Sophia, Lady Jersey, re *inter alia* Russian affairs, 1826-7, n.d. (**Acc. 510/421, 564, 664, 679; Acc. 1128/274/a-i, 284**); verses by A. Pushkin in his own handwriting, *c.* 1830 (**Acc. 1128/187/29**); press cuttings re Crimean War (**Acc. 1128/240**); letters re assistance of the Russian army in crushing the Hungarian rising, 1849 (**Acc. 1128/344-5, 349**). *See handlist for details.*

161.4 LEGGE FAMILY PAPERS (F/LEG)

Travel diaries, military notes, papers and letters covering the service of Lt-Col. Edward H. Legge in the Crimea, 1855-6 (**/896, 914, 921-7, 936-9**); TS copy of a diary of a lieutenant, RN, during the Crimean War, 1854-7 (**/954-57**); copy of a letter of thanks from Elizabeth Wilcox to the Tsar (Alexander I) for freeing her son John Duncan, taken prisoner on board ship, 2 Apr. 1804 (**/999**).

161.5 PEACHEY PAPERS (F/PEY)

Papers relating to Robert Hynam, watchmaker in St Petersburg, including correspondence with his brother William, 1778, 1792-3, 1800-1, 1813-14 (**/141, 143, 150-1, 160, 162, 164**); letters from Robert Hynam to Messrs Lamb and Webb, 4 Aug. 1778 (**/142**); copy letters from Robert to S. More and Prince Loupoukin (I. V. Lopukhin), 1797, 1799, 1800 (**/145-7**); letters from Baron de Nicoley and Gen. N. Murav'ev to Robert, 1800, 1805 (**/149, 154**); petition and copy letter from Robert to Alexander I, 1801 (**/152-3**); letters from Benjamin Hynam to William from St Petersburg, 1812-13 (**/156, 158-9, 161**); translated Russian proclamation, 1812 (**/157**); poem dedicated to Alexander I, 15 June 1814 (**/163**); letters from William Hynam from St Petersburg, 1817-18 (**/168-9, 172-4**). Letter from H. G. Peachey to Mrs A. Peachey from Kronstadt, 28 June 1900 (**/237 A,B**); letter from C. Lyons to Edward Budgen commending his services in the Crimean War, 11 Aug. 1855 (**/465 A,B**). *See handlist for details.*

161.6 ST THOMAS' HOSPITAL (H.I./ST)
The Nightingale Collection (**H.I./ST/NC**) includes: correspondence of Florence Nightingale, 1855-97, n.d. (**NC.1-2, 4-5/1-3**); letters and papers re nurses sent to the Crimea, 1854-5 (**NC.3 SU1-SU57; NC.8/1-3, 5, 14**); report by Florence Nightingale on the nursing staff situation, 18 Nov. 1855 (**NC.8/4**); accounts, receipts, expenses etc. in the Crimea, 1854-5 (**NC.8/6-11**); form of service for the end of the War, 1856 (**NC.8/12**); letter from Elizabeth Copley re her father who fought in the Crimea and who was nursed by Florence Nightingale, 10 May 1954 (**NC.8/13**); letters and lists of subscribers to the Nightingale Fund from the Turkish contingent, 1856 (**A/NFC.29/6**). *See handlist for details.*

161.7 SHORDICHE PAPERS (Acc. 762)
Notes, letters and newspaper cuttings re Adm. Sir Robert Crown, died in St Petersburg, 21 Apr. 1841 (**/10-16**). Papers of Brig.-Gen. Paul Rycaut Churchward include lecture on Afghanistan and the North-West frontier and the possibility of the invasion of India by Russia, n.d. (**2nd dep. /11**).

161.8 WOOD FAMILY OF LITTLETON PAPERS (Acc. 1302; TRI/LET/WOOD)
Letter from P. S. Wood to Col. Thomas Wood commenting on the enthusiasm for the Crimean War, 28 Apr. 1854 (**Acc. 1302/114**); drawing of Col. David Wood's hut in the Crimea, 1854 (**/115-16**); prize certificate for Thomas Wood's boat at Vyborg, 1890 (**/128**); letters from Thomas Wood from the Crimea, 1854 (**/213-41**). Transcripts of the letters of Col. (later Gen. Sir) David Wood from the Crimea, 26 Oct. 1854 - Apr. 1856 (**TRI/LET/WOOD**).

162.1-23

GUILDHALL LIBRARY

Aldermanbury, London EC2P 2EJ

Card indexes of persons, places and subjects. The information below indicates only the material which is specifically listed as relating to Russia in the card catalogue. There may be further references to Russia and the Soviet Union in the records of other London firms and banks, and in the London Diocese papers.

162.1 ASSOCIATION OF BRITISH CHAMBERS OF COMMERCE (MSS 14,476-88; 17,363-595; 18,303)
Anglo-Russian trade committee minutes, Oct. 1944 - Mar. 1945 (**MS 14,485**).

162.2 BARING BROTHERS AND CO. LTD (MSS 18,321-50)
Letter re Crimean War finances, 1853-5, and Russian railways and loans, 1858-62 (**MS 18,321/HC.1.20.5**); papers re Russian railways, 1856-60 (**MS 18,321/HC.1.20.8**); letters from Edward Charles Baring from St Petersburg, 1858-60 (**MS 18,321/HC.1.20.13**); statistics of general trade including references to Russia (**MS 18,321/HC.2**); 20 boxes of correspondence re Russia including re loans, accounts, purchases, interest rates, railways and finance and with representatives and firms in St Petersburg, Odessa and the Baltic States, 1825-*c.*1870 (**MS 18,321/HC.10**); proposals for commercial credits including references to Russia (**MS 18,321/HC.17**). *See handlist for details of correspondence in MS 18,321/HC.10.* Records of Baring Brothers may only be consulted with written permission from the owner of the records.

162.3 BINDLOSS FAMILY (MSS 19,779-84)

Letters to Arthur Henry Bindloss, 1881-5, including letters from Russia (MS 19,779, 19,781, 19,783); letters to M. M. Bindloss, 1869-89, including letters from Russia (MS 19,780); official documents and certificates of Revd Edward Bindloss including 2 passports to Russia (MS 19,782); letters to Edward Bindloss in Russia and correspondence with the Russia Company re his appointment as chaplain to the British Factory at Archangel in 1847 (MS 19,784).

162.4 CENTRAL PROVINCES MANGANESE ORE COMPANY LTD (MSS 15,907-16,143)

Reports re ore exported from Russia and elsewhere, 1929-42 (MS 16,075); agreement between companies in the USSR ('TCHEMO') and W. A. Harrison and Co. re export of manganese ore from the USSR, 1925 (MS 16,122).

162.5 COUNCIL FOR BRITISH REPATRIATED FROM RUSSIA (MSS 11,747; 11,752-3)

Accounts and correspondence, 1921-4 (MS 11,752); papers and correspondence re individual cases, 1919-32 (MS 11,753).

162.6 THE COUNCIL OF THE CORPORATION OF FOREIGN BONDHOLDERS (MSS 15,748-814)

Minute-book of general and committee meetings of holders of the city of Riga, 1934 (MS 15,798). There could also be references to Russia amongst general minute-books, ledgers and journals, 1873-1939.

162.7 E. DENT & CO. LTD (MSS 18,005-76)

Papers include in-letters re supply of chronometers to Russia and the possible establishment of a branch of the company in St Petersburg, 1845-8 (MS 18,011).

162.8 DÜNABURG AND WITEBSK RAILWAY CO. LTD (MS 19,889)

Formed in 1863 to carry out a concession from the Russian government, changed its name to Dvinsk and Vitebsk Railway Co. Ltd in 1893, and went into voluntary liquidation on 21 May 1894. Out-letter books, 1880-94.

162.9 HAMBROS BANK LTD (MSS 19,031-223)

Correspondence between C. J. Hambro & Son and the Danish Minister of Finance re payment of compensation to Denmark by Russia, 1857-9, Danish and English (MSS 19,056, 19,058); loan papers re the following: cables between Vladivostok, Nagasaki, Shanghai and Hong Kong, 1855-83 (MS 19,081); the St Petersburg-Warsaw railway, 1856 (MS 19,158); Kirsk-Charkov-Azov (*sic*) railway, 1872 (MS 19,159); the Transcaucasian railway, 1882 (MS 19,160); flotation of Russian 4% syndicate loan of 1890 (MS 19,161); mortgage bonds of the St Petersburg Noble Bank, 1897-8 (MS 19,162); Odessa harbour improvements, 1910-11 (MS 19,162); city of Moscow loan, 1912 (MS,164).

162.10 HOOKE, D. Robert (MSS 1,757-8)

Account of journey of K'ang Hsi, Emperor of China, to western Tartary, 1683; account of journey from Moscow to China, 1693-5; account of journey made by Evesco Petlin from Moscow to Tartary and China in 1620 (read before the Royal Society in 1689) (MS 1,757).

162.11 JOHN HUBBARD AND CO. (MSS 10,364; 11,759-62)

Russia merchants. Records, 1874-1948, of company and its associated companies : Anglo-Russian Cotton Factories Ltd., Petroffsky Spinning and Weaving Company, Spassky Spinning and Weaving Company and Egerton Hubbard and Co., all of St

Petersburg; Schlüsselburg Calico Printing Company of Schlüsselburg; Ultra Wood Company of Kuopio, Finland.

162.12 FREDERICK HUTH & CO. (MSS 10,700-6)

Merchants and bankers, 1814-1936. Papers re the company's investments on behalf of clients including clients in Russia (**MS 10,700**); petitions of the liquidator of the Russian Bank for Foreign Trade, 1933-4 (**MS 10,706**).

162.13 THE LONDON ASSURANCE, MARINE DEPARTMENT (MS 14,759)

Marine Department risk books covering voyages to and from Riga, St Petersburg, Archangel, Onega and other ports, giving name of vessel, voyage made, type of cargo and its value and premium, 1832, 1854.

162.14 THE LONDON CHAMBER OF COMMERCE (MSS 16,454-789; 18,312-13)

Report of proceedings at inaugural meeting and minute-book of the British-Armenian Chamber of Commerce, 1919-22 (**MSS 16,509-10**); Russian section minute-books, 1908-64 (**MS 16,556**); fur trade 'Aid to Russia' fund minute-book, 1941 (**MS 16,642**); minute-books re shipments to Archangel (**MS 16,643/8**); minute-book of Latvian section, 1922-34, and Baltic States section, 1935-8 (**MS 16,535**); Lithuanian section minute-book, 1925-33 (**MS 16,536**). There may be material under separate trade sections (fur etc.). Permission is required from the London Chamber of Commerce to consult papers less than ten years old.

162.15-19 LONDON DIOCESE RECORDS

Extensive collection of which the records from the following churches relate specifically to Russia:

162.15 BRITISH CHAPEL, LIBAU (MS 10,953 C)

Registers of baptisms, marriages and burials, 1892-1915.

162.16 BRITISH CHURCH OF ST SAVIOUR, RIGA (MS 10,953-3 B; 11,227-8)

Registers of baptisms, marriages and burials, 1830-1939 (**MS 10,953-3 B**); minutes, 1806-22, and accounts, 1806-63, of the British Poor Fund established in 1806 by the British residents in Riga (**MS 11,227**); memorandum book including appointments, lists of benefactors, property, staff and confirmations, statistics of births, marriages and deaths and memos re contemporary events, 1898-1918 (**11,228**).

162.17 BRITISH CHURCH OF ST ANDREW, MOSCOW (MSS 11,751 A, 19,890-1)

Minute-book of meetings of subscribers to the general fund, 1900-16 (**MS 11,751 A**); cash book, 1913-17 (**MS 19,890**); note re closure of the church, 1917 (**MS 19,891**).

162.18 BRITISH EMBASSY CHURCH, MOSCOW (MSS 19,891-3)

Memo re provision of church services, 1947-9 (**MS 19,891**); financial papers, 1954-62 (**MS 19,892**); correspondence files, 1953-62 (**MS 19,893**).

162.19 CHAPLAINCY OF THE BRITISH FACTORY (RUSSIA COMPANY) IN MOSCOW, ARCHANGEL, KRONSTADT, ODESSA AND ST PETERSBURG (MSS 11,192-7, 11,224 A, 11,751, 19,230, 19,891)

Registers of baptisms, marriages and burials at Moscow, 1861-1920, and other miscellaneous papers (MSS 11,192, 11,192 A, 11, 192 C, 11,193); registers of baptisms, marriages and burials at Moscow, 1706-23, Archangel, 1719, and St Petersburg, 1723-7, 1737-1815, with lists of congregations and residents (MS 11,192 B); transcripts of baptisms, marriages and burials in St Petersburg, 1816-1918 (MS 11,194); transcripts of baptisms, marriages and burials in Archangel, 1835-83, 1913-19 (MS 11,195); transcripts of baptisms, marriages and burials, 1807-94, in Kronstadt (MS 11,196); registers of baptisms, marriages and burials in Odessa, 1883-1918 (MS 11,197); correspondence re tranfer of Odessa registers from London to Gibraltar, 1942 (MS 11,224 A); chaplains' reports from Archangel and Moscow to Revd Herbert Bury in London, 1894-1917 (MS 11,751); papers re Moscow chaplaincy, 19th and 20th century (MS 19,230); history of the Anglican chaplaincy in Moscow, 1917-48 (MS 19,891). Some registers indexed in MS 15,061.

162.20 MITFORD, Michael (d. 1709) (MS 11,892 A)

Russia and Baltic merchant. Out-letter book, 1703-6.

162.21 MOCATTA AND GOLDSMID (MSS 10.399-400; 18,637-65)

Copies of contracts and signed receipts for bars of gold relating to contracts with La Représentation commerciale de l'URSS en France, 1932-3 (MS 18,656).

162.22 RUSSIA COMPANY (MSS 11,741-757; 11,893-5)

Court minute-books, 1666-1903 (MS 11,741); cash balance book, 1868-1915 (MS 11,742); cash books, 1904-43 (MS 11, 743); ledger and journal, 1914-38 (MS 11,743 A); petty cash book, 1868-77 (MS 11,744); out-letter book mainly relating to the company's chaplaincies, 1879-85 (MS 11,745); general out-letter book, 1920-8 (MS 11,746); out-letter books of G. F. Feild, 1920-30 (MS 11,747); secretary's in-letter book, 1939-43 (MS 11,748); miscellaneous papers and correspondence, 1711-1888, 1916-19 (MSS 11,749-50); stamp duty book, 1869-1947 (MS 11,754); annual reports, 1905-53 (MS 11,755); 'general reference' book, 1877 (MS 11,756); breviate book of court business transacted and accounts of payments to refugees from Russia, 1877-1946 (MS 11,757); treasurer's account books, 1699-1904 (MS 11,893); copy of charter of incorporation and extracts from Acts of Parliament re the Company (MS 11,894); copy of transl. of charter granted by Tsar Michael to Charles II on behalf of the Company, 1628 (MS 11,895). *See card index for details.*

162.23 STRATTON AND GIBSON (from 1810, STRATTON, GIBSON AND FULLER) (MSS 19,777-8)

Account books mainly re import and sale of goods from St Petersburg to London, 1798-1817.

163.1-2
HONOURABLE SOCIETY OF THE INNER TEMPLE LIBRARY

Inner Temple, London EC4Y 7DA

By appointment. J. Conway-Davies, *Manuscripts in the Library of the Honourable Society of the Inner Temple,* 3 vols (Oxford, 1972).

163.1 THE PETYT COLLECTON (MS 538)
'The Fishery Project' containing a passing reference to shipping in Russia. n.d. ?early 17th century (**Vol. 19 f. 190**).

163.2 'Sketches of the Intrinsic Strength, Military and Naval Force of France and Russia, with remarks on their present connexions, political influence and future projects' part 1, London, 1803, by F. Maseres, seemingly unpublished (**Misc. MS 142**).

164.1-27
HOUSE OF LORDS RECORD OFFICE

House of Lords, London SW1A 0PW

By appointment. The House of Lords Record Office holds the records of the House of Lords and the House of Commons. Restrictions exist for some papers. M. F. Bond, *Guide to the Records of Parliament* (1971); M. F. Bond, *A Short Guide to the Records of Parliament,* 3rd edit. (1980); P. Ford and G. Ford, *A Guide to Parliamentary Papers* (1972) describing printed papers. Recent acquisitions are noted in the Record Office's *Annual Reports.* The Record Office has published several descriptions of particular groups of records in a series of *Memoranda.* A complete list of these *Memoranda* up to 1980 can be found in Bond, *A Short Guide,* pp. 21-3, and thereafter in the *Annual Reports.*

House of Lords Papers

Memorandum no. 20, *Guide to the House of Lords Papers and Petitions*; H. S. Cobb, 'Sources for Economic History Amongst the Paliamentary Records in the House of Lords Record Office', *Economic History Review,* 2nd series, 19 (1966) pp. 158-68 (reprinted as *Memorandum* no. 50). Printed records of speeches up to 1803 can be found in the 36 vols of *Parliamentary History* edited by W. Cobbett and then in the 5 series of *Parliamentary Debates* (known as 'Hansard'). References to Russia and the Soviet Union may be found in the following classes of records:

164.1 ACTS OF PARLIAMENT
Master copies of the Acts of Parliament start as parchment rolls and continue from 1849 in book form. The appropriate indexes and calendars can be found in Bond, *Guide* pp. 97, 102-3.

164.2 COMMITTEE MINUTE BOOKS
The minute-books (1661 to date) include manuscript minutes, amendments made to private bills, resolutions and occasional original letters. The records are described in *Memorandum* 13, *The Journals, Minutes and Committee Books of the House of Lords,* and there are TS lists of all classes of committee records in the Search Room.

164.3 JOURNALS

The journals (1510 to date) give a daily record of business transacted in the House and indicate which papers were dealt with by the House in each session. The existing journals were ordered to be printed in 1767 and by 1830 the journals were being printed soon after the session to which they referred. The original early journals and minutes sometimes differ or contain additional material from the printed journals. Published calendars of manuscript papers exist for period up to 1718, starting as Historical Manuscripts Commission reports until 1693 then continuing as a House of Lords publication. References to Russia, Muscovy and the Muscovy Company can be found in the indexes to the calendars. From 1718 searchers can trace subjects considered in the House in the *General Indexes to the House of Lords Journals,* 18 vols, 1509-1649, 1660-1973 (cumulative indexes issued decennially) and subsequently in the journals themselves. There are references to trade with Russia, treaties and conventions between Russia and Britain, foreign policy and internal events in Russia and the Soviet Union. There may also be references to Russia in supplementary series to the journals, namely, draft journals, 1621-90, minute-books (manuscript, 1610-1827; printed from 1825) and clerk's assistant's sheets, 1775 to date. *Memorandum* no. 13, *The Journals, Minutes and Committee Books of the House of Lords* gives a general description of these papers.

164.4 MAIN PAPERS, OR SESSIONAL PAPERS

Most of the papers referred to in the journals can be found in this series (1531 to date) including all documents laid before the House, petitions, private and public bills, acts, judicial papers and reports. Some papers were printed from the eighteenth century; few have been printed since 1921. Manuscript papers are described in the published calendars up to 1718 (*see entry for journals*). From 1718 to 1916 the surviving Main Papers are listed in handwritten chronological lists; thereafter copies of the journals in the Search Room are stamped with the number of each surviving paper. From 1800 the printed sessional papers are listed in the *General Index to the Sessional Papers Printed by Order of Lords or Presented by Royal Command, 1801-85,* 3 vols. Separate *Tables and Indexes* exist for 1886-1920 and after 1921 the table of contents can be consulted at the beginning of each volume. Sessional papers are described in Bond, *Guide,* pp. 127-59.

House of Commons Papers

Most records were lost in the fire of 1834 although the original journals survived. Printed papers are described in *Hansard Catalogue and Breviate of Parliamentary Papers, 1696-1834* edited by P. Ford and J. Ford, and the *Catalogue of Papers Printed by Order of the House of Commons, 1731-1800.* References may be found to Russia and the Soviet Union in the following classes of records:

164.5 BILLS

Bills are indexed in *General Indexes,* 1801-52, and *Bills, Reports and Papers etc.,* 1852-99, 1900-49, 1950-9.

164.6 JOURNALS

Manuscript journals exist for the years 1547-1800; they were all printed in the mid-18th century and subsequently printed concurrently with the session. Researchers are advised to consult the manuscript originals, especially for the period 1547-1642. Papers relating to Russia and the Soviet Union can be located in the *Collected Indices of the Journal of the House of Commons* (1547 to date) and individual indexes in each volume. An introduction to the journals is given in D. Menhennet, *The Journal of the House of Commons. A Bibliographical and Historical Guide* (1971).

164.7 SESSIONAL PAPERS

Sessional papers are described in the *List of House of Commons Sessional Papers, 1701-1750* edited by S. Lambert (1968), *House of Commons Sessional Papers of the Eighteenth Century,* vols 1 and 2 (1965-6) and E. L. Erikson, 'British House of Commons Sessional Papers of the Eighteenth and Nineteenth Centuries', *College and Research Libraries,* vol. 21 (1960) pp. 343-58 (offprint available in the Search Room).

Private Papers

Memoranda no. 54, *A Guide to the Political Papers, 1874-1970, deposited by the First Beaverbrook Foundation* (1975) and no. 60. *A Guide to the Historical Collections of the Nineteenth and Twentieth Centuries Preserved in the House of Lords Record Office* (1980). Handlists of some collections.

164.8 BALFOUR PAPERS (Hist. Coll. 199)

Papers of Harold Harrington Balfour, 1st Baron Balfour of Inchrye, include: TS of his account of the Supply Mission, published as *Moscow Diary, 1941*; 'Account of some post-Moscow 1941 Government events'. HLRO List no. 122.

164.9 BEAVERBROOK PAPERS (Hist. Coll. 184, 247)

Papers of William Max Aitkin (1879-1964), 1st Baron Beaverbrook, financier, newspaper proprietor and politician include: correspondence re American spy in Russia and the Anglo-Soviet trade agreement, 1921 (**B/13-15**); correspondence with R. Bruce Lockhart, Ivan Maiskii and Averell Harriman (**C List 109**); papers and correspondence re USSR, 1941 (**D/87-108**; 1,859 documents); file on the USSR, 1944-5 (**D/295**); correspondence with A. Eden on the USSR, 1942-4 (**D/427**); articles on Russia (**D/470**); papers on the Second Front campaign (**D/454**; 196 documents); papers on the Russian Interlude (**D/471**); papers on Russia (**D/494**); papers re propaganda and possible missions to Russia, 1918 (**E/3/15, /19, /33, /48**); film records covering visit to Moscow. There could be further references to the USSR in papers re foreign affairs, 1940-5. Restrictions on some papers. *See Memorandum 54 and HLRO lists 108-112 for further details.* There are further lists in progress.

164.10 BIGGS-DAVIDSON, Sir John (Hist. Coll. 101)

3 files on communism, 1944-79; 3 files on Eastern Europe, 1962-78. HLRO List no. 78.

164.11 BLUMENFELD PAPERS (Hist. Coll. 185)

Papers of Ralph David Blumenfeld (1864-1948), journalist, include letters from: Herbert Bailey at the British Embassy in Petrograd, May 1917 (**BAI.1**); Gen. Sir Hubert Gough on the situation in the Baltic, 1919, 1935 (**GOU. 4-5, 11**); Sir William Joynson-Hicks re deportation to Russia of A. Yasvoin, June 1927 (**JOY. 13-14**); Albert Kahn re Krassin, 26 May 1920 (**KA. 1**); Sir Basil Home Thomson re Bolshevism and interview of C. A. Hill with Lenin, 1918-19 (**THOMS. 1-3**). HLRO List no. 113.

164.12 DAVIDSON PAPERS (Hist. Coll. 187)

Papers of John Colin Campbell Davidson (1889-1970), 1st Visc. Davidson, as Parliamentary Secretary to Bonar Law inlude papers on Anglo-Soviet relations, 1920-21, with particular reference to the Russian trade delegation to London in 1921. Papers only partially sorted; list in preparation.

164.13 HADEN-GUEST PAPERS (Hist. Coll. 244)

Papers of Dr Leslie Haden Haden-Guest (1877-1960), 1st Baron Haden-Guest, consist chiefly of his accounts of visits to Russia and other European countries in connection with famine relief, 1919-36.

164.14 HAINES COLLECTION (Hist. Coll. 256)
Papers of William Henry Haines, clerk in the House of Lords, include a passport granted to him by the British Ambassador to Russia, 20 Aug. 1876.

164.15 HANNON PAPERS (Hist. Coll. 189)
Papers of Sir Patrick Joseph Henry Hannon (1874-1963) include: memo on the Allied Baltic Military Mission by Brig.-Gen. Alfred Burt, n.d. (**Box 7**); statement by N. Khrushchev to C. de Gaulle, H. Macmillan and D. Eisenhower (**Box 20**); papers re Hannon's tours of the Baltic States, 1923-35 (**Box 22/1-5**); letter from Kimmens, British Legation in Warsaw, re Polish reaction to the severing of relations between the UK and the USSR, 26 June 1927 (**Box 24**). HLRO List no. 115, *Memorandum* no. 54.

164.16 HOLLAND (PERCEVAL) PAPERS
Papers of Spencer Perceval (1762-1812) include correspondence re transport of stores to Russia, July 1810, 9 Aug. 1811 (**I. 23, 28**). The papers remain in Mr Holland's possession but may be deposited in the Record Office for the use of researchers.

164.17 LAW (BONAR LAW) PAPERS (Hist. Coll. 191)
Papers of Andrew Bonar Law (1858-1923) include: papers re trade with Russia, 1901-3, 1915, 1921-2; comment on Russian railways, 1908; comments by G. N. Curzon, W. Long, Lloyd George and the British Vice-Consul at Kiev on Russia, 1911, 1914-16; Bonar Law's speech for a good understanding between Britain and Russia, 1912; papers re Jews in Russia, 1913; report of conversation between J. Baird and the Russian Ambassador on Russian policy, 1915; correspondence re Allied intervention, the dismissal of the Russian trade delegation, 1920, and the withdrawal of the British delegation from Russia, 1923. *See HLRO List no. 116, 3 vol. catalogue and card-indexes for details and further references.*

164.18 LEVY PAPERS (Hist. Coll. 107)
Papers of Benn Wolfe Levy (1900-73), dramatist and MP, include files on foreign policy, 1946-8, and the socialist states of Europe, 1947. HLRO List no. 83.

164.19 LLOYD GEORGE PAPERS (Hist. Coll. 192)
Papers of David Lloyd George (1863-1945), 1st Earl Lloyd George of Dwyfor, include: speeches mentioning Russia, 1905-8 (**A, B**) ; papers, speeches and correspondence re Russia as Chancellor of Exchequer, 1913-15 (**C**); correspondence with Russian government and British representatives in Russia, papers re Russia and papers re supplies to Russia as Minister of Munitions, 1915-16 (**D**); papers re Russia as Secretary of State for War, 1916 (**E**). Papers as Prime Minister, 1916-22, (**F**) include general papers and correspondence re Russia, papers re missions, munitions, the Revolution, Russian morale, the Russian royal family, Jews in Russia, the Allied intervention, Anglo-Russian trade, Russian refugees, Soviet relations with America, Germany, Persia and Poland, Soviet trade delegation to Britain. General papers re USSR, 1922-45, (**G**) include correspondence with Ivan Maiskii, and papers by Hilton Young, Harold Sidney Harmsworth, 1st Visc. Rothermere, Gareth Jones, and others on the USSR. *See HLRO Lists 117-18, card indexes of persons and subjects for details and further references.*

164.20 PRICE, Morgan Philips (1885-1973) (Hist. Coll. 293)
Labour MP. Copy of soundtrack of television interview 'The world turned upside down' re his experiences in the Russian Revolution, recorded for transmission in 1967.

164.21 SAMUEL PAPERS (Hist. Coll. 128)
Papers of Herbert Louis, 1st Visc. Samuel, (1870-1963) include: record of conversations and letter from I. Maiskii, 1932-3, 1937 (**A/90, /93; A/103/85**); TS article 'Britain, Russia and the World', 1942 (**E/68**). 30 year restriction on all papers. *Memoranda* nos. 35, 41.

164.22 SANDERSON PAPERS (Hist. Coll. 128)
Papers of Sir Frank Bernard Sanderson, 1st Bt., (1880-1965) include : press cuttings on the Russian loan (**Book 2, 1924-26**); Russian broadcasts (**Book 5, 1934-7**). HLRO List no. 69.

164.23 SHAW-LEFEVRE PAPERS
papers of Sir J. G. Shaw-Lefevre (1797-1879), Clerk of the Parliaments, 1855-75, include proceedings on the Crimean War, 1854-6 (**Parliament Office**). HLRO List no. 41.

164.24 STANSGATE PAPERS (Hist. Coll. 141)
Papers of William Wedgwood Benn (1877-1960), 1st Visc. Stansgate, include: papers re Soviet offer re European economic organization, 16 May 1960 (**ST/233/12**); FO dispatches from Moscow, 1 May 1945 (**ST/234/4**), and Budapest re Soviet occupation of Hungary, 9 Nov. 1945 (**ST/240/5**); papers re the Ukraine and Soviet relations with Poland, 1941-3 (**ST/241/3-4, /242/1-4, /281/9**); papers re the USSR, 1939-59, including command papers, the visit of the Supreme Soviet delegation, the printing of the Bible in the USSR, letters to Soviet Ambassadors (**ST/244**); papers re Stansgate's visits to Russia, 1926, 1956 (**ST/289**). There are some restrictions on the papers. *See Memorandum no. 56 for further details.*

164.25 STOW HILL (SOSKICE) PAPERS (Hist. Coll. 206)
Family papers of the Soskice family include: re Russia (**Trunk B**); notes by David Soskice on Russian history, economics and political situation, Russian press cuttings, family Russian financial papers and notes by Juliet Soskice on Russia (**Trunk D**). Papers of David Soskice (1869-1943), Russian émigré and writer, include: papers re the 'Free Russia' movement including correspondence, notes re speeches and publications, comments on Russia, papers re the Russian Political Prisoners and Exiles Relief Committee and Soskice's work on *Tribune* (**D.S./1**); articles, notes and press cuttings re Russia (**D.S./2**); Russian and English correspondence of David Soskice and his family, *c.* 1890-1926, including information on his experiences in Russia and the 'Free Russia' movement (**D.S./3-4**). Papers of Sir Frank Soskice (1870-1963), Lord Stow Hill, include letters from Aleksandr and Oleg Kerenskii, 1960, 1963, n.d. (**KER/1-2**) and John Max Muller re trade with the USSR, 1956 (**MAX/1-2**). *See handlist for details.* Permission to consult the Stow Hill papers must be obtained from the Hon. Oliver Soskice, 38 Marlborough Road, Oxford.

164.27 STRACHEY PAPERS (Hist. Coll. 196)
Papers of John St Loe Strachey (1860-1927), journalist, include: correspondence re Russia in Political Persons Files; correspondence re Russo-Japanese War (**S/15/4/3-4; S/15/5/10**), re political situation in Russia, 1917 (**S/18/4/33**) and re the *Spectator*'s attitude towards the Bolsheviks, Aug. 1924 (**S/19/6/27**); correspondence in Papers-Political, Russia re the Russo-Japanese War and the situation in Russia (**S/22/1/1-3**). *See Memorandum no. 54 and HLRO List no. 199, which is still in progress, for details.*

165.1-2

HUTCHINSON PUBLISHING GROUP LTD

Hutchinson House, 17-21 Conway Street, London W1P 6JD

By appointment for *bona fide* researchers.

165.1 3 files of correspondence and contract with Vassily Aksyonov and TS extracts from *The Island of the Crimea*, published by Hutchinson in 1985.

165.2 Correspondence and contract with Vladimir Rybakov and extracts from *The Burden* and *Outlines of an Autobiography*, published by Hutchinson in 1984.

166.1

THE ILLUSTRATED LONDON NEWS PICTURE LIBRARY

20 Upper Ground, London SE1

By appointment. Engravings, photographs and illustrations from 1842 to the present day, based on 8 magazines published by Illustrated Newspapers. There is a cumulative subject index for *The Illustrated London News* from 1842 and a chronological index for the other magazines, and subject files arranged by country, subjects and names. This is a commercial library and the rate card for reproduction of illustrations and for research may be obtained from the Library.

166.1 8 files of illustrative material (sketches, photographs, line engravings) relating to Russia and the Soviet Union, dating from 1844, including Russian towns and countryside, Russian customs and pastimes, military campaigns, the Tsars and their entourage and the Revolution. 16 files of illustrative material relating to the Crimean War, including copies of photographs by R. Fenton. Further material will probably be found in files relating to prominent individuals connected with Russia and the Soviet Union.

167.1-5

IMPERIAL COLLEGE OF SCIENCE AND TECHNOLOGY ARCHIVES

Room 455, Sherfield Building, Imperial College, London SW7 2AZ

By appointment. J. Perceval, edit., *A Guide to Archives and Manuscripts in the University of London,* vol. 1 (1984) pp. 36-47.

167.1 ARMSTRONG, Henry Edward (1848-1937)
Chemist. Letters to Armstrong from G. C. Foster referring to paper by D. I. Mendeleev on the expansion of liquids, 7 Apr. 1884 **(170)**, to D. I. Mendeleev, 12/24 Sept. 1889 **(299)**, and to N. A. Menschutkin (Menshutkin), 6/17 July 1891 **(300)**.

167.2 HUXLEY, Thomas Henry (1825-95)
Naturalist. Letters to Huxley from K. E. von Baer in St Petersburg and Dorpat, [1860], 1867-8 **(10.109, 188, 192)**, L. Boguslavskii in Riga, 1/12 Sept. 1888 **(11.27)**, Sir Charles N. E. Eliot at the British Embassy in St Petersburg, 28 Apr. -- **(15.175)**, Sir Robert B. D. Morier re a Siberian mining scheme, *c.* 1893 **(23.7)**, and V. V. Zalenskii in Odessa, [1883] **(29.273)**. W. R. Dawson, *The Huxley Papers* (London, 1946).

167.3 JACKSON, Willis, Lord Jackson of Burnley (1904-70)
Electrical engineer. Correspondence, reports, articles and newspaper cuttings re visit to Moscow, Nov. 1955 **(8)**.

167.4 PLAYFAIR, Lyon, 1st Baron Playfair of St Andrews (1818-98)
Chemist. Letters to Playfair from Sir James Dewar re negotiations with Rothschilds over Russian oil trade, 22 Nov. 1885 **(229)**, Thomas Cochrane, 10th Earl of Dundonald, with a

small plan of Sebastopol, 21 Apr. 1855 **(929)**, and Frederick Blackwood, 1st Marquis of Dufferin and Ava, from St Petersburg, 2 Apr. 1880 **(1052)**.

167.5 THOMPSON, Silvanus Phillips (1851-1916)
Physicist and electrical engineer. Letters to Thompson from A. Smirnov in St Petersburg, 1892 **(293-4)**.

168.1-173

IMPERIAL WAR MUSEUM

Lambeth Road, London SE1 6HZ

By appointment to all departments. Records relating to Russia and the Soviet Union can be found in the Departments of Documents, Photographs and Sound Records. Card indexes to subjects (campaigns) and persons are available. Handlists for large collections.

168.1-152 Department of Documents

168.1 AGAR, Capt. A. W. S., RN
Papers and photographs, including material from the Baltic and the Kronstadt raid, 1918-19.

168.2 AIREY, Group Capt. J. L.
Pilot's flying log-book, 2 MSS diaries and a few other papers covering his flying duties with No. 221 Squadron RAF in South Russia, Dec. 1918 - Dec. 1919.

168.3 ALLFREY, Maj. E. M.
TS diary of his service in the 46th Bn Royal Fusiliers in the Russian Relief Force on the Dvina River Front, June-Sept. 1919.

168.4 ALLHUSEN, Maj. D.
Small collection of letters covering his service as a junior officer with No. 1 Special Company King's Royal Rifle Corps in North Russia, Apr.-May 1919, with the British Military Mission to the Baltic States, Jan.-May 1920, and with a British commercial mission to Russia, Feb.-June 1923.

168.5 ANDRUS, Brig.-Gen. T. A.
Letters re his command of the 39th Infantry Bde in Persia and the Caucasus, including the reoccupation of Baku, Oct.-Dec. 1918.

168.6 ARCHER, Adm. Sir Ernest
Letters written when head of the Joint Military Mission to Russia, 1944-5.

168.7 BAKER, Lt F. A.
Account of his service in the 1st Bn The Royal Scots in the Caucasus, Jan.-May 1919.

168.8 BALFOUR, Harold Harrington, Lord Balfour of Inchrye
Microfilm copy of diary of the Anglo-American mission to Moscow, 21 Sept. - 10 Oct. 1941. *See list for details.*

168.9 BEAUMONT, Sir Henry
Microfilm copy of autobiography describing his experiences as a diplomat in St Petersburg, 1905-06.

168.10 BECKITT, R. R.
Microfilm copy of MSS diaries of his service with the ASC in Britain and North Russia, 1918-19. *See list for details.*

168.11 BERESFORD-ASH, Maj. D.
Account of service in the Baltic and the Caucasus, Oct. 1918 - July 1920.

168.12 BILNEY, Air Vice-Marshal C. N. H.
Microfilm of memoirs and log-book of service in the RNAS in British occupation force on the Caspian Sea, 1919. *See list for details.*

168.13 BOCK, Max
Carbon copy of TS diary describing his experiences as a German Jew in Berlin in April and May 1945, including description of Russian bombardment and occupation of the city, German and English transl.

168.14 BONE, Grp Capt. R. J.
Microfilm copy of TS memoirs include description of the work of the British forces in Murmansk in North Russian campaign. *See list for details.*

168.15 BOSTOCK, Cdr J.
Microfilm copy of letters written whilst serving as a Lt in HMS *Ajax* on the Mediterranean Station, describing South Russia intervention, 1920-1. *See list for details.*

168.16 BOWEN, Cdr J. H., RN
Diary covering his service in the river gunboat *Moth* in North Russian campaign, July-Oct. 1919.

168.17 BRACHER, J. H.
Diary covering service as Quartermaster Sgt, 17th Bn the King's Liverpool Regiment, in North Russia, Oct. 1918 - June 1919; TS 'Proclamation' to British troops explaining the reasons for their fight against Bolshevism; messenger's pass; ration lists; sketch map of the Dvina River Front. *See list for details.*

168.18 BREWSTER, Cdr B. T., RN
Microfilm of memoirs, 'Russian Relief Force and the Evacuation of North Russia', describing service in gunboat *Cicala* and with naval gun detachment on the Dvina River Front in North Russia, May-Oct. 1919.

168.19 BROCK, W. C.
Letters to his family whilst serving with 'Syren' Force at Murmansk, June-Sept. 1919, and with the British Legation in Finland, Jan.-Apr. 1920.

168.20 BROMHEAD, Col. A. C.
Transcript of the diaries he kept while working as a propaganda agent showing war films, and including descriptions of life in Russia and visits to the Russian front, Feb. 1916 - Jan. 1917; Apr. - Sept. 1917.

168.21 BURN, Lt-Col. A. G.
Served on Lord Milner's Committee for Russian supplies and with the North Russia Expeditionary Force. Diary (/2); MS and TS 'The Jottings of a Dug-Out in North Russia 1918-19' (/3); miscellaneous items including photographs, drawings, postcards, maps, Christmas cards (/4). *See list for details.*

168.22 BURNETT, Adm. Sir Robert
Microfilm copy of records of his command of the 10th Cruiser Squadron in defence of convoys to North Russia, Sept. 1942 - Dec. 1943. *See list for details.*

168.23 BURROUGH, Adm. Sir Harold
Microfilms of papers including material on convoys to Russia, Second World War. *See list for details.*

168.24 BUTLER, Maj.-Gen. S. S.
Microfilm copy of memoirs including an account of his service as GSOI Naval Intelligence at Constantinople where he was responsible for collecting information on Asia Minor, Eastern Europe and Russia, particularly on the White Russian forces, 1919-20.

168.25 CAZALET, Vice-Adm. Sir Peter
Some papers concerning convoys to Russia in the Second World War. *See list for details.*

168.26 CHICHESTER, Capt. R. A. A.
Miscellaneous documents re his service in North Russia in 1919 including daily intelligence summaries and reports, messages, signals, orders, communications, newsheet, Russian civilian internal passport, numerous hand-drawn maps of the area.

168.27 COURTNEY, Dame Kathleen d'Olier
Letters and diaries relating to her work with the Friends' Relief Service in Salonika and Eastern Europe, 1915-27. *See list for details.*

168.28 COX, Cdr M. L.
A few records of his service in HMS *Ceres* in the Baltic, Nov.-Dec. 1918.

168.29 CULLEN, Lt A. A.
TS memoir 'A Caucasian Adventure', describing British military intervention in Trans-Caucasia and his imprisonment by the Turks.

168.30 DALY, W.
Copy of MS autobiography including service in HMS *Barryfield* in the Black Sea.

168.31 DAVIDSON, Lt H. J., RNVR
TS account of his service as an Ordinary/Leading Seaman in several ships, 1941-4, including in the destroyer HMS *Scourge* on escort duty in the North Sea and with the North Russian convoys, Mar.-Dec. 1944.

168.32 DAWSON, R.
TS account of his service in North Russia with 2/10th Bn the Royal Scots, Aug.-Oct. 1918, and as a POW of the Bolsheviks in Moscow, Oct. 1918 - Apr. 1920.

168.33 DRAGE, Cdr C. H., RN
Microfilm copies of diaries include service in the armoured cruiser HMS *Cochrane* in north Russian waters, and in the Russian yacht *Gorislava*, 1918.

168.34 DUNNINGTON-JEFFERSON, Lt-Col. Sir John
A few TS reports and MSS letters written by Capt. G. H. MacCaw re the operations of the Russian Army on the Eastern Front, June-Aug. 1916.

168.35 DURNFORD, Vice Adm. J. W.
TS autobiography 'A Shellback Remembers' describing, service as naval adviser to the White Armies in South Russia.

168.36 DVORKOVITZ, Dr P.
Postcards and letters describing his imprisonment in Moscow, 1918-19, together with reports and correspondence re Russian flag days in England, 1915-16, and propagandist efforts to persuade Russian front line troops to continue fighting, 1916-17.

168.37 FARMBOROUGH, Miss F.
Incomplete MSS recollections of her nursing service on the Russian front in 1915 and MSS diary fragments for Jan.-Feb. 1916 and June-Sept. 1917.

168.38 GAMMELL, Lt-Gen. Sir James Andrew Harcourt
Papers re the British Military Mission to Moscow, 1945.

168.39 GAWTHORPE, Brig. J. B.
Diary, orders, intelligence reports, correspondence, memos, and notes re his service in North Russia; copies of Bolshevik newspaper.

168.40 GEDYE, George Eric Rowe
Moscow correspondent of *The New York Times.* Papers include correspondence, memoirs, press dispatches, articles, newspaper cuttings, chapters of autobiographical account *Curtain Raiser. See list for details*

168.41 GILMORE, Brig. G. H.
Memoir of his service with the North Russian Expeditionary Force, 1918-19.

168.42 GLOVER, D.
TS memoir of his experiences following his escape from an evacuation march of POWs in Poland, Jan. 1945, which involved being aided by the Russians and transported to the British Military Mission at Odessa.

168.43 GLYN, Maj. Sir R. G. C. , the Lord Glyn
Microfilm of letter to family from Mission of Arthur Paget to Russia, 1915.

168.44 GOODDEN, Lt-Col. R. B.
A collection of letters, diaries and papers re his service as Military Attaché in Eastern Europe and the Baltic States in the 1920s.

168.45 GOODNIGHT, H. F.
TS account of his experiences while serving as a gunner in the 421st Howitzer Battery in North Russia, Dec. 1918 - Sept. 1919.

168.46 GOTTO, Capt. R., RN
Midshipman's journal covering his service in the destroyer HMS *Venomous* in operations against the Bolshevik Navy in the Baltic, Oct.-Dec. 1919, and in the Battleship HMS *Marlborough* which assisted in the evacuation of White Russian refugees from ports in the Black Sea, May 1920.

168.47 GRACE, Capt. N. V., RN
Letter describing visit to Archangel in the minelayer HMS *Adventure*, 1941.

168.48 GRUNDY, Sub-Lt T., RNR
Collection of papers re service in the Caspian Sea, including Bolshevik propaganda leaflets, 1918-19.

168.49 GUNDRY-WHITE, Lt-Col. L. A.
Diary describing service as Liaison Officer with the British Military Mission to South Russia, Nov.-Dec. 1919.

168.50 HAIGH, G. E.
Diary covering his service as a signalman including in the battleships HMS *Albemarle* and HMS *Glory* in North Russia, July-Aug. 1919.

168.51 HAMPSHEIR, Sub-Lt J. W., RNR
Copy of MSS deck log-book of *CMB4* covering her transportation to the Baltic and service there with the Bolsheviks including the sinking of the cruiser *Oleg*, together with the official documents issued to him at the time of his service in the Baltic.

168.52 HARRISON, E. J.
The Times correspondent in St Petersburg, 1914-16. Account of the political background to the Russian Revolution and events in Russia in 1917.

168.53 HARRISON, Cmdr R., RNR
Records of his command of the naval detachment with Dunsterforce, 1918, and of SS *Venture* with the British naval expedition in the Caspian Sea, Sept. 1919 - Aug. 1919.

168.54 HARTLEY, Lt R. St John
Microfilm of letter to his sister re escorting of 300 Bolshevik prisoners to Finland, 11 Mar. 1920.

168.55 HAYES, Lucy
Papers re the Anglo-Russian hospital in Petrograd, 1915-17, including: papers re journey to Russia; press cuttings; correspondence, some in Russian; printed brochures and maps. *See list for details.*

168.56 HEMPEL, H.
TS account of his experiences as a POW in Czechoslovakia, May-Aug. 1945, and in the Caucasus, Aug. 1945 - Dec. 1949, following his capture while serving with an infantry unit of the German Army on the Eastern Front.

168.57 HENDERSON, Maj.-Gen. Patrick Hagert (1876-1968)
Papers and diaries covering service in South Russia and the Trans-Caspian, 1917-19.

168.58 HESKETH, Air Vice Marshal
Records of 'Kuban Group' RAF in South Russia, 1920.

168.59 HILL, Capt. D. C., RN
British Naval Attaché in Moscow, 1946-8. Collection of lectures, notes and official memoranda re life in Russia and his work; historical details on the Russian Navy.

168.60 HIRST, F.
Brief account of his journey to northern Russia with the 6th Bn Yorkshire Regiment and of a mutiny which broke out on board ship, 1918.

168.61 HODGES, Miss K.
TS memoir of her service as a nurse with a Russian unit on the Galician Front, Dec. 1916 - summer 1917.

168.62 HOWARD, Brig. T. F. K.
Microfilm of account of experiences on the North Russian Front, summer 1919.

168.63 HOWES, Maj. B. E.
Diary of his service with the 9th Bn, the Royal Warwickshire Regt, in South Russia, Dec. 1918 - Mar. 1919.

168.64 HULLS, Col. L. R.
Official and personal papers re his service with the Armoured Car Bde and Dunsterforce in South Russia, his imprisonment at Tiflis, 1918, and subsequent service as a British Liaison Officer to the Georgian government at Tiflis, 1919-20. *See list for details.*

168.65 HUTCHINGS, W. A.
Account of his experiences with the British Naval Mission, led by Cdr Bruce Fraser, which was captured by the Russians and of his time as a POW in Baku, Apr.-Aug. 1920.

168.66 JACK, A.
Letter to Brig. Marce describing the situation with the White Russians, July 1919.

168.67 JAMES, Vice-Adm. T. N.
Papers re the evacuation of Russian refugees by HMS *Cardiff*, 1920.

168.68 JENKS, Wing Cdr M. H.
Memoir of service career including with the Army of the Black Sea in 1919 and describing the evacuation of the South Russia Force.

168.69 JOWETT, R.
TS copy of a diary of his service in the seaplane carrier HMS *Pegasus* during the North Russia expedition, May-Sept. 1919.

168.70 KALLIN, Lt M., RNVR
Letters in Russian and English re his service as an interpreter in North Russia during the Second World War.

168.71 KEIGHLEY, Sub-Lt, H. S., RN
Scrapbook containing letters, press cuttings, telegrams and photographs re his imprisonment at Baku by the Bolsheviks as member of British Naval Mission under Cdr B. A. Fraser, Apr.-Aug. 1920. *See list for details.*

168.72 KERSLAKE, S. A.
Copy of memoirs covering service in the armed trawler HMS *Northern Gem* which served as an armed escort and rescue ship on convoys in the North Atlantic and on the Archangel run, Second World War (published as *Coxwain in the Northern Convoys*).

168.73 KING, Surg. Lt-Cdr W. H., RN
TS account, MSS letters and diary re his service as a medical officer with the RNAS Armoured Car Section in Russia, Nov. 1916 - Aug. 1917.

168.74 LE BRUN, G.
Notes describing experiences during First World War including the evacuation of Batum, 1919.

168.75 LIDDELL, Col. L. A.
Incomplete collection of transcripts of the daily proceedings of the trial of FM Erich von Manstein and documents produced in evidence, finding aids and summary of the course of the Russian campaign (written by von Manstein to support his defence). *See list for details.*

168.76 LOCKYER, L.
Collection of notes, papers and maps on naval operations during the Russo-Japanese War, assembled during research for a book on that war.

168.77 LODGE, Surgeon Lt W. O., RN
Memoir of service including in HMS *Curacoa* in the Baltic in May 1919.

168.78 LUPTON, A.
Diary kept while serving with the Royal Marines in the Russian ship *Slava* with the Caspian Naval Force, Aug. 1918 - June 1919.

168.79 McCALL, Adm. Sir Henry
TS account of service in the destroyer HMS *Westcott* in the Baltic, including raid on Petrograd, 1919.

168.80 MacCAW, Capt. G. H.
TS letter written to Lord Kitchener's biographer re Kitchener's relations with the Russians, 1913-16.

168.81 MacEWAN, Col. M.
Miscellaneous documents including letters, orders, photographs, notices, citation, some in Russian, re service with No. 47 Squadron RAF in South Russia. *See list for details*

168.82 MACKIE, Capt. A. C.
Letters to his family when in command of the 253rd Machine Gun Company with the North Russian Expeditionary Force, and then as Bde Maj. to the 237th Bde on the Murmansk front, June-Dec. 1918.

168.83 MacLENNAN, Capt. W. A.
Copy of a lecture which he delivered on his return from North Russia where he served as a Medical Officer in 1919 describing conditions and work of the Army medical services.

168.84 MacLEOD, Lt-Col. N.
Letters to his wife from Archangel whilst serving in the 2nd Bn Slavo-British Allied Legion in 1919.

168.85 MAITLAND-EDWARDS, Lt-Col. G.
Copy of an account of a journey to the Russian front and a tour of inspection of the battlefields during the 1917 offensive by Lt-Gen. Sir Charles Barter, British military representative to Russian HQ in the field.

168.86 MANN, E. Leslie
Microfilm of autobiographical account 'The Relief of Archangel', re service with North Russian Expeditionary Force.

168.87 MARTEL, Lt-Gen. Sir Giffard
Reports, letters and photographs from the Military Mission to Russia, 1941-4; material re the Russian Front produced by War Office, 1941-3; articles on Russian history; correspondence re Russia and communism; photographs re visit to Russia, 1936. *See list for details.*

168.88 MASON, Lt L. W.
Copy of his flying log-book with entries re the bombing raids which he carried out in the Archangel region in July 1919.

168.89 MASON-MACFARLANE, Lt-Gen. Sir Noel
Drafts of articles re British Military Mission to Russia. Publication based on documents must be approved by the donor.

168.90 MERCER, Lt H.
Observer's flying log-book covering service with No. 47 Squadron RAF in South Russia, July-Oct. 1919.

168.91 METELMANN, H. F. K.
Photocopies of account, written in 1983, of incidents during his service as a private in the 22nd Panzer Division and unnamed Kampfgruppen on the Eastern Front, *c.* 1942-4, German.

168.92 MEZMALIETIS, M.
Photocopy of account, written in 1983, describing his experiences following his arrest by the Germans in Latvia in 1943 for refusing to enlist in the German army.

168.93 MILLER, W. G.
Copies of 2 letters to relatives whilst serving as a private in the 2/7th Bn Durham Light Infantry with Elope Force in Archangel, Oct., Dec. 1918.

168.94 MOORE, Maj. M. S.
Letters home and press cuttings from North Russia, 1919, where he was serving with the 2nd Bn, the Hampshire Regt.

168.95 MOORE, W. J.
Diary as officers' steward in the armed trawler HMS *Daneman* re passage, as part of the escort force of Convoy PQ18, from Iceland to Archangel, and re her salvage and repair by the Russians after she had run aground, Sept. 1942 - Jan. 1943.

168.96 NEEDHAM, Maj.-Gen. H.
Photographs and cards re service with the North Russian Expeditionary Force in Murmansk and Archangel, Sept. 1918 - Oct. 1919.

168.97 NEWMAN, L. D.
Brief account of his experiences as PO in HMS *Edinburgh* throughout the German submarine attacks on 30 Apr. and 2 May 1942 while she was escorting a convoy off Murmansk, including a description of her sinking.

168.98 PAGE, A. S.
Miscellaneous documents re service in Macedonia and South Russia in 1919.

168.99 PARSONS, Lt J. R., RNVR
Copies of letters home and other miscellaneous records whilst assistant to Rear-Adm. Phillimore's naval mission when attached to the Tsar's court, 1915-16.

168.100 PERCIVAL, Lt-Gen. A. E.
Papers re North Russian relief force including photographs, mess book, audit books, reports, maps, official papers, receipts, bills (/7/1-24). *See list for details.* The prior written permission of Col. Percival is required to consult these papers.

168.101 PERTWEE, Capt. H. G., RN
Bound volume containing copies of all the reports of proceedings and dispatches concerning the operations of the British naval expedition in the Caspian Sea, Oct. 1918 - Sept. 1919, when Paymaster Lt Pertwee was the Commodore's Secretary; published list of merchant ships in the Caspian Sea.

168.102 PHILLIMORE, Adm. Sir Richard Fortescue
Letters home, a diary and 2 photograph albums covering service as Chief of the British Naval Mission to Russia, 1915-16; letters from Capt. F. N. Cromie RN, who was Naval Attaché in Russia, 1918.

168.103 POCOCK, L. C. and Mrs G.
Notebook containing reminiscences of Russia kept by Mrs Pocock, 1914-18, and notebook containing technical and diary notes kept by L. C. Pocock during his First World War service in an Anglo-Russian hospital.

168.104 POND, Maj. B. A.
Memoirs including his service as a signaller with 45th Bn Royal Fusiliers in the North Russia Force.

168.105 RANDOLPH, E.
Memoir including a description of the liberation of his POW camp in Austria by the Russians in Apr. 1945 and his subsequent interrogation in Odessa before being repatriated to England.

168.106 REARDON, C.
Diary, postcards, photographs and other papers re his service in Siberia with the 25th Bn, Middlesex Regt, Aug. 1918 - Apr. 1919.

168.107 REED, W.
Letters to his wife, while serving as PO with A Section of No. 3 Squadron of the RNAS Armoured Cars Section in North Russia and in the Caucasus; album of postcards from Russia.

168.108 RENDEL, F. E.
Over 80 letters, with TS transcripts, to relatives, diary and a few official documents whilst serving as a nurse with the Scottish Women's Hospitals in Russia and the Balkans, 1916-19. *See list for details.*

168.109 RENDEL, Capt. W. V.
Letters, photograph and press cutiings re his service with the North Russian Expeditionary Force, 1918-19. *See list for details.*

168.110 ROBERTS, W. G.
Memoirs including account of service as able seaman in the battleship HMS *Marlborough* in South Russia, 1919, which helped with the evacuation of the Dowager Empress and the Grand Duke Nicholas; TS of article 'Experiences in South Russia and Turkey'.

168.111 ROBERTSHAW, Vice-Adm. Sir Ballin
Microfilm of memoir covering his service on the Anglo-French military mission to Russia, Aug. 1939.

168.112 ROEBER, Capt. W. C. T.
Papers re service with North Russian Expeditionary Force include: diary, 19 Sept. - 5 Dec. 1918; field messages, official and private papers, 10 Sept. 1918 - 14 June 1919; TS copy of memoir 'Archangel with the North Russian Expeditionary Force 1918-1919' by Brig. G. H. Gilmore, 1966. *See list for details.*

168.113 ROSE, R. F.
Memoir of service as a stoker in the Royal Navy, including in the Baltic against possible Russian manoeuvres, 1919-20.

168.114 ROUPELL, Brig. G. R. P.
Microfilm documents include: account of service in North Russia at Obozerskii (/8); 'Private Reflections' on prison life in Moscow, Aug. -Nov. 1919 (/9); diary in prison, Aug. 1919 - Mar. 1920 (/7). *See list for details.*

168.115 RUBBERT, Maj. H.-J.
Letters and postcards to parents while serving with Panzer Regiment 4, 13th Panzer Division, on the Russian front, 30 May 1941 - 13 Mar. 1943.

168.116 RUDD, R.
Copy of a diary covering service in the RAMC attached to "D" Force in North Russia, Sept. 1918 - July 1919.

168.117 RUSSELL, H. V.
Copy of MS diary of his service in the light cruiser HMS *Attentive*, May-Oct. 1918, which was an initial base for the Allied Expeditionary Force in North Russia, and his period of service on the Dvina River Front.

168.118 SAMPSON, A. V. D.
Diary covering service in HMS *Kent*, sent to Vladivostok to help relieve besieged White Russian troops and evacuate refugees, Jan.-Aug. 1919.

168.119 SEDGWICK, Lt H. W.
Photocopy of a brief diary covering his service as an RAOC officer attached to the British Military Mission in South Russia, Sept. 1918 - July 1919.

168.120 SHARP, Capt. P. M.
Brief memoir covering service as an Intelligence Officer in Batum, 1919.

168.121 SHRUBSOLE, Engineer Rear-Adm. P. J.
Photocopies of letters covering service in Allied naval forces in the Black Sea and the Sea of Azov in support of the White Russian army in the Crimea, Mar. - Aug. 1919; TS transl. of a Bolshevik propaganda leaflet distributed to British sailors in 1919.

168.122 SILCOCK, Cdr R. K., RN
Midshipman's journal covering service on the Mediterranean Station, Oct. 1919 - Sept. 1921, including references to the Allied evacuation of South Russia.

168.123 SPICER, Capt. G. E.
Pocket diaries and photograph albums covering service with the 155th Field Ambulance in North Russia, May-Oct. 1919.

168.124 STEMANN, P. E. von
Berlin correspondent of the Danish newspaper *Berlinske Tidende*, 1942-5. Account includes details of his experiences while sheltered by the Russian forces in the final weeks of the war.

168.125 STEWART, Col. C. V.
Brief TS memoir of his service as a liaison officer with the Russian artillery on the Dvina River Front in North Russia, Sept. 1918 - July 1919.

168.126 STRUBEN, Cdr R. F. C., RN
TS memoirs which include his service in the destroyers HMS *Whirlwind* and HMS *Verity* during operations against the Bolsheviks in the Baltic, June-Nov. 1919, and in the auxiliary anti-aircraft ship, HMS *Ulster Queen* escorting the Arctic Convoys PQ15 and PQ12, Apr.-May 1942.

168.127 STURDY, Maj. A. E.
Gen. Ironside's original dispatches and appendices on the North Russian campaign, 1918-19; copy of the GHQ War Diary, 1918-19; letters home; miscellaneous notes on the North Russian campaign.

168.128 SWINLEY, Capt. C. S. B.,RN
Papers re service in light cruiser HMS *Ceres*, used for evacuation of the British Military Mission to the White Russians from Odessa in Feb. 1920.

168.129 TEALE, Maj. J. W.
Album containing papers and cuttings re his service in the Royal Marines at Gallipoli, in France and in North Russia, 1915-19.

168.130 THOMPSON, A. E.
Diary covering service as a wireless operator, RE, with the British forces fighting against the Bolsheviks in the Archangel area, Sept. 1918 - Aug. 1919.

168.131 THOMSON, G. E.
Account of his service with the 2/10th Bn, the Royal Scots, in North Russia, 1918-19.

168.132 THUILLER, Lt-Col. H. S.
Brief account of his service with the Royal Artillery in South Russia, 1919-20.

168.133 TYLER, Cdr T. St V. F.
Diary covers service as 1st Lt of the monitor HMS *Humber* in the Dvina River Flotilla during the final stages of the Allied intervention in North Russia, May-Sept. 1919.

168.134 WALDEN, H. J.
Microfilm of account of his experiences as POW in Germany, 1940-5, and his eventual escape through Eastern Europe and Russia in early 1945 entitled 'A Scar on my Mind'.

168.135 WALLER, A.
Diary with summary entries of his service in Russia with the RNAS Armoured Car Squadron under Frederick Locker-Lampson, 25 June 1917-9 Feb. 1919.

168.136 WATSON, Brig. H. N. G.
Unfinished account of his service as a supply officer to British troops in the Archangel area of Russia in 1917.

168.137 WEDGWOOD, J. C., Baron Wedgwood of Barlaston
Microfilm of letters, newspaper cuttings covering his service in Russia when he was sent on a secret mission to Siberia to report on the political situation, 1918-19, account 'Allied Influence in Russia'. *See list for details.*

168.138 WELLS-HOOD, Lt-Cdr W., RNVR
Copy of a lecture on his service in the RNAS Armoured Car Section in Russia, Dec. 1915 - Dec. 1917.

168.139 WILLIAMSON, A. T.
Autobiography including service in the RN as a stoker with the Mine Clearance Service in the Baltic, 1919-20.

168.140 WILLIAMSON, Brig. H. N. H.
Artillery adviser with the British Military Mission to South Russia, 1919-20. Diary and letters, reports and notes on the campaign in Russia; report on the Lienz affair when former White Russians were returned to the Red Army, 1945.

168.141 WILSON, FM Sir Henry
Papers re the British Military and Political Mission to Petrograd, Jan.-Apr. 1917, and a diary covering the same period, together with correspondence with members of the British Military Mission to South Russia, Oct.-Dec. 1919.

168.142 WILSON, Capt. J. B.
Account of his service with the Royal Engineers in North Russia, photographs and assorted documents, 1918-20.

168.143 WILSON, J. H.
Photocopy of pocket diary with brief entries covering service as PO in No. 3 Squadron of the RNAS Armoured Car Section in Russia, 1915-17, and the Caucasus, 1916.

168.144 WOOD, Maj.-Gen. G. N.
Account of his service as a subaltern on attachment to the Military Mission to the Russian forces fighting under Denikin against the Bolsheviks during the Russian Civil War, 1919-20.

168.145 WOODS, Col. F. J.
Memoirs, telegrams, orders, correspondence, petitions from the Karelians for annexation by the British, maps and photographs re his raising and command of the Karelian Regt and of the Allied forces in Kem' and Karelia, including account of operations against the Bolsheviks.

168.146 WYLD, Capt. H. W., RN
Volume of letters covering his command of HMS *Nereide* in the Black Sea supporting the White Russians against the Bolsheviks, Nov. 1918 - Jan. 1919.

168.147 YOUNGER, Maj.-Gen. J. E. T.
Letters from Moscow as representative of the British Red Cross there, 1945.

168.148 A short history of the 421st Howitzer Battery RFA in North Russia, 1918-19 (**Misc. 114**).

168.149 Joint War Committee notes on the British Red Cross Society and Order of St John in Corfu, Serbia, Montenegro, Salonika, South Russia and Rumania during the First World War (**Misc. 476**).

168.150 Personal account of a man's work with the Red Cross for Russian POWs in Germany following the Armistice in 1945, in camps of which the British assumed control, describing conditions, the prisoners' health and morale, and their attitude towards the Russian Revolution (**Misc. 544**).

168.151 Copy of the ship's log of *Olitchka* (?*Olichka*), a Russian merchant ship which was converted for use as a hospital ship by the North Russian Expeditionary Force and was used for the evacuation of casualties on the Dvina River, June-Sept. 1919 (**Misc. 549**).

168.152 **Department of Photographs**

Concise catalogue indicating classes of documents; card index to campaigns, regiments and individuals.

168.152 There are extensive collections of photographs relating to Russia and the Soviet Union, too numerous to list individually, but the following classes are particularly relevant: **CR** : includes 200 photographs from the Air Ministry re the RAF in Russia; **Q** : a class of 114,000 photographs relating to the First World War, including photographs of the Allied intervention in Russia; **RR** : 1,000 photographs re Russian forces on active service; **RUS** : 3,000 Russian official photographs covering operations and the civilian population. There are also albums of Russian tanks and aircraft, an album re the Russo-Japanese War, official German and Austrian photographs re the Eastern front in the First World War, Finnish photographs of the Winter War, German photographs of the Eastern front in the Second World War, photographs of Russian POWs in Vienna in the Second World War, of supplies to the USSR and of prominent Russian individuals.

168.153-73 **Department of Sound Records**

BBC Sound Archives in the Imperial War Museum. World War 1939-1945; *'The World at War' 1939-1945* (Thames Television Recorded Interviews); also card indexes to places and persons.

168.153 Air Vice-Marshal Bilney recording his experiences in South Russia, 1919 (**000002/08/01-04**). *See Department of Documents, Bilney, 168.12.*

168.154 Recording of experiences of RAF pilot in North Russia, 1918 (**000015/08/05-08**).

168.155 Recording of experiences RNAS observer re bombing operations in Astrakhan', 1918-19 (**000026/05/04**).

168.156 Recording of experiences of RAF pilot in North Russia and as a prisoner in Moscow, 1919 (**000301/07/07**).

168.157 Interview with Miss F. Farmborough, governess to Russian families in Kiev and Moscow, 1908-17 (**000312/17/01-09**).

168.158 Recording of experiences of Basford in HMS *Delhi* of bombardment of Kronstadt, 1919 (**000669/19/17**).

168.159 R. F. Rose broadcasting on the British fleet sent to help the Finns against Russia, 1919 (**000754/13/13**).

168.160 Patrick Curry broadcasting on the reaction to the Soviet intervention in Hungary in 1956 and in Czechoslovakia in 1968 (**000799/03/03**).

168.161 Albert Cole recalling being stationed in Vladivostok, 1928-9 (**000813/04/01,04**).

168.162 Joe Norman recalling touring in the USSR with the World Sports Federation delegation as a boxer, 1932 (**000818/04/01**).

168.163 Dr Lachman, German cavalryman, recalling service on the Russian front, 1915-17 (**004151/01**).

168.164 Recording of Mr Sagovsky on the atmosphere in St Petersburg, 1916-17 (**004221/B/B**).

168.165 Wing Cdr Jenks' recollections of Baku and Novorossiisk, 1918 (**004609/05/03-04**).

BBC recordings include :

168.166 Dispatches from Finland by Edward Ward, 15 Jan. 1940-13/14 Mar. 1940 (**/1014-/1023**).

168.167 Dispatches from the USSR (Moscow, Leningrad, Sebastopol) by Vernon Bartlett, Paul Winterton and Walter Kerr, 1940-42 (**/2111-/2118**).

168.168 Special news bulletins from the USSR, 1941, 1943, 1945 (**/2629, /2646, /2693**).

Recordings from Deutsches Rundfunkarchiv include:

168.169 Speeches of Lenin, 1919-20 (**/5279-/5283, /5292-/5296**).

168.170 Speeches of Trotskii, 1920 (**/5297-/5300**).

168.171 Speeches of Stalin, 1941, 1945 (**/5493, /8166**).

168.172 Recordings re German invasion of the USSR, 1941 (**/8170**), and air attack on Moscow, 1941 (**/8138**).

Recordings from 'The World at War' include :

168.173 Interviews re the USSR by Maj.-Gen. V. Antonov, Z. T. Bokiewicz, C. E. Bohlen, Dr J. Brauning, Dr Rolf Elble, W. Feldheim, A. Harriman, Gen. H. Hinrichs, A. Hiss, Prof. A. Iwanska, V. Klokov, Gen. N. I. Lomov, F. Luft, Gen. H. von Manteuffel, Dr E. Maurer, Gen. W. Nehring, H. Oehmichen, Col. W. Osterholz, C. Ronke, Sir John Russell, O. Rybakov, A. Schimpf, Dr H. Schmidt-Schmiedebach, Prof. G. A. Tokaty, N. Volkov, Gen. W. Warlimont.

169.1-60
INDIA OFFICE LIBRARY AND RECORDS

197 Blackfriars Road, London SE1 8NG

The India Office Library and Records is a Department of the British Library Reference Division. It holds the records of the East India Company (1600-1858), the Board of Control (1784-1858), the Burma Office (1937-48) and the India Office (1858-1947). This is the largest archive of public records in the United Kingdom relating to the Russian threat to northern India and Afghanistan, Russian Central Asia and the Caucasus. W. Forster, *Guide to the India Office Records, 1600-1858* (1919; reprinted 1961, 1966); J. C. Lancaster, *A Guide to Lists and Catalogues of the India Office Records* (London, 1966); J. C. Lancaster, 'The India Office Records', *Archivum*, XV (1965), revised form in *Archives*, IX, no. 43 (April 1970). A new *Brief Guide to the India Office Records* by M. I. Moir is under preparation and will supersede the earlier general guides. The Library and Records have produced leaflets describing some of the collections.

Public Records

Public records are covered in the guides listed above. Printed indexes and registers are available for some series of records. Manuscript indexes have been brought together to form the series Registers and Indexes, 1702-1950 (6,165 vols). The indexes in this series are arranged by the series to which they belong and have the same series mark as the series, prefixed by the letter Z. There will almost certainly be material relating to Russia in the following records which are listed by date only: Records of General Committees and Offices, 1700-1873 (**D**) (253 vols); General Correspondence, 1602-1859 (**E**) (1,597 vols); Board of Control, 1784-1858 (**F**) (2,860 vols). The manuscript registers and indexes for these series should indicate whether Russian and Soviet material exists. Records relating to Russia and the USSR are most extensive in the series Political and Secret (**P/L & S**) which for clarity of description has been subdivided.

169.1 COUNCIL OF INDIA (C)
The minutes of the Council of India, 1858-1942, (123 vols) are listed by date only in *India Office Records: C. Council of India*. A list of memoranda dealt with by the Council includes memoranda on Central Asia, 1874-5, 1878-9, (**/137-8, /141-2**), Russian Turkestan, 1874, 1877, 1879, (**/137, /140/ 142**) and Armenia and the Trans-Caspia, 1879, (**/139**), and these and similar issues are likely to be covered in the minutes.

169.2 ECONOMIC (L/E)
The series Commerce and Revenue Papers, 1921-4, (**L/E/7/1083-1171**) includes papers on commercial treaties between England and Latvia during the latter's period of independence (**/1086**) and a report by Sir Aurel Stein on his 3rd Central Asian expedition

of 1923 (**/1166**). The series Industries and Overseas Department Papers, 1921-4, (**L/E/7/1172-1322**) includes papers on Russian and Armenian refugees.

169.3 FACTORY RECORDS (G)

Series G/29 is described in *Factory Records, Persia and the Persian Gulf c. 1620-1822* by L. A. Hall. There is one reference to Russia; a letter from Sir Harford Jones at Baghdad re the wish of Russia to reach an accommodation with Persia, 20 Dec. 1806 (**/32 ff. 539-59**).

169.4 HOME MISCELLANEOUS SERIES, 1600-1900 (H)

Artificial series (847 vols) of documents from many other series. Subject index in S. C. Hill, *Catalogue of the Home Miscellanous Series* (1927) includes references to Russian-Persian relations, 1804 and 1857, and to Georgia, 1801 and 1810.

169.5 INFORMATION, 1921-47 (L/I)

Series of 149 boxes and 146 boxes of films includes material on Soviet propaganda and publicity in India and the BBC Russian broadcasts, 1946 (**/946**) and the Red Army Day celebration, 1943-4 (**/1099**) and a 'Guidance on relations with Russia', 1943 (**/1100**).

169.6 MILITARY, 1718-1948 (L/MIL)

Series of 8,736 vols and 4,500 boxes. The series are listed in A. Farrington, *Guide to the Records of the India Office Military Department* (1982), which also lists the war diaries in full. The series Compilations and Miscellaneous (**L/MIL/5**) includes: the order of the battle of the Army of the Black Sea, 1920 (**/811**); papers re the Caucasus and Central Asia, *c.* 1918-20 (**/378(32), /808, /810**); copy memo by Col. Kono, Japanese General Staff, on a proposed Anglo-Japanese intervention in Siberia, 1918 (**/743**). The series Departmental Papers, Military Collections (**L/MIL/7**) includes material on the Russian scare of 1885 (**/7261-5**) and the Bolshevik threat to the North-East Frontier, 1927 (**/19395**). The series Military Department Library (**L/MIL/17**) includes a collection of notes from war diaries relating to the campaign in the Caucasus, 1918-19 (**/17/5**), which are accompanied by a selection of maps referred to in the diaries (**/5/3892**). There may be further references to Russia and the Soviet Union in other series which are listed by date alone, in particular: Home Correspondence, 1830-81, (**L/MIL/2**); Correspondence with India, 1803-1937, (**L/MIL/3**); Military Department Internal Papers, 1858-1957, (**L/MIL/4**); Departmental Papers: Military Correspondence, 1882-1948 (**L/MIL/6**). The appropriate MS registers and indexes can be found under the series mark **Z/L/MIL** in the published Indexes and Registers.

169.7 PARLIAMENTARY BRANCH PAPERS (L/PARL)

Series (510 vols) includes: agreement with Russia as to the northern boundary of Afghanistan (**/2/88**); parliamentary papers on Central Asia, 1864-88 (**/2/88, 182-3**); paper re the agreement with Russia over the Pamirs, 1895 (**/2/284**); convention with Russia on Persia, Afghanistan and Tibet, 1907 (**/334**).

169.8-14 POLITICAL AND SECRET, 1778-1950 (L/P & S)

Series of 5,800 vols and 880 boxes consisting of archives accumulated in London by the administration of the Political and Secret committees or departments of the India Office, the Board of Control and the India Office. M. A. Moir, *A Study of the History and Organization of the Political and Secret Department of the East India Company, the Board of Control and the India Office, 1784-1919, with a Summary List of Records* (submitted as part requirement of the University of London Diploma in Archive Administration, 1966, and available in the Library); TS, *A Summary List of India Office Records P & S*. A new *Guide* to the Political and Secret Records is under preparation.

The political and secret records are listed and indexed unevenly, with detailed TS lists for the period 1912-50 only. The following series probably contain material relating to Russia but are listed by date only in the *Summary List*: Court and Committee Minutes, 1778-1867 (**L/P & S/1**); Board of Control: Secret Minutes, Political Pre-Coms and Drafts, 1785-1858 (**L/P & S/2**); Secret, Political and Foreign Correspondence with India: abstracts and notes, 1784-1858 (**L/P & S/4**); Political Correspondence with India, 1792-1874 (**L/P & S/6**); Political and Secret Correspondence with India, 1875-1911 (**L/P & S/7**); Demi-Official Correspondence, Secretary's Letters and Telegrams, 1862-1912 (**L/P & S/8**); Correspondence relating to areas outside India, 1781-1911 (**L/P & S/9**).

Specific references to Russia and the Soviet Union can be found in the following Political and Secret records:

169.8 HOME CORRESPONDENCE, 1807-1911 (L/P & S/3)
Primarily correspondence between the Home Government of India and other British Government Departments (notably the Foreign Office). The records include a section on Central Asia (/75), and there is extensive further material on Russia in the records which are indexed by date alone.

169.9 DEPARTMENTAL PAPERS: POLITICAL AND SECRET SUBJECT FILES, 1901-31 (L/P & S/10)
TS descriptions of contents of each volume. Records include volumes re the following: Russia's relations with Britain (/9, /10, /122, /125, /450, /455, /1108), with Afghanistan (/126, /141-2, /226, /315, /1116), with Persia (/450, /455, /1021, /1038, /1072, /1282) and with Tibet (/102); Central Asia (/16, /54, /741, /1032); Russia in the First World War (/526, /593); Bolshevik activities in Central Asia and Afghanistan, 1918-24 (/836-7); the Soviet threat to India, 1925-34 (/1152). *See Summary List for details.*

169.10 DEPARTMENTAL PAPERS: POLITICAL AND SECRET ANNUAL FILES, 1912-30 (L/P & S/11)
Extensive material re Russia and the USSR including Russia's relations with other powers (Asian and European), Central Asia and the Caucasus and Russian internal policies and problems. Papers are particularly numerous for the period 1918-20 and relate to the independence movements in the states of the Caucasus and Trans-Caspia, the movements of White and Red troops in the Civil War, the Allied intervention in South Russia and the victory of the Red Army. After this date the amount of material relating to Russia decreases but there are papers concerning Russian refugees, Anglo-Soviet relations and Bolshevik propaganda and intrigue. *See TS bound list of sets of papers in this series for details.*

169.11 DEPARTMENTAL PAPERS: POLITICAL EXTERNAL FILES AND COLLECTIONS, c. 1931-50 (L/P & S/12)
External files include papers re the USSR's foreign relations, internal policies and Allied policy towards the USSR during the Second World War. The Collections, 1922-50, (/4003-47) include collections on Russia relating to Soviet foreign relations, propaganda and internal policies, British subjects in the USSR, British Embassy and Foreign Office reports on the USSR, Central Asia and refugees. There is also material relating to the USSR in collections relating to Aden, Afghanistan, Aircraft and Aviation, Arabia, China, Chinese Turkestan, Communism, India, Japan, League of Nations, North West Frontier, Pakistan, Persia, Postal and Wireless, Routes, Telegraphs, Travellers, Turkey and War. *See TS bound list of vols of papers in this series for details.*

169.12 CONSUL PAPERS, 1885-1930 (L/P & S/16)
Vol., 'Russia: Consul-General at Bombay, September 1905 to February 1906' (/1).

169.13 POLITICAL AND SECRET MEMORANDA (L/P & S/18)

Subject index cites references to Russian and Soviet foreign relations, the frontier with Afghanistan, Russian advances in Central Asia, the Trans-Caspia and Trans-Caucasia railways, reports of secret agents in Afghanistan, India and Turkestan relating to Russia, Bolshevism and the Soviet system of government. Section C deals specifically with Central Asia and Persia and consists of 221 sets of memoranda, 1859-1946. *See TS subject index for details.*

169.14 POLITICAL AND SECRET DEPARTMENT LIBRARY (L/P & S/20)

Mainly printed books. Also, sets of papers re Russian foreign relations and the visit of Col. Stoddart and Capt. A. Conolly to Bukhara, 1844-5 (/A.7), military reports on Russian Turkestan, 1911, 1914 (/A.107, /A.117(1)), photographs of the Russian Pamirs, 1915 (/A.119), reports on the British Military Mission to South Russia, 1919 (/A.123(4)) and various Foreign Office correspondence and memoranda re Russia and Central Asia. *See TS index for details.*

169.15 PRIVATE OFFICE PAPERS, *c.* 1916-47 (L/PO)

Series of 26 vols and 470 boxes. There are no specific references to Russia or the USSR in the TS guide but there are papers on the defence of India, 1927-47, and correspondence concerning communists, 1928-38, both of which could refer to the USSR.

169.16 PROCEEDINGS OF THE GOVERNMENT OF INDIA AND OF PRESIDENCIES AND PROVINCES, 1702-1936 (P)

Class of 46,324 vols comprising the copies of proceedings or consultations of the presidents and councils of individual provinces which were sent to London (summaries only of routine administration from 1860). Records are listed in *List of Proceedings: India, Bengal, Bombay, Madras, Burma and Other Administrations, 1834-1936* 3 vols, and *List of Proceedings etc.: North-Western Provinces and Other Minor Administrations, 1834-99.* There are no subject headings in these indexes but material relating to Russia and the USSR will be found in the sections entitled 'India: Foreign Proceedings'.

169.17 RESIDENCIES, CONSULS AND AGENTS (OUTSIDE INDIA) (R)

The records of the British Legation in Afghanistan, 1923-48, (R/12) (21 boxes) are listed in L. A. Hall, *A Brief Guide to Sources for the Study of Afghanistan in the India Office Records* (1981), and include papers of the Soviet Union in general, and in particular on refugees, Soviet intrigue and propaganda, Soviet-Afghanistan relations and trade and agricultural agreements in the 1930s and 1940s. The guide *Political Residency and Agencies in the Persian Gulf* by P. Tusan (1979) covers the class R/15 and includes an abstract of correspondence re Russian proceedings on the Island of Ashurada, 1837-54, and correspondence on Russo-Persian relations, 1854-75 (/1/704).

169.18 WAR STAFF, 1939-46 (L/WS)

Series of 200 boxes. Papers are listed in A. Farington, *Guide to the Records of the India Office Military Department* (1982). Records include papers re the following: the Russian threat to India, 1939-40 (/1415); Russian relations with India (/12350), Persia (/12545B) and the Middle East (/18353); supplies of equipment to the USSR, 1941-2, 1944 (/15023; /2/84); the USSR in general, 1947-9 (/17161).

Private Papers

The Orme and Mackenzie collections have separate catalogues; other collections acquired up to 1937 are described in G. R. Kaye and E. H. Johnson, *European Manuscripts in the India Office Library*, vol. 2 part 2, *Minor Collections and Miscellaneous Manuscripts* (1937). Private papers acquired since 1937 can be found in the card catalogue in the Library and Records. A summary list can be found in the pamphlet *Accession of Private Collections 1937-1977*. Handlists and catalogues are available for some collections. There may be further references to Russia and the USSR in collections which are not listed or where the handlist lists material by date alone.

169.19 BAILEY COLLECTION (MSS.Eur.F.157)
Papers of Lt-Col. Frederick Marshman Bailey (1882-1967) include: letters written from Russia (/171) and Tashkent (/179); TS Russian diary, 1918-19 (/209); diaries of journeys from Kashgar to Tashkent and from Bukhara to Meshed, 1918-20 (/210); Russian vocabularies, correspondence and other documents while in Turkestan (/276); notebooks of events in Tashkent and Bukhara; papers re Austrian POWs in Russia; drafts and TS of *Mission to Tashkent*; maps of Russia and Central Asia.

169.20 CHARLES BELL COLLECTION (MSS.Eur.F.80)
Papers of Sir Charles Alfred Bell (1878-1945), Tibetan scholar, include his advice on Tibetan policy and Russian relations, Soviet treaties, 1921-5, and the Anglo-Russian agreement of 1907.

169.21 BIRDWOOD COLLECTION (MSS.Eur.D.686)
Papers of FM Sir William Riddell Birdwood (1865-1951), 1st Baron Birdwood of Anzac and Totnes, include: Kitchener-Curzon correspondence re Russian activities of the Afghan frontier, Mar. 1904 (/4); memo by Gen. Sir Beauchamp Duff on the dispatch of troops from England in the event of war with Russia, May 1906 (/39); secret memo by Horatio H. Kitchener, Lord Kitchener, on the effect of the Anglo-Russian convention, Oct. 1907 (/41); secret note by Col. Sir Arthur McMahon re possible Russian invasion of India, Sept. 1907 (/46).

169.22 BURNE, Sir Owen Tudor (1837-1909) (MSS.Eur.D.951)
Papers as Secretary of the Political and Secret Department include memos and minutes on Russia and Central Asia, 1874-86 (/24).

169.23 CAROE COLLECTION (MSS.Eur.F.203)
Papers of Sir Olaf Kirkpatrick Caroe (1892-1981), Governor of the North West Frontier Province, 1946-7, inlcude drafts and correspondence re his book *Soviet Empire: The Turks of Central Asia and Stalinism* (1953) and other writings about Russian policy in Central Asia and Afghanistan.

169.24 CHELMSFORD COLLECTION (MSS.Eur.E.264)
Papers of Frederic John Napier Thesiger, 1st Visc. Chelmsford, (1868-1933) as Viceroy of India include reports on the situation in the Caspian, Trans-Caspia and the Caucasus (/54).

169.25 CLERK COLLECTION (MSS.Eur.D.538)
Papers of Sir George Russell Clerk (1800-89) include a notebook containing comments on Russia (/6).

169.26 CUNNINGHAM COLLECTION (**MSS.Eur.D.670**)
Papers of Sir George Cunningham (1888-1964) include a duplicated copy of an analysis of Soviet publications on Kashmir and the North West Frontier by Sir Olaf Caroe, 1957 (**/33**) (**MSS.Eur.D.670**).

169.27 CURZON COLLECTION (**MSS.Eur.F.111**)
Papers of George Nathaniel Curzon, Marquis Curzon of Kedleston (1859-1925) as Viceroy in India, 1899-1905, include: MS of a paper on British and Russian commercial competition in Central Asia, 1889 (**/20**); papers re Russia, the frontiers and Central Asia (**section 2**); printed reports on Russia in Asia (**section 4**).

169.28 DAVIDSON, William Alexander (1830-85) (**MSS.Eur.A.127**)
Surgeon. Papers include notes on travels in the Crimea.

169.29 DE BRETEL, Michel Henri Fabus (d. 1796) (**MSS.Eur.F.193**)
Indigo planter. Papers include proposed route to be taken by the Russians to enter India, presented to the Tsar of Russia, n.d. (**/104**).

169.30 ELGIN COLLECTIONS (**MSS.Eur.F.84**)
Papers of Victor Alexander Bruce, 9th Earl of Elgin, (1849-1917) as Viceroy and Governor-General of India include a map delimiting the Russian and Afghan territories in the Pamirs, 1895 (**/132**).

169.31 ELPHINSTONE COLLECTION (**MSS.Eur.F.88**)
Papers of the Hon. Mountstuart Elphinstone (1779-1859) include notes on the invasion of India by the Russians (**/2 no. 25**) and notes on Central Asia (**/13**).

169.32 HAMILTON COLLECTION (**MSS.Eur.F.123**)
Papers of Lord George Francis Hamilton (1845-1927) as Secretary of State for India include papers on Russia, 1901 (**/47**) and on the Russia sanitary cordon in Persia, 1902 (**/58**).

169.33 KEYES COLLECTION (**MSS.Eur.F.131**)
Papers of Brig.-Gen. Sir Terence Humphrey Keyes (1877-1939) include: photograph album 'Journey in Russian Turkestan ... ', 1904; letters, papers and photographs from his service in South Russia, 1917-20; lectures on Bolshevism.

169.34 KILBRACKEN COLLECTION (**MSS.Eur.F.102**)
Papers of Sir Arthur Godley, 1st Baron Kilbracken of Killegar, (1847-1932) as Permanent Under-Secretary of State for India include interviews with Mr Notovich, correspondent of *Novoe vremya* and notes by Sir D. Mackenzie Wallace, 1887 (**/54, /56a**).

169.35 JOHN LAWRENCE COLLECTION (**MSS.Eur.F.90**)
Papers of Lawrence (1811-79) as Viceroy and Governor-General of India include official papers, mainly re Central Asia (**/71**).

169.36 LEE-WARNER COLLECTION (**MSS.Eur.F.92**)
Papers of Sir William Lee-Warner (1846-1914) as Member of the Council of India include printed convention between Britain and Russia concerning Persia, Afghanistan and Tibet, signed 31 Aug. 1907 (**/21**).

169.37 LINLITHGOW COLLECTION (**MSS.Eur.F.125**)
Papers of Victor Alexander John Hope, 2nd Marquis of Linlithgow, (1887-1952) as
Viceroy and Governor-General of India include maps of the Soviet Front and of Germany
and the USSR, 1941 (**/173**).

169.38 LYALL COLLECTION (**MSS.Eur.F.132**)
Papers of Sir Alfred Comyn Lyall (1835-1911) include: papers on Central Asia and
England and Russia in Asia, 1881-1907 (**/36-7**); memos and correspondence on
Anglo-Russian treaties, 1881, 1908 (**/61**); articles on Russia (**/133-4**).

169.39 THE MACKENZIE COLLECTIONS
Papers of Lt-Col. Colin Mackenzie include a reference to extracts, apparently translated
from Dutch, from *North and East Tartary* referring to treasures in Siberia and the Volga
area, a tomb near Astrakhan and petrified wood from Sumatra (**86.1**). C. O. Blagen,
European Manuscripts in the India Office Library, vol. 1, part 1: *The Mackenzie
Collections.*

169.40 McMAHON, Col. Sir Arthur Henry (1862-1949) (**MSS.Eur.B.228**)
Papers include notes on the effect on Afghanistan of an attempted Russian invasion, 1907
(**p. 7**).

169.41 MOORCROFT COLLECTION (**MSS.Eur.C.68-9; MSS.Eur.D.236-54,
256**)
Diaries of William Moorcroft (?1765-1825), veterinary surgeon and superintendent of the
East India Company, covering travels to Leh, Dras, Kashmir and Bukhara.

169.42 MORLEY COLLECTION (**MSS.Eur.D.573**)
Papers of John Morley, Visc. Morley of Blackburn, (1838-1923) as Secretary of State for
India include: letters from Sir Alfred Lyall to Morley re Afghanistan and Russia, 1906 (**/47
f. 1**); printed papers re the Anglo-Russian convention, 1906-7 (**/255**).

169.43 NAPIER COLLECTION (**MSS.Eur.F.114**)
Papers of Robert Cornelius Napier, 1st Baron Napier of Magdala and Carynton (1810-90)
as C.-in-C. in India include political reports and correspondence on the Russian position
in Central Asia, 1873 (**/5/30**).

169.44 THE ORME COLLECTION
'Extracts from letters from Gombroon, 27 January 1752 - 22 June 1753' include a letter
mentioning a report that the Russians have opened a trade in woollen goods between
Astrakhan and Organge (**211.2**). S. C. Hill, *European Manuscripts in the India Office
Library*, vol. 2, part 1: *The Orme Collection* (1916).

169.45 SHEIL, Sir Justin (**MSS.Eur.D.645**)
Papers include material on the mission to Bukhara to recover prisoners undertaken by Dr
Joseph Wolffe.

169.46 VIBART COLLECTION (**MSS.Eur.F.135**)
Papers of Col. Henry Meredith Vibart (1839-1917) include diary of the Russo-Turkish
War, 1877-8 (**/41**).

169.47 GEORGE WHITE COLLECTION (**MSS.Eur.F.108**)
Papers of FM Sir George Stuart White (1835-1912) include notes on defence against
Russian aggression, 1890-1 (**/15**). Letters from James White to his father and sister from
the Crimea, 1855-6 (**/117**).

169.48 'Mr Forster's Rout from Jumboo, in the Northern Mountains of Hindustan, to Astracan in Russia', referring to the journey of 1783-4 and similar to his later published work (**MSS.Eur.B.14**).

169.49 'Routes in Azerbaijan, Kurdistan and Armenia', 1811-29, by W. Monteith (**MSS.Eur.B.24**).

169.50 'Journal of a Tour through Azerbijan and the Shores of the Caspian', 1838-9, being a draft of the paper given to the Royal Society by W. Monteith (**MSS.Eur.B.25**).

169.51 Diary of Capt. Arthur Conolly and letters and extracts from his journal of a journey to Bukhara, 1842 (**MSS.Eur.B.29**).

169.52 Letter from Sir Harold George Grey, Visc. Howick, to Lord John Russell criticising the fears of George Eden, Lord Auckland, of Russian and Persian activities in Afghanistan, 8 Oct. 1838 (**MSS.Eur.B.198**).

169.53 Letter from William Wilberforce Bird to William Butterworth re the fear of Russian influence in Persia (**MSS.Eur.B.234**).

169.54 2 letters re *Travels in Bokhara* (London, 1834) by Sir Alexander Burnes (**MSS.Eur.B.256**).

169.55 Diaries of Maj. Ronald Sinclair (pseud.) as political agent in the Trans-Caspia, 1918-19 (**MSS.Eur.C.313**). Collection closed.

169.56 Typed folios of Capt. A. Conolly's diary covering journey to Bukhara, 1842 (**MSS.Eur.D.161**).

169.57 Confidential file containing correspondence and draft memos on Afghanistan, with particular reference to the Russian attack on Panjdeh, 1885 (**Photo.Eur.28**).

Maps

A Catalogue of Manuscript and Printed Reports,Field Books, Memoirs, Maps etc. of the Indian Surveys, Deposited in the Map Room of the India Office (1878). There is an amended, annotated copy of this catalogue in the Library and Records and a fuller list is under progress. A leaflet produced by the India Office Library and Records, *Guide to the Map Collection* provides an introduction to the collection.

169.58 'Map of Parts of Georgia and Armenia etc' by Lt-Col. W. Monteith, including a letter from Monteith forwarding a plan of the frontier between Russia and Persia as defined in 1829 (**MS 33**).

169.59 'A Sketch of a Journey from Heraut to Khiva and St Petersburgh', 1839-40, by Capt. J. Abbott (**MS 38**).

169.60 'Tabular Route from Khiva to Dusht Kulla, taken by Lt R. C. Shakespeare [Shakespear] with the Russian Prisoners' (**MS 39**).

170.1
INSTITUTE OF EDUCATION LIBRARY

Institute of Education, University of London, 11-13 Ridgmount Street, London WC1E 7AH

170.1 HANS COLLECTION
Books, papers and correspondence of Dr Nicholas Hans (1888-1969), born in Odessa, Reader in Comparative Education at King's College, London; writer on Russian and European education. Papers include: drafts of articles and books including references to Russia (**NH1**); drafts of unpublished works including 'Notes on educational reform in Poland and Russia in the Eighteenth Century' (**NH2/8**); notes on lectures etc. while at Novorossiisk University, 1907-12, Russian (**NH3/1**); folder of loose notes and papers re Russia and the USSR, English and Russian (**NH3/2/1**); correspondence with the Association of Russian Educational Organisations in Exile, 1925, Pedagogic Bureau for Russian Elementary and Primary Education in Exile, 1925, Professor D. Katsarov, 1958, Professor A. Florovskii, 1959, 1963, Professor I. A. Kairov and others mainly re academic matters, mostly in Russian (**NH4**); folder of early papers, permits and certificates, 1906-22, mostly in Russian (**NH5/1**). For details of correspondence, see *In memoriam Nicholas Hans* (Education Libraries Bulletin Supplement 19) (London, 1975).

171.1
ISLINGTON LIBRARIES DEPARTMENT

Finsbury Reference Library, 245 St John Street, London EC1V 4NB

171.1 Album of goodwill from the women of Moscow to the women of London, 1942.

KING'S COLLEGE, LONDON

See Liddell Hart Centre for Military Archives, King's College, London.

172.1-25
THE LABOUR PARTY ARCHIVE

144-152 Walworth Road, London SE17 1JT

By appointment. Research fees for users; members of the Labour Party or a Party affiliated to the Socialist International have free access. Detailed TS handlists cover many series. A pamphlet, *Labour Party: Guide to the Archives* gives an introduction to the holdings of the Archive. Documents are closed for 15 years.

Advisory Committees

172.1 ADVISORY COMMITTEE ON INTERNATIONAL QUESTIONS (**LP/IAC**)
Appeals, correspondence, memos, pamphlets, statements and resolutions re the USSR including re intervention, the blockade of the USSR, the famine, Soviet foreign relations

and internal conditions and the Ukraine, 1918-22. *See card index of questions, 1920-38, for details and further information.*

General Secretaries Papers

172.2 A. HENDERSON PAPERS (LP/HEN)
Papers of Arthur Henderson include: letters from Petrograd re the Russian situation to R. W. Raine, T. W. Dowson, G. H. Roberts, Sir Charles W. Starmer, 1917 (**/1/28-32**); letters re his desire to go on a mission to Russia, 1929 (**/1/47-58**); press cuttings re Russian situation (**/14/2, 6**); MS poems re Petrograd (**/14/3-4**); anon. memo 'England and the Russian Revolution' (**/14/7**). Papers of William W. Henderson include Labour Party memo re members who supported Soviet aggression in Finland, 20 Mar. 1940 (**/15/13-14**) and memo by Hugh Dalton of conversation with John Gunther on the Russian situation, Sept. 1939 (**/16/1**). *See handlist for details.*

172.3 J.S. MIDDLETON PAPERS (LP/JSM)
Papers of James Smith Middleton (1878-1962), General Secretary, 1934-44, include: correspondence re the Zinoviev letter (**/ACP/11-17; /ZI/1**); letter from Newcastle West Labour Party with resolution condemning the request for freeing British prisoners in the USSR, Apr. 1933 (**CP/18-20**); memo by the Voters' Council opposing alleged nationalization of women in Bolshevik Russia, Mar. 1919 (**WOR/10-13**). *See handlist for details.*

172.4 M. PHILLIPS PAPERS (GS/INT)
General Secretary, 1944-62. 3 boxes of reports, correspondence, memos, printed material and press cuttings re delegation to Moscow and China, 1954; file of correspondence re the USSR, 1940s-50s. Papers in the process of being sorted.

International Department (LP/ID)

172.5 ANCILLARY ORGANISATIONS OF THE COMMUNIST INTERNATIONAL, 1926-40 (LP/ID/CI/1-74)
Papers re the Friends of Soviet Russia, 1928-39, n.d., and the National Congress of Peace and Friendship with the USSR, 1935-7, n.d.; speeches by A. Lozovskii and G. E. Zinov'ev; newspapers cuttings re the USSR and from Soviet newspapers, 1926, 1934. *See handlist for details and further references.*

172.6 WILLIAM GILLIES CORRESPONDENCE (LP/WG)
Papers of William Gillies (1885-1958), first International Secretary of the Labour Party, 1920-44, include: papers re Palestine including re persecution of Zionist Socialists in the USSR, 1932 (**PAL/2-5**); papers re peace include memo and notes re Russia (**PCE/50-4, 95**); papers on Poland include correspondence re the Ukrainian minority in Poland, 1930-3 (**/POL/17-20**). Box of papers re Russia (**Box 9**) includes correspondence re the following: USSR in general, 1921, 1926, 1931-9, including re the visit of the Webbs to the USSR, the expulsion of Trotskii from France, cultural relations between Britain and the USSR, applications for British nationality, Soviet trade and industry, religious persecution and living conditions in the USSR, (**/RUS/1-109, /181-231**); Eva, Daniel and Mary Broido, 1935-41 (**/RUS/110-38**); the Moscow Trials, 1935-8 (**RUS/139-60**); the disappearance of Marc Rein, 1937-8 (**/RUS/161-80**); Professor G. V. Lomonosoff, 1930-1 (**/RUS/232-44**); Peter Petroff, 1934-6 (**RUS/245-57**); the Ukraine, 1932-5 (**UKR/1-11**). *See handlist for details.*

172.7 LITHUANIA, 1942-46 **(LP/ID Box 4)**
Letters from displaced Lithuanians, 1945, and correspondence re émigrés; memos re
Lithuanian co-operatives under Soviet and German occupation and the Lithuanian Social
Revolutionary Party delegation; joint declaration of the Lithuanian Political Parties and
Combat Organizations, 1944.

172.8 PAPERS ON THE INTERNATIONAL SITUATION **(LP/ID/INT)**
Letter from Adam Ciolkosz enclosing memo on Polish-Russian relations, 23 July 1941
(/12/3).

172.9 POLITICAL REFUGEES IN LITHUANIA (POLISH), 1940 **(LP/ID
Box 5)**
Correspondence re refugees.

172.10 RUSSIA, 1940-5 **(LP/ID Box 6)**
Summary of transmissions from Radio Moscow, 1940-5; correspondence re 'Help for
Russia Fund', 1919-42; note on Polish-Russian relations, 1941; papers re the USSR at war
including re deportees and refugees, the Anglo-Soviet Friendship Committee, the Soviet
TUC delegation to Britain, Soviet loans and exports and general correspondence, 1939-44;
correspondence, telegrams and statement re delegation to the USSR, 1942-5; 'Forty Two
Days in the Soviet Union' by J. Parker, 1945.

172.11 RUSSIAN FILES **(LP/ID/RUS)**
Reports by A. F. Kerenskii on international questions and the economic situation in
Russia, Jan. 1920 **(/KER/1-2)**; reports from the Kuban', the Don, the Ukraine, the Crimea,
Siberia and north-west Russia during the Russian Civil War, Denikin's system of
government and treatment of the Jews and statements by Russian Social Democrats
(/RCW/1-29); D. Sokolov's documents on conditions in post-revolutionary Russia
(/SOK/1-12); originals and translations of P. Tomskii's speeches at the XIVth Party
Congress **(/TOM/1-12)**; *Isvestiya* reports of the XIVth Party Congress **(/14C/1-5)**. Papers,
correspondence, report and printed material re the trial of members of the Socialist
Revolutionary Party in Moscow, 1922 **(/SRP/1-122)**. *See handlist for details.*

International Department Papers post 1945

172.12 ARMENIA, 1946 **(LP/ID Box 1)**
Correspondence re the Armenian Socialist Party.

172.13 BALTIC STATES, 1950-63
1 file of material re the Baltic States.

172.14 ESTONIA, 1946-7 **(LP/ID Boxes 1, 6)**
Papers re the Estonian Socialist Association in Sweden; official Soviet data on Estonian
agriculture; memos re deportations, Estonian agricultural exports and the Baltic States in
general.

172.15 FINLAND, 1946 **(LP/ID Box 2)**
Memo, 'The Carelian Question and the Peace Negotiations'.

172.16 DENIS HEALEY ARTICLES, 1946 **(LP/ID Box 3)**
TS memo, 'Russian Foreign Policy'.

172.17 HUNGARY - UPRISING
1 box of Labour Party circulars, memos, pamphlets and statements re the 1956 uprising.

172.18 LITHUANIA, 1946 (**LP/ID Box 4**)
List of and correspondence re displaced Lithuanian Social Democrats.

172.19 RUSSIA, 1946-7 (**LP/ID Boxes 4, 9**)
Newspaper cuttings and survey of the Soviet press and radio; extract from 'Russia and the Labour Party' by W. W. Miller; 'Nuremberg and the Moscow Trials'; general correspondence.

172.20 UKRAINE, 1954-6
1 file of material re the Ukraine.

172.21 USSR, 1949-64
7 boxes of material including: general correspondence; memos on Soviet foreign policy, Cominform, Soviet education, theatre, labour camps, living conditions, trade unions, collectivization, science and other topics; papers re the visit to the USSR by H. Gaitskell in 1959 and H. Wilson in 1964; papers re the dinner speech of Khrushchev and responses from members of the Labour Party and local Labour Parties, Apr. 1956.

Labour Party Subject Files

172.22 HAROLD LASKI CORRESPONDENCE, 1938-50 (**LP/LAS**)
Draft report and letters re visit to the USSR, 1946 (**/38/45-7**).

172.23 RUSSIA (**LP/RU/18, 21**
Correspondence re military intervention, 1918-19 (**/18/1-8**); correspondence and papers re resumption of trading facilities with Russia, May 1920 (**/18/9-11**); resolutions re Russian situation from local Labour Parties, Apr. - May 1919 (**/18/12-93**); file of miscellaneous correspondence re USSR including re famine relief, newspaper reporting of Soviet affairs, political trials and the 'Help for Russia Fund', 1921, 1935-8, 1941-3 (**/21/1-23**). *See handlist for details.*

Special Collections

172.24 COUNCIL OF ACTION (**LP/CA**)
Formed 9 Aug. 1920 to oppose the intervention in Russia in 1920. Administrative papers, correspondence, memos, minutes etc., Aug. 1920 (**/ADM/1-58**); papers on a special conference to obtain a mandate for the Council of Action, Aug. 1920 (**/CON/1-76**); foreign correspondence and papers, Dec. 1917 - Nov. 1920, including correspondence with Krassin, All Russian Central Council of Trade Unions delegation, the Polish Socialist Party, sympathisers in Berlin, Prague, Antwerp, Rotterdam and elsewhere, draft proposals for peace, resolutions (**/FOR/1-116**); general correspondence with local Councils of Action and individual sympathisers, July 1920 - Aug. 1921 (**/GEN/1-1132**); memoranda of resolutions, reports and instructions to local Councils of Action, meetings, press coverage and Russo-Polish relations, 1920 and n.d. (**/MEM/1-47**).

172.25 LABOUR AND SOCIALIST INTERNATIONAL (**LSI**
Correspondence, memos, speeches and resolutions re the USSR including correspondence with individual Russians, the Russian Socialist Revolutionary Party and Soviet and Estonian delegations, papers re the Union for the Regeneration of Russia, the Mensheviks, the Georgian and Ukrainian Social Democratic Parties, the nationality question in the USSR, the Allied intervention and the Baltic States, 1918-23, 1939. *See handlist for details and further references.*

173.1-27
LAMBETH PALACE LIBRARY

Lambeth Palace Road, London SE1 7JU

By appointment for *bona fide* researchers on production of a letter of introduction. H. J. Todd, *A Catalogue of the Archiepiscopal Manuscripts in the Library at Lambeth Palace* (London, 1812); E. G. W. Bill, *A Catalogue of Manuscripts in Lambeth Palace Library MSS 1222-1860, 1907-2340, 2341-3119*, 3 vols (London, 1972-83). Published catalogues and TS lists of papers of archbishops, bishops and the Society for the Propagation of the Gospel; further lists under preparation. Archbishops' papers are subject to the thirty year ruling.

Manuscript Collections

173.1 ANGLO-CONTINENTAL SOCIETY PAPERS (MSS 2908-25)
Account of the Russian Orthodox Church, and in particular the Holy Synod, *c.* 1915-20 (MS 2912 ff.298-331).

173.2 BISHOP OF FULHAM PAPERS (MSS 1847-60)
Photographs of and notes on the English Church in Moscow, *c.* 1950. (MS 1860 ff.130-3).

173.3 EELES COLLECTION (MSS 1501-51)
Collection of Francis Carolus Eeles includes: notes on the Russian and Armenian liturgies, n.d. (MS 1546 pp.80-3); 'Institutiones Theologicae ... in usum juventutis Roxoland in seminario Kolomnensi, curis auspiciis et mandato illustrissimi DD Theodosii Episcopi Kolomnensis et Kaschiviensis ...', 1779, written for a seminary of the Russian Orthodox Church at Kolomna (MS 1548); translations into English of documents relating to the Russian Orthodox Church in the 19th century by Richard White Blackmore, chaplain to the Russia Company, 1819-47 (MS 1550). *See entry in Bill's catalogue vol. 1 for further details.*

173.4 GIBSON MANUSCRIPTS
Letter from the primate of Poland to the King of Sweden about the affairs of Poland and Lithuania, n.d., late 17th, early 18th century (MS 933 f.126).

173.5 HEADLAM PAPERS (MSS 2615-50)
Papers of Arthur Cayley Headlam (1862-1947), Bishop of Gloucester, include: papers re religious persecution in Russia, 1922-3 (MS 2626 ff.246-86); report on the Russian student Christian movement, 1924-6 (MS 2626 ff.356-60); papers re Soviet invasion of Finland, 1939 (MS 2641 ff.180-9) and annexation of the Baltic States (MS 2644); letter re Russian policy in Finland, *c.* 1940 (MS 2650 f.183); G. Fedotov, 'The Russian Church in the emigration', 1942 (MS 2650 ff.201-7); anon. 'The truth about religion in Russia', 1943 (MS 2650 ff.217-19). *See Bill's catalogue vol. 3 for further details.*

173.6 JERUSALEM AND THE EAST MISSION FUND PAPERS (MSS 2327-41)
Correspondence of John Wordsworth, Bishop of Salisbury, President of the Mission, relating to relations with Eastern Churches includes letter from William John Birkbeck re dispute in the Russian Church about transubstantiation, 3 Aug. 1898 (MS 2330 ff.88-100) and letters re the Armenian question, 1892-7, 1907-8 (MS 2330 ff.111-207); correspondence of G. F. P. Blyth, Bishop in Jerusalem, includes 'Letters which have passed between the Archbishop of Canterbury and Hierarchs of the Russian Church, 1888'

(published 1896) (**MS 2333 ff.1-2v**); petition by 'Bishop' Mathew to the Holy Synod of the Russian Orthodox Church, 1910 (**MS 2333 ff.265-9**).

173.7 PAPERS CONCERNING MARSHAL AUGUST MARMONT (MS 2687)

Order from Napoleon to Marmont for cities to send delegations to Paris to report the barbarous acts and intentions of the Russians, 21 Feb. 1814 (**f.27**).

173.8 PALMER PAPERS (MSS 1861-1906, 2452-2502, 2800-57, 2965-3015)

Papers of Revd William Palmer (1811-79) include: correspondence re negotiations with the Russian Orthodox Church, ?1824-53 (**MS 1894**); petition by the Scottish Episcopalian Church to the Synod of the Russian Orthodox Church respecting union, ?1851 (**MS 1895 f.81**); copies of documents re history of the Russian Orthodox Church (**MSS 1896-1900**); Revd W. Palmer's journal of a visit to Russia, 3 Feb. - 2 May 1841 (**MS 1901**); letter from Philaret, Metropolitan of Moscow, to Revd W. Palmer, 1841, Latin (**MS 2497 f.5**); 'extracts made in Russia from Mr [Horatio] Southgate's publication' (**MS 2821 pp.197-230**); journal by Revd W. Palmer of a visit to Constantinople, southern Russia and the Crimea, 20 July - 4 Oct. ?1851 (**MS 2829**); letter from Stepan Stepanovich Dzhunkovskii, Russian priest, to Revd W. Palmer, 24 Sept. 1849 (**MS 2837 f.59**). Papers of Edwin James Palmer (1869-1954), Bishop of Bombay, include extracts from the marriage laws of the USSR, Germany and Turkey (**MS 2996 f.141-9**). *See* E. G. W. Bill, *A Catalogue of the Manuscripts in Lambeth Palace Library*, vols 2 and 3, and E. G. W. Bill, *Catalogue of the papers of Roundell Palmer (1812-1895) first Earl of Selborne* (London, 1967).

173.9 RILEY PAPERS (MSS 2343-2411)

Papers of John Athelstan Laurie Riley (1858-1945), anglican layman active in ecclesiastical affairs, include: letters to him from the following: Constantine Pobiedonostzeff (K. P. Pobedonostsev), Chief Procurator of the Holy Synod of the Russian Orthodox Church, 1890, 1901 (**MS 2343 ff.122-5, MS 2344 f.206**), Russian Academic Group in Britain, 1923 (**MS 2347 f.132**), E. Sabline, Russian refugee in London, 1934 (**MS 2348 f.129**) and William John Birkbeck, Russian scholar, 1892-1915 (**MS 2351 ff.1-95v**); copy rescript of the Episcopal Synod outside Russia, 1925 (**MS 2347 f.190**); list of Serbian and Russian ecclesiastics at Belgrade, n.d. (**MS 2353 f.291**).

173.10 SECKER PAPERS

Vol. 4 of 4 vols of papers relating to foreign Protestants, 1699-1768, includes letters and copies of letters relating to the Polish dissidents including from Mr Woide in St Petersburg and Prince Repnin, 1766 (**MS 1122/4 ff.353-92**).

173.11 WHITE PAPERS (MSS 1472-82)

Correspondence of F. A. White with Arthur Steinkopff Thompson, former chaplain at the embassy in St Petersburg, ?1880 (**MS 1480 f.369**).

173.12 Scrapbook and reports re persecution of the Jews in Poland, Lithuanian and Rumania, 1936-7 (**MSS 1716A, 1716B**).

173.13 Photograph of the St Petersburg express train, n.d. (**MS 2944 f.54**).

173.14 Letter from Charles Lindley Wood, 2nd Visc. Halifax, to William John Birkbeck, Russian scholar, 10 Dec. 1896 (**MS 3065 f.27**).

Archives

Archbishops' papers in chronological order of Archbishop:

173.15 TAIT PAPERS

Papers of Archibald Campbell Tait, Bishop of London 1856-68, Archbishop of Canterbury 1868-82. London papers include papers re chaplaincies in Moscow, 1865-8, Odessa, 1864-7 (**418 ff.**), St Petersburg, 1860-8, 1884 (**419 ff.**). Canterbury papers include correspondence re the following: interview with the Tsar, 1874 (**53 ff.4-5, 93 ff.57-8**); Russian Orthodox Church, 1869-82 (**163 ff.282-5; 226 ff.355-63; 273 ff.137-40; 287 ff.330-4**); distribution of Bibles in Russia, 1876, 1880 (**224 ff.105-10; 266 ff.234-43**); Russian burial laws, 1875 (**244 ff.59-60, 75-8, 96-101**); the persecution of the Jews, 1882 (**281 ff.232-59**).

·173.16 BENSON PAPERS

Papers of Edward White Benson, Archbishop of Canterbury 1883-96. Correspondence and papers re the following: Russian Orthodox Church (**32 ff.78-87; 71 ff.403-6; 76 ff.394-405; 80 ff.219-74; 86 ff.322-7; 100 ff.98-106; 133 ff.216-18** *passim*; **146 ff.79-86; 147 ff.82-3, 86**); Russian Jews, 1890-1 (**86 ff.295-302; 91 ff.288-368; 103 ff.226-62**); distribution of Bibles in Russia, 1891 (**93 ff.52-61**); the seaman's institute at Libau, 1891-2 (**133 ff.163-8, 177-9, 216-18** *passim*); persecution of Protestants in Russia, 1891-3 (**100 ff.96-7; 113 f.451; 126 f.17-30**); Russian lepers, 1892 (**109 ff. 190-201** *passim*); appeals to Nicholas II on behalf of the Armenian Christians, 1896 (**147 ff.260, 310-14, 317-24, 327-9; 148 ff.198-9** *passim*); the coronation of Nicholas II, 1896 (**148 ff.112-97; 157 ff.283-8** *passim*). See *Index to the letters and papers of Edward White Benson, Archbishop of Canterbury 1883-1896 in Lambeth Palace Library* (London, 1980).

173.17 FREDERICK TEMPLE PAPERS

Papers of Frederick Temple, Archbishop of Canterbury 1896-1902. Correspondence and papers re Nicholas II's call for a peace conference, 1898-9 (**14 ff.348-55; 25 ff.372-3**), rumours of Russian influence in the election of the Oecumenical Patriarch of Constantinople, 1901, and the Metropolitan of Beirut, 1902 (**32 ff.316-21** *passim*; **59 ff.6-7, 186-7** *passim*) and re the representation of the Russian Orthodox Church at the coronation of Edward VII, 1902 (**57 ff.182-3**). *See* M. Barber, *Index to the letters and papers of Frederick Temple, Archbishop of Canterbury 1896-1902 in Lambeth Palace Library* (London, 1975).

173.18 DAVIDSON PAPERS

Papers of Randall Thomas Davidson, Archbishop of Canterbury 1903-28. Correspondence and papers re the following: Russian persecution of the Jews, 1891, 1906 (**29 f.116; 120 ff.140-211**); Russo-Japanese War, 1904 (**97 ff.323-51**); the memorial to the Duma, 1906 (**120 ff.98-122**); imprisonment of N. Tchaycovsky (Chaikovskii), 1908 (**150 ff.388-94**); persecution of the Georgian Orthodox Church, 1909 (**155 ff.148-66**); Jews at Kiev accused of ritual murder, 1912 (**176 ff.199-235**); visits to Russia by Bishop H. Bury , W. H. Frere, later Bishop of Truro and George Lansbury, 1912-14, 1919-20 (**176 ff.263-4; 182 ff.371-87; 192 ff. 37-45; 197 ff. 84-112**); assistance for Prof. N. N. Glubovskii on leaving Russia, 1921-3 (**199 ff. 254-347**); assistance for Ukrainian members of the Russian Orthodox Church, 1924-8 (**204 ff. 366-404; 217 ff. 162-80**); position of the Russian Orthodox Church in the USSR, 1926 (**210 ff. 61-2**); *c.* 12 vols on Russia and the Russian Orthodox Church, 1903-28, and 1 vol. on the Church in Georgia.

173.19 LANG PAPERS

Papers of Cosmo Gordon Lang, Archbishop of Canterbury 1928-42. Papers re the following: Soviet-Finnish war, 1939-41 (**34 ff.353-455**); position of the Churches in the

USSR, 1928-34 (**73; 74; 75; 101 ff.38-56; 120 ff.51-74**); famine relief, 1933-4 (**75 ff.78-290** *passim*); treatment of Finns in the USSR, 1931, 1935 (**106 ff.60-115; 134 ff.58-100**); Russian Orthodox clergy outside the USSR, 1931-8, 1941 (**116 ff.73-100; 128 ff.22-5; 145 ff.56-98; 149 ff.323-7; 165 ff.204-6; 184 ff.254-61**); suppression of the Russian Orthodox Student Union in Latvia, 1935 (**135 ff.276-316**); imprisonment of P. A. Florenskii, Russian Orthodox priest, 1937 (**151 ff.6-14**); report on prison camps in the USSR, 1940 (**179 ff.198-202**); German invasion, 1941-2 (**186 ff.176-249**); formation of the Russian Society to promote Anglican-Orthodox relations, 1912 (**189 ff.293-302**).

173.20 WILLIAM TEMPLE PAPERS

Papers of William Temple, Archbishop of Canterbury 1942-4. Proposed statement on post-war reconstruction by Christian leaders in Britain, China, USA and the USSR, 1944-5 (**37 ff.266-309**); letter re fund for Soviet controlled areas of Poland, 1943-4 (**37 ff.109-31**); memo from Russian Orthodox Church on Nazi subversion in the Ukraine, 1942 (**38 ff.263-9**); prayers for the Russian Orthodox Church, 1943 (**38 ff.369-71**); letter re death of Sergius, Patriarch of Moscow, 1944 (**38 ff.372-68**); prayers for Red Army Day, 1943 (**49 ff.1-11**); papers re attempts to assist Poles and others deported to the the USSR, 1943-4 (**49 ff.12-105**); letter re proposed delegation from the USA to the Patriarch of Moscow, 1944 (**49 ff.409-23**).

173.21 FISHER PAPERS

Papers of Geoffrey Francis Fisher, Archbishop of Canterbury 1945-61. Papers re deportation of Poles and others to the USSR, 1945 (**3 ff.300-15; 9 ff.280-4**); criticism of attitude of Roman Catholic Church towards the USSR, 1946 (**19 ff.9-18**); proposal for appointment of a chaplain to the British Embassy in Moscow, 1947 (**31 ff.117-32**); report of a conference of the Russian Orthodox Church in Moscow, 1947 (**34 ff.112-14**); proposal for a delegation from the Lambeth Conference to visit the USSR, 1948 (**49 ff.69-72**); papers re influence of the USSR in Eastern Europe, 1949 (**69 ff.139-40**); request from Latvian Lutherans to come under the jurisdiction of the Bishop of London, 1951 (**88 ff.63-5**); papers re visits of G. E. Ingle, Revd C. E. Raven and A. M. Stockwood to the USSR, 1952-3 (**101 ff.94-5; 126 ff.75-8; 129 ff.368-71; 132 ff.63-8**).

Fulham papers (Bishops of London) in chronological order of bishops:

173.22 HOWLEY PAPERS

Papers of William Howley, Bishop of London 1813-28 include papers on Anglican chaplaincies in St Petersburg, 1818, 1825 (**4 pp.1003-34**) and Riga, 1825 (**4 pp.1035-42**).

173.23 BLOMFIELD PAPERS

Letter-books of Charles James Blomfield, Bishop of London, 1828-56, include letters re confirmation services for Anglicans in Russia (**54 ff.353, 365-6**). Letter-books available on microfiche.

Other Archive collections:

173.24 LAMBETH CONFERENCE PAPERS

MS records of conference discussions and correspondence available until 1948. The 1888 conference discussed the relations of the Anglicans with the Russian Orthodox Church and the conferences of 1897, 1908, 1920 and 1930 discussed Church unity and relations with the Eastern Orthodox Churches. The 1908 conference records include a letter from Henry Codmon Potter, Bishop of New York, to Thomas Frank Gailor, Bishop of Tennessee, re relations with the Russian Orthodox Church (**LC 74 ff. 202-3**), correspondence re the invitation to the conference of the Russian Archimandrite (**LC 75 ff. 52-9** *passim*) and correspondence with William John Birkbeck re postponement of the

National Council of the Russian Orthodox Church (**LC 79 ff. 155-9**). The records of the 1920 conference include correspondence with Sir Bernard Pares, Father Eugene Smirnoff (E. Smirnov) and others re Russian translations of the 'Appeal to all Christians' (**LC 138 ff. 97-164** *passim*).

173.25 SOCIETY FOR THE PROPAGATION OF THE GOSPEL PAPERS
Letter from John Urmston from Archangel to the Secretary of the Society with unfavourable account of religion in Russia, 1703 (**IX. f. 34**). *See* W. W. Manross, *S.P.G. Papers in the Lambeth Palace Library, Calendar and Indexes* (London, 1974).

173.26 BISHOP BELL'S PAPERS
Papers of George Kennedy Allen Bell, Bishop of Chichester, 1929-58, include correspondence of the relief of Russian clergy, the Church and communism in the USSR, Russian POWs and refugees, deportees and the USSR and the Baltic States.

173.27 DOUGLAS PAPERS
Papers of Canon John Albert Douglas, honorary General Secretary of the Church of England Council on Foreign Relations. Papers re the following: Russian Orthodox Council of Bishops in Exile, 1920, 1922-6 (**1 ff.150-8; 17 ff.464a, 466; 46 ff.1-408; 51 ff.26-30**); persecuted clergy in Russia, 1927 (**5 ff.286-94**); Russian clergy and Church Aid Fund, 1923-52 (**33 ff.245-9** *passim*; **42 ff.254, 308-10; 45 ff.126-9, 3-335; 46 ff.91-3, 98-101**); Russian Orthodoxy in Japan, America and Jerusalem, 1924-47 (**41 f.123-208; 46 ff.227-31, 248-9, 258-9; 52 ff.45-50**); Russian Orthodox Theological Academy in Paris, 1923-52 (**41 ff.265-308** *passim*; **43 ff.158-216; 45 ff.3-335**); Russian Relief and Reconstruction Fund, 1924 (**45 ff.1-2**); Russian student Christian movement, 1924, 1926-38 (**45 ff.6-7, 23-7, 336-58**). *See TS index for names of correspondents with Russian connections.*

174.1
LEWISHAM LOCAL HISTORY CENTRE

The Manor House, Old Road, Lee, London SE13 5SY

174.1 Album of goodwill from the women of Moscow to the women of Lewisham, *c.* 1942.

175.1-30
LIDDELL HART CENTRE FOR MILITARY ARCHIVES

King's College London (KQC), Strand, London WCIB 5DS

By appointment. *Consolidated List of Accessions* (1981); J. Perceval, edit., *A Guide to Archives and Manuscripts in the University of London*, vol. 1 (1984) pp. 64-85. There are handlists and summary lists for most collections. Readers wishing to publish a manuscript deriving from or quoting from papers in the Centre must submit relevant portions to the Trustees for scrutiny before publication.

175.1 ALANBROOKE, FM Visc. Alan Francis (1883-1963)
Chief of Imperial General Staff, 1941-6. Papers include: correspondence with Archibald, 1st Earl Wavell, re the Russian front, 2 Nov. 1942, re Alanbrooke's visit to the USSR and improved relations with Stalin, 1 Nov. 1944, and re the Yalta Conference, 13 Mar. 1945 (**6/D4/X/2/3, 9, 11**); TS letter from Churchill enclosing note on comments made by Stalin

about Alanbrooke, 30 July 1945 (**7/2/11**); photograph of arrival of the British party at Moscow, 1945 (**8/7/12**); photographs re journey and arrival at Moscow Conference, 1942 (**11/1/22-3**); notes on Russians, 1944-5 (**12/X/10**). There might also be references to the USSR in his diaries.

175.2 ALEXANDER, H. T.
'Russian report' re Ghana, 1961. Collection closed at present.

175.3 BENSON, Lt-Col. Sir Reginald Lindsay (1889-1968)
Anon. assessment of the regime in Russia and possible ways of successful Allied intervention, 8 Apr. 1918 (**A6/9**); TS letter from Douglas Haig, 1st Earl Haig, to Gen R. G. Nivelle re desirability of the Russians taking the offensive, 1 Apr. 1917 (**B1/24**); TS copy of directive re change of strategy owing to Russian 'defection', 17 Dec. 1917 (**B2/22**).

175.4 BONHAM-CARTER, Victor (b. 1913)
Author. Draft script on Russia in 1914-16 (**II.18**).

175.5 BURNABY, Lt-Col. Frederick Gustavus (1842-85)
Miscellaneous papers including his book *A Ride to Khiva*, 1876.

175.6 CAPPER, Maj.-Gen. Thompson (1863-1915)
Printed articles by Lt-Col. P. I. Izmet'ev, officer of the Russian General Staff, on 'The Importance of Secrecy in War', Nov. 1907 (**11/4/5**).

175.7 CLIVE, Lt-Gen. Sir George Sidney (1874-1959)
Diary of journey to Russia and start of his work as military governor in Cologne, 1917-18 (**II/4**).

175.8 COLLIER, Air Marshal S. Conrad
Photocopies of correspondence with Lt-Col. Thomas A. Julian, USAF, re Soviet Union, 1941.

175.9 DAVIDSON, Maj.-Gen. Francis Henry Norman (1892-1973)
Diary written on return to Britain from the Allied Military Mission to Moscow, July-Aug. 1939 (**A**); chapters for book re events leading to the German-Soviet pact of Aug. 1939 (**L**).

175.10 EDMONDS, Brig.-Gen. Sir James Edward (1861-1956)
Served in War Office Intelligence Division in charge of the section following the Russo-Japanese War. Memoirs include chapter covering the Russo-Japanese War (**III/4**); newspaper cuttings re Russia (**VIII/9**). There might be material in his correspondence, 1891-1954 (**II/1-2**).

175.11 ELLIOT, Air Chief Marshal Sir William (1896-1971)
Papers include: TS copy of letter to the Hon. Dean Acheson commenting on NATO and relations with N. Khrushchev, 2 July 1961 (**4/1/1**); correspondence with Frederick Wills re the Soviet invasion of Czechoslovakia, 1968 (**4/6/15, 24a, 26-7**); photographs from South Russia, 1919 (**8/4/3a**).

175.12 FULLER, Maj.-Gen. John Frederick Charles (1878-1966)
Letter to Mrs Fuller re the Russo-Japanese War, 1 July 1905 (**IV/3/127**); letter to Revd A. Fuller re the Russian Revolution, 26 July 1917 (**IV/3/216**).

175.13 GOLDSMITH, Cmdr M. Lennon
Photocopies of letters to his father while serving in the Black Sea, 1919.

175.14 GRANT, Lt-Gen. Sir Robert (1837-1904)
Memo on the Afghan frontier policy and Russian defences by Gen. Sir Frederick Roberts, C.-in-C. of Madras Army, 1885.

175.15 HAMILTON, Gen. Sir Ian Standish Monteith (1853-1947)
Papers include: correspondence on the Russo-Japanese War, 1904-10 (**7/1/9/1-13; 7/3/8/1-30; 25/12/2/34, 37**); correspondence re Russia, comprising mainly letters from Hamilton from St Petersburg and Moscow, 1909-10, 1919, n.d. (**7/3/11/1-7; 25/12/2/2-6**); extracts from 'Considerations sur la campagne de Mandchowrie' by Gen. F. Silvestre and 'L'expérience de la guerre Russo-Japonaise' by Lt-Col. A. A. Neznamov (**7/3/14/6-7**); account of the battle of the Alma, 22 Dec. [1854] (**7/5/6**); foreign manoeuvre notes on Russia, 1919, n.d. (**19/11/1-2**). *See handlist for details.*

175.16 HOWELL, Brig.-Gen. Philip (1877-1916)
TS letter from Col. W. Malleson re intelligence about Russian troop movements, 1 Aug. 1905 (**IAI/5**); photographs of the Russo-Japanese War, 1904 (**IV/D/4**).

175.17 ISMAY, Gen. Lord Hastings Lionel (1887-1965)
Deputy Secretary and Secretary of the Committee of Imperial Defence, 1940-5; Deputy Secretary (Military) to the War Cabinet, 1940-5. Papers include: account of the Tehran and Moscow Conferences (**I/5/1; II/3/193-4; II/3/220/2**); material re convoys to the USSR (**I/14/124-5; III/4/9/4**); correspondence re Chruchill's memoirs re Russia, 1948-9, n.d. (**II/3/58/1-2; II/3/115/2; II/3/171/2**); Churchill's notes on the Yalta Conference (**II/3/296**); papers re the USSR as Secretary-General of NATO, 1952-6 (**III/12/22/2; III/13/26; III/16/10, 12; III/18/3; III/20/14; III/21/5**). Correspondence re the USSR and peace conferences with the Rt Hon. A. Eden, 1943-4, 1965 (**IV/Avo/1, 3-4, 20/2**), Lt-Gen. M. Brocas Burrows, 1944-5 (**IV/Bur/1-9**), Gen. Mark W. Clark, 7 Jan. 1944 (**IV/Cla/6**), Lewis S. Douglas, 1944 (**IV/Dou/1, 5, 7**), Lord Louis Mountbatten, 1945, n.d. (**IV/Mou/2B/123/3, /125/5**), Lt-Gen. W. Bedell Smith, 1946-7 (**IV/Smi/34-35B**); printed notes of the War Cabinet re Anglo-Soviet political conversations in Moscow, 1944 (**IV/9-10**). *See handlist for details.*

175.18 KIGGELL, Lt-Gen. Sir Launcelot Edward (1862-1954)
Chief of General Staff to the British Armies in France, 1915-18. Papers include: letter from FM Sir William Robertson re the Russian débâcle, 27 July 1917 (**IV/7**); TS copy of letter from FM Earl Haig to Maj.-Gen. Sir Stanley B. Donop re supplies for Russia, 18 July 1916 (**V/28**); TS letter from Maj.-Gen. C. E. Caldwell re importance of heavy guns to the Russians, 30 Aug. 1916 (**V/36**); TS copy of 'His majesty the emperor Nicholas with the Russian armies in the field', 3 Dec. 1916 (**V/64**).

175.19 LEVER, Capt. George Harold (1892-1973)
Served with the British Military Mission in South Russia, 1919-20. Diary, Oct. 1919 - 29 June 1920 (**IV/1**); box of photographs, postcards and lantern slides (**IV/2**).

175.20 THE LIDDELL HART COLLECTION
Papers of Sir Basil Liddell Hart (1895-1970), military theorist, writer and publicist, includes many papers re the USSR including: correspondence with Lt-Gen. Sir Gifford Le Quesne Martel, Head of the Military Mission at Moscow (**1/492**); correspondence with USSR embassies (**2/99**); notes, TSS and proofs of books re the USSR (**9/24, 27-8, 31**); memos re the USSR with particular reference to Soviet army strength, 1932-50 (**11/1932/2, 6; 11/1933/43; 11/1935/159; 11/1941/40; 11/1943/71-2; 11/1948/19; 11/1950/32-3, 39**); talks with I. Maiskii, 1935-40 (**11/1935/110; 11/1938/117; 11/1939/19; 11/1940/3**); papers re mission to the USSR, 1942, 1944 (**11/1942/14; 11/1944/9, 12, 61-3**); notes and memos re the USSR at war (**11/1942/30, 48, 99-100; 11/1943/19; 11/1946/2, 6-7;**

11/1947/17; 11/1951/16); memo re Soviet demands on Finland, 14 Mar. 1940 (**11/1940/16**); memo re the Khar'kov trial, 25 Dec. 1943 (**11/1943/81**); articles re the USSR; press cuttings; pamphlets. There might also be material amongst his correspondence, interviews, talks and diaries. *See handlist for details and further references.*

175.21 LISTER, Lt-Col. Frederick Hamilton (1880-1971)
'Russian Journal' covering his service in South Russia, 1919-20.

175.22 McLEOD, Gen. Sir Roderick William (b. 1905)
Letter of 24 Oct. 1966 to Col. K. Garside re Lord Ironside's attitude to a possible war with the USSR in 1940 (**4/1**).

175.23 MANSTEIN, FM Erich von (1887-1973)
Papers re his trial for war crimes, 1949, include synopsis of the retreat of the German army from southern Russia (**9**). Non-British readers must seek the approval of the Judge Advocate before being allowed access to the papers.

175.24 MAURICE, Maj.-Gen. Sir Frederick Barton (1871-1951)
Papers include: correspondence of Sir Henry Creswicke Rawlinson re Russian campaign, 2 July 1888 (**3/4/1**); letter from Lt-Gen. Sir W. R. Marshall re the Russian army, 10 Sept. 1917 (**3/5/51**); letter from Maj.-Gen. Sir C. M. Maynard serving with the Russian Expeditionary Force, 29 Oct. 1918 (**3/5/81**).

175.25 NORTH, Maj. John (1894-1973)
Papers and correspondence re his articles on Russian and Soviet history (**IV/1C/40; IV/1C/MISC 1; IV/3/106a-d; V/3/4**); letter from North to the *Daily Mail* re the USSR, 23 Feb. 1959 (**IV/4e/48**).

175.26 PENNEY, Maj.-Gen. Sir William Ronald Campbell (1894-1963)
TS letter to Penney from Capt. D. M. MacLeod re the popularity of Russia among troops at Anzio, Apr. 1944 (**7/20**).

175.27 POOLE, Maj.-Gen. Sir Frederick Cuthbert (1869-1936)
Box of papers re the British Military Mission to Denikin's army.

175.28 ROBERTSON, FM Sir William Robert (1866-1933)
Papers include: TS lecture re Russia in Central Asia, ?1906 (**I/2/8**); reports, papers and notes re Russia from GHQ of British Expeditionary Force in France, 1915 , with particular reference to the condition of the Russian army (**I/5/11/8-14; I/9/49; I/10/17**), German policy re Russia (**I/5/11; I/9/48**), Russian plans in the Balkans (**I/9/33, 52**) and transport of Austro-Hungarian troops from the Russian front (**I/10/20**); telegrams to and from Brig.-Gen. W. H. H. Waters, British Military Mission with the Russian Imperial GHQ, 1916 (**I/14**); Robertson's secret papers for the War Cabinet re Russia, 1917 (**I/17/1, 3**); letter from Gen. Sir Charles Harington to Robertson re Adm. A. V. Kolchak, 19 June 1919 (**I/28/13**). Correspondence re Russia, 1915-17, including with the following: Sir Guy Munro (**I/32/57**); Lloyd George (**I/33/10**); Arthur John Bigge, Baron Stamfordham (**I/33/64**); Reginald Baliol Brett, 2nd Visc. Esher (**I/34/3**); Marshal Ferdinand Foch (**I/34/28**); George Francis Milne , 1st Baron Milne (**I/34/30**); Herbert Charles Onslow , 1st Visc. Plumer (**I/34/41**); Maj.-Gen. C. E. Caldwell (**I/35/20**); Sir Edward Grey (**I/35/45**); Maj.-Gen. Sir John Hanbury-Williams (**I/35/55-9**); F. O. Lindley (**I/35/67**); Adm. Sir J. R. Jellicoe (**I/36/47**); Alfred Milner, Visc. Milner (**I/36/66**). *See handlist for details and further references.*

175.29 STEPHENSON, Maj. Frederick Simeon Dauncey (1897-1975)
Account 'Ourselves and Russia', 1941-2.

175.30 WYNNE, Capt. Graeme Charmley (1914-58)
Draft text of a talk by Wynne on 'The Stalin position', n.d., probably 1941 **(9/2)**.

176.1-18
LINNEAN SOCIETY OF LONDON

Burlington House, Piccadilly, London WIV 0LQ.

By appointment. *Catalogue of the Manuscripts of the Library of the Linnean Society of London*, 4 parts (London, 1934-40). Detailed entry in *Natural History Manuscript Resources in the British Isles*, edit. by G. D. R. Bridson *et. al.* (London, 1980). Card index of manuscripts. The Linnean Society Archives are in the process of reorganization.

176.1 AMMAN, Johannes (**MSS Linn. Cat. Pl.2**)
'Flora Tatarica Orenburgensis in itinere Moscva - Ufam ... per Sibiriam et Uralenses montes Ufam peracto observata et collecta a Joanne Gottfried Heinzelmann 1736 ... Recensuerunt Dr Amman ... Dr Siegesbeck ... Dr Gerber ... Dr Schober' with annotation by C. Linnaeus.

176.2 COLLINSON, Peter (**MSS 323**)
Commonplace Book I includes letters from John Cook to Collinson and to Dr Sanches from Astrakhan', 10 June, 11 July 1744 (**pp. 203, 306-07**).

176.3 THE ELLIS MANUSCRIPTS (**MS 292**)
Papers of John Ellis (?1705-76), naturalist, include draft letter from Ellis to ?Linneaus re Dr Solander and the collection of the observatory in St Petersburg, Oct. or Nov. 1762 (**Notebook 2 40v-41r**).

176.4 FEDTSCHENKO (FEDCHENKO), Boris Alekseevich (**MSS Misc. SP 254**)
TS 'On the Tremandraceas of Asian Flora' *c.* 1908.

176.5 HOOKER, J.D. (**MSS Misc. SP 437**)
Paper 'Note on the occurence of an eatable Nostoc in the Arctic Region and in the Mountains of Central Asia' read 20 Jan. 1852.

176.6 KNOCH, F (**MSS Misc. SP544**)
Letter to Home Office from St Petersburg re travel to Lake Kubenskoe to obtain fertilized eggs of Nelma for hatching in Britain, 31 Aug. 1886.

176.7 LERCHE, Johann J. (**MSS Linn. Misc. Authors, Linn. Cat. Pl. 6, 6A**)
'Descriptio plantarum quandarum partim minus cognitarum, Astrachanensium et Provinciarum Persae, Mari Caspio adjacentium ... 1765' (**MSS Linn. Misc. Authors**); 'Plantarum Astrachanensium partim minus cognitarum, et Descriptio plantarum deserti Astrachanensia in via ad Kislar it. Hircaniae annis 1746-7' (**MSS Linn. Misc. Authors**); 'Flora Persiae et in confiniis Maris Caspii proveniens ab Astrachania transmissa a Dr Lerch, Petroburgi mense martio 1736 vom Hrn Achiatro e Collectione Heinzelmani [J.G. Heinzelmann]' (**MSS Linn. Cat. Pl.**).

176.8 LINNAEUS' CORRESPONDENCE
Letter from James Mounsey to Linnaeus from Russia, 29 Mar. 1744 (vol. X f. 276).
(Correspondence has been microfilmed.)

176.9 LINNEAN SOCIETY ARCHIVES
From 1788. The index to minute-books and general minute-books (no. 1: 1802-13 etc.) has references to Russia. There could be material relating to Russia and the Soviet Union in Correspondence, External Affairs, Certificates of Fellows, Foreign Members & Associates, Fellowship Records and Register of papers read at the Society. Archives under reorganization.

176.10 MUSEUM DARWINIANUM, MOSCOW (MS 638)
7 portfolios of photographs of exhibits in the Museum on the life and ideas of Charles Darwin, 2 portfolios on the formation of the Museum, the old and the new buildings, and the life of its founder Aleksander F. Kohts, c. 1959-62.

176.11 PULTENEY, Richard (MS 163)
'An Account of Mr Isbrant's [E. Ysbrants Ides] Journey from Moscow to China. Collected from the Life of Peter The first Emperor of Russia ... January ye 25. 1742-3', including map and pen and water colour drawings.

176.12 SCHOBER, Gottlob (MSS Linn. Cat. Pl. 7)
'Plantae in Territorio Moscoviensi crescentes ordine alphabetico designata a ... , Moscoviae 1736'.

176.13 SMIRNOVE, James (Smirnov, I.) (MSS Misc. S.P.)
Paper 'On the Locusts (species Gryllus migratorius of Linnaeus) which devastated the Crimea and the southern provinces of Russia in 1824' read 2 May 1826.

176.14 THE SMITH PAPERS (MS 301)
Papers of Sir James Edward Smith include: letter from Nicolas Joseph, Baron von Jacquin, introducing a minister of the Russian Court, 4 July 1791 (5.188); letter from John Stackhouse re being made Hon. member of Moscow Academy, 17 May 1816 (25.175); letter from Baron Otto Herman von Vietinghoff re preparatory work on rare plants of Russia, Moscow 30 Jan. 1811 (10.84); list drawn up by Matthew Guthrie headed 'Note of a Collection of Russian Minerals' sent to the Society 13 Feb. 1793 (39.184).

176.15 STEVEN, Chevalier de (MSS Misc. S.P.)
Illustrations from his published paper 'Description of 9 new species of plants from Caucasus'.

176.16 Transcribed note from The Times for 17 Mar. 1858 re ravages of Black Sea teredo at Sebastopol (MSS Misc. S.P.).

176.17 Letter in Russian from T. Riabouchinsky (T. Ryabushinskaya) inserted in a printed book, n.d. (Q 915.73 : 582 RIA).

176.18 Letter by Peter Leopold von Schrenck from the Imperial Academy of Sciences in St Petersburg inserted in his book, Reisen und Forschungen in Amur-Lande ... (St Petersburg, 1860) (Q 915.73 : 595.76 SCH).

177.1-4

LLOYDS BANK ARCHIVE

Archivist, Secretary's Department, Head Office, PO Box 215, 71 Lombard Street, London EC3P 3BS

By appointment. In general documents relating to customers and their business are not available for at least one hundred years; papers re the Bank's central policy and attitudes might be made available before this date but access is restricted. Some material in the archives relating to the USSR can be found in J. R. Winton, *Lloyds Bank 1918-1969* (Oxford, 1982).

177.1 File re 'the Holy Synod of the Empire of Russia 7% Sterling Loan' to buy wax for use in Russian churches, 1916.

177.2 Ledger, 'Foreign Credits. Russian' covering business of the City Office with merchants and financiers engaged in Russian trade, 1916-19.

177.3 File, 'Comments on Russian Economic Position, 1929'.

177.4 File re threatened action in New York State on behalf of a group of Russians in Paris claiming against the assets of the old Imperial regime, 1938.

178.1

LONDON FESTIVAL BALLET ARCHIVE

Festival Ballet House, 39 Jay Mews, London SW7 2ES

By appointment.

178.1 File of material including correspondence and production notes re 'The Snow Maiden', first performed on 17 July 1961 with Soviet choreographers and designers.

179.1-8

LONDON LIBRARY

14 St James's Square, London SW1Y 4LG

Apply to the Librarian for access; the London Library is a private library normally only open to subscribing members. M. Higgins, 'The London Library's Russian Manuscripts', *Adam* (1977) (reprinted in *The London Library*, edited by M. Grindea (1978) pp. 66-70); M. Higgins, 'The Russian Collections of the London Library', *Solanus*, 17 (1982) pp. 49-51. Manuscripts are not recorded separately and can be found in the author catalogue.

179.1 BADDELEY, John F.
Commonplace book beginning in St Petersburg, Dec. 1882 and 'Key to Kalmuk Map no. 2' (**safe 1**); 97 photographs of the Caucasus (**safe 5**).

179.2 CURTIS, Charles B.
'Journal of Travels through Russia to Constantinople in Parts of Asia Minor during the years 1815-1816', n.d. (**safe 1**).

179.3 ESENIN, Sergei (1895-1925)
MS and TS of poem 'Pugachev', 1921 (**safe 1**).

179.4 WALLACE, Sir Donald Mackenzie (1841-1919)
Journalist and author. Notes on the first and second Dumas and revolutionary movements; chronicle of events in Russia, 1861-1906 (**safe 1**).

179.5 WRIGHT, Sir Charles T. Hagberg (1862-1940)
Librarian of the London Library, 1893-1940. Vol. 1 of *Autographs, Letters etc.* includes: photograph of Lev Tolstoi and Anton Chekhov, 1902; unidentified fragment of MS by Tolstoi, before 1900; letters from Count A. K. Tolstoi to Baron F. Meyendorff, Russian Chargé d'Affaires in Weimar, 1867-9; letters from Maksim Gor'kii to Wright from Capri, 1906-7; TSS articles by Gor'kii, 1905, 1907; 2 poems by V. Brusov, 1915; letters from D. Merezhkovskii to Wright, 1920s (**safe 1**).

179.6 TS 'A Bibliographical List of English Books and Articles Relating to British Influence in Russia, 1553-1853' (1922) compiled by Vladimir Poliakoff, Paul Leon, Charles T. Hagberg Wright and with items in the London Library marked (**safe 1**).

179.7 Map of Russia, sheet 9, 1864 (**safe 5**).

179.8 Printed Russian proclamations of various parties; extracts from newspapers; TS accounts of meetings, resolutions etc. of delegates in 1905 (**safe, folio**).

LONDON SCHOOL OF ECONOMICS AND POLITICAL SCIENCE LIBRARY

See entry for the British Library of Political and Economic Science, London.

180.1-2
LONDON SCHOOL OF HYGIENE AND TROPICAL MEDICINE LIBRARY

University of London, Keppel Street, London WC1E 7HT

By appointment. Archival material listed by author not subject.

180.1 BUDD, Dr William
Correspondence includes letter from Budd to Dr A. Smith, Director-General of the Army and Ordinance Medical Department, with suggestions for preventing the spread of cholera amongst troops in the Crimea, 23 Dec. 1854, and reply, 8 Jan. 1855.

180.2 ROSS ARCHIVES
Correspondence, visiting cards, menus, newspaper cuttings etc. re visit to Russia in 1912 of Sir Ronald Ross as a member of a delegation of parliamentarians and academics. *See catalogue for details of correspondence.*

LONDON UNIVERSITY LIBRARY

See University of London Library, London.

181.1-3

MARX MEMORIAL LIBRARY

Marx House, 37a Clerkenwell Green, London EC1R 0DU

By appointment.

181.1 TS 'A Tour in Bolshevy' by O. G. S. Crawford, 1932.

181.2 TS 'Letters from a Soviet Citizen' by Ivan Lobachevskii, transl. by his wife, *c.* 1940-5.

181.3 Files of photographs re Russia and the USSR of the following: Soviet parliament delegation **(file 10)**; Anglo-Russian delegations **(file 11)**; Lenin exhibition material **(file 17)**; 1820-1920 exhibition in the USSR **(file 18)**; Marx, Lenin and Trotskii **(file 20)**; Kropotkin **(file 27)**; Workers International Relief **(file 29)**; G. Zinov'ev, M. M. Litvinov *et al.* **(file 34)**; Polish insurrection, 1863 **(file 35)**; Russian Revolution scenes **(file 36)**; Valentina Tereshkova, Moscow sanatorium, Revolution Day celebrations **(file 39)**; Central Asian republics **(file 42)**; Lenin, USSR, tributes to Lenin **(unnumbered files)**.

182.1-16

MIDLAND BANK GROUP ARCHIVES

Mariner House, Pepys Street, London EC3N 4DA

By appointment. Catalogues. Access to records relating to particular individual or corporate accounts is not normally given without the permission of the account-holders or their successors. The Bank normally asks to see the text of any research based on the Bank's archives before publication. The following items relate specifically to Russia but further references may be found in the general records of the Bank, particularly in the diaries of managing directors and joint general managers, *c.* 1905-35.

182.1 BUNKER PAPERS
Papers of F. J. Bunker as the Bank's agent in St Petersburg/Petrograd including papers re political and economic conditions and re customers and business, 1913-18 **(151/1-4)**.

182.2 Papers re Russian credit scheme, Oct. 1915 **(30/179)**.

182.3 Union Bank of Moscow papers including memos, regulations, balance sheet and correspondence between Alex Watt and Andrew Haes, 1907-9 **(30/218)**.

182.4 Annuaire Statistique de la Ville de Moscou, 1907-8, and correspondence and contract with Moscow municipality, 1912 **(30/219)**.

182.5 Printed list of shares in Russian banks, 1908-9, Russian **(30/220)**.

182.6 Printed Russian bank legislation in French and notes on the All Slav Bank, 1909 (**30/221**).

182.7 Memo by Sir Henry Burdett on the Anglo-Russian Trust Ltd, Apr. 1909 (**30/221**).

182.8 Odessa municipal loan correspondence, July-Oct. 1909 (**30/225**).

182.9 Diary of S. B. Murray's visit to Russia, with interview notes and balance sheets, Sept.-Oct. 1909 (**30/226**).

182.10 Proposals for the purchase and issue of Russian government bonds, Nov. 1909 (**30/227**).

182.11 Correspondence re Russian irrigation schemes, Nov. 1909 (**30/228**).

182.12 Estimates and correspondence re proposed loans for the Moscow-Reval railway and Donetsk railway, 1909-10 (**30/229**).

182.13 Correspondence and papers re loan to the city of Moscow, 1910 (**30/230**).

182.14 Report on 'France and England and the future Russian loans', *c.* 1910 (**20/231**).

182.15 TS agreement between Compagnie du Chemin de Fer de Kakhetie, Birch Crisp, Anglo-Russian Bank and the Anglo-Russian Trust, Feb. 1912, French (**30/232**).

182.16 Correspondence with the municipality of St Petersburg, May 1913 (**30/233**).

THE MIDDLESEX REGIMENTAL MUSEUM

See entry for Bruce Castle, London.

MOCATTA LIBRARY

See entry for University College London.

183.1

THE MUSEUM OF LONDON

150 London Wall, London EC2Y 5HN

183.1 THE PAVLOVA COLLECTION
Mainly costumes; also some documents re Anna Matveevna Pavlova (1881-1931).

184.1-2
MUSEUM OF MANKIND

Burlington Gardens, London W1X 2EX

By appointment.

184.1 Memo by H. Meyerowitz containing a report on investigations on art education in the USSR, 1936.

184.2 *C.* 12 studio portraits of Russians, with some written information on the backs. Collection uncatalogued.

185.1-201
NATIONAL ARMY MUSEUM

Department of Records, Royal Hospital Road, London SW3 4HT

Access to *bona fide* researchers on proof of identity. Tickets are issued to long-term users. Card indexes to campaigns, countries, foreign armies and photographs. Handlists of some large collections. New accessions are now entered on a microfiche catalogue, which has two indexes.

185.1 CODRINGTON PAPERS (6807-375 to -381)
Official papers of Gen. Sir William John Codrington (1804-84), C.-in-C. in the Crimea, 1855-6, include: personal papers (**-375**); Light Division papers (**-376**); inherited head-quarters' papers (**-377**); routine letters from London (**-378**); official and private correspondence, 1855-6 (**-379**); correspondence, reports, intelligence papers, papers re supplies, regimental returns, decorations (**-380**); papers re peace negotiations and evacuation of the Crimea (**-381**). *See index of correspondents.*

185.2 CODRINGTON, Gen. Sir William (7808-90)
Collection of private documents and papers re the Crimean War comprising TS transcripts of letters written to his wife during the campaign and various official and public papers. *See list for details.*

185.3 EDWARDS FAMILY PAPERS (8111-30)
Collection includes 45 letters from Col. Clement Alexander Edwards to his family from before Sebastopol, 11 May 1855 - 19 June 1856 (**-4 to- 48**). *See list for details.*

185.4 KNOLLYS, Gen. Sir William Thomas (8105-62)
Papers include 2 vols of copies of Scots Guards' Brigade Orders in the Crimea, Mar. 1855 - May 1856 (**-11,-12**); MS text of history of the Scots Guards covering the Crimean War (**-21 to -23**). *See list for details.*

185.5 PENFOLD, Capt. H. de L. (7808-94)
Papers include transl. of Special Order of the Day to troops at Baku from Lenin, May 1920; 'Narrative of Operations against Bolsheviks at Enzeli', 18 - 19 May 1920; TS copies of various orders captured from the Russians, Sept. 1920 (**7808-94**). *See list for details*

185.6 RAGLAN PAPERS (6807-279 to -305)

Crimean Head Quarters' papers of Lord Fitzroy Somerset, 1st Baron Raglan (1788-1855) include: official correspondence with Newcastle and Panmure as Secretaries of State for War (**-281 to -286**); dispatches from Alma, Balaclava, Inkerman, Kerch', Redan and siege of Sebastopol (**-288**); correspondence with S. Herbert, HQ Staff, Board of Ordnance (**-289**), Aberdeen, Palmerston, Lord John Russell, Sir John Graham, Sir Clive Wood, George William Villiers, 4th Earl of Clarendon, Foreign Office, Sir Charles Trevelyan (**-291**), Stratford Canning, 1st Visc. Stratford de Redcliffe (**-292**), principal staff officers and Florence Nightingale (**-293**), British ambassador in Paris, French generals in the Crimea (**-294**), Turkish commanders and the British Mission (**-295**), Col. Fenwick Williams (**-296**), British admirals (**-298 to -300,-302**), intelligence reports (**-301**), British consuls (**-302,-303**), Russian commanders (**-304**). *See list and index of correspondents for details.*

185.7 ROBERTS PAPERS (7101-23)

Papers of Frederick S. Roberts, 1st Earl Roberts of Kandahar, include: documents re the defence of the North-West Frontier and the threat of invasion by Russia, 1880-1900 (**-162**); printed memos re Russia (**-168, -277**); TS memo by ?Roberts re possible Russian advance in Afghanistan (**-169-5**); correspondence and papers as C.-in-C. on the North-West Frontier including material on the Russian threat to India. *See list for details*

185.8 SAVORY, Lt-Gen. Sir Reginald (7603-93, -94)

TS autobiographical account of activities in Siberia with the British Military Mission, Apr. 1919 - May 1920 ; loose photographs of scenes in Siberia, correspondence and diaries from Vladivostok, 1919-29. *See list for details.*

185.9 WARRE, Gen. Sir Henry James (7212-10)

Microfilms of papers include diaries covering his service in the Crimean War (**-12 to -15**).

Nineteenth-century miscellaneous documents

185.10 Diary of Maj. Henry Walter Bellow covering the Crimean War, 1855 (**5112-21**).

185.11 Newspaper cuttings re and letter from Col. H. Shirley to Miss Storey from the Crimea, 4 Feb. 1855; letter from Sgt M. Horgan from Sebastopol, 4 Feb. 1855; home-made playing card pack; Russian-Bulgarian phrase book (**5407-15**).

185.12 Plan of siege of Sebastopol (**5409-13**).

185.13 Printed Naval Orders for the disembarkation of the Army in the Crimea; letter from Sir Evelyn Wood to Rear-Adm. J. W. Whyte, 1854 (**5501-7, 8**).

185.14 Proof copy of critique of "Kinglake Crimea"; miscellaneous letters re the Crimean War (**5602-51**).

185.15 Souvenirs of the Jubilee and Centenary Luncheon of the Charge of the Light Brigade; typewritten account of the action at Balaclava (**5610-47**).

185.16 Plans of the positions at Sebastopol, 1854 (**5704-64**).

185.17 Documents re 'Crimean Tom', the cat brought home from the Crimea (**5803-10**).

185.18 Illuminated Turkish documents from the Crimea, brought back by Lt-Gen. W. C. Forrest (**5804-5**).

185.19 Letters and documents of Gen. W. C. Forrest including service in the Crimea with the 4th Dragoon Guards (**5802-32**).

185.20 Letters written from the Crimea by Col. P. L. Clowes (**5807-11**).

185.21 Press cutting album of W. C. Forrest includes reports of the inquiry into the state of the army before Sebastopol (**5901-3**).

185.22 Letter from Capt. A. J. Layard, RN, to his brother from the Crimea; letters re his death on board HMS *Faith*, 1855 (**5903-128-9**).

185.23 List of goods sent to the Crimea, 1854 (**5910-220**).

185.24 Typed copy of extracts from letters written by Dr John Bent from the Crimea, 1855 (**5910-304**).

185.25 Bill of exchange made out to Lord Raglan, Balaclava, 6 Feb. 1855 (**5910-329**).

185.26 Letter from Florence Nightingale to G. S. Beatson, Staff Surgeon, from Balaclava, 15 June 1856 (**5912-174**).

185.27 Certificate for rations received in transport vessel off Balaclava, 27 Aug. 1855 (**6008-86**).

185.28 Copy of a letter and accompanying sketch from Adm. M. B. Dunn to his sister from Balaclava (**6012-340**).

185.29 3 letters from Robert Bagshaw from the Crimea where he served as a ganger in the Army Works Corps (**6112-35**).

185.30 Letter from Capt. S. T. Gordon to William Hale Noble from the Crimea, 5 Nov.1854 (**6112-406**).

185.31 Account of brave conduct of two soldiers of the 47th Foot at the Alma (**6112-479**).

185.32 Letter from Pte George Savery, 38th Foot, to his father written on a Russian pass after the fall of Sebastopol, 18 Sept. 1855 (**6204-6**).

185.33 The 3 original orders for the Charge of the Light Brigade received by Maj.-Gen. George Charles Bingham, 3rd Earl of Lucan, at Balaclava (**6211-4**).

185.34 Printed pamphlet of letters received from Sgt John Hopkins during the Crimean War (**6301-89**).

185.35 Letter from Sir Henry Fowle-Smith to A. W. Kinglake describing the death of Lord Raglan, July 1877 (**6305-162**).

185.36 2 notebooks containing copies of letters from Maj. William Charles Forrest to his wife and mother from the Crimean War (**6309-5-1,-2**).

185.37 File of biographical material re VC including awards to Sgt Alfred Ablett, Sir Collingwood Dickson and Capt. Henry Mitchell Jones after action at Sebastopol (**6309-115**).

185.38 Map of Sebastopol, 1858 (**6311-55**).

185.39 Letters from Pte G. Burdis to his family, 27 Oct. 1854, and Pte Sruffe to Burdis's father, 29 May 1855 (**6311-151**).

185.40 Letter from H. Clark of the Land Transport Corps from the Crimea, 1855 (**6402-33**).

185.41 Letter from George Williams to his brother from the Crimea, 13 Dec. 1854 (**6403-17**).

185.42 General Order of 5 Dec. 1856, thanking the British German Legion on the occasion of their disbandment; newspaper cuttings re Legion (**6409-15**).

185.43 Photostat copy of documents re Trumpet-Maj. Joy, 17th Lancers, Balaclava 1854 (**6410-3**).

185.44 Diary by Hepton Bassett Scott of the Crimean War (**6508-2**).

185.45 Small envelope of letters from the Crimean War (**6509-3-3**).

185.46 Diary by Lt Col. R. H. Russell covering service in the Crimea, 1855-6 (**6509-25**).

185.47 3 letters by Capt. E. A. Perceval to his father from the Crimea, June-Aug. 1855; 4 sketches of the Crimea; bundle of Russian documents and MS sheet music, with inscription 'Taken in Tchernaya after the bombardment, 1855' (**6509-139**).

185.48 Collection of letters by Hepton Bassett Scott from the Crimea, with typed transcript, Jan.-Nov. 1855 (**6601-2**).

185.49 Map of Sebastopol showing positions of Allied armies, 1854 (**6605-42**).

185.50 2 TS copies of letters from Lt Henry B. Roberts to his family from Camp Balaclava, 27 Oct., 2 Nov. 1854 (**6702-36**).

185.51 Notebook containing MS account of the 88th Foot at the battle of Inkerman 'compiled from statements of officers present with the Rangers during that action' by Lt-Col. Nathaniel Steevens (**6706-30**).

185.52 TS copies of 4 letters written by Capt. Thomas Everard Hutton after the battle of Balaclava, Oct. 1854 (**6707-16**).

185.53 TS copy of a letter by C. H. Bracebridge from hospital in Scutari barracks, 13 Nov. 1854 (**6707-24**).

185.54 MS transl. of the private journal of a Russian artillery officer in the Crimea, the original found in Sebastopol after its capture, Jan.-Apr. 1855 (**6709-36**).

185.55 Notebooks of Canon W. M. Lummis re Charge of the Light Brigade including correspondence re casualty figures and muster rolls (**6801-25**).

185.56 Letters from Capt. Charles Milligan to his mother from the Crimea, including references to the British German Legion, July 1854 - June 1856 (**6802-4**).

185.57 Letters from A. W. Kinglake to Gen. Frederick Harris re his history of the Crimean War and including sketch maps of action in the Crimea (**6802-4**).

185.58 Map of position of the British Army before Sebastopol, 16 May 1855 (**6803-22**).

185.59 Copy of MS journal of Capt. James Armar Butler, Ceylon Rifle Regiment, who was killed whilst serving with the Turkish Army at the siege of Silistria, June 1854 (**6803-45**).

185.60 2 vols of documents re history of the Rifle Brigade comp. by Sir William Cope including: copies of letters from Sir Arthur Lawrence to his wife from the Crimea (**p. 341**); copy of Gen. F. Canrobert's General Order of 21 Nov. 1854 (**p. 397**); copies of letters written from the Crimea by Fitzroy Freemantle (**p. 443**) (**6804-2**).

185.61 Autograph letters and autographs of notable personalities connected with the Crimean War (**6804-3**).

185.62 Letters by J. H. U. Spalding from the Crimea and correspondence re his death during the siege of Sebastopol, Jan. 1855 (**6804-4**).

185.63 Diary of Mark Walker covering service in the Crimean War as Adjutant of the 30th Foot, 18 Apr. 1854 - 14 July 1860 (**6807-85**).

185.64 Letter from Lord Raglan to Lord Stratford, Sebastopol, 11 Jan. 1855 (**6807-133**).

185.65 Letter from Sup.-Gen. W. T. Doyne, Army Works Corps, to Sir Joseph Paxton, with plans of a new military road from Balaclava to Sebastopol, 14 Apr. 1856 (**6807-142**).

185.66 Recollections of the battle of Inkerman by Sir Frederick Paul Haines, R. D. Astley, J. Ayde, and Charles West, 6th Earl De La Warr, sent to A. W. Kinglake for his history (**6807-146**).

185.67 Account by Pte Daniel Bourke of his experiences in the Crimean War, written in 1910 (**6807-152**).

185.68 TS extracts by Lt (later Maj.-Gen. Sir) Thomas Townsend Pears from a journey to India via the Black Sea and Armenia, 1837 (**6807-214**).

185.69 2 TS vols by Maj. (later Sir) Lumley Graham of his Crimean journal, 3 Apr. 1854 - 29 Apr. 1855 (**6807-231**).

185.70 Leather bound notebook containing part of the journal of a British officer serving with the Turkish Army, 15 May - 15 June 1854 (**6807-232**).

185.71 MS plan of the English and French trenches at the attack at Sebastopol by Lt B. G. Humphrey, Sept. 1855 (**6807-241**).

185.72 Part of a MS notebook containing copies of letters from the Crimea by Henry Timson, 6th Dragoons, including an account of the Charge of the Heavy Brigade at Balaclava (**6807-244**).

185.73 Private journal of Surgeon C. Pine, beginning in the Heavy Cavalry camp, Balaclava, 6 Oct. 1854 (**6807-262**).

185.74 Letters and diaries of Lt-Col. G. L. Carmichael during the Crimean War and the Indian Mutiny (**6807-264**).

185.75 Bound MS containing copies of letters by Col. A. C. Sterling from the Crimea and a later commentary on the battles (**6807-270**).

185.76 Regimental Order Book of the Mounted Staff Corps in the Crimean War, 23 Sept. 1854 - 12 Aug. 1855 (**6807-354**).

185.77 Letter, with sketch, from Maj.-Gen. Charles Gordon to his brother from Sebastopol, 28 Feb. 1855 (**6807-366**).

185.78 3 forms of prayer and thanksgiving used in the Crimean War (**6807-394**).

185.79 Memorandum by Brig. R. Taylor re the assault on Sebastopol, July 1855 (**6807-449**).

185.80 Bundle of letters by the Gage family include accounts of the battles of the Alma and Balaclava (**6807-484**).

185.81 TS letters by Henry Gregory re service with the 13th Light Dragoons in the Crimean War and including an account of the Charge of the Light Brigade (**6808-8**).

185.82 Album of press cuttings of W. C. Forrest re mainly the reports of the inquiry into the state of the army before Sebastopol (**6901-3**).

185.83 Journal of Henry Ridley James re Crimean War, 14 Sept. 1854 - 21 May 1855; letter to his mother, 27 May 1855 (**6901-46**).

185.84 Letter from Thomas Smith to his brother from camp before Sebastopol, 13 Feb. 1855 (**6905-22**).

185.85 Photocopy of letter by Lt E. A. Stotherd to his brother desribing the battle of the Alma, 21 Sept. 1854 (**6905-25**).

185.86 Photocopies of letter from James Evans, 97th Foot, to friends from the camp before Sebastopol, 23 June 1855 (**6910-7**).

185.87 Diary of Maj. Edward Wellesley, 73rd Foot, covering service in the Crimea, Apr.-Sept. 1854 (**7006-8**).

185.88 TS copy of letter from L. Prendergast to Col. Williams re experiences with the Scots Greys in the Crimean War, Dec. 1906 (**7009-9**).

185.89 Letter by C. Campbell from the Crimea, May 1855; newspaper cuttings of obituaries (**7011-4**).

185.90 Letter by Sous-Officer François Lambelet, French Army, written before Sebastopol, 14 Dec. 1855 (**7201-21-2**).

185.91 Musical score,'The 7th Royal Fusiliers, A Story of Inkerman' (**7202-27-1**).

185.92 Letters, press cuttings, programmes re the bugle of Trumpet-Maj. Joy, said to have been used at the Charge of the Light Brigade (**7202-36**).

185.93 Letter from William Simpson to his wife from near Varna, 30 June 1854 (**7203-23**).

185.94 5 letters by N. Kingscote, Scots Guards, from the Crimea, Sept. 1854 - Jan. 1855 (**7205-28**).

185.95 Letter from unknown person describing conditions during the siege of Sebastopol, 6 Aug. 1855; letter from Ensign Alexander Lyon Emerson to his father from Sebastopol, 18 Apr. 1856 **(7206-22)**.

185.96 TS summary of life of William Cattell including his service with the 5th Dragoon Guards in the Crimea **(7208-4)**.

185.97 2 memos by Col. C. A. Windham after the battle of Inkerman, 6 Nov. 1854 **(7208-13)**.

185.98 Letter from Lt Alfred Howell to his brother from Kerch', 24 Nov. 1855 **(7208-51)**.

185.99 Folding, linen-backed map of the 'Theatre of War', 1853 **(7210-38)**.

185.100 TS copy of letter by 'Robert', a soldier in the 2nd Dragoons (Royal Scots Greys), describing the battle of Balaclava, 13 Nov. 1854 **(7210-68)**.

185.101 Photocopies of transcripts of letters by Capt. Emilius Delme Radcliffe to his parents from the Crimea and India **(7211-52)**.

185.102 11 letters from Sgt Robert Larke to his family from the Crimea, 1855 **(7301-56)**.

185.103 Letter, written on the back of a printed Russian form, from Staff Sgt J. Brown to his parents re fall of Sebastopol, 13 Sept. 1855 **(7304-27)**.

185.104 Photocopies of 2 letters by Capt. Soames Gambier Jenyns, describing the battle of Balaclava and the Charge of the Light Brigade **(7305-6)**.

185.105 Letters from William Archer Amherst (afterwards 3rd Earl Amherst of Arracan), Frederick Paulet, John Wyatt and H. M. Addington re the action at Balaclava and the wounding of Amherst, Oct. 1854 **(7305-75)**.

185.106 A pass allowing Capt. Warren and party to pass through the trenches and Sebastopol, 15 Sept. 1855 **(7306-11)**.

185.107 Photocopy of TS journal of Daniel William Powell covering service in Crimean War, 12 Dec. 1854 - 31 May 1855 **(7306-22)**.

185.108 MS 'The lady with a lamp, a study [of] the legendary lamp carried by Miss Florence Nightingale in the hospital at Scutari during the Crimean War' by John W. Forsaith **(7306-26)**.

185.109 'Coldstream Guards, Nominal Return of Non Commissioned Officers, Drs and Privates who died during the Eastern Campaign from 23rd February 1854 to 30th June 1856' by Sgt-Maj. E. Wallis **(7309-52)**.

185.110 Letters from Nigel Kingscote, Scots Guards, to his father re his service in the Crimean War, Feb. 1854 - June 1856 **(7311-170)**.

185.111 79 letters by James Rowe, storekeeper at the Commissariat at Scutari to friends in England and part of his memoirs of the war **(7402-22)**.

185.112 Journal by Capt. J. A. Butler whilst serving at the defence of Silistria **(7402-129)**.

185.113 TS copy of an account of the Charge of the Light Brigade by James Mustard, 17th Lancers, the last survivor, who died in Feb. 1916 **(7402-154)**.

185.114 6 maps of Turkey with items on the back re the Crimean campaign, Apr. 1854 **(7403-27)**.

185.115 Photocopy of letter from Cornet George Wombwell, 17th Lancers, to Mr Scott from the Heights before Sebastopol, 2 Dec. 1854 **(7403-124)**.

185.116 Letter by Col. John St George describing the siege of Sebastopol, 9 June 1855 **(7405-16)**.

185.117 Photograph of Henry Press Wright wearing his Crimean decorations; photocopy of letter from the Crimea **(7405-84)**.

185.118 Atlas of the 1812 Russian campaign, containing details of the strength of the French and Russian forces **(7406-42-11)**.

185.119 'A panoramic view of the Sea of Azov, Kerch....showing the positions taken by the Allies, likewise comprising the whole of the Crimea', June 1855; 'Carte des voies de Communication de la Russie d'Europe et des états voisins dressée par ordre de S.M. L'Empereur par L Sagasan',1854 **(7406-43)**.

185.120 68 letters by George Cruse, 1st Royal Dragoons, from the Crimea, May 1854 - May 1855 **(7412-76)**.

185.121 Letter from Pte E. Griffiths from camp before Sebastopol **(7501-50)**.

185.122 Petition requesting award of a VC to Col.-Sgt John Brophy for gallant action in the Crimean War, July 1846 **(7504-79-5)**.

185.123 Diary by Lt George Robertson covering service in the Crimea, 18 Dec. 1853 - 28 Mar. 1857 **(7508-61)**.

185.124 Duplicated TS transcripts of letters by Maj. G. C. Clowes from the Crimea, May 1854 - Sept. 1855 **(7509-59)**.

185.125 11 letters from Brevet-Maj. R. Poore to his parents from the Crimean War **(7509-60, -61)**.

185.126 Photograph of letter from Lt E. H. Webb to his mother from the camp before Sebastopol, 7 June 1855 **(7605-14)**.

185.127 Letter from F. ?Thorpe to his brother from the camp before Sebastopol, 3 Jan. 1855 **(7605-18)**.

185.128 Photocopies and transcripts of letter from Lt W. Drage to his parents from the Crimea, 1856 **(7605-77)**.

185.129 Journal by Lt Hugh Annesley, Scots Guards, during service in the Crimea, 1854 **(7606-10)**.

185.130 2 bound MS books containing two versions of memoirs by Cpl John Fisher of service in the Crimea, *c.* 1860 **(7606-38-9)**.

185.131 Photocopies of 3 letters from Pte James Rixon to his family describing the battles of the Alma and Inkerman, Nov. 1854, Jan., Feb. 1855 **(7607-27)**.

185.132 Photocopy of printed letter from George Greenfeld to his wife and family from the heights above Sebastopol, 24 Nov. 1854 **(7607-85)**.

185.133 Letter from Pte T. Hagger to his parents from camp before Sebastopol, 1 Dec. 1854 **(7608-32)**.

185.134 Photocopies of letters from Lt J. G. Harkness to his mother from the camp before Sebastopol, 17, 22 Oct. 1854 **(7611-37)**.

185.135 Photocopy of letter re battle of Balaclava, 8 Nov. 1854 **(7703-52)**.

185.136 Transcripts of 3 letters re death of Lt H. G. Teesdale after the battle of the Alma, Oct. 1854 **(7704-17)**.

185.137 TS account of the life of Gen. Sir Hugh Rowlands covering his service in the Crimea, comp. 1977 **(7706-12)**.

185.138 3 letters from Lt (later Sir) G. J. Young to his mother re Crimean War, Mar.-Aug. 1854 **(7706-29)**

185.139 Letter from Lt H. S. Ryder, 2nd Bn Rifle Bde, to his parents, and letters of condolence after his death during the attack on the Redan **(7712-46)**.

185.140 Photograph of a plan showing the order of disembarkation of the British Expeditionary Force in the Crimea, Varna, 2 Sept. 1854 **(7721-21)**.

185.141 Pencil sketch of Prince A. S. Menshikov's palace at Sebastopol by Maj.-Gen. Walter Newman, 13 Feb. 1856 **(-9)**; letter from the Crimea **(-22) (7801-71)**.

185.142 2 letters from Pte Robert Hull to his wife from the Crimean War, 4 May, 12 July 1854 **(7804-39)**.

185.143 2 letters by Pte Alexander Hood to his cousin from the Crimea, 15 Jan., 24 Feb. 1855 **(7805-47)**.

185.144 Certificates of French and Turkish decorations awarded to Col. Frederick Evelegh for service in the Crimean War **(7807-56)**.

185.145 Photocopy of 4 letters from Dr Alfred Roberts to his wife re visit to the Crimea and Constantinople and service at Renkoi Hospital, Aug.-Nov. 1855 **(7808-54)**.

185.146 Microfilm copies of transcripts of letters from Assistant Surgeon William Leslie from the Crimea, 18 June 1855 - July 1856 **(7808-82)**.

185.147 Microfilm copy of TS transcripts of memoirs of Gen. H. R. Browne including his service in the Crimea **(7901-78)**.

185.148 Photocopy of letter from Richard Willis to his sister from the Crimea, 6 Mar 1855 **(7902-57)**.

185.149 Transcript of 2 letters by Capt. G. C. Morgan to his father describing the Charge of the Light Brigade, 27, 30 Oct. 1854 **(7903-2)**.

185.150 TS copy of diary of Sgt James Taylor covering his service in the Crimea (**7905-51**).

185.151 TS transcript of letter from Lt H. H. Jolliffe to his father describing the Charge of the Light Brigade, 28 Oct. 1854 (**7907-148**).

185.152 4 letters from Pte Richard Morgan to his brother from Portsmouth and the camp before Sebastopol, Dec. 1854 - Mar. 1856 (**7908-6**).

185.153 Microfilm of diaries by Col. E. B. Reynardson re service in the Grenadier Guards in the Crimea, 1854-5 (**7908-56**).

185.154 Roll of the 11th Hussars at Balaclava, 15 Oct. 1854 (**7908-61**).

185.155 Photocopy of diary and notebook of Dr W. A. Barr covering voyage and arrival at Scutari, 4 Nov. 1854 - 7 Jan. 1855 (**8003-76**).

185.156 Lithographed account of the Crimean War from May 1855 onwards, describing the capture of Sebastopol, written in 1900 (**8010-12**).

185.157 Scrapbook of Bde Surgeon F. B. Baker, Scots Fusilier Guards, including papers re service in the Crimea (**8010-22**).

185.158 Diary of Lt J. C. G. Kingsley, Cape Mounted Riflemen, including voyage to the Crimea, Apr.-Sept. 1854 (**8011-9**).

185.159 6 letters from Lt H. J. Alderson to his mother during the Crimean War, Aug. 1854 - Mar. 1855 (**8011-54**).

185.160 4 letters from Veterinary Surgeon Hicks Withers to his father from the Crimea, July 1854 - Jan. 1855; MS and printed accounts of the battle of Balaclava (**8106-66**).

185.161 Photocopy of transcript of a letter from Lt H. E. Handley to his mother describing the battle of Balaclava, 27 Oct. 1854 (**8110-69**).

185.162 Photocopied transcripts of diaries and letters by Lt.-Col. C. L. Cocks from the Crimean War, 1854-6 (**8111-13**).

185.163 'Letter Book of the Provisional Battalion 11th December, 1854', containing copies of letters from Balaclava, 11 Dec. 1854 - 20 May 1856 (**8111-58**).

185.164 Photocopy of diary by Lt H. Tower, Coldstream Guards, of service in the Crimea, 1 Apr. 1854 - 9 July 1856 (**8202-18**).

185.165 Letters re mainly uniforms of the British Army including uniforms in the Crimea (**8204-734**). *See list for details.*

185.166 6 short stories on aspects of life in the Crimea and 'Recollections of events and incidents connected with my campaigning in Turkey and the Crimea' by Staff Sgt William Wharin, Mar.-Sept. 1854 (**8210-86**).

185.167 38 letters from Maj. W. P. Radcliffe to his parents whilst serving in the Crimea (**8212-29-44**). *See list for details.*

185.168 Memoirs written by an Orderly Cpl of the 49th Regiment re his service in the Crimea (**8301-7**).

185.169 Photocopy of 'Reminiscences of Twenty Five Years Service in the XCIII Sutherland Highlanders by Lt General F. W. Traill Burroughs C B 1848 to 1873' covering his service in the Crimea (**8305-24**).

185.170 Photocopies and transcripts of 11 letters from Lt Frank J. Curtis to his sister on route to and in the Crimea; letters of condolence re his death (**8307-48**).

185.171 TS transcript of letter from Sir William Gordon, Bt., to his mother describing the Charge of the Light Brigade (**8310-132**).

185.172 2 vols of letters containing copies of letters from Capt. Edward Seager, 8th Hussars, to his family from the Crimea, 5 June 1854 - 15 Aug. 1855 (**8311-9**).

185.173 Diary and letters from Capt. C. B. Phillips, 39th Regt, to his mother from the Crimea (**8311-29**). Prior permission to publish extracts from these papers must be obtained from the donor.

185.174 Microfilm copies of 54 letters from 1st Class Staff Surgeon J. S. Prendergast to his brothers and sisters from the Crimea, 31 Dec. 1854 - 1 July 1855 (**8312-7**).

185.175 Pencil sketch plan of the Charge of the Heavy Brigade by Hon. Maj. Solomon Williams, 4th Dragoon Guards (**8312-52**).

185.176 TS transcript of a letter addressed to 'Monsr le Marechel' written before Sebastopol, French, 18 Aug. 1855 (**8401-30-2**).

185.177 TS transcripts of 4 letters from Capt. Charles Glazbrook, 49th Foot, to his mother from the Crimea, 3 May - 21 Sept. 1854 (**8401-100**).

185.178 Letters to the Preston family including from their children serving in the Crimea (**8402-25**). *See list for details.*

185.179 Microfilm copy of MS memoirs entitled 'Reminiscences of the Crimean War by J. Beardsley, Late C Troop RHA' (**8405-131**). Access forbidden until 1 May 1991.

185.180 Letters from George Valentine Mundy describing his service in the Crimea, Feb. 1854 - July 1856 (**8409-31, -31 to -201**).

185.181 Letters from an unknown member of the 11th Hussars from the Heights of Sebastopol, 6 Jan. 1855 (**8503-36**).

185.182 Account of the Crimean War written by a member of the Light Company of the 38th Regt (**8504-98**).

185.183 33 letters by Sgt F. Newman, 97th Foot, during the Crimean War (**MF. 27/4**).

Twentieth-century miscellaneous documents

185.184 Letter from Petrograd re Mesopotamian campaign, First World War (**5904-198**).

185.185 Bundle of Russian propaganda posters from the Russo-Japanese War (**5905-42**).

185.186 Instructions to the British Military Mission to Finland and the Baltic States, 4 June 1919; account of operations; diary, 1919 (**6111-93**).

185.187 2 envelopes of papers re Artists Rifles in the North Russian campaign (**6112-637**).

185.188 Packet of letters from Trevor Barslow to his mother from Murmansk, 1918-19 (**6302-61**).

185.189 Map re Russo-Japanese War (**6312-260**).

185.190 2 letters; account and map of Archangel Expedition, 1918-19 (**6602-68**).

185.191 Diary of Capt. A. H. Brooke, 18th Lancers, re surveying mission on the Turco-Persian border, including reference to Russian troop build-up on the Turkish border, 1 Jan. - 14 Oct. 1914 (**6607-15**).

185.192 Vol. of TS letters by G. Uloth to his mother describing service in the 7th Light Cavalry in East Persia and Persian Baluchistan, 1915-18, and operations against the Bolsheviks in Russian Turkestan, Jan. 1918 - May 1919 (**7203-41**).

185.193 Letters by Lt-Col. Eustace Maxwell include Easter card sent to a Russian regiment by the Durham Light Infantry in 1916 (**7402-34-39**).

185.194 Letters from Lt-Col. H. K. Percy-Smith to his mother from the Black Sea, 8 Oct. 1917 - 25 Aug. 1919 (**7510-33**).

185.195 Diary by Maj. L. E. L. Maxwell including description of holiday on the southern shore of the Caspian Sea in July 1942 and comments on the Russian troops stationed there (**7603-20**).

185.196 Microfilm copy of memoir 'Adventures in Three Services' by Brig. A. R. Oram including service in Russia, First World War (**7904-48**).

185.197 Newspaper cuttings re Allied intervention in Russia and public reaction to events there (**8108-11**).

185.198 Press cuttings, orders and other items re service of Lt W. M. Beavan in a Labour Bn of the 1st Slavo-British Legion near Archangel, 1919, including information on the mutiny of the Bn (**8202-3**).

185.199 Microfilm copies of memoirs of Capt. E. H. Keeling, 119th Infantry, recounting his escape from Kut through Russia, 1917 (**8402-9**).

185.200 Notebook of Walter Harold Wilkin re his service as liaison officer with the White Russians at Archangel, 1919 (**8505-24,-8**).

Photographs

185.201 Large collection of photographs re Russia and the Soviet Union. Photographs can be found re the Crimean War (including of Balaclava, Inkerman and Sebastopol), Russo-Japanese War, the Eastern Front in the First World War, the Allied intervention in Russia and re the Russian army and navy in general. Details can be found in the card-indexes to photographs, particularly under the following headings: Crimean War, Russia, Russian Army, Russo-Japanese War, World War I Russia.

186.1
NATIONAL FILM ARCHIVE

British Film Institute, 81 Dean Street, London W1V 6AA

By appointment. The viewing service caters for private viewing by *bona fide* researchers on the Archive's premises (at least eight weeks' notice should be given) for which a small handling fee is charged. Copies of stills, posters and designs can be ordered and purchased. *Preliminary Title List*; catalogues of *Non-Fiction Films* arranged by country; card index of subjects.

186.1 Collection includes many Russian and Soviet documentary films and British documentary films relating to Russia and the Soviet Union dating from the early 20th century. *See catalogues and card index for details.*

187.1-110
NATIONAL MARITIME MUSEUM

Manuscripts Section, Greenwich, London SE10 9NF

By appointment. R. J. B. Knight, *Guide to the Manuscripts in the National Maritime Museum*, vol. 1, *The Personal Collections* (London, 1977), vol. 2, *Public Records, Business Records and Artificial Collections* (London, 1980). Records are arranged in handlists by the following sections: section 1 - Admiralty Records; section 2 - Dockyard Records; section 3 - S.N.R.A. List, Business Records; section 4 - Personal Papers; section 5 - Artificial Collections; section 6 - Single Volumes; section 7 - Single Documents; section 8 - Reproductions.

187.1 ALBYN LINE LTD (ALB)
Carried South Wales or Tyne coal to the Continent and returned with grain from Odessa. Papers include directors' and shareholders' minute books, cash books, ledgers, 1901-66; ships' voyage books, 1953-66; chief officers' log-books, 1960-66; 2 out-letter books, 1966.

187.2 ALTHAM, Capt. Edward (1882-1950) (RUSI 241)
Senior officer of the Archangel River Expeditionary Force serving in the *Fox*. Order books, 1918-19 (/2); privately printed *Bolos and Barishnyas*, an account of the North Dvina camp, 1919 (/5/5); photograph of northern Russia (/7); *The Soldiers' English-Russian Conversation Book* (/8).

187.3 ANDERSON COLLECTION (AND)
Extracts from Russian published works (/64); vol. of notes by R. C. Anderson on Russian Naval History (/72); MS vol. 'The Russian Fleet in the Baltic Sea and Mediterranean' (/170).

187.4 BAIRD, Dr William James (BGY/B)
Letters, memoranda and certificates covering his service in the Crimean War (/5).

187.5 BAYNES, Adm. Sir Robert Lambert (1796-1869) (BAY)
Served with the blockading fleet in the Baltic in 1855. Papers include official service documents, personal papers and an autobiographical outline of his career, 1810-57.

187.6 BEDFORD, Adm. Sir Frederick George Denham (1838-1913) (**BED**)
Served as Midshipman in the Crimea and the Baltic, 1854-5. Logs of HMS *Sampson*, *Victory*, *Vulture* and *Forth*, 1854-6 (/**1, 2**).

187.7 BETHUNE, Adm. Charles Ramsay Drinkwater (1802-84) (**DRW**)
Member of Embassy of the Earl of Durham to Russia to report on the naval installations in the Black Sea, 1835. Letters to his family, 1830-5 (/**4**).

187.8 BLANE, Sir Gilbert, 1st Bt (1749-1834) (**BLA**)
Physician of the Fleet. Letter from Paul I to Dr Blane, congratulating him on his book and accepting a copy of it, 1 Nov. 1799 (/**50**); letter from Count Vorontsov (?S. Vorontsov) transmitting a gold medal from the Empress of Russia to Blane, 1 Apr. 1786 (/**52**).

187.9 BRIDGES, Paymaster Lt Albert Francis Barclay (**BRG**)
Pocket diaries cover service in the Eastern Mediterranean and the Black Sea during operations against the Bolsheviks, 1918-20 (/**2, 3**).

187.10 CALDWELL, Capt. Henry (1815-68) (**CAL**)
Served in HMS *Duke of Wellington* in the Baltic during the Crimean War. Orders in the Baltic, 1855-6 (/**305**); remark book of HMS *Duke of Wellington*, 1855-6 (/**310**); orders and bills of the *Duke of Wellington*, 1856 (/**315**).

187.11 CHILDERS, Lt William Henry (1837-69) (**CHI**)
Served in HMS *Britannia* in the Crimea, 1852-4, and present at the battles of Alma and Sebastopol. Commissions, certificates, letters of appointment, orders, memoranda, 1852-69 (/**1**); letters to his parents mainly re the Crimean and Chinese Wars, 1851-63 (/**4**).

187.12 CODRINGTON PAPERS (**COD**)
Papers of Adm. Sir Henry John Codrington (1808-77) re the Crimean War include: logs of HMS *Royal George*, 1854-6 (**108/1,3-5**); signal log, 1854 (/**108/2**); signal log of HMS *Algiers*, 1856 (/**108/5**); letter-books, 1852-9 (/**109/1,2**); order-book, 1855-6 (/**109/3**); copies of certificates granted by Henry Codrington, 1853-6 (/**110/1**); sick list of HMS *Royal George*, 1854 (/**110/2**).

187.13 COLES, Capt. Cowper Phipps (1819-70) (**CCC**)
Papers re Russian navy (/**85**), Russian ironclads (/**358**).

187.14 COLLINSON, Vice-Adm. Sir Richard (1811-83) (**CLS**)
Notebook containing observations and calculations of magnetic declination made at Sitka (Russian America, now Alaska), 5 Nov. 1850 (/**26**).

187.15 COWAN, Adm. Sir Walter Henry, 1st Bt. (1871-1956) (**COW**)
Commanded the naval force in the Baltic during the anti-Bolshevik operations in 1920. Scrapbook by C. H. De Denne, Cowan's secretary, containing track chart of an engagement with the Bolsheviks, 18 May 1919 (/**23**).

187.16 DUNDAS, Adm. Sir James Whitley Deans (1785-1862) (**DND**)
In command in the Mediterranean at the outbreak of the Crimean War. Monthly returns of ships under his command, official and private correspondence, memo on the bombardment of Sebastopol, 1851-5 (/**1-11**).

187.17 EDGELL, Vice-Adm. Harry Edmund (1809-76) (**EDG**)
Out-letter book from HMS *Tribune* and *Bittern* in the Crimea, 1855-8 (/**1**).

187.18 FISHER, Adm. Sir William Wordsworth (1875-1937) **(FHR)**
In command of HMS *Iron Duke*, Mediterranean Fleet, 1919. Papers on the situation in the Black Sea and the Mediterranean, 1919-22 **(/10)**.

187.19 FRANK STAFF COLLECTION **(STF)**
Letters forwarded from St Petersburg to Philadelphia, 1823, 1828, 1837, 1840 **(Frame No. 11)**.

187.20 FRANKLIN, Sir John **(FRN)**
Letter to Mary Anne Kay describing his recent visit to Russia, 26 Oct. 1828 **(/21)**.

187.21 FREMANTLE, Adm. Sir Sydney **(FRE)**
Deputy Chief of Naval Staff, 1918-19. Papers and minutes re the Baltic provinces and North Russia, 1918-19 **(/316a, 316b)**.

187.22 GREIVE, Vice-Adm. William Samuel (*c.*1830-1892) **(WRE)**
Served as Lt in HMS *Penelope* in the Baltic during the Crimean War. Papers include log of *Penelope* **(/102)** and commissions, 1851-84 **(/104)**.

187.23 HARTWELL PAPERS **(HAR)**
Papers of Dr John Lee (1783-1866) **(/301-59)** include letters dealing with the transl. and publication in 1856 of a *Memoir* of the Russian circumnavigator, Adm. Krusenstern (I. F. Kruzenshtern).

187.24 THE HENLEY COLLECTION **(HNL)**
Voyage accounts, correspondence, bills of lading, accounts etc. re voyages of the *Ann, Anna Maria, Cornwall, Dolly, Eagle, Freedom, Heart of Oak, Henley, Holderness, Lady Juliana, London, Lord Nelson, Mary, Mary Ann, Montreal, Nelly, Norfolk, Peggy, Pitt, Polly, Queen, Star, Telemachus, Valiant, Zephyr* to St Petersburg, Riga, Archangel, Narva and Onega, 1786-1830. *See list for details.*

187.25 JENKINSON, Rear-Adm. Henry (1790-1865) **(JEN)**
3 letters to his mother from St Petersburg, Nov. 1816 - Jan. 1817 **(/4)**.

187.26 JERRAM, Adm. Sir Martyn (1858-1933) **(JRM)**
C.-in-C. of the China Station, 1915-18. Papers re the China Station include reports of an interview at Vladivostok and letters from Russian officers **(/16)**.

187.27 JOHNSTONE, Vice-Adm. Charles (1843-1927) **(JOH)**
Newspaper cuttings and accounts re Russo-Japanese War **(/38)**.

187.28 KELLOCK, C. W. & Co. **(KCK)**
Papers cover the period of the Crimean War when the Company acted as brokers and appraisers to the Admiralty and sold a number of Russian prizes.

187.29 KEPPEL, Adm. the Hon. Sir Henry (1809-1904) **(HTN)**
Served in HMS *Rodney* in the Black Sea during the Crimean War. Papers include logs, 1853-7, annual diaries, 1855-7, letters to his family during the Crimean War.

187.30 LLOYDS REGISTER OF SHIPPING **(LLY)**
Surveyors' reports and plans of foreign ports include Riga, 1889 **(/1140)**, and Sebastopol, 1891 **(/1150)**.

187.31 THE MACKINNON HOOD PAPERS (**MKH**)

Papers of Vice-Adm. Sir Samuel Hood, 1st Bt., (1762-1814), second-in-command to Adm. J. S. Saumarez in the Baltic include letters, orders and memos from Saumarez, 21 Mar.-20 Oct. 1808 (**/109**), miscellaneous papers re Hood's capture of the Russian ship *Sewolod* (*Vsevolod*), 26 Aug. 1808 (**/110**).

187.32 MARKHAM, Adm. Sir Albert Hastings (1841-1918) (**MRK**)

Album of views (photographic plates) made during the Arctic voyage of the *William Barents* 1876 including Novaya Zemlya (**/12**).

187.33 THE MARTIN PAPERS (**MTN**)

Papers of Cdr Henry John Martin (1841-76) include log-book of HM steam frigate *Curacoa*, 1854-7 (**/101-102**), letters written to his family including references to the Crimean War, 1855-61 (**/107**).

187.34 MEYNELL, Lt Francis (1821-70) (**MEY**)

Log-book of HMS *Royal George* by Capt. H. J. Codrington, illustrated by Meynell, while in the Baltic in the Crimean War, 1853-4; 11 water colour drawings and a chart of the Black Sea (**/1**); press cuttings and letters to his father during service in HMS *Royal George* in the Baltic, 1854 (**/7**).

187.35 MICHELL, Adm. Sir Frederick Thomas (*c.*1785-1873) (**MIC**)

In command of HMS *Queen* in the Crimean War. Collection of commissions, appointments and letters cover his whole career, but the Crimean papers are the most numerous, and include landing orders, 1854, and orders for the bombardment of Sebastopol.

187.36 MILNE PAPERS (**MLN**)

Papers of Sir Alexander Milne, 1st Bt., include memo on the Russian steam navy (**/142/3**), papers re transport in the Crimean War, 1854-6 (**/156**).

187.37 MONTAGU, Rear-Adm. the Hon. Victor (1841-1915) (**SAN**)

Transcript of letters from the Baltic and the Black Sea during the Crimean War (**/T/101**).

187.38 MOORE, Adm. Sir Arthur (**BGY/M**)

Papers as C.-in-C. in China, 1905-08, include papers re the visit of the fleet to Vladivostok, 1907 (**/5**).

187.39 NAPIER, Adm. Sir Charles (1786-1860) (**NAP**)

Commanded the Baltic Fleet in the 1854 campaign as Vice-Adm. Correspondence, listed by name of correspondent, 1813-60. *See list for details.*

187.40 NOEL, Adm. Sir Gerard Henry Uctred (1845-1918) (**NOE**)

C.-in-C. in China, 1904-06. Papers include reports on the Russo-Japanese War (**/20**).

187.41 NORRIS, Adm. David Thomas (1875-1937) (**NOS**)

Commanded the British naval forces in the Caspian Sea. Papers include: 'HM Sarlanza', May - Nov. 1915 ending with the ship being mined in the White Sea (**/1**); 'Caspian Letters of Proceedings once Despatches, 1918-19' (**/4**); 'Caspian Letters to R.A.B.S. and Russia 1919' (**/5**); 'Letters of Proceedings, Caspian 1918' (**/6**); 'Caspian Air Reports 1919' (**/7**); 'Dunsterforce and Oddments 1918-19' (**/8**); 'Caspian Fleet Temporary Memoranda 1919' (**/9**); 'In Signals at Baku 1918' (**/10**); 'Out Signals at Baku 1918 (**/11**); Caspian Air Photographs' (**/16**); printed *Steam Ships of the Caspian Sea* (**/18**).

187.42 PARKS FAMILY PAPERS (PKS)
Papers of Capt. Murray Thomas Parks (1862-1932) include a sketch of Maxemoff (? Vice-Adm. A. S. Maksimov), n.d. (*/4*).

187.43 PHILLIPP-CROKER COLLECTION (CRK)
Letter from Nelson to the Tsar of Russia, 1799; extract of letter to the Tsar recommending the award of the Cross of Malta to Lady Hamilton and Capt. Ball, 1799; drafts of letters from Nelson to Count P. A. von Pahlen, 16 May 1801; letter from Adm. A. G. Spiridov, 20 May 1801 (*/89/14*).

187.44 PHIPPS HORNBY PAPERS (PHI)
Papers of Adm. Robert Stewart Phipps Hornby (1866-1956) include visiting cards of Russian officers at the Mediterranean Station (*/202*) and papers re the visit of the Russian fleet to Tangiers, 1904 (*/210*).

187.45 PURCELL-BURET, Capt. Theobald John Claud (1939-50) (PUR)
Description of a tour of Russia, Poland and Czechoslovakia, 20 June - 19 July 1959, together with brochures and notes for a lecture on the tour (*/68*).

187.46 SHARPE, Vice-Adm. Philip Ruffle (1831-92) (SHP)
Personal journal while in HMS *Rattlesnake* in the Bering Straits, 1854-5 (*/4*).

187.47 SPRATT, Vice-Adm. Thomas Abel Brimage (1811-88) (SPR)
Commanded HMS *Spitfire* during the Crimean War. Autobiographical papers re the Crimean War (*/1/3,4*); report re the Bug and approach to Nikolaev (*/2/5*); letters re the Crimean War (*/3/7,8*).

187.48 STOPFORD, Vice-Adm. Sir Montagu (1798-1864) (STO)
General orders and memoranda issued to the fleet in the Crimea by Stopford as Captain of the Fleet, 1854 (*/202*).

187.49 THESIGER, Adm. Sir Bertram Sackville (1875-1966) (TGR)
Served in HMS *Calypso* in the North Sea and the Baltic, 1917-19. Journal, 1916-18 (*/4*); papers on Estonia (*/19*).

187.50 TIZARD, Capt. Thomas Henry (1839-1924) (TIZ)
Log of HMS *Dragon* during his service in the Baltic and Black Sea during the Crimean War, 1854-67 (*/1-2*).

187.51 WATERS, Capt. George Alexander (1890-1903) (WTS)
Logs of HMS *Simoom* covering his service in the Black Sea in the Crimean War, 1852-61 (*/2*).

187.52 WEBLEY-PARRY, Rear Adm. William Henry (1764-1837) (WEB)
Papers while serving in HMS *Centaur* in the Baltic include Adm. J. S. Saumarez's dispatches, 1808 (*/4*).

187.53 WHITE, Arnold (1848-1925) (WHI)
Journalist. Cuttings and 6 letters re Kishinev massacres, 1903 (*/119*).

187.54 Lt's log of the *Royal Transport*, given to Peter I by William III, 1697 (**ADM. L/T/138**).

187.55 List of French, Russian and German ships, *c.* 1880-1904 (**AFN/4**).

187.56 Letters from Adm. J. W. D. Dundas and Sir Thomas Byam to Adm. E. Hawker re the Crimean War, 1854 (**AGC/5/26**).

187.57 Holograph letter from Sir C. H. Knowles, St Petersburg, 20 Sept. 1772 (**AGC/7/15**).

187.58 Holograph letter from Edmund Lyons from HMS *Agamemnon* at Varna, 16 Aug. 1854 (**AGC/7/31**).

187.59 Report by Capt. Edmund Moubray to Capt. E. Ommanney during operations in the White Sea, 1854-5 (**AGC/7/32**).

187.60 Résumé of operations in the Black Sea by Capt. E. Ommanney, 1854 (**AGC/9/17**).

187.61 Extract from a letter from Mr Stuart to Charles James Fox as Foreign Secretary from St Petersburg, 20 Aug. 1806 (**AGC/14/15**).

187.62 Document signed by Charles Whitworth, St Petersburg, 27 Dec. 1799 (**AGC/16/25**).

187.63 Holograph letter from Capt. John Stewart to James Sykes re Turkish relations with England, France and Russia, 25 Mar. 1809; report from Capt. E. M. Lyons re attack on Kola in the Baltic campaign of 1854 (**AGC/30**).

187.64 10 letters by William Hall, English surgeon with the Russian Navy, n.d. (**AGC/36**).

187.65 Letters by Capt. E. Ommanney re the Crimean War, 1853-4 (**AGC/49**).

187.66 Letters written by J. Davison from Sebastopol, 1854-5 (**AGC/D/7**).

187.67 Correspondence of Vice-Adm. Makerov (M. K. Makarov) with Sir Evan Nepean during the Anglo-Russian blockade of the Dutch coast, 1798-1801 (**AGC/M/2**).

187.68 7 letters by James Williamson, seaman on a transport, to his sister from Balaclava, 1854-6 (**AGC/W/9**).

187.69 TS of 'The war on the Finnish coast, 1854-5' by M. Borodkin, transl. from Russian (**HIS/39**).

187.70 Account of the action at Sebastopol by W. H. Hunkin, Coxswain, written in 1889 (**HSR/C/14**).

187.71 Account by Frederick Cleeve discussing relations between the army and navy during the Crimean War, written 1895-6 (**HSR/C/15**).

187.72 TS report of the actions between the Russians and the Japanese at Chemulpo and Port Arthur, Feb. 1904 (**HSR/D/3**).

187.73 Account of a chance meeting by Col. A. F. Birch-Jones with a Russian sailor who had fought in the *Dmitrii Donskoi* at the battle of Tsushima, 1905, and who told him the story (**HSR/D/5**).

187.74 Document, signed by Peter I, containing the line of battle and order of sailing of the Russian fleet for the summer campaign against the Swedes, 21 June 1719 (**HSR/HF/7**).

187.75 Sebastopol harbour from a Russian survey with the batteries and ships as seen from HMS *Retribution*, 6 Jan. 1854 (**HSR/X/12**).

187.76 Correspondence re evacuation of Russian refugees on the *Franz Ferdinand*, 1921 (**HSR/Z/1**)

187.77 Journal kept on board *St Dinnan*, a Russian privateer, 1788 (**JOD/46**).

187.78 Journal of Revd Robert Hinds, Chaplain in HMS *Rodney* during the Crimean War, 1853-6 (**JOD/64**).

187.79 Diary and sketch-book of Revd E. L. Bowman, Chaplain in HMS *Tribune* in the Black Sea, 1855 (**JOD/93**).

187.80 Journal of Cdr C. G. Grylls serving in HMS *Sans Pareil* in the Black Sea, Sept.-Oct. 1854 (**JOD/96**).

187.81 Diary of Alfred Kneale, HM trawler *Ganton*, in the Expeditionary White Sea Squadron, June 1915 - Apr. 1916 (**JOD/131**).

187.82 Journal of Henry H. Matchett, Chaplain in HMS *Blenheim* and HMS *Exmouth* at the Baltic Station, 20 Mar. 1854 - 19 Nov. 1855 (**JOD/144/1**).

187.83 Diary of Joseph Paul Hoskins in HMS *Cornwallis* in the Baltic, 1855 (**JOD/154**).

187.84 Diary of Midshipman William S. Bailey in the Crimean War, 1855-7 (**JOD/155**).

187.85 Journal of Leading Signalman E. E. Growcroft in the Aegean and Black Sea, Oct. 1918 - Jan. 1919 (**JOD/168**).

187.86 Diary kept by a short-term member of crew of HMS *Daffodil* at the evacuation of Murmansk and Archangel, 1919 (**JOD/194**).

187.87 Copy of letter-book of Capt. E. Ommanney, 1854-5 (**LBK/14**).

187.88 Copy of the letter-book of Adm. Sir William Houston Stewart re his service in command of HMS *Hannibal* in the Crimea, 1855-7 (**LBK/42**).

187.89 Copy letterbook containing correspondence betwen Adm. Sir Charles Knowles and Catherine II re his review of the Russian Navy, 1771-4 (**LBK/80**).

187.90 Logs of merchant ships include: the *Active* on a voyage from London to Riga, 1796 (**LOG/N/12**); the *Benjamin* on 2 voyages to St Petersburg and back, 1830-2 (**/29**); the *Great Britain* on 2 voyages carrying troops to the Crimea, 1855-6 (**/30**); the barque *Arundel* on a voyage from Liverpool to Odessa and back, 1836-7 (**/36**); the brig *Sancho* on 2 voyages to Archangel, 1848-50 (**/56**); the *Unity* on a voyage from Hull to St Petersburg, 1818 (**/74**); the schooner *Claymore*, kept during a cruise in the Mediterranean and Black Sea, 1858-60 (**/79**).

187.91 Logs of Royal Navy ships during the Crimean War include: HMS *Brunswick*, 1855 (**LOG/N/5**), *Albion* and *Queen*, 1853-55 (**/11**), *Waterloo*, *Duke of Wellington* and *Geyser*, 1853-5 (**/23**), *Arrogant*, 1854 (**/A/28**), *Wellington*, 1856-7 (**/D/10**), *Furious*, 1855-6 (**/F/5**), *Orion*, 1855-6 (**/O/1**), *Simoom* and *Snake*, 1853-5 (**/S/30**).

187.92 Microfilm of log kept by Capt. Mackenzie serving in HMS *Miranda* during the Crimean War **(MRF/104)**.

187.93 Microfilm of a diary by John C. Sabbens serving in HMS *Sphinx* in the Crimea, 1854-7 **(MRF/135)**.

187.94 Transl. from Russian of a paper by P. I. Belavenets re the Baltic campaign in the Crimean War **(NOT/40)**.

187.95 Navigational workbook of Staff Officer Cdr Henry A. Moriarty kept in HMS *Duke of Wellington* in the Baltic and the Mediterranean, 1853-7 **(NVP/16)**.

187.96 Photostat of a letter re the strength of the Russian and Swedish navies in the event of war, n.d. **(PST/21)**.

187.97 A confidential report addressed to the Rt Hon. Sir James Graham, Bt., First Lord of the Admiralty, re Baltic fleet and state of defences at Kronstadt, Reval etc., 1 Oct. 1853 **(RUSI/NM/86/28)**.

187.98 Fragmentary account of the incident on board the Russian battleship *Potemkin* by K. Perelingh, Sept. 1905 **(RUSI/NM/195)**.

187.99 Papers re the service of Adm. Edward Tatham, including his service in the Crimea **(RUSI/NM/236)**.

187.100 Transcript of the correspondence of Vice-Adm. George F. Hasting re service in HMS *Curacoa* in the Mediterranean and the Black Sea in the Crimean War **(TRN/10)**.

187.101 Transcript of 5 letters from George R. Donovan to his family written on HMS *Cormorant* in the Crimea, 1855-6 **(TRN/41)**.

187.102 TS transcript of a letter from B. R. Sulivan discussing Sir Charles Napier and the Baltic operations, 17 Sept. 1855 **(TRN/65)**.

187.103 Transl. from a history of the Solovetskii monastery (published in St Petersburg 1899) of an account of the attack on the monastery by British naval forces under Capt. Erasmus Ommanney, C.-in-C. of squadron in the White Sea in 1854 **(XHIS/1)**.

187.104 Reports by S. S. Haimun for *The Times* re Russo-Japanese War, 1904 **(XHSR/Z/1)**.

187.105 Photocopy of diary of J. W. Carmichael (1800-68), marine painter, during visit to the Baltic to join the Royal Naval ships fighting in the Crimean War, May - Aug. 1855 **(XJOD/7)**.

Accessions from 1981 (temporary class marks)

187.106 Approx. 50 letters by Seymour Spencer Smith of HMS *Curacoa* re life as cadet and midshipman during the Crimean War, 1854-6 **(MS81/049)**.

187.107 Papers of Percy F. Turner re Baltic and White Sea Conference, early 1920s **(MS81/141)**.

187.108 42 letters by Felix Webber, naval cadet and midshipman, mainly to his mother, including accounts of his service in HMS *Bellerophon* in the Crimean War **(MS82/143)**.

187.109 Papers of William Pickford, 1st Lord Sterndale (1849-1923), Master of the Rolls, almost exclusively re the North Sea incident of 21-22 Oct. 1904 (the attack on Hull fishing boats by ships of the Russian Fleet) (**MS84/091**).

Historic Photographs Section

187.110 The Historic Photographs Section of the National Maritime Museum holds the following photographs relating to Russia: 2 boxes entitled "Russia" containing photographs of Russian and Soviet ships, 1876-1969, with some photographs of line engravings of an earlier date; 2 boxes relating to the Crimean War, containing mainly photographs of engravings from the *Illustrated London News*; photographs of Petropavlovsk in the 1890s; album of photographs of the British Expeditionary Force in Archangel, 1919; album of photographs re the evacuation of Odessa, Feb. 1920. This Section is open to visitors by appointment only, on Tuesdays, Wednesdays and Thursdays.

188.1-3

NATIONAL MUSEUM OF LABOUR HISTORY

Limehouse Town Hall, Commercial Road, London E14

By appointment.

188.1 Postcard to J. T. Kent from Russia, n.d. (**JK 107**).

188.2 Notes on a Special Trades Union and Labour Conference on Labour and the Russo-Polish War, 13 Aug. 1920, and accompanying ephemera (**TM 118**).

188.3 Photographs of the USSR and prominent Russians. *See catalogue for details.*

189.1

NATIONAL PORTRAIT GALLERY ARCHIVE AND LIBRARY

15 Carlton House Terrace, London SW1Y 5AH

By appointment for *bona fide* researchers. Name index for artists' files.

189.1 Photographs of portraits and engravings of some Russian sitters in foreign sitters' files, and photographs of portraits by Russian artists in files on artists.

190.1

NATIONAL UNION OF RAILWAYMEN

Unity House, Euston Road, London NW1 2BL

By appointment. *See* entry for the Modern Records Centre, University of Warwick, where the records of the NUR are kept.

190.1 Photographs re the visit of a delegation of the NUR to the USSR, 1957 (main file of records are at the Modern Records Centre).

191.1

NAVAL HISTORICAL LIBRARY

Ministry of Defence, Empress State Building, London SW6 1TR

By appointment.

191.1 Copies of documents re the service of Adm. Sir Charles Knowles in the Russian Admiralty, 1770-4 **(Ba 012)**.

192.1

THE NIGHTINGALE SCHOOL

2 Lambeth Palace Road, London SE1 7EP

By appointment.

192.1 Collection of 13 Crimean War broadsheets pasted in an album.

193.1-3

THE ORDER OF ST JOHN MUSEUM AND LIBRARY

St John's Gate, St John's Lane, Clerkenwell, London EC1M 4DA

By appointment. Catalogues.

193.1 Copy of document re establishment of the Order of St John in Russia by Paul I, *post* 1797, French **(K2/26)**.

193.2 Protest by the Priory of St John of Russia against the cowardly surrender of Malta, 26 Aug. 1798, French **(K3/7)**.

193.3 Copy of the protest made by the Priory of St John of Russia with an account of the capture of Malta, 27 Aug. 1798 **(K7/23)**.

194.1

PHARMACEUTICAL SOCIETY OF GREAT BRITAIN

1 Lambeth High Street, London SE1 7JN

By appointment for *bona fide* researchers.

194.1 'Catalogus medicamentorum sinensium quae Pekini comparanda et determinanda curavit Alexander Tatarinov', 1856 (**615.7:915.1 (074:083.8)**).

195.1-62

POLISH INSTITUTE AND SIKORSKI MUSEUM

20 Princes Gate, London SW7 1PT

By appointment. The Polish Institute and Sikorski Museum came into existence in 1945. They house the largest collection in the West of documentary material relating to the independent Polish state, 1918-39, and Polish affairs in the Second World War, much of which relates to Polish-Soviet relations. *Guide to the Archives of the Polish Institute and Sikorski Museum*, comp. by W. Milewski, A. Suchcitz and A. Gorczycki, vol. 1 (London, 1985). Two further volumes are in preparation which will cover military records, including the records of the Polish Army created by Gen W. Anders in the USSR. Inventories exist for all classes in Polish. The majority of the documents are in Polish.

Government Records

195.1 CIVIL CHANCELLERY OF THE PRESIDENT OF THE POLISH REPUBLIC, 1939-49 (**A.48**)
Documents and correspondence re Polish-Soviet relations, 1941, 1943, and visit of PM S. Mikołajczyk to Moscow, 1944 (**/2**); papers re occupied Poland and the Warsaw uprising (**/4**); papers of the Ministry of Internal Affairs and Foreign Affairs (**/7**); papers re Polish refugees and deportees (**/8**).

195.2 COUNCIL OF MINISTERS, 1939-49 (**PRM**)
Papers of the Prime Minister and the Secretariat include documents re foreign affairs and occupied Poland.

195.3 MINISTRY OF FOREIGN AFFAIRS, 1918-45 (**A.11**)
Papers re Polish-Soviet relations, the foreign policy of the USSR, frontier and territorial problems, the Soviet occupation of Poland after Sept. 1939, Poles in the USSR in camps and their enforced resettlement, Polish armed forces in the USSR, military and political agreements between Poland and the USSR, Polish embassies in the USSR, the Katyń massacre.

195.4 MINISTRY OF INFORMATION AND DOCUMENTATION, 1940-9 (**A.10**)
Articles re occupied Poland.

195.5 MINISTRY OF INTERNAL AFFAIRS, 1940-9 (**A.9**)
Reports on the Soviet occupation of Poland; papers on national minorities in Poland.

195.6 MINISTRY OF LABOUR AND SOCIAL WELFARE, 1940-9 (A.18)
Papers re the protection of and aid for the Polish population in the USSR and supplies for Polish evacuees from the USSR.

195.7 MINISTRY OF PREPARATIONS FOR THE PEACE CONGRESS, 1939-45 (A.21)
Papers re the Soviet occupation of Poland; reports re Polish-Soviet relations.

195.8 POLISH EMBASSY IN LONDON, 1919-45 (A.12)
Papers re Polish foreign policy and occupied Poland.

195.9 POLISH EMBASSY IN MOSCOW AND KUIBYSHEV, 1941-3 (A.7)
Codes telegrams; reports; dispatches; instructions to the Ministry of Foreign Affairs; documents from representatives of the Polish embassy in the USSR.

195.10 THE POLISH NATIONAL COUNCIL, 1939-45 (A.5)
Advisory body to the Polish Government in Exile. Papers re foreign affairs and occupied Poland.

Private Collections

The collections below include papers relating specifically to the USSR but there will be further references to the USSR and Soviet policy in other private collections. See the *Guide* for details. Most of the collections relate to the experience of Poles in the USSR during the Second World War.

195.11 ALEXANDROWICZ, Maj. Stanisław (KOL.127)
Memoirs cover war service in the Polish-Soviet war.

195.12 ANDERS, Gen. Władysław (KGA)
Papers re Polish-Soviet relations as C.-in.-C. of the Polish Army in the USSR, 1942-3; papers re the formation and organization of the Polish Army in the USSR.

195.13 BĄKIEWICZ, Col. Wincenty (KOL.138)
Telegrams to and from the Polish forces in the USSR, Middle East and Italy, 1941-4; reports re tracing Polish nationals in the USSR, 1941-3; documents re the Soviet occupation of eastern Poland; eye-witness reports on conditions in Soviet prisons and camps; documents re the trial of 16 members of the Polish Underground State in Moscow; documents re the Polish Army in the USSR.

195.14 BANASIŃSKI, Eugeniusz (KOL.129)
Consul. Documents and photographs re the work of the Committee of Aid for the Polish Population in the USSR and re the evacuation of Polish children from the USSR.

195.15 BISIŃSKI, Lt Jan (KOL.254)
Diary and photographs re the Polish Army in the USSR, 1941-2.

195.16 BOBER, Maj. Jan (KOL.154)
Memoirs, sketches, memos and correspondence re his time as prisoner in the USSR, 1939-41.

195.17 BRZESZCZYŃSKI, Maj.-Gen. Stefan (KOL.262)
Memoirs and correspondence covering his service as Military Attaché in Moscow, 1939.

195.18 BRZEZICKI, Sgt Roman **(KOL.155)**
Memoirs cover his deportation to the USSR and service in the Polish Army in the USSR.

195.19 CELICHOWSKI, Dr Stanisław **(KOL.151)**
Papers re his internment in the USSR, 1942.

195.20 DZIĘGIELEWSKI, Stanisław **(KOL.247)**
Documents re his service for the Polish Embassy in Tashkent, 1943-4.

195.21 GAWEŁ, Lt-Col. Władysław **(KOL.242)**
Monitorings of Soviet radio communications, 1943.

195.22 GINSBERT, Lt-Cdr Julian **(KOL.160)**
Papers re his imprisonment in the USSR, 1939-41.

195.23 GROBICKI, Maj.-Gen. Jerzy **(KOL.80)**
Memoirs cover the Polish-Soviet War, 1919-20, and his imprisonment in the USSR; correspondence from the USSR; papers re the Katyń massacre, 1942-3.

195.24 GRODZICKI-ŁADA, Juliusz **(KOL.31)**
Papers and press cuttings re Polish-Soviet relations, 1943-5.

195.25 GWIAZDOWSKI, Tadeusz **(KOL.33)**
Diplomat. Papers re Polish-Soviet relations, 1945.

195.26 HOFFMAN, Dr Jakub **(KOL.18)**
Letters from prison in the USSR, 1940-1.

195.27 JACHNIK, Col. Stanisław **(KOL.215)**
Papers re the Soviet armed forces, life in the USSR and the sovietization of Poland, 1950s.

195.28 JANKOWSKI, Jan Stanisław **(KOL.49)**
Politician. Correspondence from Lubyanka prison, 1946-9; press material re his arrest and death, 1945-64.

195.29 KIERKOWSKI, Col. Kazimierz **(KOL.34)**
Diary covering life in the USSR and the Polish Army in the USSR; photographs of the USSR, 1939-44.

195.30 KMICIC-SKRZYŃSKI, Maj.-Gen. Ludwik **(KOL.66)**
Russian family papers and documents from the 19th century; memoirs covering service in the Polish-Soviet War, 1919-20.

195.31 KOMARNICKA, Irena **(KOL.153)**
Official documents of the Polish Embassy in the USSR, 1943-4; correspondence of T. Romer re Polish-Soviet relations, 1943-57.

195.32 KOMARNICKI, Prof. Wacław **(KOL.38)**
Papers re Polish-Soviet relations, 1941, 1943-4.

195.33 KOŃCZYC, Col. Piotr **(KOL.54)**
Papers and photographs re the Polish armed forces in the USSR, 1941.

195.34 KRUPA, Dr Jan **(KOL.165)**
Memoirs cover deportation to the USSR and the Polish Army in the USSR, 1941-2.

195.35 LIBERYS, Napoleon **(KOL.234)**
Diary covering life in Latvia and in the USSR; articles re Polish life in Latvia before and after the Soviet occupation.

195.36 LIPSKI, Józef **(KOL.2)**
Diplomat. Treatises re the USSR, communism and Ukrainian issues, 1941-9.

195.37 LIS, Lt-Col. Józef **(KOL.210)**
Studies and reports on the Polish Army in the USSR; Polish-Soviet documents, 1943-5; papers re the evacuation from the USSR, 1942.

195.38 MICHUŁKA, Maj. Stanisław **(KOL.172)**
Papers re Polish POWs in the USSR, 1940-1.

195.39 MŁYNARSKI, Capt. Bronisław **(KOL.75)**
Documents and sketches re camps in the USSR, 1940-1; documents re the Polish armed forces in the USSR; papers re the Katyń massacre; correspondence with Khrushchev.

195.40 MOSZCZEŃSKI, Lt-Col. Józef **(KOL.125)**
Military historian. Papers re his studies in Kiev.

195.41 OPAŁKA, Feliks **(KOL.56)**
Papers re the evacuation of the Polish Army in the USSR, 1941; documents issued by the Soviet government to Poles, 1941-2.

195.42 PAPROCKI, Stanisław **(KOL.30)**
Lawyer. Papers re the Ukraine and Polish-Ukrainian affairs, 1943-50.

195.43 PONINSKI, Count Alfred **(KOL.29)**
Diplomat. Essays and papers re the religious question in the USSR, 1926-34; documents re the Polish Legation in Moscow, 1927-37.

195.44 RACZYŃSKI, Count Edward **(KOL.23)**
Diplomat. Papers re Poles repatriated from the USSR, 1956-9.

195.45 ROMER, Tadeusz **(KOL.5)**
Diplomat. Microfilm of papers re Poles deported to the USSR; minutes of conversations with Soviet politicians, 1941-3; papers re the Katyń massacre.

195.46 SAVORY, Prof. Sir Douglas **(KOL.9)**
Papers re the Katyń massacre, 1941-52.

195.47 SIKORSKI, Gen. Władysław **(KOL.1)**
Diary, copies of correspondence, reports, press cuttings, official and private documents re Polish affairs including relations with the USSR, 1932-43.

195.48 SKOLIMOWSKI, Maj.-Gen. Aleksander **(KOL.268)**
Educated in Warsaw and St Petersburg. Memoirs covering service in the Imperial Russian Army, mid 19th century, Russian.

195.49 SOKOLNICKI, Henryk **(KOL.180)**
Memoirs as counsellor at the Polish Embassy in Moscow, 1941-2.

195.50 SUKIENNICKI, Prof. Wictor **(KOL.214)**
Papers re the Katyń massacre and Lithuanian affairs.

195.51 ŚWIANIEWICZ, Prof. Stanisław **(KOL.260)**
Papers re the Katyń massacre and his imprisonment in a Soviet labour camp, 1943-4.

195.52 SZEMBEK, Count Jan **(KOL.85)**
Diplomat. TS papers re Soviet affairs.

195.53 WAŃKOWICZ, Karol **(KOL.227)**
Agronomist. Diary of Polish-Soviet War, 1919-20. Microfilm.

195.54 WŁODKOWICZ, Capt. Józef **(KOL.266)**
Papers in Russian, 1919.

195.55 WOŁKOWICKI, Maj.-Gen. Jerzy **(KOL.212)**
Memoirs re his service in the Imperial Russian Navy (before 1914) and re his imprisonment in the USSR, 1939-41.

195.56 WYNNE-RUSHTON, Maj. Gerald **(KOL.223)**
Papers re the evacuation of Poles from the USSR, 1942-3.

195.57 ZAWIŁO, Warrant Officer Marian **(KOL.152)**
Memoirs covering imprisonment in the USSR, 1940-1.

Subject Collections

195.58 KATYŃ MASSACRE, 1940 **(KOL.12)**
Press cuttings, minutes of hearings and statements of witnesses, reports, documents on Polish-Soviet relations, lists of victims, diaries, telegrams, papers and correspondence re POWs in the USSR, publications, photographs, maps.

195.59 LITHUANIA **(KOL.168)**
Materials re Polish-Lithuanian relations, 1918-39; treatise by A. Merkelis re the deportation of Lithuanians to the USSR.

195.60 PRESS CUTTINGS **(KOL.272)**
Press cuttings re Russia, 1940-6, Poland and Russia, 1944-5, and Poland, Britain and Russia, 1941-5.

Military Records

195.61 These will be described in the additional two volumes of the *Guide to the Archives of the Polish Institute and Sikorski Institute* which are under preparation. They include the records of the Polish Armed Forces in the USSR (**A.VII**), Polish Army in the Middle East (**A.VIII**) and the GHQ of the Armed Forces (**A.XII**).There will also be accounts and reports (approx. 20,000) written by Polish prisoners in labour camps in the USSR, 1939-43, commenting on life in central, southern and eastern regions of the USSR, approx. 250 sheet newspapers and placards, hand-drawn in the USSR by Polish prisoners, and approx. 150 war diaries of various units of the Polish Army in the USSR created by Gen. W. Anders.

Visual Material

195.62 Some Soviet newsreels and films and stills re Poles in the USSR. The film collection is in the process of being catalogued and is not available at present. Approx. 100 maps including maps of Polish territories occupied by the Soviet army and the dispersal of Poles in the USSR. Photographs of the USSR, mainly 1939-45.

196.1-31

POLISH LIBRARY

283-246 King Street, London W6 0RF

By appointment. Most of the following documents are in Polish.

196.1 TS 'I was a Russian slave' by Arthur Lorin (**194/Rps**).

196.2 TS 'Stalin's son in German captivity' by Alexander Janta, Polish (**243a/Rps**).

196.3 TS 'In Russian service' by Bronisław Grąbczewski, Polish (**246/Rps**).

196.4 TS 'The Soviet system. Marxism and Stalinism, Communism and Sovietisation' by Ryszard Wraga, Polish (**255/Rps**).

196.5 TS 'The heavy industry in the Ukraine and its importance in the economy of the USSR' by Michał Bida, Polish (**351/Rps**).

196.6 Letters to Stefania Zahorska in London sent from Soviet occupied Vil'na, 1940, and letter from Al Wat from Alma-Ata, 17 June 1942.

196.7 Papers of Jan Wilczyński re the activities of the Polish community in Kiev, 1917-18, Polish (**403/Rps**).

196.8 Album of photographs of Poles in Soviet Russia, 1939-42 (**447/Rps**).

196.9 J. Alexandrowicz papers re the cadet schools of the Polish Army in the USSR, Iran and Italy, Polish (**456/Rps**).

196.10 Account by Władysław Guziewicz, Artur Gospodarczyk, Piotr Szyndlarewicz, Tadeusz Prządko, Józef Breywo and Franciszek Chrostowski of their deportation and exile in the USSR, Polish (**521/Rps**).

196.11 Poetry by a Polish insurgent of the insurrection of 1830-1 exiled to Siberia, *c.* 1840, Polish (**531/Rps**).

196.12 Poems written in and re the USSR by Tadeusz Chróściel, 1941-2, Polish (**536/Rps**).

196.13 Memoirs and record of conversations with Soviet people by B. P. Charles (**561/Rps**).

196.14 Vols 4 and 5, 1939-43, of the memoirs of Henryk Janiszowski covering imprisonment in the USSR, Polish (**572/Rps**).

196.15 TS 'The land of slavery', by Teresa Habdan, pseud., 1946, Polish (**602/Rps**).

196.16 TS 'Public libraries in Soviet Lithuania' by Kazimierz Okulicz, London 1975, Polish (**613/Rps**).

196.17 TS 'In the land of captivity', by Stanisław Lubodziecki, 1942-3, Polish (**616/Rps**).

196.18 TS 'The social welfare of the Polish deportees in the USSR and afterwards' by Wacław Stefan Flisiński, 1974, Polish (**620/Rps**).

196.19 203 letters, postcards etc. from Poles in the USSR to the editor of the Polish weekly *Polska* in Kuibyshev, Polish (**633/Rps**).

196.20 Lectures of and documents collected by Stanisław Lubodziecki, some re Soviet concentration camps and the Russian Revolution, Polish (**659/Rps**).

196.21 TS memoirs of Bronisław Brzezicki covering imprisonment in the USSR, 1943-5, Polish (**692/Rps**).

196.22 'The one story out of a 1000', 1942, by Wiesław Samborski including coloured drawings from the USSR, Polish (**694/Rps**).

196.23 TS 'The situation is changed' by Henryk Moszczyński re the USSR, 1943, Polish (**718/Rps**).

196.24 Telegram from Major Jacyna in Kuibyshev to Alina Jezewska in Altai, 1941, Polish (**715/Rps**).

196.25 TS 'Paratroopers from Kozelsk' by Henryk Moszczyński, London, 1944, Polish (**719/Rps**).

196.26 TS 'The Road' by Abraham Inselman, Odessa, 1966, Polish (**744/Rps**).

196.27 TS 'The Soviet invasion' by Edward Dubanowicz, Polish (**756/Rps**).

196.28 Photostats of documents re the nobility of the Zdziechowski family, 1828-58, from the Central State Historical Archive (Tsentral'nyi gosudarstvennyi istoricheskii arkhiv) in Leningrad, Polish (**758/Rps**).

196.29 TS 'From liberation to freedom' by Michael Strapko referring to the USSR (**775/Rps**).

196.30 TS 'The year of the Polish-Soviet agreement' by Mieczysław Pruszyński, 1942, Polish, and 4 TS letters re this memo.

196.31 The Library also holds the archives of the Polish weekly *Polska Walcząca* (Fighting Poland), published in Britain during the Second World War. Amongst letters from over 1,500 correspondents are letters from Poles in the USSR, including letters from Teodor Parnicki in Kuibyshev, 1942-3.

197.1

PORT OF LONDON AUTHORITY LIBRARY AND ARCHIVE COLLECTION

Units 39, 41, Cannon Workshops, West India Docks, London E14

By appointment.

197.1 The Library and Archive Collection house the minute-books of the private dock companies operating in London from 1799, and the minute-books of their successor, the Port of London Authority, from 1909. The minute-books are concerned with the administration of the docks, rather than with trade, and references to Russia and Russians will be few, although there may be references to leases of property to companies trading with Russia, problems relating to Russian cargoes and the misdemeanours of Russian sailors. The Surrey docks at Rotherhithe, whose minute-books date from 1801, dealt particularly with the timber trade and Russian ports. Printed pamphlets, with manuscript additions, are retained relating to duties on timber.

198.1-4

POST OFFICE ARCHIVES

The Post Office, Room SG 26-28, Headquarters Building, St Martin's le Grand, London EC1A 1HQ

Catalogues. See TS guide to the Post Office Records no. 12 'Historical Summary' and publications relating to Russia (**FS 41**).

198.1 ENGLISH MINUTES, 1794-1920 (**Post 30**)
Minutes re wireless telegraphy development re Russia, 1906 (**/2/1321**) and proposed wireless telegraph service to Russia, 1917 (**/2/2445**).

198.2 GENERAL MINUTES, 1921-40 (**Post 33**)
Minutes re: mail and parcel post service resumed to Russia after the war (**/1/172, 256-57**); Anglo-Russian telegraphic communication cable, 1916-27 (**/1/779-81**); direct parcel post service to Russia, 1915-18 (**/1/1200**); route used for postal services to the USSR, 1926 (**/2/1683**); direct wireless services to the USSR, 1927 (**/2/2178**); telephone service to the USSR, 1929-39 (**/3/3615**); commercial treaty with the USSR, 1930-7 (**/4/4268**); parcel post agreement with the USSR, 1931-7 (**/4/4430**); enquiries re picture telegraphy service, 1929-32 (**/4/4601**); proposed introduction and draft agreement re money order service with the USSR, 1923-41 (**/4/5017**).

198.3 OVERSEAS MAILS : ORGANISATION, TREATIES, CONVENTIONS AND CONFERENCES (**Post 46**)
Agreement with Russia for the exchange of money orders, 1904 (**/45**).

198.4 PACKET MINUTES, 1811-1920 (**Post 29**)
Minutes re: particulars of early postal services to Russia, 1856 (**/1/67-9**); financial enquiry re Post Office business with Russia, 1880 (**/1/288**); Russian customs regulations, 1893 (**/1/552**); parcel post services to Russia, 1904 (**/2/823**); the establishment of money order services to Russia, 1904 (**/2/838**); parcel post services to the Far East via Siberia, 1908, and Vladivostok, 1915 (**/2/992, 1275-6**); parcel post to Russia via Sweden, 1916 (**/2/1294**).

199.1-93

PUBLIC RECORD OFFICE

Chancery Lane, London WC2A 1LR and Ruskin Avenue, Kew, Richmond, Surrey TW9 4DU

The Public Record Office is the largest record-holding institution in the United Kingdom and has the largest collection of public and diplomatic records relating to Russia and the Soviet Union. In general, records are open to inspection after 30 years, but some may be closed for a longer period. The *Guide to the Contents of the Public Record Office*, 3 vols (London, 1963-9) describes records in all departments of state and supplements bringing the information up to date are available in the Reading Rooms at Chancery Lane and Kew. An outline of the records relating to Russia and the Soviet Union can be found in N. E. Evans, 'Principal Sources in the Public Record Office for the History of Russia and of Anglo-Russian Relations', *Solanus*, no. 16 (July 1981) pp. 1-14, on which this entry is largely based. See also, G. M. Phipps, 'Manuscript Collections in British Archives Relating to Pre-Petrine Russia', *Canadian-American Slavic Studies*, vol. 6, no. 3 (Fall 1972) pp. 400-15. The Public Record Office has produced handlists and information sheets describing several categories of records.

A two-volume TS *Summary of Records* lists all the departments whose records are held, and gives the title of individual classes of records within each department, the covering dates of the records and the number of documents in each class. References in the *Summary of Records* can be followed up in the TS lists of classes of records available in the Reading Rooms. The amount of description in these lists varies, ranging from only the covering dates and volume number to a brief description of the content of each volume. Some of these lists have been published in a series of Public Record Office Lists and Indexes and Public Record Office Supplementary Lists and Indexes.

The following list indicates the main classes of records in which material relating to Russia and the Soviet Union will be found. A comprehensive description of all the public records relating to Russia and the Soviet Union has not been attempted (see introduction) and researchers should note that further material will certainly be found in other classes of records in the Public Record Office, and in particular in those whose records are listed by date and volume number alone.

Public Records at Chancery Lane

199.1 EXCHEQUER, PORT RECORDS, 1565-1798 (E 190)
Records of ports include material relating to Russian trade but are arranged by port only.

199.2 GENERAL REGISTER OFFICE (RG)
The records of the General Register Office, Office of Population Censuses and Surveys, include a class concerned with foreign deaths, 1830-1921 (RG 35) in which there are references to Russia, 1835-70 (/18-19).

199.3 HIGH COURT OF ADMIRALTY (HCA)
List of 105 prize papers concerned with the Crimean War (HCA 33).

199.4 PUBLIC RECORD OFFICE (PRO)
The class Gifts and Deposits (PRO 30) holds the following papers relating to Russia: Venetian manuscripts including an account of the origin and costumes of the Cossacks, 1656 (/25/111) and a report on Muscovy by the priest Bianchi da Belluno, 1655 (/25/133);

miscellaneous papers including papers of a French Council of War held at Paris to consider further action in the Baltic against Russia and a copy of a chart of the neighbourhood of Helsingfors, 1856 (/26/57). *See also PRO papers listed at Kew and under Private Papers.*

199.5-16 STATE PAPERS (SP)

199.5 STATE PAPERS, DOMESTIC

State papers, Domestic, are calendared in *Calendars of State Papers, Domestic Series*, 1547-1781, and *Calendar of Home Office Papers, George III*, 1760-75. After 1781 domestic papers can be found in the Home Office series. References to Russia can be found in the indexes to each volume.

199.6 STATE PAPERS, FOREIGN, GENERAL SERIES

The series State Papers, Foreign, is the main source for diplomatic records until 1782. For the period 1543-1577 the papers are arranged in a general series by reign as follows: Edward VI (**SP 68**); Mary (**SP 69**); Elizabeth I (**SP 70**). Calendars of abstracts of dispatches of English representatives abroad are available for the period 1547-77: *Calendar of State Papers, Foreign: Edward VI*, 1547-53 (1 vol.); *Calendar of State Papers, Foreign: Mary*, 1553-8 (1 vol.); *Calendar of State Papers, Foreign: Elizabeth I*, 1558-77 (11 vols). 5 Russian royal letters can be found in the class **SP 70** and have been printed in Yu. Tolstoi, *Perviya sorok let snoshenii mezhdu Rossieyu i Anglieyu* (St Petersburg, 1875) and *Oxford Slavonic Papers*.

199.7-16 STATE PAPERS, FOREIGN, (under countries etc.)

199.7 From July 1577 the papers are arranged by country, and papers relating to Russia form class **SP 91** (111 vols). Descriptions of papers in this class can be found in the continuation of the calendar series, *Calendar of State Papers, Foreign, Elizabeth I*, 1577-89 (vols 12-23), and then in the *List and Analysis of State Papers Foreign, Elizabeth I*, 1589-93 (vols 1-4). The *Catalogue of State Papers, Foreign, Poland, Sweden, Switzerland, Russia*, 1589-1665, includes a 'Descriptive List of State Papers, Foreign, Russia, 1589-1665', which gives the date, name of sender and recipient and brief description of the content of each dispatch. There are TS lists of material relating to Russia, 1704-41 (**SP 91/4-27**) in the Reading Room. A small number of documents concerning Russia are listed in the *Calendar of State Papers, East Indies, China, and Japan, 1513-1624* and in the *Calendar of State Papers, East Indies, China and Persia, 1624-34*. There will also be references to Russia in the State Papers, Foreign, of other countries, for example Germany (**SP 80**), Hamburg (**SP 82**), Saxony-Poland (**SP 88**), Prussia (**SP 90**) and Sweden (**SP 95**). The dispatches of several British ambassadors to Russia in the eighteenth century have been printed in volumes of the *Sbornik Imperatorskogo russkogo istoricheskogo obshchestva*.

The class State Papers, Foreign, Russia, (**SP 91**) and the state papers, foreign, of other countries are the main sources for diplomatic material relating to Russia before 1782, but material can also be found in the following classes of State Papers, Foreign:

199.8 ARCHIVES OF BRITISH LEGATIONS, 1568-1866 (SP 105)

There are no records of the Legation in Russia but there may be material relating to Russia in the records of other Legations for which material is arranged by date only.

199.9 CONFIDENTIAL (SP 107)

Class of 110 vols of intercepted dispatches of foreign legations in London, 1726-66, may contain material relating to Russia but is arranged by date only.

199.10 FOREIGN ENTRY BOOKS (SP 104)

References to Russia and Poland can be found in the class of Entry Books of King's Letters and Secretaries' Letters, 1674-1766 (**SP 104/118-27**), and the class Foreign Ministers in England: Russia, 1714-20 (**SP 104/254**). Material might also be found relating to Russia in the following classes: Miscellaneous (**SP 104/164, 171-5, 183**); Northern, 1747-61 (**SP 104/261**); Ambassadors' privileges (Northern), 1710-82 (**SP 104/264-7**).

199.11 FOREIGN MINISTERS IN ENGLAND (SP 100)

Correspondence of the Russian envoys in England with the Secretaries of State, 1707-80 (**/51-4**).

199.12 ROYAL LETTERS (SP 102)

47 Russian letters, 1570-1682, including some by Patriarch Filaret Nikitich (**/49**). These letters have been printed in Yu. Tolstoi, *Perviya sorok let snoshenii mezhdu Rossieyu i Anglieyu* (St Petersburg, 1875) and *Oxford Slavonic Papers*. Formal Russian royal letters, 1683-1779 (**/50-1**).

199.13 SUPPLEMENTARY (SP 110)

Class includes records of Legations. There are no records of the Legation in Russia but there may be material on Russia in the records of other legations.

199.14 TREATY DOCUMENTS (SP 108)

Original protocols and ratifications of treaties relating to Russia can be found in **SP 108/426-440** for the period 1735-66. There will also be references to Russia in the treaty documents of other countries; for example, the treaty documents for France include a Convention between Great Britain, France and the States General for the discharge of Russian troops, 1748 (**SP 108/109**).

199.15 TREATY PAPERS (SP 103)

Treaty papers relating to Russia can be found in the class **SP 103/61-3** for the period 1618-1780. There could be references to Russia in the treaty papers of other countries.

199.16 VARIOUS (SP 109)

Class consisting of drafts of letters, miscellaneous papers and précis books, Charles II - George III, may include material relating to Russia.

199.17 TREASURY SOLICITOR AND H.M. PROCURATOR GENERAL (T.S. 15)

Class includes material re prize cases during the Crimean War.

Public Records at Kew

199.18 ADMIRALTY RECORDS (ADM)

Naval records are described in the *Guide to the Contents of the Public Record Office*, in the Public Record Office Handbook no. 15, *The Second World War : Guide to Documents in the Public Record Office* and in the Public Record Office Information Leaflets no. 42, *Operational Records of the Royal Navy in the Great War, 1914-19* and no. 43, *Operational Records of the Royal Navy in the Second World War, 1939-45*. The relevant published lists are Public Record Office Lists and Indexes no. XVIII, *List of Admiralty Records,* volume 1 and Public Record Office Supplementary Lists and Indexes no. VI, *List of Admiralty Records,* volumes 1-9.

There will be references to Russia amongst the Admiralty and Secretariat Out-letters, Minutes and Memoranda (**ADM 2-3**) which are listed by date only. Ship's logs and logs by admirals, captains and masters (**ADM 50-4**) are listed under the name of the ship but will contain references to Russia. Specific references to Russia can be found in the following classes: Admiralty and Secretariat Papers (**ADM 1**) (2,774 pieces); Registers of Prisoners of War, 1755-1831 (**ADM 103**); Mediterranean Station Records, Correspondence etc., 1843-1920 (**ADM 121**); Historical Section, War Histories, 1900-24 (**ADM 137**); Papers and Cases, Supplementary Series, 1892-1951 (**ADM 178**).

199.19 AIR DEPARTMENT (AIR)

Air force records are described in the Public Record Office Handlist no. 15, *The Second World War : Guide to Documents in the Public Record Office* and in the Public Record Office Information Leaflet no. 45, *Operational Records of the Royal Air Force in the Public Record Office*. Specific references to Russia and the USSR can be found in the following classes: Chief of Air Staff, 1916-57 (**AIR 8**) and Director of Plans, 1914-47 (**AIR 9**).

199.20 BOARD OF CUSTOMS, EXCISE AND OF CUSTOMS AND EXCISE (CUST)

There could be material on Russian trade in the ledgers of imports and exports, 1697-1899 (**CUST 3-4, 8, 14**) which are listed by date only.

199.21 BOARD OF TRADE (BT)

The records are described in the Public Record Office Supplementary Lists and Indexes no. XI, *Board of Trade Records to 1913*, and in the TS *Current Guide* to the Public Record Office available in the Reading Rooms (the relevant passage is 601.1.1-601.8.3). Many of the classes are listed by date only (for example, In-letters, Foreign Office, 1924-45, (**BT 2**) and Commercial Department Out-letters, 1864-1921 (**BT 12**)) but there are specific references to Russia in the following classes: In-letters and Files, General, 1791-1863 (**BT 1**); Miscellanea, Russia and Sweden, 1817-20 (**BT 6/68**); Companies Registration Office, Files of Dissolved Companies (**BT 31**); Department of Overseas Trade, 1918-46 (**BT 59-60**); Advisory Committee to the Department of Overseas Trade, 1918-30, including reports on the economic situation in Russia (**BT 90**).

199.22 BRITISH COUNCIL PAPERS (BW)

The class British Council Files : GB Series, 1934-47, (**BW 2**) includes papers relating to an exchange of engineering students with the USSR, 1943-4, and the class British Council Files : USSR, 1941-7 (**BW 64**) consists of 8 pieces including material on films, exchanges, Russian studies in British universities, scientific collaboration and library and research facilities.

199.23 CABINET OFFICE PAPERS (CAB)

Some of the Cabinet Office papers have been published as Public Record Office Handbooks no. 4, *List of Cabinet Papers, 1880-1914*, no. 6, *List of Papers of the Committee of Imperial Defence to 1914* and no. 9, *List of Cabinet Papers, 1915 and 1916*. Cabinet Office papers are described in the following: Public Record Office Handbook no. 11, *The Records of the Cabinet Office to 1922* and no. 17, *The Cabinet Office to 1945*; Public Record Office Information Leaflet no. 59, *The Records of the Cabinet Office*. There are indexes in the Reading Room in Kew to Cabinet conclusions, 1919-37, C.P. (Confidential Print) papers, 1923-37, War Cabinet minutes, 1916-18, GT papers 1-3000 (**CAB 24**) and to classes **CAB 23, 128-9**.

No Cabinet minutes were kept until the formation of the Cabinet Secretariat in 1916. The only record of earlier Cabinet decisions is to be found in letters to the Sovereign after each meeting which are kept at the Royal Archives at Windsor. Photocopies of these letters, 1868-1916 (**CAB 41**) and of Cabinet memoranda, 1880-1916 (**CAB 37**) are available in the Reference Room at Kew. In November 1914 a War Council was set up by the Cabinet, replaced in May 1915 by the Dardanelles Committee, and in November 1915 by the War Committee. The papers and minutes of these committees form the class **CAB 22** and are reproduced as photocopies in the class **CAB 42**. The main series of papers circulated to the War Cabinet from December 1916 form the class **CAB 24** (classified as GT papers) and photocopies of the minutes and conclusions of the War Cabinet (**CAB 23**) are available at Kew. References to Russia can be found in all these classes. Further material can be found relating to Russia in the following classes: Cabinet Office Historical Registered Files, 1916-59 (**CAB 21**); Supreme War Council, 1917-19 (**CAB 25**); General Series, 1915-39 (**CAB 27**); Official War Histories, Correspondence and Papers (**CAB 45**). The main sources for the history of the War Cabinet in 1939-45 are its minutes (**CAB 65**) and memoranda (**CAB 66**), both of which contain references to the USSR. References to the USSR can also be found in the following classes: Hankey Papers, 1908-44 (**CAB 63**); Miscellaneous and General Series, 1941-7 (**CAB 78**); Commonwealth and International Conferences, 1938-45 (**CAB 99**); British Joint Staff Mission : Washington Office Files, 1940-9 (**CAB 122**); Minister of Reconstruction, 1940-65 (**CAB 124**); Ad Hoc Committees : General and Miscellaneous Series, 1945-52 (**CAB 130**); Commonwealth and International Conferences to 1945 (**CAB 133**). Photocopies of the minutes and memoranda of the Cabinet, 1945-8, (**CAB 128-9**) are available in the Reading Room at Kew. *See also CAB papers listed under Private Papers.*

199.24 COLONIAL OFFICE (CO)
Entry book for 1710-11 includes material on Russia and the Baltic trade (**CO 389/21**) and there could be further references to Russia and Russian trade.

199.25 DOMINIONS OFFICE (DO)
There are references to Russia and the USSR in this class; see TS guides and card index for details.

199.26-36 FOREIGN OFFICE (FO)

The organization of papers relating to foreign affairs underwent a change in 1782 when one of the Secretaries of State was made responsible for foreign affairs at the head of the Foreign Office (earlier diplomatic records can be found in the series, State Papers, Foreign). A summary of the contents of the Foreign Office can be found in the *Guide to the Contents of the Public Record Office* vol. 2, and the PRO Handbook no. 13, *Records of the Foreign Office, 1782-1939.* There are TS lists of Foreign Office classes of records in the Reading Rooms and published lists in the following series: Public Record Office Lists and Indexes no. LII, *List of Foreign Office Records to 1878*; Public Record Office Supplementary Lists and Indexes no. XIII, *List of Foreign Office Records* arranged in volumes as follows: *General Correspondence, 1879-1905, Japan-Saxony* (vol. 3); *Various Classes* (vol. 5, 1879-1913, vol. 12, 1914-38, vol. 26, 1939-46); *General Correpondence (except Political)* (vol. 9, 1914-38, vol. 25, 1939-46); *General Correspondence, Political* (vol. 10, 1914-29, vol. 11, 1930-8, vols 18-22, 1939-45, vol. 24, 1946, vol. 28, 1947); *Confidential Print : Numerical Series, 1829-1915* (vol. 23).

Material relating to Russia and the USSR can be found in the classes listed below. There may also be material relating to the USSR amongst the following classes of Foreign Office records: Foreign Trade Department, 1916-19 (**FO 833**); Foreign Policy Documents, 1978-82 (**FO 972**); Foreign Office, Background Briefs, 1978-82 (**FO 973**); Information Reports, 1948-51 (**FO 973**). *See also FO papers listed under Private Papers.*

199.26 FOREIGN OFFICE : GENERAL CORRESPONDENCE, 1782-1906
Until 1906 the general correspondence of the Foreign Office, consisting of drafts and copies of letters sent from London and correspondence and dispatches received from

abroad, is arranged by countries. The class **FO 65** (1,739 vols) deals with Russia, although there will also be material in the correspondence of other countries, such as Germany, Poland, Prussia, Sweden and Turkey. The lists give only a brief indication of the content of each volume; more information can be found in the original manuscript registers of the Foreign Office, 1761-1890, **FO 802**, and 1817-1920, **FO 556**, in the volumes entitled 'Russia' (also a volume entitled 'Russia. Central Asia', **FO 802**, 1858-81) which are on open access at Kew. These registers give the names of correspondents and a brief description of each letter. The class **FO 566** also includes references to the location of further correspondence on the same matter which can be found in that class. The class, Indexes to General Correspondence, 1891-1905, (**FO 804**) is a subject index for these years in which references to Russia can be found under the country, individuals and subjects; a page reference is given to the relevant page in the registers which make up class **FO 566**. The class **FO 605** consists of microfilm copies of class **FO 802** and the class **FO 738** of microfilm copies of class **FO 804**. There are also references to Russia in the class Supplement to the General Correspondence, 1780-1905 (**FO 97/340-61, 461-2**).

199.27 FOREIGN OFFICE: GENERAL CORRESPONDENCE, 1906-

From 1906, the correspondence is organized under the following headings: Commercial (**FO 368**); Consular (**FO 369**); Political (**FO 371**); Treaty (**FO 372**); Contraband, in times of war (**FO 382**); Prisoners, from 1915 (**FO 383**); News, from 1916 (**FO 395**). From 1906 to 1919, material is listed in a comprehensive card index at Kew, arranged by year and within each year by subject. The most relevant heading is 'Russia' but material can also be found under areas of the Russian Empire (Siberia, the Ukraine etc.), under other countries, and under individuals and subjects. The card index can be supplemented by reference to the Registers (**FO 566**) by noting the year and appropriate file number. From 1920, the card index is superseded by annual printed indexes forming the class **FO 409**. These have been reprinted by the Kraus-Thomson organization and are available up to the year 1951. The printed indexes are arranged in the same way as the card index. In both indexes the country to which the material relates is given a number, which for Russia is no. 38, prefixed by N for Northern Department from 1920. Papers which were considered to be particularly sensitive at the time of registration were registered separately and are known as 'green papers'. There are separate indexes for these papers from 1920 to 1940 in the printed indexes. There are also references to Russia in the classes General Correspondence, Prisoners, 1915-19 (**FO 383**) and General Correspondence after 1906, 1936-47 (**FO 850**).

The general correspondence of the Foreign Office is the main series of papers relating to diplomatic relations with Russia and the USSR, but material can also be found in the following classes of Foreign Office records:

199.28 CONFERENCES: CONTINENTAL, 1814-22, VARIOUS INTERNATIONAL, 1920-9 (**FO 92, 840**)

Both classes includes references to Russia and the USSR.

199.29 CONFIDENTIAL PRINT

The class Confidential Print, 1827-1914 (**FO 881**), is arranged by country and date and consists of papers which were printed for circulation within the Foreign Office. The class Confidential Print **FO 418** deals specifically with Russia and the USSR, 1821-1956, as does Confidential Print, Central Asia, 1834-1911 (**FO 539**). There could also be material relating to Russia in the confidential print of other countries and areas, for example Poland, 1814-1956 (**FO 417**), Scandinavia and the Baltic States, 1919-49 (**FO 419**), Eastern Europe (General), 1948-56 (**FO 472**) and Northern Affairs, 1942-5 (**FO 490**).

199.30 CONTROL COMMISSION FOR GERMANY (FO 1005)
Records Library papers include papers relating to the Soviet Zone in Germany.

199.31 EMBASSY AND CONSULAR ARCHIVES
Records of embassies and legations in the Russian Empire and the USSR form the following classes of records: Russia (**FO 181-4, 399**); Archangel (**FO 264-7**); Odessa (**FO 257-8, 359**); Leningrad (**FO 378-9**); Warsaw (**FO 392-4, 640**); Libau (**FO 396, 400, 439-40, 661**); Batum (**FO 397**); Rostov-on-Don (**FO 398**); Moscow (**FO 447-8, 518**); Vladivostok (**FO 510, 537**); Tallinn (**FO 514**); Riga (**FO 516**); Kovno and Memel (**FO 722**); Helsingfors (**FO 768**); Tammerfors (**FO 769**). There will also be references to Russia in the consular records of other countries, for example Danzig (**FO 634**) includes material relating to the British blockade of Russian ports during the Crimean War. The relevant published lists are in the following series: Public Record Office Lists and Indexes no. LII, *List of Foreign Office Records to 1878*; Public Record Office Supplementary Lists and Indexes no. XIII as follows: *Embassy and Consular Archives, 1879-1905, Japan-Saxony* (vol. 15); *Embassy and Consular Archives, 1914-38, Columbia-Estonia* (vol. 16); *Embassy and Consular Archives, 1914-38, Finland-Morocco* (vol. 16, including the consuls of Latvia and Lithuania); *Embassy and Consular Archives, 1914-38, Nepal-Yugoslavia* (vol. 17). There may be references to Russia in the class Passport Office, Correspondence with H.M. Embassies etc., 1886-1900 (**FO 614**).

199.32 FOREIGN OFFICE MAPS (FO 925)
This class is the main source for maps in the Public Record Office and includes maps of fortifications, railways and town plans. There is a card index in the map room at Kew in which references can be found to Russia in the indexes for both Europe and Asia. See also, Public Record Office Information Sheet no. 49, *Maps in the Public Record Office*. A catalogue of European maps in the Public Record Office is under preparation.

199.33 KING'S LETTER BOOKS, 1710-1828 (FO 80)
Formal Russian royal letters (/57A-59).

199.34 MISCELLANEA SERIES I & II (FO 95-6)
References to Russia and the USSR can be found in the first series, 1639-1942, (**FO 95**) under the headings Foreign Entry Books, Library, Royal Letters, Supplementary Correspondence and Treaty, and in the second series, *c.* 1700-1937, (**FO 96**) under Archives of Special Commissions, Drafts, Minutes, Royal Letter Department, Slave Trade Commission and Treaty.

199.35 PRIVATE PAPERS AND COLLECTIONS (FO 800)
Private Office Papers : Miscellaneous (**FO 800/383-**) includes papers re Russia (**/383, 385-6, 394**). Private Secretaries' Papers (**FO 800/401-**) includes records of conferences held in the USSR (**/401, 408-9, 414-15**). *See also FO 800 papers listed under Private Papers.*

199.36 TREATIES : PROTOCOLS AND RATIFICATIONS (FO 93-4)
Protocols of treaties relating to Russia, 1695-1975 (**/91**). Ratifications of treaties are arranged by year and country.

199.37 HOME OFFICE (HO)
The class Miscellaneous, Warrant Books, 1750-1934, (**HO 118**) includes the records of the Special Commission for determining prizes in hostilities with Russia and the class Broadcasting Department : Registered Files (**HO 256**) includes records of the BBC Overseas Service. There will be records relating to individual Russians who lived and settled in Britain amongst Home Office papers.

199.38 MINISTRY OF INFORMATION (INF)

Material re the USSR can be found in the following classes: Ministry of Information, Files of Correspondence, 1936-50 (INF 1); Guard Books and Related Unregistered Papers, 1939-45 (INF 2); Original Art Work, 1939-46 (INF 3); Film Production Documents, 1932-69 (INF 6).

199.39 PRIME MINISTER'S OFFICE (PREM)

References to Russia and the USSR can be found in particular in the classes Correspondence and Papers, 1916-46 (PREM 1, 4, 8) and Operational Papers, 1938-46 (PREM 3) which includes papers on the USSR in the Second World War.

199.40 PUBLIC RECORD OFFICE (PRO)

The class Reproductions of Records : Extraneous Documents (PRO 22) includes English Royal Letters in the Central State Archive of Ancient Records in the USSR (Tsentral'nyi gosudarstvennyi arkhiv drevnykh aktov) 1557-1665 (/60), and maps and plans relating to the Crimean War (/68). *See also papers from* PRO *listed under Private Papers and* PRO *papers held at Chancery Lane.*

199.41 TREASURY RECORDS (T)

Treasury records are described in the Public Record Office Lists and Indexes no. XLVI, *List of Treasury Records* and in the Public Record Office Supplementary Lists and Indexes no. XII, *Treasury Records, 1838-1938.* The class Various (T 64) lists trade returns and there are some specific references to exports to Russia (/273/45, /275/148, /241). The class Russian Accounts, 1916-28, (T 255) concerns the dues of the Imperial Russian government and the anti-Bolshevik governments of Russia and the Baltic States.

199.42 WAR OFFICE (WO)

Military records (mainly but not exclusively held in the War Office papers) are described in the *Guide to the Contents of the Public Record Office* and specifically in the Public Record Office Handbook no. 15, *The Second World War : Guide to Documents in the Public Record Office* and in the following Public Record Office Informations Leaflets: no. 39, *Prisoners of War : Documents in the Public Record Office*; no. 40, *Operational Records of the British Army in the Great War, 1914-19*; no. 41, *Operational Records of the British Army in the Second World War, 1939-45*; no. 58, *Operational Records of the British Army, 1660-1914.* The relevant published Public Record Office Lists and Indexes are no. XXVIII, *List of War Office Records, volume I* and no. LIII, *Alphabetical Guide to the War Office and Other Military Records Preserved in the Public Record Office.*

Material relating to the Crimean War can be found in the following classes of War Office papers: In-letters and Papers, 1732-1868 (WO 1); Secretary of State Out-letters, 1793-1859 (WO 6/69-80); Scutari Depot Muster Books and Pay Lists, 1854-6 (WO 14); Headquarters Records, 1746-1909 (WO 28); Commissariat Department, Accounts (WO 60); Commissariat Department, Miscellanea, 1798-1859 (WO 62); Miscellaneous Records of the Judge Advocate's General Office, including papers re an inquiry into supplies for the British army in the Crimea (WO 93). There will also be material in the class Secretary at War Out-letters, 1684-1861 (WO 4) (1,052 pieces) which is listed by date only. The class Registered Papers, General Series, (WO 32) includes material on the Crimean War, the military missions to Russia, the organization of the Red Army and Russian POWs. The class Reports and Miscellaneous Papers, 1853-1948, (WO 33) includes papers on the Crimean War, the Russian advances into Central Asia, the Russo-Japanese War, the Allied intervention in Russia and the Second World War. The First World War and the Allied intervention are covered more specifically in the following classes: War of 1914-18, War Diaries (WO 95, 154); War of 1914-18, Maps and Plans (WO 153); War of 1914-18, Correspondence and Papers of Military Headquarters (WO 158); War of 1914-18,

Miscellaneous Unregistered Papers (**WO 161**). Second World War and post-war papers relating to the USSR can be found in the following classes: War of 1939-45, Military Headquarters Papers, Military Missions (**WO 202**); Allied Forces Headquarters, 1941-8 (**WO 204**); Directorate of Military Intelligence, 1926-46 (**WO 208**); Chief of the (Imperial) General Staff Papers, 1935-54 (**WO 216**); Private Office Papers of the Permanent Under-Secretary of State and Secretary of State (**WO 258-9**).

Private Papers (at Kew)

There will also be references to Russia in the papers of Secretaries of State and Under Secretaries of State for Foreign Affairs which are listed by date only in the class **FO 800**. *See relevant list for details.*

199.43 ALLEN PAPERS (**PRO 30/2**)
Papers include list of Russian sovereigns, 9th - 11th centuries, and list of metropolitans and patriarchs, 10th - 18th centuries (**/2/23**) and Crimean map, 1854-5 (**/3/10**).

199.44 AMPTHILL PAPERS (**FO 918**)
Papers of Odo Russell (1829-84), 1st Lord Ampthill include correspondence with Russian diplomats (**/18, 26, 46**) and British diplomats in Russia (**/27-8, 35, 50, 53, 56**). *See list for details.*

199.45 ARDAGH PAPERS (**PRO 30/40**)
Papers of Sir John Charles Ardagh (1840-1907) include: notes by Ardagh on a visit to St Petersburg and Helsingfors, 1878 (**/1/327-32**); papers re Russia and correspondence from Lt-Col. W. G. Nicolson re the visit of the Tsarevich Nicholas to Britain, 3 Jan. 1891 (**/2/312-13**); correspondence with Sir Mortimer Durand re relations with Russia in Persia, 1895 (**/2/420-31**); memo re Russia in Central Asia (**/14**).

199.46 BALFOUR, Arthur James (1848-1930), 1st Earl of Balfour (**FO 800/199-217**)
Foreign Secretary and Lord President of the Council. Papers re Russia and Siberia, 1916-20 (**/205**) and miscellaneous correspondence, 1917-19 (**/214-17**).

199.47 BERTIE, Sir Francis Leveson (1844-1919), 1st Visc. Bertie of Thame (**FO 800/159-91**)
Diplomat. Papers re Russia, 1897-1918 (**/176-8**).

199.48 BLOOMFIELD PAPERS (**FO 356**)
Collection includes papers of John Arthur Douglas Bloomfield (1802-79), 2nd Baron Bloomfield, as Envoy at St Petersburg, 1840-51 (**/1-7**).

199.49 BRIDGES, Sir Edward (**CAB 127/326-37**)
Uncirculated memo by Lord Beaverbrook on policy towards the Soviet Union, 1942 (**/329**).

199.50 CARNARVON PAPERS (**PRO 30/6**)
Correspondence of Henry Howard Molyneux, 4th Earl of Carnarvon, as Secretary of State for the Colonies could include references to Russia; also War Office publications re Russia, 1873, 1877 (**/111, 117**).

199.51 CAVE PAPERS (**PRO 30/7**)
The official correspondence of Andrew Snape Douglas includes a dispatch on the intrigues of the Russian minister at the Sicilian court, 1814 (**/1**).

199.52 CHAMBERLAIN, Sir (Joseph) Austen (1863-1937) **(FO 800/256-65)**
Correspondence as Secretary of State for Foreign Affairs includes papers on Russia.

199.53 CHATHAM PAPERS **(PRO 30/8)**
Papers of William Pitt (1708-78), 1st Earl of Chatham, include diplomatic papers re Russia **(/88)**. Papers of William Pitt (1759-1806) include a file marked 'Russia and Poland; miscellaneous papers, despatches and letters from' **(/337)**. *See also Hoare (Pitt) papers.*

199.54 COLCHESTER PAPERS **(PRO 30/9)**
Papers of the Rt Hon. Charles Abbot, 2nd Baron Ellenborough include a memo re Russia's policy towards India, 1829-30 **(/4/45)**. *See also Ellenborough papers.*

199.55 CORNWALLIS PAPERS **(PRO 30/11)**
Papers of Charles, 1st Marquis Cornwallis, include a reference to peace moves in Vienna and St Petersburg, 1781 **(/6)**.

199.56 COWLEY PAPERS **(FO 519)**
Collection includes the papers of Col. Frederick Wellesley as Military Attaché in Russia **(/274-81, 302)**. *See list for details.*

199.57 CRIPPS, Sir Richard Stafford (1889-1952) **(CAB 127/57-154)**
Papers include his correspondence as Ambassador in Moscow, 1940-41, 1942-4 **(/64,75)**.

199.58 ELLENBOROUGH PAPERS **(PRO 30/12)**
Papers of Edward Law (1790-1871), Earl of Ellenborough, include correspondence re the arrest of Col. Stoddart and Capt. A. Conolly in Bukhara, 1842 **(/26/4)**; copies of secret letters re Russian aspirations in Central Asia, Persia and Turkey, 1828-30 **(/29/26)**. *See also Colchester papers.*

199.59 EYRE PAPERS **(PRO 30/46)**
Papers of Maj.-Gen. Sir William Eyre (1805-59) include re his service as commander of the 2nd Brigade, 3rd Division, in the Crimean War **(Boxes 5-8)**, and miscellaneous papers re the Crimea **(Box 9)**.

199.60 GRANVILLE PAPERS **(PRO 30/29)**
Papers of Lord Granville Leveson-Gower (1773-1846), 1st Earl Granville, include material on his embassy to the court of Russia, 1804-7 **(/10-12, 384, 388)**. Papers of Granville George Leveson-Gower (1815-91), 2nd Earl Granville, include correspondence with the British Embassy in Russia, 1870-4, 1880-5 **(/91, 97, 114, 185-6, 209)**, the Russian Embassy in London, 1870-4 **(/115)** and confidential print re Russia, 1821-73, 1879-82 **(/253-4, 325-9, 426)**. *See list for details.*

199.61 GREY, Sir Edward (1862-1932), 3rd Bt, 1st Visc. Grey of Falloden **(FO 800/35-113)**
Papers re Russia as Foreign Secretary, 1905-16 **(/72-5)**. *See MS index (/113) for details.*

199.62 HAMMOND PAPERS **(FO 391)**
Collection includes the correspondence of the Rt Hon. Edmund, afterwards Lord, Hammond (1802-90), Permanent Under-Secretary of State for Foreign Affairs, with British representatives in Russia.

199.63 HENDERSON, Rt Hon. Arthur (1863-1935) **(FO 800/280-4)**
Labour leader and statesman. Papers re Russia while Secretary of State for Foreign Affairs.

199.64 HOARE (PITT) MSS **(PRO 30/70)**
Letters from Count S. R. Vorontsov to William Pitt including a covering letter for a snuff box presented by Catherine II, 1795 (*/3/192*). *See also Chatham papers.*

199.65 ISMAY PAPERS **(CAB 127/1-56)**
Papers of Gen. Hastings Lionel Ismay (1887-1965), 1st Baron Ismay, include: records of discussions between the PM and Stalin; a copy of an *aide-mémoire* to M. Molotov, 1942 (*/23*); correspondence and minutes re 'Tolstoy', the military meetings held in Moscow in Oct. 1944 (*/34*).

199.66 JACKSON PAPERS **(FO 353)**
Collection includes the papers of Sir George Jackson (1785-1861), Secretary of the Embassy in Russia, 1816, and the correspondence of C. Whitworth and others from Warsaw and St Petersburg, 1791-2, 1802-7 (*/66, 67*).

199.67 KERR, Sir Archibald John Kerr Clark (1882-1951), 1st Baron Inverchapel **(FO 800/298-303)**
Correspondence as Ambassador to the USSR, 1942-6.

199.68 KITCHENER PAPERS **(PRO 30/57)**
Papers of Horatio Herbert Kitchener (1850-1916), 1st Earl Kitchener of Khartoum, include extensive material re Russia. The index lists material relating to Russia in general and also to press correspondents in Russia, the telegraph to Vladivostok, Nicholas II, missions to Russia, the Russo-Japanese War, Russia in the First World War, several Russian cities and Russian relations with India, Persia and Rumania.

199.69 LASCELLES, Sir Frank (1841-1920) **(FO 800/6-20)**
Correspondence of Sir Frank as Ambassador to Russia, 1894-5 (*/15, /17*). *See MS subject index (/20) for details.*

199.70 LOWRY COLE PAPERS **(PRO 30/43)**
Travel journals in Russia kept by Katherine Gertrude Robinson (née Harris), 1777-9, 1782-8 (*/10-13, 18-20*) and Harriet Mary (née Amyand), wife of the 1st Lord Malmesbury, 1777 (*/35*).

199.71 MACDONALD, J. Ramsay (1866-1937) **(CAB 127/282-95; PRO 30/69)**
Labour leader and statesman. Foreign Office telegrams to Russia **(CAB 127/293)**; papers re the Anglo-Soviet conference, 1924 **(PRO 30/69/1/22)**; Foreign Secretary papers re Russia, 1924 (*/1/104-6*); telegrams re Russia, 1924 (*/1/222*); file re the Zinoviev letter, 1924 (*/1/234*); Private Office papers re Russia, 1929-32, 1935 (*/1/266, 281, 303, 305, 325*). *See list for details.*

199.72 MACKINDER, Sir Halford John (1861-1947) **(FO 800/251)**
Geographer and MP. Papers re the mission to South Russia, 1919-20.

199.73 MANCE PAPERS **(PRO 30/66)**
Papers of Sir H. Osborne Mance (1875-1966) include papers on the re-establishment of trade with Russia and central Europe, 1919-20 (*/15*).

199.74 MILNER PAPERS (PRO 30/30)

Papers of Alfred Milner (1854-1925), Visc. Milner, include: memos and telegrams concerning the relations between the Bolsheviks and the Baltic States, 1919 (*/5*); copies of telegrams concerning the fighting between Persian and Bolshevik troops, 1920 (*/23*); papers re the Russian trade delegation, 1920 (*/25*).

199.75 NAPIER PAPERS (PRO 30/16)

Papers of Sir Charles Napier include MS plans and sketches of Hangö, Sveaborg and Kronstadt from his expedition to the Baltic in 1854. *See list for details.*

199.76 NICOLL PAPERS (PRO 30/42)

Papers of Sir John Nicholl, the King's Advocate General, 1798-1809, include references to naval provisions carried in Russian ships, 1801, (*/5/8*) and copies of letters and petitions re Russia, 1799, 1802-3 (*/23/6; /25/9; /30/7; /31/2; /32/7, 13*).

199.77 NICOLSON PAPERS (FO 800/336-81, PRO 30/81)

Papers of Sir Arthur Nicolson, 1st Baron Carnock, include his correspondence as Ambassador to Russia, 1905-6 (**FO 800/336-81**); journal as Ambassador in St Petersburg, 1906-7 (**PRO 30/81/13**) and diary and notebook written at St Petersburg, 1910 (*/14-15*).

199.78 PETTY-FITZMAURICE, Henry Charles Keith (1845-1927), 5th Marquess of Lansdowne (FO 800/115-46)

Correspondence as Secretary of State (*/115-16*); papers re Russia, 1895-1905 (*/140-1*). *See MS index (/146) for details.*

199.79 PIERREPONT PAPERS (FO 334)

Letters from Benjamin Garlike in Russia and Denmark, 1804-7 (*/13*).

199.80 RODNEY PAPERS (PRO 30/20)

Letters re the membership of Lord Rodney (?George Brydges Rodney, 1st Baron Rodney) of the Free Economical Society of Russia, 1789-90 (*/26/11*).

199.81 RUSSELL PAPERS (PRO 30/22)

Papers of Lord John Russell (1792-1878), PM, 1846-52, 1865-6, and Foreign Secretary, 1852-3, 1859-65, include extensive material on Russia. The index lists papers relating generally to Russia and the Russian Tsars and also to Russian armed forces, finances and serfs, the 1812 campaign, Central Asia, Circassia, the Crimean War, the Crimean Conference, Russia's relations with Afghanistan, Austria, the Balkans, Bulgaria, China, France, Greece, Hungary, Italy, Montenegro, Norway, Persia, Poland, Prussia, Serbia, Syria, Turkey and the USA. *See lists and index for details.*

199.82 SATOW PAPERS (PRO 30/33)

Papers of Sir Ernest Mason Satow (1843-1929) include a map of Siberia, n.d. ?17th century (*/23/7*).

199.83 SIMMONS PAPERS (FO 358)

Private papers of Lt-Gen. Sir John Lintorn Arabin Simmons (1821-1907), chiefly re the Russo-Turkish War, 1876-80. *See list for details.*

199.84 SIMON, John Allsebrook (1873-1954), 1st Visc. of Stackpole Elidor (FO 800/285-91)

Papers as Secretary of State for Foreign Affairs include references to Russia.

199.85 SPRING-RICE, Sir Cecil Arthur (1858-1918) **(FO 800/241-2)**
Correspondence as Secretary of the Embassy in Russia, 1903-6.

199.86 STRATFORD CANNING PAPERS **(FO 352)**
Collection includes papers from the mission of Stratford Canning, 1st Visc. Stratford de Redcliffe, to Russia, 1825 **(/9-10)**. There are also references to Russia in his papers concerning his missions to Turkey and Greece and miscellaneous papers. *See list for details.*

199.87 STUART PAPERS **(PRO 30/36)**
Official and diplomatic correspondence of the Hon. Sir William Stuart includes papers as Chargé d'Affaires in Russia, 1867-8 **(/4)**.

199.88 STUART DE ROTHESAY PAPERS **(FO 342)**
Papers include the correspondence of Charles Stuart (1779-1845), later Sir Charles and Lord Stuart of Rothesay, as Secretary of the Embassy and Minister *ad interim* in Russia **(/3-8)**.

199.89 VILLIERS, Sir Francis Hyde (1852-1925) **(FO 800/22-4)**
Assistant Under-Secretary of State for Foreign Affairs. Papers include letters from Sir Arthur Nicolson from St Petersburg and elsewhere, 1893-1908 **(/22)**.

199.90 WARNEFORD NIGHTINGALE PAPERS **(PRO 30/71)**
Papers of Maj. G. W. Nightingale include letters from Archangel and Tarnowitz where he was serving with the British Expeditionary Force **(/4)**.

199.91 WHITE, Sgt W. **(PRO 30/39)**
Documents of unknown ownership include a letter from Sgt White to his brother from the Crimea, 1855 **(/1/10)**.

199.92 WHITE PAPERS **(FO 364)**
Papers of Sir William Arthur White as Vice-Consul and acting Consul-General at Warsaw, 1857-64.

199.93 WOOD, Charles, 1st Visc. Halifax **(FO 800/309-28)**
Papers as Secretary of State for Foreign Affairs include references to the Baltic States, the USSR and Finno-Soviet relations. *See MS index (/327) for details.*

200.1-12

ROTHSCHILD ARCHIVES

New Court, St Swithin's Lane, London EC4P 4DU

Apply to Archivist for access with details of proposed research and names of two referees. All work based on or containing extracts from material in the Rothschild Archives must be submitted to the Archivist before publication. Access is restricted to material prior to 1914. G. A. Knight, 'Das Rothschild'sche Banken - und Wirtschaftsarchiv in London : Empfängerüberlieferung im Überblick' *Bankhistorisches Archiv*, 5, 1 (July 1979). Catalogues of records; an index to the whole collection is being entered on a computer.

Rothschild Business Archives

200.1 ACCOUNT CURRENT (I)
Russian Dividends Account Books, 1878-1932 (**/17/1-4**).

200.2 BOOK KEEPING (VI)
Journal of Prussian and Russian dividends, 1824-32 (**/4/11**).

200.3 CHEQUES, ANCIENT (IX)
Loan cheques of 1822 Russian Loan, 1825-44 (**/62/9-10**).

200.4 CORRESPONDENCE (XI)
Extensive correspondence with Russian government, firms, banks and individuals, *c.* 1823-1914, re loans, stock and bonds. Letters received include letters from the Russian government, banks in Moscow, St Petersburg and Helsinki, J. M. de Rothschild in St Petersburg, and firms in Russia including F. C. Gasser, Kapherr & Co. and Steiglitz & Co. Special correspondence includes re Russian credits, 1898. Letters received include unsorted letters from Russia and copy letter books, 1894-1922. Sundry correspondence, divided alphabetically, includes many letters from clients in Russia including banks in Moscow, St Petersburg and Warsaw and firms including Abbott & Sons, W. Anderson & Co., Achenbach & Colley, Bagge & Co., Becke & Crube, J. Gamper & Co., Krohn & Co., Lobach & Co., Meyer & Bruxner, Mollwo & Son, Schultze & Pander, Steiglitz & Co., and individuals including G. Backhausen, M. Demidov, G. Kirschten, J. Kisnich, M. and J. Krause, A. P. Neumann, T. Thorncroft and E. C. Walther. *See catalogues for details.*

200.5 LOANS (XIII)
Specimens of bonds and scrip certificates re Russian loans of 1822, 1870, 1873 and 1875 (**/206/1-2**); notarial acts for destruction of cancelled talons for the Russian loan of 1862, Apr. 1907 (**/224/1**); prospectuses re Russian loans of 1870, 1871, 1872, 1873, 1875, 1889, 1891, 1894 (**/230/69-77**); notarial acts for the cancellation of bonds for the Russian loan of 1822 (**/255/1**). *See catalogue for details.*

Rothschild Family Papers

200.6 ROTHSCHILD, Emma Louise von (**RFamC/14**)
Letter to Lionel and Charlotte Rothschild re Russian business, 31 Aug. 1868 (**/6**).

200.7 ROTHSCHILD, Evelina de (**RFamC/6**)
Letter to Lionel Rothschild re the Russian loan, 1863 (**/36**); letters to Charlotte Rothschild with references to Russia, 1866, n.d. (**/90, 92-3**).

200.8 ROTHSCHILD, Ferdinand de (**RFamC/8**)
Letters to Lionel and Charlotte Rothschild from St Petersburg, Moscow, Rostov and Sebastopol, 1867 (**/18-26**).

200.9 ROTHSCHILD, Baroness Leonora (**RFamC/17**)
Letters to Lionel and Charlotte Rothschild re the Empress of Russia and Russian Princesses, ?1867 (**/78-9, 111, 173**) and re Russian affairs and personalities, n.d. (**/123, 129, 210, 280, 301, 319, 339, 384, 388, 413**); letter to Alfred Rothschild re dinner party at the Russian Embassy, n.d. (**/292**). *See catalogue for details.*

200.10 ROTHSCHILD, Leopold (**RFamC/5**)
Letters to Lionel Rothschild from Moscow, St Petersburg, Nizhnii Novgorod, Saratov, Kazan', Rostov, Taganrog, Yalta, Sebastopol and other Russian towns, 1867, n.d. (**/111, 115-42, 286**). *See catalogue for details.*

200.11 ROTHSCHILD, Baron Lionel (**RFamC/4**)
Letters to Leopold Rothschild on business matters re Russia and Russian finances and scrip, 1863, 1870, n.d. (**/225, 227, 240-1, 247, 353, 425**). *See catalogue for details.*

200.12 MISCELLANEOUS ROTHSCHILD FAMILY CORRESPONDENCE (**RFamC/12**)
Letter from Beatrice Rothschild from St Petersburg, n.d. (**/17**); letter from Adelina Patti Nicolini to Rothschilds & Sons, 1 Jan. 1891 (**/91**).

201.1-9
ROYAL AIR FORCE MUSEUM

Aviation Records Department, Hendon, London NW9 5LL

By appointment. There may be further material on the intervention period in collections listed under unit, station or aircraft type.

201.1 Citation in Russian for awards made to members of 47 Squadron by the White Russians, 1919, with transl. (**A338**).

201.2 2 documents in Russian made out to Lt W. J. Daddo-Langlois, 1919 (**A427**).

201.3 Photograph album of the RAF in South Russia, 1919 (**B896**).

201.4 Pilot's flying log-book of Flt Lt S. D. Culley covering operations in Russia, 25 May 1917 - 20 Dec. 1927 (**B990**).

201.5 Pilot's flying log-book of Lt W. J. Daddo-Langlois covering operations in Russia, 1919 (**B1070**).

201.6 2 files of correspondence, reports, minutes and memos on the supply of British and American aircraft and equipment to the USSR, on the organization of the RAF Mission and technical assistance parties to the Red Air Force and the business transacted between the Mission and the Red Air Force liaison committee, 1941-2 (**B1147**).

201.7 Report on a visit to Red Air Force base Ivanovo by Wg/Cdr H. H. Hilliar and Flt Lt G. Crichton, 27-29 May 1942 (**B1149**).

201.8 Notes on the organization and administration of the RAF in the USSR, 1942 (**B1150**).

201.9 Pilot's flying log-book of Marshal of the Royal Air Force Sir Neil Cameron covering operations in the USSR, 13 May 1939 - 29 Dec. 1944 (**M10,153**).

202.1
ROYAL ANTHROPOLOGICAL INSTITUTE OF GREAT BRITAIN

Photographic Collection, 56 Queen Anne Street, London W1M 9LA

By appointment.

202.1 38 photographs of Russians, 1870s-1890s; 33 photographs of models of ethnic groups at the Moscow Ethnographical Exhibition in 1867.

203.1-46
ROYAL ARTILLERY INSTITUTION

Old Royal Military Academy, Woolwich, London SE18 4JJ

By appointment.

203.1 ADYE, Gen. Sir John Miller (**929**)
2 letters from Adye to Bingham from the Crimea, 7 Sept. 1854, 21 Jan. 1855 (**/1, 3**); sketches of action in the Crimea and account of the battle of the Alma, 20 Sept. 1854 (**/2**).

203.2 ARBUTHNOT, Maj. George Holme (**MD/1212**)
15 photographs of memorials and fortifications in the Crimea, taken in 1910.

203.3 BENT, Surg. John (**MD/1293**)
Letters and reports re service in the Crimea, 1855.

203.4 BROWN, Sgt (**MD/646**)
TS photocopy of account of experiences in the Royal Artillery, mainly in the Crimea and the Indian mutiny, 1854-66.

203.5 BUNBURY, Lt-Col. Henry William (**MD/480**)
Copies of 65 letters from the Crimea.

203.6 CAMPBELL, Maj.-Gen. Sir John William Loudun (**MD/1187**)
TS memoirs 'My Soldiering Days' covering service in the Crimean War.

203.7 CATOR, Gen. Sir William (**MD/893**)
'Siege of Sebastopol - Showing the Armament of the English Batteries at the commencement of each Bombardment, and the expenditure (Navy included) during each bombardment 1854-55'.

203.8 CLAYTON, Lt-Col. E. (**MD/1452**)
Papers mainly re Poland and the Polish army include a draft report on Vil'na, *c.* 1923.

203.9 DACRES, Gen. Sir Richard (**B2/4542**)
Orders and memos connected with the Crimean campaign.

203.10 DICKSON, Gen. Sir Collingwood (**MD/100**)
'A Reminiscence of General Sir Collingwood Dickson, VC, GCB, in the Crimea' by Maj.-Gen. C. H. Owen, with correspondence relating to it.

203.11 EVERARD, G. (**MD/1258**)
2 letters from Everard to his brother from before Sebastopol, 1855.

203.12 FITZMAYER, Maj.-Gen. Sir James (**MD/941**)
Pamphlet and letters re the responsibility for 18-Pounders at the battle of Inkerman (**/2**); 'Weekly Sick Report' from Camp Varna, 20 Aug. 1854 (**/3**); return of casualties and rounds fires at the battle of the Alma (**/5**); 3 passes in the name of Col. Fitzmayer issued for the French trenches before Sebastopol, 1855 (**/6**); Russian papers found in Sebastopol by Fitzmayer (**/13**).

203.13 GARDINER, Gen. Sir Robert William (**MD/1178**)
Letters from the Crimea (**/28**).

203.14 GEARY, Lt-Col. John Alexander (**MD/1146**)
Letters from Alfred Geary from before Sebastopol, 1856 (**/5**); Crimean War diary of ?Alfred Geary, 1855-6 (**/6**).

203.15 HARISON, Capt. Nathaniel Evanson (**MD/174**)
Letter by Harison from Camp Varna in the Crimea, 24 July 1854 (**/1**).

203.16 HEADLAM, Maj.-Gen. Sir John (**MD/183**)
Report on a visit to the Russian Front, 1917 (**/5**).

203.17 LAUDER, Lt J. J. (**MD/398**)
Account of 55th Field Battery's campaign in North Russia, 1919 (**/1**); news communiqués from North Russia, 1919 (**/2**); withdrawal and operation orders from North Russia (**/3-4, 6**); miscellaneous messages and maps from North Russia (**/5, 8**); letters from Lauder to his mother from North Russia (**/7**); Russian currency notes (**/9**).

203.18 LAWSON, Surg. G. (**B2/410e**)
Account covering service in the Crimean War.

203.19 LEFROY, Gen. J. H. (**MD/1101; MR/46, 55**)
Collection of documents re the history of the Crimean War including memos and returns by Sir George Maclean, 1855-6 (**MD/1101**); reports on hospitals etc. in the Crimea by Maj.-Gen. Stocks and Lefroy, 1856 (**MR/46**); papers of Lefroy re the 'Mission to the East, 1855-6', including correspondence, reports and returns from his tour of the Crimea (**MR/55**).

203.20 LOWE, Maj. Francis Manley (**MD/190**)
Notes and correspondence of *c.* 1890-1930 re graves in the Crimea.

203.21 MACLEOD, Col. Roderick William **(MD/1150)**
Letters from Gen. W. E. Ironside to MacLeod from North Russia (/6).

203.22 MACMUNN, Lt G. F. **(MD/845)**
Hospital requistion of a Field Battery at Sebastopol by MacMunn, 1855.

203.23 MAUDE, Capt. (later Col. Sir) George Ashley **(MD/1286)**
Printed booklet containing 27 letters written by Maude to his wife from the Crimea, 1854.

203.24 MAULE, Maj.-Gen. Henry Barlow **(MD/562)**
25 vols of his journal, 1855-93, covering service in the Crimean War (/1-25); TS copies of 36 letters from the Crimea (/26); book of range tables with MS notes giving range of guns in use during the Crimean War (/28).

203.25 MITCHELL, Cpl Thomas **(MD/1061)**
17 letters from the Crimea, 1854-6.

203.26 MOIR, Lt-Col. (Revd) Malcolm Edward **(MD/802)**
Diary covering his service in D/177 Bde in North Russia, July-Oct. 1919.

203.27 MONTGOMERIE, D. **(MD/178)**
Sketches, illustrations and correspondence re Russian guns, 1854-5.

203.28 MUNTON, John **(MD/1641)**
Autobiography of service in the Royal Artillery covering service in the Crimean War.

203.29 NICOLLS, Maj.-Gen. O. H. A. **(D2/242)**
Diary covering service in the Crimean War.

203.30 RAMSDEN, Capt. John Charles **(MD/1185)**
Diary of service in the Crimea and India, 1855-7 (/1).

203.31 RICHARDS, Capt. William Powell **(MD/263)**
Letter from Richards to his aunt from before Sebastopol, 1854 (/1); notebook containing fair copies of his Crimean War letters, 1854-5 (/2); TS copies of his Crimean War letters (/3).

203.32 SMITH, Gunner Mark **(MD/253)**
Account book covering service in the Crimea.

203.33 TAYLOR, Asst.-Surg. Arthur Henry **(MD/274)**
TS copies of letters from Taylor to his parents from the Crimea, 8 Oct. 1854 - 14 Mar. 1856.

203.34 TEESDALE, Maj.-Gen. Sir Christopher Charles **(MD/1125)**
2 journals covering the siege of Kars in the Crimea, 1854-6 (/2).

203.35 WIGHTMAN, James William **(/679)**
Account of the Charge of the Light Brigade as a participant and of his experiences as a Russian prisoner (published in 1892).

203.36 WILLIAMS, Lt-Gen. Sir William Fenwick **(MD/917)**
Commissions and dispatches from Kars, 1855 .

203.37 WILSON, Gunner Edward (**MD/332**)
Letter from Wilson to his brother from the Crimea, 29 Dec. 1854.

203.38 WINDHAM, Maj.-Gen. A. C. (**MD/165**)
Memo on the stealing of horses in the Crimean War, 13 May 1856.

203.39 Chart showing returns of ordnance, ammunition and casualties at the siege of Sebastopol, 1854-5 (**MD/273**).

203.40 Detail of ordnance, ammunition and stores forwarded as a battery train for service in the East (the Crimea) in March 1854 (**MD/892**).

203.41 Detail of a battery of 32 pounders equipped for field service in the East (the Crimea), 1854 (**MD/894**).

203.42 Muster roll of the Royal Artillery in the Crimea,1855-6, copied from War Office Records (**MD/938**).

203.43 Order book of No. 2 Co., 11th Bn, Royal Artillery from the camp before Sebastopol, Nov. 1855 - Feb. 1856 (**MD/1048**).

203.44 Garrison and regimental orders of the Royal Artillery in the Crimea, 3 May 1856 - 3 Oct. 1856 (**MD/1059**).

203.45 Nominal roll of officers, non-commissioned officers and soldiers of the Royal Regt of Artillery entitled to receive a medal for service in the Crimea (**MD/1067**).

203.46 Royal Artillery returns prepared at Woolwich, 1854-6 (**MD/1084**).

204.1-2

ROYAL COLLEGE OF MUSIC

Parry Room Library, Prince Consort Road, South Kensington, London SW7

By appointment.

204.1 Letters from A. K. Glazunov to Sir Hubert Parry, 3-4 June 1907, 7/20 May 1909 (**MSS 3000-3002**).

204.2 Letter album of Sir Charles Villiers Stanford includes letters from A. K. Glazunov, 22 Apr. 1921, and P. I. Tchaikovsky, 21 Feb., 11 Mar. 1893 (**MS 4253 nos. 146, 158-9**).

205.1-2

ROYAL COLLEGE OF PHYSICIANS

11 St Andrews Place, Regents Park, London NW1 4LE

By appointment.

205.1 Photocopies of Thomas Dimsdale's letters on the inoculation of Catherine II and her son, 1768-81. *See Appendix 2, Unrecorded Papers in Private Ownership, Dimsdale Papers, for originals.*

205.2 Journal of J. F. Payne in Russia, 1879.

206.1-9

ROYAL COLLEGE OF SURGEONS OF ENGLAND

35-43 Lincoln's Inn Fields, London WC2A 3PN

By appointment.

206.1 Letter from Catherine Herbert, Countess of Pembroke, to Samuel Bentham inviting him to Vorontsov's (?S. R. Vorontsov or M. S. Vorontsov) birthday dinner, 30 May n.y.

206.2 Letter from Sir Robert Murray Keith, Ambassador at Vienna, to Charles Whitworth, Ambassador at St Petersburg, 8 Oct. 1790.

206.3 2 letters from Count C. Lieven, Russian Ambassador, to Gen. Samuel Bentham, 22 Sept. 1827, 5 Feb. 1828.

206.4 Letter from Count Orloff (? Vladimir Grigor'evich Orlov) to Dr Matthew Baillie, 8 Oct. [1821].

206.5 Letter from N. V. Sklifossovsky (Sklifosovskii) to [Alban Doran], n.d.

206.6 Letter from Adm. Tchitchazoff (P. V. Chichagov) to Gen. Samuel Bentham, [1806].

206.7 2 letters from Count Woronzov (S. R. Vorontsov), Russian Ambassador, to Samuel Bentham, 1799, 15 Apr. 1800.

206.8 3 unrelated documents in Russian, presumably picked up by Dr Blenkins in Sebastopol, being: a case report on Andrei Kartovskii, sailor, 27 Aug. 1851; a request for hospital supplies, received 4 Mar. 1854; a request for leave, 8 Feb. 1841.

206.9 Photographs of B. P. Petrovskii and S. S. Yudin, both Honorary Fellows of the College.

207.1

ROYAL COMMISSION ON HISTORICAL MANUSCRIPTS

Quality House, Quality Court, Chancery Lane, London WC2A 1HP

207.1 The Royal Commission on Historical Manuscripts acts as a central clearing-house for information about the nature and location of historical manuscripts and papers outside the public records. Several private collections which include papers relating to Russia are listed in the National Register of Archives at the Royal Commission and details of these can be found in Appendix 1. The Royal Commission held the papers of the Broadlands Archives Trust (Palmerston Papers) until September 1984 when they were tranferred to Southampton University Library (see entry for Southampton University Library), although a catalogue of these papers is retained by the Commission.

208.1-2

ROYAL COMMONWEALTH SOCIETY

Northumberland Avenue, London WC2N 5BJ

By appointment. D. H. Simpson, edit., *The Manuscript Catalogue of the Library of the Royal Commonwealth Society* (1975).

208.1 Account by S. Forbes White of visits to Siberia, 1904-18.

208.2 Account by Charles Edward Jewel Whitting of a visit to Russia and Central Asia, Aug. 1960.

209.1

ROYAL ENTOMOLOGICAL SOCIETY OF LONDON

41 Queen's Gate, London SW7 5HU

By appointment.

209.1 MS of a paper by Jacob Hübner on the Lepidoptera of the Ukraine, *c.* 1787-8.

210.1-86
ROYAL GEOGRAPHICAL SOCIETY

1 Kensington Gore, London SW7 2AR

Access is normally restricted to Fellows of the Society. Applications from non-Fellows should be addressed to the Director and Secretary. There are author and geographical card indexes, TS catalogues, and lists of correspondence from the foundation of the Society in 1830 to 1920. A list of correspondence 1921-40 is in progress. There is a published handlist compiled by C. Kelly, *The RGS Archives* (1977).

Correspondence (letters to the Society unless stated)

210.1 Letter from Sir J. E. Alexander from the Crimea, 1 June 1856.

210.2 Letter from John Arrowsmith re map of Georgia and Armenia, 21 June 1833.

210.3 2 letters from Professor Baer re geography in Russia and the Russian expedition to Khiva, Feb.-Apr. 1840.

210.4 Letter from M. S. Bentham re the invention of an amphibious carriage by Gen. Sir Samuel Bentham and his use of it in travels in Russia, 22 June 1855.

210.5 Letter from Mrs Isabella Bishop from Peking re her travels in Korea, China and Russian Manchuria, 5 Oct. 1894.

210.6 Letters from Oswald W. Brierly re his Crimean War sketches, n.d.

210.7 Letter from Richard Francis Burton from the Crimea, 18 Aug. 1855.

210.8 Letters from Maj. F. C. H. Clarke, 1876-80, contain references to the Congress of Orientalists at St Petersburg.

210.9 Letter from Richard Collinson re the threat of Russian expansion around the Amur, n.d., received 4 Oct. 1858.

210.10 Letter from Lt A. Conolly advising against travel to Khiva, n.d., received 1838.

210.11 Letter from Ney Elias re Russian consul at Kashgar, 20 Dec. 1879.

210.12 2 letters from Professor A. Erman re Yakutsk and Kamchatka, 5 Mar. 1838, 26 Feb. 1839, French.

210.13 Letters from the Foreign Office re Russian expedition to Novaya Zemlya, 15 Aug. 1837, re Finland, 31 May 1840, re the Russian exploration of the Aral Sea, 17 May 1851, re the expedition of 1715 to Khiva, 27 Apr. 1853.

210.14 Letter from Prince E. M. Galitzin (Golitsyn), n.d., *c.* 1850.

210.15 Letter from M. Gamazov from St Petersburg, 29 Aug./10 Sept. 1876.

210.16 Letter from Lt A. C. Glascott from St Petersburg re maps of the Turco-Persian frontier, 2 Dec. 1862.

210.17 6 letters from Col. G. Helmerson from St Petersburg re geographical progress in Russia, 1842, 1845-9.

210.18 30 letters from Ellsworth Huntington re his travels in the Transcaspia and his projected expedition to Tibet, 1902-5.

210.19 Letters from the Imperial Russian Geographical Society on behalf of N. Khanikov, 1850s.

210.20 3 letters from Col. J. R. Jackson from St Petersburg re Siberian rivers and the levels of the Caspian and Black Sea, May-June 1836.

210.21 76 letters to Sir John Keltie from Prince Petr Kropotkin, 1880-1917, and 6 letters to the same from Gen. Yu. M. Shokal'skii, 1915-18.

210.22 Letters from N. Khanikov, 19 Oct. 1844, 12 May 1862, French.

210.23 15 letters from Prince Petr Kropotkin, 1913-14.

210.24 15 letters from Adm. P. I. Krusenstern (Kruzenshtern) from St Petersburg mainly re publications and Russian expeditions, 1837-40, 1842, 1844-5.

210.25 14 letters from A. T. Kupffner from St Petersburg mainly re books and periodicals, 1836-8, 1842, 1844-6 French.

210.26 2 letters from Adm. Lutke (Count F. P. Litke or Lütke) from St Petersburg and Estonia, 19 Sept./1 Oct. 1856, 26 Aug./7 Sept. 1858, French.

210.27 12 letters from Kate Marsdon referring to her work in Siberia, 1911-20.

210.28 Letters from E. Delmar Morgan referring to Russian translations and publications, 1876-8.

210.29 3 letters from Roderick Impey Murchison re N. Khanikov, 3 Dec. 1841, 22 Sept. 1844, 11 Nov. 1851; draft of a letter to Grand Duke Constantine of Russia, 6 Nov. 1851; notes on the Russian opposition to Lt Pim's plan, 5 Jan. 1852.

210.30 3 letters from Sir William Rawson re maps of the Trans-Siberian railway, Oct. 1895.

210.31 23 letter from Gen. Yu. M. Shokal'skii mainly re news of the Imperial Russian Geographical Society, 1911-17.

210.32 Letter from Capt. C. Stoddart re survey of road to Khiva and Bukhara, 14 Mar. 1837.

210.33 Letter from Dr J. D. Thompson requesting introductions for his proposed visit to Russia, 15 Mar. 1853.

210.34 Letter from Vrontchenko (M. V. Vronchenko) from St Petersburg, 23 Oct. 1844.

210.35 3 letters from John Walker re the preparation of Col. W. Monteith's map of Armenia, 17 Feb. 1831, 7, 17 Jan. 1832.

210.36 Letters from Dr G. Wallin from Finland, 1851-2; extract from the Council Minutes of the Imperial Russian Geographical Society, 14 Sept. 1851; extracts from documents of the Russian Society relating to Wallin; copy of letter from Wallin to the same.

210.37 Letter from Joseph Wolff re his invitation to travel to Russia, 30 Mar. 1850.

210.38 4 letters from Adm. N. Wrangel (Vrangel') from St Petersburg, 1837, 1840, German and French.

210.39 Letter from S. Zelenoi re monument to Adm. P. I. Krusenstern (Kruzenshtern), 24 Oct./5 Nov. 1872.

210.40 Letters and papers re the Royal Geographical Society and schemes of transliteration of Russian, Persian, Greek and other place names.

Library MSS, Journal MSS and Observations Files

210.41 RAWLINSON, Sir Henry Creswicke
Papers include notebooks containing extracts and notes on the antiquities of Central Asia, and a large number of parliamentary papers and confidential India Office papers, 1869-93, concerning relations with Russia on the Persian and Afghan frontiers.

210.42 Journal by A. R. M. on board HMS *Adelaide* sailing from Plymouth to the Crimea, 28 Dec. 1854 - 13 Feb. 1855.

210.43 Collection of MS and printed material of John F. Baddeley re the Amur river and to his journeys in the Amur region in 1900, 1907, 1909-10, Russian and English.

210.44 Transl. by J. Michell of an article by Karl Baer published by the Imperial Russian Geographical Society on scientific observations on the Caspian and its neighbourhood, 1860.

210.45 Photocopy of record left on Novaya Zemlya in 1597 by William Barents and Jacob von Heemskerk.

210.46 Report by Capt. Francis Beaufort on Col. W. Monteith's map of Armenia, 1831.

210.47 W. G. Blackie, 'Recent acquisitions made by Russia at the expense of the Chinese territory of Manchuria with some account of the Amur river'.

210.48 James Brant, 'Journey through part of Armenia and Asia Minor', 1836.

210.49 MS article by Maj. C. D. Bruce, 'A thousand miles across Asia from Pekin to Lake Baikal', 1907; typed copies by Bruce of route reports on a journey through Tibet, Central Asia and China, 1905-6.

210.50 Notes on the Caucasus by Capt. C. D. Cameron, 1862.

210.51 Observation file and computations of heights in Central Asia by Douglas Carruthers, 1910.

210.52 Margaret A. Chambers, 'The lure of the Caucasus : sketches in prose and paint of travels under the old regime, 1912-13'.

210.53 Folder of notes by A. E. Coates and photographs concerning the Museum Darwinianum, Moscow.

210.54 R. P. Cobbold, 'Journey in Central Asia', 1898.

210.55 Transl. by Col. Henry Yule of A. P. Fedchenko, 'Visit to the Altai steppe', 1874.

210.56 Travel diary of Capt. W. J. Gill in India, Persia and Russia, 1880-1.

210.57 Lt Adam Gifford Glascott, 'Notes made during an excursion along the coast of the Black Sea from Trebizond to Batoom', 1839.

210.58 C. M. Grant, 'Notes on a journey from Pekin to St Petersburgh across the desert of Gobi', 1863.

210.59 Professor J. von Hamel, 'On the height of the city of Moskow', 1838.

210.60 Col. J. R. Jackson, 'On various heights in Russia', 1837.

210.61 G. Kuhlewein, 'News of some European travellers who perished in central Asia within the last twenty years', 1861.

210.62 A. M. Lomonosov, 'Trans-continental European Pacific rail-road', 1873.

210.63 Abstract of a report by S. V. Martinova on an expedition organized by P. Ushakov to the Pechora region in 1903, Russian.

210.64 Transl. by E. Delmar Morgan of an article by N. A. Mayev from the Proceedings of the Imperial Russian Geographical Society on the valleys of the Vaksh and Kafirnahan, 1872, and a report by the same on an expedition to the Hissar country, 1876.

210.65 A. Michie, 'Travelling notes on China, Mongolia and Siberia', 1864.

210.66 Positions, levels, meteorological observations in Azerbaijan by Col. W. Monteith, 1818-20.

210.67 Capt. J. Wolfe Murray, 'Theory of Mr Tchaikovsky concerning the course of the ancient Oxus', 1885.

210.68 Travel journals of Miss E. F. Noel in Finland, 1906, and in the Caucasus, 1913.

210.69 Transl. by E. Delmar Morgan of the journal of the Archimandrite Palladius of an expedition through Manchuria, from Peking to Blagoveshchensk.

210.70 Journal by le Chevalier de Paravey, 'Mémoire sur les anciennes navigations dans la mer du nord de l'Asie...'.

210.71 Journal by Lt B. C. T. Pim, 'Plan for an investigation of the northern coasts of Siberia in search of the missing expedition under Sir John Franklin', 1851.

210.72 Transl. by R. Michell of a report by G. I. Radde to the Imperial Russian Geographical Society on explorations in south-eastern Siberia, 1855-9.

210.73 Transl. by A. M. Lomonosov of an address by N. Severtsov to the Imperial Russian Geographical Society on a journey in Fergana and the Pamirs in 1877-8.

210.74 A sketch map by R. B. Shaw to illustrate a proposed article on a prince of Kashgar's account of the geography of Turkistan and a tracing of a Chinese map of Turkistan, 1876.

210.75 Yu. M. Shokal'skii, 'The discovery of the eastern point of Asia and the work of Semen Dezhnev', 1908.

210.76 Col. H. Solomon, 'Report on a journey from London to the Lena goldfields' mine headquarters at Nadiezhdinski', n.d.

210.77 Transl. of L. Starokadomskii, 'Across the Arctic Ocean from Vladivostock to Archangel', 1916.

210.78 Edward Stirling, 'An account of the accidents which befell Mr Moorcroft [W. Moorcroft] and the party with him in Turkestan as given by Luskeree Khan, one of his servants...' n.d.

210.79 Route reports of the University of Bristol Rover Crew on the Russia-Lapland expedition, 1961.

210.80 Albert Upmalis, 'The Latvian Republic', 1932.

210.81 A. Vambéry, 'A journey to Khiva, Bokhara and Samarkand', 1864.

210.82 Account by Col. W. Venyukov of the work of Russian sailors in the northern ocean in 1895, and of the hydrographic expedition to the mouth of the Yenisei and Ob' and part of the Kara Sea in 1896, Russian; transl. of notes to Venyukov's map 'Russian explorations in Asia 1854-74'.

210.83 Journal by Joseph Wiggins, 'Proposed further expedition to open trade with Russia via the Obi river', 1875.

210.84 Lt John Wood, 'The fall and rapidity of the Oxus and of other rivers compared with the Oxus', n.d. ?1840.

210.85 Barometrical heights in Armenia, 1830-4.

210.86 Letter book of the *Orient* while stationed off Scutari, 1854.

211.1-7

ROYAL INSTITUTE OF INTERNATIONAL AFFAIRS

Chatham House, 10 St James's Square, London SW1Y 4LE

By appointment for *bona fide* researchers. Registers of each section of the archives of Chatham House. Sections of the archives dealing with purely internal Chatham House affairs are closed indefinitely; other sections of the archives are closed for thirty years although records of general meetings are open from June 1973. All meetings of the Institute and account of research in progress can be found in the *Annual Reports* from 1920 to date.

211.1 THE FOUNDATION OF CHATHAM HOUSE; RESEARCH POLICY AND ADMINISTRATION (section 2)
Correspondence re Russian and International Law Studies at Chatham House, 1944-9 (/1/10).

211.2 CORRESPONDENCE WITH INDIVIDUALS (section 4)
Correspondence with Sir Ivison Macadam re his visits to Latvia and the USSR, 1932 (/MACA/h-i).

211.3 MEETINGS (section 8)
Texts of talks, and occasionally texts of questions, 1920 to the present, relating to many aspects of the USSR, including general impressions and comments on the USSR, Anglo-Soviet relations, Soviet foreign relations with the China and the West, Soviet internal policy, Soviet leaders, Second World War conferences and treaties, SALT negotiations, trade and commerce with the USSR, the Soviet invasions of Czechoslovakia and Afganistan, Soviet policy towards the non-Russian republics, life in the USSR including the Church, labour camps, economic conditions, agriculture, social conditions, the legal system, political trials and human rights. *See register for details.*

211.4 STUDY GROUPS (section 9)
Papers presented, reports, correspondence etc re the USSR from the following study groups: Committee on Reconstruction : Anglo-Soviet Relations Group (/26); Joint Group with the Institute of Industrial Administration on Industrial Management in the USSR (/27); Chatham House Memoranda Sept. 1939 - Jan. 1940, papers presented at Balliol College (/36j, q, z, dd, nn); Study Group on the Soviet Union, 1967-8 (/72); Study Group on the Soviet Union, 1969-71 (/81); Study Groups on East-West Relations, 1968-73 (/82); Energy as a Factor in Soviet Policy, 1974-6 (/99); Changing Patterns in Eastern Europe, 1979-80 (/126); The Soviet Union and the Countries of the 'Arc of Crisis', 1980-1 (/130); Soviet Policy in the Far East, 1982 (/133); The Sino-Soviet Dispute and International Security, 1980-2 (/137). *See register for details.*

211.5 CONFERENCES (section 10)
Papers and correspondence of the following conferences: Conference of Teachers and Research Workers on the USSR, 1964-6 (/21); Anglo-Soviet Journalists' Conference, 1967 (/30); EEC and Eastern Europe, 1973 (/54); Anglo-Soviet Round Table Conferences, 1975-7 (/72).

211.6 COURSES (section 11)
Courses re the USSR, 1942, 1944-6, 1948, 1951, 1955 (/1/1-3, 22, 24, 35, 43, 56, 68, 70, 83).

211.7 DEFENCE SEMINARS (section 21)
File of papers re seminar on European policy options in the light of the USA and USSR détente, 2-3 May 1974 (**/1a**).

212.1-6
ROYAL INSTITUTION OF GREAT BRITAIN

21 Albemarle Street, London WIX 4BS

By appointment for accredited researchers. Permission to consult recent records and private collections must be sought from the Librarian. A handwritten index is available of the minutes of Managers Meetings and General Meetings, 1799-1929, and of lectures delivered, 1800-1929. The minutes of Managers Meetings, 1799-1903, have been reproduced in a facsimile edition and each volume is indexed. The minutes are indexed on cards for the period 1929-67, and from 1967 are indexed from computer records and available as a computer print-out. The series Royal Institution General MSS, comprising mainly correspondence, runs from 1799. There is an incomplete card index for this series. Handlists and card indexes cover most of the collections of private papers.

212.1 MEETING OF MANAGERS' MINUTES
Minutes include references to Russians who became subscribing and honorary members of the Institution. For example, in the nineteenth century there are references to Prince E. A. Baratynskii, Prince V. Gagarin, N. N. Novosil'tsev, Count G. Orlov, Prince P. M. Volkonskii and Count Vorontsov (S. R. or M. S. Vorontsov). The Grand Duke Nicholas was made an honorary member in 1817 (**vol.VI pp. 151-2**) and visited the Institution when Tsar in 1844 (**vol. IX p. 310**). References to Professor D. I. Mendeleev mainly concern his Faraday lecture given in 1889 (**vol. XIV pp. 164, 168, 175, 191, 268, 283, 295, 301**).

212.2 ROYAL INSTITUTION GENERAL MSS
Correspondence includes: letter from George John Spencer, 2nd Earl Spencer, to Grand Duke Nicholas re his election as honorary member, 10 Mar, 1817 (**84**); letters to D. I. Mendeleev, 1904 (**111/17**); letter from Mendeleev to Sir Frederick Bramwell, 14/26 May 1891 (**Box XVIII file 228**).

212.3 LECTURES
Lectures concerning Russian topics were given by C. E. Turner in 1881, 1883 and 1888, by S. Graham in 1917 and 1920 and C. A. Beazley in 1917 (cited in the MS index to lectures delivered). In recent years lectures have been given by Dr S. S. Medvedev and Professor P. L. Kapitsa.

212.4 BRAGG PAPERS
Papers of William Henry Bragg (1862-1942), crystallographer, include correspondence re the invitation of the Soviet scientists, B. P. Orelkin and T. T. Wassilieff (Vasil'ev), to work in his laboratory, 1923-4, 1926-7 (**WHB 27A/2o-28, 33-7; 27B/24, 74-80**). Papers of (William) Lawrence Bragg, crystallographer, include correspondence re his proposed visit to the USSR, 1966, 1968 (**WLB Box 34 File C**).

212.5 DAVY PAPERS
Papers of Sir Humphry Davy include letter to him from Prince C. Lieven, 22 Jan. 1827 (**Box 9/I**).

212.6 TYNDALL PAPERS
Papers of John Tyndall include correspondence with N. de Khanikof (N. V. Khanikov) **(25/28)** and Olga Novikov (née Kireev) **(26/F11-27/B11; 28/B3; 29/B8; 30/E8-12, F3-4)**.

213.1

ROYAL OPERA HOUSE ARCHIVE OFFICE

Covent Garden, London WC2E 7QA

By appointment. Card indexes for operas and ballets list material relating to Russian and Soviet works under the name of the opera or ballet and under individual performers.

213.1 The archive consists mainly of photographs of performances, sets and costumes designs, programmes and press cuttings and includes material relating to Russian and Soviet composers, companies, choreographers, producers and performers. There are also photographs of and material relating to Russians (for example P. I. Tchaikovsky, M. Musorgskii, Mikhail Baryshnikov, George Balanchine, Rudolph Nureyev and Fedor Chaliapin (Shalyapin)) in connection with Covent Garden and other performances. There is material relating to Russian ballet companies which have appeared at Covent Garden, for example Diaghilev's Ballets Russes, the original Ballet Russe of Col. de Basil, the Ballet Russe de Monte Carlo, the Kirov and the Bolshoi, as well as some general material on ballet and opera in Russia.

214.1-11

THE ROYAL REGIMENT OF FUSILIERS

City of London Headquarters, The Royal Regiment of Fusiliers, H.M. Tower of London, London EC3N 4AB

By appointment. Manuscript material received before 1968 is arranged by subject; records acquired after this date are arranged by name of donor. There are subject indexes to material received before and after 1968 and also to articles in the *Royal Fusiliers Chronicle*.

Archives, 1685-1968

214.1 Photographs of the painted panorama of Sebastopol; 2 photographs of memorials to British soldiers who died in the Crimean War; 7 letters from and relating to the Crimean War; newspaper cuttings **(C-37)**.

214.2 TS, 'Some Experiences of a Regimental Surgeon during the Crimean War, 1854-55' by Surgeon-Maj.-Gen. Alfred Malpas Tippetts, written 1897 **(E-3)**.

214.3 TS of part V of diary by Asst.-Surgeon T. E. Hale in the Crimea, Nov.-Dec. 1856 **(H-9)**.

214.4 TS, 'Her Majesty Queen Victoria and the War in the Crimea' by K. R. Wilson **(W-12/3)**.

Archives, 1968- (arranged by name of donor)

214.5 Photograph of painting of the 7th Royal Fusilers Regiment in the Crimea (**Forbes**).

214.6 TS copies of letters from Col. C. A. L. Shipley to his mother from the Crimea (published in the *Royal Fusiliers Chronicle*) (**Shipley**).

214.7 Photocopies of letters of Richard Saville from the Crimea (**Thompson**).

214.8 Correspondence re Crimean War grave marker, 1978-82 (**Titchener**).

Photographs

214.9 3 albums and 1 scrapbook of photographs including the Crimean War.

214.10 5 albums of photographs compiled by F. Moore including photographs of the 7th Machine Gun Corps in Archangel, 1917-19.

214.11 Photographs of the 45th Bn in Russia, 1919 (**B-35, B-35 (Annexe)**).

215.1-56
ROYAL SOCIETY

6 Carlton House Terrace, London SW1Y 5AG

By appointment. J. O. Halliwell, *A Catalogue of the Miscellaneous Manuscripts Preserved in the Library of the Royal Society* bound with W. E. Shuckard, *Catalogue of the Manuscript Letters in the Possession of the Royal Society* (London, 1840); A. H. Church, *The Royal Society. Some Account of the 'Classified Papers' in the Archives with an Index of Authors* (Oxford, 1907); A. H. Church, *The Royal Society. Some Account of the 'Letters and Papers' of the Period 1741-1806 in the Archives with an Index of Authors* (Oxford, 1908); R. K. Bluhm, 'A Guide to the Archives of the Royal Society and to Other Manuscripts in its Possession', *Notes and Records of the Royal Society of London*, vol. 12, no. 1, August 1956, pp. 21-39. TS 'The Revised Catalogue of the Manuscripts (General)'; card catalogue of correspondence and other manuscript material.

215.1 BAWDEN, Sir Frederick Charles
Plant pathologist; treasurer of the Royal Society, 1968-72. Papers re secondment of staff and visits to the USSR, 1958-64, 1967, 1971 (**D.40**).

215.2 BLACKETT, Patrick Maynard, Baron Blackett of Chelsea (1897-1974)
President of the Royal Society, 1965-70. Papers include: letter from J. Chadwick re visits to the USSR, [1945] (**D.190**); folder of notes and graphs, 'USSR - USA Total Man Power', *c.* 1961 (**F.84**); papers re the Anglo-Soviet Conference, Feb. 1961 (**G.99**); correspondence re and TS of lecture for Rutherford Centenary Celebrations, Moscow, Aug. 1971 (**G.125**); correspondence with P. L. Kapitsa, 1966, 1971, 1973-4 (**J.46**); papers re the Pugwash conferences and discussion meetings in Moscow and elsewhere, 1961 (**J.67**).

215.3 BOYLE COLLECTION (**BP, BL**)
Collection of Robert Boyle includes letters to him from Samuel Collins from Vologda, 20 Nov. 1663 (**BL.2.32**) and from Dr Laurentius Rinhuber, physician to the Tsar, re Russian matters, 24 Sept. 1683, Latin (**Bl.42-4**).

215.4 DALE, Henry Hallett (1875-1968) **(93 HD)**
President of the Royal Society, 1940-5. Correspondence re Anglo-Soviet co-operation, 1941-5 **(8.8)**; correspondence and report of the Anglo-Soviet Medical Society, 1941-6 **(8.9)**; British Council correspondence and papers re the USSR, 1942-5 **(14.11)**; correspondence and papers re the USSR Academy of Sciences, 1947-65 **(16.8)**; membership of the USSR Academy of Sciences, 8 Mar. 1942 **(138.2)**. The permission of the family is required to consult these papers. Apply to Librarian or Archivist.

215.5 FLOREY ARCHIVES
Papers of H. W. Florey, President of the Royal Society, 1960-5. Papers re his visit to the USSR, 1943-4 **(47)**; diary of A. G. Saunders of visit to the USSR with Florey, 1943-4 **(48)**; diploma of foreign membership of the USSR Academy of Sciences, 1966 **(271)**. The permission of the family is required to consult these papers. Apply to Librarian or Archivist:

215.6 SABINE, Edward **(Sa)**
President of the Royal Society, 1861-71. Letters from M. Rikatcheff (?Rikachev) to Sabine, 4/6 Feb., 18 Feb./1 Mar. 1868 **(1082-3)**; 'Report of the Committee ... appointed for the purpose of communicating to the Russian Government the opinion of the British Association ... ' re the question of a magnetic observatory at Tiflis, n.d. **(1218-9)**. There might be further references to Russia in his correspondence.

215.7 WAGNER, L. R. **(LW)**
Papers re geological visitors to Britain from the USSR, 1961-4 **(/14/86)** and a visit by Wagner to the USSR, 1962 **(/14/87)**. The permission of the family is required to consult these papers. Apply to Librarian or Archivist.

The following letters and documents have been arranged alphabetically owing to the complexity of the different series under which they are listed. Letters with a class mark consisting of a single letter (corresponding to the first letter of the surname of the author) followed by numbers can be found in Shuckard's catalogue (for example, Bayer, N. S.); other letters and documents can be found in the card catalogue in the Library under author or corresponding institution.

215.8 2 letters from N. S. Bayer to Sir Hans Sloane from St Petersburg, 20 June 1733, 17 Aug. 1736 **(B.3.36, 47)**.

215.9 Letter from Theophilus S. Bayer to Dr C. Mortimer, St Petersburg, 24 Aug. 1737, Latin and English transl. **(B.3.48-9)**; copies of letters from Bayer to the Royal Society from St Petersburg, 1733, 1735-7 **(LBC.21.87, LBC.22.293, 295, LBC.23.71-2, LBC.24.76)**.

215.10 Letter from the Bibliothèque Impériale Publique (Imperatorskaya publichnaya biblioteka), St Petersburg, 10/22 Jan. 1864, French **(MC.7.7)**.

215.11 Letter from Breinius to Sir Hans Sloane, St Petersburg, 28 Sept. 1735 **(B.3.45)** (published in *Philosophical Transactions*, vol. 40, 1737); paper on observations on the mammoth's bones and teeth found in Siberia, read 1735 **(LBC.22.35)**.

215.12 Letter from G. B. Bulfuiger to Dr Jurin, St Petersburg 1728, French **(B.2.39)**.

215.13 Letters from J. Nicholas L'Isle from St Petersburg to Dr Jurin, 31 Dec. 1728, French **(I.2.7)**, to Mr R. Nettleton, May 1737, French **(I.2.26-7)**, to Dr Mortimer, 16 July 1737 **(I.2.29)** and to Dr J. Bevis re the late comet, 1/12 June 1742 **(L&P.I.115)**; 'Projet de la mesure de la Terre en Russie', St Petersburg 1737, read 23 June 1737, French **(Cl.P.II.39-40)**.

215.14 Diary and notebook of Dr Robert Erskine (d. 1718) and *c.* 40 letters to Erskine from various correspondents, transcibed from the USSR Academy of Sciences, Leningrad **(Box 48)**. The microfilm Cabinet 'Erskine' has letters to Erskine from Golitsyn (?Prince M. M.) and A. Menshikov.

215.15 Paper by Robert Erskine (namesake of above) 'Of a centrifugal engine for raising water' read 24 Jan. 1756 **(L&P.IV.243)**.

215.16 Copy letter and paper by Leonhard Euler from St Petersburg , 24 Oct. 1751, 21 Oct./1 Nov. 1768 **(L&PC.II.230, L&PC V.60)**.

215.17 Letter from Christian Goldbach to the Royal Society, St Petersburg, 11 Oct. 1726, Latin **(G.2.5)**.

215.18 Papers by M. Guthrie, 'Of the antiseptic regimen of the natives of Russia', read 3 Apr. 1778 **(L&P.VII.38)**, 'Of the plan to recover people in Russia apparently deprived of life by the burning of charcoal', read 4 Mar. 1779 **(L&P.VII.93)**, 'Of the congelation of quicksilver at St Petersburg, 23 Jan. 1783', read 25 Mar. 1784 **(L&P.VIII.68)**, 'Education of female nobility in Russia', 10 Oct. 1781 **(L&P.VII.256)**; letter from Guthrie to the Royal Society containing a report of the description by P. S. Pallas of Crimean volcanoes, 2 Jan. 1795 **(L&P.X.120)**.

215.19 Letters and papers from the Imperial Academy of Sciences, St Petersburg, 11 Oct. 1726, Latin, 8 Feb. 1732/3, 1755, 23 Apr. 1761, 18/39 Mar. 1876, 9 Jan. 1899, n.d. (2) **(LBC.19.358, RBC.18.123, L&P.II.468, L&P.III.240, L&P.IV.72, MC.10.378, MC.17.211, RS.3.1, L&P.IV.128)**.

215.20 Paper by Pere Jartoux, 'The Tartarian plant called Gin-seng extracted from printed Jesuit letters of 1713', read 4 Mar. 1713/14 **(CLP.X(1).42)**.

215.21 Letters from Kazan' University, 31 Jan/12 Feb. 1863, n.d., Russian and English transl. **(MC.6.301, MC.17.338)**.

215.22 Letters from Nikolai Khanikov to J. F. W. Herschel, 23 Sept. 29 Dec. 1864 **(HS.11.80-81)**, and to E. Sabine, 17 Oct. 1870 **(Sa.750)**.

215.23 Letters from Prof. A. O. Kovalevskii re paper on osteology of hypotanidae, Munich, 6 May 1872, 15 May 1873 **(MC.9.547, 554; RR.7.250-1)**, and to the Royal Society from Algeria, 6 May 1886, French **(MC.14.127)**.

215.24 Letters from A. T. Kupffner mainly to E. Sabine from St Petersburg, 1829-30, 1836, 1840-59 **(AP.16.21, HS.11.94, MM.3.108, MM.4.139, 292, MM.10.35, 41-8, 50-65, MM.11.161, 179)**.

215.25 Draft and 2 fair copies of Prince A. Menshikov's diploma as a Fellow of the Royal Society, 21 Oct. 1714 **(DM.5.56-58)**.

215.26 Letter from Metchnikoff (Dr I. I. Mechnikov), 1906 **(MC)**.

215.27 Letter from the Ministère de la Marine Impériale (Morskoe ministerstvo), 10/23 June 1906 **(MC)**.

215.28 2 letters from the Ministry of War (Voennoe ministerstvo), St Petersburg, 20 Apr., 22 Jun. 1909 **(CD)**.

215.29 Letters from G. Müller from St Petersburg to Dr C. Mortimer, 30 June 1733 **(M.3.18-19)**, and to Sir Hans Sloane, 30 June 1733 **(M.3.20)**; letter re Kamchatka expedition, 30 June 1733, Latin and French **(LBC.20.250, 252)**.

215.30 Letters from the Musée Publique, Moscow (Moskovskii Publichnyi i Rumyantsevskii Muzei), 5/17 Oct. 1866, 9/21 Dec. 1894 **(MC.7.364, MC.16.168)**.

215.31 2 letters from the Observatoire Physique Centrale de Russie (Glavnaya Fizicheskaya Observatoriya), St Petersburg, 10/22 June 1874, 7 Feb. 1876, German and French **(MC.10.346)**.

215.32 Papers by P. S. Pallas, 'On the cold in St Petersburg in the winter of 1762-3' **(L&P.IV.143)**, 'Of iron ore in Siberia' read 16 May 1776 **(L&P.VI.181)**.

215.33 Letter by Prof. I. P. Pavlov, 9 Dec n.y. (early 20th century) **(MC)**.

215.34 Copy of letter from Mark Popovskii re N. I. Vavilov, 21 Jan. 1966 **(Box File LXXII.d.13(7))**.

215.35 Diploma and seal awarded to Joseph Priestley in 1780 by Catherine II **(655 LXXI.d.7, 656 XIII.a.8)**.

215.36 Count G. Razumovskii, 'Mémoire sur l'Origine des bitumes solides ou concrètes, & particulièrement du Charbon Minéral' ?1784 **(AP.5.18)**.

215.37 Letters from P. J. Rocquette to the Royal Society, St Petersburg, 1732 **(Q.R.1. 76-82)**.

215.38 Letter from S. Rumovskii to I. H. de Magdellean (J. H. de Magalhaens) re observation on the transit of Mercury at St Petersburg, 1786 (published in *Philosophical Transactions* 77) **(L&P.IX.8)**.

215.39 3 letters from the Russian Ambassador (Count A. Benkendorff), 1905-06 **(MC)**.

215.40 Letter from the Russia Company, 1847 **(LUB.R.398)**.

215.41 3 letters from the Russian Embassy, Dec. 1915 **(MC)**.

215.42 Copy letter from I. de Schouvallow (I. Shuvalov), May 1758 **(L&P.III.338)**.

215.43 Letter from the Société Impériale de Minéralogique (Imperatorskoe Mineralogicheskoe Obshchestvo), St Petersburg, 15 May 1890 **(MC.15.77)**.

215.44 Letter from the Société Impériale des Naturalistes (Imperatorskoe Obshchestvo lyubitelei estestvoznaniya, antropologii i etnografii), Moscow, 24 July/5 Aug. 1855, 28 Jan./7 Feb. 1859, 3/15 July 1873, 1/14 Feb. 1911 **(MC.5.208, MC.6.10, MC.10.2, MC)**.

215.45 Letter from P. Tchebitchef (Prof. P. L. Chebuyshev) to the Royal Society, St Petersburg, 11/23 Mar. 1878, French **(MC.11.191)**.

215.46 Letter from C. Tcheffkine (?Chefkin, K.) to E. Sabine, St Petersburg, 21 Aug. 1841 **(MM.10.79)**.

215.47 Letter by Prof. K. A. Timiryazov, 4 Dec. n.y. (early 20th century) (**MC**).

215.48 Letters from Capt. North Vigor to Mr S. Collinson, St Petersburg, 22 Nov. 1737 (**V.58** and copy of the same **LBC.24.139**), 11 Mar. 1738 (**LBC.24.357**).

215.49 Copy letter from Richard Waller to Prince A. Menshikov, 21 Oct. 1714 (**LBC.15.140**).

215.50 C. Whitworth, 'About the Russia Enquiryes', London, 7 Mar. 1712/13 (**LBC.16.25**).

215.51 Paper by Sir Peter Wyche, 'Concerning the way used in Muscovy to keep their grain' read 14 July 1670 (**CLP.X(3).15**).

215.52 Inquiries made to the Royal Society re Moscovia, 23 Jan. 1671/2, n.d. (*post* 1692) (**XIX.71, 98**).

215.53 Extract of History of Muscovy, n.d. *c.* 1670, Dutch (**CLP.XVI.20**).

215.54 Description of Tobol'sk and part of Siberia, n.d. *c.* 1675, Dutch (**CLP.VII(1).16**).

215.55 Description of the Somoiddes (Samoyeds), n.d. *c.* 1675, Dutch (**CLP.VII(1).17**).

215.56 Meteorological Archives include observations on St Petersburg, 1725 (**MA.54**).

216.1-7
ROYAL SOCIETY FOR ASIAN AFFAIRS
42 Devonshire Street, London W1N 1LN

Access by appointment for *bona fide* researchers.

216.1 SHAKESPEAR, Sir Richmond Campbell (1812-62)
1 box of papers include: letters and copies of letters mainly to his sisters written during his mission to Khiva and journey through Russia to St Petersburg, 1838-40; 2 journals and draft of journal of his journey through Russia, May-Oct. 1840; papers re the Khiva mission including a list of the released Russian prisoners and 2 letters in Russian, 1840; memo on the release of the Russian prisoners from Khiva; memo on the Russian invasion of India, written at Kabul.

216.2 WHEELER, Col. G. E.
Military Attaché in Iran and Iraq, 1926-31, in General Staff (Intelligence) HQ, India, 1935-40, Information and Oriental Counsellor in British Embassy in Tehran, 1946-50, Director of Central Asia Research Centre 1953-68. Unpublished memoirs describe his experience of Soviet policies and activities in Asia. They are in Col. Wheeler's possession but will ultimately be deposited in the Royal Society for Asian Affairs.

216.3 Articles by C. H. Ellis on Central Asia and the Great Game etc. 2 files, 1 vol. and notes.

216.4 TS extract from account by Lt (later Maj.-Gen. Sir) Thomas Townsend Pears of overland journey to India via Constantinople, Armenia and Persia, 1837.

216.5 Memoirs of Kashgar by Dr S. G. Tscherbakoff (?Shcherbakov), Mar.-Apr. 1932.

216.6 Photographs, 'Duplicates of Official Pictures', of Dunsterforce campaign.

216.7 Miscellaneous collection of printed photographs of different races including Russian, Georgians, Turks, Arabs and Chinese, late 19th century.

217.1-8
ROYAL SOCIETY FOR THE ENCOURAGEMENT OF ARTS, MANUFACTURES AND COMMERCE

John Adam Street, Adelphi, London WC2N 6EZ

By appointment. Card indexes of correspondents, authors of papers, and subjects.

217.1-5 CORRESPONDENCE
There may be letters from and relating to Russia in the following series of correspondence: Loose Archives (chiefly letters received), 1754-1851, Guard Books (chiefly letters received), vols. I-XII, 1754-67, vols. A and B, 1759-79, Letter-books (copies of letters received), 4 vols., 1767-78, Letter-Books (copies of letters sent), 4 vols., 1770-97, 1816-50. *See card index of authors.* Miscellaneous correspondence *c.* 1854-*c.* 1887 is deposited in the Greater London Record Office. The following letters are listed under Russia in the card-index:

217.1 Letter by Mathew Guthrie re method of painting in egg on the special form of cement or glue used by the Turks, St Petersburg, received 27 Dec. 1792 (**C4/56 f.2**).

217.2 Letter by Mathew Guthrie re Siberian hemp and referring to his publications in the *Bee*, St Petersburg, 2 May 1793 (**C5/36 f.2**).

217.3 Letter from L. Waxell enclosing an account of the 'adjudication' with a proposed new question by the Imperial scientists at St Petersburg, 24 July 1807 (**D1/165 ff.2, 6**).

217.4 Letter by James Heard re wooden pavements, St Petersburg, 16 Sept. 1839 (**F1/352 f.2**).

217.5 Letter from James Mounsey, Moscow, 7 Nov. 1759 (**RSA GB II f.27**).

217.6 MEMBERSHIP LISTS
The Signature Book, 1754-64, and MS Subscription Books, 1755-1856, will record Russian visitors and subcribers to the Society, including Father Ya. I. Smirnov, Russian Chaplain in London, who visited the Society on 21 Mar. 1782 (**RSA MSS Subscription Book 1773-92**).

217.7 MINUTES
MS Society minutes run from 1754, MS Committee minutes from 1758 and MS Council minutes from 1846. There will be references in the Society minutes to Britons in Russia and Russians who were elected as members of the Society, including: Dr James Mounsey (**RSA Soc Min, 30 Apr. 1755**), Dr John Rogerson (**RSA Soc Min, 18 & 25 June 1766**), Count A. de Moussin Pouschkin (Musin-Pushkin) (**RSA Soc Min, 29 Mar. 1775**), Count I. G. Chernyshev (**RSA Min, 24 & 31 May 1769**), Father A. A. Samborskii (**RSA Soc Min, 21 Mar. 1774**), Grand Duke Nicholas (Nicholas I) (**RSA Soc Min, 9 Apr. 1817**). Father Ya. I.

Smirnov's attendance at the Society's Committee on the Polite Arts is recorded in Committee Minutes (**RSA Min Comm (P.A.)**).

217.8 TRANSACTIONS
There will be references to papers relating to Russia in MS Transactions, 1770-1862, including papers by various authors relating to Siberian barley (**Trans. Agric. 1770-1, 1771-2, 1772-3**). Papers relating to Russia will also be found in the printed *Transactions of the Society* vols. I-LVII, 1783-1851.

218.1-3

ROYAL SOCIETY OF MEDICINE

1 Wimpole Street, London W1M 8AE

The Library is normally open only to members of the Society; researchers who are not members of the Society should apply to the Librarian for access.

218.1 2 genealogical charts by William Bulloch tracing the incidence of haemophilia through the European royal families, including the Romanovs.

218.2 2 papers by ?Wilhelm Heinrich, chief physician of Sebastopol Naval Hospital and Medical Inspector of the port: 'Descriptio lithotomiae feliciter die XIX men[s] Augusti anni MDCCCXLI in nosocomio maritimo quod Sebastopoli floret ... factae'; 'O raznykh sposobakh lecheniya breda ot p'yanstva ...', 1841 (**MS 509**).

218.3 Case-note by P. Lomovitskii of Tomsk on acromegaly, 6 Dec. 1928, Russian (**in Acromegaly MSS 536-7**).

219.1

RUSSIAN REFUGEES AID SOCIETY

Nicholas House, 27 Blenheim Road, Bedford Park, London W4 1ET

219.1 Originally the British branch of the Russian Red Cross, the Society changed its name in 1920 to the Russian Benevolent Society and in 1978 to the Russian Refugees Aid Society. The Society exists 'to promote in the United Kingdom the welfare and relief of aged, poor, sick and otherwise needy refugees from the area which was formerly part of the Russian Empire and their families' and runs residential homes for elderly Russian refugees. The Society has extensive archives, dating from about 1921, concerning Russian refugees in the United Kingdom but holds no Red Cross documents. The Society cannot allow scholars personally to consult the archives, but the General Secretary is prepared to assist accredited scholars with specific enquiries. The Society is a registered charity and scholars would be expected to make a donation for the information supplied, proportionate to the extent of the work required. Enquiries should be made to the General Secretary.

220.1-3
THE SALVATION ARMY

International Headquarters, 101 Queen Victoria Street, London EC4P 4EP

By appointment. Files containing material relating to the international work of the Salvation Army, arranged by country. Card index of references to Russia and the Soviet Union in the following Salvation Army publications: *All the World*, *Vanguard*, *War Cry*, the Salvation Army *History*, the Salvation Army Year-Books.

220.1 Four files of miscellaneous material relating to Russia including: photographs; extracts from Salvation Army publications; xerox copy of the first issue of *Vestnik spaseniya*, July 1913, and *Vpered*, that is, *War Cry*, published in Paris for the White Russian émigré community, Mar. 1926; TS translations of published accounts of Salvation Army work in Russia, including *The Smallness of Man - the Greatness of God* by Nadja Konstantinova-Sundell, *Ten Years in Russia* by K. Larsson, *Prisoner in Petrograd* by Clara Becker, *She was a Pioneer in Russia* by Commissioner Tor Wahlström.

220.2 File on Estonia including: photographs; extracts from *War Cry*; letter inviting the Salvation Army to work in Estonia, 9 Apr. 1927.

220.3 File on Latvia including: pamphlets; photographs; extracts from Salvation Army publications; copy of letter re the Salvation Army in Latvia; TS memoirs *The Salvation Army in Latvia* by Maj. Balshaitis.

221.1-8
SCHOOL OF ORIENTAL AND AFRICAN STUDIES LIBRARY

Malet Street, London WC1E 7HP

Handlists of collections; card catalogue of individual manuscripts in the main Library catalogue. J. Perceval, edit., *A Guide to Archives and Manuscripts in the University of London*, vol. 1 (1984) pp. 86-99.

Archives

221.1 COUNCIL FOR WORLD MISSION (CWM)
Archives of the London Missionary Society and the Commonwealth Missionary Society, now the Council for World Mission. Papers concerning Europe include letters, Europe and Russia, 1822-34 (**box 1**). Papers concerning Russia comprise: outgoing letters, India and Russia, 1831-43 (**boxes 2-6**); incoming letters, Russia, 1804-48 (**boxes 1-3**); journals from Russia, 1818-27 (**box 1**). Incoming letters from Russia from the following missionaries: J. Abercrombie, J. C. Brown, T. S. Ellerby, F. Gellibrand, P. Gordon, J. Hands, E. Henderson, R. Knill, A. Merrielees, J. Paterson, C. Rahmn, W. Ropes, E. Stallybrass, W. Swan, J. Venning, R. Yuille from St Petersburg, Novgorod, Tiflis, Sarepta, Kyakhta, Khodun' and elsewhere. Missionaries' journals include those of R. Knill, C. Rahmn, E. Stallybrass, W. Swan, R. Yuille. Papers concerning North China include incoming letters with references to Russia, the Siberian Mission and Mongolia. Home Personnel papers include the papers of Dr Ralph Wardlaw Thompson which include correspondence with Paterson, Swan and Yuille re the Siberian Mission, 1801-44. *See handlists for details.* C. S.

Craig, *The Archives of the Council for World Mission (incorporating the London Missionary Society) : an Outline Guide* (London, 1973).

221.2 METHODIST MISSIONARY SOCIETY (MMS, WMMS)

European correspondence includes correspondence with D. Macpherson and R. Ross in Astrakhan', 1822, 1824, P. Batchelor, J. McCourtie, J. Ross and J. Thorn in the Crimea, 1854-6, and M. Eck in St Petersburg, 1875 (**MMS.2B. Box 50**). There may be material in the Synod minutes re Europe of the Wesleyan Methodist Missionary Society, 1823-1945 (**WMMS.Europe. Boxes 51-6**). *See TS guide and handlists for details.*

221.3 THE UNITED SOCIETY FOR CHRISTIAN LITERATURE (USCL)

Founded in 1935 when the Religious Tract Society and the Christian Literature Society for India and Africa merged. Correspondence, Foreign, of the Religious Tract Society includes copies of letters to Russia, 19th century (**/152-170, 176-7, 179, 186-93**).

Manuscripts

221.4 DURAND PAPERS (MS. 257247)

Papers of Sir Henry Mortimer Durand (1850-1924) include correspondence on Japanese-Russian mediation (**/14b**) and translations from Russian into English (**/17c**).

221.5 MAZE, Sir Frederick (MS English 285232)

Official of the Chinese Imperial Maritime Customs. Semi-official letters from Tientsin, 1915-17, include references to Russian employees (**II/4**). Papers listed in *Papers Relating to the Chinese Maritime Customs, 1860-1943* (London, 1973).

221.6 PAGET PAPERS (PP.MS.4)

Papers of William Paget (1637-1713), 6th Lord Paget, may include references to Russia in papers connected with his ambassadorial service in Constantinople and Vienna, 1688-1706.

221.7 ROBINSON, A. F. (MS.380052)

Official in the Chinese Salt Revenue Department, 1919-29. Papers re a 5% reorganization loan from the Russo-Asiatic Bank.

221.8 'Kankai-ibun-ki',

being a description of a sailor's travels from Nagasaki to South America, England and Russia, 1793-1805, transcribed by Otsuki Shigetada (10 vols), early 19th century, Japanese (**MS. 55942**).

222.1-56

SCHOOL OF SLAVONIC AND EAST EUROPEAN STUDIES LIBRARY

Senate House, Malet Street, London WC1E 7HU

By appointment. Brief lists for some collections; more detailed list of Pares papers.

222.1 AMFITEATROV, Aleksandr Valentinovich (1862-1938)

Journalist and popular novelist. Letters to him mainly re the affairs of the Brotherhood of Truth (Bratstvo russkoi pravdy), 1920s-30s.

222.2 ANGLO-RUSSIAN LITERARY SOCIETY, subsequently ANGLO-RUSSIAN SOCIETY
Founded 1893 with the aims of promoting the study of Russian language and literature and friendly relations between Great Britain and Russia; renamed 1930. Papers and correspondence, chiefly 1904-35. *See list for details.*

222.3 BEVAN, Daisy (Mary Waldegrave, Mrs Edwyn Bevan) (b. 1871)
TS 'Odd Memories of an Ordinary Person' includes references to visits to Russia in 1878-9 and 1890.

222.4 BLOCH, J. & Co.
9 photographs of the showrooms and offices of the firm in Moscow, *c.* 1900.

222.5 BLOCK, Alexander
TS essay 'Russia's Contribution to the New Social Order' re consequences of the Russian Revolution, written *c.* 1944-5.

222.6 BRASOVA, Countess Natal'ya Sergeevna, née Sheremetevskaya (1890-1952)
14 photograph albums depicting life of Mme Wulfert, afterwards Countess Brasova, with Grand Duke Michael, 1909-13; annotated *Pamyatnaya knizhka na 1909 god*; 3 other papers. *See list for details.*

222.7 BROMHEAD, Lt-Col. Alfred Claude (1876-1963)
Diaries, papers and photographs re his visit to Russia as a member of the Special Mission to the Russian Armies to show British propaganda films, 1916-17.

222.8 BUXTON, David Roden
Xerox of TS article 'A Russian village before the five-year plan'.

222.9 CARNEGIE ENDOWMENT FOR INTERNATIONAL PEACE
TSS (mostly unpublished) submitted to their series for the Economic and Social History of World War I. *See list for details.*

222.10 CHICHAGOV, Adm. Pavel Vasil'evich (1767-1849)
TS memoirs 'Horatius of the Beresina' transl. and annotated by Dinah Dean.

222.11 COMMITTEE FOR THE CONSTRUCTION OF AN ORTHODOX CHURCH IN BRUSSELS AS A MEMORIAL TO THE MARTYR CZAR NICHOLAS II
Appeal literature, 1930.

222.12 DEANE, John
MS 'History of the Russian Fleet during the Reign of Peter the Great' (published by the Navy Records Society).

222.13 GALTON, Dorothy
Papers re the School of Slavonic and East European Studies, the Anglo-Russian Literary Society and Slavic studies in the USA and Canada in 1945. *See list for details.*

222.14 GOLOVIN, Orest, i.e. Roman Brandt (1853-1920)
MS 'Shekspirovskie stikhi', transl. of some of Shakespeare's sonnets.

222.15 HARE, Hon. Richard Gilbert (1907-66)
Photographs of Russian silver, porcelain etc.

222.16 HESSEN, Prof. Sergius (1887-1950)
Autobiography, bibliography, correspondence, TS articles.

222.17 KEATING, Daniel F.
Certificates and plans re gold mines in Tomsk, 1911.

222.18 LIEVEN, Prince Paul Ivan (1875-1963)
MS copy of his memoirs, 'Dela davno minuvshikh let i teni tekh, kogo uzh net, 1875-1925', written 1954.

222.19 LOEWENSON, Lev Sergeevich (d. 1968)
Librarian of SSEES. MS slips for a Russian-English military dictionary, bibliography of books and articles in English on Russia, correspondence, notes and photostats of documents. 11 boxes. *See list for details.*

222.20 LUCKYJ, George and RUDNYCKYJ, Jaroslav
TS 'A Handbook of Ukrainian', n.d.

222.21 MACARTNEY, George, Earl Macartney (1737-1806)
MS draft of part of his *An Account of Russia MDCCLXVII* with some differences from the published version.

222.22 MATTHEWS, Prof. William K. (1901-58)
60 notebooks, 20 files, 2 diaries, folders and envelopes of papers include material re Russian language and literature. *See list for details.*

222.23 MEYENDORFF, Baron Alexander (1869-1964)
TS bibliography of English books on Russia.

222.24 MILLER, Margaret S.
Notes, MSS and TSS, with some correspondence, on aspects of the Russian and Soviet economy; correspondence re visit to the USSR in 1968; papers re the Old Students' Association of the School of Slavonic and East European Studies; proofs of *Economic Devolution in Eastern Europe* by Ljubo Sirc; pamphlets.

222.25 MOLLO, Evgenii Semenovich (1904-85)
Military historian and artist. Correspondence, chiefly in Russian, re mainly Russian military history and militaria; notes and documents re mainly orders and uniforms; genealogical notes and correspondence. *See list for details.*

222.26 MURRAY, Lt-Gen. Sir James Wolfe (1853-1919)
Album of mementoes re the visit of the British delegation to Russia, 22 Jan. - 6 Feb. 1912.

222.27 MUSIN-PUSHKIN, Count Aleksei Semenovich (1730-1817)
Photostats of dispatches by Musin-Pushkin from the archives of the Russian Ministry of Foreign Affairs, 1772-3.

222.28 PARES PAPERS
Papers of Sir Bernard Pares (1867-1949), Professor of Russian Language, Literature and History, Director of the School of Slavonic and East European Studies, include: material

re SS *St Kilda*, 1904; diary of Pares and Samuel Northrup Harper in Russia, 1907; dispatches from Russia and the Russian front, 1914-18; TS memoirs of a journey to Russia after the Revolution; papers re the Civil War; reports, diary, memos from Siberia, 1919; papers re Russian refugees, relief organizations, and Russian Clergy and Church Aid Fund; papers of Anglo-Soviet Public Relations Committee/Association, 1941-2; material re Russian studies in the UK; general correspondence, press cuttings, pamphlets, MS copies of historical writings. 53 boxes, 7 envelopes, 5 bundles, 5 cartons, 2 books of press cuttings. *See list for details.* Access on the authority of the Director of the School of Slavonic and East European Studies.

222.29 PARTIYA NARODNOI SVOBODY
1 box of minutes of meetings of the Paris Democratic Group of the Party of National Freedom, 28 July 1921 - 21 Sept. 1922.

222.30 PAVLOVSKY, G. A.
TS paper on the problem of currency reconstruction in Russia, 1921.

222.31 PETRAZYCKI, Leon (1864-1931)
Professor of Jurisprudence at the Universities of St Petersburg and Warsaw. Appreciations of Petrazycki by G. K. Gins and A. Meyendorff.

222.32 PODKOMISSIYA PO POL'SKOMU VOPROSU
3 memos by V. M. Fel'kner re Russian and Polish national debt, railways and taxes and finances, 1919.

222.33 PUSHKIN, Aleksandr Sergeevich
84 photographs from an unidentified Soviet exhibition of Pushkin's literary entourage, title-pages of his works, illustrations of productions and sketches for productions of his works.

222.34 RICHARDSON, Edmund W.
Collection of picture postcards of and about Russia, mostly early 20th century.

222.35 RUSSIAN STUDENT CHRISTIAN MOVEMENT OUTSIDE RUSSIA
Illustrated report on the work of the Movement in the Baltic States, 1929-30; memos on its work in Europe and France, 1930.

222.36 SETON-WATSON, Robert William (1879-1951)
Masaryk Professor of Central European History in the University of London. Papers include 1 box of correspondence, memoranda and reports chiefly on the Carpatho-Ruthenians and Ukrainians in Poland, 1919-39 (**box 30**). *See list for details.* Access on the authority of Mr Christopher Seton-Watson.

222.37 SOKOLOV, B. N.
TS carbon copy of 'Kamennougol'naya promyshlennost' Rossii v 1914-1917 godakh' (161 pages plus tables).

222.38 SOVET RUSSKIKH CHASTNYKH ZHELEZNYKH DOROG
2 duplicated memos from Belgrade, Dec. 1922.

222.39 STAKHAVICH, M.
MS 'Nochnoe. Stsena iz russkago byta'.

222.40 TOOGOOD, Henry Foster
Photographs from Russia, 1923, 1925.

222.41 TREVOR-BATTYE, Aubyn Bernard Rochfort (1855-1922)
Xerox of journal kept on the Island of Kolguev in Barents Sea, 1904.

222.42 WARDROP, Sir Oliver (1864-1948)
MS transl. into English of account of shamanism in Siberia and European Russia by V. M. Mikhailovskii.

222.43 WHARTON, Leonard C. (1877-1943)
Papers and correspondence re Slavonic studies in Britain, 1921-34.

222.44 WOLF, Lucien (1857-1930)
Correspondence re his editorship of *Darkest Russia: a Weekly Record of the Struggle for Freedom*, 1911-14, 1916, 1928; correspondence, pamphlets and press cuttings re the murder of the imperial family.

222.45 ZISSERMAN, N. V.
TS 'Rukovodyashchie nachala kolonizatsii Sibiri i Priamurskogo kraya' (after 1937).

222.46 Letter to the President of the Osobyi komitet po delam russkikh emigrantov v Latvii in London, 27 Aug. 1920.

222.47 Duplicated notes entitled 'Otryvki i doksografiya drevneishikh grecheskikh filosofov', n.d., before 1917.

222.48 Visitors' book and list of titles from exhibition of Soviet art books at the National Book League, 1978.

222.49 Album of photographs of Russian icons with introduction and notes by A. Anisionov, ?1929.

222.50 Album of photographs entitled 'Centrosoyus 1932' of buildings and activities of Soviet co-operatives.

222.51 Photograph album of Moscow and rural scenes made by pupils of School No. 14, Moscow, *c.* 1960.

222.52 Album of photographs of Norway and Russia, end of 19th century.

222.53 31 photographs by Soyuzfoto of Moscow, Livadiya (near Yalta) and Tadzhikistan, 1934-5.

222.54 Album of photographs entitled 'Tolstovskii muzei, Yanvar' 1912 g.'.

222.55 Album of photographs entitled 'Vidy Moskvy i eya okrestnostei', n.d., before 1917.

222.56 Album of illustrations from the *Illustrated London News* entitled 'Russo-Turkish War, 1876' (*sic*).

223.1-5

SCIENCE MUSEUM LIBRARY

South Kensington, London SW7 5NH

By appointment. Card index arranged by name, location and subject; handlists for individual collections.

223.1 FIELD COLLECTION (FIELD)
Papers of Joshua Field (1787?-1863), engineer, include letter from William Handyside to probably Field or Henry Maudslay from St Petersburg re business in Russia, 23 May 1823 (2/8).

223.2 GILL COLLECTION (GILL)
Papers of Stanley Gill (1926-75), computer scientist, include correspondence, notes and journal re Gill's visit to the USSR, 1968-9 (C.32).

223.3 NILSEN COLLECTION (NIL)
Collection of MS notes on coinage and the production of precious metals, 1830-60, including 3 vols of notes on Russia (21-3).

223.4 PEARSON COLLECTION (PEAR)
Business records of S. Pearson and Son Ltd, contractors with extensive interests in the oil industry, include: reports and memos on petroleum fields in Russia, 1886, 1907-27, papers re contracting and industrial enterprises in Russia/USSR, 1916-17, 1927, and reports by E. L. Ickes on minerals in Novaya Zemlya (C.8); papers and maps re oil and mining propositions on Sakhalin Island, 1914-22 (C.15).

223.5 YOUNG COLLECTION (YOUNG)
Papers of Christopher Alwyne Jack Young (1912-78), pioneer of instrumentation and process control systems, include correspondence re the visit to the Central Instrument Research Laboratory by Vladimir G. Lazarev and V. A. L'vov from the USSR, 1972 (B.135).

224.1-3

THE SCOUT ASSOCIATION'S ARCHIVES

The Scout Association, Baden-Powell House, Queen's Gate, London SW7 5JS

By appointment.

224.1 Report on Lt-Gen. R. S. S. Baden-Powell's visit to Russia, 1910.

224.2 Log-book and photographs of the 1st Archangel Scout Troop, 1918-19.

224.3 Photograph album of Adm. B. Thesiger including some pictures of Russian Scouts.

225.1

SOCIALIST PARTY OF GREAT BRITAIN

52 Clapham High Street, London SW4 7UN

By appointment; limited research facilities.

225.1 MS minutes of the Socialist Party of Great Britain run from 1904 and will contain references to Russia and the USSR; also collection of pamphlets and copies of *The Socialist Standard* from 1904.

226.1

SOCIETY OF ANTIQUARIES OF LONDON

Burlington House, Piccadilly, London WIV 0HS

By appointment. H. Ellis, *Catalogue of the Manuscripts in the Library of the Society of Antiquaries* (1816). Accessions since 1816 are listed in three handwritten volumes.

226.1 Permit issued by the St Petersburg customs department to William Long to trade in Russian goods, ?1718, Russian (**MS 206.18**).

227.1-2

SOCIETY FOR CULTURAL RELATIONS WITH THE USSR

320 Brixton Road, London SW9 6AB

By appointment; limited research facilities.

227.1 RECORDS OF THE SOCIETY
Most of the papers of the Society (founded 1924) have been dispersed but the following items remain: telegram from Aleksandr Fadeev to the Society on the death of G. B. Shaw, 3 Nov. 1950; postcard from Shaw re the royalties on his plays performed in the USSR; TS article by A. Surkov, 'On False and Real Truth in Art'; TS letter by Ralph Parker, 'Letter to the Editor - Literaturnaya Gazeta'; 6 scrapbooks of newspaper cuttings re the Society, 1924-39, 1942-4, and some loose cuttings re the visit of Yurii Gagarin to Britain in 1961.

227.2 VISUAL AIDS
Extensive collection of photographs, film strips, slides, maps and charts covering various aspects of life in the USSR and prominent personalities. Lists of all visual material are available.

228.1-12

SOCIETY FOR PROMOTING CHRISTIAN KNOWLEDGE ARCHIVES

Holy Trinity Church, Marylebone Road, London NW1 4DU

By appointment. The class marks stand for the following: **Mins** for minutes of the Society; **ALB** for Abstract Letter-Book volumes containing the summaries of letters received; **AR** for Annual Report; **CS2** and **CN** for 2 series of letter-books of drafts of outgoing letters from the Secretary of the Society; **PF** for Publications Committees, Foreign Translations.

228.1 Report from H. W. Ludolf in The Hague re the lack of a Patriarch in Moscow and the tutoring of the Tsarevich by Jesuits, 1701 (**ALB. 1. 349**).

228.2 Report by Robert Hales from Berlin including request for names of good authors for use of the preceptors of the Tsar's son and an account of the state of Protestantism in Lithuania and Samogitia, 1704 (**Mins. 1. 287/8**), with the response from the Society with suggestions of authors (**Mins. 1. 289**).

228.3 Letter reported from Robert Hales in Dresden to John Hodges re Roman Catholic activity in Russia and reaction to it, with suggestion for action by the Society, 1706 (**Mins. 1. 399-400**).

228.4 Report from Robert Hales in Zell re translations into German, Czech and Russian, 1707 (**Mins. 2-4. 61**).

228.5 Postscript to the Annual Report of 1711 on Charity School developments referring to the Tsar's zeal in setting up schools in his dominions (**AR. (1711)**).

228.6 Report from Herr Neubauer, Overseer of Charity Houses in Halle, re Society's Charity School literature being dispersed as far as Moscow and the resulting donations from Russia, 1712 (**ALB. 3. 3061**).

228.7 Correspondence between Provost von Platen of Wolgast and John Holling in Hanover re the former's appeal for gifts for his fund for repairing Muscovite damage in Pomerania, 1714 (**ALB. 5. 3853; CS/2. 4. 9a**).

228.8 Letter from Henry Newman, Secretary of the Society, to the Most Revd Hugh Boulter, Archbishop of Armagh, re the cause of distressed Lithuanian Protestants, 1725 (**CS/2. 16. 31**).

228.9 Report from the Revd Caspar Matthias Rodde of Narva re Arabic Psalters for Persian prisoners in Russian garrisons, 1728 (**Mins. 12. 187; ALB. 14. 9942**) and Henry Newman's reply, 1729 (**CS/2. 20. 43; PF/1. CS/2. 22**); further correspondence on the Arabic scriptures sent to Rodde for distribution in Russia, 1736-42 (**ALB. 20. 14750-1, 15231; ALB. 21. 16011, 16050; CN/2. 3. 43; CN/2. 8. 80-1; Mins. 19. 68, 72, 76; PF/1. CS/2. 22**).

228.10 Minutes and correspondence re raising money for distressed English and Scottish Protestants in Lithuania, 1730 (**Mins. 13. 217; ALB. 15. 10927/37/50; CS/2. 21. 62/4; CS/2. 22. 12; CN/3. 3. 57**) and thanks from representative in Lithuania, 1731 (**ALB. 16. 11381**).

228.11 Contemporary report on the the presence of Alexander I and other dignitaries at the Anniversary Service of Charity School Children in St Paul's Cathedral, 1814.

228.12 Appeal from Memel for an English church and grant voted, 1858 (**AR. (1858). 62; Mins. 47. 273**).

229.1-51

SOCIETY OF FRIENDS' LIBRARY

Friends House, Euston Road, London NW1 2BJ

The Library is open to members of the Society of Friends and to other *bona fide* researchers by appointment. Card indexes and TS lists of manuscripts. Documents less than fifty years old and unlisted manuscripts are not normally made available.

Central Archives

229.1 LONDON YEARLY MEETING

The annual assembly of British Quakers; the body which oversees policy. *Proceedings* including minutes are printed from 1857. MS minutes, 1668-1857, include reference to Russia in vol. 26, 1847-56, p. 543. Indexes available, 1668-1974. Handlist 'International Affairs and Service' gives the following references to Russia in London Yearly Meeting records: reports on Russia by the Friends Relief Committee, Friends Service Council, Friends Committee for International Service; papers re training school for nurses in Russia, 1927-8; papers of the Committee on Relations with Russia, 1927-8; reports on religion in Russia, 1930-2; report on Quaker couple to live in Russia, 1956-7; papers of the Soviet Union and Eastern Europe Working Group, 1966, 1972; papers re study exchanges with USSR, 1969. *See list for details.*

229.2 MEETING FOR SUFFERINGS

The standing executive committee of the Yearly Meeting. Indexes of minutes, 1700-1857. Miscellaneous material relating to Russia includes: account of visit to Russia by Stephen Grellet and William Allen, 1819 (**Casual Correspondence 103-125**); material re burial ground in Leningrad, 19th century (**Trust Property Book 2 of the Meeting for Sufferings p. 15, Meeting for Sufferings Box, bundle 10**).

The following are Standing Committees of the Yearly Meeting or Meeting for Sufferings in which material relating to Russia and USSR will or might be found:

229.3 CONTINENTAL COMMITTEE (**Temp MSS 91-2**)

Papers re visit of Joseph James Neave and John Bellows to Russia, 1892-3, papers re bibles for Russia, 1893-5, and papers re J. Carl Hohenberg in Russia, 1882-4 (**Temp MSS 91/6**).

229.4 COUNCIL FOR INTERNATIONAL SERVICE (1919-27)

Russia and Poland Committee records from *c.* 1920 including: papers re relief, Nov. 1927 - Aug. 1940; Russia and Poland Friends Council for International Service papers, Jan. 1924 - Nov. 1927; papers re 'The Czar 1935' and Lithuania, *c.* 1935 (**E/1**); correspondence to and from Moscow, 1921-31 (**RU/1**); 18 issues of the information sheet of the Comité International de Secours à la Russie, 1921-22 (**RU/2**); box of slides re Russian famine.

229.5 EAST-WEST RELATIONS COMMITTEE (1950-51, 1955-65)
The aim of this committee was to ease tension between East and West. Minute books, 1950-65, newscuttings and photographs re a visit to USSR, July 1951 **(SR 4)**.

229.6 EMERGENCY AND WAR VICTIMS RELIEF COMMITTEE (1914-24)
Russia Committee (afterwards Poland and Russia Committee) minute books, 1918-23; negatives of Russian famine photographs, 1920-23; papers re Friends Relief Mission in Russia, 1920-25, including administrative records, general correspondence, papers re visits and conditions in Russia and details of mission work. *See TS file list for details.*

229.7 FRIENDS COMMITTEE FOR REFUGEES AND ALIENS (1942-3, 1948-50)
Known as Germany Emergency Committee, 1933-42, and as the Refugees and Aliens Section of Friends Relief Service, 1943-8. There might be material concerning Russian refugees, POWs and deportees in the minutes of these committees. The permission of the Recording Clerk is required to see these records.

229.8 FRIENDS SERVICE COUNCIL (1927-78)
There might be material re Russia in the minutes of the following sub-committees: Europe Committee, 1939-78; Central and Eastern Europe Committee, 1945-8; Poland Advisory Group, 1948-9; East European Committee, 1974-8. The Librarian is to be consulted about the use of any of these documents.

229.9 QUAKER PEACE & SERVICE (1979-)
Successor body to Friends Service Council. *Reports* to Yearly Meeting can be found in the annual indexes to Yearly Meeting *Proceedings*.

229.10 PEACE COMMITTEE (1888-1965)
The committee's minutes deal with *inter alia* the Tsar's Peace Manifesto of 1898. Subjects dealt with by the committee include: Meeting for Sufferings visit to Russia, 1951, 1954-6; visits of Russians to England including Khrushchev and Bulganin; Moscow Youth Festival, 1958; delegation to USSR of peace organizations in the UK, 1958-9; Leningrad Burial Ground reports, 1962. *See TS list for details.*

229.11 PEACE & INTERNATIONAL RELATIONS COMMITTEE (1965-78)
Successor body to Peace Committee. *Reports* to Yearly Meeting can be found in the indexes to Yearly Meeting *Proceedings*.

229.12 RUSSIA FAMINE FUND COMMITTEE (1910)
Minutes and accounts.

Manuscript Collections

229.13 ALLIS MSS (MS Vol. 215)
Extract of a letter giving an account of Alexander I's visit to the Westminster Meeting, 19 June 1814 **(pp. 107-09)**; address of the Society of Friends to Alexander I **(p. 109)**; account of Thomas Clarkson's conversation with Alexander I at Paris, 1815 **(pp. 114-19)**.

229.14 RICHARD REYNOLDS BALL MSS (Temp MSS 486)
13 letters from Russia, 1916-18 (/4); Friends War Victims Relief Committee report of visit of investigation to East Galicia and West Ukraine, n.d., visit of Cuthbert Clayton to East Galicia and West Ukraine, 4-23 Jan. 1920, and extract from minutes of meeting of the

Russia and Poland sub-committee of the Friends War Victims Relief Committee, 7 Apr. 1920 (**/8**).

229.15 FLORENCE BARROW MSS (Temp MSS 590)

Letters from Russia from Florence Barrow, Anna Wells and various correspondents, 1916-17; reports on Russian refugees, 1917, 1919; TS 'Stray Memories of Buzuluk 1916-1918' by Barrow; anon. TS 'Memories of Russia 1916-17 with the Friends War Victims Relief Unit'; TS 'Extracts from Emilie's letters' i.e. E. C. Bradbury, 1917; photographs of relief work in Russia; letters from Margaret Barber from USSR, 1949.

229.16 EDWARD BERNSTEIN MSS (Temp MSS 592)

Notes, transcripts, translations, news cuttings, bibliographies, commentaries, printed pamphlets re Russia especially re religious sects, mainly compiled *c.* 1918-20. 2 boxes, 1 vol.

229.17 CATHERINE L. BRAITHWAITE COLLECTION (Temp MSS 10A, 11-16, 57)

Extract from letter describing Alexander I's visit to the Westminster Meeting, 1814 (**Temp MSS 10A/6**); letters to William Allen from Odessa, 1825 (**Temp MSS 11/9**); letter from John Bellows to J. B. Braithwaite on Armenian relief, n.d. (**Temp MSS 13/6**); account of visit of Edmund Wright Brooks and Francis William Fox to Russia, 1891-6 (**Temp MSS 13/9**); letters of Edmund Wright Brooks from Russia, 1892-5 (**Temp MSS 13/13**); letters from Daniel Wheeler re Russia (**Temp MSS 57/8**).

229.18 DOUKHOBORS (DUKHOBORS) PAPERS (MS Box C, Temp MSS Box 0.2)

Material re Russian Dukhobors includes: extract from Russian archives re Dukhobors; copies of letters from Robert Pinkerton and John Paterson to Richard Phillips re them; 'Some Aspects of the Society of Dukoborsty' *c.* 1805, Russian (**MS Box C**); Doukobortsi [*sic*] Committee papers, *c.* 1896-1906, correspondence re emigration of Dukhobors to Canada and Cyprus, 1898-1913 (**MS Box 0.2**).

229.19 GEORGE FOX PAPERS (MS Box C)

Report of death of 60 "Quakers" in Russia executed for not uncovering before the Tsar, n.d.

229.20 GURNEY MSS (Temp MSS 434)

Letters from Thomas Shillitoe to Germany and Russia, May 1824 (**2/285**).

229.21 J. J. NEAVE MSS (MS Box 5)

Letters from Russia from J. J. Neave to F. Hopkins, 1893 (**/13/7-9**).

229.22 RICHENDA SCOTT MSS (Temp MSS 591)

2 folders of research notes and correspondence for her *Quakers in Russia* (London, 1964).

229.23 STACEY MSS (Temp MSS 130)

Letter from John Barclay to Lydia Barclay re Clarkson's MS of visit to Alexander I, 16 Nov. 1818 (**/457**); report of the committee appointed to present the address of the Meeting for Sufferings to the Emperor of Russia, 1814 (**/18/8**); copy of report of the visit of Stephen Grellet, William Allen and John Wilkinson to Alexander I, 21 June 1814 (**/18/9, 10**); copy of extract of letters from Stephen Grellet to --- from the Crimea, 2 May 1819 (**/19/3**) and re Dukhobors, 16 May 1819 (**/19/4**).

229.24 JOHN THOMPSON MSS
Papers re visit of Alexander I to Nathaniel Rickman (**/120**) and Westminster, 1814 (**/441**); correspondence of Alexander I with Massachusetts Peace Society, 1817 (**/399**); Thomas Clarkson's interview with Alexander I, 1815 (**/480**); address by Daniel Wheeler from Russia to Balby Monthly Meeting, 1821 (**/615**).

229.25 DANIEL WHEELER MSS (**Temp MSS 366**)
Notebook of letters from St Petersburg and 'Shoosharry' farm near St Petersburg, 1832-3; MS maps of Shoosharry Farm, n.d., Ochta (Okhta), 1820 and Volkova, 1823 and n.d.; 2 etchings of Wheeler's grave near Leningrad; vol. of letters, 1817-24, including from Okhta and Shoosharry; vol. of 'Minutes of Friends constituting the Meeting at Ochta near Petersburgh', 1818-38, including addresses to Balby Monthly Meetings. Vol. of letters, and papers relating to the Wheeler family including: Daniel Wheeler's account of voyage from England to Russia and life in St Petersburg, 1817; account of the Spiritual Christians (Dukhobors) in Russia, 1835; copy of report submitted to Alexander I re contract and salary of Daniel Wheeler, 1836; notification by Military Governor of St Petersburg that the police should assist Daniel Wheeler in his work, 1837; notification of appointment of A. D'junkovsky (Dzhunkovskii) as manager, 1839; notification by A. Golitsyn of Alexander's approval of Daniel Wheeler jun.'s reports; copy of grant of land for Quaker cemetery, 1840; account of privileges to Englishmen who come to work at Tammerfors, 1840; obligation of John Muller re transfer of duties to him, 1840; bills, balance of accounts, customs certificates, receipts. *See list at beginning of vol. for details. See also* **portfolios 8, 39, 41, 42, Temp MSS 407, John Thompson MSS** *and* **MS Box X.**

229.26 WILKINSON MSS (**Temp MSS 128**)
Papers include the following letters: William Knight to Thomas Wilkinson re medallion of Alexander I, 1817, Anne Knight to --- mentioning Stephen Grellet, William Allen and Joseph Foster on their way to Russia, 9 Aug. 1818 and William Knight to --- re Alexander I's conversion, 14 Jan. 1818 (**/7**); Dorothy Parker to Thomas Wilkinson re Neva flood, 6 Jan. 1825 (**/18/32**); Joseph Marriage to Thomas Wilkinson re opening for a manager of an estate in Russia, 19 June 1823 (**/22/79**).

229.27 ALEXANDER C. WILSON PAPERS (**Temp MSS 192**)
Envelope re his son marked 'Geoffrey from Russia 1941-42' with some later letters (**Box D/18**).

229.28 Account of the Tsar of Russia and Prince Galliczin (A. Golitsyn), 1846 (**MS Box X**).

229.29 Letter from the Russian Ambassador to R. Forster acknowledging address to Alexander II, 24 June 1861 (**MS Box 11.5 (3)**).

229.30 Letters from Elihu Burritt to Anna Mary Southall re spread of Olive Leaf Mission to Russia and Spain, 2 Oct. 1851, and deputation sent by Friends to the Tsar, 10 Apr. 1854 (**MS vol. S.101**).

229.31 Scrapbook compiled by Patrick O'Brien Baker of Meeting for Sufferings Quaker Mission to Moscow, 1951 (**MS vol. 201**).

229.32 Letter from Russia from Joseph Cooper to Isaac Robson, 2 Dec. 1873 (**Port.D.54**).

229.33 Letter from Daniel Wheeler from St Petersburg to ---, 25 Jan. 1832 (**/137**); ukaz to Synod in Moscow forbidding 'unbecoming praise' of Tsar, 1817 (**/159**) (**Port.8**).

229.34 Account of visit of Alexander I to Westminster, 1814 (**Port.17/88**).

229.35 Account of Thomas Clarkson's interview with Alexander I, 1815 (**Port.18/138**).

229.36 Address to Alexander I by the Society of Friends, 1815 (**Port.20/8**).

229.37 Letter from Peter Bedford to J. Hodgkin referring to a delegation to Nicholas I, 1854 (**Port.38/62**).

229.38 Letters from Daniel Wheeler from Moscow to Mary Saunderson, 4 Apr. 1821 (**/21**) and to William Hargreaves, 16 Apr. 1823 (**/67**) (**Port. 39**).

229.39 Letters from Russia from the following: Sarah Wheeler to S. Singleton, 10 Aug. 1818 (**/143**); Daniel Wheeler to ---, 22 Nov. 1824, to John Edmondson, 1 Apr. 1820, to David Mallinson, 18 Feb. 1821, 13 Jan. 1821, to George Edmondson, 10 Nov. 1824, 27 Jan., 12 Oct. 1825, 13 Oct. 1826, 19 Oct. 1831, to --- 11 Oct. 1824 (**/145, 169, 176, 178-9, 181, 183-6**); George Edmondson to John Edmondson, 1818-19 (**/148, 150, 152, 177**); George Edmondson to William Singleton, 1818, 20 Oct. 1819, 23 Jan. 1823 (**/149, 151, 155, 172**). Also paper re arrangement for the work near Okhta for 1825 (**/142**) (**Port. 41**).

229.40 Letters from Daniel Wheeler to Thomas Shillitoe, 28 Feb. 1826 (**/15**) and extract to --- re death of Alexander I, 13 Dec. 1826 (**/33**) (**Port.42**).

229.41 Letters to William Allen from St Petersburg from Walter Venning, 7 Mar. 1819 - 13 June 1819 (**/2**) and from John Venning, 1819-25 (**/3**) (**Temp MSS 4**).

229.42 Letter from R. R. Tatlock from Moscow to Friends War Victims Relief Committee, 1917, and extract from letter from Mr Patterson to --- re Dukhobors, 1813 (**Temp MSS 4A/10**).

229.43 Thomas Clarkson's account of his conference with Alexander I, 1815 (**/7**); insertion in letter from Dr James Hamel to A. C. re Alexander I (**/10**); copy of Address of Society of Friends to Alexander I and Frederick William III of Prussia, 1814 (**/14**); narrative by William Allen of his interview with Alexander I and others in London, June 1814 (**/15**); anecdote of Alexander I (**/18**); ukaz by Alexander I to the committee for clerical schools in Russia (**/31**) (**Temp MSS 5**).

229.44 Letter from John Bellows to J. B. Braithwaite re immigration of Dukhobors to Cyprus, 20 Aug. 1898, and postcard from Edmund Wright Brooks to J. B. Braithwaite from the Russian frontier, 3 Mar. 1896 (**/1**); copy letters from John Bellows to Edmund Brooks from St Petersburg, 11 Dec. 1892, and from J. J. Neave to --- from St Petersburg, 17 Dec. 1892 (**/4**) (**Temp MSS 7**).

229.45 Report on Russian burial ground by G. Macmaster,n.d. (**Temp MSS 9/4**).

229.46 Letter from John Yeardley to Elizabeth Clibborn with account of visit to Russia, 1853 (**Temp MSS 10/1**).

229.47 Russian documents, letters, papers and passport of Theodore Rigg, 1916-19 (**/7**); papers re mission to Moscow, 1918-19 (**/8**) (**Temp MSS 86**).

229.48 Papers of Lydia Rickman re visit to Russia, 1928 (**Temp MSS 87/8**).

229.49 Letter from Thomas Shillitoe to Thomas Christy describing visit of Daniel Wheeler to St Petersburg, 20 Sept. 1924 (**/5**); extract from letter from Sarah Kilham to Hannah

Kilham describing floods in St Petersburg, 21-30 Nov. 1824 (*/6*); note to Shillitoe informing him of appointment to see Tsar, 24 Dec. 1824 (*/7*); letter from Basil Passof (?Vasilii Passov) to Shillitoe re audience with Alexander I, 21 Jan. 1825 (*/8*); letters from Daniel Wheeler from St Petersburg to Shillitoe, 21 July 1825 (*/9*) and to David Mallinson, 10 July 1826 (*/10*) (**Temp MSS 407**).

229.50 Newspaper cuttings from the *Manchester Guardian* containing articles by John Rickman and W. T. Goode on the Friends War Victims Relief Committee work in Russia, Jan. - Oct. 1919 (**Temp MSS 416**).

229.51 TS 'Auch Russen menschenfreundlich', German transl. of *Those Human Russians* by W. R. Hughes (**Temp MSS 510**).

230.1
TATE GALLERY ARCHIVE

The Tate Gallery, Millbank, London SW1P 4RG

By appointment.

230.1 MICHAEL SADLER PAPERS (**Acc. no. 8221**)
Letters from Vasilii Vasil'evich Kandinskii (1866-1944) to Michael Sadler. Papers not yet available; apply to Archivist.

231.1-31
THE TIMES ARCHIVE

Times Newspapers Ltd, P.O. Box 7, 200 Gray's Inn Road, London WC1X 8EZ

By appointment; apply in writing to the Archivist. Research facilities are limited. All papers are closed for thirty years; in addition there are collections of 'Confidential Memoranda' relating to countries and other subjects which are closed for fifty years. Card indexes of persons and subjects are available. Papers are arranged in boxes and folders alphabetically by subject or person but, with a few exceptions, the papers within a folder or box are not sorted or listed.

Subject Folders

Countries are treated as subjects, and the main source for material on Russia and the USSR are the folders entitled 'Russia' and the 'Crimean War'. Papers concerning Russia can also be found in the subject folders on other countries, such as Afghanistan, Czechoslovakia, Finland, Hungary, Poland etc., but much of this material is classified as Confidential Memoranda and is therefore closed for fifty years.

231.1 RUSSIA
9 folders of material, 3 of which are numbered. Folder 1 comprises the following: a letter from R. A. Wilton to Wickham Steed re censorship of *The Times* in Russia, May 1915; miscellaneous letters, newspaper cuttings and telegrams re Russia; list of expense allowances in Moscow; 'Peace Letters' written to *The Times* by Russians in 1980. Folder 2

comprises letters from and concerning correspondents in Russia, mostly from the 1960s, and therefore closed for thirty years. Folder 3 comprises the following: correspondence 1917-42, including reports on the policy and attitude of *The Times* towards Russia; paper, 'Conversations between the British Ambassador and M. Litvinov', 21 Apr. 1933; a speech by Vladimir de Markozov, 1923; TS of an article by G. A. Pavlovskii on the New Economic Policy. A folder of correspondence re Russian Supplements to *The Times*, 1911-17; a folder containing extracts from the memoirs of Anastas Mikoyan, *The Road of Struggle*, and correspondence re the memoirs; a folder of correspondence re the Russo-Japanese War, including letters from Capt. Brinkley, Lionel James, David Fraser and others; a folder re Khrushschev, 1970, closed for thirty year; 3 folders of Confidential Memoranda, 1952-, closed for fifty years.

231.2 CRIMEAN WAR
A folder of papers including: a TS account of events; correspondence re *The Times'* Crimean Fund; letters to *The Times* in response to the public report on the plight of the British sick and wounded; a letter from and letters to Florence Nightingale.

Personal Folders

There is a card index of past and present employees of *The Times* which includes the names of some, but not all, Russian correspondents. Researchers should note that this is an index of personnel and not primarily a guide to the content of the archive. Not all the people in the index have left papers and an annotation on the card (usually 'See Archives folder or box') indicates that papers exist. Frequently the papers of foreign correspondents consist merely of financial arrangements and conditions of service and contain little or no information about Russia or the USSR. The following correspondents have left some material relating to Russia or the USSR and, unless stated otherwise, their papers are kept loose in folders under the name of the correspondent and are unlisted. It is likely that there will be references to Russia and the USSR in the papers of foreign correspondents of other countries, for example, those of Afghanistan, Austria, the Balkans, China, Czechoslovakia, Finland, Germany, Hungary, Poland and the USA. There will also be material relating to Russia and the USSR in the papers of proprietors, editors and foreign editors of *The Times* in addition to those listed below (Delane, Harmsworth and Walter).

231.3 BALMFORTH, C. E.
Correspondent in Odessa, 1895-1902. Letters from Odessa.

231.4 BONAVIA, David
Moscow correspondent, 1969-72. Papers closed for thirty years.

231.5 BOURCHIER, James David (1850-1920)
Balkans correspondent. Letters from Bucharest, 1910-18, refer to Russia; letters from Odessa, 1917-18.

231.6 BOURNE, Eric
Contributer from Moscow, 1955. Papers closed for thirty years.

231.7 BROWN (BRAUN), Dr Constantine
Correspondent in Russia, 1917. Letters from Bourchier in Odessa re Brown, 1917.

231.8 CANG, Joel
Occasional correspondent in Poland, 1946. Papers from Poland refer to the USSR.

231.9 DAVY, Richard William (b. 1936)
Special writer on East European affairs, 1970. Papers closed for thirty years.

231.10 DELANE, John Thadeus (1817-79)
Editor of *The Times*, 1841-77. There is a card index of Delane's correspondence, arranged alphabetically by the name of correspondents. The correspondents include Russell in the Crimea and there might be further material relating to Russia.

231.11 DOBSON, George
Correspondent in St Petersburg, 1876-1901. Letters from St Petersburg.

231.12 FARMBOROUGH, Miss Florence
Occasional correspondent in Russia, 1918. Notes concerning her work in the Russian Red Cross in the First World War.

231.13 FRASER, David Stewart (1869-1953)
Special correspondent in the Russo-Japanese War and in Siberia, 1918-19. Letters relating to the Russo-Japanese War and from Siberia.

231.14 HARMSWORTH, Alfred Charles William, Visc. Northcliffe (1865-1922)
Proprietor of *The Times*, 1908-22. There is a partial index to Northcliffe's correspondence which includes 2 letters from him to John Walter on Walter's visit to Russia, Nov. and Dec. 1913, and a letter to him from Cecil Harmsworth re an exchange of prisoners with the Russians, 12 Nov. 1919.

231.15 HARRISON, E. J.
Correspondent in Vladivostok, Aug. 1914, and in the Baltic States, 1920. Letter to Harrison re German colonists in Russia.

231.16 JAMES, Col. Lionel (1871-1955)
Correspondent in the Russo-Japanese War. Papers re his career.

231.17 KAZARINE, S. de
A Russian who worked in the Baltic States, 1922-3. Letters by H. G. G. Daniels from Berlin referring to the USSR.

231.18 KOROSTOVITZ, V. de
Worked for H. G. G. Daniels in Germany, *c.* 1923, and supplied the Berlin office with Russian news. A paper by Korostovitz concerning Ukrainian refugees.

231.19 LUMBY, Christopher Ditmar Rawson (1888-1946)
Warsaw correspondent, June 1919. Letters from Poland refer to Russia.

231.20 PARKER, A. Ralph
Correspondent in the USSR, Sept. 1941 - Mar. 1947. Box of papers include: a translation of Parker's article on Shostakovich in *Literaturnaya Rossiya*, 1964; papers re his book *Behind the Scenes of British Diplomacy*; TS of his article 'Deinocephalion fauna of the Middle Volga'; TS 'Czechoslovak Diary in July 1945'; letters from Moscow.

231.21 REDFERN, Gilbert (b. 1887)
Commercial attaché in Warsaw; Warsaw correspondent, 1934-8. Paper concerning minorities in Poland, including Russians and Belorussians.

231.22 RUSSELL, Sir William Howard (1820-1907)
War correspondent in the Crimean War. 3 boxes of miscellaneous papers, correspondence and press cuttings and a photograph of Russell in his tent. The correspondence is in bound volumes and there is card index of correspondents.

231.23 SAUNDERS, George (b. 1859)
Correspondent in Paris and Berlin. There is a card index of his correspondence which indicates that several letters refer to Russia including a letter to G. G. Robinson re Franco-Russo-Turkish relations and Austro-Russian relations, 23 July 1913, and to Wallace re Anglo-Russo-German relations and Russia and the USA, 2 Feb. 1897.

231.24 SCOTT, Capt. G. A.
Assistant correspondent in St Petersburg, June 1914 - Oct. 1915. A brief account of his experiences in Russia.

231.25 TIDMARSH, Kyril (b. 1931)
Moscow correspondent, 1965-8. Papers closed for thirty years.

231.26 URCH, Reginald Oliver Gilling (1884-1945)
Riga correspondent for Soviet affairs, 1922-39. Large collection of letters and memos from Riga.

231.27 WALLACE, Sir Donald Mackenzie (1841-1919)
Correspondent in St Petersburg, 1877-8; director of the Foreign Department of *The Times*, 1891-99. Papers include: 'Rough notes on the foreign policy of Russia during the reign of Nicholas II', 1903; 'Conversation with Prime Minister Stolypin', 1908; 'Conversation with the Emperor', 1908; letters to Francis Knollys, 1st Visc. Knollys, from St Petersburg, 1903.

231.28 WALTER PAPERS
Proprietors of *The Times*, 1785-1966. A TS loose index gives a partial guide to the correspondence of the Walters which includes: letter from Vincents, at the Foreign Office, to John Walter I re the reports of Russian victories, 1812; letters from John Walter III to his mother describing the visit of the Grand Duke of Russia to Oxford, 24 May 1839, and to Delane re the Crimean War, Jan., Nov. 1855; letter to A. F. Walter re the trial of Russian nihilists, 4 July 1890; letter from John Walter V to R. M. Barrington-Ward re the policy of *The Times* towards Spain, Russia and Czechoslovakia, Oct. 1948.

231.29 WASHBURN, Col. Stanley
Correspondent with the Russian armies, 1914-18. Reports and sketches of troop movements.

231.30 WILTON, Robert Archibald
Correspondent in Russia, 1905-21. Papers include: letters from St Petersburg, 1913-17, and from Omsk, 1919; notes on a trip to the Russian front, 1915, on the battle of Platonovka and on the death of Rasputin.

Letter-Books

231.31 There are 2 series of Managers' Letter-Books covering the period Aug. 1847 - Feb. 1848, May 1849 - Feb. 1915, consisting of copies of out-letters, which in the early volumes are hand-written and almost illegible. The letters are mainly acknowledgements and courtesy letters but there are some letters to Russian correspondents, for example a letter to R. Wilton and Vladimir Kokovtsov re the Russian Supplements to *The Times*, Mar.

1913 (**vol. 57, new series**). There are 3 general indexes of correspondents to the letter-books and indexes in each volume. The general indexes refer to the second series (new series) of letter-books, but one volume has additions in green ink which refer to the first series. The indexes can be supplemented by use of the index of persons (*see personal folders*) in which the annotation 'M.L.B.' on cards indicates that there is a reference to this person in the letter-books.

232.1-16
TRADES UNION CONGRESS ARCHIVE AND LIBRARY

Congress House, Great Russell Street, London WC1B 3LS

232.1-5 Archive (Filing Department)

Access by permission of the Deputy General Secretary to whom applications should be made. All documents are closed for thirty years. Material is arranged under subjects; some major subjects, such as countries, have several sub-divisions. Papers, usually TS papers and memoranda of which there are sometimes several copies, concerning Russia and the USSR can be found under the following subject headings, but there may be additional material under other headings.

232.1 FINLAND (948.7)
TS papers re Soviet attack (**948.7/510**).

232.2 INTERNATIONAL TRADE UNION AND LABOUR MOVEMENT (910)
TS paper on communist infiltration (**910.31**).

232.3 PEACE AND DISARMAMENT (906)
TS paper on the USSR and USA in the League of Nations, 1934 (**906.13**).

232.4 REVOLTS AGAINST OPPRESSION (914)
TS papers on anti-Soviet uprisings in Hungary and Poland, 1956 (**914.1**). Not available until 1987.

232.5 USSR (947)
The section USSR-General comprises 10 boxes of miscellaneous papers, mainly TS, including correspondence, press releases and cuttings, reports, memos, notes and articles on many aspects of Soviet life including foreign relations, agriculture and industry, trade, trade unions, prisoners, refugees, famine relief, persecution and case histories of individual Soviet citizens. In addition to general material, USSR is subdivided into sections relating to various aspects of the USSR as follows: Trade Union Unity (Anglo-Russian Committee) (**/220**); Anglo-Soviet Trade Union Committee (**/230-2**); Anglo-Russian Trade Union Council (**/233**); Hospitality and Entertainments (**/234**); Trading Regulations - General (**/400**); Trade Embargo, 1933, and English prisoners (**/410**); ARCOS (**/420**); Political (Zinoviev) (**/500**); Kirov Assassination Deputation, 1934 (**/512**); German Attack on Russia, 1941 (**/520**); Delegate Conferences (Empress Hall) (**/523**); Speakers and Meetings (**/524**); Aid Russia Fund (**/525**); GB-USSR Association, 1958- (**/614**) (closed until thirty years has expired); Anglo-Russian Parliamentary Committee (**/612**); Congress of Peace and Friendship with Russia (**/613**); Anglo-Soviet Committees and Societies (**/619**); Prisoners (**/700**); Delegations (**/910-16**); British Council Soviet Relations Committee, 1955 (**/935**); Monthly Report, 1936- (**/991**). Material relating to

non-Russian Soviet republics can be found in the following sub-divisions of USSR: Lithuania **(947.3)**; Latvia **(947.4)**; Estonia **(947.5)**; Georgia **(947.9)**.

232.6-16 Library

By appointment; apply to Librarian. The Library collection comprises mainly pamphlets but some TS material relating to Russia and the USSR (press releases, correspondence, reports etc.) can be found in the following sections and there could be further material under other subject headings, such as the foreign relations of other countries and trade union delegations. Large sections are subdivided usually by covering dates and subjects.

232.6 COMMERCE. RUSSIA (**HF 2667**)
TS report on Soviet trade, 1927 (**General. 1925-**).

232.7 COMMUNISM. RUSSIA (**HX 724**)
Regulations and resolutions of the 9th Congress of the Communist Party of the USSR, 1920; copies of speeches, resolutions and proceedings of the 20th Congress, 1956; draft programme of the Party, 1961.

232.8 CONSTITUTIONAL HISTORY. USSR (**JN 6581**)
TS bulletin, *Les Echos de Russie*, 1918.

232.9 ECONOMIC CONDITIONS. RUSSIA (**HC 333**)
TS material can be found in the following boxes (arranged by covering dates and subjects): report on Soviet economic situation (**1928-31**); reports on Soviet rural and urban life (**1936-57**); monthly economic statistics for the USSR, 1926-9 (**Economic Statistics**); reports and press releases re Russian famine, 1921 (**Famine**).

232.10 HISTORY. BALTIC STATES (**DK 511**)
TS report on Baltic workers under Soviet rule, 1949.

232.11 HISTORY. RUSSIA (**DK 266**)
TS material can be found in the following boxes (arranged by covering dates of material and subjects): translations from the Soviet press and memo on the economic blockade of the USSR (**1920-24**); press cuttings, 1927 (**1925-9**); reports on Soviet rural and urban life, administrative structure and Soviet affairs (**1946-54**); notes on the USSR by John Jagger and F. W. Pethick-Lawrence and interview with William Pearson (**Delegations. Visits. 1920-50**); reports of delegations to the USSR (**Delegations. Visits. 1951-**); abstract re charges against Trotskii at the Moscow trials, 1937 (**Trials. 1936-8**).

232.12 HISTORY. UKRAINE (**DK 508**)
TS petition from the Political Committee of the Bukovina, 1924; reports from prisoners of Perm' concentration camp, 1975.

232.13 INTERNATIONAL RELATIONS. FOREIGN RELATIONS. RUSSIA (**JX**)
TS reports re the arrest of British travellers, the present position of Anglo-Soviet relations, and M. Litvinov's reply to the British note, 1923 (**General**); TS reports re exchange of notes between Indonesia and the USSR, 1956, and the new organization to control 'Friendship', 1958 (**1955-**).

232.14 LABOUR. RUSSIA (**HD 8521**)
Press release and United Nations' report on forced labour in the USSR, 1950 (**1950-52**).

232.15 TRADE UNIONS. RUSSIA **(HD 6732)**
TS report of a Norwegian delegation to the USSR **(to 1947)**; TS report on the activities of Soviet trade unions **(1970-)**.

232.16 PHOTOGRAPHS
Photographs relating to the USSR can be found under te following subject headings: Trade Unions-USSR; TUC Delegation-USSR; USSR.

233.1-6

UNITED GRAND LODGE OF ENGLAND LIBRARY

Freemasons' Hall, Great Queen Street, London WC2B 5AZ

Access to the Library by non-members of the Order is by arrangement with the Librarian.

233.1 ELAGIN, Ivan Perplench (known in England as John Yelagin)
Appointed Provincial Grand Master of the English Provincial Grand Lodge of Russia, 28 Feb. 1772. 3 letters from St Petersburg, 1776; letter-book of copies of 9 letters to Elagin in St Petersburg, 1772-8.

233.2 APOLLO & CASTOR LODGES, RIGA
Joint letter from Lodges, 1792.

233.3 ASTRAEA LODGE, RIGA
Petition for, draft warrant and Warrant Book entry, 1787; dispensation to hold meetings in Courland, 1787.

233.4 GRAND LODGE OF ASTRAEA
Letter with printed letter explaining its origin and history, 1817; printed calendar and list of members, 1817, 1818; 4 MS and engraved certificates issued by the Grand Lodge and a subordinate lodge.

233.5 LODGE OF PERFECT UNION, ST PETERSBURG
Contemporary copy of minutes, 1771-2; letter-book copies of 4 letters to the Lodge, 1772-4.

233.6 GRAND LODGE OF THE UKRAINE
2 blank, engraved certificates, *c.* 1917-20.

234.1-6

UNITED SOCIETY FOR THE PROPAGATION OF THE GOSPEL ARCHIVES

USPG House, 15 Tufton Street, Westminster, London SW1P 3QQ

By appointment. Card indexes to subjects and to the Society's early correspondence.

234.1 ANNUAL REPORTS
Letter from Revd A. B. Turner from Newchwang in Manchuria referring to the Russian presence, 26 Nov. 1900, published in *Report* for 1900.

234.2 CONTINENTAL CHAPLAINCIES COMMITTEE
Vols of minutes and MS correspondence, 1862 to early twentieth century, with foreign chaplaincies including chaplaincies at Memel and Odessa. *See index to each volume for details.*

234.3 CORRESPONDENCE
Correspondence re the Chaplaincy of the Muscovy Company in the early eighteenth century including: letter from William Lloyd and Robert Mainwaring from Moscow to Mr R. Harwood, mentioning that the Tsar had given the Company some ground on which to build a church, 10 Mar. 1703 (**A.1./85**); letter from Revd John Urmston to Archdeacon Stubbs from Archangel including comments on the customs and manners of the Russians and the religious policy of Peter I, 30 Sept. 1703 (**A.1./138**). *See also Journals.*

234.4 CRIMEAN MEMORIAL CHURCH
Papers, correspondence etc. re Crimean Memorial Church in Constantinople.

234.5 CRIMEAN WAR CHAPLAINS' PAPERS
Papers include: correspondence re applications and appointment of chaplains; correspondence with the War Office; papers re fund for sending chaplains to the Crimea and the Nightingale Fund; papers re the Scutari hospital; correspondence from individual chaplains in the Crimea. *See files on individual applicants for details.*

234.6 JOURNALS
MS Journal (i.e. the Society's Minute Book) vol. 1 records letter from William Lloyd and Robert Mainwaring to Mr R. Harwood mentioning that the Tsar had given the Company some land on which to build a church, 18 June 1703 (**f.110**). *See also Correspondence.*

235.1-28

UNIVERSITY COLLEGE LONDON

Gower Street, London WC1E 6BT

235.1-16 The Library, Manuscripts Room

D. K. Coveney, *Descriptive Catalogue of Manuscripts in the Library of University College London* (London, 1935); *Manuscript Collections in the Library, a Handlist* (1978); J. Perceval, edit., *A Guide to Archives and Manuscripts in the University of London* (1984), pp. 100-38. Handlists and card indexes of correspondents for some collections.

235.1 BEESLY PAPERS
Papers of Edward Spencer Beesly (1831-1915), Professor of History at University College, 1860-93, and editor of the *Positivist Review*. Correspondence (**5**) includes with N. Ryazanov (pseud. of D. B. Gol'dendakh), M. M. Stasyulevich and I. S. Turgenev. *See card index to correspondents.*

235.2 BENTHAM PAPERS
Papers of Jeremy Bentham (1748-1832), philosopher, include: letter to Adm. P. Tchitchegof (P. V. Chichagov), 28 Nov. 1820 (**x.30-31**), and projected letter to Catherine II, probably 1776, French (**clxix.13**). A. Taylor Milne, *Catalogue of the Manuscripts of Jeremy Bentham in the Library of University College, London*, 2nd edit. (London, 1962).

235.3 BENTHAM, Sir Samuel (1757-1831) (**MS ADD. 94**)
1 vol. of MS memoirs in a series of letters, copied from originals, covering his journey to Russia, 1779-80.

235.4 BRIGHT, John (1811-89) (**MS OGDEN 65**)
Politician. Letters to his wife, Margaret Elizabeth, née Leatham, include references to the Crimean War, 1854-5 (**65/167-71, 178, 184, 212, 222, 224, 238**). *See calendar for details.*

235.5 BROUGHAM PAPERS
Papers of Henry Peter Brougham (1778-1868), 1st Baron Brougham and Vaux, include unsigned memo on Russo-Turkish relations, n.d., endorsed 1853 (**11.959**). Correspondence includes with the following: Thomas Kraskowski, including a copy of a memo on the Russian, Polish and Lithuanian nations, Jan. 1842, and a copy of a letter addressed to Robert Peel re Tsar Nicholas I, 27 May 1842 (**40.670, 40.673**); Princess Dorothea Lieven (67 letters), 1834-53, n.d. (**40.768-834**); Fitzroy James Henry Somerset, Baron Raglan, re the death of 'young Spalding' before Sebastopol, 22 Jan. 1855 (**43.235**). *See card index of correspondents.*

235.6 CHADWICK PAPERS (1800-90)
Papers of Sir Edwin Chadwick (1800-90), sanitary reformer, include: report, 'Condition of Sanitation in Russia' by René La Vallée, 1884 (**61**); 2 letters from Thomas Banfield from Balaclava, 15, 27 Sept. 1855 (**236/13-18**); letter from Osbert Chadwick to his father from Odessa, 27 Jan. 1877 (**467/1-8**); 2 letters from Sir Robert Rawlinson from Balaclava, 7, 26 May 1855 (**1645/138-45**); letters from Dr John Sutherland from Constantinople, Mar.-July 1855, and from Balaclava, 13 Aug. 1855 (**1920/327-47**). *See card index of correspondents for further references.* J. Percival, comp., *The Papers of Sir Edwin Chadwick (1800-90)* (1983).

235.7 ECONOMIC TRACTS

2 letters from Prince Petr A. Kropotkin to Thomas Hutchinson, 3 Oct. 1893, 14 Dec. 1898, one sewn into *The Place of Anarchism in Socialist Evolution*, 1886 (**B 92**), and the other into a pamphlet *The Commune of Paris*, 1891 (**B 93**).

235.8 GALTON PAPERS

Papers of Sir Francis Galton (1822-1911), founder of the Eugenics Laboratory at University College, include correspondence with P. Boborykine (Boborykin), 30 Nov. 1880 (**152/6A**); and Vice-Adm. J. Likhatchof (I. Likhachev), 7 Nov. 1901 (**276/2**). M. Merington and J. Golden, comp., *A List of the Papers and Correspondence of Sir Francis Galton (1822-1911)* (1978).

235.9 GARDNER, Ernest Arthur (1862-1939) (**MSS ADD. 82**)

Yates Professor of Archaeology at University College. Journal of travel to Russia, 1895.

235.10 GREENOUGH PAPERS

Papers of George Bellas Greenough (1778-1855), President of the Geological Society and Geographical Society, include: notes, fragments and printed matter concerning Russia, 1819, 1836 (**16/33**); bound notebook entitled 'Russia', [1811] (**16/34j**). J. Golden, *A List of the Papers and Correspondence of George Bellas Greenough (1778-1855)* (1981).

235.11 HUTH, Frederick and HUTH COMPANY (**L.A.B.A**)

London merchant bankers, dissolved in 1936. Foreign correspondence in-letters includes 4 letters from Russia, Oct. 1842 - Oct. 1843 (**Box 2**). 4 boxes of files, 1914-32, relating to British banks in Russia and Russian banks of commerce in St Petersburg and Moscow and firms in St Petersburg, Moscow, Odessa and Narva including J. & V. Bergman, Wogau & Co., Reichert & Meyer, Industrial & Commercial Society, Tea Trading Society, Schlossberg Brothers, Petrograd Metal Works, N. N. Chlebnikoff (?Khlebnikov), M. Kirschakoff (?Kirshakov) & Sons, N. G. Smirnov & Co., Tentelev Chemical Works, E. M. Meyer & Co., James Beck Cotton Spinning Co., Narva Cloth Manufacturing, A. & E. Guinard. *See handlist for details and covering dates.*

235.12 PEARSON PAPERS

Papers of Karl Pearson (1857-1936), Professor of Applied Mathematics and Mechanics, 1884-1911, and then of Eugenics, 1911-33, at University College. MS of 'Women in Old Russia' by N. Tchaykovsky (Chaikovskii) with notes, 1886 (**10/5**); 5 letters from Chaikovskii including one to Maria Sharpe Pearson, 1887-8 (**10/55**); MS paper on biometrical studies of Russians including photographs and a map by E. Tschepourkowski (?Cheporkovskii), 1923, and letters from the same, 1913, 1923 (**451**); letter from the Soviet Academy of Sciences, 1926 (**511**); letter from the General Secretary of the Hermitage, Leningrad, 1936 (**555**). General correspondence includes letters from I. I. Orlov, 1913-14 (**776/8**), V. Romanovskii, 1924-5 (**/831/3**), the Russian Anthropological Society, 1904 (**834/9**), S. Stepnyak, [1885]-92 (**861/7**), N. W. Tchaykovsky (Chaikovskii), 1888 (**/874/5**), E. Tscheporkowski (?Cheporkovskii), 1930 (**874/6**). *See card index of names.* M. Merrington *et al.*, comp., *A List of the Papers and Correspondence of Karl Pearson (1857-1936)* (1983).

235.13 RAMSAY PAPERS

Papers of Sir William Ramsay (1852-1916), Professor of General Chemistry, University College, 1887-1912. Correspondents include Prince B. B. Golitsyn, 3 June 1894 (**vol. 6(ii) p. 290**), D. I. Mendeleev, 23 Sept. 1905 (**vol. 14(i) p. 72**) and A. Mendeleev, 15 Feb. 1907 (**vol. 14(i) p. 121**). *See handlist and card index.*

235.14 THE ARCHIVES OF ROUTLEDGE & KEGAN PAUL LTD
(ROUTLEDGE ARCHIVES)
Papers, 1853-1973, including correspondence, proofs of books and accounting records
include references to books on Russia and Russian authors. For details see, G. Forlong,
The Archives of Routledge & Kegan Paul (1978) and *Index of Authors and Titles : Kegan
Paul, Trench, Trubner & Henry S. King, 1858-1912* (1974).

235.15 SOCIETY FOR THE DIFFUSION OF USEFUL KNOWLEDGE
(S.D.U.K. PAPERS)
Founded 1826. MS of *Geography of Russia* by Wilhelm Wittich (6 vols), *c.* 1832 (**133a-f**).

235.16 WOODWARD, Sir Arthur Smith (1864-1944)
Keeper of the Geological Department, British Museum (Natural History), 1901-24. Letter
from Lev Simonovich Berg to Woodward, 13 Feb. 1937, pasted in Berg's *Classification of
Fishes both Recent and Fossil*, Moscow 1940.

235.17-28 Mocatta Library

By appointment; apply to the Librarian of University College Library for permission to
use the Library. Opening hours are limited. The Mocatta Library is the library of the
Jewish Historical Society of England and houses the Mocatta Library collections and the
Anglo-Jewish Archive. The Gaster papers are stored in the Mocatta Library but were
donated to University College Library and are not strictly part of the Mocatta Library
collections. Card indexes for the manuscript collections of the Mocatta Library and the
Anglo-Jewish Archive; handlists of most collections of the Anglo-Jewish Archive.

235.17 THE GASTER PAPERS
Papers of Dr Moses Gaster (1856-1939), scholar and rabbi. Correspondence, 1870-97,
with many correspondents in Russia including Hayyim Berlin, Abraham Bik, Reuben
Brainin, Reuben Asher Braudes, Daniel Chwolson (Khvol'son), Isaac Dembo, Alexander
Harkavy (Garkabi), Edward Delmar Morgan, Isaac Perkov, Leon Pinsker, Baer Ratner,
Moses Reines, Samuel Benjamin Schwarzberg, Alexander Zederbaum (Tsederbaum); also
with the Russo-Jewish Committee, Russo-Jewish Fund, *Ha-Meliz* in St Petersburg.
Correspondence, 1898-1939, with Yehezkiel Abramskii, Meir Dizengov, Zalman David
Levontin, Max Emmanuel Mandelstam, Menaham Mendel Ussishkin, Chaim Weizmann.
See handlist for details. Press cuttings re persecution of Jews in Russia and elsewhere,
1886-1906 (**A/2A**). Cataloguing still in progress.

Mocatta Library Collections

235.18 Holograph letter from Sir Moses Montefiore to J. A. Franklin re *inter alia* the
sufferings of the Jews in Russia, 8 Sept. 5603 (?1843) in Picciotto, *Sketches of
Anglo-Jewish History* (**BA 5 PIC**).

Anglo-Jewish Archive

235.19 ANGLO-JEWISH ASSOCIATION PAPERS (AJ/37, 95)
Foreign Affairs Committee papers include: printed League of Nations report by Lucien
Wolf on Russian Jewish refugees, 1923 (**AJ/37/6/5/36**); subject-file on anti-semitism in
Eastern Europe, 1951-4 (**/6/6/1**); printed reports on Jews in Estonia etc., 1955 (**/6/6/6**).
Correspondence, press cuttings, articles re the USSR (**AJ/95/80**); memo on Jews in
Eastern Europe, 1950 (**/ADD/19**).

235.20 BRODETSKY, Selig (1888-1954) (AJ/3)
Mathematician and Zionist leader. Letter from H. Kobold of Kiev to Brodetsky, 29 Apr. 1910 (/16b); cables from Riga, 23-4 Dec. 1939 (/75, 77).

235.21 BRYNMAWR JEWISH COMMUNITY (AJ/277)
Copy of passport of Moiser Dovidov Goldin, 16 Oct. 1901, Russian with English transl. (/C/1); diploma issued by the Gomel' general craft guild to Goldin to practise as a qualified watch and clock repairer, 7 Dec. 1900, Russian with English transl. (/C/2).

235.22 HERTZ, Joseph Herman (1872-1946)
Chief rabbi of the United Hebrew Congregation of the British Empire. Papers uncatalogued and as yet unavailable, but may contain letters from correspondents in Russia.

235.23 LAZARUS, Harris M. (AJ/27)
Letter and pamphlet re Russian atrocities demonstration, 16 Nov. 1905 (/A/1-2).

235.24 MACCOBY, Chaim Zundel (AJ/63)
Letters to Maccoby, the so-called Kamenitzer Maggid, from J. Arlowitz from Vilkomier (Vilkomir), 1895 (/21), Isaac Rabinowitz from Lithuania, 1886 (/23); card from R. Brainin from Minsk, 1888 (/49); receipt from Riga, 1886 (/51).

235.25 STETTAUER PAPERS (AJ/22)
Papers of Carl Stettauer (1859-1913) re mainly his visit to Russia in 1905 to organize relief work after the pogroms. **Portfolio A**, 'Newspaper Cuttings. Photographs. Letters. etc. 1905-6', includes cuttings re his visit, financial records, resolutions and reports of meetings protesting against the pogroms, letters to Stettauer, photographs of the Kiev pogrom. **Portfolio B**, 'Pogroms I', and **Portfolio C**, 'Pogroms II', include German TSS reports, newspaper cuttings, correspondence, tracts, petitions, eye-witness accounts etc. re pogroms in Bryansk, Kiev, Siedlitz (Sedlets), Kiev, Bohopol (Bogopol'), Rostov, Vyaz'ma and elsewhere and re the Jewish question and way of life. **Portfolio D**, 'Literature', consists of printed reports and publications re the Jews in Russia. **Portfolio E**, 'Letters and Accounts' includes accounts of the Russo-Jewish Committee, 1905-7, reports on the pogroms and on Jews in Russia. **Portfolio F**, 'Reports', includes Stattauer's letter-books, 1905, correspondence re his visit to Russia, diary of Jack M. Myers covering journey to Russia, 1905, report of D. Feinberg, Dr Paul Nathan and Stattauer on their visit to Russia, 1905. *See handlist for details.*

235.26 Passport and laisser-passer of Isaac Mejzner (or Meisner), *c.* 1868, Russian (AJ/137).

235.27 First part of an autobiographical sketch of childhood by Abraham Weiner covering emigration from Lithuania to Wales in the 1880s (AJ/249).

235.28 Russian passport of J. Podgeur, 1895 (AJ/272).

236.1-10

UNIVERSITY OF LONDON LIBRARY

Senate House, Malet Street, London WC1E 7HU

R. A. Rye, *Catalogue of the Manuscripts and Autograph Letters in the University Library ...* (London, 1921), and *Supplement, 1921-30* (London, 1930); M. Canney, J. M. Gibbs, R. Watson, *Catalogue of the Goldsmiths' Library of Economic Literature*, vol. 3 (London, 1982); J. Perceval, edit., *A Guide to Archives and Manuscripts in the University of London*, vol. 1 (1984), pp. 139-53. TS handlists of additional manuscripts since 1930 and individual collections; card index of manuscripts on microfilm.

236.1 BROMHEAD, Lt-Col. Alfred Claude (1876-1963) (MS 817)
Member of special mission to Russia to show and distribute propaganda films to the Russian forces, 1916-17. Diaries in Russia, Feb. 1916 - Jan. 1917, Apr.-Sept. 1917; TS carbon copy of unpublished edition of the diaries; 3 photographs and 2 plans from Russia.

236.2 THE DUCKWORTH PAPERS
Records of the publishing house of Duckworth. Correspondence with the Friends of the Soviet Union, the Soviet Embassy, re royalties in the USSR and re publications concerning Russia and the USSR. *See handlist for details.*

236.3 TOLANSKY, Professor Samuel (1907-73) (MS 827)
Physicist. Correspondence with E. Stuart Kirby re a Russian translation of Tolansky's *Modern Revolution in Optics* and Kirby's proposed book on diamonds in the USSR, 1972-3 (**H.100**).

236.4 Commonplace book including 'The copye of the Emperor of Russia or Muscovy his stile' from a letter sent to Edward VI (**MS 187 f. 129v**).

236.5 Letter from I. M. Maiskii to H. W. R. Greaves, 20 Nov. 1942 (**MS 822/6**).

236.6 Copy of précis of Napoleon I's statement made before Prince A. B. Kurakin, Russian Ambassador in Paris, ostensibly proposing a basis for negotiations with Alexander I, 15 Aug. 1811, French (**MS 831**).

236.7 Copies of letters from Charles XIV, King of Sweden and Norway, to Alexander I, 10 June 1813, French (**MS 832**).

236.8 Agreement between Albert Rumball, Thomas Rumball, Joseph Rivolta, John Septimo Rivolta and Vincent Wanostrocht to share the expenses of a journey to St Petersburg by Albert Rumball and re the profits should licences be obtained to form the Azov and Don Gas Company, 23 Oct. 1868 (**MS 857**).

236.9 4 boxes of copies (positive prints) of Foreign Office papers in the Public Record Office relating especially to China (FO 17) but also to the USA (FO 5) and to Russia (FO 65), *c.* 1897-1904 (**MS/F. 162**).

236.10 Microfilms from the US National Archives including material relating to the German offensive against the USSR (**MIC. 166**).

237.1-11
VICTORIA AND ALBERT MUSEUM

South Kensington, London SW7 2RL

237.1-8 Library

By appointment. Card catalogue for manuscripts; subject index of printed holdings includes references to manuscripts.

237.1 Grant by Paul I confirming the starostvo of Bludno and Malich to Petr Pastukhov, the Tsar's former tutor, St Petersburg, 22 Feb. 1797 (**MS.L.133-1980**).

237.2 'Drevnosti Kavkaza' by V. V. Vasil'ev, being an album with drawings and watercolours of Caucasian art and architecture, 1881-4 (**MS.L.184-1980**).

237.3 TS 'Istoriya russkoi zhivopisi ot Petra I do nashego vremeni, 1700-1917' by Petr Petrovich Pertsov, *c.* 1920-6 (**MS.L.17-1981**).

237.4 TS translations into English by N. W. Wilson of 3 novels by Konstantin Georgievich Paustovskii based on the lives of the painters Orest Kiprenskii, Isaac Levitan and Taras Shevchenko (**MS.L.47-1982**).

237.5 Grant by Catherine II to Maj.-Gen. Simeon Zorich of estates and 4 orders including those of St George and Aleksandr Nevskii, St Petersburg, 20 Dec. 1778 (**MS.L.31-1983**).

237.6 Letters of Peter I to Johann Wilhelm, Count Palatine of the Rhine, requesting protection for Israel Orii, Moscow, 23 Jan. 1704, Russian (**MS.L.47-1984**).

237.7 Letters and notes of Mikhail Larionov and Natal'ya Goncharova, 1912-27, with a TS article by Larionov, 'A propos du Rayonnisme' (**Box V.36.F, xii-xiii**).

237.8 Vol. of papers concerning the reproduction of art objects in Russia for the South Kensington Museum (now the Victoria and Albert Museum), including: copies of official letters about the visit to Russia of Sir Philip Cunliffe Owen, Robert H. Soden Smith and Wilfred Cripps; a printed *Summary of the List of Art Examples Selected as Suitable for Reproduction* with MS notes; 32 letters from Alfred Maskell to Owen re art collections in Russia and re plaster casts of Russian works of art, 1880-81 (**86.0.31**).

237.9 Prints and Drawings Department

By appointment.

237.9 Sketchbook with pencil drawings and landscapes by Natal'ya Goncharova and loose papers including: draft of an article on art theories, *c.* 1915-16; proofs of Aleksandr Rubakin's *Gorod* (Paris, 1920); report to the Union of Russian Painters in Paris, *c.* 1920; postcard from S. Konovalov to M. Larionov, 31 Oct. 1919 (**E.964-1961**).

237.10-11 Theatre Museum

By appointment.

237.10 Designs, press cuttings, posters and programmes of performances by the Ballets Russes and Diaghilev Ballet, 1909-29.

237.11 Correspondence, music and libretti for 'Chauve Souris', *c.* 1924-9.

238.1

WARBURG INSTITUTE

University of London, Woburn Square, London WC1H 0AB

238.1 YORKE COLLECTION
Papers re the visit of Aleister Crowley to Moscow in 1913 as manager of the Ragged Ragtime Girls on tour at the Aquarium, Moscow. Restricted access; apply to Librarian.

239.1-47

WELLCOME INSTITUTE FOR THE HISTORY OF MEDICINE

183 Euston Road, London NW1 2BP

Access for *bona fide* researchers by written application to the Librarian. Persons wishing to publish manuscripts or autograph letters must obtain the prior written permission of the Librarian of the Institute. S. A. J. Moorat, *Catalogue of Western Manuscripts on Medicine and Science in the Wellcome Historical Medical Library*, 3 vols (London, 1962, 1973). Card indexes of autograph letters. *Contemporary Medical Archives Centre. Consolidated Accession List* (London, 1982).

239.1-41 The Library

Western Manuscript Collection

239.1 BARNES, Robert (1817-1907) **(MS 5188)**
Diploma of honorary membership of the University of Khar'kov, 30 Jan. 1867.

239.2 BERNARD, J. F. **(MS 1143)**
'A Relation of Grand Tartary, drawn up from the Original Memoirs of the Suedes, who were Prisoners in Siberia, during the War between Sueden and Russia' transl. by William Farrington, 1738.

239.3 BRICE DE BEAUREGARD **(MS 1355)**
Notes and extracts on crystal-gazing in Russia, on the cabbalistic mirror, invocation of spirits, ceremonial magic etc., 1844-6. French.

239.4 FOLKES, Martin (1690-1754) **(MS 2391)**
Collection includes a holograph work on Siberia by John Fothergill, 1748 (published in *Philosophical Transactions of the Royal Society* vol. 45, (1748), pp. 248-62).

239.5 GRIGOROVICH, Hilarion **(MS 2633)**
'Philosophia Christiano-Aristotelica Roxolanae juventutis proposita ... In Collegio Tychorsciano Charkowiensi ...1729...'. An unnamed student's notes of lectures on philosophy given by Grigorovich at a Jesuit college in Khar'kov, 1729-30.

239.6 KALINOVSKII, Stepan (MS 3100)
'Naturalis scientia videlicet Physica, una cum scientia Metaphysica. Tradita est a Reverendo... Patre et Ordinario Philosophiae Professore Stephano Kalinowski. In Collegio Mohyleano Kyowiensi, finita ... 1731'. An unnamed student's notes of lectures given by Kalinovskii at Kiev, 1731.

239.7 LARREY, Baron Dominique Jean (1766-1842) (MS 3172)
Journal includes references to his experiences in the Russian Campaign of 1812.

239.8 LEE, Robert (1793-1877) (MSS 3213-3220)
Obstetric physician and gynaecologist. Diary in Russia as personal physician to the Vorontsov family, 29 Oct. 1824 - 10 July 1825; diary of Russian travels, 14 Oct. 1825 - 6 Jan. 1827; transcripts by Lee's son of the travel diaries (MS 3220).

239.9 PAYNE, Joseph Frank (1840-1910) (MS 3821)
Physician and medical historian. Paper on the epidemic of plague in the province of Astrakhan' in the winter of 1878-9, written 1880.

239.10 PROUT, John (MS 4010)
Staff surgeon in the Russian Army, private physician to the Vorontsov family, became Collegiate Assessor in 1839. Collection of medical notes and extracts includes 'Private notes of the late John Prout Esqr, M.D. Odessa : S. Russia', n.d.

239.11 TORRIANO, Charles Edward (1833-1908) (MS 4820)
Notebook containing notes of lectures on military subjects, artillery, explosives etc. with a fragment of a diary from 21 - 30 July 1855 written in the Crimean War.

239.12 TOUX, Jean Louis Lucas de et al. (MS 4828)
'Collectanea, versiones et scripta rarissima, a quodam Theophilo, Hermeticae Philosophiae scrutatore sedulo, hoc in libro propria manu referta et multis elucidata ... anno ... MDCCXXX' by J. L. L. Toux. Contains additions by Theodor Karzavin in Latin and Russian including 'Processus utilis' (pp. 250-63), table of alchemical signs (pp. 238-43), Rosicrucian parable (pp. 250-63), 'Clavis signorum' (pp. 288-90), alchemical notes (pp. 404-12, 442-53).

239.13 WYLIE, Sir James (1768-1854) (MS 5098)
Physician to Alexander I and President of the Medical Academy of St Petersburg. 'Geschichte und Verlauf der Krankheit von welcher Seine Kayserlich Majestät Alexander I gestorben sind', Taganrog 1825, being a transl. of the Latin original by Conrad Hoffregen.

239.14 ZUROVSKII, T. (MS 5119)
'Animus chyr[ur]gicae juvent[u]tis normae formularum addictus : in duplici systemate quorum Imum Theoriam, aliud Praxim in se compraehendunt. Fundatus curiosis alumnis sincere oblatus Moscuae in Noscomio Augustano...', Moscow 1724.

Autograph Letters Collection

The order of the following letters corresponds to their alphabetical arrangement, usually but not always by author, in the card catalogue of autograph letters in the Reading Room. There are no MS numbers but a catalogue is under preparation.

239.15 Ivan Bogdanovich Auerbach, geologist and mineralogist, to --- re fossils near Moscow, Moscow 30 July 1881.

239.16 Adriano Balbi, geographer, to Yakov Nikolaevich Tolstoi, *c.* 1829.

239.17 George Eleazor Blenkins to T. M. Stone from Sebastopol, 1856.

239.18 Sergei Petrovich Botkin, Professor of Medicine in St Petersburg, to Dr H. Cazales, 14 Nov. 1866.

239.19 Feodor Aleksandrovich Bredikhin, astronomer, to Professor C. A. Young, 1881.

239.20 Sir James Mackintosh to James Currie referring to Russia, 6 Feb. 1808.

239.21 Jean-Baptiste-Henri Durand-Brager, painter attached to the French Black Sea Squadron in the Crimean War, to Jean Z. Amussat, 1855.

239.22 Johann Nepomuk von Fuchs, botanist, to Professor Deleuze, from St Petersburg, 24 May 1825.

239.23 Carlo Giuseppe Gené to M. Menetries, conservator of the Museum of the Imperial Academy of Sciences in St Petersburg, 13 Aug. 1839.

239.24 Jonas Hanway, traveller and philanthropist, to Revd Forster, from St Petersburg, 12 Apr. 1746.

239.25 Moritz Hermann Jacobi, physicist and engineer, to ---, from St Petersburg, 24 Dec. 1869, 5 Jan. 1870, 16 Feb. 1870, 22 Mar./3 Apr. 1870.

239.26 Medical certificate, signed by Joseph Karrass, for Phillipe Germain de Galland, Moscow, 8 Aug. 1818.

239.27 August Friedrich Ferdinand von Kotzebue, notes on the botany of Tyumenville (Tyumen'), Siberia, *c.* ?1800.

239.28 Diploma from the Imperial University of St Vladimir, Kiev, for Joseph, 1st Baron Lister, 2 Oct. 1884.

239.29 Professor A. F. Marion to ---, re Professor A. O. Kovalevskii, zoologist, 8 May 1885.

239.30 13 letters of Ilya Ilyich Metchnikoff (Il'ya Il'ich Mechnikov), biologist and bacteriologist, 1902-06.

239.31 Extract of letters from James Mounsey to Henry Baker re everlasting sacred fire in Persia and black naptha, Riga, 24 Feb. 1748.

239.32 Letters re Napoleon's campaign in Russia in 1812 including re organization of hospitals in Vil'na, 24 Sept. 1812.

239.33 5 vols of letters of Florence Nightingale to various correspondents, 1829-1905. No list.

239.34 Copies of letters from the Nomographic Societies of Moscow and Leningrad to Professor Maurice d'Ocagne, 16 June 1934, 15 Jan. 1935.

239.35 Peter Simon Pallas to --- from St Petersburg, 25 Dec. 1779, 12 Jan. 1782, 4 Jan. 1791, from Simferopol', 16 Jan, 1805.

239.36 Nikolai Ivanovich Pirogoff (Pirogov), military surgeon, to Dr Wenzel Leopold Gruber, 1 Jan. c.1846, and to ---, 31 Jan. n.y., n.d.

239.37 Ludvig Puusepp, Estonian neurosurgeon, 'A la question de la localisation du signe du petit orteil par les cas des tumeurs de corps strié', *c.* 1890.

239.38 Friedrich Theodor Schubert, Director of the Observatory of the Academy of Sciences, St Petersburg, to Hofrath Tilesius von Tilenau, 19 June 1814.

239.39 Peter von Tchihatchef (Petr Aleksandrovich Chikhachev), Russian geologist and naturalist, to ---, n.d. late 19thc.

239.40 Arnim Vambéry to --- re travels in Central Asia, n.d. late 19thc?

239.41 Sergei Voronoff (Voronov) to ---, n.d. early 20thc?

239.42-7 **Contemporary Medical Archives Centre**

239.42 ABORTION LAW REFORM ASSOCIATION (SA/ALR)
Scrapbook 'Abortion Laws Russia, 1930-1937' by Janet Chance (**E.2**).

239.43 CHAIN, Sir Ernst Boris (1906-1979) (**PP/EBC**)
Biochemist. Correspondence with Soviet scientists and the USSR Academy of Sciences, 1975-9. *See index of list.*

239.44 GARNHAM, Professor P.C.G. (1901-) (**PP/GAR**)
Protozoologist. Correspondence with parasitologists and protozoologists in the USSR (**C.34-40**).

239.45 HILL, Prof. Archibald Vivian (1866-1977) (**Acc. 180**)
Physiologist. Correspondence includes 2 letters from I. P. Pavlov, 29 Nov. 1925, 13 Feb. 1929, and letters from Leon Abarovich Orbeli, neurophysiologist, 1930, with copies of later correspondence relating to Orbeli's 75th birthday celebrations, 1957.

239.46 MELLANBY PAPERS (**Acc. 178**)
Papers of May Mellanby (1882-1978) include photographs and postcards of Russia, and in particular of oil fields in the Caucasus, late 19th and early 20th centuries. Papers as yet uncatalogued.

239.47 SHARPEY-SCHAFER, Sir Edward Albert (1850-1935) (**PP/ESS**)
Physiologist. Correspondence with Russian scientists in Section C; file 'Russian Scientists', mostly re position of scientists after the Revolution (**E.16**); 3 letters from Ivan Petrovich Pavlov (**E.3/30, E.16/1, E.18/20**).

240.1-15

WESTMINSTER DIOCESAN ARCHIVES

Archbishop's House, Ambrosden Avenue, London SW1P 1QJ

By appointment through written application to the Archivist. All documents are closed for thirty years. Material relating to the USSR can be found during the period of office as Archbishop of Westminster of Cardinal Bourne (1903-35) (archive reference **Bo.**), Cardinal Hinsley (1935-43) (**Hi.**) and Cardinal Griffin (1943-56) (**G.**). Subject indexes indicate material, mainly pamphlets and press cuttings but also manuscript material, relating to the USSR in the following files.

240.1 ANGLO-GEORGIAN SOCIETY (**Bo. 5/57b**)

240.2 ANGLO-UKRAINIAN COMMITTEE, 1949-50 (**G. 1/43f**)

240.3 ASSOCIATION OF UKRAINIANS IN GREAT BRITAIN, 1948-64 (**G. 4/22**)

240.4 BALTIC STATES, 1942-51 (**G. 2/135**)
Material relates mainly to Lithuania and includes: pamphlets; letters from the Lithuanian Association of Great Britain; telegrams from Lithuania, 1944; TS English transl. of memo from the Lithuanian bishops to the German Occupation authorities, 13 Oct. 1942.

240.5 BOLSHAKOFF, Dr Serge (Sergei Bolshakov) (**G. 1/35g**)
Copies of *The Bulletin*; correspondence re the Church in the USSR, 1944-9.

240.6 COMMUNISM (**Hi. 2/55**)
Pamphlets and leaflets re Soviet Russia; TS memos and notes on the religious policy of the USSR by Mrs James Purdey, Duchess of Atholl, 1932; TS 'Summary of propaganda ... carried on in England for the Soviet Government ... ', 25 Mar. 1930.

240.7 EASTERN CHURCH (**Hi. 2/71**)
Letters, memos etc. re relations with the Orthodox Churches, mainly Italian.

240.8 LATVIAN CATHOLIC ASSOCIATION, 1948-59 (**G. 1/42a**)

240.9 RUSSIA, 1918-39 (**Hi. 2/188**)
Pamphlets; general correspondence; letters from the Catholic Relief Committee for Russia re deported and imprisoned Russian clergy, 1938; letters from prisoners in the USSR; appeal for the Russian Clergy and Church Aid Fund, 1930.

240.10 RUSSIA, 1920-22 (**Bo. 5/36b**)
TS memo re the Catholic question in Russia by Philip Leigh Smith, 1921; letter re Catholics in the USSR, 1921, Russian and English transl.; protest re the removal of relics from Vladivostok, 1921; Russian and English transl.; pamphlets, printed reports, letters etc. re famine and famine relief in the USSR.

240.11 RUSSIA, 1944-48 (**G. 3/8**)
Pamphlets; booklets; newspaper cuttings; TS memo 'Can Russia be believed?'.

240.12 UKRAINE, 1922 (**Bo. 5/56b**)
Printed pamphlet, 'The Case for the Independence of Eastern Galicia', 1922, and letters re the same, mostly French.

240.13 UKRAINE, 1946-55 (**G. 2/30**)

240.14 UKRAINIAN EXARCHATE, 1957-63 (**G. 2/131**)

240.15 UKRAINIAN STUDENTS, 1946-47 (**G. 3/10**)

241.1
THE WERNHER COLLECTION

Luton Hoo, Luton, Bedforshire LI1 3TQ

By appointment.

241.1 The Wernher Collection includes many photographs of the members of the Russian Imperial family who were relations of Lady Zia Wernher, daughter of the Grand Duke Michael of Russia, *c.* 1890- *c.* 1914, and also an unautographed MS of Pushkin's poem 'Freedom'.

242.1
THE LATVIAN LEGATION ARCHIVE

Catthorpe Manor (Latvian Welfare Fund), near Lutterworth, Leicestershire

By appointment.

242.1 THE LATVIAN LEGATION ARCHIVE
Records of the Latvian Legation from 1918. Apply to Archivist for conditions of access.

243.1-30
KENT ARCHIVES OFFICE

County Hall, Maidstone, Kent ME14 1XQ

F. Hull, *Guide to the Kent County Archives Office* (1958) and *Supplements*, 1971 and 1981. TS lists of collections; card indexes of persons and places. There are separate indexes to the De L'Isle, Stanhope and Sackville catalogues.

243.1 AMHERST MSS (**U1350**)
Letters from Sir Joseph Yorke, Baron Dover, to Sir Jeffrey Amherst the following subjects: Russian claims in the Baltic, 4 June 1757 (**C41/11**); Franco-Russian relations, 1757, 1768 (**C41/38-9**); Mr Fawkener, recommended by Catherine II, 8 Feb. 1771 (**C41/40**); partitions of Poland, 1772-3 (**C41/40, 47, 57**); Russo-Turkish war, 1774 (**C41/50-2, 54**); Russian position re America, 1 Apr. 1777 (**C41/95**). Treaty between Russia and Prussia, 12 June 1762 (**O41/23**). *See catalogue for details.*

243.2 BEST MSS **(U480)**
Papers of Mawdistley Gaussen Best include diaries covering Crimean War **(F56-7)**.

243.3 CHAPMAN MSS **(U619)**
Letters from E. F. Chapman re his mission to Odessa, 1804 **(C6)**.

243.4 COBB MSS **(U1453)**
Papers of Francis Cobb include: correspondence re insurance of cargoes to Riga, 1822 **(B5/4/488)**; letters re voyage round the world by Lutke (Fedor Petrovich Litke), Russian captain, 1829 **(B5/4/819)**; shipping records re Russia, 1804, 1830 **(B5/4/998, 1363)**; letter from John Mortlock re meeting in support of Russia, 1812 **(C181)**; letters from the Russian embassy in London, 1781, 1783, 1785 **(O82/1-5)**.

243.5 COLLET MSS **(U1287)**
Collet family papers include: letters from James Collet and agents, mainly to Mark Wilks Collet, from Archangel or referring to trade there, 1820, 1832, 1834-6, 1846 **(C2; C5; C11, C14/1; C18; C39/2, 8; C57; F24)**; letter from Collet to his cousin re hopes for establishment of agency in Liverpool for his Archangel and St Petersburg houses, 1835 **(C18)**; letter to Collet re mission from Russia for marine steam machinery **(C64)**; letter re Russian admiral seeking to employ marine engineer **(C73)**; copy letter from Collet to Rothschilds re the Russian and Mexican loans, 1864 **(C79/3)**; part of a letter re coinage, apparently from an official in the Russian mint, *c.* 1890 **(O7)**. *See catalogue for details.*

243.6 DE L'ISLE MSS **(U1475)**
Papers of Sir Robert Sidney, 1st Earl of Leicester, (1529-86) include letter from Sir William Browne, lieutenant-governor of Flushing re rumours of Polish victory over Russia, 20 Sept. 1610 **(C8/856)** and letter from Joachim Camerarius re peace between Poland and Russia, 28 Mar. 1582, Latin **(C22/1)**. Permission to use this collection must be obtained from Lord De L'Isle, Penhurst Place, Penhurst, Tonbridge, Kent.

243.7 GARRETT FAMILY MSS **(U888)**
Papers of Sir Robert Garrett include: letter from Garrett to Charlotte Bentinck re rumours of war between France and Russia, Oct. 1811 **(C11/17)**; TS extract from letter by Garrett from the Crimea, 1855 **(C37)**; sketch from the Crimea and 2 copies of letters from Gen. Wesselitskay (S. G. Veselitskii), 1855-6 **(O11)**.

243.8 HALLETT & CO., ASHFORD **(U1045)**
Papers of the Billington family include letter from George [Billington] to his father from the Crimea, 1856 **(F9)**.

243.9 HARDINGE MSS **(U927)**
Papers of Charles, 1st Baron Hardinge of Penhurst, Ambassador to St Petersburg, 1904-6, include: papers re negotiations for an agreement with Russia, 1906 **(O1)**; FO reports including Russia, 1907-9 **(O3; O6; O9)**; copies of treaties with Russia **(O4; O20)**; letter to Sir Eyre A. B. W. Crowe re negotiations with the Soviet government, 28 Nov. 1922 **(O29/20)**; correspondence re Edward VII's visits to the German, Austrian and Russian Emperors, 1906-9 **(O21)**; letters re relief for Russian refugees, 30 Aug., 23 Sept. 1924 **(O30/24, 28)**. *See catalogue for details.*

243.10 HARRIS MSS **(U624)**
Papers of George, 1st Baron Harris, include: letter from Sir Stephen Lushington re probability of war between Russia and Turkey, 1821 **(C67/118)**; copy of news from Russia etc., 1799 **(O659)**.

243.11 HUBERT HALL MSS (**U890**)
Letter from Beatrice Webb to Dr Hubert Hall re Russia, 6 Dec. 1932 (**F4/10**).

243.12 KNATCHBULL MSS (**U951**)
23 letters from Richard Astley Knatchbull-Hugessen to his family from the Crimea, 1854-5 (**C6**).

243.13 KNOLLYS MSS (**U1186**)
Papers of Sir William Knollys (1797-1883) include letters to him from Henri d'Orléans re revue of troops who served in the Crimea, 28 July 1856 (**C16**) and Sir Andrew Buchanan from St Petersburg, 5 Dec. 1866 (**C20**); letter from Princess Dagmar of Denmark, the future Empress, to the Tsarevich (Alexander III), 29 Oct. 1866 (**C32**).

243.14 MAIDSTONE MUSEUM COLLECTIONS (**U1823**)
Passports for Julius Lucius Brenchley in China, Russia and Hawaii, 1855-6 (**O2**).

243.15 MANN (CORNWALLIS) MSS (**U24**)
Letters from Fiennes Wykeham-Martin mainly to his brother from the Crimea, 1854-5 (**C6**).

243.16 MASTER MSS (**U119**)
Letters to Richard Master as merchant in Riga, early 18th century (**C4**).

243.17 NORMAN MSS (**U310**)
Claims by Norrisson Covardale for money for information re Danish ships importing timber from Riga, 1762 (**B28**); letters from George Norman to his stepmother from Russia, 1784 (**C3**); letters from Capt. Herman Norman to his family from the Crimea, 1854-5 (**C45; C57; C123/1**); letters and papers re death of Herman Norman in the Crimea, 1855-6 (**C59; C123/2; F33**).

243.18 NORTH (WALDERSHIRE) MSS (**U471**)
'Great Ledger' of Sir Dudley North including accounts of trading in Archangel and journal of correspondence, 1680-1705 (**A244-5**); supplementary ledgers and correspondence, 1705-23 (**A246-7; A257; A259**); letter from St Petersburg, 1815 (**C132**).

243.19 OSBORNE MSS (**U771**)
Letters from William Bland to his father re Napoleon's desperate situation in Moscow, 1812 (**C25**); account of the Alexander column at St Petersburg, 1834 (**C39**).

243.20 PRATT MSS (**U840**)
Papers include: letter from Sir Henry Hardinge, 1st Visc. Hardinge, to John Jeffreys, 2nd Earl and 1st Marquis Camden, re Russian aims and the Polish question, 1814 (**C51/2-3**); memo from Castlereagh to Alexander I, 1814 (**C51/4**); letter from Alexander I to Charles, Lord Stewart, 27 Sept. 1813 (**C91/8**); letters to Sir J. J. Pratt from Castlereagh and Pitt re Russia, 1808, 1796 (**C98/14; C123/9**) and from Thomas Reynolds re the Polish rising, 1831 (**C256/34-7, 46, 48**); letters from Herbert Murray to his mother from the Crimea (**C544/1-15**). *See catalogue for details.*

243.21 RECORDS OF THE ROYAL WEST KENT REGIMENT (**WKR**)
Correspondence and papers re the Crimea include: letters from Capt. A. C. K. Lock, Richard Sutcliffe and Lt Anderson (**B1/Z6A, Z6B; BM/Z4**); papers re awards of the Victoria Cross (**B2/Z13**); photographs, print and newscuttings (**B2/Zp2, Zp12; B2/Z8**); papers of M. A. Clarke re Crimean War including account of captivity in Russia (**BD/Z1**);

printed general order for the embarkation of the Army from the Crimea, 1856 (**BM/Z2**). *See catalogue for details.*

243.22 SACKVILLE OF KNOLE MSS (U269)

Papers of Charles Whitworth (1675-1725) include full powers to Russia, 1709, 1711 (**O174/1-2**). Papers of Charles Whitworth (1752-1825), Minister in St Petersburg 1789-1800, contain many references to Russia including: full power as plenipotentiary, 1791, 1793, 1799 (**O195/1-3**); diplomatic papers re Russia, 1798-1800, including letters from Daniel O'Bayley in Revel, papers re Paul I's awards of the Order of St John of Jerusalem and the Order of Malta, instructions from the British government to Whitworth and letters from the British colony at Riga and the British factory in St Petersburg (**O196/1; 0197/1-2, 5-6, 8-9**); papers re Whitworth's financial affairs in Russia, 1797-1801, 1808 (**O196/1-6**); drafts of letters and memos by Whitworth, 1798-1800 (**O197/8**); letters from Count Panin, 1800-2 (**0197/11**); letter from Alexander I, 1814 (**O226/5**). Sackville family papers include bill for carriage of pictures from St Petersburg, 1805 (**A252/16**). *See catalogue for details.*

243.23 SMITH-MASTERS MSS (U1127)

Merchant's ledger including trade with Archangel, early 18th century (**A32**); letter from Lady Nelson re HMS *Samson* at Sebastopol (**C91**).

243.24 STANHOPE OF CHEVENING MSS (U1590)

Letters from Percy C. S. Smythe, 6th Visc. Strangford, from St Petersburg to Philip, 4th Earl Stanhope, 1825-6 (**C138/3**); letters of Lady Griselda Teckell (née Stanhope) to an unknown correspondent in Russia, 1820-1 (**C254**); correspondence of Philip Henry, 5th Earl Stanhope, with Carlyle re relations between Frederick II and Catherine II, 1864 (**C470/64**); letters and copy letter by Catherine II, 1790, n.d. (**C472/9; C477/7; S3/C10/21-2**); Russian passport, 1909 (**C654**); letter from Gen. Rudolf de Salis to the 5th Earl from the Crimea, 1854 (**C714/40**); papers of Hon. Edward S. Stanhope re Russian policy in Afghanistan, Persia and the Trans-Caspia, 1878-9 (**O233/1; O236; O238-9**). *See catalogue for details.*

243.25 STREATFIELD MSS (U908)

28 letters from Henry Armytage to his family from the Crimea, 1854-6 (**C106**).

243.26 J. T. THOMAS MSS (U1625)

Labour MP. Letter to Thomas from the UK delegation at the Imperial Economic Conference in Ottawa re proposed increase of credit to Russia, 1932 (**O37**).

243.27 VON ANACKER MSS (U1036)

Passport issued to Johan Leonte Frelick to travel in Russia, 26 Nov. 1786, German and Russian (**F9/1**).

243.28 WEIGHALL MSS (U1371)

Letters from John Fane, 11th Earl of Westmorland, to his wife Priscilla, Countess of Westmorland, referring to Alexander II and Russian influence in Wurtemberg, 1858, 1865 (**C13; C20/10, 12, 54**); correspondence of Lady Westmorland with various people including references to the Crimean War (**C25; C30; C42; C44**), and to Lady Rose Weighall re the death of Nicholas I (**C53/17**); letter by Francis W. H. Fane, 12th Earl of Westmorland, from the Crimea, 1855 (**C54**); memoir of Lady Rose Weighall including account of meeting the Tsar of Russia (?Alexander II) (**F18**). *See catalogue for details.*

243.29 WOOD MSS (U1390)

Notes in a diary of a voyage and visit to Russia by Revd Warne, 1887 (**F1-2**).

243.30 WOODGATE FAMILY MSS (**U1050**)
An account of Lord Raglan's proceedings in the Crimea, *c.* 1857 (**F57**).

244.1-3

CO-OPERATIVE UNION LTD LIBRARY

Holyoake House, Hanover Street, Manchester M60 0AS

By appointment.

244.1 HOLYOAKE COLLECTION
Correspondence and documents of George Jacob Holyoake include: letter from John Wilson re notification of a committee set up to agitate for a war with Russia, 12 July 1853 (**/578**); letter from T. Thomasson re ceasing to read the *Reasoner* since it supported the Russian war, 7 Jan. 1858 (**/992**); letter from J. G. T. Sinclair re letters to Gladstone and *The Times* re Russo-Turkish relations, Mar.-Apr. 1877 (**/2392-2396**); letter from Holyoake to Gladstone thanking him for the speech which corrected anti-Russian feeling, 11 Feb. 1878 (**/2437**); letter by Holyoake and J. S. Stansfeld re Turkish question, Feb., Mar. 1878 (**/2440, 2442**).

244.2 ROBERT OWEN DOCUMENTS
Letter from Owen to the Russian ambassador telling him of his vision in the hope that it would prevent hostilities between principles of aristocracy and democracy, 3 Jan. 1854 (**/2178**); letter from Owen to Tsar Nicholas re his spiritualistic experiences, 20 Nov. 1854 (**/2218**).

244.3 Fraternal addresses from Tsarist and Soviet Co-operative organizations to the British Co-operative Congress (**Co-operative Congress Reports**).

245.1

COSTAIN PETROCARBON LTD

Petrocarbon House, Sharston Road, Manchester M22 4TD

For access, apply in writing to Mr P.J. Hoare, Director and General Manager, Nuclear Engineering Division, Costain Petrocarbon Ltd.

245.1 The firm, previously known as Petrocarbon Developments Ltd, was involved in the design and erection of chemical plants in the USSR (in Mogilev, Omsk and Volgograd) in the late 1960s and early 1970s. Records remain relating to the project for a high base calcium sulphanates plant in Omsk including TS preliminary and final contracts, commercial documents, insurance documents, correspondence and newspaper cuttings.

246.1-2
GREATER MANCHESTER MUSEUM OF SCIENCE AND INDUSTRY

Liverpool Road Station, Liverpool Road, Castlefield, Manchester 3 4JP

By appointment. Handlists.

246.1 THE BEYER, PEACOCK COLLECTION
The firm of Beyer, Peacock and Co. of Gorton were locomotive manufacturers and supplied Russia with locomotives from the 1860s. Copies of order-books, some details of the costs of orders and official photographs of the locomotives supplied.

246.2 CRAVEN BROTHERS COLLECTION
Machine tool builders who supplied the USSR with tools for a plant for the production of railway axles in 1933-4. Correspondence, some costs, details of orders and references in the minute-books to this contract.

247.1-17
THE JOHN RYLANDS UNIVERSITY LIBRARY OF MANCHESTER

Oxford Road, Manchester M13 9PP

By appointment. The English manuscripts have been listed in a series of *Handlists*, and there are individual handlists (published and typescript) of large collections. Accessions are noted in the *Bulletin of the John Rylands Library*. With the exception of the *Manchester Guardian* records, the collections listed below are housed in the original John Rylands Library building in Deansgate. In addition to the documents listed below the Library holds 22 Armenian documents, mainly gospel books which are described in F. Taylor, 'The Oriental Manuscript Collections in the John Rylands Library', *Bulletin of the John Rylands Library*, vol. 54, no.2 (1972).

247.1 ALAD'IN PAPERS
Papers of Aleksei Alad'in are partly listed and sorted. A list is available of his TS articles commenting on Russia, his exile and other political issues. Correspondence of Alad'in with Constance Nightingale and letters from Alad'in to David Russell, 1917-27, contain references to Russia and are listed. The remainder of the collection (6 boxes and approx. 40 packets) is unsorted but contains material relating to pre- and post-revolutionary Russia. Apply to Archivist for conditions of access.

247.2 AUTOGRAPH COLLECTION
Includes: engraving of St Petersburg and letter from Prince A. N. Galitzin (Golitsyn) from St Petersburg, 14/26 Feb. 1831 (**348(278)**); letter from Count L. Tolstoi to G. T. Sadler, 16 Dec. 1898 (**740(1)**).

247.3 BAGSHAWE MUNIMENTS (B)
14 letters from the Revd Arthur Young to his parents and wife from Russia and the Crimea, where he farmed, 1805-20 (**22/6/2-15**). Extracts published in the *Bulletin of the John Rylands Library*, vol. 38 (1955-6).

247.4 HENRY BAKER CORRESPONDENCE (Eng MS 19)
Letters from James Mounsey, 1747-70, including some from St Petersburg (**vols. 3-8**).

247.5 THE BROMLEY DAVENPORT MUNIMENTS
Diary of William Davenport Bromley of a journey to Russia through Germany, 1844 (**3/23**); his Crimean diary, 5 Dec. 1854 - 17 May 1855, with a TS copy (**3/24**).

247.6 CRAWFORD MUNIMENTS
Copies of letters written by Robert Lindsay from the Crimea, mainly to his parents, 2 vols, 1854-6 (**42/3/5**); letters by the same from the Crimea, 1854 (**73/1C**); 'Campaign on the Moselle under Count Seckendorff. 1735', English and French (**76/1/1**); journal of John Lindsay, 20th Earl of Crawford, (d. 1749) re his service with the Russian army including copies of letters to the Duke of Newcastle, accounts and extensive notes on Russian military disciplines and tactics (**76/1/2**). *See* G. A. Matheson, F. Taylor, *Handlist of Personal Papers from the Muniments of the Earl of Crawford and Balcarres Deposited in the John Rylands University Library of Manchester* (1976). Permission must be sought from Lord Crawford to consult this collection.

247.7 BASIL DEAN COLLECTION
List of correspondents includes Moscow theatres including the Moscow Jewish Theatre, 1927; envelope of articles on the theatre in England and Russia.

247.8 E. A. FREEMAN ARCHIVE
Historian. Correspondence includes references to Russian involvement in the movements for independence in the Balkans and the Russo-Turkish War of 1877-8. Collection in the process of being listed. Apply to Archivist.

247.9 GUARDIAN ARCHIVES
W. P. Crozier archives (**145**) include contributions from A. Alad'in, 1942-3 (**145/1/1**). Correspondence with Igor B. Vinogradov, 1931-56 (**B/V49A/1-89**); documents re Poland, especially re alleged persecution of Ukrainians, 1930-32 (**223/37/1-70**); TS articles by A. Ransome re the Polish War (with maps) and the C.-in-C. of the Russian Red Army, list by Ransome of generals of the old Russian Imperial Army now holding posts in the Red Army, covering letter by Ransome re above from Reval, 6 May 1920 (**223/48/1-7**); *Manchester Guardian* supplements, notes, correspondence etc. re Russia, 1917, 1932, 1934 (**259/15-16, 285/1/26**). Correspondence, 1872-1929, includes with Latvian Legation, Ivan Maiskii, V. N. Polovtsev, M. Philips Price, A. Ransome, D. Soskice, L. Trotskii, Princess N. Trubetskoi, I. Vinogradov. C. P. Scott correspondence includes with M. Litvinov, M. Philips Price, A. Ransome, D. Soskice, Sir Paul Vinogradov. Correspondence, 1932-56, includes with British-Soviet Friendship Society, Soviet War News, B. Temkov. *See handlist for details.*

247.10 HIBBERT-WARE PAPERS (Eng MSS 989-1038)
TS letters from Capt. G. H. Hibbert-Ware to his mother from the Crimea, 2 Dec. 1854 - 23 May 1856 (**MS 1027**).

247.11 HOLMAN HUNT MSS (Eng MS 1275 no.5)
Letter from Michael Frederick Halliday to William Holman Hunt from Sebastopol, 4 Jan. 1856.

247.12 JODRELL BANK ARCHIVES
Correspondence re International Astronomical Union, Moscow, 1958. Provisional list.

247.13 STANLEY CORRESPONDENCE (**Eng MSS 1092-5**)
Letter from Augustus Lane Fox (later Lt-Gen. Lane Fox Pitt-Rivers) to his wife from Balaclava, 28 Sept. 1854 (**MS 1093/87**).

247.14 Genealogical tables showing Russian descendants of 'Sigurd Ring von Norwegen, 695-730' to the middle of the nineteenth century by C. Hopf (**German MS 6**).

247.15 Letter to an unknown correspondent by F. M. Dostoevskii, 1863 (**Box RU**).

247.16 Studies on the probable course and result of a war between Russia and England and other papers re Britain's relationship with Russia, Turkey and Afghanistan, part MS, part printed, 1878-80 (**Manuscript cupboard**)

247.17 *Sandan*, written in Kalmuck with an inscription in the hand of Johann Jaehrig (d. 1795), translator of Mongolian for the Tsar (**Rylands Mongolian MS 2**).

248.1-21

MANCHESTER CITY ARCHIVES DEPARTMENT

Central Library, St. Peter's Square, Manchester M2 5PD

Handlists and card indexes.

248.1 MILLICENT GARRETT FAWCETT PAPERS (**M50/**)
Suffragist. Papers on the International Women's Suffrage Alliance include letters from Carrie Chapman Catt re the Russian Revolution, 19 Mar. 1917 (**2/22/212-13**). Letter from Prince Petr and Princess Sofiya Kropotkin, May 1917 (**7/5/19**); letter from Lev Tolstoi to Russian conscientious objectors (**7/5/20**).

248.2 LIGHTFOOT FAMILY PAPERS (**M75/**)
Swatch book of John Lightfoot of Broad Oak Print Works, Accrington, for work done in Russia, 1868-9 (**44**).

248.3 MANCHESTER REGIMENT COLLECTION (**M25/**)
Regimental diaries, 1758-1945 (**1**) and digests of service, 1758-1939 (**2**) cover service of the regiment in the Crimean War. List of killed, injured and missing of the 63rd Regt of Foot at Scutari, 1854 (**7/1**); correspondence of Ensign Hulton Clutterbuck, 63rd Regt (**23**).

248.4 MANCHESTER, SALFORD AND DISTRICT JOINT DISARMAMENT COUNCIL (**M313/**)
Draft of speech, 'Russia, Japan and China in Manchuria', n.d. ?1930s (**3/5**).

248.5 RECORDS AND ACCOUNTS OF THE MANCHESTER, SALFORD AND DISTRICT SOUTH AFRICAN WAR FUND (**M21/**)
Letter to the Fund questioning payment to the Crimean and Indian Mutiny Veterans' Association, 1919-23 (**3/11,13,15**); press cuttings re application from the Veterans' Association for a grant, 1907 (**4/8**).

248.6 MASON, John (**L29/**)
Letters from Grenville Withers, engineer in St Petersburg, to John Mason of Globe Works, Rochdale, machine maker, re efforts to sell textile machinery in Russia, *c.* 1849-55 (**Box 1**).

248.7 MORRIS, Henry Isadore (MISC/ 786/)

Photocopies of identity certificates of Henry Isadore Morris (born Beerz in Kovno district, Russia) in Yiddish and Russian with English transl., 1893, 1896, 1915, 1918 **(1-4)**; letters from Lithuanian Legation and Russian Consulate re loss of his passport, 1922-3 **(9,10)**; letters from friends and relations in Riga, 1912, 1926, 1939 **(15,19,25)**.

248.8 THE NATIONAL (FORMERLY LANCASHIRE) PUBLIC SCHOOL ASSOCIATION (M136/)

Letters during the Crimean War expressing the view that war is occupying the public mind to the exclusion of other questions such as education, 1854 **(2/3/428, 629, 1204, 2656, 3107)**.

248.9 PAPERS OF THE NICHOLSON FAMILY (C17/)

Letters from Richard Wood of Macclesfield mentioning that his son is in St Petersburg, 1843-4 **(2/23/4,5)**.

248.10 REDFERN COLLECTION (MS F O91.5 Re 1)

Papers of Percy Redfern, co-operative movement journalist, include letters from Lev Tolstoi, n.d.

248.11 PAPERS OF WRIGHT ROBINSON (M284/)

Pacifist, later Lord Mayor of Manchester. 3 leaflets supporting the Russian Revolution, 1917 **(Box 7)**.

248.12 ST PAUL'S LITERARY AND EDUCATIONAL SOCIETY, MANCHESTER (M38/)

Essays and articles include 'A War Aspect', 1856 **(4/2/2)**, 'A Bennett St Lad in the Crimea', 1858 **(4/2/4)**, 'Reminiscences of a Balaclava Hero', 1890 **(4/2/36-7)**, 'Tolstoi - novelist' **(4/2/45)**, 'Notes in Russia', 1913 **(4/2/59)** and 'The Downfall of Russianism', 1922 **(4/2/68)**; letter from Elizabeth Thompson saying she is to be introduced to the man who sounded the Charge of the Light Brigade, 1879 **(4/2/25)**; letter from Mackenzie Wallace, *The Times* correspondent in St Petersburg, 1878 **(4/2/26)**; letter from Prince P. Kropotkin to C. Rowley, 1889 **(4/2/36)**; photographs of Tolstoi and Prince Kropotkin **(4/2/57)**.

248.13 SIMON ARCHIVES (M11/)

University papers of Ernest E. D. Simon, 1st Baron Simon of Wythenshawe, include section on Russia (interview with Sir Henry Tizard, 1944) **(1/24)**; papers re nuclear disarmament include correspondence re Russia **(8/15)**; diary of a visit by Michael Simon to Russia, 1936 **(15/11)**.

248.14 WATKINS FAMILY PAPERS (M219/)

Letters from John Bright re his attitude to the Crimean War, 4 Nov. 1854, 2 May 1855 **(2/3-4)**.

248.15 THE GEORGE WILSON PAPERS (M20/)

Letter from Tsar Nicholas I, 3 Mar. 1855. **(22)**.

248.16 Evangelia Slavonicae. Illustrated MS of the New Testament written by a Russian monk, 1793-1800, with letters from J. W. Koch of the Commercial Union in St Petersburg and Robert Mackay also in St Petersburg to Sam Hanson of London re the work, 1866 **(MS F 091.B13)**.

248.17 Russian call up certificate, 1884 **(MISC/617)**.

248.18 Autograph book of good wishes from the Soviet Union to the people of Manchester on the occasion of a civic visit to Leningrad, 1956 (**MISC/652**).

248.19 Letter from Elizabeth Gaskell re departure of Florence Nightingale to take over the hospital at Scutari, 1854 (**MISC/710/5**).

248.20 Autobiography of Esther Segal, born 1910 in Belorussia, written 1979 (**MISC/801**).

248.21 Passport in Ukrainian, 28 Oct. 1898, for Hyman Ordman, born 1880 (**1**); certificate of naturalization of Hyman Eli Ordman, 23 Apr. 1947, born in Russia in 1880 (**2**) (**MISC/857/**).

249.1

MANCHESTER CITY ART GALLERY

Mosley Street, Manchester M2 3JL

249.1 Album of 206 photographs compiled by J. H. Abbot Anderson, 3rd Bn, Manchester Regt, *c.* 1903-10, includes photograph of a funeral of a Russian officer.

250.1

ROYAL NORTHERN COLLEGE OF MUSIC LIBRARY

124 Oxford Road, Manchester M13 9RD

By appointment. Access to the Brodsky collection is by permission of the Librarian.

250.1 ADOLPH BRODSKY COLLECTION

Russian musician, born in Taganrog 1851; Professor of Violin and Principal of the Royal Northern College of Music. Collection includes: letters in Russian including: 13 letters and 1 telegram from P. I. Tchaikovsky to Adolph and Anna Brodsky, 1882-1891, n.d.; letter from P. I. Tchaikovsky to L. Kupernik, 1 Dec. ?1882; 3 letters from Modeste Tchaikovsky to Anna and Adolph Brodsky, 1908; 3 letters from Kupernik to Adolph and Anna Brodsky, 1889, n.d.; 3 letters from Ivan Turgenev to Adolph Brodsky, n.d.; 2 letters from Adolph to Anna Brodsky, 1887, 1907; letter from Secretary of Moscow Concerts Society to Adolph Brodsky, 1909; letters, mainly in French, from Anna Brodsky's sister Olga giving accounts of life in Russia in the period immediately following the Revolution of 1917; collection of over 200 photographs including signed photographs of Tchaikovsky, O. Gabrilovich and L. V. Afanas'ev and postcards of Moscow; drafts of speeches given at the Royal Manchester College with annotations in Russian; concert programmes; press cuttings. A card catalogue of the collection is in progress and a published catalogue is envisaged for the future.

251.1

WORKING CLASS MOVEMENT LIBRARY

111 Kings Road, Old Trafford, Manchester M16 9NU

251.1 4 photographs of the British Labour Delegation to Russia, Apr. 1917.

252.1

DERBYSHIRE RECORD OFFICE

County Offices, Matlock, Derbyshire DE4 3AG

By appointment.

252.1 FITZHERBERT OF TISSINGTON COLLECTION (**D239**)
Papers of Alleyne Fitzherbert (1753-1839), Lord St Helens, as Ambassador to Russia, 1801-2, include copies of letters and dispatches, notes and observations on Russia, letters of credential and safe conduct; also correspondence and diplomatic papers re Russia, 1781-1813 (**M/0424-868**). Papers of Joseph Ewart, Minister Plenipotentiary at Berlin, 1786-91, include considerations on discussions between the Allies and Russia (**M/0756-95**). *See handlist and index for details.*

253.1

THE HANCOCK MUSEUM

Newcastle upon Tyne NE2 4PT

253.1 Notebook of Abel Chapman (1851-1929), 'On a trip to East Finmark and part of Russian Finland, Spring and Summer 1884'.

254.1

NEWCASTLE UPON TYNE CENTRAL LIBRARY

Newcastle upon Tyne NE99 1MC

254.1 ARMSTRONG-WHITWORTH COLLECTION : 'BAIKAL'
Album of photographs of the firm of Sir W. G. Armstrong Whitworth and Co. Ltd, shipbuilders, relating to the construction of the ice-breakers/train ferries *Baikal* and *Angara* for use on Lake Baikal, 1896-9.

255.1-3

NEWCASTLE UPON TYNE UNIVERSITY LIBRARY

Newcastle upon Tyne NE2 4HQ

Prior notice is required for access to collections; apply in writing to the Special Collections Librarian.

255.1 RUNCIMAN PAPERS

Papers of Walter Runciman (1870-1949), 1st Visc. Runciman of Doxford, Liberal statesman, include: Cabinet papers relating to Russia, 1911-16 (**WR 50, 58, 78, 99, 139**); correspondence re Russia when he was at the Board of Trade, 1914-16 (**WR 115, 117-18, 126-8**); papers re Russian railways, 1915-20 (**WR 146**); correspondence including references to Russia, 1919-20 (**WR 177, 185**); letters and papers re Anglo-Russian relations including the Temporary Commercial Agreement of Feb. 1934 (**WR 270**). *See*, A. Elliot and G. Williams, *Catalogue of the Papers of Walter Runciman, 1st Viscount Runciman of Doxford (1870-1949)* (1973).

255.2 C. P. TREVELYAN PAPERS

Papers of Sir Charles Philips Trevelyan (1870-1958), Liberal and later Labour MP and Cabinet Minister, include: a letter from Sir Charles' cousin, M. Philips Price, from Russia in 1917 and 3 documents by Price written in Russia in 1917 describing aspects of the Revolution (**CPT 69**); MS notes for speeches relating to Russia, 1924, 1939-44 (**CPT 111, 184-9, 194**); Cabinet papers and other official documents on communism and Soviet organization and personnel, 1929-30 (**CPT 140**); 6 letters from Sir Charles from Russia, and copies of the same, 1939 (**CPT 155, 213**); miscellaneous letters, notes and press cuttings on Russia, 1936-44 (**CPT 207**); press cuttings on Russian relations. The subject index indicates another 38 packets which contain unspecified references to Russia, mostly in correspondence and official papers (**CPT 16, 46, 52, 70, 83, 100, 102-3, 105-6, 108, 113-22, 127, 137, 140, 149-50, 153, 159-60, 163, 173, 194, 201, 207, 213-14, 240, 264**). *See*, A. Elliot and G. Williams, *Catalogue of the Papers of Sir Charles Philips Trevelyan (1870-1958)* (1973). Permission to photocopy or to quote from the papers must be sought from the Trevelyan family; details from the Special Collections Librarian, Newcastle University Library.

255.3 WILCOX PAPERS

Papers (1 box) bequeathed by Edwin H. Wilcox, newspaper correspondent in Russia during the Revolution and Civil War, consisting mainly of TS articles re Russia but also some correspondence, including a letter from A. I. Guchkov to Wilcox on the death of Guchkov's brother, 1935, and rare pamphlets. Collection uncatalogued.

256.1-4

NORTHUMBERLAND COUNTY RECORD OFFICE

Melton Park, North Gosforth, Newcastle upon Tyne NE3 5QX

256.1 BRANDLING MSS (**ZBG**)

3 letters from John Brandling in the Crimea, 1854 (**19/1-3**).

256.2 ST PAUL BUTLER (EWART) MSS (ZBU)
Papers of Count Horace St Paul Butler who served in the Austrian Imperial Army 1756-70, include letters and papers re the Seven Years war including notes about an attack on the Russians by the King of Prussia at Loebus, 12 Aug. 1759 (B.2/3/36) and a note of pay and subsistence of officers and men in the Russian army, n.d. (B.2/3/72).

256.3 CARR ELLISON MSS (ZCE)
Account books and letter-books of William Coatsworth and Ralph Carr, merchants of Gateshead and Newcastle, *c.* 1709-1804, may include references to Russian and Russian ports in connection with their Baltic trade.

256.4 RIDLEY (BLAGDON) MSS (ZR1)
*C.*50 letters from Lt-Col. William John Ridley, Scots Foot Guards, and Col. Charles William Ridley, Grenadier Guards, from the Crimea, 1854-6 (26/13).

257.1-8

TYNE AND WEAR ARCHIVES DEPARTMENT

Blandford House, West Blandford Street, Newcastle upon Tyne NE1 4JA

257.1 BLACK, D. F. and A. (696)
Papers relating to shipbuilding include: photographs of the Imperial Russian armoured cruiser *Russic* and of models of Russian train ferries; printed invitation to the launch of the Russian Volunteer Fleet steamer *Saratov*; publicity brochure issued by Sir W. G. Armstrong Whitworth Co. Ltd entitled *Some Examples of Ice Breaking Steamers*, 1872-1952.

257.2 COWEN, Joseph (634)
Liberal MP for Newcastle. Papers include letters and newspaper cuttings, 1841-1900, re the Balkans, the Treaty of Berlin, trade with Russia, the Crimean War, foreign policy towards Russia, the treatment of the Jews in Russia, Russian internal affairs and Poland.

257.3 MERZ AND MCLELLEN (1325)
Electrical engineers of Newcastle upon Tyne. Photographs of railways in the USSR, *c.* 1951-60.

257.4 RENDEL, Lord Stuart (31)
Partner and later director of Sir W. G. Armstrong Whitworth and Company, armament manufacturers of Newcastle upon Tyne. Papers include correspondence concerning Russian contracts, 1910. Restricted access to papers; apply to the County Archivist, Tyne and Wear Archives Department.

257.5 WARDROPPER FAMILY PAPERS (809)
Facsimile and typed transcript of diary of Thomas Wardropper re his journey to Russia to demonstrate the Stephenson locomotive, 1836-7 (/1); typed transcript of log of a journey from St Petersburg to England and back by Thomas and Mary Wardropper, 1851 (/2); photocopy of letter from Alice Wardropper from St Petersburg to her uncle, 1913 (/3); photocopy of extract from letter of Thomas Wardropper from St Petersburg to Tom Fender, 1917 (/4); photocopy of Russian passport of Mary Hamilton, 28 Aug. 1857 (/7).

257.6 Copy of an account by Thomas Diamond of North Shields of the voyage of the *Lily* from Cardiff to Vladivostok, Nov. 1904 - May 1905, undertaken on behalf of the Russian government during the Russo-Japanese War **(1116)**.

257.7 'G.A.F.', the Gazette of the Archangel Force, 7 June 1919 **(1686/1)**.

257.8 In addition to the collections listed above, the Department holds extensive collections of shipbuilding and engineering companies which include references to trade with Russia and the USSR. A search of the catalogues of these collections and of the documents themselves would be necessary to trace such references but major collections of this type include: Sir W. G. Armstrong Whitworth and Company (later Vickers Ltd), engineers, 1847-1960 **(130, 450, 1027)**; Austin and Pickersgill Ltd, shipbuilders of Sunderland, *c.* 1920-60 **(937)**; Hawthorn Leslie Ltd, engineers and shipbuilders, 1883-1956 **(962)**; Redheads, shipbuilders of South Shields, 1863-1902 **(1061)**; Stag Line, shipowners of North Shields, 1864-1970 **(628)**; Tyne Tees Steam Shipping Company, 1864-1957 **(92, 882)**.

258.1
NEWPORT CENTRAL LIBRARY

John Frost Square, Newport, Gwent NP9 1PA

258.1 HANBURY WILLIAMS, Sir Charles (1708-59)
Approx. 22 vols of diplomatic correspondence and journals, 1730s to late 1750s, covering his mission to Dresden, and positions as Envoy Extraordinary at Berlin and Ambassador in St Petersburg.

259.1-26
NORTHAMPTONSHIRE RECORD OFFICE

Delapre Abbey, Northampton NN4 9AW

Handlists; name, place and subject card indexes. Reference numbers beginning with **X** refer not to the number of the collection but to the number of the box in which the record can be found.

259.1 BADBY PARISH REGISTER **(22P)**
Memo by Thomas Coxe of his baptism of Princess Bariatinsky (Baryatinskaya), daughter of Prince Ivan Bariatinsky (Baryatinskii), at Altona, Denmark, 1807 **(/6)**.

259.2 BATEMAN-HANBURY (KELMARSH) **(BH(K))**
Lease of home in Soho Square, London, lately occupied by the Russian Ambassador (A. S. Musin-Pushkin), 1770 **(/1107)**.

259.3 BRUDENELL MSS **(Bru)**
Copy of instructions from Lord Raglan to the Earl of Cardigan during the Crimean War **(N.iv.2-5)**; letters re the Crimean War, 1855, 1861-2, 1865 **(N.iv.6-9)**; papers re the Balaclava and Calthorpe case **(N.iv.31, N.vi.60b, N.xv.1-16)**.

259.4 CARTWRIGHT (AYNHO) (C(A))

Letter from Thomas Cartwright to his father, William Ralph Cartwright, re struggle in Poland, June 1831 (/8183); extracts from official communications made to the Russian Ambassador (S. R. Vorontsov), London, 19 Jan. 1805, May 1815 (/8288); letter from Charlotte Cartwright to William Ralph re his visit in the train of Prince G. A. Potemkin, 21 July 1791 (/8402); letter from M. Cartwright to William Ralph re Mr Monier arrived from St Petersburg, 31 Dec. 1792 (/8404). Memo re A. A. Cartwright, killed in the Crimea (**Box 53**). Papers of Sir Fairfax Cartwright, diplomat, include many references to Russia , 1900-14, but are as yet uncatalogued.

259.5 FINCH HATTON (FH)

Account of a dispute at cards signed by E. Finch, Minister to Russia, at St Petersburg, 1740 (**/3848**).

259.6 FITZWILLIAM CORRESPONDENCE

Letter from M. Nikolai about the education of the future Paul I of Russia, 1770 (**X.1603**); letter from Tiflis describing Georgia, 1814 (**Drawers 82/49**).

259.7 GOTCH (KETTERING) (G(K))

Eyewitness account of the retreat from Moscow dictated by M. Corbin, 1821 (**/1076**).

259.8 GRAFTON COLLECTION (G)

Rhyme, 'from Potterspurg' praising someone for fighting for his country abroad (probably refers to the 7th Duke of Grafton in the Crimea) (/3939); letter from C. W. Strong to "FitzRoy" from before Sebastopol (/3948/3); account of the state of mind of an injured man near death (probably refers to the 7th Duke of Grafton's injuries at the battle of Inkerman, 1854) (**/3948/4**).

259.9 HENLEY (WATFORD) (Acc. 1967)

Notes on a housing tour in Russia by a member of the Henley family, 1935 (**/118**).

259.10 KNIGHTLEY COLLECTION (K)

Letters to Lady Knightley from E. T. Gage and P. Amy from Sebastopol, 1854-5 (**/2823-4**).

259.11 LANGHAM (COTTESBROOKE) (L(C))

Printed plan of retreat from Moscow, 1812 (**/388**).

259.12 LEWIS, Alderman Walter (ZB.49)

Letter from R. T. Paget to Lewis re Father Galvin's need to find a centre for Ukrainians to meet at, Nov. 1952, and reply (/19); papers re Lewis's attendance as Mayor of Northampton at reception given by Bulganin and Khrushchev, 1955-6 (/24); notes on Russia and the Russian attitude to war, 1941-2 (**/43**).

259.13 ROUGHTON (KETTERING) COLLECTION (R(K))

Letter from George Greaves in Archangel to William Roughton with news from St Petersburg; extracts from his notebook about his work as a clergyman at Archangel, 28 July/9 Aug. 1824 (**/95**).

259.14 SOTHERBY (ECTON) COLLECTION (X.1077)

Letters from J. Sotherby to his mother from the Crimea, 1855 (**bundle 8**).

259.15 WARD HUNT (WADENHOE) (WH)

14 letters from Sir James Graham to Sir Charles Napier re naval policy in the Gulf of Finland, Mar.-May 1854 (**/368**).

259.16 WESTMORLAND (APETHORPE) COLLECTION (W(A))
Letters from Francis W. H. Fane, 13th Earl of Westmorland, to his mother, Priscilla Anne, Lady Westmorland, from the Crimea, 1854-5 (**Misc. vol. 54**).

259.17 Plans of Sebastopol by James Wyld, 1855 (**Maps 822,827**).

259.18 Photocopies of letters from Philip Pratt to his father, 1855 (**Photocopy 1471/4-7**).

259.19 3 letters in Russian, taken from Sebastopol (**X.2631**).

259.20 First report of the Great Britain-USSR Association and prospectus, 1959-61 (**X.6443**).

259.21 References to Latvian refugees in Lübeck camp, 1956 (**X.7110**).

259.22 Newspaper and magazine extracts re Crimean cemeteries and 'Russia and her Church' in scrapbook of Revd H. Bigge (**YZ.665**).

259.23 Diary by Dr Barr of journey to the Crimea, Nov. 1854 - Jan. 1855 (**YZ.7037**).

259.24 2 letters to Lord Charles Lennox Fitzroy from Sebastopol and various military papers relating to him, 1853-5 (**ZA.4126**).

259.25 Christmas card depicting 'Peter the Great visited by William III at Deptford Dockyard 1697' by Bernard F. Gribble (**ZA.7759**).

259.26 Letter from William Wing to the Revd John Hunman re rejection of 3 points by the Russians, 29 Apr. 1855 (**ZA.7916**).

259.27 Journal of W. S. Strong covering the Crimean War (**ZA.8547**).

259.28 Notes on the Soviet attitude to the war, 1941-2 (**ZB49/43**).

260.1-16

NORFOLK RECORD OFFICE

Central Library, Norwich, Norfolk NR2 1NJ

260.1 AYLSHAM COLLECTION (AYL)
Travel diary of W. H. Scott of Aylsham in the Crimea, 1855, with sketches (**729**).

260.2 BOLINGBROKE COLLECTION (BOL)
Diary of Revd D---, including copies of letters from Thomas Towner, Pte in the 95th Light Infantry, written from Russia, 1853-5 (**234**).

260.3 BRADSER-LAWRENCE COLLECTION (B-L)
Agreement by William and Thomas Bagge, shippers of King's Lynn, to carry iron and deals from Kronstadt, 24 May 1783 (**VIa (XIII)**); 5 letters to and from James Christie re the valuation of the Houghton pictures belonging to George Walpole, 3rd Earl of Oxford, proposed for sale to Catherine II, Sept., Nov. 1778 (**VIb (VI)**); anon. papers re 'Manning the Czar's fleet at Petersburgh', 'Short Informations as to the present State of Muscovy', 'Cloathing the Czars Army', [1710] (**Xb (2)**).

260.4 GREAT YARMOUTH BOROUGH ARCHIVE (Y)

Letter from an unknown person to Col. Sir John Cowell describing the battle of Sveaborg, 1855 (**/D27/14**).

260.5 HOBART OF BLICKLING COLLECTION

Papers of John Hobart, 2nd Earl of Buckinghamshire, as Ambassador to Russia, 1762-5. 2 vols of letters to his aunt, Henrietta Howard, Countess of Suffolk, and his wife, 1762-8, include letters from his embassy at the Russian court, 1762-5, including an analysis of the character of Catherine II (**MC/284-5**); letter from Alexander I to Emily, Marchioness of Londonderry (**MC 3/293**); bundle of correspondence sent to Hobart, largely during his stay in Russia, dealing with political intelligence in London and Norfolk, 1757-69 (**NRS 14626**); bundle of accounts and miscellaneous papers re the embassy to Russia (**NRS 16389**); letters from George Grenville to Hobart during his embassy to Russia and papers re the negotiation of the Treaty of Commerce with Russia, 1763-4 (**NRS 21089**); diplomatic papers re the embassy to Russia, 1762-4 (**NRS 21121-2**); letter-books containing letters sent by Hobart from St Petersburg, 1762-5 (**NRS 21408-9**); catalogue of Hobart's dispatches and correspondence during his embassy to Russia, 1762-8 (**NRS 21410**); foreign correspondence and other papers of Hobart as Ambassador to Russia, 1762-4 (**NRS 23488**).

260.6 JEWSON PAPERS

Diary of a visit to Russia with a parliamentary delegation by Percy William Jewson, 1945 (**accn. 17.4.73, S 192 D**).

260.7 KETTON CREMER COLLECTION (WKC)

Letter from P. Kasturin to Revd Johns on types of ?sandpiper found in Russia, 1747 (**7/43**); 'Relation de la révolution en Muscovie', 1741 (**7/67**).

260.8 KIMBERLEY PAPERS (KIM)

Papers of John Wodehouse Kimberley (1826-1902), 1st Earl of Kimberley, include miscellaneous bills and account re household, clothing, entertainment and transport costs in St Petersburg and other places while he was British Ambassador to Russia, 1856-8 (**32-3**), and 2 letters to Kimberley re the trial of Prince P. Dolgorukov, 1861 (**34**).

260.9 LE STRANGE OF HUNSTANTON COLLECTION

Reminiscences of William Veasey covering the Crimean War, written 1894 (**39c**).

260.10 WALSINGHAM COLLECTION (WALS)

Letter addressed to Thomas de Grey, 6th Earl Walsingham, re the purchase of 2 grey mares from Prince Vladimir Galitzine (Golitsyn), 3 Dec. 188? (**LXVIII/28/53**).

260.11 Letter by Daniel Anguish from the Crimea, 1855-6 (**MC 20/40**).

260.12 Journals, with sketches, by Charles William Quevillart covering the Crimean War, 1854-6 (**MC 24/2-3**).

260.13 Travel diary of E. A. Field in Russia and Central Europe, 1901 (**MC 57/19-20**).

260.14 18th century transcript of 'Observations on 17 years of Russian travel 1573-90' by Sir Jerome Horsey (**MS 4496**).

260.15 Journal, correspondence, photographs and pamphlets of T. D. Copeman as a Quaker relief worker in Russia, 1921-2 (**MC 81/59-69; MS 10990**).

260.16 3 letters from J. T. Hasfeld in St Petersburg to George Borrow, 1844, 1854, 1875 (**MS 11322 P 138 C (Box IV)**).

261.1

THE ROYAL NORFOLK REGIMENT ASSOCIATION

Britannia Barracks, Norwich, Norfolk NR1 4HJ

By appointment.

261.1 5 letters from Col. (later FM) Colin Campbell to Capt. William Seward re his promotion and the fighting in the Crimea, *c.* 1853-5 (**44**).

262.1

NEWSTEAD ABBEY

Enquiries to: The Keeper, Castle Museum, City of Nottingham Arts Department, Nottingham NG1 6EL

By appointment.

262.1 THE GOODLAKE COLLECTION (**NA**)
Papers of Col. Gerald Goodlake in the Crimea include: commissariat account book, 1855-6, with loose papers (**213**); notebook and memorandum books containing notes on the war (**214-7**); Russian ledger of a chemist's list of supplies, 1850 (**219**); Russian day book of work done and goods received, 1851 (**220**); maps and plans, some published, of the Crimea (**221, 228-32, 234**); weekly labour account and returns of men of various divisions of the army, 1856 (**233**).

263.1-8

NOTTINGHAM UNIVERSITY LIBRARY

Manuscripts Department, University Park, Nottingham NG7 2RD

By appointment.

263.1 BATES, Leslie Fleetwood (1897-1978)
Physicist. Correspondence re International Conference on Magnetism, Moscow, 22-28 Aug. 1973 (**E.47**).

263.2 LAVRIN PAPERS
Papers of Janko Lavrin, Professor of Russian at University College, later University of Nottingham, 1918-52, are unlisted but include TSS of some of his published work on Gogol' and Dostoevskii, MS notes and other writings.

263.3 MANVERS COLLECTION (M)
Bundle of correspondence, agreements and bills of lading re the sending of goods and livestock to Elizabeth Chudleigh (styled Duchess of Kingston) on her model farm in Narva, late 18th century (**4148**).

263.4 NEWCASTLE COLLECTION (Ne)
Papers of Henry Pelham (1696-1754), First Lord of the Treasury, include letters from James O'Hara, 2nd Baron Tyrawley, from Moscow, Riga and Königsberg, 1744-5 (**C 279-88**) and papers re ambassadors' allowances and payments to Russia, *c.* 1748-51 (**C 847-52**), and there may be further references to Russia in his extensive diplomatic correspondence (**C 36-1533**). Papers of Henry Pelham Clinton (1811-64), 5th Duke of Newcastle, when Secretary of State for War include extensive papers relating to the Crimean War including: letters from Lord Raglan, Lord Aberdeen, Lord Palmerston, Visc. Hardinge, James Graham, the Earl of Clarendon, Lord John Russell, Gen. Sir George Brown and others (**C 9,788-10,865, 10,883**); letters from his brother, Lord Robert Clinton, from a tour of the Crimea, 1855 (**C 10,866-8**); TS copy of journal by Pelham Clinton of a tour to the Crimea and 61 photographs of the Crimea, 1855 (**C 10,884a-b**). There may be further references to Russia in his papers as Colonial Secretary and his general political papers.

263.5 PORTLAND COLLECTION (PW)
Papers of Lord William Bentinck, 2nd son of the 3rd Duke of Portland, include many references to Russia in correspondence and official papers. There are references to Russian affairs in the Napoleonic Wars in his papers as Ambassador Extraordinary in Sicily, 1811-14, (**Jd 1-6270**), in particular: papers re the French invasion of Russia, 1812 (**Jd 695-8, 2353, 3359, 2822, 3102-4, 3110, 3144**); Russo-Turkish relations (**Jd 2337-8**); extracts from letters of Adm. P. V. Chichagov and M. I. Kutuzov (**Jd 3109, 3118, 3124-5, 3139**); 'Return of the prisoners made by the ... 1st Russian army ...' since 1812 (**Jd 3121**); correspondence with Sir Robert Wilson, 1814 (**Jd 5486-5521**). Bentinck's papers as Governor of Bengal and Governor-General of India (**Jf 1-2966**) will contain references to Russia in his correspondence; in addition there are 4 memos and 1 letter re Russian policy in Asia and the possible threat to India, 1830, 1834 (**Jf 2288, 2304, 2655, 2720-1**). Miscellaneous vols entitled 'Literary Manuscripts' include diplomatic correspondence from Vienna and the Treaty of Ryswick which may include references to Russia, 1697-1704 (**V 65-8**), and 'Reflections on the Practicability of an Invasion of British India by a Russian Army' (**V 136**). Papers of Robert Harley, 1st Earl of Oxford, include: correspondence with A. Matveev, Russian Ambassador in London, 1704-11, including lists of Russian generals who conducted the siege of Narva, copy of a decrees by Peter I re the Dukedom of Livonia, 1704, memo re military affairs from Astrakhan', 1706, speech to Her Majesty by the Muscovite Ambassador, 1707, and list of sailors from Muscovy to be appointed to the Navy, 1708 (**2 Hy 1234-1308**); letter from B. F. von Baron de Schack, Minister of the Tsar, 1713 (**2 Hy 1312**); letters from Charles Whitworth, English Ambassador in Moscow, 1704-14 (**2 Hy 1313-37**); letter from Robert Jackson, Envoy to Sweden, including information on Swedish and Russian navies, 9 May 1714 (**2 Hy 1358**); copy of a speech made by the Tsar of Muscovy (Peter I) to William III, n.d. (**2 Hy 1400**); extracts from letters of ministers in St Petersburg, Dresden and the Hague, 1714 (**2 Hy 1413-5**).

263.6 STEINITZ PAPERS
Papers of Benno Steinitz, Austrian Reserve Officer who was captured in Galicia in 1915 and held in POW camps in Russia until 1920, include: letters from him to Felix and Rolly Steinitz from Tobol'sk, POW camps and Vladivostok, 1915-20 (**C 1720-8**); diaries and journals, 1915-20 (**D 8-18**).

263.7 WRENCH COLLECTION **(Wr, Wre)**
Letters from Asst Surg. Edward Mason Wrench mainly from the Crimea, 1854-8 **(Wr C 1-335, 345-64)** and copies of the same **(Wre C 1-15/1)**; letters from John Henry Kirke from the Crimea **(Wr C 336-44)** and copies of the same **(Wre C 16/1-13; Wr Kri C 1-3)**; diaries of Wrench in the Crimea, 1856-7 **(Wr D 1-2)**; letters re Lt John Eschalaz of the 55th Regt of Foot **(Wre C 17/1-21)**; letters re Crimean War hospitals and charities, 1855-6 **(Wre C 18/1-27)**; miscellaneous papers re the Crimean War **(Wre X)**.

263.8 Collection of Soviet Second World War posters, mainly *post* 1943.

264.1

NOTTINGHAMSHIRE RECORD OFFICE

County Hall, High Pavement, Nottingham NG1 1HR

P. A. Kennedy, *Guide to the Nottinghamshire County Records Office* (1960).

264.1 THE SAVILE COLLECTION **(DDSR)**
Collection includes letters to John Savile, 1854-68, from Sir George Hamilton Seymour, Envoy Extraordinary and Minister Plenipotentiary in Russia, 1851-6, Sir John Fiennes Twistleton Crampton, Envoy Extraordinary and Minister Plenipotentiary in Russia, 1858, and Sir Andrew Buchanan, Ambassador in Russia, 1864 **(226)**.

265.1-7

THE SHERWOOD FORESTERS MUSEUM

Regimental Headquarters, The Worcestershire and Sherwood Foresters Regiment, Triumph Road, Lenton, Nottingham

By appointment.

265.1 Diary of Lt Braybrookes covering his service in the Crimean War, 17 July - 20 Sept. 1854.

265.2 Letter from Sgt J. Gooding to his uncle from Scutari, 31 May 1855.

265.3 TS reminiscences of Maj.-Gen. E. Davison Smith covering the Crimean War and the Indian Mutiny.

265.4 Transcripts of letters written to H. C. Wylly while writing the history of the 95th Regt in the Crimean War.

265.5 Nominal roll of the 95th Regt at the battle of the Alma.

265.6 Monthly return of the 95th Regt at Sebastopol.

265.7 Album of 12 photographs of the Crimean War.

266.1
UPPERMILL BRANCH LIBRARY

St Chads, High Street, Uppermill, Oldham

By appointment.

266.1 HEWKIN COLLECTION
Collection of local books and documents includes letter-book of James Lees re the wool trade including copies of his letters to his representatives in St Petersburg, 1840s **(MS 18)**.

267.1
THE ASHMOLEAN MUSEUM

Department of Western Art, Oxford OX1 2PH

By appointment.

267.1 TALBOT COLLECTION
Extensive collection of maps, prints and drawings re the topography of Russian cities, and especially St Petersburg from its origins to *c.* 1900, with some portraits.

268.1-2
BALLIOL COLLEGE LIBRARY

Oxford OX1

By written appointment with the Librarian.

268.1 MORIER, Sir Robert Burnett David (1826-93)
Ambassador in Russia, 1884-91. 76 boxes of material many of which contain extensive material on Russia including: correspondence from St Petersburg with Benjamin Jowett, Edward H. Stanley, 15th Earl of Derby, Archibald P. Primrose, 5th Earl of Rosebery, Robert A. T. Cecil, 3rd Marquis of Salisbury, Sir Stafford H. Northcote, 1st Earl of Iddesleigh, and others, arranged in boxes by date; 2 boxes labelled 'Mission to Russia, 1885-6' including vol. 'Mission to Russia. Correspondence with H.M. Secretaries of State, 1885 and 1886' and general correspondence with the Foreign Office; box labelled 'Salisbury' containing correspondence with Lord Salisbury from St Petersburg; box labelled 'Private Correspondence' 1888-90 from St Petersburg; box labelled 'Russia-Siberia, 1890-92 containing 5 files of private and official correspondence; correspondence, memos, maps, printed material and photographs re Siberia and the possibilities of British trade there; correspondence with the Anglo-Siberian Trading Syndicate Ltd, 1889 and other companies re potential trade in Siberia; file re the journey of the Tsarevich Nicholas to India, 1891; notebooks and diaries covering period in Russia.

268.2 THE URQUHART BEQUEST
Papers of David Urquhart (1805-77) include: correspondence re Russia in the papers of the Working Men's Committees, 1857-9 **(I.G.4(b), 5/3, 11/14, 16, 17/4)**; foreign politics letters re Russia include a letter from Karl Marx and correspondence with George, 2nd

Duke of Cambridge (**I.J.1**); foreign politics letters re Circassia including with the Circassian Committee at Constantinople, Ismael Effendi and a German traveller in the Caucasus, and a history of the Circassian War, 1844 (**I.J.9/1-11**), foreign politics letters re Turkey and the East include papers on commerce, Russian policy and the possibility of establishing a council for 2 Crimeas under the Porte, 1838 (**I.J.II/C/2, 4, 11**); foreign politics papers, loose papers include papers re Circassia (**I.J.III.5**), the Crimean War (**I.J.III.12a, 26**), and Russian policy in Greece (**I.J.III.13**), Moldavia and Rumania (**I.J.III.20**).

269.1-161
BODLEIAN LIBRARY

Broad Street, Oxford OXI 3BG

269.1-154 Department of Western Manuscripts

W. H. Black, comp., *A Descriptive, Analytical, and Critical Catalogue of the Manuscripts Bequeathed unto the University of Oxford by Elias Ashmole* (Oxford, 1845); *Catalogi Codicum Manuscriptorum Bibliothecae Bodleianae* (part 4 covers Tanner MSS, part 5 (4 vols) covers Rawlinson MSS) (Oxford, 1853-98). Western manuscripts acquired up to 1915 are listed in *A Summary Catalogue of the Western Manuscripts in the Bodleian Library at Oxford* (7 vols) (Oxford, 1895-1953); acquisitions since 1915 are described in typescript catalogues available in the Library. Card indexes of persons and places. J. D. A. Barnicot, 'Slavonic Manuscripts in the Bodleian', *Bodleian Library Record*, I, (1938), pp. 30-3. Manuscripts with a shelfmark including the word 'dep' are not the property of the Library but have been placed there on recoverable deposit.

Ashmolean MSS

269.1 'The title of the Emporoure of Russia. *The most highe mightie* etc.', n.d. (**MS. Ashmole.38 f.116**).

269.2 'A Voiag of ambasad [to Russia] undertaken by the right honnorable Sr Dudlie Diggs, in the year 1618' being a narrative of the voyage round the North Cape to Archangel (**MS. Ashmole.824 ff.175-186v**).

269.3 'The translation of the Emperour of Russia his l're sent to her M^{a}ie Ao 1589, touching Doctor Ridley', dated Moscow May A.M. 7107 (**MS. Ashmole.826 f.21**).

269.4 'A true historicall relation of the horrible tumult in Moscaw (ye cheife citie in Moscovia) on the 22 of June 1648, caused by the intolerable taxes and contributions layd on the commonaltie ...' (**MS. Ashmole.826 ff.17-18v**).

269.5 Transl. of letter from Olexeye Michaylowiche (Tsar Alexis) to Charles II, 31 July 1662 (**MS. Ashmole.862 ff.255-60**).

269.6 Representation by Evan Offonasyeve (Ivan Afanas'ev) and Ivan Davidov, Russian Ambassadors, for the banishment of an imposter in London, calling himself Prince of Belorussia, *c.* 1660 (**MS. Ashmole.862 ff.263-8**).

269.7 'A draught of one halfe of the Emperour of Muscovies great Seale, the other halfe being like unto it. 1663' (**MS. Ashmole.1121 f.469**).

269.8 'The translation of two of the seales of the Emprour of Muscovy, performed by Mr Frese, interpreter to the Muscovy Embassador ... ', 31 May 1594, 12 June 1602; transl. 4 July 1663 (**MS. Ashmole.1131 ff.125a, 127a**).

269.9 Letters from the Tsar of Russia (Boris Godunov) to Elizabeth I, June 1602, Russian (**MS. Ashmole.1538**).

269.10 Letter from the Tsar of Russia (?Boris Godunov) to her Majesty (?Elizabeth I), 14 Oct. n.y., Russian (**MS. Ashmole.1539**).

269.11 A drawing of the great seal of the Tsar of Muscovy, n.d. (**MS. Ashmole.1540**).

269.12 'Hir Maties l'res [to William Cecil, Lord Burghley, permitting] 23000 weight of bell-mettell to be sent by ye Moscovie marchantes into Moscovy', 7 May 1597 (**MS. Ashmole.1729 f.23a**).

269.13 2 letters from the Tsar of Russia to Elizabeth I, n.d. (**MS. Ashmole.1763 ff.47a, 48a**).

269.14 Drawing of the great seal of the Russian Tsar, and copy of inscriptions around the seal, n.d. (**MS. Ashmole.1763 ff.48b, 49a**).

269.15 Letters from the Tsar of Russia to Elizabeth I, n.d. (**MS. Ashmole.1763 ff.51b-2a, 53a, 54a**).

269.16 A scroll of articles, 16th or 17th century, Russian (**MS. Ashmole.1774**).

269.17 Letters missive of Charles I to Tsar Michael recommending Richard Smith as agent for English affairs and commerce, 31 July 1634 (**MS. Ashmole.1781**).

Rawlinson MSS

269.18 ROBINSON, Bp John (**MS. Rawl.A.285-6, B.376, C.391-3**)
Correspondence during the negotiations at Utrecht include: letter from James Jefferyes, with an account of the capitulation of the Muscovite army to the Turks, 27 July 1711 (**f.15**); intelligence from Hamburg re movements of Russians, 9 Feb. 1711/12, French (**f.58**); copy letter by St John with account of the Tsar's marriage, 2 Mar 1712 (**f.67**); 4 letters from Charles Whitworth from St Petersburg and Berlin, Mar.-Oct. 1712 (**ff.72, 100, 136, 145**); letters from James Scott, Envoy in Poland, re Russia, 1712-13 (**ff.151, 439**) (**A. 286**). Papers re Treaty of Utrecht include copies of 2 dispatches from Charles Whitworth, partly in cipher, Mar.-June 1712 (**C.392 ff.301, 304**).

269.19 THURLOE, John (**MS. Rawl.A.1-67**)
Various letters of intelligence on Russian affairs, 1654-8, many printed in Dr Birch's collection (published London 1742). Unprinted letters include: extract from a letter of intelligence respecting the proceedings of the Russians against the Swedes, 1655 (**A.26 p.374**); news from Riga, 18 Oct. 1656 (**A.43 p.75**); extract of a letter from Riga, 18 Jan. 1658 (**A.57 p.108**); copy of letter from Tsar Alexis to the King of Poland, 1658, Latin (**A.58 p.333**). *See catalogue for details.*

269.20 ZOLLMAN, Philip Henry (**MS. Rawl.D.870**)
Secretary to Stephan Poyntz, 1724-30. Series of copies of newsletters from St Petersburg, 7 Oct. 1724 - 23 Aug. 1727, including list of the fleet in the Baltic, 1725 (**ff.19-208, 392**).

269.21 Copy letter from Charles II to the Tsar, with the credentials of his ambassador, J. Hebdon, 16 Sept. 1676 (**MS. Rawl.A.256 pp.115, 117**).

269.22 'Itinerarium Mundii, that is, a memoriall or sundry relations of certaine voiages, journeies, ettc., passed and performed into some parts of England, Holland ... Polonia, and Moscovia or Russia, to the north side of the world, from ao.1639 to 1648; by Peter Mundy' (**MS. Rawl.A.315**).

269.23 'Of the horrible tyranny of Ivan Vaslowich emperor of Moscovia', 1533-84 (**MS. Rawl.B.158 p.83**).

269.24 Notes of the embassies of Sir Peter Wyche to Moscow and to Warsaw, 1669-70 (**MS. Rawl.C.233**).

269.25 Outline of the history of Moscovia and Russia, 1630-68 (**MS. Rawl.C.734 f.375**).

269.26 Rough first copy of *A history of Russia from the earliest times to the death of Ivan IV in 1584'* (published 1720) including a 'translation of Mr [Gottl. Sam.] Treuer's Introduction to the Russian history, in High Dutch' (**MS. Rawl.D.29 f.130**).

269.27 Transl. of letter of credentials from Tsar Michael to Charles I on behalf of his physician, Dr Arthur Dee, 19 Dec. A.M. 7135 (**MS. Rawl.D.391 f.31**).

269.28 'Forma gymnasii academiae Petropolitanae et leges tum magistriis gymnasii tum discipulis datea' n.d. (**MS. Rawl.D.566**).

269.29 'Relatione del regno di Moscovia', n.d. (**MS. Rawl.D.605 f.1**).

269.30 'Relatione del regno di Moscovia', n.d. (**MS. Rawl.D.635 f.339**).

269.31 *Adversaria* of Michael Maittaire including letter from Empress Anne of Russia to the primate of Poland against the election in 1734 of Stanislaus as King, French; copy of 'mémoire présenté par les ministres de l'Emp. de Russia et Pologne aux États Généraux', 15 June 1735 (**MS. Rawl.D.728 ff.206, 208**).

269.32 Style and title of Tsar Theodore, end of 16th century (**MS. Rawl.D.867 f.216**).

Tanner MSS

269.33 Letter from Dr Isaac Basire to Dr John Barwick re doctrines of the Russian Church, 19 Dec. 1662 (**MS. Tanner 48 f.76**).

269.34 Collection of letters and papers during the years 1559-69 include: motives for keeping an English agent in Russia (**f.137**); copy of the embassage of Ivan IV to Elizabeth I, 1569 (**f.140**); 'A note of such things as are graunted in the privledge geuen by the emperour Majestie of Russia to the marchaunts, etc.' (**f.144**); transcript letter from the English ambassador (probably Sir Thomas Randolph) to Ivan IV, 1569 (**f.146**); requests made by the Russia Company to the Emperor of Russia (**f.150**); speech of the English ambassador to the Tsar of Russia (**f.155**) (**MS. Tanner 50**).

269.35 Transcript of letter from both Houses of Parliament to the Tsar of Russia, Feb. 1645/6 (**MS. Tanner 60 f.407**).

269.36 Letter from Sir Dudley Digges from Archangel to the Marquis of Buckingham re the seige by the Poles of Moscow, 31 July 1618 (**MS. Tanner 74 f.121**).

269.37 Collection of letters and papers of the reign of Elizabeth I include: letter from Tsar of Russia to Elizabeth I, n.d., Russian (**f.7**); grant made by Frederick II, King of Denmark, of a free passage to the Muscovite Company, 2 June 1583, Latin (**f.199**); explanation of the agreement made between Elizabeth I and Frederick II for a free passage to Russia, 12 Oct. n.y., Latin (**f.204**) (**MS. Tanner 79**).

269.38 'Relatione della Moscovia, l'anno 1560' (**MS. Tanner 231 f.65**).

Other Collections

269.39 ADDISON PAPERS (**MSS. Addison dep.**)
Papers re supply of munitions for Russia, 1915-16 (**Boxes 9, 28, 48**); report on progress of Russo-American contracts, 1917 (**Box 28**); folder entitled 'Russia 1917' (**Box 29**); letter from Christopher Addison, 1st Visc. Addison, to W. A. Burton re offer of a post on the Anglo-Russian sub-committee, 1917 (**Box 54 no.111**); letter from Addison to Count P. N. Ignat'ev re French steel for the Russians, 1917 (**Box 54 nos.530-1**). The box numbers are temporary and will be discarded when the collection is catalogued and new numbers allocated.

269.40 ASQUITH PAPERS (**MS. Asquith**)
Copy of telegram from Nicholas II, 1915 (**4 f.169**); letter from Lloyd George urging need of a special mission to Russia, Sept. 1916 (**30 f.239**); memo by Herbert Henry Asquith, 1st Earl of Oxford and Asquith, of conversations re Russia, July-Aug. 1917 (**32 f.176**); memo by L. B. Franklin on the Russian treaty, Oct. 1924 (**34 f.193**); letter criticizing the King's decision in making the Tsar an honorary Admiral of the Fleet without consulting the goverment, 1908 (**46 f.25**). A form has to be signed before access is given and permission to quote from the papers must be obtained from Mr Mark Bonham Carter, 13 Clarendon Road, London W11.

269.41 ATTLEE, Clement Richard, 1st Earl Attlee (**MS. Attlee dep.**)
Notes for a broadcast after the German attack on USSR, 1941 (**3 ff.17-25**); papers re a statement on the Russo-German war by V. Suchomlin (Sukhomlin), 13 Oct. 1941 (**4 ff.29-34**); notes for the House of Commons' debate on the Crimea Conference, 1 Mar. 1945 (**17 ff.69-82**); telegrams to and from Ernest Bevin in Moscow, Apr. 1947 (**51 f.164; 52 f.12**).

269.42 BAKER PAPERS (**Dep.b.136, c.263-72, d.215-18, e.52-64, f.26-7**)
Papers re Greek Boundary Commission include letters from Col. A. de Scalon, the Russian Commissioner, to Col. George Baker (**Dep.c.269**), map of the Ottoman Empire, the Black Sea and the frontiers of Russia and Persia (**Dep.c.272**).

269.43 BARLOW PAPERS (**MS. Barlow**)
Privileges granted to English merchants at Archangel by the Russian Tsar, *c.* 1642-3, Russian (**52**).

269.44 BOLSHAKOV, Sergei (**Dep.b.115-35**)
Russian émigré. Access to papers only with the permission of the owner, Mr Evan Davies, P.O. Box 324, Lamesa, New Mexico 88044, USA.

269.45 BRIDGES, Robert Seymour (1844-1930) (**Dep. Bridges**)
Poet Laureate. Note by Bridges on Ramsay MacDonald and the Zinoviev letter, 1924 (**71 f.35**).

269.46 BRYCE, James, Visc. Bryce of Dechmont **(MS. Bryce)**
Many references to Russia in his correspondence, 1876-1917. Bryce Papers (English) include references to Russia amongst correspondence between Bryce and Arthur Cohen, Dicey (?A. V. Dicey), Edward Augustus Freeman, William Ewart Gladstone, Sir Courtenay Peregrine Ilbert, Goldwin Smith and Sir George Otto Trevelyan. Bryce Papers (U.S.A.) include references to Russia amongst correspondence between Bryce and Charles William Elliot, James Levi Barton, Charles Francis Adams II, Wendell Phillips Garrison, Laurence Godkin, John Franklin Jameson, Henry Cabot Lodge, Seth Low, James Ford Rhodes and Elihu Root, and in miscellaneous correspondence and Embassy papers. Topics covered include diplomatic relations, the threat of Russian dominance in Asia, persecution of the Jews, the Russian Revolution and the Allied intervention. *See handlists for details.*

269.47 BURGES, Sir James Bland (1752-1824) **(Dep. Bland Burges)**
Letters to Burges from St Petersburg from William Eton, 1795 **(34 ff.107-27)**, Sir Charles Whitworth, 1789, 1794-5 **(44 ff.156-76; 59 pp.11-14)**, Count S. Vorontsov **(44 ff.156-76)** and Robert Adair, 1791 **(62 pp.1-18)**; copy of trans. of Chinese document sent to Russia, 21 Jan. 1789 **(51 ff.1-3)**; papers re and notebooks of Richard C. Etches, Russian commissary general of the Marine, 1789-90, n.d. **(51 ff.12-40; 52 ff.60-6, 107; 53-56)**; copies of letters re Robert Adair's visit to Russia, 1791 **(51 ff.93-7)**; commission to David Williams signed by the commander of Russian squadron in Copenhagen, 1789 **(52 f.109)**; observation by Joseph Ewart on Anglo-Russian relations, 1791 **(58 pp.45-59)**; account by Robert Keith of the revolt of 12 July 1762 **(58 pp.11-14)**. *See index.*

269.48 CARTE PAPERS **(MS. Carte)**
' ... Remarques ... sur les moeurs, habillements, religions, etc. de quelques peuples qui sont sous la domination de Muscovie' *c.* 1724 **(262 f.13)**.

269.49 THE CHURCH'S MINISTRY AMONG THE JEWS **(Dep. C.M.J.)**
Papers re mission work in Russia, 1884-1901 **(d.50/10-11)**. The papers cannot be consulted or quoted from without the permission of the Secretary of the Society.

269.50 CLARENDON PAPERS **(MSS. Clar. dep)**
Correspondence of George William Frederick Villiers (1800-70), 4th Earl of Clarendon, as Foreign Secretary include many letters to and from Russia, 1853-4, 1865-6, 1868-70 **(c.8 ff.1-413; c.37 ff.1-147; c.57 ff.1-297; c.71 ff.312-834; c.86 ff.83-193; c.102 ff.1-196; c.209-10; c.475; c.482; c.496; c.510)**; letters to and from Turkey during the Crimean War and miscellaneous Crimean papers **(c.22-3; c.38; c.40-1; c.60 ff.1-254; c.559 fld. 2; c.560)**; letters on travels in Russia from W. Spottiswoode, 1856-7 **(c.274)**; draft and declaration of a convention on maritime law involving Britain and Russia, 24 Feb. 1857 **(c.275 f.312)**; treaty of Neuchâtel signed by Britain, Russia *et al.*, 26 May 1857 **(c.278 f.41)**. Papers of Katherine , Countess of Clarendon, are uncatalogued but include accounts of the Crimean War.

269.51 CLARK PAPERS
Include papers of Lord George Macartney including copies of letters from Macartney to Lady Holland from St Petersburg, 1766 **(MS.Eng.lett.d.374 ff.37-41)**; notes on Russia **(MS.Eng.misc.b.162 f.18)**; notebook 'no.6' containing general observations on Russia, 1786 **(MS. Eng.misc.e.879)**.

269.52 G. N. CLARK PAPERS
Envelope entitled 'Frontiers of Russia' **(107)**; folder entitled 'Geographical Russia' **(151)**.

269.53 THE ARCHIVES OF THE CONSERVATIVE PARTY
There could be material relating to the USSR in the minutes, resolutions and agenda of the Office of the National Union (NUA), in the uncatalogued papers of the Conservative Overseas Bureau/International Office (**CCO 140, 507**), and in the papers of the Conservative Research Department relating to foreign affairs and industry and trade (**CRD 1/75, 19, 22**). Records are open until 1964.

269.54 COULSON, Charles Alfred (1910-74) (**MS. Coulson**)
Chemist. Papers re visit to USSR, Jan. 1963 (**8 A.8.1**); correspondence with Society for Cultural Relations with the USSR, 1950 (**139 F.7.7**); Correspondence with Soviet scientists. *See index of correspondents.*

269.55 CRAMPTON, Sir John (1805-86)
Ambassador in St Petersburg, 1858-60. Papers are uncatalogued but include some items relating to his time in Russia.

269.56 CRAWFORD, O. G. S. (1886-1957) (**MSS. Crawford**)
Archaeologist. Vol. of photographs and papers re Crawford's visit to Russia in 1932 (**127-8**).

269.57 CURZON COLLECTION (**MS. Curzon**)
Autograph collection includes autograph piece by Catherine II, n.d., letter from Catherine II to G. A. Potemkin, 1783, 2 letters by Prince A. Czartoryski, 1771, 1806, letter from Paul I, 1789, 2 letters by Alexander I, 1804, n.d., letters by Prince A. B. Kurakin, Princess T. B. Potemkina and Count Romantzov (?N. P. Rumyantsov).

269.58 DARLINGTON PAPERS
Papers of C. D. Darlington contain extensive correspondence, reports, press cuttings, drafts and offprints of articles re N. I. Vavilov, T. D. Lysenko and the controversy over genetics. *See catalogue for details.*

269.59 DASHWOOD FAMILY PAPERS (**MS. D.D. Dashwood/Bucks**)
Papers of Sir Francis Dashwood, 2nd Bt, include papers re treaty with Russia, 1747 (**B.6/2-3**) and his diary of journey to Russia, 1733 (**B.12/1**).

269.60 DE MICHELET, Charles Eastland (1810-98)
British Consul in St Petersburg, 1849-66. Papers uncatalogued but include his diaries and some printed Russian proclamations. Papers not yet available to readers; apply to Keeper of Western Manuscripts.

269.61 DUCANE, Sir Edmund F. (1837-1903) (**MSS.Eng.hist.c.647-50; Eng.lett.c.313, d.334-5; Eng.misc.b.113-14, g.78**)
Correspondence with B. Kokhanovskii, 1st Secretary of Russian embassy in London, 1873 (**MS.Eng.hist.c.647 f.147**).

269.62 ELKIN, Boris Issakovich (**MS.Russian d.3-12**)
Letters to Elkin, 1923-4, 1939-63, from V. A. Maklarov (**d.3-6**), M. Aldanov (**d.7**), Mrs L. Dan (**d.8**), C. Kuskova-Prokopovich (**d.9-10**), Sir Bernard Pares (**d.11 f.11**), Sir Harold Beeley (**d.12 ff.48, 70**) and E. H. Carr (**d.12 f.80**).

269.63 ENSOR PAPERS
Papers of Sir Robert Ensor, journalist and historian. Memo on Russian situation, 1919; memo on Poland and Lithuania, 1920; papers re Anglo-Soviet Relations Committee; papers re protest meeting against the Tsar, 1905.

269.64 GIBBES, Charles Sydney (1876-1963)
English tutor to the Tsarevich Alexis; later known as Father Nicholas. Papers not yet catalogued but include diaries, notebooks, correspondence, passes and permits, reports, memos, drafts of articles and other papers of and re Gibbes during and relating to his experiences in Russia, 1908-61. *See preliminary list for details.*

269.65 GROSVENOR, Lord Robert, 1st Baron Ebury (**MSS. Eng.lett.c.439-41; Eng.misc.c.667-8**)
Letters giving detailed accounts of actions in the Crimean War, 1855 (**MS Eng.lett.c.441 ff.129-40**).

269.66 HARCOURT PAPERS (**MS. Harcourt dep.**)
Papers of Lewis Harcourt, Visc. Harcourt, include cabinet memoranda re Russia, 1907-13 (**587, 589**).

269.67 THE HEMMING COLLECTION
Papers of Francis Hemming re the International Council for Non-intervention in Spain include letters re USSR ceasing to pay towards expenses of the Observation Plan, 1937-8, and letters re USSR withdrawing its representation on the Committee, 1939 (**item 13**).

269.68 HERRICK FAMILY PAPERS (**MSS.Eng.hist.c.474-84, b.216**)
Account of transaction in stock of the Russia Company, 1589 (**c.477 f.105**).

269.69 THE HUGHENDEN PAPERS
Papers of Benjamin Disraeli (1804-81), Earl of Beaconsfield, include: papers on Poland, 1863 (**A/X/A/52**); official papers, correspondence, telegrams, memos, pamplets etc re the Eastern Question (899 items) (**B/XVI/A-F**); papers re the Berlin Congress (273 items) (**B/XVII**); papers re foreign affairs including re Russia, Russia in Asia and Russia in the Balkans (**B/XVIII/A**) and re Afghanistan, the Indian frontier and Russia in Asia (**B/XVIII/B**). There could be further references to Russia in his major correspondence (8,250 items) (**B/XX**) and general correspondence (9,516 items) (**B/XXI**).

269.70 INVERCHAPEL, Archibald Clark Kerr, Baron Inverchapel (1882-1951) (**Dep. Inverchapel**)
Ambassador in USSR, 1942-6. General correspondence and papers, 1901-51.

269.71 JAMES PAPERS (**MS. James**)
Papers of Richard James, who went to Russia as chaplain to Sir Dudley Digges. Latin verses include 'in sortes amicarum die Valentini A.D. 1618 in civitate Moscua' (**13 p.236**) and 'To Mr Daniel Clutterbrooke uppon occasion, keepinge himself a ship boarde in the haven of Archangell in Russia in a Hamborow ship' (**13 p.256**); travel notes of James's Russian journey, 1618-19 (**13 p.251**).

269.72 JOHN JOHNSON COLLECTION
Includes album of 99 Russian postcards of the early 1900s (**no.51**).

269.73 KAY-SHUTTLEWORTH, Selina (**MSS.Eng.lett.c.514, d.479; Eng.misc.d.1198, e.1302**)
Journal of Ronald O. L. Kay-Shuttleworth in Poland, Russia and the Middle East, 18 July - 28 Aug. 1939 (**Eng.misc.e.1302**).

269.74 KONOVALOV, Prof. Sergei (1899-1982)
Professor of Russian at the University of Oxford. Unsorted papers.

269.75 MALONE PAPERS (MS. Malone)
Papers about the disposition of Sir Joshua Reynolds' pictures include a letter from Sir Joshua's executors to Catherine II, 17 Jan. 1793, French (41 f.3).

269.76 MENDELSSOHN, Kurt Alfred Georg (1906-80) (MSS. Eng.misc.b.361-88)
Physicist. Papers include: correspondence and photographs re conferences in the USSR, 1957, 1966 (368 C.4; 380 E.131; 388 J.7); notes for lectures and broadcast on Russian science (368 C.34, C.41); correspondence re Russian editions of his works, 1969-71 (369 D.15, D.20); correspondence with Russian scientists including P. Kapitsa (372 D.74; 375 E.13; 380 E.133; 387 H.43); correspondence re conferences in USSR. Not all the material is available for consultation; apply to the Keeper of Western Manuscripts. *See index of correspondents.*

269.77 MIERS, Sir Henry Alexander (MSS.Eng.misc.c.539, f.415-17, g.79-96)
Papers include diaries in Russia, 1899 (f.415-16) and Sweden and Russia, 1892 (g.79).

269.78 MILNER, Alfred, Visc. Milner (1854-1925) (MSS. Milner Dep.)
Cabinet minister. Documents re the negotiations preceding the war, published by the Russian government (133 item 11); official telegrams re Russia, 1918 (141; 364 ff.1-282; 366 ff.1-493; 367; 369); reports on allied action in Russia, 1918-19 (365 ff.283-427); memo on political situation in Russia, 1917 (372 ff.130-3); notes on Milner's defence of the policy of the Allies in Russia, 1918 (372 ff.238-44).

269.79 MONCKTON, Walter Turner, 1st Visc. Monckton of Brenchley (1891-1965) (Dep. Monckton 1-53; Dep. Monckton Trustees 1-89)
Cabinet minister. Correspondence of Monckton with Stafford Cripps, as Ambassador in Moscow, and Ivan Maiskii (Dep. Monckton Trustees 2-6).

269.80 MONK BRETTON PAPERS (Dep. Monk Bretton)
Papers of John George Dodson, 1st Baron Monk Bretton, include: letters of Henry Campion from the Crimea, 1855 (38); notes on Russian finance, 1876, and the cost of the Afghan and Crimean Wars, 1877-8 (44). Papers of John William Dodson, 2nd Baron Monk Bretton, include blue book, 'Convention between the United Kingdom, France, Greece and Russia, to facilitate the conclusion of a loan by the Greek Government', Mar. 1898 (83).

269.81 MONTAGU PAPERS (MS. Montagu)
Autograph letters of eminent foreigners include notes in French stated to be in the hand of Catherine II (d.20 f.3) and Alexander I (d.20 f.38).

269.82 MÜLLER, Prof. Friedrich Max (1823-1900) (Dep.a.28, b.112-24, c.253, d.149-203, e.85, g.1-2)
Journal of Mrs Müller covering the Crimean War (Dep.d.198); patent of honour conferred on Müller from the Lithuanian Literature Society, 1879 (Dep.a.28); copies of letters from soldiers serving in the Crimea, 1854-5 (Dep.d.201).

269.83 NEVINSON, Evelyn Sharp (1869-1955) (MSS. Eng.lett.c.277-9, d.276-80; Eng.misc.b.102, c.499, d.667-73, e.630-41, f.403-11, g.76)
Author, journalist and suffragette. Letters from Prince P. A. Kropotkin to Henry Wood Nevinson, 1909 (MSS. Eng.lett.c.278 f.47); photographs re Russian famine relief work, Jan.-Feb. 1922 (MS.Eng.misc.d.673); Russian diaries, Jan.-Feb. 1922 (MS.Eng.misc.d.667, e.632).

269.84 NORTH FAMILY PAPERS (MSS. North)
Papers of William North (1678-1734), 6th Baron North, 2nd Baron Grey, include papers re the enlarging of the Russia Company, 1699-1701 (**b.1 ff.331-3**). Transcript of a history of Russia under Peter the Great, 1817 (**g.2 p.201**).

269.85 PEIERLS, Sir Rudolf (Ernst) (b.1907) (MS. Eng.misc.b.197-226)
Physicist. Correspondence with Soviet scientists including D. M. Blokhintsev (**203 C.28**) and P. L. Kapitsa (**209 C.162**), L. D. Landau (**210 C.179**); unpublished article by Peierls, 'Russian Science', 1957 (**218 D.10**); correspondence re his book *Soviet Physics*, 1956, 1965-6 (**219 D.17**); correspondence re conference on Low Temperature Physics, Moscow, 1966 (**222 E.10**). *See index of correspondents.*

269.86 PIGOTT PAPERS (MS. Pigott)
3 views of Peter I's cottage at Zaandam in Holland (**b.2. f.72**).

269.87 PONSONBY, Arthur Augustus William Harry, 1st Baron Ponsonby of Shulbrede (1871-1946) (MSS.Eng.hist.a.20, c.651, d.363)
Private secretary to Sir Henry Campbell-Bannerman. Papers re the controversy over the parliamentary vote on the King's visit to Russia (**c.657 ff.64, 89, 119**); copy of letter by Morgan Philips Price from Tiflis re Russian politics (**c.664 f.67**); letters arising from the culmination of negotiations with the Soviet government, Aug. 1924 (**c.669 f.17**).

269.88 RADCLIFFE TRUST (MS. Radcliffe Trust)
Dissertation by J. F. Payne, 'On the epidemic of plague in the province of Astrakhan, 1878-9' (**d.35**).

269.89 RAMSAY FAMILY PAPERS (Dep.a.29)
7 letters by Caroline, wife of Sir John Borlase Warren, from St Petersburg, 1802-03.

269.90 RUMBOLD, Sir Horace George Montagu, 9th Bt (1869-1941) (MS. Rumbold dep.)
Correspondence as diplomat in Warsaw, 1919-20 (**26-7**).

269.91 SAVILE PAPERS (MS. Savile)
A diploma conferring on Professor James Bradley, Astronomer Royal, the membership of the Imperial Academy of Sciences at St Petersburg, signed by Count Kirill Razumovskii, 23 Sept. 1754 (**MS.Savile e.11**).

269.92 SELBORNE PAPERS (MS. Selborne)
Papers of William Waldegrave Palmer, 2nd Earl of Selborne, include: letter describing conditions in Russia, 1917 (**93 ff.214-16**); papers re Russo-Japanese War, 1904-5 (**154-5**); papers re treaty with Russia, 1924 (**215**).

269.93 SELDEN PAPERS (MSS.Arch.Selden, Selden Superius, Selden Supra)
Specimens of Russian calligraphy, introducing the name and titles of the Tsar Michael and forms of address, first half 17th century (**MS.Arch.Selden A.72(5)**); a short account of the nations of Europe and their finances chiefly based on Relazioni by Venetian ambassadors and including Tartary, late 16th century, Italian (**MS.Arch.Selden B.12**); a collection of Russian documents including the *Sudebnik* of Ivan IV, 1549 and a list of patriarchs of Constantinople (**MS.Selden Superius 112 ff.3, 79**); 'Leges Jo. Basilidis [Ivan IV] anno 7058 [1549] eaedem cum praecedenti', ?late 16th century (**MS.Selden Superius 113**); 'An Abridgement of the Russe Sowdebnik or Law Booke', second half 16th century (**MS.Selden Supra 59**); an English version of the *Sudebnik* and list of 'Courtes and Officers', *c.* 1600 (**MS.Selden Supra 60**).

269.94 SHERARD MSS (MSS. Sherard)
Papers belonging to Oxford University Department of Botany include plates and annotated copy of *Historia Muscorum*, 1740 (**13/207 f.10, 210**) and diploma conferred on H. Sibthorp by the Empress of Russia, 1754 (**20/259**).

269.95 SIMON, John Allesbrook, 1st Visc. Simon (MSS. Simon)
Cabinet Minister. Memo, 'The mystery of Burgess and MacLean', June 1951 (**99 ff.141-7**).

269.96 SMITH, Rennie (1888-1962) (MS.Eng.hist.c.467-9, d.286-302, e.230-9, f.14-20)
TS copy article, 'Great Britain, Russia and Germany, 1945' (**c.467 f.33**); photograph of Lenin, n.d. (**c.468 f.57**); lecture notes by Smith re USSR, 1943, 1945 (**d.292 ff.1-2**).

269.97 SODDY, Prof. Frederick (1877-1956)
Chemist. Invitation to visit the USSR Academy of Sciences, 1945 (**249**). *See index of correspondents.*

269.98 SOMERVILLE COLLECTION
Correspondence of the Woronzov Greig family, 1st half of nineteenth century, consists mainly of family correspondence but also includes: 2 statements signed by Baron (?M. I.) Pahlen, St Petersburg 1839-40 (**Fld MSFP-50**); petition to the Tsar about claim against Woronzov Greig's inheritance, 12 Oct. 1829 (**Fld MSFP-53**); draft and copy of letter from Mary Somerville to the Tsar, 5 Sept. 1832, 24 Mar. 1834 (**MSDIP-9**); correspondence and papers relating to Samuel Greig including letters from Catherine II and Paul I (**Fld MSFP$_2$-70, 71**). Permission to consult these papers must be obtained from Mr G. L'E. Turner, Museum of the History of Science, Oxford. *See handlist for details of Woronzov Greig family correspondence.*

269.99 STEIN, Leonard Jacques (Stein boxes 1-139)
Research notes, corrigenda and Russian translations (**67, 72**); papers re Russian Jews and pacifism, 1917 (**117**).

269.100 STOKES, Richard Rapier (1897-1957) (Dep. Stokes)
Cabinet minister. File re Russian tour, 1934 (**Box 20**). Permission to consult these papers must be obtained from Mr J. Hull, 23 Edwards Square, London W8.

269.101 TOYNBEE, A.J.
Box of papers re atrocities and refugees from Anatolia, Smyrna, Bulgaria and Georgia.

269.102 UNBEGAUN, Prof. Boris O. (1898-1973)
Professor of Comparative Slavonic Philology at the University of Oxford. Unsorted papers.

269.103 UNIVERSITY COLLEGE MANUSCRIPTS
'Of the Russe Commonwealth' being a description of Russia, its government and customs etc. by Giles Fletcher (**CXLIV**). H. O. Coxe, *Catalogus Codicum MSS qui in Collegiis Aulisque Oxoniensibus hodie Adservantur* (Oxford, 1852)

269.104 WHITE, Eric Walter (MSS.Eng.lett.c.413-17; Eng.misc.c.638-51)
Material re I. F. Stravinskii including correspondence re White's books, articles, press cuttings, lecture note, letters and copies of letters from Stravinskii (**MS.Eng.misc.c.645-51**).

269.105 WILBERFORCE FAMILY PAPERS (**MS. Wilberforce**)
Letter from Alexander I to William Wilberforce, 1822 (**d.13 f.1**).

269.106 WOOLTON PAPERS
Papers of Frederick James, 1st Earl of Woolton, include a comparison of civilian food supplies during the Second World War when Woolton was Minister of Food.

269.107 WORTHINGTON-EVANS, Sir Laming, 1st Bt (1868-1931) (**MSS. Eng.hist.c.890-940, d.424-7, e.319-20, f.26**)
Secretary of State for War, 1921-2. Letter from R. S. Hoare to Worthington-Evans urging that the negotiations with the Russian be conditional on an end to Bolshevik propaganda, 22 Apr. 1922 (**MS Eng.hist.c.930 ff.53-4**).

269.108 ZIMMERN, Sir Alfred (1879-1957) (**MSS. Zimmern**)
TS 'Essential Russian' n.d. by Stefan Osusky (**164**).

269.109 Letters patent of Elizabeth I to Boris Godunov, 1600 (**Dep.c.544**).

269.110 Copies of letters by Roger Fenton from the Crimea, Apr.-June 1855 (**Dep.d.579**).

269.111 Letter from Bishop Gilbert Burnet describing his interview with Peter I, 19 Mar. 1698 (**MS.Add.D.23 f.10**).

269.112 A safe-conduct from the Tsar Michael to Arthur Johnson and his two nephews to return from Moscow to England, 19 Dec. 1626, Russian (**MS.Add.D.75 f.3**).

269.113 Signatures of Catherine II and Alexander II (**MS.Autog.c.24 ff.430, 437**).

269.114 'Discorso della Moscovia' by the Venetian ambassador, late 16th century (**MS.Bodl. 880 f.523; 911 f.320**).

269.115 Letters from Vladimir Kokovtsov, 1915 (**MS Don.c.155 ff.17-18**).

269.116 Notes on Russian foreign policy by Maj. Francis D'Arcy Bacon, 1826 (**MS.Don.e.13**).

269.117 Notes by Sir Robert Ker Porter chiefly on military colonies in Russia and the situation in Persia in 1820, written *c.* 1820-4 (**MS.Eng.hist.c.409**).

269.118 Letter from B. Chaikovskii to Arthur Ponsonby, 1912 (**MS. Eng.hist.c.659 f.68**).

269.119 Passage in clerical hand, 'The Emperor of Russia [Michael] his Privileidge to the English Muscovite merchants', 28 June 1628 (**MS.Eng.hist.c.712 pp.736-9**).

269.120 Report on Russian trade with directions for Robert F. Falk when about to travel in Russia by H. E. Falk, Dec. 1861 (**MS.Eng.hist.d.150 ff.94-110**).

269.121 English transl. of *Die letzte Tage des unvergesslichen Monarchen des hochseligen Kaisers Alexander I* (**MS.Eng.hist.d.263**).

269.122 3 journals kept by Sir Thomas Villiers Lister during diplomatic missions to Moscow, 1856 (**MS Eng.hist.d.483 ff.16-168**).

269.123 Crimean War diary of Lt (later Maj.-Gen.) Charles Henry Owen of the 12th Bn, Royal Artillery, July 1854 - Nov. 1855 (**MS.Eng.hist.e.219**).

269.124 Letter from Heinrich Schliemann to Baron Nikolai Bogoushefsky (Bogushevskii), 8 Oct. 1879 (**MS. Eng.lett.c.199 f.123**).

269.125 Letters from Sir Paul Vinogradoff to Reginald Leslie Hine, 1925 (**MS.Eng.lett.c.213 f.26**).

269.126 Letters from C. W. Strong to his sister Fanny mainly from the Crimea, 1852-5 (**MS.Eng.lett.c.408**).

269.127 3 letters from Cecil H. R. Barnes, an officer serving with the British Military Mission in southern Russia to Mrs C. Hicks-Austin, 1920 (**MS.Eng.lett.c.462 ff.181-9**).

269.128 Letter from Prince P. A. Kropotkin to Margaret Woods, 1894 (**MS.Eng.lett.d.183 f.33**).

269.129 Printed document entitling a sailor to a day's rations 1849, taken at Redan in 1855, Russian (**MS Eng.lett.d.193 f.197**).

269.130 34 letters from Olga Novikov to F. Chesson, 1877-8, n.d. (**MS.Eng.lett.d.222 f.208**).

269.131 31 letters and photographs of Olga Tolstoi, daughter-in-law of L. Tolstoi, to Gertrude Ellen Cornelia Russell, 1905-36 (**MS.Eng.lett.d.269 ff.38-143**).

269.132 Letter from R. H. Binnington to his brother and sister from the Crimea , 1855 (**MS.Eng.lett.e.141 ff.222-3**).

269.133 116 photographs taken during the Soviet invasion of Czechoslovakia, 1968 (**MS.Eng.misc.a.27**).

269.134 Letter re the retreat from Moscow in 1812 (**MS Eng.misc.b.162**).

269.135 Miscellaneous papers re the Crimean War (**Eng.misc.b.163 ff.6-9; b.165 ff.73-82**).

269.136 TS set of 'Stories to kindle Patriotism, written for Japanese Boys during the Russo-Japan War' trans. by Revd L. B. Cholmondeley, 1909 (**MS.Eng.misc.c.45**).

269.137 Account of Russia's debts and the bond of the emperor granted to Messrs. Hope and Co., 1 Jan. 1798 (**MS.Eng.misc.c.143 f.273**).

269.138 Journal of travels of Sir Charles Stuart, Baron Stuart de Rothesay, through northern Europe to St Petersburg and from there to Vienna, July-Sept. 1801 (**MS.Eng.misc.c.256**).

269.139 Copy 'Ordonnance de Sa Majesté Impériale l'Empereur & Autocrate de toutes les Russies, addressée au Sénat dirigeant', 30 Nov. 1806 (**MS.Eng.misc.c.292 f.67**).

269.140 150 letters from William Thomas Stead to Olga Novikov (née Kireev) (**MS.Eng.misc.d.182**).

269.141 'The journey of Elizabeth, 3rd wife of the first Baron Dimsdale, on a Journey to Russia in the year 1781' (**MS.Eng.misc.d.354**).

269.142 Unpublished MS of Professor Samuel Dobrin's *Towards a Study of Soviet Law and Government,* 1956-8 (**MS. Eng.misc.d.521**).

269.143 Epitaph of Peter I, Latin and French (**MS. Eng.misc.f.79 pp.89-91**).

269.144 Review by Catulle Mendes of the play 'Catharine de Russie', late 19th century (**MS.French d.18 f.159**).

269.145 Letters from the Swedish, Danish, Dutch, Saxon, Spanish and English residents at St Petersburg to Frederick Christian Weber, Hanoverian Resident at St Petersburg, 1718 (**MS.French d.35**).

269.146 Letter to Anastasia Mikhailovna Shcherbinina, French; letter from V. A. Zhukovskii to Prince Nikita Grigorevich, n.d., Russian (**MS.Ital.c.77**).

269.147 Scribbles in Russian apparently by a Cossack soldier from Orenburg, 1914-15 (**MS.Lat.misc.d.88**).

269.148 Extracts of letters from Humphrey Sibthorp, Prof. of Botany, to Count Kirill Razumovskii and Stefan Petrovich Krachennikov (**MS.Lat.misc.e.109**).

269.149 Album Amicorum of I. C. Falck kept in various places in Germany and Russia, 1773-6 (**MS.Mus.e.35**).

269.150 Russian fables in rhyme by N. Vinogradov,1895-6, Russian (**MS.Russ.c.2**).

269.151 Poems by N. Vinogradov, 1897, Russian (**MS. Russ.c.3**).

269.152 Draft of preface to *Tsarstvo bozhie vnutri vas* by L. N. Tolstoi, 1813, with fragment of an unidentified work with corrections in Tolstoi's hand (**MS.Russ.c.4**).

269.153 Literary pieces by N. Vinogradov including poems, 1889 (**f.4**); extracts from his diary, 1859-72, written in 1892 (**f.56**); essay on A. Plestcheeve (Pleshcheev) of Orenburg, 1893 (**f.100**), Russian (**MS.Russ.d.1**).

269.154 Various drafts of the anonymous memoirs of a member of the Narodnaya Volya party, *c.* 1880-91, Russian (**MSS.Russ.d.2, e.2-8**).

269.155 'An Account of the Visit of ... the Prince Regent, the Emperor of Russia, the King of Prussia, Prince Blucher, etc. etc., to the University and city of Oxford, June 1814' differing from the printed accounts (**MS.Top.Oxon.c.1**).

269.156 Department of Oriental Manuscripts

D. Barrett, *Catalogue of the Wardrop Collection and of Other Georgian Books and Manuscripts in the Bodleian Library* (Oxford, 1973); S. Baronian, F. C. Conybeare, *Catalogue of the Armenian Manuscripts in the Bodleian Library* (Oxford, 1918).

269.156 THE WARDROP COLLECTION (**MS. Wardr.**)

The collection includes many historical documents from the early nineteenth century including: papers re petitions from Georgia 1905-07 (**c.1(9, 32-34, 36, 38, 41-2)**); circulars of the Georgian Information Bureau, 1918 (**c.1(13-14)**); land lease in Georgian and Russian, 1815 (**c.1(17)**); notes on the condition of Georgia by Prince and Princess Tcherkesoff (?Cherkesov) 1921 (**c.19**); memos on the Declaration of the Georgian Republic, 1918-19 (**c.23(1-3)**); papers re Georgia, 1916-31 (**c.25**); correspondence and papers of J. O. Wardrop re Georgia (**c.27, d.23, d.25, d.29, d.38-9**); articles etc. re Georgia (**c.29, d.40/4**); transcriptions and copies of historical documents (**d.3, d.24, e.8**); correspondence of Marjory Wardrop re Georgia (**d.16, 20, 26**). *See catalogue for details.*

269.157-61 Map Room

Topographical card index.

269.157 'A sketch exhibiting the movements of the principal French & Russian Corps between the rivers Vistula & Oka... from 10th June 1812 to the 17th February 1813' by Maj. Blacker, 1813 (**MS.C40:6(90)**).

269.158 'Isle de Retusari ou des Lievres ... près de Petersbourg dans la mer Baltique' *c.* 1750 (**MS.C40:21(7)**).

269.159 'Dwina fluvius', *c.* 1650 (**MS.Ashm.1820b**).

269.160 'Kaminiec Podolski. Plan de la ville de Kaminiec dressé sur le lieu par Cyprien Tommaszevicz', 1672 (**Sutherland 144(196)**).

269.161 View of Moscow, *c.* 1700 (**MS.Draw.Gen.a.5(19)**).

270.1-2

CHRIST CHURCH LIBRARY

Oxford OX1 1DP

By appointment.

270.1 DRAGE, Geoffrey (1860-1955)
Conservative MP, publicist and writer. 15 packets of diplomatic correspondence mainly concerning Germany, Austria and Russia including 17 letters from W. J. Birkbeck re Russia and in particular the Church in Russia, 1905-15, 16 letters to Drage re Russian affairs, 1891-1929, and 11 letters from Stackelberg re the Bolsheviks taking his estates, (**Box no.2/1-2, 9**); papers re the commonwealth and the Far East include letters from Sir Ernest Satow, Minister in Peking during the Russo-Japanese War (**Box no.3/2**); miscellaneous diplomatic correspondence re Eastern Europe including material on Poland in the 1920s with references to Russia and reports on Bolshevism (**Box no.6/Ib, d**).

270.2 DRIBERG, Tom, Lord Bradwell
Labour MP and journalist. Correspondence with Guy Burgess in Moscow, press cuttings re Burgess and MS of Driberg's interviews with Burgess (**B10**); letter from A. Kerenskii to Driberg, 1 Oct. 1952 (**K6**); notes by Driberg on an interview with N. Khrushchev (**K11**); dinner invitation from T. Samarin, Soviet Military Attaché (**S39**).

271.1

CONTEMPORARY SCIENTIFIC ARCHIVES CENTRE

16 Wellington Square, Oxford OX1 2HY

271.1 The Contemporary Scientific Archives Centre was established in 1973 to locate, sort, index and catalogue the manuscript papers of distinguished contemporary British scientists, engineers and medical men. The Centre does not retain the collections but places them in an appropriate national or university library after they have been catalogued. Copies of all the catalogues are kept at the Centre and may be purchased from the Centre. The catalogues are available for consultation at the British Library, the Bodleian Library, Cambridge University Library, London University Institute of Historical Research, the John Rylands University Library of Manchester, the National Library of Scotland, the Scottish Record Office, the National Library of Wales, the Public Record Office of Northern Ireland, the Royal Society, Imperial College of Science and Technology and the Science Museum, London.

The Centre holds papers while they are being catalogued but research access to these papers is not normally granted. The papers of C. D. Darlington, which include references to the Lysenko controversy, were tranferred from the Centre to the Bodleian Library in 1985. Information concerning cataloguing completed and in progress can be found in biannual *Progress Reports*.

272.1-7

EDWARD GREY INSTITUTE OF FIELD ORNITHOLOGY, ALEXANDER LIBRARY

Department of Zoology, South Parks Road, Oxford OX1 3PS

By appointment.

272.1 'Benefit and Harm Caused by Birds of the Family Lariformes in Volga and Kuban Fisheries' by T. L. Borodulina, n.d.

272.2 Notebook, 'Journey across Siberia to China' by A. J. Crosfield, 1903-22.

272.3 'Menzbierm als Zoogeograph, und Probleme der Weiterentwicklung der Sovietischen Zoogeographie' by I. Pusanov, n.d.

272.4 Report on a visit to the USSR on behalf of the Scott Polar Research Institute by B. Roberts and T. Armstrong, 28 May - June 1956.

272.5 'Die ökologisch-morphologischen Untersuchungen der Vogel im Institut für Morphologie der Tiere der Akademie der Wissenschaften von der USSR' by G. S. Schestakowa.

272.6 'Birds of the Ussuri Region' by K. A. Vorobuev, 1954.

272.7 'About spreading some birds in Georgia' by R. Zhordania, 1960.

273.1

MAGDALEN COLLEGE LIBRARY

Oxford OX1 4AV

By prior arrangement with the Librarian. Henry O. Coxe, *Catalogus Codicum MSS qui in Collegiis Aulisque Oxoniensibus hodie Adservantur* (Oxford, 1852) vol. 2.

273.1 Letters (nos. 1-3, 11-18) to Martin Joseph Routh, President of Magdalen College, include letters from William Palmer or from his father, before and during the former's visit to St Petersburg and Kronstadt, 1840-3, in connection with the proposal for the union of the Anglican and Russian Orthodox Churches (**Magdalen College MS 485**).

274.1-3

MERTON COLLEGE LIBRARY

Oxford OX1 4JD

Access by arrangement with the Librarian. Henry O. Coxe, *Catalogus Codicum MSS qui in Collegiis Aulisque Oxoniensibus hodie Adservantur* (Oxford, 1852) vol. 1.

274.1 Letter from Prince C. Lieven, Russian Ambassador, re a gift of a vase to the College by Alexander I after his visit to Oxford in 1814 to receive an honorary degree (**E.1.21**).

274.2 Russian passport, 19th century (**E.1.32**).

274.3 3 boxes of letters by James Harris (1746-1820), 1st Earl of Malmesbury, from St Petersburg during the time of his embassy, 1777-83, mainly French (**F.3.3.**).

275.1-2

MUSEUM OF THE HISTORY OF SCIENCE

University of Oxford, Old Ashmolean Building, Broad Street, Oxford OX1 3AZ

By appointment.

275.1 Letter from James Donn to Dr Fischer at Count Razumovskii's residence in Moscow, 1808, re seeds sent from Russia (**MS Gunther 16, item 16**).

275.2 'A Treatise on Cholera containing the authors experience of the epidemic known by that name, as it prevailed in the city of Moscow in autumn 1830 & winter 1831 ...' by Professor James Keir, Moscow, 1831 (published in Edinburgh, 1832) (**MS Museum 99**).

276.1-3
NEW COLLEGE LIBRARY
Oxford OX1 3BN

Henry O. Coxe, *Catalogus Codicum MSS qui in Collegiis Aulisque Oxoniensibus hodie Adservantur* (Oxford, 1852) vol. 1; F. W. Steer, *The Archives of New College, Oxford* (Oxford, 1974).

276.1 MILNER PAPERS (9,127)
Papers of Alfred, Visc. Milner, (1854-1925) include a photograph of a group of military figures including the Tsar, n.d.

276.2 SMITH PAPERS (9,242)
Papers of Alic Halford Smith (1883-1958), Vice-Chancellor of the University of Oxford, 1954-7, include papers re his visit to Moscow as a member of the University delegation, 1956.

276.3 Photographs of a visit to New College by Bulganin and Khrushchev in 1956 (**14,531; 14,470**).

277.1-9
NUFFIELD COLLEGE LIBRARY
Oxford OX1 1NF

Apply to Librarian for access; letters of introduction are required. Lists produced by the National Register of Archives for Cherwell, Emmott, Fabian and Seely collections; rough handlists for other collections.

277.1 CHERWELL, Frederick Alexander Lindemann, Visc. Cherwell of Oxford (1886-1957)
Papers include: letter from P. L. Kapitsa, 1933 (**E.108**); report on Soviet tanks, July 1944 (**G.370**); notes on the Soviet Air Force, 1942, n.d. (**G.540**); correspondence and papers re the exchange of scientific information with the USSR, 1943-5 (**G.545-6**); minutes, correspondence, statistics etc, re supplies of raw materials and armaments to the USSR, 1941-5 (**H.140-3**); article 'My visit to Russia' by Mrs Clementine Churchill as Chairman of the British Red Cross Aid to Russia Fund, May 1945 (**J.61**).

277.2 CLAY, Sir Henry (1883-1954)
Articles by Clay and others, mainly re tours to the USSR in the early 1930s.

277.3 COLE, George Douglas Howard (1889-1959)
2 articles issued by the Ministry of Economic Warfare re the economic conditions in occupied Russia, 1942-3 (**B.3/3/E Box 2**).

277.4 CRIPPS, Rt Hon. Sir Richard Stafford (1889-1952)
MP; British Ambassador in Moscow, 1940-2. Speeches re the USSR and Anglo-Soviet relations, 1942-4, n.d. A large number of the Cripps papers are in the possession of Mr M. Shock who is writing a biography of Cripps. *See card index for titles of speeches.*

277.5 EMMOTT, Alfred, Lord Emmott (1858-1926)
Correspondence of Emmott with the Foreign Office as Chairman of the Committee to Collect Information on Russia, 1920-1 (**Boxes 7-8**).

277.6 THE FABIAN SOCIETY
Correspondence re translations of Tolstoi by Aylmer Maude (**A 8/2**); conference reports of the International and Commonwealth Bureau of the Society including reports on American-Soviet relations in 1947 (**J 62/1**) and Anglo-Soviet relations in 1951 (**J 63/3**). The papers have been partially indexed; several boxes of papers since 1974 are still to be sorted and listed and more will be deposited in the Library.

277.7 SEELY, John Edward Bernard, Baron Mottistone (1868-1947) (**MS Mottistone**)
War Office paper on the military situation between Russia, Austria and Montenegro, May 1913 (**20 ff. 221-31**).

277.8 TANNER, Jack (Frederick John Shirley) (1889-1965)
Trade unionist. A few papers re the Friends of Soviet Russia including the constitution, circulars etc. of the group as well as reports on national and international conferences.

277.9 13 boxes of left-wing and Trotskyist articles by various authors, 1930-54. *See list for details.*

278.1

PITT RIVERS MUSEUM, BALFOUR LIBRARY

University of Oxford, South Parks Road, Oxford OX1 3AP

Access for *bona fide* researchers on written application to the Librarian. Unpublished list of collection; full catalogue in progress.

278.1 Ethnographic photographic collection including photographs of the following: a Samoyed, 1861 (**PRM.NY.15-23**); Crimean 'types', 1862 (**PRM.NY.24-7**); Lithuanian 'types', 1864 (**PRM.NY.48-70**); Siberian peoples from the 1914 Yenisei expedition (*c.* 200 prints and negatives) (**PRM.B59/20-32, 37**); peoples of the Soviet Union, *c.* 1865-1900 (*c.* 200 photographs).

279.1-2

THE QUEEN'S COLLEGE LIBRARY

Oxford OX1 4AU

By appointment; apply to Librarian. Henry O. Coxe, *Catalogus Codicum MSS qui in Collegiis Aulisque Oxoniensibus hodie Adservantur* (Oxford, 1852) vol. 1; *Catalogue of MSS Acquired by the Queen's College Oxford since the Publication of H. O. Coxe's Catalogue of the Oxford College MSS.*

279.1 'Of the mission of Charles Howard, 1st Earl of Carlisle, ambassador to the Russian court', 1663 (**MS 284 f. 39**).

279.2 'A charter conveying the privilege of free trade granted by the emperor Demetrian [Dmitrii], unto the English merchants trading to Moscow', 10 Dec. 1602 (published in V. N. Aleksandrenko, 'Materialy po smutnomu vremeni na Rusi XVII v.', *Starina i novizna* 14 (1911) pp. 235-8) (**MS 384**).

280.1

RHODES HOUSE LIBRARY

South Parks Road, Oxford OX1 3RG

Researchers holding a Bodleian Library ticket may use the Library.

280.1 BRITISH AND FOREIGN ANTI-SLAVERY SOCIETY ARCHIVES (**MSS Brit. Emp. s. 22**)
2 minute-books and other papers of the British Armenia Committee, *c.* 1915-38 (**G 506**).

281.1-28

ST ANTONY'S COLLEGE

Oxford OX2 6JF

By appointment to all departments.

281.1 Main Library

281.1 FARREN PAPERS

TS copies of letters from Gen. Richard Thomas Farren to his mother covering his service in the Crimean War.

281.2-21 Middle East Centre

Published list of the holdings of the Middle East Centre (1979); more detailed handlists of some collections.

281.2 BARBOUR, Nevill
Articles on a visit to Uzbekistan, 1960, and religion in the USSR (**Box II file 1**).

281.3 BOWEN, H. C.
Part of an account in Church Slavonic of a pilgrimage to Jerusalem on behalf of the Tsar (**Box 4 (xi)**).

281.4 CLAYTON, Brig. Iltyd N.
Correspondence between Clayton and Sir Arthur Smith includes comments on Russian aims in Palestine, 1944-5 (**Box II file 1**).

281.5 CUNNINGHAM, Sir Alan
Memo on Russia and Palestine by R. Newton, Dec. 1945 (**Box IV file 3**).

281.6 DUNLOP-SMITH, Sir James
Note by A. Verrier re British attempts to come to terms with Russia, May 1968.

281.7 EDMONDS, C. J.
Reports on the Shahsevan and Shaghaghi tribes and the tribes of Azerbaijan by M. S. Hayem, 1919, report on the political situation in Caucasian Azerbaijan by Edmonds, 1919, and report on Azerbaijan by E. Bristow, 1920 **(Box VI file 5)**; notebook and tour notes in the Caspian by Edmonds, 1919 **(Box VIII file 3)**; 'The ancient languages of Azerbaijan' by W. B. Henning **(Box XVII file 6)**; correspondence and press cuttings re the possible appearance of Tsarevich Alexis in Iraq, 1965-72 **(Box XIX file 2)**.

281.8 EVERETT, Sir William
Sketch map to illustrate the probable concentration and lines of operation in the event of an occupation of Asia Minor by Russia, 1876, general map of Armenia, map of the eastern part of Turkish Armenia and Transcaucasia, 1877, sketch map of the Russo-Turkish frontier in Asia, 1878, map of Caucasia, 1855 **(Box 1 file 4)**; notes by Everett on Aleksandropol', Tiflis and Erevan **(Box 2 file 1)**; correspondence re famine relief in Armenia, 1881, and the Anglo-Russian frontier commission, 1879-83 **(Box 2 file 4)**.

281.9 FARRELL, Jerome
'Pedagogue's progress' being reminiscences of Mesopotamia, Transcaucasia and Palestine.

281.10 HAMILTON, J. A. de C.
MS and TS copies of diary of events in north-west Persia and Baku, 1918-19.

281.11 INGRAMS, William Harold
Cabinet paper on counter-measures against Soviet propaganda in the Middle East, 1947 **(Box VIII file 4)**.

281.12 JERUSALEM AND THE EAST MISSION
Correspondence re the Armenian Church, 1922-44 **(Box XX file 1)**; correspondence re the Russian Clergy and Church Aid Fund, 1935-49 **(Box XX files 3-5)**. Permission of the Secretary of the Jerusalem and the Middle East Church Association is required to consult the papers.

281.13 MONROE, Elizabeth
Translations of documents from the Russian archives on the break-up of the Ottoman Empire, 1914-15.

281.14 MORRISON, Revd M. E.
MS copy of book by his daughter on his work as a missionary in Central Asia and the Middle East, with related articles and press cuttings, 1877-1917.

281.15 PHILBY, H. St J.
Notes and views on the Armenian and Kurdish questions, 1919, by Sir A. Hirtzel and Sir A. T. Wilson **(Box VI file 4)**; letter re the economic position in Saudi Arabia and possibilities for trade with the USSR, 31 May 1946 **(Box XXXII file 4)**.

281.16 PRICE, Morgan Philips
Memo sent to the Russian Embassy and the Foreign Office re the Russian presence in Iran, 1946 **(Box 2 file 1)**; articles, correspondence and press cuttings re Armenia, 1963-70 **(Box 8 file 1)**; articles, book reviews, maps and press cuttings re the USSR, 1949-71 **(Box 8 file 2)**; articles, correspondence and press cuttings re Kazakhstan, 1952-67 **(Box 8 file 3)**; 'Turkic

languages of the USSR' by G. K. Dulling, anon., 'A note on the history of the Turco-Caucasian border', and 'Georgia and Turkey - the historical background' by O. N. Kazara (**Box 8 file 4**).

281.17 RAPP, Sir Thomas
Unpublished memoirs covering his service in the Canal Zone, Arabia, Morocco and Persia, 1920-52, including some details of the wartime supply route to Russia and the Kurdish Republic of Mahabad.

281.18 ROSS, Henry
Letters from Samsoon, 1855-6, include references to the Crimea.

281.19 SYKES, Sir Percy M.
Letter from Allenby (? Edmund Henry Hynman, 1st Visc. Allenby) re a Soviet attempt to involve him in embroiling Japan with Britain, 1934; letter from V. Minorskii re 'Peter the Great's will', 1945; miscellaneous writings on British and Russian relations and policy in Persia.

281.20 TWEEDY, Owen
Diaries, 1926-52, include references to Russia in the diary for 1928.

281.21 WHEELER, Col. Geoffrey
Article on orientalists in the USSR, 1960.

281.22-28 Russian Centre

The following papers are stored in a metal cupboard in the Russian Centre office.

281.22 CONFERENCE PAPERS
Papers given at conferences on 'Changes in Soviet Society', n.d., and 'Soviet Literature 1917-1962', 1962; *Seminar notes* from the Harvard University Russian Research Centre, 1964-5, 1971-2; 'The Economic Burden of Soviet Involvement in the Middle East' by Gur Ofer.

281.23 MAX HAYWARD PAPERS
MSS of publications by various authors (**M.A.**); press cuttings re dissidents and the defection of Svetlana Allilueva (**M.B.**); correspondence with Ivy Litvinov (née Moss) and material for her autobiography (**M.C.**); tapes (**M.D.**).

281.24 HUNGARY 1956
UN Security Council verbatim reports, General Assembly reports and resolutions, background information from Radio Free Europe and Hungarian and Soviet commentaries (**H.A.**); press cuttings (**H.B.**); press and Radio Free Europe documents (**H.C.**).

281.25 GEORGE KATKOV PAPERS
Papers on trials in the USSR; offprints and miscellaneous papers; Radio Liberty transcripts, *Vospominaniya o Revolyutsii 1917 goda*.

281.26 MS copy of TS held in Columbia University Russian Archive of *Antonovshchina (Iz vospominanii Antonovtsa)* by Mikhail Lidin (M. Fomichev).

281.27 MS 'Arest-obysk' re workings of the Soviet Secret Police.

281.28 Press cuttings re Czechoslovakia, 1968.

282.1-2
ST JOHN'S COLLEGE LIBRARY

Oxford OX1 3JP

By appointment; apply in writing to the Librarian. H. O. Coxe, *Catalogus Codicum MSS qui in Collegiis Aulisque Oxoniensibus hodie Adservantur* (Oxford, 1852), vol. 2; H. M. Colvin, *Summary Catalogue of Manuscripts 213-310 being a Supplement to Coxe's Catalogue of 1852* (1956); *Supplementary List of Manuscripts Acquired or Listed since 1956*; *Manuscripts Acquired or Listed since 1979* (1981).

282.1 Letter from Tsar Michael to Charles I, 4 Mar. 1631 (printed in S. Konovalov, 'Twenty Russian Royal Letters (1626-34)' *Oxford Slavonic Papers* 8 (Oxford, 1958) pp. 117-56) **(MS St John's 253 f. 9)**.

282.2 TS 'Forty two days in the Soviet Union' by John Parker, 1945 **(MS St John's 332)**. Access restricted; apply to Librarian.

283.1-16
SOCIETY FOR CENTRAL ASIAN STUDIES

19a Paradise Street, Oxford OX1 1LD. Postal address: PO Box 131, Oxford OX1 2NJ

Access to *bona fide* researchers by written appointment. The Library also holds some theses relating to Central Asia and TS translations of German and Soviet articles on Central Asia.

283.1 TS bibliographies of books re Central Asia by several authors.

283.2 Anon., TS 'Handbook of Tajikistan', n.d.

283.3 Anon., TS 'Journey to Siberia and the Pacific', n.d.

283.4 Anon., TS 'Memorandum on the Peoples of the Caucasus with special reference to the Tribes of Dagistan and an Excursus on Communism and Philology', n.d. *post* 1949.

283.5 Anon., TS 'Moscow School (Internat) No. 11', 1962.

283.6 Anon., TS notes on visit to Central Asia, 1968.

283.7 Anon., TS 'Notes on Visit to Kazakhstan and Uzbekistan', 11-18 July 1962.

283.8 Anon., TS 'A Visit to Central Asia, 1964'.

283.9 Anon., 'A Visit to Yakutsk and Verkhoyansk'.

283.10 TS 'Caucasia : Notes on Political and Economic History, 1920-39' by W. Allen.

283.11 TS 'The Türkmen Tent', by P. and M. Andrews, n.d.

283.12 TS chapter 3 of 'Service in Western Siberia, 1859-75' by I. F. Babkov.

283.13 TS 'Afghanistan between East and West' by Peter G. Franck, 1958.

283.14 TS 'Notes made during a Mission of the International Institute for Educational Planning to the USSR' by M. C. Kaser, 1965.

283.15 TS 'Iran in World War I' by Lev Ivanovich Miroshnikov, being 3 lectures given at the Russian Research Center and Center for Middle Eastern Studies, 1962.

283.16 TS 'Notes on Caucasian Turkish and the Turkoman Dialect' by Capt. M. P. O'C Tandy.

284.1-8
TAYLOR INSTITUTION LIBRAY

Slavonic and Modern Greek Department, 47 Wellington Square, Oxford OX1 2JF

By appointment. *Catalogue of Autograph Material Acquired by the Library During the Years 1950-1970.*

284.1 AUTY, R. (1914-78)
Professor of Comparative Slavonic Philology at the University of Oxford. Unsorted collection of *c.* 30 boxes of correspondence, papers and MS copies of published works.

284.2 FORBES, Nevill (1883-1929)
Professor of Russian at the University of Oxford. Unsorted collection comprising mainly books but also administrative papers on university matters and examination papers.

284.3 MORFILL COLLECTION (**Morf.**)
Collection of W. R. Morfill includes Russian MS, presumed in Morfill's hand (**DK4.C4(1880,3)**), and MS of 4 lines of verse, presumed a transl. of a Ukrainian poem (**PG 3972.V6.Ed.1.**).

284.4 PENNINGTON, Anne (1934-81)
Professor of Comparative Slavonic Philology at the University of Oxford. Unsorted collection of *c.* 12 boxes of correspondence, papers and MS copies of published works.

284.5 2 postcards from St Petersburg to Kapellmeister Fielder in Hamburg, 23, 26 Jan. 1898 (**C.A.CUI**).

284.6 Photostats of Pushkin texts which appeared in *Moskovskii vestnik* I-XII with notes by Valentine Glasberg.

284.7 MS list of Russian literature translated into Welsh by T. Hudson-Williams, 1950.

284.8 Note from F. P. Marchmont to H. Krebs at the Taylor Institution re Russian teaching matters.

UNIVERSITY COLLEGE

Oxford OX1 4BH

University College manuscripts are on deposit at the Bodleian Library and may be consulted there (*See*, Bodleian Library, *269.103*).

285.1-16
THE BLACK WATCH MUSEUM

Regimental Headquarters, Balhousie Castle, Hay Street, Perth PH1 5HR

By written appointment.

285.1 'Orders for the Valley Guard' issued by the Highland Bde in the Crimea, 13 May 1855 (**530**).

285.2 TS copies of diaries including 'Account of the Royal Highlanders at Alma' by Sgt McSally, 1854 (**640**).

285.3 Account of the Crimean War and the Indian Mutiny by J. Bryson, 1848-61 (**1026**).

285.4 TS copy of diary of Pte David McAusland, 42nd Regt, containing an account of the Regt's activities in the Crimean War and the Indian Mutiny, 1848-60 (**1026**).

285.5 Memoirs of the Crimea by Charles Dunsmore Wilson, *c.* 1855 (**1026**); 'An account of the 42nd Regiment's operations in the Crimea' probably written by Wilson (**File H-5. Section C**).

285.6 Copy diary of Sgt George Rankin, 42nd Regt, covering his service in the Crimean War (**1051/ii**).

285.7 Regimental order book of the 42nd Regt, 1854-60 (**2270**).

285.8 Vol. of photographs, letters, invitations, newspaper cuttings etc., 1900-35, belonging to C. B. Henderson who served in South Africa, India, Scotland, France, Mesopotamia, Palestine and Russia (**2376/4**).

285.9 Diary of Capt. T. H. Montgomery, 42nd Royal Highlanders, comprising copy letters re the Crimean campaign, 1854 (**2384**).

285.10 'My Military Life', being the memoirs of Lt (later Capt.) Sir P. A. Halkett, re mainly the participation of the Black Watch in the Crimean campaign (**3234/1**); sketchbook of Halkett including sketches of the Crimea, 1854 (**3635**).

285.11 Letter from Hector John McDonald to Harvey including references to the battle of the Alma, written 1895 (**File H-4. Section M**).

285.12 TS copy 'The Royal Highlanders at Alma, by one of then', n.d. and photograph of the Black Watch piper who took part in the battle (**File H-5. Section A**).

285.13 Letters from Lt Joseph Charles Ross Grove, 42nd Regt, to his parents from the Crimea, 1854-5 (**File H-5. Sections G-H**).

285.14 Reproductions of photographs of Sebastopol, *c.* 1855 (**File H-6. Sections V-W**).

285.15 Papers of Maj. Charles C. Graham (Graham Stirling of Craigbarnet) include diary kept in the Crimean War and letters to Mrs A. G. Stirling describing military life in the Crimea.

285.16 TS list of men, with brief biographies, who joined the 42nd from the 92nd Depot Companies to make up numbers for the Crimea, 1973.

286.1

DEVON RECORD OFFICE, WEST DEVON AREA

Unit 3 Clare Place, Coxside, Plymouth PL4 0JW

286.1 Diary of Capt. Stephen Chapman, 20th Regt, covering his service in the Crimean War, 1854-5 (**94/190**).

287.1

THE KING'S OWN YORKSHIRE LIGHT INFANTRY MUSEUM

Wakefield Road, Pontefract, West Yorkshire WF8 4ES

By appointment.

287.1 Album of photographs including photograph of a Russian naval machine gun team at a guard post during the 1912 Chinese rebellion in Hankow (**L50/641**).

288.1-18

ROYAL NAVAL MUSEUM

Library and Archives, HM Naval Base, Portsmouth, Hampshire PO1 3LR

By appointment.

Crimean War material

288.1 Notes from the log of HMS *Terrible* during the Crimean War compiled by Valentine Rickord, clerk, 1854-5, and pass to the French trenches issued to Rickord, 14 Dec. 1855 (**RNM 135/56**).

288.2 Engravings taken from the *Illustrated London News*, 1855-6 (**RNM 155/56**).

288.3 Correspondence, printed by order of the House of Commons, of Vice-Adm. D. Dundas re the Russian firing on a Flag of Truce, the blockade of the Sea of Azov and the bombardment of Odessa, 1855 (**RNM 173/82; 1021/81**).

288.4 Holograph notes re arrangements for the disembarkation of troops in the Crimea under the orders of Rear-Adm. E. Lyons (**RNM 195/83**).

288.5 Sketch map of the bombardment of Bomarsund, 16 Aug. 1854 (**RNM 243/56**).

288.6 Letter from Ernest Cochrane serving in HMS *Edinburgh* off Helsingfors, 2 July 1855 (**RNM 291/84(16)**).

288.7 TS extract from the diary of Paymaster H. F. Pullen describing the explosion of a Russian 'Infernal Machine' on board HMS *Exmouth*, 21 June 1855 (**RNM 510/81**).

288.8 Journals kept by F. C. Corbet, Master's Assistant, while serving in HMS *Gladiator* and in HMS *Apollo* in the Black Sea, 1853-7 (**RNM JB8 60/78; JB9 61/78**).

Twentieth-century material

288.9 Service pass, Archangel, and treasury bill for 50 roubles, payable 15 Feb. 1919 (**RNM 87/79**).

288.10 10 rouble note issued to G. Jones, 1919 (**RNM 282/81**).

288.11 Account by R. M. Edmonds of the journey of HMS *Jupiter* to Archangel in Feb. 1915 (**RNM 461/76**).

288.12 Annotated map of Caucasia showing British assistance in operations against the Bolsheviks, 1918-19 (**RNM 715/82**).

288.13 Photograph of illustrated address of thanks issued to HMS *Kent* for assistance to Russia in the Far East, 1919 (**RNM 718/81**).

288.14 Printed letter of appreciation addressed to the officers and sailors of the British Navy by Lt-Gen Borovskii, May 1919 (**RNM 731/81**).

288.15 Photograph album of Japan compiled by James Somerville while serving in HMS *Sutlej*, 1905, and Japanese postcards commemorating the war with Russia (**RNM B25 119/81**).

288.16 Photograph album of China, 1905-6, including photographs of the aftermath of the Russo-Japanese War (**RNM B53 273/81**).

288.17 Journal kept by Midshipman G. E. Sutcliffe on HMS *Leviathan* while shadowing the Russian Baltic Fleet, 4 Nov. 1904 (**RNM JC36 36/80(b)**).

288.18 Journal kept by Midshipman A. M. Pilling while serving in HMS *Benbow* and HMS *Montrose* in the Black Sea, Nov. 1919 - Nov. 1920 (**RNM JD33 1283/83**).

289.1-9

LANCASHIRE RECORD OFFICE

Bow Lane, Preston, Lancashire PR1 8ND

289.1 ASHWORTH, George (DDX 1237)
Papers include Ashworth's diary, Russian vocabulary notebook and photographs when based in Vladivostok with the Allied intervention forces, 1918-19 (/3/7, 4/12-13, 4/17).

289.2 ATHERTON BROS LTD, PRESTON (DDAt)
Textile machinery manufacturers. 7 foreign letter-books re overseas orders, 1900-30, including Russian orders (/3/1-7).

289.3 BRYAN BLUNDELL MSS (DDBb)
Journal of 3 voyages of the *Cleveland* between Liverpool and Archangel, 1709, 1711, 1713 (/8/4).

289.4 GARNETT, William J. (DDQ)
Letters while Secretary of the British Embassy in St Petersburg, 1903-11, including: descriptions of a tour in the Crimea, 1903, and journey from Peking to Moscow, 1908; miscellaneous letters from Russia addressed to Garnett; the loyal address to George V from the English residents in St Petersburg, 1910. The collection is uncatalogued but temporary box numbers are 28, 64, 69, 80-1.

289.5 SIR CUTHBERT GRUNDY PAPERS (DDX 207)
Letter from L. Lardner to Richard Cook mentioning the church at Riga, 15 Aug. 1766 (/62(3)).

289.6 PARKER OF BROWSHOLME COLLECTION (DDB)
Anon. journal and draft letters describing a tour of Europe including Russia, with sketches, n.d., *c.* 1800 (/74/42).

289.7 PLATT-SACO-LOWELL COLLECTION (DDPSL)
Textile manufacturers of Hemshore, Accrington, Bolton and Oldham. References to Russia and the USSR may be found in Foreign Books and correspondence files from the late 19th century and under the names of the original firms which amalgamated to form Platt-Saco-Lowell as follows: Platt Brothers and Co. Ltd of Oldham : agreement re erection work in the USSR, July 1933 (/1/106/70); Dobson and Barlow Ltd of Bolton : references to Russia in contract summary books, 1881-1941 (/2/3/10, 15, 17-21), and circulars re orders for polyester fibre plant, 1967 (/2/38/23); Howard and Bullough Ltd of Accrington : overseas order books, 1871-1920 (/3/4/1-2), file on Russian delegation visit to the firm, 1961 (/3/38/68); Tweedales and Smalley Ltd of Castleton : Russian orders and prices book, 1893-1938 (/5/2/22); Platt International : box of papers re visit to Russia and Russian collaboration, 1905-73 (/14/12/35) and box of correspondence from and re the USSR, 1970-3 (/14/12/41). Permission is required to consult records under 40 years old.

289.8 TURNER AND SMITH OF PRESTON, SOLICITORS (DDTs)
Log of voyage of the *Anne Shepherd* between Liverpool and St Petersburg, 1862 (temp. box no. 15).

289.9 Letter from Lt E. M. Alderson from Sebastopol to Charles W. Swainson, 24 Aug. 1855 (DDX 230/1).

290.1-2

REGIMENTAL MUSEUM OF THE QUEEN'S LANCASHIRE REGIMENT

Regimental Headquarters, Fulwood Barracks, Preston, Lancashire PR2 4AA

By appointment.

290.1 136 letters from Gen. Richard T. Farren, 47th Lancashire Regt of Foot, to his mother from the Crimea, 20 Mar. 1851 - 1 Dec. 1856.

290.2 36 lithographs of the Crimea during the War.

291.1-13

BBC WRITTEN ARCHIVES CENTRE

Caversham Park, Reading, Berkshire RG4 8TZ

By appointment only. Government papers are subject to the 30 year rule; staff papers are closed for 70 years. Other papers, unless stated, are open until 1962 but not all papers since 1954 have yet been transferred to the Centre. The Centre also holds a collection of press cuttings, which is indexed, and scripts of broadcasts relating to the USSR, some of which have been reprinted in *The Listener*. Broadcast scripts are available mainly on microfilm. The material listed below consists mainly of memoranda, reports and correspondence and is listed by file titles within the original file sections. Additional material relating to the USSR may be found in the Contributors section. All copies are subject to copyright restrictions.

Overseas (E)

291.1 COUNTRIES (E1)
USSR: Anglo-Soviet programmes, 1945-6 (*/1261*); BBC monitoring reports, 1950-1 (*/1262*); British embassy, Moscow, 1954 (*/1263*); broadcasting in the USSR, 1936-52 (*/1264*); broadcasting in the USSR, 1941-54 (*/1265*); exchange of programmes and material, 1939-45 (*/1266*); John Fisher, 1942-4 (*/1267*); Foreign Office, 1951-4 (*/1268*); magazine programme, 1942 (*/1269*); material for use in programmes, 1941-3 (*/1270*); Moscow News Talks, schedule of transmissions, 1944 (*/1271*); Moscow Telecommunications Conference, 1946-7 (*/1272*); news, 1941-5 (*/1273*); Radio Centre, Moscow, 1945-53 (*/1274*); reception, 1941-6 (*/1275*); Russian broadcasts, 1948-54 (*/1276*); Russian intercepts, 1940-41 (*/1277*); Russian material for BBC programmes, 1943-5 (*/1278*); Russian propaganda, 1930-31 (*/1279*); Russian Service, 1945-54 (*/1280*); policy, 1939-44 (*/1281*); Soviet intake reports, 1946 (*/1282*); Soviet Union, general, 1941-54 (*/1283*); television, 1947-51 (*/1284*); visits, 1936-54 (*/1285*).

291.2 FOREIGN GENERAL (E2)
Anglo-Soviet co-operation, 1950-57 (*/33*); Armenian, 1942 (*/42*); counter propaganda to USSR satellites, 1949-56 (*/119*); Soviet war news, 1943-5 (*/298*); Russia: listening conditions and jamming, 1950-54 (*/525*); Leonard Schapiro, 1952-3 (*/531*); Ukrainian broadcasts, 1949-54 (*/560*).

291.3 AUDIENCE RESEARCH (**E3**)
USSR, 1947-53 (**/32**); USSR, 1946-8 (**/106/1-4**); Estonia, 1953-4 (**/127**); USSR, 1952-4 (**/131**).

291.4 PUBLICITY (**E12**)
British embassy, Moscow, 1942-6 (**/61**).

291.5 TRANSCRIPTIONS (**E17**)
Russia, 1942-7 (**/183/1-6**).

291.6 TANGYE LEAN'S OFFICE (**E20**)
Red Army Day celebrations, 1942-3 (**/80**); Russia: Free Germany Committee, 1943-5 (**/82**); Russian radio, 1939-49 (**/83**).

Radio (R)

There might also be material in Board of Governers minutes, 1927-75 (**R1**) and, Board of Management minutes (**R2**).

291.7 GOVERNMENT COMMITTEES (**R4**)
Beveridge Committee: The Soviet Idea, 1948 (**/6**).

291.8 ENTERTAINMENT (**R19**)
Russian Night, 1943 (**/1064**); Russian Revolution, 1937-8 (**/1065**).

291.9 MUSIC: GENERAL (**R27**)
Red Army Day, 1943-5 (**/441**); Russian music, 1941-3 (**/449**); Russian musicians, 1946-7 (**/450**); Stalin's Birthday Concert, 1941-2 (**/488**).

291.10 NEWS (**R28**)
Soviet view, 1948-54 (**/254**).

291.11 POLICY (**R34**)
Anniversary of the Nazi-Soviet pact, 1949 (**/222**); communism, 1940-55 (**/313**); broadcasts to the forces, Russia, 1942-3 (**/387**); Russia: Anglo-Soviet organizations, 1941-7 (**/866**); Bulganin/Khrushchev visit, 1956 (**/1000**).

291.12 TALKS (**R51**)
Language talks: Russian lessons, 1942-6 (**/292**). Russia, 1929-54 (**/520/1-2**).

Television (T)

291.13 COUNTRIES (**T8**)
Moscow radio and television, 1946-54 (**/55**); Russian embassy, 1952 (**/56**); Soviet contacts (lists), 1954 (**/57**); Soviet delegation, 1954 (**/58**); television development, 1954 (**/59**); Russia A-Z (**/60**).

292.1-4
BERKSHIRE RECORD OFFICE

Shire Hall, Shinfield Park, Reading, Berkshire RG2 9XD

292.1 DUNDAS FAMILY PAPERS (D/EDd)
4 letters to *The Times* re Adm. James Whitely Dundas and his conduct as C.-in-C. of the Black Sea Squadron, 1854 (**F6**).

292.2 EWEN PAPERS (D/EE)
Letters from Arthur J. A. Ewen, including some from the Crimea (**C2/1-27, C4**).

292.3 PLEYDELL-BOUVERIE PAPERS (D/EPb)
Character studies of notables to whom W. Pleydell-Bouverie, Earl of Radnor, was presented on a tour of Russia, 1797-8 (**F29**).

292.4 VAN DE WEYER PAPERS (D/EB 1089 VdW)
Correspondence on the Grand Russian Railway Co, 1864-8 (**F6 (1-5)**).

293.1-7
INSTITUTE OF AGRICULTURAL HISTORY AND MUSEUM OF ENGLISH RURAL LIFE

PO Box 229, University of Reading, Whiteknights, Reading, Berkshire RG6 2AG

By appointment. The holdings of the Library, Archive and Photographic collection are listed in the *Guide* to the Institute; farm business records are described in a summary catalogue, *Historical Farm Records*.

293.1 CLAYTON & SHUTTLEWORTH LTD
Agricultural steam engineers of Lincoln. Registers of engine and thrashing machines include references to Russia under the name of the agent or importer.

293.2 JOHN FOWLER & CO. (LEEDS) LTD
Agricultural steam engineers whose Russian business was conducted via an agency in Kiev. Power of attorney to Ladislas de Klupffel in St Petersburg, 1873; papers of the Baku-Batoum Pipe Line Syndicate Ltd, 1886-9; 2 advertising leaflets in Russian for gyrotillers, 1929, 1932; engine registers including references to Russia usually under name of agent or importer.

293.3 HUNTER, Herbert (1882-1959)
Agricultural scientist. Papers re the proposed appointment of Hunter as Agricultural Attaché at the British Embassy in Moscow, 1942-4 (**6**); correspondence with N. I. Vavilov re Hunter's proposed visit to the USSR, Sept. 1939 (**28**); TS transl. of 'On the Genetic Nature of Winter and Spring Varieties of Plants' by N. I. Vavilov and E. S. Kuznetsov, 1926 (**34**).

293.4 MARSHALL, SONS & CO. LTD
Agricultural steam engineers of Gainsborough. Agency books, 1870s-1910s, comprise summaries of worldwide agency agreements including Russian agencies in St Petersburg,

Rostov, Omsk, Minsk and Riga; engine registers including references to Russia usually under name of agent or importer.

293.5 NALDER & NALDER LTD

Agricultural engineers of Wantage. Correspondence with agents in Odessa, late 19th and early 20th centuries; thrashing machine and screen registers including references to Russia usually under name of agent or importer.

293.6 THE NITRATE CORPORATION OF CHILE LTD

File of papers concerning the marketing and promotion of and experiments with agricultural fertilizers, chiefly nitrates, in Russia, 1895-1917.

293.7 RANSOMES, SIMS & JEFFERIES LTD

Agricultural engineers of Ipswich. Russian agency book, 1861-86, covering agencies in Beltz (?Bel'tsy), Khar'kov, St Petersburg, Samara, Saratov and Taganrog and comprising historical notes, details of agreements, sales and quantity of goods sent; vol. of financial statements for the Odessa branch, 1892-1919; advertising and technical literature in Russian, 1860s-1910s; show certificates from various Russian towns; engine registers including references to Russia usually under the name of agents or importer; unpublished history of the firm, written 1928-30, including information on Russian business.

294.1-11

READING UNIVERSITY LIBRARY

Department of Archives, Manuscripts amd Rare Books, Whiteknights, Reading, Berkshire RG6 2AE

By appointment. J. A. Edwards, *A Brief Guide to Archives and Manuscripts in the Library, University of Reading* (Reading, 1983).

Modern political papers

294.1 ASTOR, Nancy, Visc. Astor (1879-1964) (MS 1416)

MP. Papers include files on Russia among her political and parliamentary papers, 1926-37, and on communism, 1924-7.

294.2 ASTOR, Waldorf, 2nd Visc. Astor (1879-1952) (MS 1066)

MP. File on Russia, 1930-1 (*/1/781*) and communism, 1931-2 (*/1/782*).

294.3 KLEIN, Viola (1908-73) (MS 1215)

Sociologist. Papers include notes on marriage and the family in the USSR, 1950 (*/10/1*).

294.4 ROBERT HARBOROUGH SHERARD (MS 1047)

Writer. Correspondence includes letters to Sherard from Serge Cheremetiev (Sergei Sheremet'ev), 1934, 1937.

294.5 SIR ALFRED WOOD COLLECTION (MS 1087)

Correspondence with Fen Fibre Co. re Russian hemp seed, 1917-20 (**D/20:2/8**).

Records of British publishers

The collections of several publishers have not yet been catalogued, including Routledge and Kegan Paul Ltd (**MS 1489**) and Secker and Warburg Ltd (**MS 1090**), and may contain references to Russian and Soviet authors and publications.

294.6 GEORGE BELL AND SONS LTD (**MS 1640**)
Correspondence with A. L. Pasternak, 1972-3 (**4498, 4546**) and V. V. Nabokov, 1926 (**5160**) and re publication by A. P. Sokol'skii, 1967-9 (**4619**).

294.7 BODLEY HEAD (**MS 2606**)
Contracts include with N. S. Leskov (**Box 9**), L. Trotskii (**Box 14**), Yu. N. Tynyanov (**Box 14**) and L. Leonov (**L2**); correspondence re publications by A. I. Solzhenitsyn (**692-3, 795-6, 856-9, 1210-15**), A. P. Chekhov (**842**), M. Sholokov (**1383-5**), A. Zinov'ev (**1576-8**) and others. Permission of the publisher must be sought by prospective users.

294.8 JONATHAN CAPE LTD (**MS 2446**)
Book files on publications by V. V. Mayakovskii, V. P. Nekrasov, E. P. Zamyatin and Yu. Zhukov; correspondence re publications by M. Gor'kii, L. N. Tolstoi and E. A. Yevtushenko, V. V. Nabokov and others. Permission of the publisher must be sought by prospective users.

294.9 CHATTO AND WINDUS, HOGARTH PRESS (**MS 2444**)
Hogarth & Chatto records include author and book files on A. P. Chekhov and I. S. Turgenev. Hogarth Press records include correspondence re the publication of works by I. A. Bunin, A. P. Chekhov, F. M. Dostoevskii, M. Gor'kii and L. N. Tolstoi. Permission of the publisher must be sought by prospective users.

294.10 LONGMAN ARCHIVES (**MS 1393**)
Notebook kept by C. S. S. Higham during a visit to the Baltic States, 1934 (**II.148/56**). Collection of contracts may include contracts with Soviet authors.

294.11 MACMILLAN AND COMPANY LTD (**MS 1089**)
Card index of in-letters includes Russo-Manchurian Bank Trade Co., 1929 (**127/43**) and A. N. Tolstoi, 1934 (**154/53**) and there may be further references to Russian correspondents.

PUBLIC RECORD OFFICE

Ruskin Avenue, Kew, Richmond, Surrey TW9 4DU

See entry for the Public Record Office, London.

295.1-15
ROYAL BOTANIC GARDENS ARCHIVES

Kew, Richmond, Surrey TW9 3AB

Access by written application to the Archivist; there are limited research facilities. See description of the library and archives in *Natural History Manuscript Resources in the British Isles* edited by G. D. R. Bridson *et al.*, (London, New York, 1980) pp. 242-61. There are name indexes on cards for correspondence and miscellaneous reports. H. Hooker, *Letters to Sir W. J. Hooker*, 2 vols, gives references to letters to Hooker in the Directors' Correspondence.

Directors' Correspondence

Bound volumes of original letters to directors arranged geographically by the country or area referred to in the letter or from which the letters were sent. Letters relating to Russia may be found in any volume but are particularly likely to be found in the following series of volumes:

295.1 CHINESE AND JAPANESE LETTERS
Letter to the director from S. G. R. Littledale re plants in Mongolia and Siberia, 1898 (**vol. 151 f. 821**). There may be further references to Russia in the letters of other correspondents.

295.2 CHINESE, JAPANESE AND SIBERIAN LETTERS
Letters to the director concerning Siberia including from the following: Miss Close re her collection of Siberian plants, 1908-9 (**ff. 308-9**); P. Krylow (Krylov), Tomsk, 1906 (**f. 310**); W. R. Price re Siberian travels, 1911 (**ff. 314-16**); J. Williams re Siberian travels, 1911 (**ff. 319-26**); S. G. R. Littledale re his Siberian collections, 1901-2 (**ff. 171-3**). There may be further references to Russia in the letters of other correspondents.

295.3 EAST INDIA, CHINA, MAURITIUS LETTERS
Letters to W. J. Hooker from C. Cocks, Sebastopol, 1856 (**vol. 55 f. 67**). There may be further references to Russia in the letters of other correspondents.

295.4 FRENCH, DUTCH LETTERS
Letters to W. J. Hooker from A. Richter, Moscow, 1844 (**vol. 47 f. 381**). There may be further references to Russia in the letters of other correspondents.

295.5 GERMAN LETTERS
Letters to W. J. Hooker from: N. Amenkople, Moscow, 1857 (**vol. 48 f. 165**); H. Bunge, Dorpat, 1836-59 (**vol. 48 ff. 171-5; vol. 50 ff. 26-9; vol. 51 ff. 46-9**); H. W. Crowe, Helsingfors, 1857-8 (**vol. 48 ff. 185-7**); A. de Berg, St Petersburg, 1856 (**vol. 48 ff. 266-7**); E. L. Regel, St Petersburg, 1857-60 (**vol. 48 ff. 312-9**); W. Besser, Kiev etc., 1828-37 (**vol. 49 ff. 5-18, 264**); F. E. L. Fischer, St Petersburg, 1828-53 (**vol. 49 ff. 39-55; vol. 50 ff. 30-54; vol. 51 ff. 104-59**); Prof. C. F. Ledebour, Dorpat, 1828-35 (**vol. 49 ff. 152-63; vol. 50 ff. 185-8**); H. G. Bongard, St Petersburg, 1835-8 (**vol. 50 ff. 13-16; vol. 51 ff. 20-3**); J. H. Brandt, St Petersburg, 1837 (**vol. 50 f. 25**); G. S. Karelin, St Petersburg, 1838 (**vol. 50 f. 176**); G. von Liphert, Dorpat, 1851 (**vol. 51 f. 351**); C. Meyer, St Petersburg, 1836-53 (**vol. 51 ff. 374-7**); I. Renard, Moscow, 1841 (**vol. 51 f. 409**). There may be further references to Russia in the letters of other correspondents.

295.6 MISCELLANEOUS FOREIGN LETTERS

Letters to W. J. Hooker from F. E. L. Fischer, St Petersburg, 1824-7 (**vol. 43 ff. 42, 68, 118-20, 136, 178-84**); and Prof. C. F. Ledebour, Dorpat, 1827 (**vol. 43 f. 129**). There may be further references to Russia in the letters of other correspondents.

295.7-10 NORTH EUROPEAN LETTERS

This is the main series of Directors' Correspondence in which letters from and concerning Russia can be found.

295.7 NORTH EUROPEAN LETTERS, 1845-1900 A-G (**vol. 135**)

Letters to directors including from the following: Henry Wemyss Feilden re expedition to Novaya Zemlya, 1845-1900 (**ff. 97-9**); A. F. Batalin, St Petersburg, 1892-6 (**ff. 128-36**); A. Becker, Sarepta, 1889 (**f. 140**); A. de Berg, Consul-General for Russia in London, 1868-74 (**ff. 145-52**); E. Bretschneider, St Petersburg, 1883-9 (**ff. 264-73**); V. F. Brotherus, Helsingfors, 1890-9 (**ff. 289-304**); A. von Bunge, Dorpat and Revel, 1860-6 (**ff. 307-19**); A. Fischer de Waldheim, St Petersburg, 1897-1900 (**ff. 644-8**). There will be further references to Russia in the letters of correspondents writing from outside Russia.

295.8 NORTH EUROPEAN LETTERS, 1845-1900 H-M (**vol. 136**)

Letters to directors including from the following: F. Kamienski (Kamenskii), Odessa, 1889 (**f. 950**); N. Kauffengauz, Moscow, 1870 (**f. 952**); V. Kiela, Kazan', 1880 (**f. 959**); S. O. Lindberg, Helsingfors, 1866-84 (**ff. 1019-1045**); S. G. R. Littledale re expedition to Kamchatka, 1900-1 (**ff. 1086-7**); H. C. Marval, St Petersburg, 1893-4 (**ff. 1118-21**); Charles Maximowicz (K. I. Maksimovich), St Petersburg, 1865-90 (**ff. 1122-86**). There will be further references to Russia in the letters of correspondents wrting from outside Russia.

295.9 NORTH EUROPEAN LETTERS, 1845-1900 N-Y (**vol. 137**)

Letters to directors including from the following: W. Nylander, Helsingfors, 1861-3 (**ff. 1420-5, 1431-5**); E. L. Regel, St Petersburg, 1862-91 (**ff. 1514-1646**); R. E. von Trautvetter (Trautfetter), St Petersburg, 1866-70 (**ff. 1786-92**). There will be further references to Russia in the letters of correspondents writing from outside Russia.

295.10 NORTH EUROPEAN LETTERS, 1901-1914 (**vol. 138**)

Letters to directors including from the following: G. I. Anderson re journey to Russia, 1907 (**f. 233**); A. Creswell, Kashgar, 1912-14 (**ff. 237-40**); A. Fischer de Waldheim, 1912-14 (**ff. 242-8**); O. Fedtschenko (Fedchenko), 1903, 1906 (**f. 249**); B. Fedtschenko (Fedchenko), 1905 (**f. 250**); Prof. F. Kamienski (Kamenskii), Odessa, 1908 (**f. 254**); S. G. R. Littledale re plants from the Caucasus (**f. 256**); W. Lipsky (V. I. Lipskii), St Petersburg, 1906 (**f. 257**); N. Monteverde, St Petersburg, 1913 (**f. 258**); John Palabin (I. V. Palibin), St Petersburg, 1911 (**ff. 259-60**); E. L. Regel, St Petersburg, 1902 (**f. 261**); D. Sireitschikoff (D. P. Syreishchikov), Moscow, 1910 (**f. 265**); I. Serebrianikow (?Serebryanikov), Yaroslavl', 1910-11 (**ff. 266-8**); P. Sinzov (?Sintsov), Perm', 1912 (**f. 269**); P. M. Sykes, Transcaspia (**f. 270**); G. Woronov (Voronov) (**f. 272**). There will be further references to Russia in the letters of correspondents writing from outside Russia.

Other Collections

295.11 BANKS CORRESPONDENCE

Letters to Sir Joseph Banks from the following: Sir Charles Blagden mentioning *inter alia* that Maskelyne has tested a timepiece for the Empress of Russia, 30 Sept. 1785 (**vol. 1 p. 207**); Anton Pantaleon Hove from St Petersburg, 20 Sept. 1795, and Odessa, 15 Aug. 1796 (**vol. 2 pp. 128, 147**); N. Novossiltzoff (Novosil'tsev) conveying the Tsar's thanks for

Banks' assistance in making purchases of sheep and cattle for export to Russia (**vol. 2 p. 275**). *The Banks Letters* edited by W. R. Lawson (London, 1958).

295.12 LETTERS TO I. H. BURKILL

Letter from Henry Wemyss Feilden referring to plants from the Urals and Siberia, 25 Feb. 1898 (**f. 55**). There may be further references to Russia in the letters of other correspondents.

295.13 LETTERS TO J. D. HOOKER

Letters from Henry Wemyss Feilden re plants from Novaya Zemlya and his expedition there, 1898-9 (**vol. 8 ff. 97-9**). There may be further references to Russia in the letters of other correspondents.

295.14 LINDLEY LETTERS

4 letters from J. D. Prescott to John Lindley from St Petersburg, 1823-9 (**ff. 95, 733-46**).

295.15 MISCELLANEOUS REPORTS : RUSSIA

Vol. of miscellaneous correspondence and printed matter concerning Russia, 1857-1913, divided into sections as follows: antisophia austriaca, bark bread, catalogue of plants (Finland), grass seeds, karaff, kefir, liquorice, polygonum sachalinense, St Petersburg Botanic Garden. The vol. consists mostly of consular reports from J. P. Carruthers in Taganrog, 1878, and A. Murray in Batum, and of newspaper cuttings and other printed material.

296.1-8

THE GREEN HOWARDS REGIMENTAL MUSEUM

Richmond, Yorkshire DL10 4QN

By appointment.

296.1 Copies of dispatches from war correspondents re the battle of Inkerman (**165**).

296.2 2 photographs by Roger Fenton of the Crimea (**277**).

296.3 Sketches of Russian uniforms of the Crimean War period (**349**).

296.4 Russian regimental orders found in Sebastopol after the final assault, 8 Sept. 1855 (**382**).

296.5 Booklet entitled 'Position on the Alma' including 7 sketches by Maj. E. W. B. Hamley (**402**).

296.6 TS copy of medical notes on Lt Massey after the battle of the Alma (**405**).

296.7 Photograph album inscribed 'B. L. Maddison, August 1908' including photograph of a visit of the Russian fleet to a troop ship, *c.* 1910.

296.8 Miscellaneous papers and photographs belonging to F. Neesam of the Green Howards in connection with Archangel, 1918-19 (**319**).

297.1
BRIAN O'MALLEY CENTRAL LIBRARY AND ARTS CENTRE

Walker Place, Rotherham, South Yorkshire S65 1JH

297.1 TS of autobiography 'We tread but one path', written in 1966 by T. H. James, member of the Communist Party, including an account of the 18 months he spent in the USSR.

298.1-4
CLWYD RECORD OFFICE, RUTHIN BRANCH

46 Clwyd Street, Ruthin, Clwyd LL15 1HP

298.1 GLYNDWR MSS (**DD/G**)
Correspondence and papers re a journey to Russia undertaken to establish links in the leather trade and including a survey of Russian tanneries, *c.* 1890-1910. Collection in the process of being catalogued.

298.2 LLANTYSILIO HALL MSS (**DD/LH**)
Report on a trade mission to Russia by members of the Board of Becos Traders Ltd, 1923 (**/458**).

298.3 PLAS HEATON MSS (**DD/PH**)
Coloured lithograph of panoramic view of Sebastopol, 1855 (**/372**).

298.4 Photograph album including views in the Crimea, 1919-20 (**DD/DM/222/15**).

299.1-4
ST ANDREWS UNIVERSITY LIBRARY

North Street, St Andrews, Fife KY16 9TR

299.1 FORBES, George (**MS Deposit 7 Box XI.12**)
Scientist. Account of freeing Josef Szlenker from exile in Siberia, *c.* 1873.

299.2 FRIPP, Alice (**MS DK 508.6F8**)
Diary and letters written in the Ukraine, 1886-7.

299.3 PHILP, William (**MS 36981**)
Lawyer. Recollections of a voyage to the north of Europe (Riga) in 1822.

299.4 THOMPSON, Sir D'Arcy Wentworth (**MSS 9013-29950, 40500-48539**)
Scholar. Papers include: references to Russian Behring Sea fur seal fishery, 1896-7; files of miscellaneous notes and printed matter collected on a trip to Russia in 1925; correspondence with Sir Maurice Drummond Peterson, British Ambassador to Moscow, and with academics at Soviet institutions including L. S. Berg, A. P. Dobroklonskii, G. von Doepp, D. M. Fedotov, F. F. Kavraiskii, N. M. Knipovich, A. Lebedintsev, K. A.

Mekhonoshin, N. Miller, G. Yu. Roskin, Yu. M. Schokalsky (Shokal'skii), B. N. Shvanvich, V. A. Steklov and P. Sushchinskii (**MSS 42341, 42359-60, 43793-800, 46230**).

300.1
SOCIÉTÉ JERSIAISE, LORD COUTANCHE LIBRARY

Société Jersiaise, The Museum, 9 Pier Street, St Helier, Jersey

By appointment.

300.1 Log-book entitled 'Return of troops marched in and out of Barracks...' including references to Russian troops involved in the Dutch Expedition, 1799-1800.

301.1
SALFORD ARCHIVES CENTRE

658/662 Liverpool Road, Irlam, Manchester M30 5AD

301.1 Ledger of Royles Ltd, steam appliance manufacturers of Manchester, including references to trade with S. G. Martin and Co. of Moscow, 1903, and Robert Kölbe in St Petersburg, 1905-6 (**U117/F3/2**).

302.1
NATIONAL UNION OF MINEWORKERS

St James' House, Vicar Lane, Sheffield, South Yorkshire S1 2EX

By appointment.

302.1 The Union holds documentation relating to exchange visits between the UK and the USSR involving mineworkers, including a trade union delegation from the UK to the USSR in 1947.

303.1-17
SHEFFIELD CITY LIBRARIES, ARCHIVES DIVISION

Central Library, Surrey Street, Sheffield S1 1XZ

303.1 BAGSHAWE COLLECTION (**Bag. C.**)
Correspondence with Japanese Ambassador about the Russo-Japanese War, 1905 (**778(V)**).

303.2 RECORDS OF BALFOUR DARWINS LTD (**B.D.R**)
Steel manufacturers of Sheffield. Daybooks, 1869-70, 1874-5, and European daybooks, 1879-81, 1885, 1889-90, 1899-1901, 1905-6, 1910-11, 1914-19, 1930-33, include trade to

Russia (**1-3, 24-8, 30-1, 33, 35, 37, 39**), including large consignments to the Russian Central War Industries Committee in 1916 (**37**).

303.3 CARPENTER COLLECTION (**Carpenter MSS**)
Correspondence of Carpenter with Russian and Bulgarian translators and publishers, 1901-14 (**270/152-60**); letters to Edward Carpenter including from Max Flint from Slobodka near Kovno (Kaunas), 1893-1901 (**364/1-25**), George Tchitcherine (Georgii Chicherin), A. L. Pogoskii and P. D. Ouspensky (Uspenskii) (**382/1-16**) and Prince Petr Kropotkin, 1888, 1912 (**386/26, 209**).

303.4 RECORDS OF HENRY FISHER AND CO. (**M.D.**)
Steel and file manufacturers of Sheffield. Letter-books, 1904-9, comprising letters and memos sent to Hugo Grunert, Fisher's agent in Odessa (**6675-6**); correspondence including letters from Russia re goods supplied before the Revolution, 1915-19 (**6748**).

303.5 JACKSON COLLECTION (**J.C.**)
Note that Daniel Wheeler relinquished his post under the Tsar of Russia to go to Australia as a preacher, and a poem written after his death (in 1840) (**1367/135**).

303.6 NICHOLSON PAPERS
Papers of Owen's Patent Wheel, Tire and Axle Co. Ltd of Rotherham include records re legal cases re contracts for supplying wheels and axles to companies and persons in Russia and correspondence with Messrs C. Wachter and Co. of St Petersburg, the firm's Russian agents, 1870s.

303.7 OBORNE RECORDS (**O.R.**)
Accounts of Walter Oborne (d. 1778) and Thomas Gunning as partners in the hardware trade, 1758-68, including trade with St Petersburg (**3**).

303.8 PAPERS OF JOHN OSBORN (**M.P.C.**)
MP for Sheffield. Papers re visits to the USSR as a member of the Technical Delegation from the British Steel Founders Association, 1962, the Anglo-Soviet Parliamentary Group, 1963 (**65**) (papers closed for 30 years from the date of the last entry) and the Inter-Parliamentary Union delegation, 1968, 1974 (**66**) (papers closed for 30 years).

303.9 H. SHAW (MAGNETS) RECORDS (**H.S.M.**)
The earlier daybooks from 1870 include information on magnets supplied to Moscow in the late 19th and early 20th centuries (**1-5**).

303.10 SHEFFIELD CHAMBER OF COMMERCE (**L.D.1986**)
Vol. for 1908-11 includes papers re the Russian tariff on high-speed steel (**/7**); vols for 1931-2, 1932-3 and 1944-5 include references to Soviet trade (**/16-17, 29**); vols for 1936-7 and 1939-40 include a Russian section (**/21, 24**).

303.11 RECORDS OF THE SHEFFIELD SOCIETY OF FRIENDS (**Q.R.**)
Letter requesting information for a testimony to the late Daniel Wheeler who lived in Russia, 20 Nov. 1840 (**71**).

303.12 SPEAR AND JACKSON LTD (**S.J.C.**)
Sawmakers of Sheffield. Schedules and ledger of account sheets re debts of persons and firms in Russia, 1915-30, with correspondence and forms re their claims, 1930-6 (**74**); papers, copies of correspondence and statements of accounts with Carl Pfeiffer, agent in Russia, 1913-41 (**75-6, 78, 120**); detailed consignment accounts for goods sent to Russia

and Eastern Europe, 1916-17 (**77**); invoices and correspondence re exports to the USSR, 1931-6 (**117**).

303.13 THORNCLIFFE RECORDS (**T.R.**)

Records of Newton Chambers and Co., Chapletown, include: plan and elevation of a gasometer and circular condenser to be supplied to Messrs Le Jersey and Co. of Manchester for installation at Moscow, 1859 (**613-15**); plan of part of gasworks for Messrs Le Jersey and Co. for installation at Moscow, 1870 (**638**).

303.14 WENTWORTH WOODHOUSE MUNIMENTS (**Bk; F; R; W.W.M.**

Burke papers include: 5 letters from Count S. R. Vorontsov, 1791, 1793 (**Bk. 1/2524, 2528, 2537, 2794, 2800**); MS copy of a letter from Catherine II to Elzéar-Ferdinand-François, Comte de Broglie, 22 Oct. 1791 (**Bk. 1/2566**). Papers of William T. Spencer, 4th Earl of Fitzwilliam, include: copy of letter from Catherine II to George III re Adm. C. Knowles and copy of the King's reply, 11 Mar. 1774 (**F. 65/120**); letters and papers re Russian trade and the possible effects of a war, 1791 (**F. 65e**); copy of letter from Catherine II to Count S. R. Vorontsov, 28 Apr. 1791 (**F. 115/22**). Papers of Charles Watson-Wentworth (1730-82), 2nd Marquis of Rockingham, include: copy of a treaty of commerce with Russia, 1765 (**R. 68**); 2 letters from Sir Charles Knowles to the Marquis from Russia, 1771-2, 1777, and copy letter from the Marquis to Sir Charles, *post* 1771 (**R. 148/1-3; R1/1355, 1405, 1431-2, 1745**); letters from various correspondents to the Marquis re events in Russia, 1757-9, 1762 (**R1/108-9, 122, 140, 146-8, 271, 274, 286**); letter from Prince Dmitrii Golitsyn, 23 Mar. 1772 (**R1/1401**); letters from Prince L. A. Naryshkin, 1773-5 (**R1/1436, 1597a-b**); correspondence between the Marquis and Prince and Princess M. O. Naryshkina, mainly re horses and racing, 1773-80 (**W.W.M. R 195 c (70-131)**).

303.15 YORKSHIRE ENGINE COMPANY RECORDS (**Y.E.C.**)

Records and photographs relating to locomotives and tenders supplied to the Moscow and Ryazan' Railway and the Tambov and Kozlov Railway, 1869, the Lemberg and Czernowitz Railway, *c.* 1869, the Poti and Tiflis Railway, *c.* 1869 and 1870, and the Transcaucasian Railway, *c.* 1873 (**1: E 8-12, 14, 16-17, 41; 2-3; 5-6**).

303.16 Russian passports of S. F. Ibberson and his wife, 1869 (**M.D. 1624**).

303.17 Copy of a letter from Robert Hadfield to his son Samuel re *inter alia* commerce with Russia, [1798] (**M.D. 6627/22**).

304.1

SOUTH YORKSHIRE COUNTY ARCHIVES SERVICE

Cultural Activities Centre, Ellin Street, Sheffield S1 4PL

304.1 JOHN KENYON & CO. (**244/B**)

Saw manufacturers of Sheffield with a large trade with Russia and the Baltic States. Records include minute-book of board meetings and general meetings, 1909-30 (**1/1**), financial records including accounts, bills, transfers of cash and analysis of accounts, 1911-30 (**2/1-6**) and receiver's records, 1929-30 (**4/1-2**).

305.1-4

SHROPSHIRE RECORD OFFICE

Shirehall, Abbey Foregate, Shrewsbury SY2 6ND

M. C. Hill, *A Guide to the Shropshire Records* (1952).

305.1 LLOYD JONES OF SHACKERLEY COLLECTION (SRO 1781)
Journal by Daniel Jones, member of a family of ironmasters, of his travels in Russia in the summer of 1852 (*/5/6*) and 2 letters re his proposed visit to Moscow, July 1852 (*/5/27, 29*). The journal may be consulted at the discretion of the County Archivist and none of the personal material may be published.

305.2 LEIGHTON OF SWEENEY COLLECTION (SRO 1060)
Account by Thomas Browne Parker of his tour in Russia, 1825-6 (*/232*); letters written by Parker from Russia, 1825-6, and typed transcripts of the same (*/264-77, 281-9, 295*); passport to go from Sweden to Russia issued in Berlin, 23 May 1825 (*/293*).

305.3 MR RENSHAW'S COLLECTION (SOLICITOR) (SRO 2937)
Journal by Augustus Thursby-Pelham of a cruise to St Petersburg for the coronation of the Tsar, 1896 (*/1*).

305.4 MRS TURNBULL'S COLLECTION (SRO 1502)
Block of shares in the Nicholas Railway from St Petersburg to Moscow, 1867 (*/105*).

306.1

SOUTHAMPTON CITY RECORD OFFICE

Civic Centre, Southampton, Hampshire SO9 4XL

306.1 BOARD OF GUARDIANS' RECORDS
Papers, mainly official correspondence re the arrival in Southampton of a party of 90 Russian émigrés of German descent who had emigrated to Brazil and were trying to return to Russia, Dec. 1879 - Jan. 1880 (SC/AG. 14/15).

307.1-3

SOUTHAMPTON UNIVERSITY LIBRARY

Southampton S09 5NH

By appointment.

307.1 HANSARD FAMILY PAPERS
Papers of Gen. Sir John Saint George (1812-1891), who served in the Crimean War and visited St Petersburg in Oct. 1868 as British delegate to a conference on explosive bullets, comprise memoirs (5 vols), 1812-91, diaries (2 vols), 1851-8, diary and notebook as an artillery officer in the Crimea, 6 Aug. - 15 Oct. 1855, and travel journals (5 vols), 1860-90 (A 528).

307.2 PALMERSTON (BROADLANDS) PAPERS

There are extensive references to Russia in the correspondence of Henry John Temple (1784-1865), 3rd Visc. Palmerston including with the following: George Hamilton-Gordon, 4th Earl of Aberdeen; George Douglas Campbell, 8th Duke of Argyll; George Eden; Sir Frederick James Lamb, Baron Beauvale; the Hon. John Duncan Bligh; the Hon. John Arthur Douglas, 2nd Baron Bloomfield; Baron François de Bourqueney; Baron Ernst Phillipp Brunnow; Andrew Buchanan; Sir Stratford Canning; Henry Wellesley, 1st Baron Cowley; Hugh Richard Charles Wellesley, 2nd Baron Cowley; John George Lambton, 1st Earl of Durham; Prince A. M. Gorchakov; Count Nikolai Keselev; Prince C. A. Lieven; Princess Dorothea Lieven; Charles Eastland de Michele; Adm. Sir Charles Napier; Henry Pelham Pelham-Clinton, 5th Duke of Newcastle; Count K. R. Nesselrode: Prince A. F. Orlov; John Ponsonby, 2nd Baron Ponsonby; Sir Hugh Henry Rose; Lord John Russell; Count M. S. Vorontsov; Nicholas I. Also, memos and drafts re Russia and foreign affairs from the War Office, *c.* 1830-60. *See handlist and index for further correspondents and details.*

307.3 WELLINGTON PAPERS

Papers of Arthur Wellesley (1769-1852), 1st Duke of Wellington, include: memo on Russia, 1818 (**1/609**); papers re Russo-Turkish affairs, Jan.-Feb. 1822 (**1/698, 701**); memo on the war in Russia in 1812, written 1826 (**1/873**); papers re St Petersburg brouillons, 1826 (**1/878**); correspondence re his emissary to St Petersburg, Feb.-Apr. 1826, with a register of correspondence for the same period (**5/1/3**); lithographed plan of the 'Passage du Caucase par le Colonel Rottiers, 1820' (**15/51**). There are references to Anglo-Russian relations in other papers but only papers of the period 1833-52 have been catalogued in detail and include: papers re Russian influence on the Porte and Anglo-Russian relations, Jan.-Feb. 1835; papers re resignation by Charles W. Stewart, 3rd Marquis of Londonderry, of his embassy to Russia, Mar. 1835; Afghanistan and relations with Russia, Oct.-Dec. 1838, Dec. 1839 - Mar. 1843. C. M. Woolfar, *A Summary Catalogue of the Wellington Papers* (Southampton, 1984).

308.1-14

STAFFORDSHIRE RECORD OFFICE

County Buildings, Eastgate Street, Stafford ST16 2LZ

Handlists. Card indexes to persons, places and subjects.

308.1 BAGOT PAPERS (D3259)

Letters to William Bagot, 2nd Baron Bagot, from his brother, Sir Charles Bagot, from St Petersburg, 1821-3 (**/15/1**), and his son, William, describing his Russian tour, 1839 (**/21/2**).

308.2 BRADFORD PAPERS (D1287)

Letters from Col. J. Macdonald to Selina, Lady Newport, from the Crimea, 1854-6 (**/10/1**); paper re quality of Russian soldier, *post* 1777 (**/10/3**). Collection in the process of being catalogued. Apply to Archivist.

308.3 CONGREVE PAPERS (D1057)

Letter from Tsarevich Nicholas to Sir William Congreve with copy letter from Congreve re the grant of the Order of St. Anne, 1801 (**M/F/47/1-4**).

308.4 DARTMOUTH PAPERS (D(W)1778)

Letter from William Legge, 1st Earl Dartmouth, to Queen Anne referring to the Tsar's threats, 20 Aug. 1712 (*/I/ii/338*); letter from the Earl of Dartmouth to Charles Townshend, 2nd Visc. Townshend, re Russia's foreign policy, 22 Feb. 1724/5 (*/III/164*); letter from Henry Howard, Earl of Suffolk, to William Legge, 2nd Earl of Dartmouth, re Russia's policy towards Sweden, 6 Sept. 1772 (*/III/277*); observations of the Board of Trade on proposed new treaty of commerce with St Petersburg, 1 Mar. 1765 (*/V/228A*); copy journal of William Davidson who served on a Russian privateer, 1789 (*/V/953*). *See catalogues for details.*

308.5 ELD COLLECTION (D798)

Correspondence between Annie Cecilia Eld and Frederick Eld while he was in the Crimea, *c.* 1854-6 (*/3/1/28*); letter re the grant of a medal to Col. Eld from the Sultan for service in the Crimea, 1868 (*/3/3/7*).

308.6 HATHERTON COLLECTION (D260)

Documents of Lord Henry Hugh Manvers Percy include: correspondence from Robert Blane from St Petersburg (*/M/F/5/70*); documents and passports in Russian, 1864 (*/M/F/5/71*).

308.7 JERNINGHAM PAPERS (D641/3)

Copy dispatches of G. S. S. Jerningham from Stuttgart, including re Crimean War, Eastern Question and attitudes to Russia, 1854-9 (*/N/6/7*); letter from Clarendon, Foreign Secretary, to Jerningham re Russia's military position in the Crimea, 1855 (*/N/6/14*). Collection in the process of being catalogued. Apply to Archivist.

308.8 KINVER PARISH RECORDS (D1197)

Minutes of meetings, list of subscribers and collectors' accounts for various districts for the Patriotic Fund, 1854 (*/8/10*).

308.9 RECORDS OF J & N PHILIPS & CO. (D644)

Four small notebooks containing note of sums collected for the Patriotic Fund for the relief of widows and orphans of soldiers in the Crimea, 1854 (*/10/4*).

308.10 SUTHERLAND PAPERS (D593)

Letter from W. E. Gladstone to Harriet Leveson-Gower, Duchess of Sutherland, giving views on the outbreak of the Crimean War (*/P/20b*). Papers of George G. Leveson-Gower, 2nd Duke of Sutherland, include: 3 letters from the Duke of Argyll re employment of mercenaries in the Crimean War, *c.* 1854-5 (*/P/22/1/3/9*); letter from his son (3rd Duke) with brief account of the Tsar's coronation, 1856 (*/P/22/1/8*); notes re political affairs and the death of Lord Frederick Leveson-Gower in the Crimean War, *c.* 1855-6 (*/P/22/1/30*). Account of the visit by George G. W. Leveson-Gower, 3rd Duke of Sutherland, to Moscow for the coronation, 1856 (*/P/24/7/7-8*); documents re the operation of the Stafford House Committee for the Relief of the Sick and Wounded Turkish Soldiers, wounded during the Russo-Turkish War, 1877-8 (*/P/26/2*). Deputy Lieutenants' papers include letter from Sir Thomas Smythe, Ambassador to Russia, to Sir John Leveson from Russia discussing the possibility of selling pearls on Sir John's behalf in Russia, 6 Aug. 1604 (*/S/4/69/19*).

308.11 PAPERS OF THE UNETT AND RELATED FAMILIES (D3610)

Journal of a visit to France by Richard Wilkes Unett including a review of the Russian army, 1815 (*/13/1*); Crimean journal and sketchbook of Lt-Col. Thomas Unett, 1854-5 (*/16/1,2*).

308.12 WILSON, Benjamin (**D3233**)
Brewer of Burton on Trent. Correspondence re trade with suppliers of grain, hops and timber, including suppliers from Memel and St Petersburg, 1796-1801.

308.13 Letter-book of Samuel Barrett & Co., tinplate manufacturers of Kings Bromley, includes references to trade with Holland and Russia, 1796-1803 (**D872**).

308.14 Handbill giving notice of a meeting in Hanley to celebrate the Russian Revolution, Apr. 1917 (**D1486**).

309.1-9
ARGYLL AND SUTHERLAND HIGHLANDERS REGIMENTAL MUSEUM

Regimental Headquarters, The Castle, Stirling FK8 1EH

By appointment. The manuscripts are in the process of being re-catalogued; new class marks are given where they exist, in addition, class marks in round brackets indicate class marks allocated in the National Register of Archives (Scotland) report and class marks in square brackets are the original reference numbers to the inventory of the Regimental Records.

Crimean War records

309.1 Regimental order book of the 93rd Highlanders, 1800-91, covering the Crimean War (**N-93 (R26)**).

309.2 Diary of Pte Robert Sinclair, 93rd Highlanders, covering the Crimean campaign, 1854-6 (**N-C93.SIN (43)**).

309.3 Crimean diary of Daniel or Donald Cameron, 93rd Regt, veteran of Balaclava, 14 Sept. 1854 - Sept. 1855 (**N-C93.SIN (159)**).

309.4 Photographs of Crimean War and Indian Mutiny veterans of the 93rd Highlanders taken in 1910 (**(49)**).

309.5 File containing letters written by S. A. Stotherd, 93rd Regt, while stationed at Balaclava and Scutari to his father and brother, 1854 (**(166) [L1]**).

309.6 Letter from Spencer Ewart to Gen. Henry F. Compton Cavendish re a water-colour of the battle of the Alma, and letter possibly from a trooper in the Scots Greys to his family from the Crimea, 13 Nov. 1854 (**(169) [L8]**).

309.7 MS notebook of 'A Private Soldier of the 93rd Sutherland Highlanders in the Crimea' (**[SB17]**).

Post-Crimean War records

309.8 Russian first-aid certificate, 1920 (**(9b) [SB56]**).

309.9 Photograph of the guard found by the 1st Bn at General HQ of the Army of the Black Sea, 1919 (**(221) [P21]**).

310.1-5

THE SHAKESPEARE BIRTHPLACE TRUST

The Shakespeare Centre, Stratford-upon-Avon CV37 6QW

Documents relating to the Shakespeare Memorial Theatre and the Royal Shakespeare Company are held in the Royal Shakespeare Theatre Collection of the Shakespeare Centre Library, and other records are held in the Shakespeare Trust Records Office, both located in the Shakespeare Centre. Catalogue cards and indexes are held in in the Shakespeare Centre Library.

310.1 Diary of Charles and Sarah Flower in Russia, 1-29 June 1869 (**DR 195**).

310.2 Passports and safeconducts issued to Sir William Chatterton for Russia, *c.* 1815 (**DR 495**).

310.3 Prompt books of productions, photographs and newscuttings re visits to the USSR by the Shakespeare Memorial Theatre, 1958-9, and the Royal Shakespeare Company, 1964, 1967.

310.4 Costume designs by Theodore Komisarjevsky (F. P. Komisarzhevskii) for *The Merry Wives of Windsor*, Moscow, 1918.

310.5 Production records relating to productions of plays by Russian dramatists by the Royal Shakespeare Company.

311.1-135

PETER LIDDLE'S 1914-18 PERSONAL EXPERIENCE ARCHIVES

Sunderland Polytechnic, St Mary's Building, Chester Road, Sunderland SR1 3SD

By written appointment; limited research facilities. TS summary lists of collection are available and material relating to Russia can be found mainly in the lists for Russia and for Dunsterforce, Caspian Naval Force and Persia and in the General Section. This is a private archive and a support donation is requested from researchers who are not students.

311.1 ALBERY, Pte W. J.
Recollections of service in South Russia with the Royal Berkshire Regt.

311.2 BALL, 2nd Lt H.
Photograph album covering service in the 46 Bn Royal Fusiliers in North Russia, 1919; tape recording of his experiences (**no. 595**).

311.3 BANNERMAN, Sir Donald
TS recollections of service as 2nd Lt with the Queen's Own Cameron Highlanders in North Russia.

311.4 BARKER, Gen. Sir Evelyn
Photographs covering his service as Capt. in the 60th Rifles, King's Royal Rifle Corps, in South Russia; tape recording of his experiences (**no. 467**).

311.5 BARNETT, C. M.
Recollections of service in North Russia.

311.6 BEEVERS, H., RN
Memoirs of service in the Caspian Naval Forces and tape recording of his experiences (**no. 387**).

311.7 BENTLEY, D. R. B.
Recollections of service in the RAF in North Russia.

311.8 BILNEY, Air Vice-Marshal C.
Log-book covering his service in the RAF in the Caspian; tape recording of his experiences (**no. 419**).

311.9 BINSTEAD, Pte C.
Recollections of his service with the Hampshire Regt in North Russia.

311.10 BISHOP, B. C.
Diaries, papers and photographs re his service as wireless operator on HMS *Transport* at Archangel; tape recording of his experience (**no. 314**).

311.11 BLACKLOCK, Capt. R. W., RN
TS memoirs re Royal Navy service in the Baltic, 1914-15; tape recordings of his experiences (**nos 445, 449**).

311.12 BOUSTEAD, Col. Sir Hugh
TS letters and recollections for his autobiography refer to training the Whites in South Russia; tape recording of his experiences (**no. 361**),

311.13 BRAYSHAW, Cpl L.
Recollections of his service with the 6th Bn Yorkshire Regt in North Russia.

311.14 BREWSTER, Cdr B. T., RN
TS recollections and photographs covering his service in North Russia and elevation sketch map.

311.15 BROWN, Pte G. W.
Tape recording of his experiences while serving with the Cameronians in South Russia (**no. 432**).

311.16 BRUCE, Capt. R.
Letters while serving with the Cameron Highlanders in South Russia.

311.17 BUCHANAN, Sir Charles
Tape recording of his experiences while serving in North Russia (**no. 377**).

311.18 COGHLAN, 2nd Lt G. E.
Photographs and maps covering his service with the Royal Engineers in North Russia.

311.19 COHEN, Cdr K., RN
Diaries (7 vols) and photographs covering his service as a Midshipman in the Black Sea; tape recording of his experiences (**no. 613**).

311.20 COLLINGRIDGE, Brig. H. V.
Tape recording of his experiences while serving with the 6th Gurkhas in South Russia (**no. 553**).

311.21 COLLINGWOOD, Anna, née Koenig
Tape recordings of her recollections of life in St Petersburg before and during the Revolution (**nos 669-70**).

311.22 COLLINGWOOD, L.
TS diary as interpreter in North Russia, 1919.

311.23 COUPE, Ordinary Seaman H.
Diary and sketches covering service in HMS *Glory* in North Russia.

311.24 CRAWFORD, Capt. J. S., RN
Recollections, scrapbook and photographs covering his service in HMS *Windsor* in North Russia; tape recording of his experiences (**no. 502**).

311.25 CULLEN, Lt A. A.
TS 'A Caucasian Adventure' re his service in the RAF.

311.26 DAVIDSON, Lt J. A.
Recollections of service with the 11th Royal Sussex Regt in North Russia.

311.27 DAVIES, Pte W.
Recollections of his service with the 7th Bn Machine Gun Corps in North Russia.

311.28 DAVIS, Adm. Sir William
Xerox copy of log as Midshipman and memoirs while serving in HMS *Neptune* and HMS *Barham* in the Baltic, 1918-20; tape recording of his experiences (**no. 490**).

311.29 DICK, Rear-Adm. R. M.
Xerox of papers covering service as Lt, RN, in HMS *Attentive* in North Russia; tape recording of his experiences (**no. 465**).

311.30 DRAGE, Cdr C.
TS xerox of diary (2 vols) covering service as Sub-Lt, RN, in North Russia; tape recording of his experiences (**no. 72**).

311.31 DRUCE, Maj. A. F.
Tape recording of his experiences while serving with the Surrey Yeomanry in Tiflis (**no. 533**).

311.32 DUNCAN PORTEOUS, Dr L.
Correspondence covering his service in South Russia and the Black Sea.

311.33 EDWARDES, Dr H. V.
Tape recording of his experiences while serving as a RN surgeon in HMS *Vindictive* in the Baltic (**no. 608**).

311.34 EVANS, Sister E. G.
Letter from a British Red Cross Unit in Odessa, 23 July 1917.

311.35 FARMBOROUGH, Miss F.
Photographs re her work as nurse on the Eastern Front; tape recording of her experiences (**no. 302**).

311.36 FARTHING, Lt-Col. C. H.
Recollections of his service in Siberia.

311.37 FENTON, Pte R. L.
Contemporary account of service in North Russia.

311.38 FOSS, Miss J.
TS account of journey through Russia, 1914.

311.39 FRASER, Adm. Bruce Austin, 1st Baron Fraser of North Cape
Tape recording of his experiences as Lt-Cdr, RN, in the Caspian, including his capture by the Bolsheviks (**no. 576**).

311.40 GAWTHORPE, Brig. J. B.
Tape recording of his experiences while serving in North Russia (**no. 519**).

311.41 GIBSON, William, 2nd Baron Ashbourne
Tape recording of his experiences while serving in the Baltic and the Black Sea (**no. 627**).

311.42 GILL, D.
Letters, recollections and TS diary re his work as mining engineer in Russia in 1914 and in the North Russian Expeditionary Force, 1919-20.

311.43 GILLESPIE, R. D.
Tape recording of his experiences as interpreter to the British Mission in Siberia and Vladivostok (**no. 643**).

311.44 GILMORE, Brig. G. H.
TS recollections and papers covering his service as Maj. in North Russia, 1918-19.

311.45 GILRUTH, Dr J. G.
Tape recording of his experiences while serving in the Black Sea in HMS *Lord Nelson* including an account of the rescue of Prince F. F. Yusupov and the Grand Duke Nicholas (**no. 607**).

311.46 GOLDSMITH, Vice-Adm. Sir Lennon
Letters covering his service as Cdr in HMS *Montrose* in the Black Sea.

311.47 GOODES, Lance Sgt A. G.
Recollections covering his service with the Royal Scots in North Russia and including his capture by the Bolsheviks.

311.48 GREENSLADE, Brig. C.
Papers and MS and TS account re his service as Capt. with the 10th Devonshire Regt in the Baltic States; tape recording of his experiences (**no. 546**).

311.49 GRIFFITHS WILLIAMS, Brig. E. L. G.
Tape recording of his experiences while serving in North Russia (**no. 440**).

311.50 GRINDLE, Capt. J. A., RN
Tape recording of his experiences while serving in the Baltic (**no. 512**).

311.51 GUNN, Capt. P. L., RN
Unpublished memoirs covering his service in the Baltic; tape recording of his experiences (**no. 470**).

311.52 HAIGH, Lt-Col. J.
Field messages, maps, diary, papers and recollections re his service with the 9th Royal Warwickshire Regt in South Russia; tape recording of his experiences (**no. 44**).

311.53 HAKEWILL-SMITH, Maj.-Gen. Sir Edmund
Letters re the evacuation of the British Military Mission in South Russia; tape recording of his experiences (**no. 406**).

311.54 HALE, F. E.
Papers and photographs covering his service in the RAF in North Russia, 1918-19.

311.55 HARRIS, Cdr G. C., RN
Papers and photographs re his service as Midshipman in the Baltic; tape recording of his experiences (**no. 296**).

311.56 HARRIS, PO J. J., RNAS
Papers, photographs and xerox copies of correspondence re his service in North Russia.

311.57 HELYAR, P.
TS extracts from his letters as Consul in Petrograd and Odessa, 1916-17.

311.58 HENSON, PO W. T., RN
Recollections and photographs re his service in South Russia.

311.59 HINES, C. P.
Tape recordings of his experiences while serving in the medical services in North Russia (**nos 612, 666**).

311.60 HOLME, B.
Letters from Russia where he worked as a tutor, 1914.

311.61 HOOPER, 2nd Lt A.
Letters covering his service with the Queen's Own Royal West Kent Regt in South Russia.

311.62 HULTON, Col. J. M.
Papers re his service with Maj.-Gen. Sir Alfred Knox's Mission in Siberia.

311.63 HUNTER, C.
Tape recording of his experiences in North Russia, 1918-19 (**no. 313**).

311.64 INGLIS, Maj.-Gen. Sir Drummond
Tape recording of his experiences while serving as Capt. with the Royal Engineers in the Caucasus (**no. 466**).

311.65 JACQUES, Pte L. W., RAMC
Diaries covering his service in North Russia, 1917-19.

311.66 JAMESON, Maj.-Gen. T.
TS recollections and photographs covering his service as Capt. with the Royal Marines in Siberia and Georgia; tape recording of his experiences (**no. 433**).

311.67 JARVIS, Maj. T. S. W.
Recollections and xerox copies of papers re his journey from Petrograd to Persia, 1918; tape recording of his experiences (**no. 411**).

311.68 JENKINS, J.
Tape recording of his experiences while serving in North Russia (**no. 144**).

311.69 JENKS, Wg/Cdr M.
Papers and recollections covering his service as Lt with the 7th Bn Gloucestershire Regt in Persia and South Russia; tape recording of his experiences (**no. 635**).

311.70 JONES, 2nd Lt E. C. J.
Papers covering his service with the Bedfordshire Regt in North Russia.

311.71 KEMP, L. H.
Tape recording of his experiences while serving with the RNAS in South Russia (**no. 14**).

311.72 KENNEDY, W., RN
Diary of service in HMS *Attentive* in North Russia.

311.73 KERR, Dr J. H.
TS recollections and diary covering service as RN surgeon in the Baltic and the Black Sea.

311.74 KERSHAW, C. A. N., RN
Recollections of service in HMS *Canterby* in North Russia.

311.75 KING, Cpl V. F.
Recollections and papers re his service with the 1st Bn the Royal Welch Fusiliers in North Russia; tape recording of his experiences (**no. 268**).

311.76 KOE, Brig. A. R.
Papers and photographs re his service as 2nd Lt with the Hampshire Regt in North Russia; tape recording of his experiences (**no. 624**).

311.77 LATIMER, 2nd Lt R. L.
Papers, recollections, diary, maps and photographs relating to his service in North Russia; Red and White propaganda; official report of the evacuation of North Russia; tape recording of his experiences (**no. 526**).

311.78 LAVRIN, Prof. Janko
TS recollections of his work as a Russian War Correspondent; tape recordings of his experiences (**nos 517, 529, 540**).

311.79 LAWFORD, F. J. C.
Photographs covering his YMCA work in North Russia, 1918-19.

311.80 LAWSON, J.
Photographs covering his service in South Russia; tape recording of his experiences (**no. 18**).

311.81 LEE, Capt. A. G., RN
Papers, letters, photographs and memoirs covering his service in the Caspian Naval Force; tape recording of his experiences (**no. 305**).

311.82 LONGDEN GRIFFITHS, Cdr C. H., RN
Recollections of service in the Black Sea.

311.83 McCALL, Adm. Sir Henry
Tape recording of his experiences as Lt, RN, in the Baltic (**no. 403**).

311.84 MACKAY, Maj. M. K.
2 accounts of his service with the Royal Army Medical Corps in South Russia.

311.85 MARQUAND, Pte W. J.
Copies of letters from North Russia where he served with the 238 Special Bde.

311.86 MASTERS, PO B. M.
Correspondence re Masters who served on coastal motor boats and took part in the Kronstadt Raid of 1919.

311.87 MISSEN, 2nd Lt L. R.
Papers and tape recording re his experiences while serving with the 7th North Staffordshire Regt in South Russia.

311.88 MONEY, Maj.-Gen. R. C.
Photographs re his service as Capt. with the Cameronians and Durham Light Infantry in South Russia; tape recording of his experiences (**no. 447**).

311.89 MURRAY, Col. W. A. K.
Photographs of Service as Capt. in North Russia.

311.90 NEVILLE, Lt-Col. Sir J. E. H.
Recollections and TS of letters to his father and sisters from North Russia where he was serving with the Oxfordshire and Bucks Light Infantry; tape recordings of his experiences (**nos 373, 407**).

311.91 NICORY, Dr C.
Recollections of his service with a British Medical Unit in Rumania and South Russia from 1916.

311.92 NORRIS, Sir Alfred
Papers covering his service as 2nd Lt with the 9th Bn King's Own Lancaster Regt in South Russia and the Transcaspia.

311.93 NORRIS, Adm. Sir Charles
Tape recording of his experiences in the Caspian Naval Force (**no. 545**).

311.94 OLDFIELD, Lt-Col. R. W.
Photographs, notes and military sketches re his service as Capt in the Baltic.

311.95 PARGITER, Maj.-Gen. R. B.
Tape recording covering his liaison work in Lithuania (**no. 466**).

311.96 PEARCE SMITH, Brig. K.
Tape recording of his experiences while serving with the Royal Berkshires in North Russia (**no. 646**).

311.97 PENDRED, Lady
Tape recording of recollections of Tiflis (**no. 442**).

311.98 PENFOLD, Capt. H. de L.
TS recollections of his service with the 9th Gurkhas in South Russia.

311.99 PERTWEE, Capt. H. G.
TS recollections and slides covering his service in the Caspian Naval Force; tape recording of his experiences (**no. 504**).

311.100 PHILLIPS, Rear-Adm. O. W.
TS recollections of his service as Lt-Cdr, RN, in the Baltic; tape recording of his experiences (**no. 544**).

311.101 POOLE, Maj.-Gen. F. C.
Copy of Maj.-Gen. Poole's report of a visit to the HQ of the Volunteer Army in South Russia, Dec. 1918 - Jan. 1919.

311.102 ROBERTS, Lt L. E.
TS recollections, papers, diary and photographs re his service with the 17th Bn King's Liverpool Regt in North Russia.

311.103 RODGER, Cdr R. H. S., RN
Recollections as Midshipman in HMS *Agamemnon* in the Black Sea, 1919.

311.104 ROGERS, Col. J. W.
Tape recordings of his experiences while serving as a 2nd Lt with the 9th Royal Warwicks in South Russia (**nos. 86, 91**).

311.105 ROUPELL, Brig. G. R.
TS of prison diary after capture in North Russia while serving as Capt. with the 1st Bn East Surrey Regt, 1919-20; tape recordings of his experiences (**nos 16, 29**).

311.106 ROWELL, Capt. R. A. M. C.
Photographs and various papers re his service in North Russia.

311.107 SAVORY, Lady P. M.
Tape recording of life in Russia during the Revolution (**no. 47**).

311.108 SAVORY, Lt-Gen. Sir Reginald
TS of diary and recollections while serving as Capt. with the 14th Sikhs in Vladivostok, 1919-20; tape recording of his experiences (**no. 47**).

311.109 SCHUSTER, Sir George
TS recollections of his service in North Russia; tape recordings of his experiences (**nos 524, 527**).

311.110 SHORTREAD, T.
Recollections of his service in North Russia; tape recording of his experiences **(no. 418)**.

311.111 SINCLAIR, G. F.
Tape recording of his experiences while serving in the Baltic **(no. 605)**.

311.112 SODEN, Capt. F. O.
Papers and photographs re his service in North Russia.

311.113 SPUY, Maj.-Gen. K. R. van der
Papers re service with the RAF in North Russia.

311.114 STEELE, Cdr G. C., RN
Tape recording of his experiences as Lt, RN, in the Baltic **(no. 504)**.

311.115 STURDY, Maj. A. E.
Papers re GHQ in Archangel; report of operations, 1 Oct. 1918 - 26 May 1919; report on operations of Gen. Ironside, 27 May - 27 Sept. 1919; Bolshevik pamphlets and propaganda.

311.116 SWINLEY, Capt. C.
Tape recording describing the evacuation of refugees from Odessa **(no. 586)**.

311.117 SYDNEY, Miss A.
Tape recording of her experiences working for famine relief in Russia after the Civil War **(no. 622)**.

311.118 SYKES, Lt R.
Copy of TS letter re his service in North Russia.

311.119 SYMONS, Lt-Col. J.
Official papers on ordnances services in South Russia.

311.120 THEODORE, F.
Papers and diary re his service in HMS *Marlborough* in the Black Sea, 1919-20.

311.121 THORNHILL, Midshipman P.
TS memoirs 'Scapa Flow to Caspian Sea'; TS of official dispatch for the Caspian Naval Forces.

311.122 THURSTAN, Violet
Papers, copies of letters and photograph album of postcards re her service in the Red Cross in Russia, 1914-15.

311.123 TINSON, G.
TS summary of voyage of the *Svyatogor* in the Baltic, 1919.

311.124 TORLESSE, Rear-Adm. A. D.
Letters, Midshipman's log and photographs re his service in the Black Sea; tape recording of his experiences **(no. 512)**.

311.125 WADE, Maj.-Gen. D. A. L.
Recollections and photographs re his service in South Russia; tape recording of his experiences (**no. 557**).

311.126 WAKEFORD, Brig. J. C. B.
Recollections and photograph albums re his service a Lt in the Royal Engineers in North Russia; tape recording of his experiences (**no. 540**).

311.127 WALSH, Mr
Tape recording of his experiences in Armenia (**no. 614**).

311.128 WELLER, Pte J. W.
TS recollections covering his service with the 46th Bn Royal Fusiliers in North Russia; pay-book and Russian money.

311.129 WHEELER, Lt C. G.
MS and TS recollections, copies of letters and photographs re his service with the Machine Gun Corps in North Russia; tape recordings of his experiences (**nos 45, 48**).

311.130 WILLIS, Capt. W. J. A.
Tape recording of his experiences while serving in the Royal Navy in the Baltic and supporting the Kronstadt raid (**no. 470**).

311.131 WILSON KNIGHT, Prof. G. R.
Tape recordings of his experiences as a dispatch rider in South Russia (**nos. 436, 439**).

311.132 WIMBERLEY, Maj.-Gen. D. N.
Tape recording of his experiences as a Capt. with the 1st Queen's Own Highlanders and Machine Gun Corps in North Russia (**no. 443**).

311.133 WOOD, Maj.-Gen. G. N.
Tape recording of his experiences while serving in South Russia (**no. 452**).

311.134 WOOLLEY, Lt Charles
Papers covering his service with the South Wales Borderers in the Caucasus; tape recording of his experiences (**no. 385**).

311.135 2 telegrams out of Petrograd, Mar. 1917.

312.1-2

SWANSEA CITY ARCHIVES OFFICE

The Guildhall, Swansea SA1 4PE

By appointment.

312.1 CHIEF EXECUTIVE AND TOWN CLERKS'S DEPARTMENT, CORRESPONDENCE FILES (T.C. 54)
Several files dealing with correspondence from the Ministry of Information during the Second World War re Soviet allies.

312.2 SWANSEA CHAMBER OF COMMERCE
There will be references to trade with Russia amongst the records. *See* E. P. Jones, *Commercial Year Book of the Swansea Chamber of Commerce* (London, 1915).

313.1-7

UNIVERSITY COLLEGE OF SWANSEA LIBRARY

Singleton Park, Swansea SA2 8PP

Prior notification of visits is preferred.

313.1 ROYAL INSTITUTION OF SOUTH WALES
Letters to A. W. Hatchett from Count Apollon Musin-Pushkin, 30 Dec. 1799, 3 Nov. 1803 **(Hatchett Letters, 4, 7)**.

313.2-7 SOUTH WALES COALFIELD ARCHIVE

D. Bevan, *Guide to the South Wales Coalfield Archive* (1980).

313.2 R. CORNELIUS PAPERS
Medical Aid to Russia Committee of Nantymoel documents including minute-book, cheques and letters from the Soviet Ambassador, 1942-4, 1951-3 **(1-7)**.

313.3 S. O. DAVIES PAPERS
Letters, postcards and telegrams re Davies's speeches defending the Soviet action in Berlin, 1953 **(A.19)**.

313.4 DAVID FRANCIS PAPERS
Report on the situation in Hungary, 1956 **(E.5)**; report of an NUM delegation visiting the USSR, 1961 **(F.13)**.

313.5 E. M. JONES PAPERS
Documents re the Pontardulais Russian Aid Committee including subscription books, expenses, notebooks and miscellaneous papers, 1941-2 **(7-26)**.

313.6 H. MORGAN (ABERTILLERY) PAPERS
Information Special re the invasion of the USSR, 25 June 1941 **(1)**.

313.7 D. J. WILLIAMS PAPERS
Diary of visit to the USSR as a member of a workers' delegation, 29 Oct. - 30 Nov. 1932 **(A.3)**; postcards and photographs of the USSR, 1939 **(A.4)**; notes for a course of lectures on the Russian Revolution and the USSR, *c.* 1926-32 **(B.13)**; notes for speeches on the USSR and China, *c.* 1962 **(C.9)**; press cuttings re Khrushchev's speech attacking Stalin, 1956 **(C.21)**.

314.1-2
SOMERSET LIGHT INFANTRY

Light Infantry Office (Somerset), 14 Mount Street, Taunton TA1 3QE

By appointment.

314.1 Diary of John F. Everett, 13th Somerset Light Infantry, from leaving Gibraltar to the taking of Sebastopol, June-Sept. 1855 (**X14**).

314.2 TS copy of letter believed to be from Pte James Sellick, 13th Light Infantry, to his parents from before Sebastopol, 17 Nov. 1854.

315.1-4
SOMERSET RECORD OFFICE

Obridge Road, Taunton TA2 7PU

315.1 DICKINSON MSS (DD/DN)
Letter-books, 1712-45, and accounts, 1728-40, of Graffin Prankard, Bristol merchant, giving details of trade with St Petersburg (**423-9, 433-40**).

315.2 HYLTON MSS (DD/HY)
Accounts re the estate of Samuel Holden, merchant trading with Russia, include references to his Russian trade, 1740-5 (**Box 45**).

315.3 MEDLYCOTT MSS (DD/MDL)
Journal (2 vols) of service in the Black Sea including action of Odessa and Alma by Mervyn Bradford Medlycott (1837-1908) (**Box 12**).

315.4 STRACHEY MSS (DD/SH)
Letters by Richard Charles Strachey (1781-1847) while travelling overland from India to England via Russia (**C/1189/7**) and diary of the journey bound with official Russian documents (**C/1189/8**).

316.1
ANGUS FIRE ARMOUR LTD

Thame, Oxfordshire

By appointment. The documents are at present held by Lord William's School, Oxford Road, Thame, Oxfordshire but will eventually be returned to the firm.

316.1 Material re the Reddaway family including: family letters; letters concerning the Bazhanovs; memoirs of Russia in 1917 and 1924; report on the Reddaway works in Moscow, 1924; report on the possibilities of trading with Russia, 1924; report on general conditions of life in Moscow; family photographs in Russia; photographs of Russian scenes; photograph of Rasputin; postcards; Russian bank notes; Russian will, 1917. *See handlist prepared by the School for details.*

317.1-3
WILTSHIRE RECORD OFFICE

County Hall, Trowbridge BA14 8JG

317.1 LONG, Walter Hume (**WRO 947**)
MP. Correspondence and minutes re a request by Long to the Foreign Office and the War Office for information re 2 Russian generals, Gourko (Gen. Vassilii I. Gurko) and Dessin, resident in Britain, Nov. 1918 (**/522**); intelligence report on 'Bolshevism in Russia' submitted to Long, Oct.-Dec. 1918 (**/595**).

317.2 WILTON HOUSE MSS (**WRO 2057**)
Box of letters and business papers re Count Simon Vorontsov, his son Prince Mikhail Vorontsov and his daughter Catherine, Countess of Pembroke, 1812-43 (**/F4/48**). Some estate and family papers are still in the possession of the family.

317.3 Letter from P. P. Loder to Giles Loder in St Petersburg re family matters and business affairs, 1836 (**WRO 1173/2**); letter from William Loder to his mother, probably in St Petersburg, re personal matters and business affairs, 1838 (**WRO 1173/3**).

318.1-4
CORNWALL RECORD OFFICE

County Hall, Truro TR1 3AY

By appointment; at least three weeks notice of a visit should be given. *Cornwall Record Office: A Brief Introduction to Sources* (1979); *List of Accessions 1981-1982, 1983-4, 1984-5* (1982-5).

318.1 THE CAREW POLE MUNIMENTS
Papers re mainly the visit of Reginald Pole Carew to Russia in 1781 and correspondence during and after the visit including: letter books, 1783-1809 (**CC/G3/1-4**); letters to Carew, 1780-2, including from Sir James Harris and Archdeacon Coxe (**CC/J/9**); miscellaneous correspondence, 1784-1804 (**CO/Q/7**); miscellaneous papers re foreign affairs including memo on Russian visit, travel impressions, anecdotes, letters from G. A. Potemkin and other papers re his Russian visit (**CO/R/3/1-248**). The collection is privately owned by Sir John Carew Pole, Antony House, Torpoint, Cornwall, and researchers wishing to use the collection must apply to Sir John for permission and arrange with the County Archivist for a temporary transfer of documents to Truro. A catalogue of the collection is available at the National Register of Archives.

318.2 PENDARVES-VIVIAN MSS (**DD.PD.**)
Diary by Sir Arthur Pendarves Vivian of a journey in East Prussia and Russia, 10 Aug. - 9 Sept. 1864 (**20**).

318.3 STEPHENS MSS (**DD.ST.**)
Letters by Gertrude Dziewicka from her travels in Russia as an English teacher commenting upon Russia and Russian society and mainly written from and about Moscow, 1894-1904 (**823-4**).

318.4 TWITE, Reginald (**DDX.497**)
Mining engineer. *C.* 100 letters from Twite in Russia to his parents, 1901-4 (**/15**).

319.1-3

WAKEFIELD DEPARTMENT OF ARCHIVES AND LOCAL STUDIES

Library Headquarters, Balne Lane, Wakefield, West Yorkshire WF2 0DQ

The following collections all form part of the John Goodchild Loan MSS, which is on deposit in the Library and may be consulted by appointment.

319.1 ALDAM MSS
Account book (beginning in 1716) of Walter Midford of Newcastle-upon-Tyne, tanner, leather merchant and ship owner, refers to a profit upon the ship the *Indeavour* on a voyage to Russia in 1707.

319.2 BACON FRANK MSS
Accounts of Matthew Ashton, Yorkshire merchant in Hamburg, 1681-85, 1702-3, refer *inter alia* to bags of Russian money, to Russian hides and to periwigs and lace exported to Archangel.

319.3 T. & J. SHACKLES OF HULL MSS
Accounts of T. & J. Shackles, whale oil merchants, 1838-47, refer to trade to Kronstadt.

320.1

WEST YORKSHIRE ARCHIVES SERVICE

Registry of Deeds, Newstead Road, Wakefield WF1 2DE

320.1 JOHN CROSSLEY AND SONS LTD (**C300**)
Carpet manufacturers of Halifax. Papers re the Russian Carpet Company, 1887-[1933], a separate company, the majority of shares of which were held by the directors of John Crossley and Sons Ltd. Papers (approx. 2 metres of shelving) relate mainly to the organization and accounts of the factory at Station Zavidovo and comprise inventories, returns of wages, memos of costs and prices, warp order books, memo of agreement with English overlookers of the works, plan of the factory at Zavidovo, letters re the construction of a new mill, 1913, details of claims lodged in 1918, and a memo on Anglo-Soviet trade, 1920-8. There will also be references to Russia and Russian customers in the general ledgers and shipping registers of the firm. The collection is subject to a 30 years' closure period but certain personal papers are closed for 50 or 100 years. Collection is available by appointment.

321.1

THE QUEEN'S LANCASHIRE REGIMENT

Regimental Headquarters, Peninsular Barracks, Warrington, Cheshire WA2 7BR

321.1 Xerox copy of a letter from Surg. John Wood to his brother from Balaclava Heights, 9 Nov. 1855.

322.1-13

WARWICKSHIRE COUNTY RECORD OFFICE

Priory Park, Cape Road, Warwick CV34 4JS

Card indexes for persons, places and subjects.

322.1 ATHERSTONE AND MANCETTER PARISH RECORDS **(CR 1907)**
Congratulatory message sent to Mr and Mrs Bracebridge on their return from 'a mission of mercy in the East' in connection with the Crimean War, 1855 **(/1)**.

322.2 DORMER OF GROVE PARK MSS **(CR 895)**
Letters from Gen. the Hon. J. C. Dormer to members of his family, 1853-88, covering his service in the Crimean War **(/90-3)**; packet containing 3 notebooks and papers re Gen. Dormer largely re military affairs, *c.* 1848-93 **(/94)**.

322.3 FEILDING OF NEWNHAM PADDOX MSS (DENBIGH MSS) **(CR 2017)**
Papers of Basil Feilding (d. 1674) 2nd Earl of Denbigh include a letter to him from 2 clerks in Holy Orders from Russia, *c.* 1634-40 **(/C101)**. Letter-books of Basil Feilding (1719-1800), 6th Earl of Denbigh include correspondence re the Russo-Turkish War, 1771-2 **(/C243 pp. 297-8, 318, 224)**, Anglo-Russian relations, 1779 **(/C244 p. 208)** and Russian policy in the war against France, 1793, 1799 **(/C244 pp. 433, 571, 587, 590)**. Vols of autographs include letters from the Tsarevich Paul, 29 Feb./11 Mar. 1780 **(/C329/114)**, Princess D. Lieven, 4 Sept. 1840 **(/C329/128)** and from Sir Colin Campbell in the Crimea to the Hon. Percy Feilding, Oct. 1855 **(/C330/93)**. Letters to Rudolph, Visc. Feilding, from the Hon. Percy Feilding and the Hon. William Henry Adelbert Feilding in the Crimea, 1854-6 **(/C420/3-10; C423/2; C450)**, Father Gagarin, a Russian convert in Paris, 1856 **(/C441/1-2)** and Gen. A. E. Codrington re William Feilding in the Crimea, and reply, 1928 **(/C998/1-2)**; letter from Gertrude Towse to Cecilia, Countess of Denbigh, re the return of Russians to Archangel from America and Canada, n.d. *temp.* First World War **(/C959)**; copy of petition to the city governor of Kiev from Miss O. Golenbetskaya re request for renewal of attestation of her maiden status so that she could marry, 7 Oct. 1842, Russian **(/N2)**. Papers of Gen. the Hon. William Feilding include letters by him from the Crimea, 1855-6 **(/W2)** and diary while on travels in the Crimea and other places, 1856-66 **(/W4)**. *See catalogues for details.*

322.4 GREVILLE OF WARWICK CASTLE MSS **(CR 1886)**
Papers of Brig.-Gen. Leopold Guy Francis Maynard Greville, Lord Brooke, include: Russo-Japanese War album, 1904 **(Box 621)**; sketches of Russia etc, early 19th century **(Box 624)**; map of the seat of war in Russia, early 19th century **(Box 740/4)**; licence for

Lord Brooke to wear the insignia of the 2nd Class of the Order of St Stanislaus of Russia, 6 Apr. 1916 (**Box 797A/36**).

322.5 LEAMINGTON HASTINGS PARISH RECORDS (DR 112)
Register of burials, 1813-1910, includes 'a man unknown, supposed a Russian', died 14 Oct. 1814 (**/4**).

322.6 MILLER AND CAREY FAMILIES MSS (CR 1374)
Account by Lt (afterwards Lt-Col.) Frederick Miller re his experiences at the battle of Inkerman, 1854 (**/3**).

322.7 MILNE PHOTOGRAPHS (CR 1894)
Box of mounted photographs including photographs of Estonia and Latvia, 1922 (**/65**).

322.8 NEWDEGATE OF ARBURY MSS (CR 136, 764, 1841)
Diary of Sir Lynedock Gardiner covering his voyage to the Crimea and service there, 1854-5 (**CR 136/A/283**); accounts, roll of officers etc of the Coldstream Guards at Scutari, 1856 (**/B/4823-4988**); printed map of a journey to eastern Europe ,made by Sir John Sinclair, 1786-7 (**/M/90**). Papers of Sir Edward Newdigate-Newdegate include: letters from Capt. Edward Newdigate (afterwards Sir Edward Newdigate-Newdegate) to his father from the Crimea, 21 Feb. 1854 - 27 June 1855 (**CR 764/223/7**); rough sketch plan of the successive English positions in front of the Redan, 1855 (**/239**); note of gratuity for wound received at Inkerman on 5 Nov. 1854 (**/252**); extracts of the above letters from Capt. Newdigate to his father from the Crimea (**CR 1841/62-3**).

322.9 THE PENNANT PAPERS (CR 2017)
Papers of Thomas Pennant (1726-98), traveller and naturalist, include: loose notes on birds including the Siberian bunting, 18th century (**/TP66/1-7**); letter from Robert Pennant to his grandmother on his return from a voyage to Archangel, 5 July 1717 (**/TP114**); letters to Pennant from A. Blackburne, 11 Jan., 18 Apr. 1778, and Edward William Bootle, 22 Feb. 1792, both from St Petersburg (**/TP177/1-2; TP179**).

322.10 SEYMOUR OF RAGLEY MSS (CR 114A, 713)
Papers of Sir George Francis Seymour (1787-1870) include: journal of voyage to Russia in HMS *Briton*, 1827 (**CR 114A/377**); chart of the Black Sea, 1836 (**/446**); map of the fleets attacking Sebastopol, 1854 (**/471**); letters by Sir George re the Crimean War, 1854 (**/526/8; /533/12**); 3 patronage-seeking letters by Mohan Lal (Agha Saheb) volunteering information about Russian advances in Afghanistan, 1875-6 (**/705**); letters, copies of letters and dispatches re the Crimean War, 1855-9 (**/715/2**); correspondence re Crimean War cemetery, 1883-4 (**/715/8**). Additional papers include letter from Adelaide, Duchess of Clarence, to Mrs Seymour, later Lady Seymour, thanking her for a vase from Russia, 1828 (**CR 713/13**). *See catalogues for details.*

322.11 SHIRLEY OF ETTINGTON MSS (CR 229)
Letter informing Sewallis Evelyn Shirley of his election as honorary life member of the Moscow Gun Club, 1899 (**/212**); maps of Russia, 1812, Sebastopol and the Caucasus, 1854 (**/218**).

322.12 SOUTHAM PARISH RECORDS (DR 583)
Register of burials, 1867-1924, includes Seth Bond, a survivor of the Charge of the Light Brigade, died 19 Dec. 1902 (**/8**).

322.13 WALLER OF WOODCOTE MSS **(CR 341)**
95 letters from Lt G. H. Waller in the Crimea, 1854-6 **(/324)**; rough plan of the fleet before landing at Alma, 1854, and other papers and letters connected with Maj.-Gen. G. W. Waller, 1856-91 **(/339)**; newspaper cuttings re the Crimean War **(/340)**.

323.1-8
HAMPSHIRE RECORD OFFICE
20 Southgate Street, Winchester SO23 9EF

323.1 BONHAM CARTER MSS **(94M72)**
Letter to Gerard Bonham Carter from the Under-Secretary of State refusing him permission to wear the Order of the Russian Red Cross, 1924 **(/F320)**; 'Scutari and Its Hospitals' by Revd Sydney G. Osborne, 1855 **(/F602)**; anon., 'Scutari and Its Objects of Interest', 1855 **(/F603)**.

323.2 CLARKE-JERVOISE MSS **(18M64)**
Letters (24 packets) written by H. Clarke Jervoise to his parents and brother from the Crimea, June 1854 - May 1856 **(Box 23)**.

323.3 HEATHCOTE MSS **(18M54)**
Letters to William Heathcote from St Petersburg and Moscow, 1716-17 **(Coffer 2 Box A Packet K)**.

323.4 MALMESBURY MSS **(9M73)**
Papers of James Howard Harris (1807-89), 3rd Earl of Malmesbury, include: file of letters including from Russia, 1852 **(1852/3)**; letter-books for Russia, Turkey etc, Feb.-Dec. 1858 **(1858/1-2)**; letters and memos to Harris re Russia and Russian foreign policy, 1858-9 **(1858-9/2)**; letters and dispatches to and from Russia to Harris and Granville George Leveson-Gower, 2nd Earl of Granville, 1852 **(2/3)**; letter-book from John Wodehouse, 1st Earl of Kimberley, in Russia to Harris, 1858 **(2/11)**; political diary of Harris, 1852-75. The permission of the depositor, to be obtained through the County Archivist, is required to consult these papers.

323.5 NORMANTON MSS **(21M57, 34M69)**
Posters and report re the Crimean Army Fund, 1854-5 **(21M57 Box B/14)**. Letters from Charles Agar on his voyage to the Crimea to James Charles Herbert Welbore Ellis, Visc. Somerton, 1854-5 **(34M69 J5-6)** and re the death of Agar in the Crimea, 1855 **(J7-8)**; letters from Charles Welbore Herbert to Herbert Welbore Ellis Agar re and from the Crimea, 1854-5 **(H3-4, H7, H10-30)** and letters re the death of Herbert in the Crimea **(H31-2)**.

323.6 RYDER CORRESPONDENCE **(Photocopy 381)**
Plea that the Emperor of Russia should grant monetary aid to M. de Puget **(/9)**. Originals kept by the Harrowby MSS Trust.

323.7 TIERNEY MSS **(31M70)**
Letter from George Tierney to Sir Thomas Maitland re the Russian position on Napoleon, n.d. **(/50g)**; letter from Samuel Whitbread to Tierney re the Peninsular War and the Russian position, 21 Dec. 1807 **(/72b)**; printed instructions to the Duke of Wellington on proceeding to St Petersburg, 1826 **(/88)**.

323.8 WICKHAM MSS **(38M49)**
Correspondence (20 items) between William Wickham and Sir Charles Whitworth in St Petersburg, 1799, 1800 **(/51)**; papers (45 items) re Marshal A. V. Suvorov, 1799 **(/90)**; 16 copies of papers re Russian politics, 1801 **(/125)**.

324.1-8

MUSEUM OF THE ROYAL GREEN JACKETS

Peninsular Barracks, Winchester SO23 8TS

Strictly by appointment; limited research facilities. Letters, accounts and miscellaneous documents are unlisted but kept in envelopes roughly according to subject (3 envelopes contain material relating specifically to the Crimean War). Bound MS diaries are shelved separately.

324.1 Envelope **20** contains miscellaneous material relating to the Crimean War including: letters from the Crimean War by Thomas Harvey Bramston, Capt. William A. MacKinnon, John B. C. Reade, W. A. Fyers, John Hanwell, Henry Hert, Mitchell-Innes and others; TS copies of letters from Raglan in the Crimea; TS account of service of John Sinton in the Crimea; MS index of extracts from the journal of Gen. Sir William Norcott in the Crimea.

324.2 Envelope **24** contains miscellaneous material relating to the Crimean War including: notes on the assault on a rifle pit by the 1st Bn Rifle Bde at Sebastopol by Col.-Sgt John Fisher; copies of letters from Sir William Norcott to Col. George Lawrence from the Crimea; letter from Gen. Sir George Brown from the Alma, 1854; TS copy of paper, 'Through the Crimea War with the 2nd Rifles' by W. Long; copy of extract from dispatch by Lord Raglan re the battle of the Alma; anon. account of the Crimean War; newspaper cuttings.

324.3 Envelope **27** contains miscellaneous material relating to the Crimean War including: anon., 'A Short account of the career of a Rifleman in the Crimea' with letter to his mother; TS extracts from the diary of Capt. E. A. Somerset, 3 Jan. 1854 - 8 Nov. 1855; extracts from letters of Sir Edward Newdigate-Newdegate, 2nd Bn Rifle Bde, in the Crimea; copies of extracts from the letters of Lt-Gen. Sir William Augustus Fyers from the Crimea; return of casualties from the Crimean War.

324.4 Diary by Lord Alexander Russell of the Rifle Bde covering his service in the Crimean War, 1855-6 **(221)**.

324.5 Diary of Lt David Alexander Gordon, 1st Bn Rifle Bde, covering the Crimean War, with sketches and loose letters from the Crimea **(256)**.

324.6 Diary of Thomas Harvey Bramston covering the Crimean War **(257)**.

324.7 6 vols of diaries of Sir William Norcott covering the Crimean War and including many drawings and sketches **(260-3)**.

324.8 MS official war diary of the King's Royal Rifle Corps covering their service in North Russia in 1919.

325.1-4
THE ROYAL HAMPSHIRE REGIMENT

Regimental Headquarters, Serle's House, Winchester SO23 9EG

By appointment.

325.1 Albums of photographs of the 2nd Bn The Royal Hampshire Regt in Murmansk and Archangel, May-Oct. 1919 (**120, 156, M347, M/582/1/82**).

325.2 Albums of photographs of the 1st/4th Bn The Royal Hampshire Regt in Baku, Krasnovodsk and the Transcaspia, Aug.-Sept. 1918 (**141-2, 147**).

325.3 Album of photographs of the 1st/9th (Cyclists) Bn The Royal Hampshire Regt in Vladivostok, Omsk and Ekaterinburg, Nov. 1918 - Aug. 1919 (**M348/79**).

325.4 War diary of the 1st/9th (Cyclists) Bn The Royal Hampshire Regt in Russia, 1918-19.

326.1-4
THE ROYAL HUSSARS (PAO) MUSEUM

Peninsular Barracks, Winchester, Hampshire SO23 9EG

Strictly by appointment only; limited research facilities. The Museum holds material relating to the 10th and the 11th Royal Hussars (Prince Albert's Own). There is no archive list but material is arranged in boxes by name of collection or by subject headings (Individuals, Miscellaneous Documents etc).

326.1 LOY SMITH COLLECTION
2 boxes of papers of and relating to Sgt-Maj. George Loy Smith (*c.* 1817-88) of the 11th Hussars. Miscellaneous letters re the Loy Smith collection, photographs and MS list of Russian trophies and relics which Loy Smith brought home from the Crimea (held in Sheffield City Museum) (**Box 1**); TS copy, with hand-drawn maps, of account of the Charge of the Light Brigade by Loy Smith, based on his diaries and letters but written in 1883, and 6 diaries of Loy Smith of which nos 5 and 6 cover the Crimean War (**Box 2**).

326.2 LUMMIS PAPERS
7 boxes of papers, press cuttings and biographical information collected by Revd Canon W. M. Lummis relating to the Crimean War and in particular to the participation of the 11th Hussars in the Charge of the Light Brigade. Press cuttings, TS muster rolls and medal roll of the 11th Hussars and correspondence re his collection (**Box 1**); lists, accounts, photographs and correspondence relating to survivors of the Charge and TS paper re 'Crimean Bob', an old troop horse (**Box 2**); papers, photographs and press cuttings relating to Maj.-Gen. James Thomas Brudenell, 7th Earl of Cardigan, and his part in the Charge and transcripts of his correspondence (**Box 3**); TS biographical information re members of the Hussars who took part in the Charge (**Boxes 4-6**); recent correspondence relating to the collection (**Box 7**).

326.3 INDIVIDUALS : 10TH HUSSARS
2 boxes containing mainly TS biographical information, correspondence with relations and press cuttings re members of the 10th Hussars who took part in the Crimean War.

326.4 INDIVIDUALS : 11TH HUSSARS

2 boxes containing mainly TS biographical information, correspondence with relations and press cuttings re members of the 11th Hussars who took part in the Crimean War. There are also some original letters and copies of letters from the Crimea.

327.1-4

HOUSEHOLD CAVALRY MUSEUM

Combermere Barracks, Windsor, Berkshire

By appointment.

327.1 Unpublished TS 'A Crimean Veteran' on the life of Capt. George Clements of the Royal Dragoons.

327.2 Sketch-book of Capt. Sandermann of the Royal Dragoons including photographs of the Crimean campaign.

327.3 Unpublished TS diary of Capt. Stocks of the Royal Dragoons covering his service in the Crimean War.

327.4 Photograph album of officers of the Royal Dragoons in 1858 including those officers who served in the Crimean War.

328.1-4

THE BRITISH RED CROSS SOCIETY ARCHIVES

Barnett Hill, Wonersh, Surrey GU5 0RF

By appointment.

328.1 MSS re the work of the Society in South Russia and Rumania, 1916.

328.2 Papers re the setting up and running by the Society of the Anglo-Russian Hospital in Petrograd, 1916-17.

328.3 Short accounts for the Society's *Journal* of relief given to civilian refugees, Constantinople, 1920.

328.4 Papers re the work of the Aid to Russia Fund, 1939-45.

329.1

ST HELEN'S RECORD OFFICE

Fish Street, Worcester WR1 2HN

329.1 PAKINGTON MSS
Letter from J. T. Austen to ?Sir John Pakington on the government's mismanagement of
the Crimean campaign, 10 Jan. 1855, letter from Sidney Herbert to Sir John re Florence
Nightingale and the Nightingale fund, 24 Nov. 1855, letter from Ralph Earle to Sir John re
foreign policy and the end of the Crimean War, 5 Dec. 1855 (**705:349 BA4732/2(vii)**).
Permission is required from Lord Hampton for original documents to be consulted; a
microfilm copy of archives is available at the Record Office and prior notice of a visit to
consult this is advisable.

330.1

FLEET AIR ARM MUSEUM

Royal Naval Air Station, Yeovilton, Somerset BA22 8HT

By appointment.

330.1 Log-book of B. G. Blandfield of service in Russia, 1919.

331.1

THE BORTHWICK INSTITUTE OF HISTORICAL RESEARCH

University of York, St Anthony's Hall, York YO1 2PW

By appointment. *Guide to the Archive Collections in the Borthwick Institute of Historical
Research* (1973) and *Supplementary Guide* (1980).

331.1 THE HICKLETON PAPERS
Papers of Sir Charles Wood (1800-85), 1st Visc. Halifax, include letters to Wood from the
following: T. G. Baring, 1st Earl of Northbrook, re the crisis with Russia, 1885 (**A4.54A**);
Lord John Russell and the 4th Earl of Clarendon re Russia and the Crimean War, 1853-6
(**A4.56-7**); the 3rd Visc. Palmerston, Gen. Charles Grey, Fox Maule, 2nd Baron Panmure,
Queen Victoria and the 1st Baron Raglan re the Crimean War (**A4.63-5, 73, 77**); the 8th
Duke of Argyll re Turkey and Russia, 1853 (**A4.82**); the 15th Earl of Derby re Russia, 1885
(**A4.87**). 'A description of the Forts at Cronstadt...' by Lt Louis Reynolds, 1856 (**A7.10**);
account by Sir Edmund Lyons of the expedition to Sebastopol (**A8.1.4**). *See catalogue for
details.*

332.1-63

Appendix 1

PRIVATELY HELD PAPERS DESCRIBED IN THE PRINTED REPORTS OF THE ROYAL COMMISSION ON HISTORICAL MANUSCRIPTS, OR LISTED IN THE NATIONAL REGISTER OF ARCHIVES AND THE NATIONAL REGISTER OF ARCHIVES (SCOTLAND)

Enquiries concerning papers in private ownership described in the published reports of the Historical Manuscripts Commission (**HMC**) and the unpublished lists of the Commission's National Register of Archives (**NRA**) should be made in writing to the owners of the collections at the address given at the end of the entry unless otherwise stated. Where an Historical Manuscripts Commission report has been superseded by a National Register of Archives list only the latter is cited. The unpublished National Register of Archives lists can be consulted in the Commission's searchroom, Quality House, Quality Court, Chancery Lane, London WC2A 1HP. Researchers should note that the location and ownership of private collections may change; the Commission updates this information on its NRA lists and for its printed reports and attention should also be paid to its publication, *Guide to the Locations of Collections Described in the Reports and Calendars Series, 1870-1980* (Guides to Sources for British History, 3) (London, 1982). Preliminary enquiries concerning papers described in the unpublished lists of the National Register of Archives (Scotland) (**NRA(S)**) should be made to the National Register of Archives (Scotland), PO Box 36, HM General Register House, Edinburgh EH1 3YY. Copies of the National Register of Archives (Scotland) lists are also filed in the National Register of Archives in London.

The following list is not exhaustive; further references to collections containing Russian-related material may be found in the personal and subject indexes to the National Register of Archives. Source lists have been prepared covering the early reports of the National Register of Archives (Scotland) and the following are of particular relevance to Russia and the USSR: no. 1, Military Subjects; no. 2, Naval and Maritime; no. 20, Middle East; no. 22, India and Far East; no. 25, European; no. 26, Travel Letters and Diaries. It should be stressed that papers are made available to researchers at the discretion of the owners and that access may not always be granted.

332.1 ARDTORNISH ESTATE OFFICE (NRA(S) 0656, NRA 16119)
Letters from S. O. Lindley to Owen Hugh Smith describing the political situation in Russia and the events leading up to the Revolution, 1915-17 (**Box 51**).

332.2 ATHOLL MSS (NRA(S) 0980, NRA 19071)
Papers of Katherine, Duchess of Atholl, include: papers on Czechoslovakia and Yugoslavia including references to the USSR, Aug. 1938 (**16/4**); notes on conversations with I. Maiskii, 14 Nov. 1938 (**26/2**); file on 'Communist Party' including references to the USSR (**34**).

332.3 BAGOT (LEVENS HALL) MSS (NRA 6234)
Papers of Sir Charles Bagot include: Series I Russia, being 6 vols of official and private correspondence with the Secretary of State for Foreign Affairs and the Imperial Secretaries of State, 1820-4; bound vol. of letters to Prince A. B. Kurakin, 1814 (**Muniment Room H**).

Enquiries to: The County Archivist, Cumbria Record Office, County Offices, Kendal LA9 4RQ.

332.4 BALFOUR PAPERS (NRA(S) 0012, NRA 10026)

Papers of Arthur James Balfour, 1st Earl Balfour, include: note of the conversation of the German Emperor (William II) with Balfour re Russia, 1 Dec. 1899 (**15**); correspondence with William W. Palmer, 2nd Earl Selborne, re the Russian crisis of 1904 (**18**); correspondence with Walter Eliot re Russian films, 1927, and with Sir Henry Page Croft re Russia, 1919 (**24**). Papers of Gerald Balfour (1853-1945), 2nd Earl Balfour, include letters to Balfour from the following: Sir C. Spring-Rice, mainly from St Petersburg, 1904-5 (**116**); J. S. Sanders referring to the purchase of Chilean warships by Russia (**122**); Henry C. K. Petty-Fitzmaurice, 5th Marquis of Lansdowne, re Russian foreign policy (**123**); Frederick S. Roberts, 1st Earl Roberts, re the Russo-Japanese War (**126**). Additional Balfour MSS include: copies of letters of Alexander Leslie-Melville, Visc. Balgonie, from the Crimea, 1854-6 (**138**); letter from Margot Asquith re the action of the Tsar and Anglo-French relations, n.d. (**166**); letter from Mrs Hilda Wynne re events in Petrograd, July 1917.

332.5 BALFOUR OF FERNIE MSS (NRA(S) 0494, NRA 14146)

Letter from Francis Balfour to his father from Scutari, 24 May 1854 (**Black Trunk Bundle 1**).

332.6 BATH (LONGLEAT) MSS (HMC 3rd report, pp. xiii-xiv, 180-202; 4th report pp. xii-xiii, 227-51; 16th report pp. 56-9; 17th report pp. 35-45; 18th report pp. 85-9; 19th report p. 7; 23rd report p. 8; Bath I-V (serial no. 58))

Report to the Lords Justices re trade between England and Russia, 10 Aug. 1697 (**3rd report p. 193**); copy of a letter from the Tsar of Muscovy (Alexis) to the Emperor and reply, 27 Apr. 1668 (**4th report p. 249**). Matthew Prior papers are calendared in **Bath III** and include: letters from Prior to Sir William Trumbell, William Aglionby and others re the visit to Peter I to Holland and England with particular reference to the tobacco trade, 1697 (**Bath III X.330, X.336, X.341, X.353, X.378, XVI.81**); journal and memoirs of Prior re the Treaty of Ryswick including references to the Tsar (**XVI.nos.86-9**); copy of letter from Sir William Trumbell to William Blathwayt re the Russia merchants, 6 Aug. 1697 (**XVII.no.30**); petition to the King from the Russia merchants re the tobacco trade and Russia (**XVII.no.34**); paper of the Commissioners of Trade and Plantations to the Lords Justice re trade to Russia, 10 Aug. 1697 (**XVII.no.33**); instructions for negotiations with Russia, 26 Aug. 1697 (**XVII.no.35**); memoir delivered by Prior to the Secretary of the Russian Ambassadors, 24 Oct. 1697, Latin (**XVII.no.36**). Enquiries to the Marquis of Bath, Longleat, Wiltshire.

332.7 BOWER OF KINCALDRUM MSS (NRA(S) 0631, NRA 15459)

Letter from A. Bower St Clair while living in Russia re his life there and giving an account of the Polish method of hunting wolves, 6/18 Dec. 1843.

332.8 BROWN-LINDSAY OF COLSTOUN MSS (NRS(S) 0336)

Copy of letter from Charles I to the Tsar of Russia in favour of Lt-Col. James Bamatyne, 4 May 1632 (**Bundle 3**); letters from Sir O. Burne to the Hon. E. R. Bourke re the Eastern Question, Kabul and the Russo-Turkish War, 1877 (**Bundle 20**).

332.9 BUCCLEUCH MUNIMENTS (NRA(S) 1275, NRA 6184)

Papers re treaties between Britain and Russia etc., 1742-62 (**Box VIII Bundle 29**); miscellaneous treasury papers re Russia etc., 1710-53 (**Box VIII Bundle 30**). Letters from Charles, Earl of Dalkeith, to his sister re his travels in Italy, Germany and Russia, 1790-2 (**Bundle 1206**); letters from Charles, Earl of Dalkeith, to Henry Scott, 3rd Duke of Buccleuch, describing his travels, 1791-3 (**Bundle 1209**).

332.10 BUCHANAN, Maj. Sir Charles (NRA 8677)

Copies of letters of Sir Andrew Buchanan (1807-82) as Secretary of the Legation at St Petersburg to Lord Aberdeen, Lord Palmerston and others, 1844-9 (3); letters re Sir Andrew's appointment to St Petersburg (5); copies of letters from Sir Andrew to Lord Clarendon from Copenhagen before and during the Crimean War, 1853-6 (7); letters from naval officers in the Baltic, 1854-5 (10); letters to Sir Andrew from Sir Charles Napier at the Embassy in St Petersburg, 1863-4 (25). Enquiries to: Maj. Sir Charles Buchanan, St Anne's Manor, Sutton Bonington, Loughborough, Leicestershire.

332.11 BURNETT OF KEMNAY MSS (NRA(S) 1368, NRA 10119)

Letters to Alexander Burnett from the following: Lord Cathcart, British Ambassador to Russia, and K. Ostrov, 18 Feb. 1771 - 28 June 1772 (Bundles 54, 78); Trevor Curry, British Consul in Danzig, re Russian troops there, 30 Jan. 1765 - 30 Apr. 1766 (Bundle 59); Sir George Macartney, Ambassador at St Petersburg, 12 July 1765 - 3 July 1766 (Bundle 61).

332.12 DR C. C. BURT MSS (NRA(S) 0891, NRA 17643)

Papers of Andrew Burt, mining engineer in China, include postcards of the construction of the Trans-Siberian railway, 1901, and of the Russian contingents in the Boxer Rebellion, 1901-2.

332.13 CAMPBELL OF KILBERRY (NRA(S) 0886, NRA 10124)

Letter from Archibald Campbell to Col. John Campbell re the Russian Revolution, 27 Apr. 1919 (Green Deed Box Bundle 4); letter from Chander Shum Shere to Sir Edward Durand re the Anglo-Russian treaty, 13 Jan. 1908 (Black Deed Box "Kilberry" No. 4 packet 3); copy of some observations made by Lord Raglan to Sir John McNeil re the Crimean War (packet 14).

332.14 LT-COL. ROBERT CAMPBELL-PRESTON MSS (NRA(S) 0934, NRA 8146)

Correspondence of Col. Alexander Campbell re the French invasion of Russia, 1812 (Bundles 132, 161).

332.15 CATHCART PAPERS (NRA 3946)

Papers of Charles, 9th Lord Cathcart, include: journal of Jane Hamilton, Lady Cathcart, covering her stay in Russia, 1745-71 (A.66); account books of Cathcart as Ambassador in St Petersburg, 1767-71 (A.71); correspondence of Cathcart with the secretaries of state while Ambassador in St Petersburg, 1768-71 (A.72-4); instructions and letters of Cathcart while in Russia, 1768 (C.6). Papers of William, 10th Lord Cathcart, include: letters to Cathcart from the Foreign Office during his ambassadorship in Russia, 1812-18 (A.95-6); letter from Cathcart at St Petersburg, mainly to Lord Castlereagh, 1815-18 (A.97); letters and drafts of dispatches by Cathcart from St Petersburg, 1812-20 (C.42-9, 51-73). Papers of Sir George Cathcart include: notes re the campaign in Russia in 1812 by Cathcart (Box 21/2); letters and papers re Cathcarts's Crimean exploits (Box 21/65); 26 maps of Russian frontiers and Persia, c. 1800 (Box 21/72); plans of battles during the French campaign in Russia, 1812-13 (Box 21/74-5); 11 photographs of the Crimea (Box 21/3). Enquiries to: Maj.-Gen. the Earl Cathcart, 2 Pembroke Gardens Close, London W8.

332.16 COLVILLE OF CULROSS PAPERS (NRA(S) 0039, NRA 10112)

Diary of the Hon. Sir William Colville during the Crimean War, 1854-5 (Compartment 3).

332.17 COLVIN MSS (NRA(S) 0872, NRA 17560)

Letters from Lt C. M. Colvin to his mother from Russia, June-July 1886 (12b).

332.18 DE BUNSEN MSS (NRA 20352)

Papers of Sir Maurice William Ernest de Bunsen (1852-1932) include letters to him from Russia etc., 1873-8 (**MB/I/b**), from Japan referring to an attempt on the life of the Tsarevich (Nicholas), 1891 (**MB/I/s**) and from Paris referring to the French belief in eventual Russian victory against Japan, 1904 (**MB/I/ff**). Enquiries to: Lady Salisbury-Jones, Mill Down, Hambleton, Portsmouth, Hampshire.

332.19 DE SALIS PAPERS (NRA 0206)

Letters and papers of Gen. Rudolph de Salis from the Crimean War (**8**). Enquiries to: Lt-Col. Fane de Salis, Bourne House, East Woodhay, Newbury, Berkshire.

332.20 DE SAUSMAREZ MSS (NRA 0730)

Dossier on the trial between creditors re a ship under Russian colours which had a case of plague on board, n.d. Enquiries to: Brig.-Gen. C. H. de Sausmarez, Sausmarez Manor, St Martins, Guernsey.

332.21 THE DEVONSHIRE PAPERS (NRA 20594)

Papers of William George Spencer Cavendish (1790-1858), 6th Duke of Devonshire, include: correspondence including with Lady G. D. Morpath, Princess D. Lieven, Naryshkin (?A. L.), Count R. Nesselrode, Mrs Henry Cavendish, J. Abercromby, Sir Alexander Crichton, the Grand Duke Nicholas and George W. F. Villiers in St Petersburg, 1817-21 (**D 215-6, 219-20, 222-3, 229-38, 246, 309, 314, 533, 535, 556**); documents re Cavendish's mission to Russia as Ambassador Extraordinary for the coronation of the Tsar Nicholas I, Feb.-Dec. 1826 (**D 1287-1360**); letters from Thomas Anderson, Richard Seymour Conway, 4th Marquis of Hertford, Countess Hélène Zavadovskii and others in St Petersburg, 1827-33 (**D 1447, 1512, 1514-15, 1870, 2856**). *See reports for details.* Enquiries to: The Trustees of the Chatsworth Settlement, Chatsworth, Bakewell, Derbyshire DE4 1PP.

332.22 EARL OF DUNDONALD MSS (NRA(S) 0081, NRA 8150)

Letters from Sir Alexander Malet to Lord Cochrane, 10th Earl of Dundonald, re peace between Turkey and Russia and the prospects of Greek independence, 1828-32 (**Box 4**); papers on the actions of Britain and Russia re Greek independence, 1827 (**Box 8, XX**); letters from Capt. Chrouschoff (?Khrushchev) on a Russian frigate, 1827-8 (**Box 8, XXI**).

332.23 THE EARL OF DUNMORE MSS (NRA(S) 0796, NRA 17664)

Letter from Lord Salisbury to Charles Adolphus Murray (1841-1907), 7th Earl of Dunmore, re Russia and northern India, 11 July 1894 (**/14**).

332.24 EWART OF CRAIGCLEUCH PAPERS (NRA(S) 1054, NRA 11854)

Letters from Gen. Ian Hamilton to Gen. Sir John Alexander Ewart re the Russo-Japanese relations, 1900 (**52**); service papers of Col. J. A. Ewart re the Crimea (**71**); correspondence of Sir James Harris from St Petersburg to Sir John Stepney, 1782-3 (**129**). Letters to Joseph Ewart from the following: Charles Henry Fraser from St Petersburg, 1787-9 (**130, 152**); Lord Carmarthan re proposed British mediation between Sweden and Russia, 15 Aug. 1788 (**131**); William Eden, 1st Baron Auckland, re Russian policy in the Crimea, 1790-1 (**132**); W. Fawkener in St Petersburg, 1791 (**132**) and Copenhagen re Russia (**133**); Francis Jackson re the Russo-Turkish War, 1791-2 (**148**); Charles Whitworth from St Petersburg, 1788-90 (**148, 150, 154**); John Joshua Proby, 1st Earl of Carysfort, from St Petersburg, n.d. (**148**); D. Hailes from Warsaw re Russian policy in Poland, 1788-91 (**149, 154**); J. Rogerson from St Petersburg, 1789 (**153**). Letters from J. A. Ewart from the Crimea, 1854 (**136**); copy of reply by Catherine II to a letter from the Prince de Ligne, 12 Nov. 1790 (**155**).

332.25 FARQUHARSON OF INVERCAULD MUNIMENTS (**NRA(S) 0061, NRA 9958**)
Letters from Robert Keith, in the service of the Russian Tsar, to George and John Keith, 11 Aug. 1734, 28 Apr. 1736 (**Bundle 15**).

332.26 FULWAR COVENTRY MSS (**NRA 0598**)
Lines by George Marent on the Crimean War, Apr. 1854 (**38(41)**). Enquiries to: Mrs Fulwar Coventry, Holy Well House, Malvern Wells.

332.27 GLASGOW RANGERS FOOTBALL CLUB LTD (**NRA(S) 1867, NRA 22250**)
Vol. of press cuttings and photographs of the Rangers versus Moscow Dynamo match, 28 Nov. 1945.

332.28 GORDON OF LETTERFOURIE (**NRA(S) 0096, NRA 10154**)
Letters from Francis Gordon re his service in the Russian navy, 1770 (**Green Deed Box**).

332.29 GOUROCK ROPE CO. LTD (**NRA(S) 0282, NRA 10832**)
Copies of letters sent from the continent, mainly from Amsterdam and St Petersburg, 15 Aug. 1815 - 31 Dec. 1816.

332.30 EARL OF HADDINGTON MSS (**NRA(S) 0104, NRA 10114**)
MS vols containing notes on the history and geography of the Scandinavian and Baltic states, Muscovy, Hungary, Silesia, Poland etc., *c.* 1720 (**Library cupboard 3 shelf 4**).

332.31 HADDO HOUSE MSS (**NRA(S) 0055, NRA 9758**)
Letters from the Chancellery of St Petersburg, 16 May 1840, French (**1/2 Bundle 1**); anon. letter to the 4th Earl of Aberdeen criticizing his Russian policy (**1/2 Bundle 2**); I. A. Krilov's *Fables* in verse, transl. by Sir J. G. Shaw-Lefevre (**1/3**); letter from W. E. Gladstone to G. J. Shaw-Lefevre re Stepnyak, 5 Dec. 1893 (**1/8 Bundle 4**); letters re the Crimean War (**1/12 Bundle 2**); letters from G. J. Shaw-Lefevre from the Crimea, 1855 (**1/47 Bundle 2**).

332.32 DUKE OF HAMILTON PAPERS (**NRA(S) 2177, NRA 10979**)
Papers of Alexander Hamilton Douglas (1767-1852), 10th Duke of Hamilton, include: letters from Rodrigo Navarro d'Andrade, William Adam, C. Zecalewsky and Matthew Anderson in St Petersburg, 1808, 1812, copy of letter from the King of Sweden to the Tsar of Russia, 7 Sept. n.y., printed material re Russia (**Bundle 698**); letters from Sophie Potocka and Matthew Anderson in St Petersburg, 1813-14 (**Bundle 706**); letters from Prince C. Czartoryski, 1835 (**Bundles 706, 709**); letter from Charles Grey, 2nd Earl Grey, referring to Napoleon in Russia, 1812 (**Bundle 754**); letter from Charlotte Leon in St Petersburg, 26 Sept. 1812 (**Bundle 766**). *See report for details and further references.*

332.33 HARROWBY MSS TRUST (**NRA 1561**)
Index to the first series lists dispatches to and from Russia, 1804, papers re Russia, 1805, correspondence with Benjamin Garlike and Granville in Russia, correspondence with A. Czartoryski and the letters and papers of Gen. Tolstoi. Index to the second series lists correspondence with A. Czartoryski and L. Czartoryski. *See indexes and reports for details.* Enquiries to: the Earl of Harrowby, Sandon Hall, Stafford.

332.34 HOBBS (VILLIERS) MSS (**NRA 12033**)
Letter from James Howard Harris, 3rd Earl of Malmesbury, to Lord Clarendon re accounts of a Russian force having got out of Sebastopol and landed on the coast of Circassia, Mar. 1854 (**I/10/1**); letter from G. T. Staunton to J. Magrath recommending M.

A. Tourgueneff (Turgenev), 8 Jan. 1831 (**I/65**); letter from Thomas Slingsby Duncombe to Lord Clarendon re his desire to give an address on Russia and Turkey, 20 Oct. 1853 (**I/76/5**); letter from Count Orlov (?A. F.) to ---, 25 Nov. [1851] (**I/94/3**); letter from N. Ogarev to ---, 16 June 1853 (**I/96/3**); letters from Philipp Brunnow, Russian Minister in London, to Lord and Lady Clarendon, 1853-4 (**I/99/6-7; I/100/5**); letter from Gen. M. E. P. M. MacMahon to --- re an incident at Fort Malakoff, 27 Dec. n.y. (**II/91/2**). *See index of correspondents.* Enquiries to: Capt. M. Hobbs, Proverbs Green, High Roding, Dunmow, Essex.

332.35 BARON HOME OF THE HIRSEL (NRA(S) 0859, NRA 10169)
Papers of Cospatrick Alexander Home (1799-1881), 11th Earl of Home, include: transcript of letter by Lady Mary Coke re the murder of Tsar Peter III, 1762 (**Box 104/1**); letters from Home to his parents written during his visit to Russia with the Duke of Wellington, 1822-3, 1826 (**Box 191 Bundle 5; Box 192 Bundles 5, 8; Box 193 Bundles 2, 7**); 3 letters from Princess E. R. Dashkova to Elizabeth, Duchess of Buccleuch, 1780 (**Box 192 Bundle 9**); letters from George ?Boudier to Home from the Crimea, and from Home to his parents from St Petersburg, 1822 (**Box 193 Bundle 10**).

332.36 HOPETOUN MSS (MARQUIS OF LINLITHGOW) (NRA(S) 0888, NRA 17684)
Letter from Henry Dundas to Lord James Hope, 3rd Earl of Hopetoun, re the difficulty of the union of Prussia and Russia, 16 Oct. 1787 (**Bundle 220**); regulations in English and Russian '... for all masters of ships and other persons sailing and comeing in merchant men to any ports or harbours belonging to the Empire of Russia ...', 1771 (**Bundle 1603**); views of Moscow and St Petersburg, *c.* 1862 (**Tea Chest "Pertabgur UK 18"**).

332.37 HUNTER OF HUNTERSTON (NRA(S) 0852, NRA 18276)
Letter from Mary, Lady Palmerston to John George Lambton, 1st Earl of Durham, Ambassador at St Petersburg, 1837, and letter from J. Savile Quinley to H. I. Sobyus describing a trip to Russia, *c.* 1837 (**Bundle 192**).

332.38 KIMBERLEY MSS (NRA 1274)
Papers of John Wodehouse (1826-1902), 1st Earl of Kimberley, include copies of dispatches from St Petersburg, 1856-8, diplomatic correspondence re Russia, 1894-5, and maps of Central Asia and Afghanistan, 1867-94. The papers remain in family possession and are not available for research.

332.39 LAMBTON PAPERS (NRA 11184)
Papers of John George Lambton (1792-1840), 1st Earl of Durham, include: papers re his embassy to Russia (**Box I**); bundle marked 'Trade with Russia' and various papers re his embassy to Russia (**Box II**); vol. entitled 'St Petersburgh, March 1836' (**Box III**); correspondence, dispatches etc. re his embassy to Russia (**Boxes VI, XI, XIV-XV, XX**); notes by Louisa, Countess of Durham, on Russia, 1836 (**Box VII**); Lambton's visiting book in Russia, 1835-7 (**Box IX**); letter-book and official diary of mission to Russia (**Box XVII**); Lambton's journal in Russia (**Box XVII/1**); letters and dispatches from Consul Gen. James Yeames at Odessa to Lambton and replies, Oct. 1835 - Apr. 1837 (**Box XX**); private letters by Lambton from St Petersburg, 1836-7 (**Box XXII**). *See report for details.* Enquiries to: The Estate Agent, Lambton Estate Office, Lambton Park, Chester-le-Street, County Durham.

332.40 LAURIE MSS (NRA 5405)
Letter from Edward B. Rice to his brother written from HMS *Leander* at Balaclava, 1856 (**112**); correspondence of J. M. Fector re Spanish, Russian and Egyptian affairs, 1836-40

(121). Enquiries to: Maj.-Gen. Sir John Laurie, Bt, CBE, DSO, Maxwelton, Moniaive, Dumfries.

332.41 LEFROY MSS (NRA 8549)

Letter from M. ?Queru to Gen. Henry Lefroy from St Petersburg, 30 Mar./10 Apr. 1870 (**34**); correspondence re Florence Nightingale at Scutari, 1856 (**72-3**); letter from Florence Nightingale at Scutari, 15 Dec. 1855 (**75**); TS copies of letters from Florence Nightingale to Col. J. H. Lefroy from Scutari (**207**); end of a letter from Sidney Herbert to Col. Lefroy re Florence Nightingale at Scutari (**208**). Enquiries to: Mrs J. L. Knyvett, Littlemore Cottage, Church Road, Sunningdale SL5 0NJ.

332.42 LOUDOUN PAPERS (THE MARQUIS OF BUTE) (NRA(S) 0631, NRA 15459)

Letters to Sir John Stuart (1713-92), 3rd Earl of Bute, from the following: Mrs Anderson re the possibility of the Russian fleet sailing for the Mediterranean, 22 Aug. 1769 (**Box 1768-71 Bundle 1**); Lord Cathcart in St Petersburg, 6/17 Dec. 1770 (**Box 1768-71 Bundle 3**); Lt-Col. William Dalrymple re Russia etc., 1774 (**Box 1772-5 Bundle 6**). Letters to Francis Rawson-Hastings (1754-1826), 1st Marquis of Hastings, from the following: Thomas Rowcroft from St Petersburg, 25 Aug. 1818 (**Box 1725-50 Bundle 7**); Frederick William, Duke of Brunswick, re request of the King of Sweden to visit Russia, 15 May 1811 (**HASTINGS Box 21 Bundle 22**); Sir Henry Ellis re the Russian threat to India, n.d. (**Box 22 Bundle 24**); Capt. M. Stewart re Russo-Turkish relations, 23 Dec. 1815 (**Bundle 31**); Sir T. S. Raffles re Russia and the Sandwich Islands, 29 Jan. 1819 (**Bundle 45**); Lt-Col. J. C. Doyle re Russian policy in Persia, 23 Jan. 1821 (**Bundle 59**); Robert Saunders Dundas, 2nd Visc. Melville, re Russian claims on Moldavia and Wallachia, 9 Jan. 1822 (**Bundle 63**); P. C. S. Smythe re negotiations re Turkey and Russia, 25 Aug. 1824 (**Bundle 71**). *See report for further references.*

332.43 McLEA PAPERS (NRA(S) 0876, NRA 17575)

Letters from Duncan M'Lea from Russia, 1812-13, 1821 (**15**).

332.44 MACPHERSON-GRANT MSS (NRA(S) 0771, NRA 17173)

Letter to James Grant re the movement of the Russian fleet, 4 Oct. 1769 (**Bundle 267**).

332.45 MAITLAND MSS (NRA 3640)

Early photographs and other papers re the Crimean War. Enquiries to Cdr J. W. Maitland, RN, Harrington Hall, Spilsby, Lincolnshire.

332.46 MALCOLM OF POLTALLOCH MSS (NRA(S) 0642, NRA 15645)

Papers of Sir Ian Zachary Malcolm include correspondence re his appointment as British Red Cross commissioner to Russia, Oct.-Dec. 1915, with miscellaneous correspondence and documents concerning the appointment (**vol. 'The War. British Red Cross Mission to Russia, Oct.-Dec. 1915'**).

332.47 MALET MSS (NRA 18542)

Copy of letter from Lt H. C. E. Malet from Balaclava, 8 June 1855 (**PPC/1/12**); letter from Lord Cathcart, Ambassador at St Petersburg, to Brook Taylor, 21 June 1815 (**C/2**). Enquiries to: Col. Sir Edward Malet, Bt, OBE, Chargot, Watchet, Somerset.

332.48 EARL OF MANSFIELD MSS (NRA(S) 0776, NRA 10988)

Papers of David Murray (1727-96), 2nd Earl of Mansfield and Visc. Stormont, diplomat, include extensive diplomatic correspondence re Russia including: letters from Sir Charles Hanbury Williams in St Petersburg and correspondence re Russia, 1756-9 (**Boxes 1-8**); minutes of Cabinet meetings re Russia, 1779 (**Box 13**); letters to Murray from George III re

Russia (**Box 14**); correspondence, mainly diplomatic, of Murray including references to Russia, 1763-81 (**Boxes 15-16, 18-19, 22**); state papers addressed to Murray including references to Russia from various embassies and individuals including: H. S. Conway; Thomas Thynne, 3rd Visc. Weymouth; John Montagu, 4th Earl of Sandwich; Thomas Robinson, 2nd Baron Grantham, 1765-78 (**Boxes 23-5, 28-6, 38-42, 48-50, 53-7**); correspondence of Murray with Sir R. M. Keith, Sir Joseph Yorke and Sir James Harris referring to Russia, 1779-81 (**Boxes 58-60**); drafts by Murray to various authorities including references to Russia, 1780-1 (**Boxes 61-4**). 2nd series includes diplomatic correspondence re Russia including correspondence with Lord Cathcart, Keith and Harris, 1771-80 (**/585, 625, 629, 637-40, 651, 661, 674, 681-5, 687-8, 690-1, 693-4, 700, 1418, 2350**). *See report for details.*

332.49 WALTER MITCHELL & SONS LTD (NRA(S) 0747, NRA 17516)
Proceeds from home and imported pigs including pigs from Siberia, *c.* 1926 - *c.* 1935.

332.50 MORAY MSS (NRA(S) 0217, NRA 10983)
Letter re the defeat of the Swedes by the Muscovites, 1719 (**VII/827**); note on the murder of Rasputin (**part 4 bundle 9**).

332.51 PENNINGTON-RAMSDEN MSS (NRA 24077)
Correspondence between Benjamin Disraeli and E. A. Seymour, 12th Duke of Somerset, re appointment of Frederick Temple Hamilton-Temple Blackwood, 1st Marquis of Dufferin and Ava, to the St Petersburg embassy, 1879 (**Library**). Enquiries to: Sir William Pennington-Ramsden, Bt, Muncaster Castle, Ravenglass, Cumbria.

332.52 RIDGEWAY MSS (NRA 6957)
Papers of Sir Joseph West Ridgeway (1844-1930) include: letter re Russian policy towards Afghanistan, 17 Mar. 1885 (**26**); memos 'Is an invasion of India by Russia possible' and 'What are Russia's vulnerable points' by F. Roberts, 1883, 1885 (**43, 51**); report by Salisbury on Anglo-Russian negotiations on the Afghan frontier (**55**); letter from C. Bayley to Sir Joseph re the Russian government and the claim of the villagers of Bosagha, 16 Jan. 1891 (**101**); TS autobiography by Sir Joseph on his work with the Russo-Afghan Boundary Commission, n.d. (**109**); letter from Sir R. B. Morier to Sir Joseph from St Petersburg, 19 Oct. 1887 (**128**); letter from the Foreign Office to Sir Joseph re negotiations over an acknowledgement of a British sextant used as a pretext for Russian espionage, 29 Aug. 1887 (**268**). There will be further references to Russia in Sir Joseph's correspondence re the Afghan Boundary Commission. Enquiries to: The Rt Hon. Lord Tollemache, Helmingham Hall, Stowmarket, Suffolk.

332.53 EARL ST GERMANS MSS (HMC 1st report pp. x, 41-4)
Papers of Sir John Eliot include letters to Sir John Norris re the Tsar from Secretary James Craggs and Lord Cathcart, 1719 (**1st report p. 41**). Enquiries to: Earl of St Germans, Port Eliot, Cornwall.

332.54 SALISBURY MSS (HMC 3rd report pp. xii-xiii, 147-80; 4th report pp. xii, 199-227; 5th report pp. vii, 261-94; 6th report pp. 250-77; 7th report pp. xiii, 182-96; 12th report pp. 23-34; 13th report pp. 26-31; 14th report pp. 16-23; 15th report pp. 21-7; 16th report pp. 48-56; 17th report pp. 28-34; 18th report pp. 34-57; 19th report pp. 9-10; 21st report p. 12; 22nd report p. 10; 23rd report p. 8; Salisbury (Cecil) I-XXIV (serial no. 9); NRA 9226)
The early Salisbury papers are calendared in 24 vols (**Salisbury (Cecil) I-XXIV (serial no. 9**) and contain many references to Russia, 1557-1611, in correspondence, instructions to envoys and petitions. There are copies of letters between Ivan IV and Elizabeth I. *See indexes to calendared vols for details.* Private and Foreign Office correspondence of

Robert, 3rd Marquis of Salisbury, **(NRA 9226)** includes: in-letters Russia, 1878-80 **(14/1-81)**; out-letters St Petersburg, 1878-80 **(31/1-25)**; in-letters Russia, Turkey, 1885-6 **(39/34-44)**; out-letters Russia, 1885-6 **(44/22-6)**; out-letters Russia, 1887-92 **(73/1-91; 74/1-100)**; out-letters Russia, 1895-1900 **(129/1-108)**. Correspondence concerns Russia foreign policy, Russian relations with Turkey, Russian policy in Central Asia and towards Afghanistan, Russian policy in the Balkans and letters from the Russian Embassy in London. There are also references to Russia in the in- and out-letters of other countries such as Austria, Germany and Turkey. *See reports for details.* Enquiries to: Archivist, Hatfield House, Hatfield, Hertfordshire.

332.55 SCOTT OF GALA MSS **(NRA(S) 0181, NRA 10544)**

Diaries (4 vols) of Capt. (later Adm.) Henry Jenkinson and Althea and Sophia Jenkinson while on visits to St Petersburg and elsewhere in Europe, 1817-19 **(Deed Box 2 Bundle 1)**.

332.56 SEATON MSS **(NRA 5288)**

Copy of memo on Russian affairs in the Crimea and the Caucasus by John Ponsonby, Visc. Ponsonby, 1834 **(E)**. Enquiries to: Mrs K. C. Mackrell, Beechwood, Sparkwell, Devon.

332.57 SOMERSET MSS **(NRA 1252)**

Letters by William Cecil Pechell from the Crimea, 1854-5 **(7)**. Enquiries to: J. F. Somerset, Holt Farm House, Clapham, Worthing, Sussex.

332.58 STEWART-MEIKLEJOHN OF EDRADYNATE MSS **(NRA(S) 2307, NRA 10186)**

Letters from Lt (later Capt.) Robert C. Cuninghame of the 42nd Highlanders to the Robertson family and his sister from the Crimea, and papers re his death **(Bundles 55-8)**.

332.59 STRATHEDEN AND CAMPBELL MSS **(NRA(S) 0579, NRA 14813)**

Warrants for affixing the Great Seal to the ratification of the Paris Convention by Prussia, France, Austria and Russia, 1861, and notes for speech against Gladstone's alleged Russophile policy, 25 Nov. 1885 **(Box 1 Bundle 1)**; letter from L. Kossuth on Russia's policy in Bulgaria, India and Persia, 20 Dec. 1877 **(Box 1 Bundle 2)**; letter by Lord Salisbury re his belief that Bismarck would not join an alliance to hinder a Russian advance on Constantinople, 19 Sept. 1880 **(Box 1 Bundle 3)**.

332.60 STUART MSS **(HMC 16th report pp. 12-14; 17th report pp. 13-19; 18th report pp. 102-6; 19th report pp. 22-5; Stuart I-VII (serial no. 56))**

The Stuart papers, 1579-1718, are calendared in 7 vols **(Stuart I-VII)**. There are many references to Russia, 1716-18, re mainly diplomatic instructions to British envoys in Russia, the foreign relations of Russia, Peter I's domestic policy and trade between Britain and Russia, and including copies of letters from and to Peter I. *See reports and calendars for details.* Access to the Royal Archives is restricted and preliminary enquiries should be addressed to the Archivist, the Royal Archives, Windsor Castle, Berkshire.

332.61 VERNEY FAMILY PAPERS **(NRA 21959)**

Vol. of notes on Florence Nightingale by her sister Frances Parthenope chiefly re her work in Scutari **(Cupboard I)**; TS recollections of the Crimean War by Sir E. H. Verney, 3rd Bt, 1899 **(Cupboard III)**; letters from friends and relatives praising Florence Nightingale's Crimean work **(Cupboard V)**; letters from well-wishes of the Scutari Hospital, 1854-5 **(Cupboard VI)**. Enquiries to: Sir Ralph Verney, Bt, KBE, Claydon House, Middle Claydon, Buckinghamshire.

332.62 EARL OF WEMYSS MSS (NRA(S) 0208, NRA 10743)
Letters from Francis Wemyss-Charteris-Douglas, 9th Earl Wemyss, from the Crimea, 1854-5 (**Drawer 33**); portfolio of letters from the Crimea, 1854-5 (**Drawer 48**).

332.63 IVISON S. WHEATLEY MSS (NRA(S) 0362, NRA 11848)
Letter to E. Viale, Sicilian Consul at Gibraltar, from FM HRH Edward, Duke of Kent, with hopes for the success of Viale's memorial to the Tsar of Russia, 3 May 1807 (**2**).

333.1-18
Appendix 2

UNRECORDED PAPERS IN PRIVATE OWNERSHIP

There has been no systematic attempt to locate unrecorded collections of Russian-related material in private ownership. The following list is not exhaustive and does not necessarily describe the most significant private collections in the United Kingdom since only collections which came to light in the course of the survey are recorded. Researchers should apply in writing to the owner of the collection at the address given at the end of each entry. It should be stressed that papers are made available to researchers at the discretion of the owners and access may not always be granted.

333.1 BAILEY, Lt-Col. Frederick Marshman (1882-1967)
TS of Bailey's *Russian Diary, 1918-20* covering his political service in Russian Central Asia and escape from the Bolsheviks with some differences from the published version; photograph album covering his experiences in Tashkent, Bokhara and Central Asia, Apr. 1918 - Feb. 1920. Enquiries to: the Hon. Mrs Bailey, Warborough House, Stiffkey, Wells-next-Sea, Norfolk.

333.2 BOBRINSKOI FAMILY MSS
TS 'Vospominaniya, rasskazannye moim detyam o pokhode v vostochnyyu Persiyu v 1916 godu' by Countess Sofiya Alekseevna Bobrinskaya with related photographs and poems; TS 'Vospominaniya gr. Alekseya Alekseevicha Bobrinskago' with a synopsis in French; TS broadcasts for the BBC, some not given, by Count Aleksei Bobrinskoi; family photographs. Enquiries to: Mrs B. Cherbanich, c/o Countess Bobrinskoy, 1 North End Road, Fitzjames Avenue, London W14.

333.3 BUXTON, David Roden
TS 'A Russian Village Before the Five-Year Plan' by D. R. Buxton recounting his experiences of village life in 1928. Enquiries to: D. R. Buxton, Old Ellwoods, 55 Bridleway, Grantchester, Cambridge CB3 9NY.

333.4 CHRISTIAN, Professor R. F.
Personal collection of documents include: letters of Gen. Jomini; MSS of stories and poems by I. A. Bunin, A. M. Remizov, D. S. Merezhovskii, Z. N. Gippius, N. Berdyaev and others; poems by N. Bakhtin (published in *Oxford Slavonic Papers*); notebooks and essays by Bakhtin; letter by M. N. Zagoskin (published in *The Slavonic and East European Review*); letters by members of the Tolstoi family; 19th-century documents emanating from Russian ministries, and particularly from the Ministry of Foreign Affairs, originally in the possession of the Russian Embassy in The Hague; collection of pre-revolutionary

postcards. Enquiries to: Professor R. F. Christian, Department of Russian, St Salvator's College, University of St Andrews, St Andrews, Fife KY16 9AL.

333.5 DAVIS, Lt-Col. Peter G.
Correspondence, papers and translations and extracts from published works relating to his research on the British campaign in the Caspian and Transcaspia, 1918-20. Enquiries to: Lt-Col. (Retd) Peter G. Davis, 39 Manor Road, Eastcliffe, Bournemouth, Dorset BH1 3EU.

333.6 DIMSDALE PAPERS
Bound vol. (54 fols) of documents connected with Dr (Baron) Thomas Dimsdale's visits to Russia to carry out smallpox inoculations including letters to Dimsdale from Catherine II, the Tsarevich Paul, Count S. Vorontsov, Princess Dashkova and others, letters from Dimsdale and medical notes, 1768-1804; correspondence of members of the Dimsdale family with Catherine II, the Tsarevich Paul, Count Vladimir Orlov, Count N. Panin, Count S. Vorontsov, Count A. Vorontsov, A. Samborskii and others, 1744-1853. *See lists for details.* Journal by Charles Hatchett of journey to Russia, 1790-1, and letters from Moscow to his father re orders for coaches. Enquiries to: R. E. Dimsdale, Barkway House, Barkway, Royston, Hertfordshire.

333.7 GAGARIN FAMILY MSS
Drawings and lithographs by Prince G. Gagarin, 1830s; papers of Prince B. Gagarin re the history of the family; MS of a novel by Prince B. Gagarin 'Ot poslednyago samoderzhavnogo tsarya – do Lenina. Roman. Istoricheskaya byl' v 3-kh chastyakh'; family and other letters of Prince Grigory Gagarin (great-grandson of the G. Gagarin cited above) from 1927; diary kept by Prince Gregory Gagarin during a visit to the USSR in 1982. Enquiries to: Prince G. B. Gagarin, Gagarino, Kiln Park Road, Narberth, Dyfed SA67 8TX.

333.8 GLOVER, Douglas G.
C. 660 photographs and 470 colour transparencies of the Imperial Russian Armed Forces including orders and decorations. Enquiries to: D. G. Glover, Wayside, Login, Whitland, Dyfed SA34 OUX.

333.9 HUDSON, Maj. Miles
Papers relating to his research on the North Russian campaign include: a chapter of an unpublished book by Maj. Odell on his experiences in North Russia; interviews with Charles Painter and H. L. Carr who served in North Russia; memoirs of Mr Pond and Bde Maj. C. E. Hudson who served in North Russia. Enquiries to: Maj. M. Hudson, The Priors Farm, Mattingley, near Basingstoke, Hampshire.

333.10 IRONSIDE, William Edmund (1880-1959), 1st Baron Ironside
Diaries covering his service in Archangel as Chief of the General Staff of the Allied forces. The diaries are not generally available to researchers but enquiries may be made relating to their content to Lord Ironside, The House of Lords, London SW1A 0PW.

333.11 LEEPER, Sir Reginald A.
Papers of Sir Reginald include: extract from minutes of a meeting of the War Cabinet re the exchange of Maksim Litvinov for Bruce Lockhart, 13 Sept. 1918; report on Litvinov's departure, 27 Sept. 1918; letter from Litvinov to Sir Reginald, 11 June 1933; unsigned draft of a report to the Foreign Office of an interview with Litvinov; brief account by Lady Leeper, Sir Reginald's wife, of her husband's relations with Litvinov. Enquiries to: Lady M. P. Leeper, Southward, Rambledown Lane, West Chiltington, Pulborough, West Sussex RH20 2NW.

333.12 LINDLEY, Sir Francis Oswald (1872-1950)

Papers of Sir Francis as Commissioner and Consul-General in Russia, 1918-19, include: diary kept in Russia, mainly in Petrograd, Oct. 1915 - 2 Sept. 1917; correspondence of Sir Francis when in North Russia with Sir George Clerk, Charles, 1st Baron Hardinge, G. W. Balfour, Earl of Balfour, E. Drummond, Philip Kerr and others (list available); orders of the GHQ of the Allied forces and of Maj.-Gen. Poole in North Russia, 1918-19; memo on the withdrawal of the Allied troops; memo on the distribution of food to the civilian population; papers re Russian banks and the feasibility of loans to Russia; memo by Col. Keyes on the Russian banking system; cheque book belonging to Sir Francis for the Russian and English Bank, Petrograd. Enquiries to: Lady B. McEwen, Marchmont, Greenlaw, Berwickshire TD10 6YN.

333.13 PEARCE, Brian

Papers relating to his research include: TS copy of report by Maj. H. B. Suttor, serving with Dunsterforce in the Caspian, of fighting at Baku on the 14 and 15 Sept. 1918; letters from the historian A. D. Lyublinskaya to Pearce discussing *inter alia* historical questions, 1964-80 (a selection of these letters are being prepared for publication); 2 letters from A. M. Pankratova, editor-in-chief of *Voprosy istorii*. Enquiries to: B. Pearce, 42 Victoria Road, New Barnet, Hertfordshire EN4 9PF.

333.14 PRICE, Morgan Philips (1885-1973)

Papers of Price, correspondent for the *Manchester Guardian* in Russia, Dec. 1914 - Dec. 1918, include: originals and copies of letters and cables from Russia, 1914-18; 3 engagement books, 1914-18; TS notes and correspondence re interview with Lenin, 1918; papers, press cuttings and pamphlets re the Allied intervention; notes re railways and troop movements in Russian Central Asia, 1910-11; papers re his travels in Russia before and after the Revolution; lecture notes on Russia; copies of newspaper articles, articles, TS copies and drafts of publications by Price re Russia; 2 boxes of glass slides of Finland, 1908, and Russia, 1917-18; 3 albums and loose photographs of Russia, Russian Turkestan, the Caucasus, Siberia and Mongolia, 1910-14; press cuttings and printed material re Russia. The papers are being used for research by his daughter and will not be available until the research is completed but enquiries may be made to: Tania Rose, 36 South Hill Park, London NW3 2SJ.

333.15 POUSTCHINE (Pushchin) (née Tatarinova), Aleksandra Feodorovna

TS memoir 'Looking Back' written in the 1960s and covering her life in Orel province, political events, the outbreak of war and the overthrow of the Tsar. Enquiries to: Lady M. Williams, 1 Morland Close, Hampstead Way, London NW11 7JG.

333.16 VILCINSKAS, Juozas

Collection relating to his political interests and research including: correspondence with leading Lithuanian politicians including S. Kairys and Kipras Bielinis, mainly re the Lithuanian Social Democratic Party; research notes, TS and printer's proofs of publications, TS underground publications and booklets re Lithuania with particular reference to the Labour movement and the Lithuanian Social Democratic Party. Enquiries to: J. Vilcinskas, 5 Holmside Road, London SW12 8RJ.

333.17 YOUNG, Harry

TS autobiography of Harry Young who was in Russia, 1922-9, as a British delegate to the Young Communist International and served on the executive of the Red International of Labour Unions and Finance Commission. The autobiography comments on life in Russia and includes sketches of prominent individuals. Mr Young hopes that the text will be published but enquiries may be made to: H. Young, 1A Eton Avenue, Sudbury, Wembley.

333.18 ZINOV'EV FAMILY PAPERS

MS memoirs of Aleksandr Zinov'ev, Marshal of the Nobility, Governor of St Petersburg guberniya and member of the State Council; MS memoirs of his son Lev Zinov'ev, Marshal of the Nobility and member of the 4th Duma. Enquiries to: K. FitzLyon, 2 Arlington Cottages, Sutton Lane, London W4 4HB.

INDEX

The index refers to entries in the text (the number of the repository followed by the number of the entry within the repository). Introductory material is not indexed. Collections of papers are indicated in bold type; repositories are in capitals. Russian names are given in British Standard transliteration (without diacritics) in the modern form of the name where identified. Where individuals and places have not been identified they appear as listed in the repository. As a result, some individuals may appear in more than one form. Similarly, some places which have changed their name frequently may occur only in the form in which they are found in the original document.

A

A la question ... du petit orteil ... (Puusepp), 239.37

A propos du Rayonnisme (Larionov), 237.7

Abbotsford Collection, **82.8**

Abbott, Capt. James, 62.2, 169.59

Abbott, Keith Edward, 146.247

Abbott & Sons, 200.4

Abercairny MSS, **86.4**

Abercrombie, J. (missionary), 221.1

Abercromby, J., 332.21

Aberdeen, George Hamilton-Gordon, 4th Earl, **146.4**, 146.61, 146.456, 185.6, 263.4, 307.2, 332.10, 332.31

ABERDEEN CENTRAL LIBRARY, 1.1

ABERDEEN CITY DISTRICT ARCHIVES, 3.1

ABERDEEN UNIVERSITY LIBRARY, 2.1-2.9

Abernon, Edgar Vincent d', Baron then Visc., **146.5**

Abinger Observatory, 102.4

Ablett, Sgt Alfred, 185.37

Abortion Law Reform Association, **239.42**

Abortion Laws (Chance), Russia, 239.42

About the Russia Enquiryes (Whitworth) 215.50

About Spreading Some Birds in Georgia (Zhordania), 272.7

Abramskii, Rabbi Dayan, 143.3

Abramskii, Yehezkiel, 235.17

Abridgement of the Russes Sowdebnik ..., 269.93

Académie des Beaux-Arts, 144.3

Academy of Sciences, (Imperial) Russian, 81.1, 86.45, 102.3, 146.34, 146.152, 176.18, 215.19, 239.23, 239.38, 269.91

Academy of Sciences, USSR, 30.2, 38.3, 38.22, 46.3, 47.4, **82.62**, 215.4-5, 235.12, 239.43, 269.97

Account of the Accidents which Befell Mr Moorcroft ... (Stirling), 210.78

Account of the 42nd Regiment's Operations in the Crimea (Wilson), 285.5

Account of Mr Isbarant's Journey from Moscow to China ..., 1742-3, 176.11

Account of the Royal Highlanders at Alma (McSally), 285.2

Account of Russia 1767 (Macartney), 146.85, 146.376, 222.21

Account of Some Post-Moscow 1941 Government Events (Balfour), 164.8

Account of the Visit of ... the Emperor of Russia ..., 1814, 269.155

Achenbach & Colley, 200.4

Acheson, Hon. Dean, 175.11

Acland of Killerton papers, **88.1**

Acquaviva, Cardinal, 146.175

Across the Arctic Ocean from Vladivostok to Archangel (Starokadomskii), 210.77

Active, merchant ship, 187.90

Acton Collection, **38.1**

Adair, Robert, 269.47

Adam, William, 332.32

Adams, Charles Francis II, 269.46

Adams, Lt-Col. Frank, 97.1

Adams, Jane, 125.23

Adamus Tracigerus, Chancellor of Holstein, 146.327

Addington, Charles, 88.5 *see also* Sidmouth

Addington, H. M., 185.105

Addington, Henry, *see* Sidmouth, Visc.

Addison, Christopher Addison, 1st Visc., **269.39**

Adelaide, HMS, 210.42

Aden, 169.11

Adiornish Estate Office papers, **332.1**

I

J

L

O

W